*American History*

*and the*

*Social Sciences*

# American History

# and the

# Social Sciences

### Edited by Edward N. Saveth

 *The Free Press, New York*
*Collier-Macmillan Limited, London*

Copyright © 1964 by The Free Press of Glencoe
A Division of The Macmillan Company

Printed in the United States of America

Collier-Macmillan Canada, Ltd., Toronto, Ontario

Library of Congress Catalog Card Number: 64–20308

*Second Printing March 1966*

*To Allan Nevins*
*Distinguished Narrative Historian*

# Contents

## Part IV—Quantification and Machine Processes

## Part V—Beyond Social Science

# Part I

# Introduction

# The Conceptualization of American History / *Edward N. Saveth*

## Historian and Social Scientist

Admittedly puzzled, Professor Richard Hofstadter found difficulty in systematizing or formalizing "what it is that I owe, as an historian, to the social sciences."[1] Rather than answer the question inherent in Hofstadter's dilemma—what is the difference between conventional historiography and a social science approach—scholars tend to debate the alternatives. In his presidential address before the American Historical Association in December, 1962, Dr. Carl Bridenbaugh warned historians against the "dehumanizing methods of social sciences" and against the social scientists' lack of "human understanding which is the first requirement of the good historian." He accused social scientists of neither understanding nor caring "about chaps." He stated: "They deal in statistics, with units and trends, hoping to deduce laws of society; their works are primarily systematic, reveal little in any historical sense, and they ignore chronology." In contrast, he continued, the historian views facts as unique in character, space, and time, and this has "restrained him from trying to fit them into a rigid theory or fixed pattern."[2]

Historians traditionally have been uncertain about the usefulness of theory in the writing of history. They make the bold affirmation, "History is unthinkable without theory," and the equally bold denial, "It is the task of the historian to tell a story and leave theory to others." History continues to struggle between the polarities noted by Huizinga: "Does history strive after knowledge of the particular or of the general, of the concrete or of the abstract, of the unique or of the repetitive? Does historical knowledge consist in graphic presentation or in concepts? Is the aim of historical method analysis or synthesis?"[3] The historian's response to these questions has bearing upon his attitude toward social science techniques. Huizinga's conclusion that it is the task of the historian to both present and synthesize data is not entirely acceptable to all historians. Much depends upon the kind of synthesis.[4]

Historians, according to Arthur Schlesinger, Jr., are less likely to deny the value of empirical social research than the value of some elaborate claims made for it. One of these Schlesinger described as the belief that social science methods were "not one of several paths to social wisdom, but the central and infallible path." Extreme claims made for quantification by social scientists are opposed by historians skeptical of social science methods.[5] Nor are historians likely to adopt the more extravagant claims of behavioralism, a recent manifestation of social science theory. Behavioralist goals such as "a general theory of action; [including] *systems* . . . beginning with the smallest cell in the human body . . . and working up through ever more inclusive systems such as the human being as an organism, the human personality, small groups, broader institutions, societies, and collections of societies," of behavior in these systems as governed by "homologous processes"—[6] appear somewhat fanciful to historians conditioned to the uniqueness of historical events. The historian tends to respond to the behavioralist's vision of "common macrotheory" and "system analysis" with a shrug. In the long history of historiography such general theories have been encountered before, and the historian has developed professional skepticism toward them.

There was a time when historians were brought close to theory by the belief that knowledge of the past would enable them to understand the present and, perhaps, to glimpse the future. This theme, in recent years, has been less recurrent in historiography, as if the past were receding rapidly from the present and becoming increasingly irrelevant to it. There is a parallel trend toward ahistoricity in social science.

Nineteenth-century political science for example, was historically oriented owing to the influence of Eichorn and Savigny, which was manifest particularly in the writings of John W. Burgess. The historical approach is still employed in political science—notably by Leo Strauss[7] and Howard White[8]—but the current emphasis is less historical than "analytic, prescriptive and descriptive taxonomic."[9] Hannah Arendt is uncertain of what history can contribute to an understanding of contemporary politics.[10] Peter Odegard hailed "the queen of the sciences—the science of politics" as "no longer a hostage to history" as it seeks to explain "why we behave like human beings."[11]

Culture, described by A. L. Kroeber as a "crucial concept" in social science analysis and a "major concept" in a possible eventual unified science of human behavior, is an example of a concept which, in recent years, has been drained increasingly of its historical content. Analysis of the definitions of culture advanced by social scientists between 1930 and 1940, compared with definitions in the ten years after 1940, revealed decline in references to history.[12]

There are some social scientists who view their problems in historical perspective. Professor Dahl's study of government power structure in New Haven[13] has adopted a developmental approach. Dahl's emphasis is upon current and recent developments in New Haven and his treatment of the early years is rather thin.[14] It was C. Wright Mills who, in calling for a genetic approach to sociological problems, warned against that "dull pudding called sketching in the historical background."[15]

Historians have attacked social scientists for stuffing their concepts with the kind of historical data that "proved" their theses.[16] Gardner Lindzey, writing in 1954, found the psychoanalysts eager and willing to apply their theories to history, but the historians inclined to hold back lest they be placed in the position of supplying data for preconceptions.[17] (This situation has altered in recent years with the eager—perhaps too eager—acceptance by a number of historians of psychological and psychoanalytical concepts.[18])

Historians and social scientists are separated by the fact that historians know too little social science and social scientists know too little history. This is an inevitable consequence of the departmental system in graduate and undergraduate schools and of the demand for intensive specialization. A recent survey pointed out that "history graduate students need more undergraduate study in related disciplines than they commonly acquire."[19] Dr. David Potter has likened academic training to industrial processes which "are largely governed by their tooling. . . . The system of departmental organization and the transmission of 'discipline' from teacher to student constitutes a machinery which tends very strongly to turn out a uniform type product until retooling does ultimately take place."[20] This volume might be considered a contribution to the process of retooling.

Some historians complain of the simplistic and reductionist approaches to data by social scientists, and of their use of slick journalese to express only a limited grasp of complex problems. Conversely, some object to the tendency of social scientists to write abstractly in a jargon which the uninitiated, including historians, find difficult to grasp.[21] There seems to be a difference between the professional climates of history and the social science disciplines. The latter are geared more intimately to business and government. There may be personality differences between historians and social scientists.[22]

These are some of the factors that separate historians from social scientists. What brings them together? There has been, for some time, an organizational interest in the relationship between history and the social-science disciplines. The Social Science Research Council has a committee on the problem which has issued publications dealing directly with this subject, and others that display marginal interest.[23] The Bureau of Applied Social Research is seeking "to adjust to historiography procedures developed in other disciplines,"[24] and the Center for Advanced

Behavioral Studies has been active in this area. A purpose of the Norristown study, directed by Professor Thomas C. Cochran, was to provide
interdisciplinary training.[25]

The American Studies movement aspires to extend the study of history
in the direction of the social sciences and the humanities. On November
6, 1962, a meeting of American Studies people expressed concern
over the possibility that history might be losing ground in relationship to
other disciplines and urged a social science approach. It is true that this
meeting reflected American Studies opinion rather than that of the historical guild itself. However, in commenting upon the proceedings, Dr.
Boyd C. Shafer, then executive secretary of the American Historical
Association and managing editor of the *American Historical Review,*
noted that in 1960, the American Historical Association had appointed a
committee on research needs and this developed plans for working
models of studies based upon concepts.[26]

As long as historians are discontented with what Professor David
M. Potter has described as "the inadequacy of their traditional method
(which was, in fact, more a technique for verifying data than a system
for interpreting them)," there will be the "desire to profit by the insights
which social scientists have gained as to the nature of man as an individual or as a member of society."[27] This again raises the problem of what
is involved in a social science approach.

## Teleology and the Social Science Approach

For a long time the social science approach to history was confused
with law and teleology in history. By teleology is meant "the study of
purposes, ends, goals, final causes or ultimate values."[28] In 1908, George
Burton Adams took issue with political scientists, geographers, sociologists, social psychologists, and advocates of an economic interpretation of
history for conceiving of the social science disciplines "as of a higher
type, more truly scientific, and more nearly final in character" than history. Adams' attack upon the social sciences encompassed, as well, the
extraneous issue of historical teleology.

Long before the rise of the social sciences, historians were concerned
with teleological history: the relationship between history and theology
and history and science; with God-determined and science-determined
history. The conception of history as the will of God, advanced by
George Bancroft before the American Historical Association in 1886,
was part of a pattern in American historical writing that went back to
the Puritan historians of the seventeenth century.[29]

At the same time that Bancroft was still expressing something of the older theological view, new intellectual impulses, centered in natural science, caused Andrew D. White, among others, to seek "a philosophical synthesis of human affairs . . . in accordance with the general laws of development in animate nature."[30] On occasion, the teleologies of religion and natural science were combined so that historical explanation, in accordance with a universal governing law, embraced and attempted to reconcile science and theology. This was true of Social Darwinism, preached by John Fiske, whose God created the laws of the natural universe, society, and history.[31] As Simon E. Baldwin said in 1906: "we may call it Nature, or call it God. What we know is that it speaks by laws—invariable laws."[32]

Early proponents of a social science approach to history contributed to the confusion. Rejecting the teleologies of religion and science, they subsumed the social science approach under the teleology of presentism. The latter was the belief, as Carl Becker said in 1912, "that society can, by taking thought, modify the conditions of life, and thereby indefinitely improve the happiness and welfare of all men." Presentism found expression "in the imperative command that knowledge shall serve purpose, and learning be applied to the solution of the 'problem of human life.' And so there comes, ever more insistently, this question: What light does the past throw on the present and the future? The answer is what our age demands of the social sciences."[33]

Historical presentism had a parallel in the "social science movement" which, as it developed in the early twentieth century, had strong reformist overtones. "The idea of the identity of the philosophy of history with Social Science . . . was slow to die," and equally durable was the relationship between social science and social reform.[34]

While in America the social science approach to history was linked with presentism and social reform, in Germany the historian Wilhelm Dilthey, by the use of psychology sought to develop history's unique subject matter as unrelated to theology, natural science, and a universal system of philosophy. To history's distinctive data Dilthey urged application of descriptive and analytical psychology "with special emphasis upon the dynamic interconnections of psychological processes, upon meaningful patterns in perception, thought and behavior and upon structural units and types as the characteristic modes of mind."[35]

Excluding the element of presentism from Carl Becker's position circa 1912, his outlook is not far removed from Dilthey's. It is questionable whether Becker knew Dilthey. He was not mentioned in Becker's fascinating survey of aspects of European social thinking, although he was known to Becker's colleague at Cornell, George Lincoln Burr.[36] The European scholar who seems to have most impressed Becker was Karl Lamprecht who, like Dilthey, sought historical synthesis in psychology. To those "interested in guarding frontiers," Becker left the problem of whether Lamprecht was an historian or a sociologist. Unlike Ferrero, Becker stated, Lamprecht did not come to the study of history as a psychologist. He came as an historian who sought syntheses in psychological concepts.

"It is for psychology to say whether there is a soul of society," said Becker, following Lamprecht, "to define the concept with as much precision as possible, to determine the process by which it operates, and to formulate methods for detecting and measuring its influence." Research, Becker continued, should focus upon the nerve centers of society wherein the "real substance" of history was to be sought. Psychology was to serve the historian as scalpel.[37]

In Becker's scheme, the application of psychology and other social sciences to history was to serve social reform. Contemporary social issues provided direction for historical research, and since society was changing along with the historian's impression of it, relativistic impressions could be formulated rather than reality being perceived. "The historian and his concepts are part of the very process he would interpret; the end of that process is ever changing, and the historian will scarcely avoid changing with it . . ."[38]

This introduced yet another extraneous factor into the relationship between history and the social sciences. Relativism joined with presentism and the problem of historical teleology to confuse the debate over the role of the social sciences in historiography. The inherent value of the social sciences as analytical devices was less important than broader themes. The fires surrounding the issues of reform and relativism had to be banked, before the relationship between history and social science could come under objective scrutiny. As late as 1939, however, Read Bain clung to the identification of social science with social amelioration.[39]

In time, the parallel between social science and social reform dropped out of Becker's thinking. His *Heavenly City of the Eighteenth-Century Philosophers*, published in 1932, "scarcely touches upon one of the really central and pivotal aspects of the Enlightenment—its social science." Becker became less willing to reduce history to psychology. In a review of Harry Elmer Barnes's *The New History and the Social Studies*, Becker said: "Knowing the newer sciences of geography, anthropology, psychology, sociology, politics, economics and ethics, or some part of them, may indeed be useful. But the systematic mastery of so many disciplines is not for all." Becker concluded that what "the historian will chiefly need in order to write a good book is intelligence, experience of men and things, insight into human conduct, literary ability, and last but not least knowledge (the more the better, whether of the newer or the older sciences of mankind), knowledge of the subject matter first of all, and then of anything in heaven or earth that may have a bearing on it."[40] In addition, Becker suggested that Barnes should actually prepare a new history based on a social science approach "instead of writing more articles and books telling us how to write the new history."[41]

More recently, Karl Popper has developed elaborate safeguards against teleology entering into a social science approach to history. Popper would confine social science explanation to process rather than trend; to the answering of "how" rather than "why" questions; to nominalist rather than essentialist formulations. This reflects Popper's overall view that social law, relativism, and teleology in history jeopardize not only the freedom of historiography but prepare the way for totalitarian society.[42] This is the current expression of an older point of view that had sources in Dilthey, Edward Spranger, and Georg Simmel. It was advanced in this country as early as 1917 by George Clinton Burr.[43]

## Concepts Prior to Social Science

Divorced from the element of teleology, the social science approach to history emerged from the first decade of the twentieth century with characteristics noted by Frederick Jackson Turner:

that no satisfactory understanding of the evolution of this American people is possible without calling into cooperation many sciences and methods hitherto but little used by the American historian. Data from studies of literature and art, politics, economics, sociology, psychology, biology and physiography, all must be used. The method of the statistician as well as that of the critic of evidence is absolutely essential.[44]

In terms of method, these factors were involved in a social science approach: the view of history as a problem, the conceptualization of data, and the borrowing of concepts from related fields. None of these methods represented a radical departure from traditional historiography. Once the field advanced beyond mere chronology it inevitably became concerned with the problem of why events happened as they did. Borrowing concepts from related fields also had a long tradition in American historiography. Theology and philosophy were the great givers to early American historiography. Toward the middle of the nineteenth century, concepts were taken over from philology and from the natural sciences. John W. Burgess, representative of an historical orientation against which Frederick Jackson Turner consciously rebelled, was no less certain than

Turner of the importance of history borrowing from other fields. According to Burgess, history was to be valued less for the brilliance that fiction and rhetoric lent to it than for the "productiveness" that was the result of integration with logic, philosophy, and ethics.[45]

Since Burgess' time, the historian has borrowed less from these fields than from the social sciences. But the basic idea of borrowing and conceptualizing from the data of history remained the same. An interesting research project would be the review of early American historiography to determine the extent to which current social science concepts were anticipated by historians writing in terms of what A. L. Kroeber has described as "nontechnical generic experience and common understanding," expressive of preformulated concepts in "the language of total and dignified communication of that day, without technical terms or jargon."[46]

Part of the answer to Professor Hofstadter's query—what do historians owe to the social sciences and, I might add, what do the social sciences owe to history—centers in the concept. As I have suggested, certain concepts have been formulated in historiography, albeit rudimentarily, prior to explicit statement in social science theory. The concept of type offers an example. Independent of its development in social science theory, especially by Max Weber, type was used in American historiography as an instrument of synthesis and analysis—as "both a historical phenomenon and a literary device." In the writings of the mid-nineteenth century romantic historians, the type epitomized the "ideally representative man . . . the incarnation of the People. He represented national ideals. He acted in the name of the People, and they acted through him. The relationship was emotional, often even mystical."[47]

Henry Adams portrayed Randolph, Jefferson, Madison, and Gallatin as "types of character" that were representative of sections and populations and that also embodied contrasts. Adams conceived of history as force, and his types represented the people in whom force resided. The types, however, were abstractions from history and without force in themselves.[48] External to the historical process, Adams' types resembled Weber's "ideal type." This too was "not a description of reality" but aimed "to give unambiguous expression to such a description." Adams' description of Randolph as representative of Virginia society at a particular time approaches in some respects Weber's "conceptually pure type" from which "factors of deviation" can be traced: "the mental perfection of what in reality exists only in tendency; the distortion and extension of reality, one-sidedly exaggerated, that is a fixed point of reference in the flow of history."[49]

The comparative method also has a history prior to the rise of the social sciences. Toward the middle of the nineteenth century, the comparative method was taken from the philologists by political historians and applied to the study of political institutions. Even as the philologists used comparisons to trace word relationships and origins, so by the same technique political historians sought to trace institutional relationships and origins. The English historian Edward Augustus Freeman wrote of the comparative method as opening a new world to the historical investigator "and that not an isolated world, a world shut up within itself, but a world in which times and tongues and nations which before seemed parted poles asunder, now find each one its own place, its own relation to every other, as members of one common primaeval brotherhood."[50]

The comparative method was pressed into the service of teleology. Resemblances were discovered between the political institutions of ancient Germany, late nineteenth-century Germany, England, and the United States. The conclusion followed that these institutions were related historically and that a shared racial heritage was responsible for institutional similarity. That American institutions were Teutonic in origin was almost universally accepted by American historians during the last two decades of the nineteenth century.[51]

Long after the Teutonic hypothesis was recognized as nonsense, the comparative method continued to be enlisted in the service of teleologies. Marc Bloch warned against abuse of the comparative method in the forming of analogies "even of inventing such analogies by arbitrarily postulating some kind of necessary parallelism between various social developments"—which was precisely the error of the Teutonists. Bloch was hopeful that recognition of institutional relationships by means of the comparative method would bring mankind closer together.[52] Similarly, Henri Pirenne believed that "the comparative method alone can diminish racial, political and national prejudice among historians."[53]

In its most recent use, the comparative method has been stripped of teleological overtones. The comparative method is now employed as an analytical device which "strives toward a definition of a political system, identifies the most important structures through which a system functions, and studies differences and similarities. It purports to establish general propositions about political behavior" stated in the form of hypotheses. Compared to the encompassing role Edward Augustus Freeman assigned the comparative method a century before, its present role is limited to merely adding "to our knowledge of the conditioning factors whose presence or absence account for the validation or the rejection of our hypotheses."[54]

Among other concepts that have developed in American historiography before evolving as social science techniques, is career line analysis. This device, useful in the study of group structure and group behavior, originated, according to Sir John Neale, in Charles A. Beard's efforts in 1913 to reveal the "economic biographies" of those involved in the adoption of the Constitution of the United States.[55] Another such concept, quantification, should be viewed in the perspective of Henry Adams' interest in statistics at a time when statistical methods were not as well developed as they are today,[56] and of George Bancroft's service as first president of the American Geographical and Statistical Society.[57] Much of the method of the *Wisconsin Domesday Book*[58] is anticipatory of the current concept of microanalysis. One could go on documenting preformulations of other concepts illustrated in Sections Three and Four of this volume.

## Concepts: Implicit and Explicit

With the advance of social science, concepts familiar to historians assume deeper meaning because of their theoretical development. Moreover, older concepts go out of fashion and are succeeded by new ones. The older political historiography, for example, was synthesized around such concepts as freedom, liberty, democracy, and will, among others. These have been succeeded by newer concepts such as decision-making, voting behavior, power, cultural federalism,[59] interest group, and leadership. The earlier concepts of political history were linked frequently to teleologies: Bancroft's "liberty" was part of God's design; Von Holst's "freedom" was an integral part of the "Times Spirit"; Parkman's "democracy" was inseparable from the destiny of the Anglo-Saxon peoples. The newer concepts may be less teleological, partly because they have less overall historical context. Sometimes an older concept will alter in meaning owing to further development in theory. The concept of liberty is being subjected at present to a kind of analysis that would not be readily comprehensible to nineteenth-century historians.[60]

As in the case of political history, contemporary economic history enlarges and refines old concepts like choice, scarcity, human wants, economic change, and growth, in addition to adding others such as entrepreneur, model, case study, and administration.[61]

Social history swung, in the late nineteenth century, from the primitive syntheses of McMaster to the meta-generalizations of Henry Adams, which were centered in the concept of force.[62] In the early 1930s, social history became oriented to goals such as discovery of "the behavior patterns of society" and "the working of processes." At least, these were the aims set for it by Professor A. M. Schlesinger, Sr.[63] More recently, J. H. Hexter[64] and Roland Berthoff[65] in this country, and H. J. Perkin and Peter Laslett in England,[66] have expressed similar views of social history.

Professor Berthoff has identified social history with sociology, "a quite specific area of human affairs which, as it happens, has already been conveniently marked out for study by the sociologists; that is, the social order—the structure of society—and the fundamental interplay of the various institutions and popular groups that make it up."[67] Berthoff fixed upon mobility as a central and synthetic concept for social history. Social order was "the proper concern of social history," and mobility was "the central theme in American social history."[68]

Yet, should social history be identified as closely with sociology and mobility as Dr. Berthoff suggested? Professor J. H. Hexter has argued that the synthetic principles of social history should be derived from the data of history itself. Even these data syntheses Hexter regarded as contingent, amounting to "a tentative scaffolding easily extended or torn down and reconstructed to help us in handling our materials, as we learn more about what we can do with those materials." Hexter concluded that "the way social change in fact took place is something we may find out by *using* our framework; it is not and *ought not be* something to be found in the framework."[69]

By deriving syntheses from the data of history, Hexter hoped to avoid imposition of dogma from outside history's realm upon the historical process. Specifically, he aimed to exclude the thrust of Marxism into historiography, as did Popper. Hexter has approached English social history in terms of "overmighty subjects" constituting a "framework" for social history.

But what of the concept of mobility as applied by Berthoff to the data of American social history? Would Hexter regard this as an "overmighty subject," or is this, like Marxism, something that is imposed upon data and alien to what Hexter considers a proper framework for social history. Berthoff's virtual equation of social history with sociology is echoed by Peter Laslett who suggests that historians "learn from sociologists" and that they "become sociological historians."[70] Laslett does not define "sociological historian" and this is unfortunate because one would like to have Hexter's reaction to the term. The answer might provide a clue as to whether Berthoff's and other social science approaches are inside the framework of social history, as defined by Hexter, or external to it.

Implied in Hexter's overmighty subject is the concept of mobility. Indeed, it is difficult to contemplate the fate of the English landed class over several centuries—this is one of Hexter's overmighty subjects—without thinking in terms of mobility. Similarly, Professor R. R. Palmer views social science concepts as implicit in historical generalization; as arising "in close conjunction with the empirical material itself." According to Palmer, concepts derived from "social psychology, the sociology of the family, social stratification, the theory of power and authority, of decision-making, law, moral philosophy and much else . . . are rarely explicitly canvassed. The historian's use and awareness of questions like these . . . appear in the quality of his judgments and the connections he makes in dealing with his empirical material—that is, his story."[71]

To leave concepts undefined has been traditional practice in American historiography—a practice which has not been without criticism. Turner has been attacked for not defining the frontier concept and related terminology;[72] Beard has been criticized for the inadequacy of his definition of class and for the manner in which he related the class concept to political results.[73] However, to make concepts explicit is not easy because each concept has wide ramification.[74]

It is use of the concept, that is to say its context, that helps to fix its meaning. Concerning the concept of power, Professor Dahl has said: "We are not likely to produce—certainly not for some considerable time to come—anything like a consistent, coherent 'Theory of Power.' We are much more likely to produce a variety of theories of limited scope, each of which employs some definition of power that is useful in the context of a particular piece of research or theory but different in important respects from the definitions of other studies."[75]

With the definition of concepts allied closely to application—a point reiterated in the introductions to the concepts whose use is illustrated in Sections Three and Four of this volume—there are limits to the meaningfulness of conceptual theory. Professor David Potter has said that the integration of history and social science centers not in bringing "into conjunction bodies of knowledge which lie at separate areas on the same plane, but . . . establishing relations between bodies of knowledge which lie on different planes."[76] One plane assists in the definition of the other. That is, theory achieves focus in the historical research problem. It is content that defines a situation in which fact and theory seem to be continuous.

Some concepts, such as class, power, and role have had extensive development in theory. Others, like family culture, have been less attractive to theorists. However, the problem that confronts the historian in the use of concepts is not so much making himself master of conceptual theory but determining which aspect of theory is relevant to his research. How much of the enormous theoretical literature on motivation, for example, need the historian know to use the concept intelligently? A definition of motivation that is universally applicable would be most helpful. But there is none, no more than there is a precise and accepted definition of such concepts as group, role, public opinion and leadership. Theory may develop and elucidate concepts, sometimes at wearisome length; but the transition to application is by no means automatic. Definition is the creature of application and that is why the fact-finding of historiography is crucial to social science.[77]

## Nature of the Concept

Concepts, in their theoretical development, have considerable sprawl and transcend disciplinary boundaries. This complicates Professor Thomas C. Cochran's attempt to fix concepts within disciplinary frameworks; to identify some concepts as sociological, others as political, and still others as economic.[78] Such an attempt overlooks the fact that the disciplinary divisions between history and the social sciences, and among the social sciences themselves, are less inherent than they are consequences of "historical accident" perpetuated "partly by vested interests and natural inertia . . . partly by the suggestive power of verbal symbols and traditional labels."[79]

In the same volume in which Professor Cochran sought to relate the concept to the discipline, Mrs. Jeanette Nichols attacked "disciplinary fragmentation." She then went on to describe a social science approach as more characteristic of certain areas of historical inquiry than it was of others. Among those fields conducive to "disciplinary mergers" were community studies, studies of entrepreneurship, and studies of economic development.[80] She also included geographic area studies—the kind of urban history that Dr. Eric Lampard has recently stressed[81] and the ecological approach which James C. Malin has pursued with reference to the grasslands.[82]

It is my belief, however, that neither the discipline nor the area are as basic to a social science approach as is the concept, which transcends limits of discipline and field. A single concept can have theoretical development in more than one discipline and its reference to a particular discipline or field can be incidental. The concept of class, for example, defined psychologically will differ from its definition by a sociologist or a political scientist. From discipline to discipline, the definition of the concept will alter, sometimes slightly and sometimes a great deal. Even within the structure of one discipline there are variations in the meaning of the concept. One zealous investigator was able to discover seventeen different meanings ascribed to power, by scholars in the field of international relations.[83] The problem of defining concepts is complicated further by combination of disciplines. Thus, Neil J. Smelser has written

*The Sociology of Economic Life* and William Kornhauser, *Political Sociology.*

Once the priority of the concept to the discipline is recognized, much of the argument among educators as to the relationship between history and the disciplines and the proper way of integrating them in school curricula is beside the point. Current efforts to cope with curricula, especially in the high schools, generally result in a tug of war between teachers of history and teachers of the social sciences, and also among the teachers of the social sciences themselves, as to how much of the subject matter of history and the disciplines is to be included. The premises of this argument are false once the concept is understood as being, by its nature, interdisciplinary and having a theoretical development in more than one social science. Much more could be accomplished if the social science teachers recognized that they were teaching concepts rather than disciplines and that the concept is illustrated best by concrete historical problems.

Apart from the concept being interdisciplinary and transdisciplinary, what are its other distinguishing traits? Ranke's idea of the "inner connectedness" of facts is the core of conceptualization.[84] Croce has dealt with the role of the concept in a variety of fields.[85] Becker has examined the relationship between facts and concepts and has concluded that concepts are no less relative than the facts from which they are derived.[86]

None of this establishes the meaning of the concept. History lacks a dictionary of its terms, and social science dictionaries define the concept from the point of view of each discipline.[87] Heinrich Rickert's complaint about the natural sciences, that there is lacking a *"fixed tradition* in terminology," is even more relevant to history and the social sciences. Rickert went on to observe that definition was remiss particularly with "respect to the word 'concept' which is employed for both 'ultimate elements' of scientific propositions, i.e., those not further reducible, and for the most complicated scientific constructs, in which many elements are combined."[88]

We are perhaps justified in venturing a tentative definition of the concept as prior to and transcendent of the discipline; a nuclear factor in integration among the social sciences and history; the "'ultimate element' . . . not further reducible which enters into larger units of abstraction called generalizations. Concepts are "particles, as it were, out of which all social behavior is formed."[89] The relationship between the generalization and its conceptual components is a theme that has not been pursued with vigor in a recent volume of essays devoted to the generalization in the writing of history.[90]

Are there essential differences between natural science, social science, and historical concepts? According to Ernest Nagel, supported by Carl Hempel, "in its method of articulating its concepts and evaluating its evidence" social science is "continuous with natural science."[91] This contrasts with Rickert's opinion that the concepts of natural and social science represent two separate orders of data.[92] My own preference for the position of Hempel and Nagel over that of Rickert does not overlook difficulties in establishing the ultimate validity of either position.

The argument of Hempel and Nagel represents an extension of what was said earlier concerning the intermingling of fact and theory in conceptual definition and the transcendence of disciplinary boundaries by concepts.[93] If it is true that history and social science represent a data continuum, should we continue to think in terms of "borrowed" social science concepts which are "applied to history"? Is there difference between data concepts such as liberty, bank, slavery, and Jacksonian democracy—all of which have significant developments in theory—and social science concepts?[94]

Emphasis upon the concept as a nuclear and interdisciplinary factor in historical and social science analysis is suggestive of the behavioralist trend in social science and, particularly, in political science. This theory stresses the role of certain hard core disciplines—psychology, sociology, and anthropology—in the explanation of political behavior. Transcending these disciplines are concepts such as voting behavior, decision-making, and those associated with psychology and psychoanalysis, which are used to explain past and current political behavior. The understanding by the behavioralist of "political life as a system of behavior operating within and responding to its social environment,"[95] bears some resemblance to Professor R. R. Palmer's view of political history as expressive of overall historical trends.[96] Other historians whose work has certain parallels with political behavioralism[97] include the late L. B. Namier[98] and W. O. Aydelotte,[99] both of whom, Aydelotte with reservation, employ the concept of career-line analysis to explain past political behavior.

## Further Research

Insofar as behavioralism aspires to macrotheory, it has slight parallel in historiography. Such progress toward macrotheory as can be made in history or social science is contingent upon knowledge of the "anatomy" of the concept. As this introduction has tried to show, knowledge of the concept is uncertain and research is needed into its nature, theory, and application. Such research should center on the following problems.

1. What is a concept and how is it related to larger units of explana-

tion, such as the generalization and the theory? The concept, as Arnold Brecht and Talcott Parsons have recognized, is a building block of theory. How the concept enters into theory and, as a nuclear factor, becomes involved in explanations of causation, social action, and behavioralism is a relatively unexplored theme. Both Brecht and Parsons have stressed the need of inquiry into this problem.[100]

2. Sections Three and Four of this volume illustrate the application of a number of concepts to the data of American history. How can this list of concepts be modified and extended? What meaning did these concepts assume in their implied use in American historiography prior to the rise of the social sciences? What has been their subsequent development in social science theory? What are the relationships among these concepts in social science theory and how do they enter into causal explanations in American history?

3. What are the differences, if any, between the so-called theoretical concepts of social science and such substantive concepts as bank, slavery and Jacksonian democracy?

4. Uncertainty surrounds classification and use of concepts, as it does types and uses of generalization.[101] Concepts may be classificatory or labeling devices, essentially taxonomic and descriptive; components of causal sequences, essentially explanatory; and, finally, descriptive of method.

Concepts as classificatory devices relate intimately to perception and the categorizing of the objects perceived. These include concepts of the most elementary sort: chair, table, or radio. Concepts of the second order enter into explanations and the construction of causal sequences and theories. Finally, many of these same concepts—class is a good example—are methodological. Class is both causal and technical in relationship to historical method, but not necessarily at the same time. Again, it is the application of the concept that determines whether it is primarily causal or explanatory or methodological. However, much more work remains to be done in the evolution of a scheme of conceptual classification.

5. What of the concept as microunit?[102] The concept has been tentatively defined as a basic unit in the integration of history and social science. Certain concepts are essentially composite in that they embrace other concepts. (Frontier is a composite concept, as are family culture and reference group.) Is there a parallel, insofar as reduction of composite concepts is possible, between natural science and social science concepts? Assuming the wisdom of fragmentation, how are so-called nuclear elements to be reintegrated? While it is relatively easy to reduce composite concepts like frontier and reference group, reintegration of component elements is a more formidable task.[103]

To question the advisability of microanalysis, or the fragmentation of data and the search for more basic elements, is tantamount to heresy in an era marked by nuclear fission. Yet, is emphasis upon the microunit the path to knowledge, as its current vogue would imply? (This theme is considered further on in this volume, in the editor's introduction to the concept of status politics.)

Recently, local history (the historical counterpart of community sociology and area studies) has assumed importance not given it since the last two decades of the nineteenth century, when Herbert Baxter Adams' seminars at Johns Hopkins planned to study institutions locally, so that a broader teleological purpose might be served.[104] Even the analogy with natural science method—given free reign eighty years ago—has a contemporary echo. Doctor E. W. Phifer, a physician, introduced his account of slavery in Burke County, North Carolina, by stating the intention "to focus down upon a high-power field and examine the cellular structure of this sociopathological process, hoping that an understanding of slavery may be reached in this painstaking fashion after grosser methods have failed."[105]

To what extent is knowledge of the microunit a clue to developments in the broader field? Does the microunit have a necessary counterpart in macrostructure? There is a fuller discussion of this in the section devoted to microanalysis.

The weaknesses of conceptual theory are reflected in the organization of this volume. The emphasis of Section Two on the discipline is not meant to establish it as a conceptual macrounit. It is, instead, recognition of a situation in which, regardless of whether the present disciplinary divisions amount to historical anachronisms, they exist along with the idea of a distinctive disciplinary contribution to historiography. The selections in this section have been chosen less for their relationship to American history specifically than for their bearing upon history and a particular discipline.

A central organizational problem of this section is definition of a social science. What is a social science and what is not? Should genealogy—that toy of filiopietists and consolation of maiden ladies—be included as a social science? There is some justification for doing so in Schumpeter's advocacy of the uses of genealogy in the study of mobility[106] and in the intimate relationship between genealogy and the concept of family culture. Should archaeology be included as a social science? Here, too, it is possible to argue both ways.[107] What is a social science has not been established. Mr. Sheldon's definition of social science as "concerned with activity as related in some manner to things outside the organism itself

—activity in terms of *principles of relationship*—and its basic task is to discover such principles and to develop them into a coherent body of science,"[108] covers a great deal of ground. So do the definitions of social science in the various disciplinary dictionaries.[109]

In Section Two views are presented by representives of the disciplines on the relationships between their particular fields and history. It is the social scientist rather than the historian who speaks. Such discussions vary quantitatively and qualitatively from field to field. More seems to have been done in relating economics to history than in relating any other discipline. *The Journal of Economic History* has been particularly sensitive to this problem in connection with the relationship between history and the study of the entrepreneur, history and the case method as applied to business enterprise, developmental factors in business administration, and decision-making in business.

Geographers, anthropologists, and archaeologists have also committed themselves. Psychoanalysts are aware of the problem to the point of eagerness, but they are not too well informed about historiography. Other psychologists have not manifested much interest. Important contributions were made, mainly in the nineteenth and early twentieth centuries, to the relationships of sociology with history and political science with history. More recently, empirical sociologists and political scientists, while not necessarily averse to employing the empirical data of history, have not written, to any great extent, on the theoretical implications of what they have been doing.

The dearth of material on the relationship between political science and history and sociology and history helps to explain the choice of the selections dealing with these subjects reprinted in Section Two. Inclusion of Karl Deutsch's analysis of the sociological writings that Joseph Schumpeter published earlier in this century is an expression of editorial judgment about sociological writing of more recent vintage in this particular area.

Escape from the ahistoricity of contemporary political science leads back to the late nineteenth and early twentieth century writings of John W. Burgess and James Bryce, especially the latter's interesting presidential address before the American Political Science Association in 1909 entitled "The Relations of Political Science to History and to Practice." Today it is mainly the political philosophers who are concerned with history although Leo Strauss would insist that the values of political philosophy transcend time and place. This concern raises the question of the relationship between political science and political philosophy; whether, in fact, there is a practical science of politics apart from the ideals of political organization. The selection by Kurt Riezler is representative of that point of view which sees no strict separation between political science and political philosophy and stresses the importance of an historical approach to both.

Sections Three and Four illustrate use of specific concepts in the writing of American history. Introductions by the editor to concepts whose use is illustrated in these sections illustrate aspects of the theoretical development of concepts related to application. These supplementary introductions are necessary because of their specific character and because they would serve only to burden the overall introduction. Supplementary introductions are not necessary in Sections Two and Five, and have not been included.

In Section Three, many concepts were excluded for reasons of space and others because, thus far, they have no application in American historiography. So vital a concept as decision making, described by David Easton as "the most generalized new concept in political research," has not been applied to the data of American history. Using game theory and operational analysis is it possible to structure a conventional historical problem, such as Douglas' decision regarding the Kansas-Nebraska Bill, into a decision-making problem in social science context? Is it possible for Lincoln's decision to supply Sumter or McKinley's decision to ask for a declaration of war against Spain to be analyzed as a problem in "the logic of choice as expressed in game theories"?[110] Or, considering Schlesinger's testimony, from a high position in the Kennedy administration, on the agony of decision-making, is it wise to conceive of decision in these terms?[111]

Section Four deals with quantitative concepts and machine processes applied to historical research. Concerning this development in historiography, the conclusion of Bernard and Lotte Bailyn is much to the point: "We found that machine tabulation opened important areas for historical investigation, but we found also that it was full of unexpected problems whose solutions were exceedingly time-consuming and not always completely satisfying." At the same time, the Bailyns admit that their analysis of the Massachusetts Register of Shipping would have been impossible without machine tabulation.[112]

Quantification is by far the most controversial element in the relationship between history and the social sciences. In this introduction, I have tried to present the social science interpretation of American history as an extension of the traditional process of conceptualization. If I have not distinguished sharply between traditional historiography and the use of social science methods by historians, it is because the border between the two is vague and uncertain. Involved in this interpretation are the familiar arguments over the relationship between history and theory and between fact and interpretation. The aspect of quantification which holds that all human relationships can be expressed numerically is something else again. But no reputable historian or social scientist holds to this point of view and it is a mistake to judge quantification in terms of its most extreme manifestations.

This introduction does not regard the social science approach to American history as an aspect of "the great mutation," as Professor Carl Bridenbaugh considered it. The introduction can be considered supportive of J. G. A. Pocock's quest for "a specialized art or craft of historical criticism; one which would devote itself to investigating, not specific historical problems, but the historian's use of his concepts and the success or failure of his efforts to keep them free from confusion and ambiguity."[113]

There is, however, more to historiography than conceptualization. Beyond the concept are the problems of value in history and of all that is comprehended in narrative and descriptive historiography. Section Five deals with the limits of a social science approach. In some respects, it is the historian's response to aspects of what social scientists have said in Section Two about the integration of social science and history. The overall position of this section is that the kind of conceptual refinement called for by Pocock and stressed by this introduction represents a phase of historical inquiry rather than the sum of it. Once elimination of "confusion and ambiguity" from concepts is accomplished—no small task—the historian will still have to deal with unique events, values, and narrative description. History is more than the sum of conceptual parts; it embraces social science and also transcends it.[114]

The major task of this volume is in keeping with Professor Potter's conclusion that "the historian really cannot abstain from generalization and cannot escape theory. The choice before him is not between a 'factual' and a 'theoretical' approach but between, on the one hand, theoretical assumptions which have been recognized and, so far as possible, made rational and explicit and, on the other hand, unrecognized, half-hidden assumptions which remain unordered and chaotic."[115]

Nevertheless, it is in light of the data of history that concepts are explicated; one must never lose sight of the importance of historical data in the definition of concepts, nor of the indeterminate elements in narrative history.

# Part II

# History and the Disciplines

# Economics / *W. W. Rostow*

I DO NOT much hold with ardent debate about method. A historian's method is as individual—as private—a matter as a novelist's style. There is good reason for reserve—even reticence—on this subject, except insofar as we seek to share each other's unique professional adventures and to listen occasionally, in a mood of interest tempered with skepticism, to such general reflections as we each would draw from those adventures.

Moreover, as a practical matter, no good cause is likely to be served by further exhortation to the historian to use more theory or to the theorist to read more history. Progress in this old contentious terrain is made only by meeting a payroll; that is, by demonstrating that something interesting and worthwhile can be generated by working with historical data within a conscious and orderly theoretical framework, or by adding to the structure of theory through historical generalization. The present paper is thus justified if at all only to the extent that it sets down some tentative and interim personal reflections drawn from practical work; for I take it to be agreed that man has open to him no alternative but to use theoretical concepts in trying to make sense of empirical data, past or present; I take it to be agreed that, as Keynes said in the preface to the blue Cambridge economic handbooks, "The Theory of Economics . . . is a method rather than a doctrine, an apparatus of mind, a technique of thinking" rather than "a body of settled conclusions"; in terms of this definition I take it to be agreed that we all wish to bring to bear in our work the most relevant "technique of thinking" available and would be pleased to use the corpus of received economic theory for all it is worth. The real questions are how, if at all, the theoretical structures developed in modern social science can be used by the working historian and how, if at all, the historian should link his insights to the bodies of theory developing in the social sciences which surround him.

My own answers to these questions are directly colored by a pleasant but somewhat bizarre education. As a relatively innocent sophomore student of modern history at Yale in the autumn of 1934, I was first introduced to an important philosophical notion. This event can hardly be

W. W. Rostow, "The Interrelation of Theory and Economic History," *The Journal of Economic History*, XVII (December, 1957), 509–23. Reprinted by permission.

ranked as revolutionary, since the notion has been part of the received Western tradition for some twenty-five centuries; namely, that human perception works through arbitrary abstract concepts and therefore the reality of what we call facts is not without a certain ambiguity. If historical narration of the most responsible and professional kind was thus shot through with implicit, arbitrary theory, why not make it explicit; and, since I was then beginning to study economics, why not see what happened if the machinery of economic theory was brought to bear on modern economic history.

This line of reflection soon opened up two quite distinct areas for experiment: the application of modern economic theory to economic history; and the application of the modern social sciences to the interaction among the economic, political, social, and cultural sectors of whole societies. I was drawn to this latter area in part because I was repelled by Marx's economic determinism without, however, finding a satisfactory alternative answer to the question he posed—an omission not yet repaired in Western thought.

In one way or another I have been experimenting ever since with these two issues; that is, with the reciprocal relations of economic theory and dynamic economic data and with the effort to analyze whole societies in motion. They have given a private unity to study ranging from the study of the Great Depression after 1873 to the selection of bombing targets in World War II; from the likely consequences of Stalin's death to the pattern of the British take-off in the 1780s and 1790s; from the historical application of the National Bureau method of cyclical analysis to the formulation of some general hypotheses about economic growth.

What I have to say about the reciprocal relations of theory and history flows directly from these and similar exercises. As befits a working paper of this kind the argument will take the form of a few concrete, arbitrary, possibly useful assertions which aim partially to answer these questions from one arbitrary and personal perspective. The assertions are essentially three: first, the problem is the most useful link between theory and empirical data; second, of the nature of an economic historian's problems he is fated to be mainly a theorist of the Marshallian long period; and third, of the nature of the Marshallian long period, the economic historian can avoid only with great difficulty being something of a general dynamic theorist of whole societies. From these assertions I derive a final proposition; namely, that in our generation the most natural meeting place of theory and history is the study of comparative patterns of dynamic change in different societies, focused around the problems of economic growth.

## II

The problem approach to history can have two meanings. It can mean that history is viewed (and rewritten) in the light of contemporary problems of public policy—as, for example, Pigou reviewed the adjustment of the British economy after November 1918 during World War II, or, in the shadow of impending legislation O. M. W. Sprague examined crises under the National Banking Act. Or the problem approach can mean that history is re-examined to throw light on an unresolved intellectual problem of contemporary interest—as, for example, Schumpeter's hypothesis about entrepreneurship in a capitalist society is now being historically tested. The two meanings are generally related because most of the intellectual issues within the social sciences, no matter how antiseptic their scientific form and articulation, are at no great remove from debate over public policy.

Economic history, as a field of academic study, is peculiarly associated with the problem approach in both senses. Thumbing through the files of our journals or the listing of doctoral dissertations one can still detect the series of fighting issues, arrayed in geological layers, out of which we have evolved. There is first the argument over the universal wisdom of free trade in which the German scholars, then Cunningham and Thorold Rogers evoked historical evidence against the repeal of the tariffs.[1] The debate quickly broadened to embrace the legitimacy of state intervention into the workings of the economy, the legitimacy of social welfare legislation, the legitimacy of labor unions. Then economic history was pushed into narrower and more technical areas by the debate over monetary and trade policy (and theory) in the 1920s and by the concern of the 1930s with the cause and cure for the business cycle. At the same time longer term reflections about the historical evolution and viability of capitalism stirred by the cloudy interwar years—notably those of Schumpeter—opened up the thriving field of entrepreneurial study, bringing *inter alia* a phalanx of economic historians to debate against their naughty muckraking parents (or occasionally against their libertine youth). And it is not too much to say that a good part of the contemporary effort in economic history is directly shaped by the concern with public policy designed to accelerate growth in the underdeveloped regions of the world, which emerged in the decade after World War II.

Although it is no great trick to identify the historical foundations of our respective interests as economic historians, the conventions of academic life tend to conceal our origins in the rude forum of social and political conflict and policy formation. American graduate schools—their methods and their manners—have a peculiar power to denature problem-oriented thought (in either sense) and to tame it to departmentally organized disciplines; for a real problem, involving whole people, rarely if ever breaks down along the lines into which the study of human affairs is professionally fragmented.

In history what begins as an analytic insight of some power and subtlety often ends in the second and third generations as a flow of monographs, high in empirical content, but increasingly divorced from the living problem that opened up the new terrain. Turner's essay on the frontier, for example, has served as the intellectual basis for two further generation's study. The frontier process has now been explored by regions, by states, and occasionally by counties. Few of these empirical exegeses have, however, added anything of analytic importance to Turner's formulation. Despite a massive empirical effort, the great historical watershed of the 1890s—a part (but only a part) of whose meaning Turner sensed—remains still to be dealt with analytically. And it is often true that in general the academic approach to history tends to divest propositions of their analytic content as rapidly as possible and to convert them into respectable, institutionalized specialties within which graduate students can be safely encouraged to write doctoral dissertations, researchable within a year after their general examinations have been completed.

There is, of course, another side to the medal. However much the historian may be (consciously or unconsciously) guided by abstract conceptions, his profession requires that, for a considerable portion of his working life, he pore over data, sort out reliable from unreliable sources, and (whatever the philosophical ambiguities) assemble facts. No man can be a historian unless he has at least a touch of the antiquarian about him, unless he derives some simple-minded satisfaction from knowing how things really were in a part of the past. Whatever his loyalty to the creation of generalized knowledge, he must derive some sly pleasure at the exception to the broad historical rule. Moreover, even if one acknowledges that the economic historian's activity should in the end be related to the solution of general problems, and even if one accepts the duty of economic history to contribute to the formation of a wiser public policy, these higher order activities need not concern the economic historian all the time, nor need they concern every economic historian. There is room for students of every bent and taste within our field over the spectrum from pure theory to statistical compilation.

When all this is said, I would still assert that economic history is a less interesting field than it could be, because we do not remain sufficiently and steadily loyal to the problem approach, which in fact underlies and directs our efforts. Take a favorable case: the studies in the transfer problem and in the balance of payments under inflationary conditions, inspired by Taussig. Here clear issues were posed, capable of orderly empirical examination; the results could be brought directly into the main stream of one of the oldest and most mature branches of economic thought, foreign trade theory; and in the post-1919 world of reparations and inflation the results bore directly on major issues of public policy. It is no accident that Taussig's inspiration yielded four of the best works in economic history ever written by Americans; that is, the balance of payments studies of Williams, Viner, Graham, and White. And if it is objected that we all have not been regularly favored with doctoral students of this quality, the answer in part is that economic history has not regularly posed to its students issues as clearly relevant to major problems of theory and public policy.

Take a case closer to us, the modern study of entrepreneurial and business history. All the returns are by no means in. We cannot firmly judge the net contribution to knowledge of the enormous postwar effort in this area. Several things can, however, be said with confidence. First, there has been a considerable amount of low-order effort, where the authors have lost touch with their problems, where the analytic terms of reference derive mainly from a firm's books and where the results can be meaningfully linked to no generally useful bodies of knowledge. Second, the most interesting efforts have been those which sought actively to overcome the built-in tendency to antiquarianism and to relate conclusions about entrepreneurship to problems within two quite distinct general bodies of knowledge: either to the process of capital formation as a whole; or to the social structure and values of the society and period whose entrepreneurs were examined. Third, the final evaluation of the worth of this effort is likely to be made not in terms of the number of firms studied—or the empirical gaps "closed"—but in terms of the extent and the character of the problems it solves and the general insights it provides or fails to provide into the workings of economic and social processes that transcend but embrace the field of business history.

What I am asserting, then, is that a heightened and more conscious loyalty to the problem could strengthen in several dimensions the relations between theory and history. The problem helps prevent the historian from becoming the prisoner of a received theoretical hypothesis; for by definition he is dealing with a question unresolved in theory, policy, or both. At the same time, by giving the historian a point of departure independent of his data, the problem helps prevent him from accepting in a fit of absent-mindedness the categories and analytic concepts built into his data. And, finally, the problem—if it is well and carefully defined—provides an area of common discourse, of useful, professional communication between the historian and the theorist, where results can be compared, where the historian can learn how the theorist poses the question and the historian can teach the theorist how things really worked. And should the latter statement be regarded as a mere verbal courtesy to our profession, it should be recalled that the classical concept of the movement of the terms of trade in consequence of capital flows never recovered from even moderately systematic historical inquiry, and that Clapham's pointed questions about empty boxes led directly (on one side of the Atlantic) to the upsetting of perfect competition as the theorist's norm. Seriously undertaken—that is, focused around clearly defined problems of common interest—the relationship between theorists and historians can be a two-way street.

### III

Having held up the bright vision of theorist and historian solving problems in cheerful, productive collaboration I come to the lion in the path to its attainment: the theorist has generally been uneasy if not awkward if forced to work outside Marshallian short-period assumptions; the historian—like the human beings he writes about—cannot avoid working in a world of changing tastes and institutions, changing population, technology, and capacity.

The difficulty goes deep. The weakness of economic theory derives from its main strength; namely, that it is the most substantial body of useful thought about human behavior that is Newtonian in character. It represents the logical elaboration of a minimum number of basic assumptions that of their nature permit of maximization propositions and thus permit static equilibrium situations to be rigorously defined. Value and distribution theory are essentially an extensive development of one proposition about man, another about his environment; that is, they derive from the laws of diminishing relative marginal utility and from diminishing returns. And these propositions remain essential, even, in modern income analysis, in the elegant world of interacting multiplier and accelerator.[2]

In both major branches—value theory and income analysis—long-period factors must be handled on an extremely restricted basis if the structure of theory is to retain its shape. As Marshall perceived, the independence of demand and supply is lost in the long period and with it the powerful tool of static analysis.[3] For a theorist it is fair enough to say, as Marshall did, that a case of increasing return is "deprived of practical interest by the inapplicability of the Statical Method"; but this is a curiously chill definition of practical interest for a historian. Similarly, in modern income analysis, when efforts are made to introduce changes in population, technology, entrepreneurship, and other long-period factors, they are made on so formal and abstract a basis as to constitute very little change from the older conventional assumption that they were fixed and constant. To Keynes's famous dictum—in the long run we are all dead—the historian is committed by profession flatly to reply, Nonsense; the long run is with us, a powerful active force every day of our lives.

Indeed the long series of debates between classical theorists and their more empirical opponents reduces substantially to a difference between those committed to the primacy of short-period factors and those who held that long-period factors might be dominant over particular short periods of time: so it was between the authors of the Bullion Report and its opponents in explaining the wartime rise in prices; between free traders and the would-be protectors of infant industries, between the opponents and advocates of legal limitation on hours of work; between those who advocated large-scale government intervention to deal with unemployment and those who feared its revolutionary long-run consequences.[4] In one sense this issue is at the core of the ideological race between Indian and Chinese Communist methods for takeoff: will victory go to the system which uses force to constrain consumption and to maximize the short-period volume of investment or to that which creates a long-run setting of human incentives and institutions more conducive to spontaneous self-sustaining growth, designed to yield (through normal plow-backs and a democratically controlled national policy) levels of investment and productivity adequate substantially to outstrip population growth? (I might say parenthetically that whatever the outcome of this competitive historical exercise, the structure of modern income analysis, as applied to economic growth, biases the case unrealistically in favor of the Chinese Communist method.)

Are we to conclude, then, that because of the nature of their professions the economic theorist and the economic historian are doomed to work different sides of a street so wide that it is hardly worth shouting across? Should the theorist, equipped with powerful mechanisms for analyzing economies under short-period assumptions, be left to deal with problems where such assumptions are useful and relevant, leaving the historian and other less disciplined but less inhibited investigators to handle the murky world of long-period change? After all, that is roughly the way our textbooks are written and our courses set up; and there is often wisdom in apparently irrational arrangements that persist.

On the whole, I would take the view that such complacent (or pessimistic) conservatism is both inappropriate and unnecessary.

It is inappropriate because whether we look to the underdeveloped areas, caught up in the early stages of the process of growth, or to the industrial societies that have learned to vote themselves chronic full employment, the economic problems of the foreseeable future, both of policy and of intellectual interest, requires the systematic understanding and manipulation of long-period factors. This is self-evident in the underdeveloped areas, where new economic institutions must be created, skills and attitudes appropriate to growth imparted, capacity expanded in appropriate balance, the possibilities of external economies examined and exploited. Even the most classically short-period of economic activities —fiscal policy—must, in the underdeveloped areas, be touched with an acute awareness of changing capital—output ratios, with the need to transfer income flows from traditional to modern sectors, and with other long-period considerations which assume a peculiar urgency in the transition to self-sustaining growth. The industrialized societies are only a little less obviously enmeshed in long-period problems: radical shifts in birth rates, with important consequences for the structure of the population and the working force; radical changes in technology and in the sectoral composition of output; the deepening commitment to make an overt political distribution of resources as among security outlays, social overhead capital, and the private sector; and so on.

In short, if the work of the economist is to be relevant, he must work to an important degree outside the theoretical structures that have mainly interested him since, say, J. S. Mill.

There is, however, no need for pessimism if one looks not merely to the formal structure of theory but also to the total capabilities of economists; and if one looks to the whole long tradition of economic thought, not merely to the theorems of greatest interest in the past several generations. Economists, it is true, receive their contemporary training and develop their professional virtuosity mainly by manipulating a relatively narrow range of propositions; but it has long been in the best tradition of economists to go forth into the world as it is, full of long-period forces; to analyze whole problems; and to prescribe for them. Sometimes those analyses and prescriptions have exhibited the bias of a training disproportionately devoted to the manipulation of short-period forces in static equilibrium situations. On the whole, however, the ablest economists transcended the limits of their most refined tools: from Marshall's testimony on the Great Depression to the Paley Commission Report; from D. H. Robertson's study of industrial fluctuations to the contemporary pilgrimage of Western economists to New Delhi.

Once out in the real world, what relation does economic theory bear to the virtues of economists when they perform virtuously? Are they merely smart fellows, handy to have around when considering a tough practical problem; or does the structure of their formal thought have a useful as well as an inhibiting effect? Put another way, what are the uses of economic theory in analyzing problems where long-period factors are important, particularly problems in history?

Theory can be useful in three distinguishable ways. First, in defining the problem. Although the best-developed areas of theory take the form of short-period propositions, economics offers an orderly way of looking at and defining the totality of factors at work in an economic system. Formal economics can help map a problem, even if it has little to suggest by way of a solution. It can help pose the questions and set up empty boxes in fields as remote from the main streams of theoretical effort as population change, the generation of new technology, and the quality of entrepreneurship. Although economists may have done little in modern times to analyze long-period factors, they are well trained in listing exhaustively the factors they are assuming fixed; and this is most helpful.

Second, although the nature of long-period change may make impossible the development of a long-period economic theory—for example, a theory of economic growth—it by no means bars the development of important theoretical propositions about long-period change. For example, income analysis has been successfully adapted as a rough-and-ready but indispensable aggregative framework for the planning of economic growth;[5] the classical analysis of factor proportions in the theory of production has been adapted to throw important light on certain growth problems;[6] and, in general, the familiar technique of isolating one variable or relationship in movement, within a system otherwise held constant, while inappropriate for the general treatment of a whole interacting historical process, can be an extremely fruitful partial technique of analysis.[7] In short, there are many more uses for theory in dealing with long-period problems than have yet been developed. Neo-Marshallian pessimism on this score—a conviction that rigor had to be abandoned when the economist departs from the short-period, that there is no middle ground between geometry and description—can easily be overdone.

There is a third role for economic theory and theorists in history; that is, to contribute actively to the systematic organization of knowledge about the past in terms of analytic categories that permit cross-comparison and generalization. This role requires that economists, in addition to maintaining and developing the Newtonian sectors of their science, begin to take seriously the biological strands in their heritage embedded in the *Wealth of Nations,* evoked in our time by Mitchell's leadership and by Schumpeter's fruitful suggestions. It is only in terms of some such grand conception focused around some clear concrete problems shared between economists and historians that the full possibilities of interrelationship can be developed. And it is to some of its implications —which most obviously bear on the study of economic growth—that I now turn.

## IV

In one sense it is distinctly anticlimactic to suggest that the major common task and meeting place of economists and historians is the analysis of economic growth; and that the systematic isolation of similarities and differences among national patterns of growth is likely to be the most productive method jointly to pursue. What, after all, have we been doing in recent years? A high proportion of recent articles in the economic history journals has been designed to translate aspects of national economic history into the more universal language of economic growth; and articles on economic growth—in fact or in name—have hit the economic journals like a biblical plague. Papers prepared for special meetings—such as the 1954 conference on capital formation—indicate not merely a convergence of interest among historians, statisticians, theorists, and functional specialists but the beginning, at least, of an ability to communicate when a problem as relatively clearcut as capital formation is explored.[8] Moreover, comparative analysis of national growth experiences is increasingly a feature of the landscape from, as it were, our little family difficulty with nineteenth-century France and Germany to the study of Brazil, Japan, and India.[9] Indeed, we need look no farther than to the sessions which have preceded us, over the past several days, reflecting the progress under way in providing a statistical bone structure for comparative growth analysis, and to the subject of tomorrow's meeting.

We have found, it might appear, an optimum focus for our efforts as economic historians: economic growth permits us to use in a shapely way much of the cumulative work of our predecessors; it provides a problem area in both policy and problem senses; in the analysis of growth the Marshallian long period, in whose treatment we historians enjoy a comparative advantage, cannot be ignored; and since by definition growth takes place over long periods of time, the economist must either study history or call us in on a basis of equal partnership at least.

But I would make two final observations before agreeing that the golden age of economic history and of collaboration between theory and history has already arrived.

First, I do not believe that the efforts now going forward, from many technical perspectives, focused around economic growth are going to yield as usable body of biological theory unless a conscious effort is made to develop that theory. I do not believe that the organization, side by side on a country basis of statistical data, industry analyses, entrepreneurial studies, and monographs on technology, with experts in Harrod-Domar models benevolently looking on, is going to yield automatically, by osmosis, the corpus of organized concepts we shall require if the golden age is to come to pass. In the three quarters of a century or so since we created our graduate schools, and the professional study of history and the social sciences, based on German models mixed with native American empiricism, we have managed to create many barren acres of factually accurate volumes, bearing on interesting issues, in which the authors left the problem of intellectual synthesis to someone else. Ironically this persistent philosophical disease—apparently a disease of modesty and intellectual scruple—has left American academic life, by default, particularly vulnerable to the brilliant, casual, and not wholly responsible insights of a Veblen, a Beard, or a Schumpeter who did not fear to generalize.

The disease can be seen in the state of American history as a whole, not excluding economic history, the latter being a peculiarly shapeless affair; it can be seen in the trailing away without adequate issue of the institutionalist school; it can be seen even in one of the most successful of these native empirical exercises, the National Bureau of Economic Research, whose monographs have enormously enriched our knowledge of limited aspects of the past and present, without, however, fulfilling the grand vision of synthesis among theory, history, and statistics that inspired Mitchell and the institution he founded. Only where the special rigors and risks of synthesis were consciously and boldly faced—as in Abramovitz' study of inventory cycles—can one perceive something of what we have all been hoping for.

I would warn, then, on the basis of our common experience and our ingrained national style, against assuming that theoretical synthesis comes about without special, conscious effort.

But to what kind of synthesis should we look? What kind of framework is capable of posing researchable questions for historians that, if answered, permit empirical results to be compared and generalized and also permit easy and useful intercommunication with the theorist?

Each answer to this question will inevitably be shaped by unique interests and experiences; mine is affected in particular by the job of trying to teach coherently the story of the evolution of the world economy over the past two centuries. I have leaned, as some of you know, to a concept of historical stages held together by a bone structure of more conventional dynamic theory. In a recent article I suggested that it may be useful to regard the period, after a relatively static traditional society begins to break up, as divisible into stages of preconditions, take-off, and sustained growth. And I have been experimenting in my seminar over the past several years with some subdivisions of the sustained growth stage, notably with substages of technological maturity and of dominance by durable consumers' goods and services, both of which are, I believe, capable of reasonably precise definition and approximate historical dating for those societies which have experienced them. (It may be that after the age of durable consumers—when diminishing relative marginal utility has set in sharply for the extra car or portable TV—that babies take over as a leading sector; but it is a bit too soon to lay this down as immutable natural law.) I doubt that stages by themselves in the old German style will serve our purpose; but if we can link them to a modified corpus of conventional economic theory—and especially provide some definitions that are at least conceptually quantitative and permit reasonably accurate dating—we may generate something of intellectual power and utility.

I would certainly not be dogmatic about the forms of synthesis likely to prove most useful; but I would urge with some confidence that, as we gain an increasing knowledge of each other's work, and as the data pile up, we must allocate more time to building and applying a synthesis than we have in the past.

I come now to a final observation. It is quite simply that the explicit analysis of growth is likely to force economic history in somewhat new ways into the analysis of politics, social structure, and culture. A glance at our textbooks indicates that economic historians are not strangers to these fields. Clapham's affectionate and precise evocation of the round of British life at various historical epochs is as good as anything social history affords; and the role of the state in economic life has embedded us all in the study of politics at one time or another. It is, indeed, possible to criticize much of conventional economic history as too political and social and not sufficiently economic. My point is that the systematic treatment of growth will pose some new problems of relationship between economic and other factors and some old problems in new forms.

The comparative study of periods of preconditioning for takeoff must, for example, focus sharply in most cases around two related questions: the formation of an effective, modern central government capable of exercising fiscal power over old regionally based interests; and the emergence of a group (or usually a coalition) with vested interests in the development of an effective national government and the technical talents and motivation to operate the modern sectors of economy. From post-medieval western Europe to contemporary Egypt and India, from Canada to the Argentine, from Japan to Turkey, the political and social patterns that have accompanied the stage of preconditions have, of course, varied, and yet they have been shot through with recognizable common features. The orderly sorting out of both common features and variations, in their relations to more familiar patterns of economic change, will prove, I believe, an essential aspect of the development of a general biological theory of economic growth. (If we move in this direction we should, incidentally, be able to get much assistance from the current generation of political scientists who are increasingly committed to the study of comparative politics in non-Western societies.[10]) Nor will these extraeconomic concerns end when we have seen our respective countries into sustained growth; for social structure, politics, and culture are not the monopoly of economically underdeveloped areas. As time goes on we shall, I suspect, be studying differences in the sociological bases and political consequences of growth stages dominated by heavy as opposed to light engineering industries, not excluding the significance of the differences within Communist societies; we shall be exploring the social and cultural, as well as the economic anatomy of the durable consumers' and service stages, which we entered in the 1920's and the entrance into which of western Europe and Japan constitutes one of the most surprising and revolutionary features of the postwar decade; and we may even learn a little about the dynamic determinants of the birth rate.

In short, in accepting economic growth as a central problem we shall, from one perspective, be forced to become general theorists of whole societies; for the motives of men and the human institutions and activities which bear directly and technically on the rate of increase of output per capita are not narrowly limited. And our loyalty should be to the problem of economic growth, wherever it may take us, not to the bureaucratic confines of economic history or of economics as they are presently consecrated in our graduate schools.

All this talk may seem heady stuff, perhaps appropriate once in a while at an annual meeting, when the members of the club gather away from their desks and filing cards, but not to be taken seriously. By Monday we shall all be back grappling with our familiar piece of the elephant. And in one sense I would agree, recalling my introductory statement that method is not an appropriate subject for serious debate and certainly not for harangue.

In a larger sense, however, the vision of how we should tackle the problem of economic growth, of where economic history fits, and how it should relate to theory are important questions. They are important because, I would guess—as a matter of prediction rather than special pleading—we are in fact going to do something about them over the next generation of work. In many areas of natural and social science the cast of American intellectual life has radically shifted in the past twenty years or so. We are no longer a nation incapable of creating new abstract concepts nor are we as awkward as we once were in dealing with them. The old generalization that Americans derive their basic science and fundamental inventions, intellectual or otherwise, from abroad requires substantial modification. I do not believe that economic history will prove to be exempt from this national process of emergence into intellectual maturity.

The problem of interrelating theory and history around the problem of growth does indeed require for its solution a difficult merger—a merger of our old national gift for the energetic pursuit of fact, with a new sustained and orderly effort to build an intermediate structure of abstraction and generalization. Our still young field of economic history, full of essential knowledge and accumulated wisdom about the way different societies have handled their economic activities, already responding with vigor to the policy and intellectual challenges of the problem of economic growth, can—and I believe will—play a strategic, indeed an indispensable, role in this merger.

# Geography / *Carl O. Sauer*

## *Apologia*

THESE REMARKS are directed to the nature of historical geography and to some of its problems. By preference I should present data and conclusions from my own work in Mexico. On second thought, however, I am moved to do what has been done so often in the annual address before this body, to set forth in some manner a confession of the faith that has stood behind one's work.

It is obvious that we who call ourselves geographers do not at present understand each other very well. We have more fraternal feeling of belonging together than common intellectual ground, on which we meet freely and easily. We can hardly claim to be getting our chief intellectual stimulus from one another, to be waiting impatiently on the research of colleagues as needed for our own work. We are of various minds as to the fields in which we are engaged. As long as we are in such a condition of uncertainty about our major objectives and problems, attempts must be made from time to time to give orientation to ourselves along a common course.

## *An American Retrospect*

This will not be another design for the whole of geography, but a protest against the neglect of historical geography. In the nearly forty years of existence of this Association, there have been but two presidential addresses that have dealt with historical geography, one by Ellen Semple and one by Almon Parkins.

A peculiarity of our American geographical tradition has been its lack of interest in historical processes and sequences, even the outright rejection thereof. A second peculiarity of American geography has been the attempt to slough off to other disciplines the fields of physical geography. Hartshorne's recent methodologic study is an interesting illustration of both these attitudes. In spite of basing himself strongly upon Hettner, he does not take into account the fact that Hettner's own contributions to knowledge have been chiefly in the field of physical geography. Nor does

Carl O. Sauer, "Foreword to Historical Geography" *Annals of the Association of American Geographers*, XXXI (March, 1941), 1–24. Reprinted by permission. Presidential address delivered before the Association of American Geographers at Baton Rouge, Louisiana, December, 1940.

he follow Hettner into his main methodologic position, namely that geography, in any of its branches, must be a genetic science, that is, account for origins and processes. Hettner's students have made many of the important contributions of late years to historical geography. Hartshorne, however, directs his dialectics against historical geography, giving it tolerance only at the outer fringes of the subject. I have cited this position because it is the latest and, I think, best statement of what is in fact, if not by avowal, a pretty general viewpoint in this country.

Perhaps in future years the period from Barrows *Geography as Human Ecology* to Hartshorne's late résumé will be remembered as that of the Great Retreat. This retraction of lines began by the pulling apart of geography from geology. Geography, of course, owes its academic start in this country to the interest of geologists. Partially in order to gain administrative independence in the universities and colleges, geographers began to seek interests that geologists could not claim to share. In this process, however, American geography gradually ceased to be a part of Earth Science. Many geographers have completely renounced physical geography as a subject of research, if not entirely as one of instruction. There followed the attempt to devise a natural science of the human environment, the relationship being gradually softened from the term "control" to "influence" or "adaptation" or "adjustment" and finally to the somewhat liturgical "response." Methodical difficulties in finding such relationships led to a further restriction, to a non-genetic description of the human content of areas, sometimes called chorography, apparently in the hope that by and by such studies would somehow add up to systematic knowledge.

This thumb-nail sketch of our generation, as to its dominant motifs, is simplified but, I hope, not distorted. Throughout this time, the desire has been to limit the field in order to secure its domination. There has been the feeling that we were too few and weak to do all the things which had been done in the name of geography and that a sufficient restriction would mean better work and the freedom from trespass quarrels.

Whichever way he has turned, the American geographer has failed to locate the uncontested field in which only professionally certified geographers might be found. Sociologists have been swarming all over the precincts of human ecology. Odum and his North Carolina associates have been exploring with success the connotations of region and regionalism. Economic geography has been approached from new angles by economists like Zimmermann and McCarty. Land planning can certainly not be claimed as the geographer's discipline, nor as a discipline in any sense, since it must obviously be primarily projected from a specific theory of the state. These errant years have not led us to the desired refuge.

We shall not find our intellectual home in this sort of movement away from our heritage.

The American geography of today is essentially a native product; predominantly it is bred in the Middle West, and, in dispensing with serious consideration of cultural or historial processes it reflects strongly its background. In the Middle West, original cultural differences faded rapidly in the forging of a commercial civilization based on great natural resources. Perhaps nowhere else and at no other time has a great civilization been shaped so rapidly, so simply, and so directly out of the fat of the land and the riches of the subsoil. Apparently here, if anywhere, the formal logic of costs and returns dominated a rationalized and steadily expanding economic world. The growth of American geography came largely at a time when it seemed reasonable to conclude that under any given situation of natural environment there was one best, most economical expression of use, adjustment, or response. Was not the Corn Belt *the* logical expression of soil and climate of the prairies? Did not its capital, Chicago, show in the character and energy of its growth the manifest destiny inherent in its position at the southern extremity of Lake Michigan, toward the eastern margin of the Prairies? Did not the green sea of corn that overwhelmed the native prairie grasses represent an ideal realization of most economical use of a site, as did the bending of the strands of communication to meet at the dynamic center of Chicago? Here the growth of centers of heavy industry at points of most economic assembly of raw materials was an almost mathematical demonstration of function of ton-miles, somewhat conventionalized in terms of freight rate structures.

And so, in the simple dynamism of the Mid-West of the early Twentieth Century, the complex calculus of historical growth or loss did not seem particularly real or important. Was it, in view of such "rational" adjustment of activity and resource, being very realistic to say that any economic system was nothing but the temporarily equilibrated set of choices and customs of a particular group? In this brief moment of fulfillment and ease, it seemed that there must be a strict logic of the relationship of site and satisfaction, something approaching the validity of natural order. Do you remember: the studies that related land use to numerical sums expressing natural environment, that related intensity of production to market distance, that planned the "best" future use of land and "most" desirable distributions of population? Actors in the last scenes of a play that had begun in the early Nineteenth Century, they were largely unaware that they were part of a great historic drama. They came to think that human geography and history were really quite different subjects, not different approaches to the same problem, the problem of cultural growth and change.

For those who would not follow in this train, the last twenty years of American geography have not been heartening. Those who found their work in fields of physical geography often have felt themselves scarcely tolerated. Particularly depressing has been the tendency to question, not the competence, originality, or significance of research that has been offered to us, but the admissibility of work because it may or may not satisfy a narrow definition of geography. When a subject is ruled, not by inquisitiveness, but by definitions of its boundaries, it is likely to face extinction. This way lies the death of learning. Such has been the lingering sickness of American academic geography, that pedantry, which is logic combined with lack of curiosity, has tried to read out of the party workers who have not conformed to prevalent definitions. A healthy science is engaged in discovery, verification, comparison, and generalization. Its subject matter will be determined by its competence in discovery and organization. Only if we reach that day when we shall gather to sit far into the night, comparing our findings and discussing all their meanings shall we have recovered from the pernicious anemia of the "but-is-this-geography" state.

## A Three-Point Underpinning for Geography

The business of becoming a geographer is a job of life-long learning. We can teach a few skills such as the making of maps of various kinds, but, mostly, in the instructional period, the best we can do is to open doors for the student.

1. One of these, which is not sufficiently often thrown wide, is that of the history of Geography. There is available a fine and great intellectual heritage to us. This is not simply the study of our subject as it has shaped up at various periods of its history, though this is stimulating enough. No one is likely to regret, for instance, becoming familiar with Greek thought in geography, as a background for his own thinking. Of especial value, however, to the development of the student is the first-hand-study of the individual great and genial figures of our past. A student can hardly immerse himself for a period in following through the intellectual history of a Ritter or Humboldt without seeing wide horizons open up. This sort of thing, however, involves learning to know these men through the whole range of their work, not by way of some one else's critique. A good knowledge of the work of one or more of our major

personalities is about as important an induction into geography as I am
able to suggest.

The list of these will vary with individual opinion. I should, however,
like to bespeak a place on this shelf of classics for Eduard Hahn, as well
as for Ratzel. Ratzel is best known to us, and that mostly at second hand,
for the first volume of his *Anthropogeographie*. There is far more in the
unknown Ratzel than in the well publicized one. Hahn is our forgotten
classic. For the view-point that I wish to develop in later paragraphs, he
is perhaps the most important person in our history. At this point, I shall
simply submit the opinion that Hahn made of economic geography an historical science, that he opened up unimagined vistas of the origin and
spread of cultures, and that he penetrated farthest, as well as first, into
the concept of the economic region. From England I should like to nominate Vaughan Cornish and from this country George Marsh for full
length biographical inquiry. The half dozen names offered will in themselves provide a truly liberal geographic education, provided each is taken
as a whole, and not skimmed eclectically in terms of pre-arranged views
as to what is and is not geographic.

2. American geography cannot dissociate itself from the great fields of
physical geography. The ways that Davis, Salisbury, and Tarr so clearly
marked out must not be abandoned. A geographer, I submit, may
properly be a student of physical phenomena without concerning himself with man, but a human geographer has only limited competence
who cannot observe as well as interpret the physical data that are involved in his studies of human economies. It is a puzzling fact that American environmentalists have reduced attention to surface and soils, to
climate and weather to most inadequate terms, whereas those who see
in geography more than the relation of man to environment have continued to support by inquiry these physical observations. In addition,
climatology, ecology, and geomorphology serve important methodologic
purposes as disciplines of observation, the techniques of which may be
applied to human geography.

3. Lastly, the human geographer should be well based on the sister
discipline of anthropology. Ratzel elaborated the study of cultural dif-
fusions which has become basic to anthropology, both as a means of inspection and as theory. This is essentially a geographic method. Its influence can be traced as a dominant theme through anthropology for
the past half century, down to the current concern with the *Kulturkreis*
and "culture area" concepts. Swedish geography gains part of its strength
from the formal association with anthropology in the joint national so-

ciety. In England the influence of Fleure and Sir Cyril Fox is that of a bond between both disciplines, strongly shown by the active generation of geographers in that country.

Methodologically, anthropology is the most advanced of the social sciences, and one of its best developed methods is that of geographic distribution. Sten De Geer's essay on the nature of geography is *de facto* a statement of a method in continuous use in anthropology. The forms of material culture with which the anthropologist deals are identical with those of human geography. His observations of culture traits, his synthesis of these into culture complexes or areas are, or should be, entirely familiar to us. His use of occurrences, discontinuities, losses and origins of culture traits in terms of their localization as diagnostic of what happened to a culture is actually a mode of geographic analysis for genetic ends. It is precisely the same method of inferring cultural movement from distributions that August Meitzen introduced into continental historical geography many years ago. It is also used in plant and animal geography to trace dispersals, retreats, and differentiations.

## The Geographic Method: Terrestrial Localization

The ideal formal geographic description is the map. Anything that has unequal distribution over the earth at any given time may be expressed by the map as a pattern of units in spatial occurrence. In this sense geographic description may be applied to an unlimited number of phenomena. Thus there is a geography of every disease, of dialects and idioms, of bank failures, perhaps of genius. That such form of description is used for so many things indicates that it provides a distinctive means of inspection. The spacing of phenomena over the earth expresses the general geographic problem of distribution, which leads us to ask about the meaning of presence or absence, massing or thinning of any thing or group of things variable as to areal extension. In this most inclusive sense, the geographic method is concerned with examining the localization on the Earth of any phenomena. The Germans have called this the *Standortsproblem*—the problem of terrestrial position—and it represents the most general and most abstract expression of our task. No one has yet written this philosophy of geographic localization, but we all know that this is what gives meaning to our work, that our one general problem is in the differentiating qualities of terrestrial space. Might one hazard the statement that in its broadest sense the geographic method is concerned with terrestrial distance? We are not concerned with universalized economic man, family, society, or economy, but with the comparison of localized patterns, or areal differentiations.

## The Content of Human Geography

Human geography, then, unlike psychology and history, is a science that has nothing to do with individuals but only with human institutions, or cultures. It may be defined as the problem of the *Standort* or localization of ways of living. There are then two methods of approach, one by the study of the areal extension of individual culture traits and one by the determination of culture complexes as areas. The latter is the general objective of these continental geographers who speak of *genre de vie* and of the English who lately are using the term "personality" as applied to a land and its people. Much of this sort of inquiry lies as yet beyond any systematic means of development.

We have available, however, an immediately useful restriction to the material culture complex that is expressed in the "cultural landscape." This is the geographic version of the economy of the group, as providing itself with food, shelter, furnishings, tools, and transport. The specific geographic expressions are the fields, pastures, woods, and mines, the productive land on the one hand, and the roads and structures on the other, the homes, workshops, and storehouses, to use the most generic terms (introduced mainly by Brunhes and Cornish). Though I should not argue that these terms include all of human geography, they are the core of the things that we know how to approach systematically.

## The Historical Nature of Culture

If we are agreed that human geography is concerned with the areal differentiation of human activities we are at grips at once with the difficulties of environmentalism. Environmental response is the behavior of a given group under a given environment. Such behavior does not depend upon physical stimuli, nor on logical necessity, but on acquired habits, which are its culture. The group at any moment exercises certain options as to conduct which proceed from attitudes and skills which it has learned. An environmental response, therefore, is nothing more than a specific cultural option with regard to the habitat at a particular time. If we may redefine the old definition of man's relation to his environment as the relation of habit and habitat, it is clear that the habitat is revalued or reinterpreted with every change in habit. Habit or culture involves attitudes and preferences, which have been invented or acquired. There is no general environmental response in the wearing of straw hats. In Chicago they may belong to the summer wardrobe of the well-dressed man. In Mexico they are the distinctive badge of the *peón* in all weather, and the unmodified Indian wears no hat at all. Like every other culture trait, the straw hat depends on the acceptance by a group of an idea or mode, which may be suppressed or substituted by another habit. The design of science that Montesquieu, Herder, and Buckle forecast, failed because we know that natural law does not apply to social groups, as Eighteenth Century Rationalism or Nineteenth Century Environmentalism had thought. We have come to know that environment is a term of cultural appraisal which is itself a "value" in culture history.

We know that habitat must be referred to habit, that habit is the activated learning common to a group, and that it may be endlessly subject to change. The whole task of human geography, therefore, is nothing less than comparative study of areally localized cultures, whether or not we call the descriptive content the cultural landscape. But culture is the learned and conventionalized activity of a group that occupies an area. A culture trait or complex originates at a certain time in a particular locality. It gains acceptance, that is, is learned by a group, and is communicated outward, or diffuses until it encounters sufficient resistance, as from unsuitable physical conditions, from alternative traits, or from disparity of cultural level. These are processes involving time and not simply chronologic time, but especially those moments of culture history when the group possesses the energy of invention or the receptivity to acquire new ways.

## Human Geography as Culture-Historical Geography

The culture area, as a community with a way of living, is therefore a growth on a particular "soil" or home, an historical and geographical expression. Its mode of living, economy, or *Wirtschaft*, is its way of maximizing the satisfactions it seeks and of minimizing the efforts it expends. That is perhaps what adaptation to environment means. In terms of its knowledge at the time, the group is making proper or full use of its site. However, these wants and efforts need not be thought of in monetary or entirely in energy terms, such as units of labor performed. I daresay that every group of men has built its habitations in the spot that for them has been most suitable. Yet to us (that is, for our culture) many such sites appear queerly selected. Therefore, as preliminary caution, every culture or habit must be appraised in terms of its own learning, and also habitat must be viewed in terms of the occupying group. Both requirements place a severe tax on our ability as interpreters.

Every human landscape, every habitation, at any moment is an accumulation of practical experience and of what Pareto was pleased to call residues. The geographer cannot study houses and towns, fields and factories, as to their where and why without asking himself about their origins. He cannot treat the localization of activities without knowing the functioning of the culture, the process of living together of the group, and he cannot do this except by historical reconstruction. If the object is to define and understand human associations as areal growths, we must find out how they and their distributions (settlements) and their activities (land use) came to be what they are. Modes of living and winning a livelihood from their land involves knowing both the ways (culture traits) they discovered for themselves, and those they acquired from other groups. Such study of culture areas is historical geography. The quality of understanding sought is that of analysis of origins and processes. The all-inclusive objective is spatial differentiation of culture. Dealing with man and being genetic in its analysis, the subject is of necessity concerned with sequences in time.

Retrospect and prospect are different ends of the same sequence. Today is therefore but a point on a line, the development of which may be reconstructed from its beginning and the projection of which may be undertaken into the future. Retrospection is concern with origins, not antiquarianism, nor do I have sympathy with the timorous view that the social scientist may not venture to predict. Knowledge of human processes is attainable only if the current situation is comprehended as a moving point, one moment in an action that has beginning and end. This does not involve commitment as to the form of the line, as to whether it has cyclic qualities or shows no regularity, but it does guard against overemphasizing the importance of the current situation. The only certain advantage of studying the present scene is that it is most fully accessible to inspection. Yet out of the contemporary data in themselves it is not possible to find the means of selecting what is diagnostic of important process, and what is not. I am inclined to say that geographically the two most important events of my life-time have been the settlement of the last of the prairie lands and the coming of the Model T Ford, one an end, the other a beginning of a series of cultural processes. Yet how well did we, whose business it was to do so, pick out these critical processes at the time of their happening, or link them with the changes derived from them? And why did we miss them, if not because we were unaccustomed to think in terms of processes?

## Historical Geography Demands Regional Specialization

The reconstruction of past culture areas is a slow task of detective work, as to the collecting of evidence and weaving it together. The narrative historian may accept anything out of the past as grist at his mill, but not so the culture historian, and I wish to reckon historical geography as a part of culture history. Our obligation is to glean classified data on economy and habitation so that a valid filling of gaps of area and of time can be made. Let us take, for example, the reconstruction of Mexico at the moment of the Spanish conquest. Here we need to know as well as is possible the early Sixteenth Century distribution of population, urban centers, urban economies, types of agriculture, sources of metal and stone, provision of plant and animal materials from wild lands, and lines of communication. The early authors who drew a picture of pre-Spanish, as against Spanish conditions, such as Torquemada's famous Monarquia Indiana, unfortunately made general, rather than localized statements, or took a situation that was true of one place and applied it as though it was general. One cannot rely, therefore, on most of the accounts that were intended to be synoptic, but must turn to the minor records that give local data. The reconstruction of critical cultural landscapes of the past involves a) knowledge of the functioning of the given culture as a whole, b) a control of all the contemporary evidences, which may be of various kinds, and c) the most intimate familiarity with the terrain which the given culture occupied.

The historical geographer must therefore be a regional specialist, for he must not only know the region as it appears today; he must know its lineaments so well that he can find in it the traces of the past, and he must know its qualities so well that he can see it as it was under past situations. One might say that he needs the ability to see the land with the eyes of its former occupants, from the standpoint of their needs and capacities. This is about the most difficult task in all human geography, to evaluate site and situation, not from the standpoint of an educated American of to-day, but to place one's self in the position of a member of the cultural group and time being studied. It is, however, a rewarding experience to know that one has succeeded in penetrating a culture that is removed in time or alien in content from ours.

Such work obviously cannot be done by sample studies ranging widely, but may require a life-time given to learning one major context of nature and culture. One may thus extend his learning outward to the limits of a culture area and explore the contrasts on the other side of the boundary line. Or one may undertake excursions to areas characterized by important kindred qualities. But always there must be the base of the area for which the observer is making himself the expert. The human geographer cannot be a world tourist, moving from people to people and land to land, and knowing only casually and doubtfully related things about any of them. I doubt whether a human geographer can ever be a continental authority. Should we not get rid of the habit of writing regional textbooks about areas we don't know, with materials we copy from secondary sources that we are unable to evaluate? Nor are a thousand so-called type studies, individually quasi-photographic records of spots on the earth, likely to add up to anything significant. We recognize expertness among ourselves in physical geography, but do we have anything of the sort in human geography? If we do not, is not the difficulty that we have been concerned with nongenetic forms of presentation rather than with intensive and analytical observation? We have a full company of Ph.D.'s duly trained in human geography, teaching hundreds of classes to thousands of students, but how little are they adding to the substances of the science they represent!

Historical regional studies of the manner indicated are in the best and oldest geographic tradition. Cluverius in the Seventeenth Century did some extraordinarily acute reconstructions of ancient Germany and Italy, skillfully uniting knowledge of the classics and knowledge of the land. Humboldt's *Essay on New Spain* is still the classic of historical geography on Mexico. The stimulus of Humboldt and Ritter was pointed up through the work of Meitzen in the mid-Nineteenth Century into an adequate discipline of historical geographic study. Meitzen's approach affected all continental geography greatly. Historical regional specialization is well expressed in the great repository of the *Forschungen zur Deutschen Landesund Voltskunde*. The influence of Fleure and Miss Taylor is evident in the studies of the younger English geographers. It is about time that we in this country become actively conscious of this, the great tradition in human geography.


## The Nature of the Culture Area

In all regional studies—and we equate regional geography and historical geography—a serious problem is in the definition of the term "area." There has been so much inconclusive discussion of the term "region" or "area" that apparently no one definition suffices.

Most commonly the attempt has been to proceed from the "natural area." Yet it is hard to know what constitutes a natural area, unless it be an island, for climates, land forms, and soil provinces are likely to diverge widely. Hence the preference for the study of islands and areas that simulate insular conditions in their sharpness of outline. If we can agree on what is a natural region, we are still faced by the fact that cultural units are likely to straddle the boundary zones of physical contrasts. Boundaries rather than centers of physical regions are likely to be centers of culture areas.

We often employ the term "natural region" to designate any areal division of simple habitat qualities that may facilitate study by reducing complexity. Quite subjectively we indicate that "natural" region A is a coniferous forest land, that region B is characterized by a certain climate, that area C is a land of mountains, that region D is a province of coal and oil. Consistently we mix terms in designating natural regions, selecting a major quality of habitat for each. We are therefore likely to conceal, rather than to answer, the dilemma of area by calling it a natural unit.

In human geography we are mainly interested in the connotation of the cultural area. The unit of observation must therefore be defined as the area over which a functionally coherent way of life dominates. The most satisfactory illustration we have to date is in Eduard Hahn's basic economic regions of the world. We are, however, still far from knowing how to determine a culture area beyond saying that it has intimate interdependence of living. Nevertheless we have a simpler task than the anthropologist in his all-inclusive culture areas, though perhaps we too in the end must build up our areas by finding a sufficient accordance of common traits. A culture area of one order may be recognized by the dominance of a single economic complex. A culture area of a superior order may be determined by the interdependence of a group of areal economies. The traits of making a living for us are the dominant things to observe. Until we know much more about them we do not need to concern ourselves much with other qualities of culture.

Economic areas rarely have fixed or sharp boundaries. Historically they may experience shifts of centers, peripheries, and changes of structure. They have the quality of gaining or losing territory and often of mobility of their centers of dominance. They are fields of energy, within which changes in dynamism may show characteristic directional shifts. It is also possible to imagine a culture area which in the course of time shifts away completely from an earlier location and still maintains organic continuity.

We are interested in the origin of a cultural system as to place of birth. This we may call the theme of the culture hearth, the inquiry into the localization of culture origins. The classical formulation of the problem still is that of the places of origin of agricultural systems. Next, we are concerned with the energy that a growing culture shows as to manner and rate by which it occupies land, including the nature of the extending frontiers. Next, we are interested in the manner of stabilization of one culture area against another. Finally there are the problems of decline or collapse and of succeeding cultures. The homologues of all these questions are well known from plant ecology in the study of plant societies.

## The Relevance of All Human Time

A dissent may now be registered against that view of geography which considers geography as exclusively or peculiarly concerned with present economies or cultures. One of the fundamental questions in all social study is how to account for the rise and loss of institutions and civilizations. The birth or fall of a great state or culture will always claim the attention of students of civilization. One is no less a geographer if he is engaged in knowing the rise and passing of a culture that lies back at the dawn of history, than if he is concerned with the growth of industrial Chicago. There may be as important things to learn about human geography in the archeology of the Mississippi Delta as in its fields of sugar cane. Any topic in the social sciences is important, not by reason of its date, but by the light it throws on the nature of culture origins and changes. This assertion is basic to the present position. If it is correct, all human time is involved in the field, and any predilection to consider the present as intrinsically most important misses the expressed aim of human geography as a genetic science.

Here and there geographers have concerned themselves with prehistoric settlements and culture. In Louisiana, Kniffen and Ford are providing a good illustration of what may be learned by archeo-geographic study. There is, indeed, a specifically geographic dimension to archeology, that of the complete distribution of the traces of a culture, so as to reconstruct its population pattern and its economic geography. Even in our best known area, that of Pueblo culture, this approach has been carried out only once, by Colton and his associates at the Flagstaff Museum, an approach which I should like to recommend as a model of workmanship. English geography is today most largely indebted to Fleure, who has concerned himself primarily with the farthest corridors of time. In this field there is hardly a question of continuity with the pesent culture area, but an approach to the general problem of the specialization and viability of culture. To some of us, at least, the geography of Basketmaker Man or of the Bell-Beaker Folk is as revealing and absorbing as anything in the present-day world. Those of us who are completely historical geographers are concerned with human origins and changes throughout all human time. Let no one think, therefore, that we are in any sense off-side from the main theme if we work at the farthest reaches of time, the childhood of our race. We think rather, that the human geographer who works on the short-time dimension of the contemporary scene is held by a peculiar obsession.

## The Archive in Historical Geography

The first step in reconstruction of past stages of a culture area is mastery of its written documents. The discovery of contemporaneous maps is the first thing hoped for, but rarely realized. We have, however, scarcely exploited the documentary possibilities in the United States of old land surveys as to notations on the character of vegetation and of "improvements" early in the period of settlement. There is a fair amount of valuable material in the Land Office plats and in the older records of land grants that gives glimpses of the pioneer landscape. Factual data, precisely localized, of enumerations of persons and goods, of land titles, assessments, production, lie neglected in various archives to await exploitation. There is an embarrassment of such riches in the old Spanish records through successive stages of its history. Familiarity with such records, for New Spain, from parish records up to summary reports that were sent to the king in Spain. There are diaries and accounts of early explorations, the *visitas* made by inspecting officials who reported in detail on condition of the country, letters of missionaries, the so-called geographic relations ordered for all Spanish America at several times in the Sixteenth and Eighteenth Centuries, records of payments of taxes and tributes, data on mines, salines, and roads. Perhaps no other part of the New World has as elaborate a documentation on settlements, production, and the economic life of every part as do the Spanish colonies, but it is certainly an exceptional area for which documentary sources will not yield a large part of the data needed to reconstruct the geographic pattern of living however, takes much time and search.

## Field Work in Historical Geography

Let no one consider that historical geography can be content with what is found in archive and library. It calls, in addition, for exacting field work. One of the first steps is the ability to read the documents in the field. Take into the field, for instance, an account of an area written long ago and compare the places and their activities with the present, seeing where the habitations were and the lines of communication ran, where the forests and the fields stood, gradually getting a picture of the former cultural landscape concealed behind the present one. Thus one becomes aware of nature and direction of changes that have taken place. Questions begin to take shape as to what has happened to local site values. It is real discovery thus to take old documents into the field and relocate forgotten places, to see where the wilderness has repossessed scenes of active life, to note what internal migrations of inhabitants and of their productive bases have occurred. There comes a time in such study when the picture begins to fit together, and one comes to that high moment when the past is clear, and the contrasts to the present are understood. This, I submit, is genetic human geography.

This may be hard and often difficult work physically, because there are trails that must be followed if one is to get the answers. One must go over the ground of former activity, no matter what its present accessibility or facilities, or lack thereof, for the comfort and health of the student. It isn't a question of learning to know a country by modern means of transport. There is an exaction of intimacy with out-of-the-way places which historical geography often imposes that modern economic geography does not do. This sort of inquiry demands that the field worker go where the evidence requires him to go. Hence the importance of those brief and precious younger years when he is physically able to follow his clues through the chosen area. There are all too few field seasons that will be available to him. At best, when the days of insufficient physical strength come upon him, he will wish that he had been in the field longer and more often, to secure the observations which he needs.

The first objectives of historical field work are to value the habitat in terms of former habit, and to re-locate the former pattern of activity as indicated in the documentary record. To these are added more specific tasks of field observation. The chief of these may be called the location of the cultural relicts and fossils.

Cultural relicts are surviving institutions that record formerly dominant, but now old-fashioned conditions. Familiar illustrations are 1) types of structures, 2) village plans, and 3) field patterns surviving from former days. Every student of European geography knows how house type, settlement plan, field systems have yielded knowledge of the spread of different kinds of settlement forms, often where the written record is silent. Scofield, Kniffen, and Schott have well shown how such data may be used in this part of the world. 4) Some of us have been engaged in tracing the distributions of varieties of native crop plants as indicators of cultural spreads. Similar work remains to be done with Old World plant and animal domesticates to trace routes of cultural dissemination. 5) Little has been done in the study of old forms of plant and animal husbandry. We lack inquiries into native hoe husbandry or *milpa* agriculture, into old traits of backwoods farming still surviving among us, into the old basic elements of our stock ranching, into the historic functions of the barn, into types of different immigrant agricultures. Such type studies, recording in faithful detail the year-round calendar of old-fashioned agricultural communities, would be of great value, especially if they can be carried out so as to show what modifications have come in with time. 6) Similarly, there still are archaic forms of placer, pit, and even lode mining, and 7) old ways of felling lumber and getting out logs. All such archaisms which help to understand former processes operative in localizing settlement and use of resource should be recorded while they still exist. 8) The old-fashioned water and animal-powered mills, and 9) the survival of old transport methods by water and land are other instances in point.

It may be objected that such inquiries are technologic and not geographic. However, every organized activity is a skill that has been learned or developed by a group or community, without the understanding of which the geographer cannot interpret the productive occupation of his area. If there is no such thing as direct adaptation in human geography, there can be no human geography that does not concern itself with communities as associations of skills. The field geographer then must observe the expression of such skills in the cultural objectives of a group occupying a given site, and the historical geographer must recover the survivals of old skills that explain older dominant forms of land occupation.

Moreover, the geographer as field worker has the opportunity to make observations on how material cultures worked that other social scientists are not likely to secure, because mostly they are not accustomed to field observations. Not even anthropologists give attention to the husbandry of their primitive peoples in the sense that should be expected from a geographer observing the same people. It is difficult to imagine a human geography that fails in expertness in the processes of getting a livelihood. If pack trails are geographic phenomena, the pack trains that use them are also; the feeding places that the animals use involve a knowledge of the fodder or forage on which they depend; then why not also the utility of the animal as to distance it can cover and load it carries, and the whole process of loading and driving? Let protest fall where it may, I should not be interested in historical geography or in human geography except as helping to understand the differentiation of cultures, and I cannot get understanding of this sort except by learning the ways and devices men have used for making a living out of their homelands.

Fossil forms may be considered those that are no longer functioning, but which still exist, either obsolete or as ruins. The field study of ruins is important, for it alone will show in some cases localization of production or settlement that has failed. There are the the direct ruins of habitation that give clues as to why people once lived there, from hearth places to early man to abandoned farmsteads. There are the curious and persistent alterations of soil where once an earthen floor stood, or the refuse of settlement was dumped, often expressed by characteristically different vegetation. There are the escaped plants of the household that may propagate themselves indefinitely in its vicinity, the lilac bushes of the northeast, the Cherokee rose of the southeast, pomegranate and quince in Spanish American lands. There are ruins of land use in abandoned fields that may be identified from prehistoric surfaces of tillage to the boom agriculture of two decades ago. The evidence may be in particular plant succession, in changes in the soil, even in ancient furrows. In the Old South, it is well known that the exact limits of old fields may be determined by stands of old field pine, and the time of abandonment approximated by the age of the trees.

There are lesser lines of historical field work, the place names that have connotations of olden days, folk customs and dialectic turns that reveal traditions of times when tradition was a living part of the economy, the memories that still belong to the oldest members of the group. The oddments one thus turns up by living with a people are not inconsiderable, and occasionally there is a lead that is most revealing. I may refer to the illumination that Eduard Hahn got out of considering unconsidered trifles about food and drink habits in Europe, especially vestigial mannerisms that no one had considered before him.

In all historical geography, field work demands most acute observation, constant alertness to clues, flexibility in hypothesis. It is not comfortably routinized as may be the mapping of current land utilization.

There is urgency in such field observations. Year by year the sweeping hands of modern industry and commerce brush away more and more of what is old. Traditions die with the old people; documents are destroyed; weather, storm, and flood erase the physical remnants; science and market standardization destroy old crops. Now is a better time than will ever be again for both students and the records, before the years invalidate both.

Thus a science of comparative regional geography may grow up among us, which will shun the following fallacies: 1) That geography has substance as a science of contemporaneous activity, 2) that historical geography can be done by adding the missing environmental notations to the works of historians, 3) that historical geography is only library work,

4) that a geographer can acquire expertness by knowing a little about a lot of unrelated localities, 5) that descriptive studies, done without regard to process, *i.e.*, genesis and function, can add up to a science, either physical or social, 6) that geography can deal with relations of culture and site without understanding the nature of cultural process, growth, and differentiation, and 7) that there is some way of compensating lack of curiosity and dearth of knowledge by devices of style and organization.

## Some Themes in Historical Geography

A number of general problems are suggested as the sort of comparative knowledge we should be advancing:

1) Certain processes of physical geography, involving secular change, may effect man. a) The most important is the problem of climatic changes or cycles. The other sciences of man expect us to get the answers as to facts, nature, and direction of climatic alteration in human time. The areally specialized geographer has the opportunity to shed light on the controversial subject. In all the dry margins of the world, this topic is of major concern; especially, have their boundaries expanded since the beginning of agriculture? Methods and results in using non-instrumental climatologic data might well constitute a recurrent symposium at meetings of this association. b) In part connected with this question is the problem of natural changes in vegetation since glaciation; few problems should be more interesting to the geographers of the interior United States than that of the prairies, or of the humid grasslands in general. c) Another topic is that of natural changes of coast line and drainage in the period of human occupation. In these meetings, Russell has pointed out drainage changes of the Mississippi, some since the crossing of De Soto. Marsh's classic *Man and Nature* outlines a lot of such problems.

2) Man as an agent of physical geography. a) At present, we incline to deny all effects of settlement and clearing on climate, in contrast to the attitude of an older generation, as shown by the literature of early American forestry. Indeed the science of forestry began largely on the hypothesis that trees diminished climatic extremes. We are hardly sufficiently well informed to dismiss this topic entirely. There is, in terms of our present information, no assurance that in certain climatic tension zones, as of dryness, radical alteration of the ground cover cannot affect critical relations of temperature, humidity, and moisture availability at and near the ground level. I should not be entirely sure that man has not extended the limits of deserts by altering the climatic condition of the

lowest film of the atmosphere, which may be called the intra-vegetational climate.

b) Geographers have given strangely little attention to man as a geo-morphologic agent. Soil erosion is the popular name for the processes of surface removal that man has released or accelerated. The incidence of soil erosion may be a major force in historical geography. Did soil losses sap the Mediterranean civilizations? Were the Virginians great colonizers because they were notable soil wasters? Geographical field work should embrace thorough search for full, original soil profiles and not the characteristic diminution or truncation of soil profiles in fields and pastures. Thus only can an understanding of the age, nature, and extent of wastage of productive surfaces be secured, and thereby the changing fortunes of human agricultural regions registered. The strange blind spot of geography to this, one of its most basic problems, may illustrate the result of dodging historical approach.

The aggradation of waste on surfaces below the slopes of cultural denudation is, of course, the complementary part of the situation. Gullies mostly are advanced, acute symptoms of soil erosion, including some that have served in text-books as illustrations of normal youthful valleys. How often have geographers distinguished between natural ravines and man-induced gullies, or found the latter of interest as to their incidence and life history? Surely nothing could be more geographic than critical studies of the wastage of surface and soil as expressions of abusive land occupation. On the one hand, are the pathologic physical processes; on the other, the cultural causes are to be studied. Next come the effects of continued wastage on survival of population and economy, with increasing tendency to degenerative alteration or replacement. Finally, there is the question of recovery or rehabilitation.

The theme was clearly indicated as a formal problem of geography three-quarters of a century ago by Marsh. Geographers have long given lecture courses on Conservation of Natural Resources and considered the evils of soil erosion. But what have they done as investigators in the field, which may lie actually at the doorsteps of their classrooms? Is the answer that soil students should study sheet wastage, geomorphologists gullies, agricultural economists failing agriculture, rural sociologists failing populations, and the geographer prepare lectures on what others investigate?

c) All results of destructive exploitation must be regarded as involving changes in habitat. The presence of civilized man has often meant changes in the regimen of streams and of underground charge of water. Irrigated areas show here and there the creeping paralysis of alkali accumulation, or of water logging. The forms of dissipation of natural capital are many, their causes are cultural, their results are slow crises in the affected areas, their connotation is therefore a matter of human geography.

d) A special problem of the alteration of the land by man is the relation of culture to plant and animal ecology. There are questions in this field that may be reserved to the plant or animal specialist. The historical geographer, however, must take this topic into account in so far as he is able to deal with it and, since he works deliberately with historical data, he may encounter evidence that the ecologist will not. In Mexico, for instance, it is apparent that civilized and primitive men have modified the vegetation rather differently. Primitive husbandry was far less bound to low slopes than is modern agriculture. Given certain conditions of climate and soil, hoe agriculture was in effect a long-term forest-crop rotation, usually on hill and mountain slopes. Under such a system, in effect as it has been for thousands of years, the whole of the present wild flora may represent locally a type of old field succession. The coming of the white man introduced in certain areas a new form of pressure on the native vegetation through heavy grazing. About the mines in particular, he effected complete deforestation through the needs of wood and charcoal in the mines, as well as by persistent pasturing of stock about the mining camps. The old mining camps may now be surrounded by open country for many leagues where once there were forests and brushlands.

These are some of the themes which the historical geographer may well develop. In the process he will probably learn somewhat about the suppression of certain vegetation elements because of their superior utility to man, or because of their low ability to reproduce, or because of their sensitivity to an ecologic balance. There is nothing particularly esoteric about learning the important constituents of a native flora, or even in observing their habits of reproduction and growth. One observer may go farther with this theme than another, but its appropriateness can hardly be questioned, and the cultural approach may sharpen observation of the biotic association as to time elements. In climatic tension zones in particular, it is possible that human interference may operate characteristically to displace widely former vegetation boundaries. Any area with a long grazing history, in particular, should be examined in this respect as to the replacement of palatable browse and grass by unpalatable, probably woody or bitter, succulent elements. The role of fire, especially in the hands of primitive man, needs much additional observation, undertaken with the knowledge that long-continued burning may have opposite effects on vegetation from those that result from a short series of burnings.

3) Sites of Settlement. The location of a settlement records the particular preferences as to habitat that concerned the founders. Since a settlement once established is not readily transferred, subsequent culture

changes alter the site value, and confront the people of the town with the alternative of moving or of meeting developing handicaps. Perhaps if we were locating our cities *de novo,* we should place relatively few of them in the exact site which they occupy. Consider the towns that grew up on once navigated streams, on portages, and under other site selections that have lost their significance, but which have imposed repeated problems on later generations as transport, supply, and municipal services have changed. If California were being settled today, San Francisco would probably be a middle class suburb of a major city across the bay. Yet in the 1840's, San Francisco was the most eligible site for a port at which ocean and river transport met. It has successfully maintained a large number of urban functions in which it acquired initial dominance, and has on the whole overcome the handicaps of a transverse peninsular position as these have developed.

At the time a settlement is made, it may generally be regarded as combining in its site the best means of satisfying the wants of the founding group. It is necessary, therefore, to regard the site in terms of the original wants. In one case, protection may be important, in another indifferent. Food and domestic water needs and transport advantages vary with the founding culture. Site classifications in terms of cultural attitudes at the time of origin of settlement have been rarely made, yet here is the basic chapter in a science of urban geography. Next would come site revaluations and accommodations under change of culture—the site viewed under successive stages.

4) Settlement Patterns. We do not have a great deal of comparative historical knowledge about a) dispersal or agglomeration of habitation, or b) about the spacing and size groups of settlement clusters that develop under particular cultures, or c) of the functional specialization as between town and town within one culture area, or d) of functional differentiation within a major town. These are some of the most obvious problems of localization of habit that need inquiry in historical and regional terms.

5) House Types. Americans have given little attention to the unit of dwelling, which commonly approximates the social unit, or the family in its inclusive connotation, rather than in the marital sense. Is the dwelling unit single or multi-family, does it provide for its dependents and retainers, does it include arrangements for the domestic animals? Does it include formal provisions for the storage of primary necessities or for the exercise of crafts or trades? What is the functional generalization of the house plan? The study of house types basically is the study of the smallest economic unit, as that of village or town is that of an economic community. In both cases description seeks the meaning of structure in rela-

tion to institutionalized process, as an expression of the culture area. Houses are historical geographic records. They may date from a former historical stage, or they may, as current buildings, still preserve conventional qualities which once were functionally important (fireplaces, porches, shutters, on American houses).

6) Land occupance studies with regard to the historic structure of the culture area. At any given time, in theory, there is a momentary equilibrium of habitat evaluation and habit wants. Environmental advantage or disadvantage should then always be relative to the moment or stage of the particular culture, and land use an accommodation of the wants and energies of a community, that changes as these change. To change, however, usually involves considerable lag, partly because of the difficulty of revising property lines. The rationalization of land use meets the opposition of the design of fields and other land holdings of earlier days. At any one time land rights and land use are likely to conserve a good deal of the past. Settlement patterns, house types, field systems and land ownership are the best recognized observational items used in reconstructing changes and continuities.

7) What of cultural climaxes? Is there in human societies something like an ecologic climax, a realization of all the possibilities inherent in that group and its site? What of limits of population growth, of production attained, of accumulation of wealth, even of increment of ideas beyond which the matured culture does not go? We may be skeptical of the more extreme hypothesis of the cyclic character of all culture, but we too are concerned with the recurrence of cultural peaks, or stabilization, and of the cultural decline. The rise and fall of cultures or civilizations which has interested most historically minded students of man cannot fail to engage the historial geographer. A part of the answer is found in the relation of the capacity of the culture and the quality of the habitat. The case is relatively simple if destructive exploitation can be shown to have become serious. There is also the knotty problem of overpopulation (which may be very much a reality in the culture historical sense though a heresy to the theoretical social scientist), involving diminishing opportunity and sharing for the individual. There may arise loss of productive energy by mal-distribution of population as between country and town, between primary producers and these who are carried as leisure class. There may be shift of comparative advantage to another people and area. A melancholy and stimulating subject is this scrutiny of the limits of culture.

8) Cultural receptivity. A new crop, craft, or technique is introduced to a culture area. Does it spread, or diffuse vigorously, or does its acceptance meet resistance? What are the conditions that make a certain group

eager to accept innovations, whereas another chooses to continue in its old ways? This is a general problem of social science, which in part can be examined by geographic studies.

The geographer, in the first place, is best able to determine the existence of physical barriers or corridors. Perhaps a crop does not spread because it encounters an unsuited climate, perhaps because the soil which it requires is not of a type that a particular husbandry has learned to utilize.

In the second place, the geographer presumably has kept track of the presence or absence of material culture traits. He should know whether a crop or a skill is confronted by a satisfactory alternate already established in the area. The dissemination of wheat growing in Latin America has been considerably affected by the food habits of the people with regard to other starch and proteid crops. It is only true in terms of world markets and hence strictly commercial production, that the yield of a given plot as to wheat or corn will determine which will be grown. I should like to add that even the current world market price is only an expression of cultural demand from a dominant purchasing group, not a real expression of utility of the several grains.

It may well be remembered that Ratzel founded the study of the diffusion of culture traits, presented in the nearly forgotten second volume of his *Anthropogeographie,* and that Eduard Hahn came upon the great problem of his life work by asking himself why some people engaged in dairying and others would have nothing to do with milk or its products.

9) The distribution of energy within a culture area. Here we may refer to the great thesis of Vaughan Cornish, that of the cultural "march." His view is that every growing civilization has had an active frontier—an actual frontier on which the energies of the people become massed, where power, wealth, invention are most highly developed. This has some resemblance to Turner's thesis of the frontier, though it does not involve the necessity of continued expansion. It begins with expansion, but the energies of a culture once localized on such a border may continue to manifest themselves by leadership in many ways long after expansion has ceased. Historically, therefore, it is not in the central parts of a cultural area that the great developments take place, but on what was both the most exposed and the most alluring border. There is a lot to be done in considering the dynamic fields (*Kräftezentren*) within the whole expanse of a given culture area. There is much to be said for the thesis of Cornish. The dynamic front of Mexico, *e.g.*, has been the northern border throughout its history. Archeology, in both New and Old World, shows many illustrations of the flowering of culture at the far margins of a culture complex.

10) Cultural stages and succession. Turner made an unfortunate error when he accepted an ancient, deductive view that human progress advances through an identical series of stages, which he thought he could recognize as general stages of the American frontier. We know that there is no general cultural succession, but that each culture must be traced separately through its history of acquisitions and losses. Hahn's great work, in particular, warns against deductive approaches to cultural stages, as, for example, by his denial that pastoral nomads derived from hunters rather than from older agricultural backgrounds. Since cultural change by no means follows a general or predictable course, it is necessary to trace back each culture through its historical steps.

It is not generally appreciated that the first and dominant pattern of Spanish settlement of the New World was the formal organization of all Spaniards into town corporations and their permanent domiciling in such a *villa* or *real*. From this basic knowledge that the Spanish pioneer was a member of a town corporation at all times, the nature of Spanish penetration and economic organization acquires a very different form from that of the settlements by the other colonial powers of the New World. On our American frontier, there was no such uniformity as in Spanish America, but a considerable number of first stages from North to South, dependent on colonizing group, nor was there one type of frontier in the Westward movement. Might it not be time for geographers to try to characterize the culture complexes and successions in the settlement of the United States? It should provide substance for some of the future meetings of our Association.

11) The contest for area between cultures. Certain cultures have been notably aggressive; some such can be determined for almost any part of the human past. The contest for dominance in the meeting zones of cultures, the manner in which a balance is established and a boundary takes form, express cultural energy and adaptability. Ratzel had in mind this sort of study in his political geography, which stressed the historical struggle for space. Whether by conquest, absorption, trade, or superior adaptability, all cultures have been marked by ground-gaining or ground-losing qualities.

## Conclusion

The human geographer has the obligation to make cultural processes the base of his thinking and observation. His curiosity is directed to the circumstances under which groups of cultures have diverged from, or been assimilated to, others. Most of the history of man has been a matter of differentiation of culture and of reconvergences. We cannot even point to a uniform human culture back in the dawn of Paleolithic time. The Tower of Babel is almost as old as man. In the literal meaning there are very few "common-sense" qualities about living habits, that is, things that are most sensibly done in one way only, general logical or psychological necessities. I fear that the more theoretical social sciences—like economics—are likely to lose sight sight of this truth. In this country, we are likely to forget this because we happen to be part of a tremendously vigorous and widespread culture, so confident of itself that it is inclined to regard other ways as ignorance or stupidity. The terrific impact of the modern Western world, however, does not repeal the old truth that the history of man has been markedly pluralistic, and that there are no general laws of society, but only cultural assents. We deal not with Culture, but with cultures, except in so far as we delude ourselves into thinking the world made over in our own image. In this great inquiry into cultural experiences, behaviors, and drives, the geographer should have a significant role. He alone has been seriously interested in what has been called the filling of the spaces of the earth with the works of man, or the cultural landscape. His primarily is the difficult job of discovering the meaning of terrestrial distributions. The anthropologists and he are the principal social scientists who have developed field observation as a skill.

The themes suggested for our work may represent a task beyond our immediate individual or joint ability, but they are at least a design of the quality of knowledge we seek. Our several efforts may build consciously toward the understanding of the differentiation of the earth at the hands of man. We shall not get far if we limit ourselves in any way as to human times in our studies. Either we must admit the whole span of man's existence or abandon the expectation of major results from human geography. Either we must produce, or warm over what others have prepared. I see no alternative. From all the earth in all the time of human existence, we build a retrospective science, that out of this experience acquires an ability to look ahead.

# Sociology / *Karl W. Deutsch*

THE COLLECTION of major essays by the late Joseph Schumpeter in the field of sociology, recently published in Germany,[1] represents a significant contribution to the social sciences and in particular to economic history. Scholars may find in it a tempting invitation to reappraise Schumpeter's contribution to a wide range of sociological and historical analysis. For Schumpeter insisted that in the search for insight into the social process two things would remain inseparable and indispensable: an analytical interest in precise and meaningful concepts, and a broad empirical familiarity with historical facts.

The essays in this volume testify that their author maintained the standards he had set himself. Schumpeter's was a truly first-rate mind, bold, incisive, and creative. These essays show him accurate in his scholarship and realistic in many of his judgments; impatient with the shallow and the trite; and profoundly convinced of the task of social science to cut through the level of accident and gossip to the basic processes of change that underlie the broad trends of past history and present politics and economics. Together, they testify to Schumpeter's intellectual stature, his broad learning, and his analytic power. There have been few men in any generation who had so much to say on so many vital topics, and who said it with such clarity and freshness.

Each of these essays is alive today. The first, a discussion of "The Crisis of the Tax-Collecting State," illuminates an important area of economic and social history at the turn from the Middle Ages to the Renaissance. It offers an intriguing development of R. Goldscheid's concept of a "sociology of finance"; and it says some important things about the continuing vitality and the unexhausted capabilities of the "tax-collecting state" and its corollary, the private enterprise system, under twentieth-century conditions and in the aftermath of total war.

Schumpeter's theory of imperialism, which is given in the second of these essays, already has become a minor classic. It offers a potentially fruitful alternative both to optimistic complacency and to Marxian near-determinism. Both this and the following essay in the German collection have been available for some time in a somewhat simplified English translation[2] which gives a fair picture of their main points but loses many of the subtleties and ironies of Schumpeter's characteristic German style.

Karl W. Deutsch, "Joseph Schumpeter as an Analyst of Sociology and Economic History," *Journal of Economic History*, XVI (March, 1956), 41–56. Reprinted by permission.

Many scholars may appreciate, therefore, the opportunity to read Schumpeter's view of imperialism in its original version, and they may find that his theory deserves careful re-examination in the light of present-day conditions.

The discussion of the nature of social classes, presented in the third essay, is again a major contribution to its subject. It, too, opens perspectives for new research and analysis which thus far have been by no means exhausted. (Professors Bendix and Lipset deserve thanks for having included two brief portions of this essay in their useful reader on "Class, Status, and Power,"[3] but these fragments are, of course, in no way a substitute for the original text of almost 70 pages.)

The last essay in the book, written in 1927, on "The Social Characteristics of Germany," contains some fascinating methodological suggestions, particularly on the sociological aspects of "national spirit" or "national character." In its conclusions, however, the essay demonstrates strikingly the pitfalls of partial insights and the dangers of short-range judgments based on broad statistical abstractions—even by such an outstanding analyst as Schumpeter himself.

Each essay offers important substantive propositions, as well as significant contributions to analytic method; and each should amply repay closer study and discussion.

## I

The first and earliest of these essays, "The Crisis of the Tax-Collecting State" (*"Die Krise des Steuerstaates"*), was addressed to a contemporary occasion, but reveals much of the basic thinking of its author. Written in the summer of 1918 and published in the journal *Zeitfragen aus dem Gebiete der Soziologie* before the end of the year, it dealt with the impending defeat of the Central Powers, the approaching collapse of Austrian public finance, and the socialist assertion that these events signified the collapse not merely of the political institutions of Austria, but rather of the entire institution of the "tax-collecting state," that is, the state depending for its income in the main upon taxes collected from private enterprises, such as businesses or farms. Such a state, some socialists claimed, was inherently incapable of coping with the vast financial burdens implicit in the sheer magnitude of war damage and needed economic reconstruction.

Dealing with this contemporary problem, Schumpeter found it necessary to discuss three broader questions: *a*) the relation of any tax-collecting state to the rest of the national economy; *b*) the recovery of any na-

tional economy severely depleted by war; and *c*) the possible existence
of historical limits to the private enterprise system.

As a method for the study of the first of these questions, Schumpeter
advocated a development of what R. Goldscheid had called the "sociology
of finance" through careful analysis of budgets and other data of public
expenditure, and through estimates of the financial needs implicit in the
commitments of the state in each particular epoch. He cited with approval
Goldscheid's characterization of the budget as "the skeleton of the state,
stripped of deceptive ideologies"; and he urged sociologists and historians
to pay far more attention to the analysis of budgetary data. In studying
history, financial data may be looked upon both as causes and as symptoms. The financial demands of governments have shaped, and sometimes
misshaped, the economies on which they were imposed; and the changing
patterns of taxation and expenditure often have been telltale indicators
of impending political events (pp. 4–6). "Anyone skilled in reading
budgets," Schumpeter added in a note, "who also followed attentively
the events on the international money market, could forsee the coming of
the [First] World War since at least ten years" (p. 58, note 3).
Schumpeter's points here may well be debatable in detail, but his plea
for a wider and more adequate use of budgetary data in historical and
sociological analysis still remains to be heeded.

Applying this approach, Schumpeter saw the rise of the modern state
as a consequence of the preceding breakdown of the feudal state, or of
its subtype, the "fief-granting state" (*Lehensstaat*), under a growing
burden of inevitable financial overcommitment. Princes had to induce
recalcitrant nobles to reside at court through offering them higher incomes and levels of luxury; and they had to meet the ever growing costs
of mercenary armies. Here, in Schumpeter's characteristic reasoning, an
economic process met with a change in social psychology. While princes
had to ask ever greater services and levies of their vassals, the latter underwent a process of "patrimonialization of personality," that is, they came
to think of themselves increasingly as private agents, and of the lands
and services they controlled as private property, and thus became ever
more reluctant to give to the prince what he demanded. Thus the house
of Hapsburg managed to extract about the year 1500 from its Austrian
hereditary territories the annual sum of about 300,000 florins Rhenish.
This was more than the aggregate revenues of the electoral principalities
of Cologne, Mainz, Trier, and Brandenburg, which then amounted to
110,000, 80,000, 60,000 and 40,000 Rh. fls. respectively, but it would have
paid for only 6,000 foot soldiers, or 2,500 "equipped horse," for one year
—a figure dwarfed by the large man-power needs of the Turkish wars
(pp. 6–14, with notes on pp. 59–66).

Everywhere princes had to turn to the estates of their territories—their nobles and cities—in order to ask their consent and support for the introduction and collection of taxes. By the second half of the sixteenth century, a tax organization based on the estates was flourishing in many regions, and the estates endeavored to keep in their own hands the control of the tax administration and state machinery which they had created. "Everywhere in Europe," says Schumpeter, "the princes took up the struggle for the conquest of this state. In England it ended on the scaffold of Charles I. Everywhere else it ended with the victory of the prince . . . [who] took from the estates the sharp weapon 'state' which they had started to create" (p. 16). Thus arose the bureaucratic state of the prince, and it was this state which eventually became everywhere on the European continent the bureaucratic state of modern democracy.

The tax-collecting state that emerged in the course of these developments is the indispensable counterpart of the private enterprise economy. Where all persons work for public ends, no state need be distinguished from the rest of the social order; the two would be identical. No primitive horde, no thoroughgoing feudal organization, and no people organized in a socialist economy thus can have a state in Schumpeter's sense of the word (pp. 18–19). "Only where the life of each individual carries its center of gravity within itself, where its meaning rests within the individual and his personal circle, where the fulfillment of personality is an end in itself—only there can the state exist as a real phenomenon" (pp. 19–20). Once economic life becomes private, however, no activity finds economic support unless it coincides with the purpose of some individual. The modern state, therefore, begins by making financial demands which are its "first utterance of life," even though later the state machinery with its personnel and associated interests tends to outgrow the realm of mere finance, and to reduce the latter to its instrument (p. 21).

This basic situation sets inescapable limits to the taxing power of the state. Taxation, Schumpeter insisted, must not destroy the incentive function of incomes on which the functioning of the economy depends. Wherever this incentive is impaired, tax yields are likely to decline as tax rates rise. This is true of both indirect and direct taxes, but according to Schumpeter—who here refines an otherwise familiar argument—it is particularly true of entrepreneurial profit, which is the specific reward of innovation, and which constitutes the most vital form of income in a free enterprise economy. This profit can be overtaxed only at the peril of stagnation. Entrepreneurial profit is distinct in principle, however, from interest on capital, premiums of risk, and wages of management, with all of which it often is confused, but all of which can bear higher burdens with less danger. Land rent and monopoly profits can safely bear still higher taxes, but even these "ideal" tax objects are limited in extent and yield. Finally, state-owned enterprises, so long as they do not make up the bulk of the economy, and thus are still conducted within the framework of a free enterprise economy, must copy the data and methods of private firms. They cannot yield, therefore, substantially more income to the state than could be obtained by their taxation under private ownership (pp. 24–31).

Schumpeter's discussion of these problems is classically lucid and incisive. He gave here in 1918 a clear-cut distinction between the superficially similar but essentially different institutions of "state capitalism" and "socialism," which were to cause so much confused discussion in subsequent decades.

The financial limits upon the capabilities of a tax-collecting state are thus much more severe than they would be upon those of a socialist economy. The establishment of the latter, however, would require according to Schumpeter a basic change in the popular will and the political power behind it, leading to a growing allocation of economic means to purposes for which they had never been accumulated by private individuals. This would require ultimately a change in the basic culture and in the prevailing motivations for economic activity. Such basic changes could occur and drive the tax-collecting state beyond the edge of breakdown; but neither World War I nor any other war seemed likely to Schumpeter to produce any such result.

Particular states might go bankrupt, but the institution of the tax-collecting state, Schumpeter felt certain, would survive the crisis of 1918, just as it had survived and grown during the wars and bankruptcies of four preceding centuries. Even the Bolshevik revolution, Schumpeter wrote in 1918, was certain to lead to the early restoration of the tax-collecting state (p. 34)—an odd prediction that was to find some partial confirmation in Russia's temporary "New Economic Policy" a few years later.

Even in Austria, the weakest and most impoverished of states, the tax-collecting state could liquidate the monetary costs of the war and start the recovery of the production of goods and services by private enterprise. War expenditures in real terms, Schumpeter argued, would be substantially completed by the end of hostilities: as after a fire, the physical damage would be done. All that remained would be the monetary claims left by the Austrian war policy of paying for goods and services not out of higher current taxes—as had been done to some extent in England—but almost entirely out of war loans and inflated currency. These inflated paper claims, however, could now be retired by means of a property levy, and recovery resumed on a sounder basis (pp. 35–51).

The essential task of any postwar recovery, as Schumpeter saw it, was "recapitalization"—the rebuilding of the depleted and undermaintained stock of capital goods and productive equipment. This required essentially a reduction of deferment of current consumption claims in favor of capital goods which would produce consumer goods and services only in the more distant future, and thus an essentially unpopular task of saving imposed upon the community as a whole (p. 53). Much of Schumpeter's argument here has remained pertinent to some of our present-day discussions not only about postwar recovery but about the economic development of underdeveloped countries, and about the comparative economic growth patterns of different countries in the Free World and behind the Iron Curtain. While an able contemporary writer such as Samuel Lubell clearly distinguishes only between "guns" and "butter,"[4] i.e., between military and civilian end products, neither of which contribute directly to subsequent production, Schumpeter in 1918 stressed the critical importance of capital goods, which cannot be classed as either "guns" or "butter," but which can be used to produce at a later time goods and services of either kind.

In the Austria of 1918 this task of saving and recovery could best be carried out, in Schumpeter's view, by private enterprise. Such enterprise had always succeeded in accumulating and concentrating resources for investment; and it alone had the experience and skill—and, Schumpeter hinted, perhaps the "desperate energy"—needed to obtain necessary raw materials in a competitive world market (pp. 54–56).

In the conclusion of his essay, Schumpeter epitomized a highly personal philosophy of social evolution. The "concrete historical moment" of 1918, he felt certain, was the moment of the business class. "They can do," he said, "exactly what must be done now." He reminded his socialist opponents that "it is the first precondition for a socialist commonwealth that capitalism has done its work, and that there exists an economy saturated with capital and rationally organized by the brains of entrepreneurs, so that we can face wih equanimity the slowing down of merely economic development, which is inevitable under socialism—for socialism means the liberation of life from economics, a turning away from economic problems. This hour has not yet come. The war has deferred it. . . . But that hour will come. Gradually private enterprise will lose its social meaning through economic development, and through the widening of the orbit of social sympathies concomitant with it. . . . Society is growing beyond private enterprise and the tax-collecting state, not because of the war, but in spite of it" (pp. 57–58).

In this characteristic extrapolation of economic and psychological

trends from past history, Schumpeter sketched a challenge to both Marxism and laissez-faire, and indicated something of the approach that
would lead him many years later to write his book on *Capitalism, Socialism and Democracy*. His conclusions of 1918 may find few champions
today. Socialism now seems less gradual and less inevitable, even in the
economically most advanced countries. None of these countries, including the United States, seems today much more "capital-saturated" than
it did forty years ago. In many underdeveloped countries, on the other
hand, private businessmen as a group have failed to display that accumu-
lative thrift, innovating enterprise, and "desperate energy," which Schumpeter ascribed to them. In his view of economic institutions, Schumpeter
remained on the whole most closely within the orbit of the ideas of
1918. It was in his perceptions of the functional requirements of economic
growth that he went furthest beyond them. Particularly in this latter
field, some of the questions and methods of his essay still offer to students of economic development a major opportunity for fruitful discussion
and research.


## II

The second essay in the book, "On the Sociology of Imperialisms"
(pp. 72–146) presents the thesis that imperialism is essentially the conduct of a military policy of aggression, expansion, and conquest, under
the domestic political pressure of a military establishment—a "war
machine"—which may owe its origin to quite different conditions such
as a war of defense or independence, but which, once established,
dominates the further political and military decisions of the state. Thus
Schumpeter found an imperialistic period in the history of ancient Egypt,
during which "war became the normal condition alone conducive to the
well-being of the organs of the body social as they now existed. . . .
*Created by a war for which it had been needed, the war machine then
created the wars which it needed for its own purposes.*"[5] These purposes
are essentially the same at any time and in any country: once warlike
and aggressive behavior patterns have been learned by the population,
or by important groups, and once they have become emobdied in important social institutions, then these patterns will be likely to be acted
out in warfare, in large part regardless of the merits or profits of any
particular war.

Hence imperialism often has an element of apparent irrationality.
"A sweeping will to conquest, with no definable limit, advancing into
manifestly untenable positions—this is typical imperialism" (p. 89). Its

warfare serves no rational goal except that of its own self-perpetuation as a going practice, and the perpetuation of the influence of its practitioners over the body politic.

A conspicious example cited for such imperialism was that of the ancient Assyrians. Their ceaseless attacks on neighboring peoples were caused, according to Schumpeter, not by economic or religious motives, but by a habit of large-scale hunting and warfare that had become for them both play and obsession. "Foreign peoples were the favorite game, and towards them the hunter's zeal took on the shape of ferocious national hatred and religious fanaticism. War and conquest were not means but ends: this was imperialism stark and naked. . . ." A warlike religion is thus a symptom of imperialism—such as that of the Assyrians, or that of Islam which Schumpeter discusses in this context (pp. 96–102)— rather than a cause. If it is popular then it must have expressed pre-existing needs and habits of the populations that accepted its first preachings. It is this social acceptability of their message that has distinguished the "true" from the "false" prophets in history (pp. 99–100).

Later and more elaborate societies may overlay and rationalize the crude pattern of imperialistic behavior based on acquired habits and established institutions of warfare, but "in its innermost essence the imperialism e.g. of Louis XIV corresponds thoroughly to that" of the Assyrians. As to the imperialism of Rome, which had its most expansive period between the Punic Wars and the time of Augustus—the Caesars, according to Schumpeter in the main rather strove to preserve the empire that had already been conquered—we are offered this characterization:

The policy of this epoch . . . is the classic example of that untruthfulness in matters of foreign policy—and, of course, in domestic affairs as well—which characterizes not only the avowed motives of action, but most likely already those motives of which the actor himself is aware. It is that policy which professes to strive for peace and unerringly produces war, the policy of perpetual preparation for war, the policy of ever-busy interventionism. No corner of the known earth, where there is not some interest injured or attacked. If these are not interest of one's own, then they are those of an ally. If one has no ally, then some alliance has to be contrived. And if for once no interest whatever can be construed, then it is simply a matter of national honor. Always one is merely contending for some legal or moral right, always one is being attacked by some evil-minded neighbor, always fighting for mere breathing space. The world abounds with enemies, and it is a matter of plain duty to take measures in advance against their undoubtedly aggressive plans. . . . Even less than in the other cases discussed thus far can these wars of conquest here be understood in terms of concrete causes or objectives. . . . And since we are dealing here neither with a people of warriors, nor in the early stages, with a military despotism or an aristocracy of specifically military orientation, we can seek for

understanding only through the scrutiny of domestic political and social interests—through the question: who stands to gain?

Certainly not the Italian peasant. . . . The situation of the Roman proletariat was different. It did indeed get much of the booty. . . . But the existence of
this proletariat, in such large numbers, as well as its political importance, in
turn were themselves the consequence of a social process that also explains the
policy of conquests. . . . The latefundian landowners were, of course, deeply
interested in war. . . . The alternative to war was agrarian reform. . . . [This]
landed aristocracy . . . rested solely on control of the state machine Its only
protection lay in national glory, in the continual play with the necessities of
foreign policy which remained a mystery to the citizen.

This does not mean that the individual Senator was always thinking of this
entire situation when he pleaded for a new war. Men are never clearly aware
of such matters. A precarious social structure of this kind merely creates a
general disposition to look out for causes for war—causes often held to be
adequate in good faith—and to turn to questions of foreign policy whenever
the discussion of social problems at home becomes too insistent . . . (pp.
108–9).

The irony in Schumpeter's language was obvious and deliberate, but
it should not obscure the analytic power of his underlying concept. For
imperialistic behavior was a function of domestic political and social
structure rather than of rational objectives in foreign policy; then even
explicit verbal professions of imperialistic policies would not be followed
up by deeds to their ultimate consequences, if there was no domestic
structure of powerful social classes irrevocably committed to warfare behind them. Thus, Schumpeter explicitly denied that English "imperialism" in the nineteenth and early twentieth centuries was either genuine
or deep-rooted. On the contrary, after examination he dismissed the
policies of the age of Cecil Rhodes and Joseph Chamberlain as a matter
mainly of political histrionics and mere verbiage (pp. 75–87). This view
is, of course, in striking contrast to that of Lenin who saw in England
the country of imperialism *par excellence*, and who asserted that no
ruling class would give up its positions without the extreme violence
of revolution or civil war. But it is Schumpeter's view of the superficial
and shallowly rooted nature of British "imperialism" which seems to
have found partial confirmation on an impressive scale by the nonviolent
retreat of British imperial power from India and Pakistan, as well as from
Iran and Egypt, during the thirty-five years since Schumpeter's essay was
originally published.

A few years before his death, Schumpeter was heard to disclaim all
contemporary relevance for his own theory: it had ceased to be applicable, he said, with the end of the nineteenth century or at the latest
with World War I. His listeners on that occasion were not certain whether
he spoke jokingly or in earnest. A critical look at the theory today might

suggest that it has several distinct implications which should be evaluated separately.

First there is the suggestion that imperialism is simply atavism, a leftover of feudal and aristocratic patterns of behavior in an essentially peaceful business age. This view, which suggests that commerce somehow necessarily implies a more peaceful way of life, already was explicitly rejected by Alexander Hamilton in *The Federalist* papers; it does not look much more convincing now. And the warlike and expansive policies of modern totalitarian dictatorships show few if any major ties to the aristocratic militaristic past of their countries; rather they appear to draw their main strength, political and military, from the new strata and regions to whom they brought gains in power, and from the new industrial and technological agglomerations which they have constructed or enlarged. A theory of militarism or imperialism as a kind of simple atavism would indeed be almost irrelevant for understanding the potentialities for imperialistic behavior in our time.

However, Schumpeter's theory has a second and more dynamic implication. Whenever new social changes create a set of military habits, politically influential groups or classes, and important social institutions, all dependent for their continued functioning on sustained policies of warfare or at least war preparations, there the pattern of seemingly irrational imperialistic behavior—in the crude Assyrian or the more polished Roman manner—may come to be acted out all over again. Where such warlike habits and institutions have once again been developed, rational discussion of aims of foreign policy might once again come to be beside the point. Only domestic changes in the distribution of economic and political influence and in popular habits of political behavior might then be able to deflect or reverse the drift to unending armed conflicts. Since institutions of authoritarian government, vast state bureaucracies, military establishments, and military elites all may be formed under a wide variety of ideological pretexts and at any level of technology now known, eternal vigilance in domestic affairs may well be the price of a nonwarlike policy, just as it long has been the price of freedom.

Just as habits can be learned, however, so they can be unlearned. As groups and institutions can harden into one pattern of interests and actions, so they can sometimes change toward the acceptance of new roles, new social functions, and new patterns of organization. This is a third, and perhaps most interesting implication of Schumpeter's approach: where Marx stressed the aspects in which he believed the social classes in different countries to be essentially alike, there Schumpeter stressed the way in which investigation shows each social class in one country to be significantly different even from its closest opposite numbers abroad. Some classes learn easily, others hard or not at all. Some classes or elite groups readily take over new social functions, where others resist all change. Some elites prosper by adaptation, other perish in defiance. Schumpeter's own remarks on the broadly recruited, adaptable, and relatively nonmilitaristic nobility of England, in contrast to their more rigid brethren on the continent, have been borne out by a flow of substantial, though presumably as yet incomplete, research results, such as those by David Landes on the contrast between French and American entrepreneurs. On this level, Schumpeter's analysis of imperialism leads to the analysis of changes in elite habits and elite structures, and of changes in the relationship of elites to the whole of the society in which they operate and on whose passive compliance or active consent they depend for their power.

## III

There is thus an intellectual as well as a personal connection between Schumpeter's theory of imperialism and his theory of social classes: the first leads to the second, and the second is already in part implied in the first. Schumpeter's third essay in the volume, entitled "Social Classes in an Ethnically Homogeneous Environment," was conceived by him in 1910. He worked long on it between 1910 and 1916, never ceased entirely to work on it until its elaboration in 1926 and its first publication in 1927. He referred at that time to "the unevenness and incompleteness of this presentation, which contrast so regrettably with its long period of maturation and the amount of labor spent on it" (p. 147).

It, too, is available in the same useful but somewhat simplified English translation by Norden and Sweezy, which was commented on above.

According to Schumpeter, social classes are an objectively given fact in social and economic life, which should not be confused with such mere classifactory constructs of economic theorists as the owners of "land," or "labor," or "capital." The confusion of these two concepts of class in much of the everyday usage of such terms as "landowners" is, to Schumpeter, a sure sign of inadequate analysis. The most clear-cut symptom of a genuine common class relationship among a number of families is the existence of the *connubium*, that is, the right of intermarriage, among them, not merely in legal terms but as a matter of social expectations and actual probabilities. In addition to this criterion of the connubium, also mentioned by Max Weber, there is the matter of mutual understanding and communication among members of the

same class: "They are in closer association with one another; they understand each other better; they act more readily in concert; they close
ranks and maintain barriers against the outside; they look into the same
segment of the world, with the same eyes, from the same viewpoint,
in the same direction. . . . Social intercourse within the class differs as
much from intercourse across class lines as swimming with the stream
differs from swimming against it." The criterion of intermarriage and,
we may add, of ease of social contact (Schumpeter does not use the word
"communication" although he clearly refers to the process) "is particularly
useful for our purposes, since we limit our study to the class phenomenon
in a nationally or ethnically homogeneous environment, and thus eliminate the most important of all other obstacles to intermarriage" (pp.
152–53).

Beyond the mere identification of classes by symptoms of this kind,
Schumpeter's analysis undertakes to answer four kinds of questions: 1)
the nature of class, including its function in the life of the society; 2) the
problem of class cohesion; 3) the formation of classes and the causes of
the existence, according to Schumpeter, of social stratification in all
times and societies; 4) the specific causes and conditions giving rise to
a concrete class structure at a particular time and place.

Essentially, a class, for Schumpeter, is a gradually changing collection of
families. "The family, not the physical person, is the true individual of
class theory" (p. 158. Schumpeter makes it clear that he is referring to
extended family, including more distant relatives). Each of these
families enters the class, or remains and rises within it, because of the
special aptitude of its members to fulfill the particular social functions
exercised by this class at that time. Fluidity, or permeability of class
boundaries, and mobility within each class, are thus of the essence of
the class phenomenon. Within each class, families rise or decline, enter
or drop out, and it is the process which maintains each class as the
collection of those families most fitted by property, experience, connections—but mainly by aptitude and inclination—to play the roles and
fulfill the social function from which their class derives its continued
existence.

In the long run, a princely house will keep its rank only if it continues
to excel in the arts of politics and warfare; and a family of bourgeois
entrepreneurs will only retain its social position if they continue to be
thrifty and, above all, enterprising. If a family of capitalists would actually
behave as the Marxian theory suggests, that is, if they would merely copy
the average behavior of their class, making average investments in the
expectation of average profits to be realized by the exercise of an average
effort at routine management, they would be, according to Schumpeter,

on a slow but certain road to ruin. Like the average of such business families over a period of several generations, they would eventually be crowded out of business by fitter and more energetic newcomers to their class (p. 164).

Classes thus tend to outlast the changing sets of families that make up their membership at each particular time. Instances of the unchanged class status of a family for several hundred years are deceptively conspicuous, for they are extremely rare exceptions (pp. 170–71). Thus, while physical persons are born into particular classes, families are not, and they are characteristically able to cross class barriers by the same processes by which they rise or decline in status within each class.

Not only the composition of each class, but also its relative position *vis-à-vis* other classes is continually changing. The class structure of every society is liable to change as the functions change which are required or rewarded by its environment, its technology, economy, or culture, or its political or military situation. The position of each class within the whole structure then depends on two groups of variables: the importance that is ascribed by the rest of the society to the particular social function which this class has been performing; and the extent to which the class continues to fulfill this function successfully. As its previous functions become obsolete, a class will either decline in power, or else acquire new functions to replace—perhaps even with a gain in power and prestige—the functions lost or in decline. The prestige of the new social function, like that of the function previously exercised, will depend not only on its intrinsic "technical" importance, but also on the degree of more general social leadership that has come to be associated with it.

Classes are thus essentially groups of families distinguished by differences in aptitude for the exercise of those social functions which have become "socially necessary" in a particular environment, and which are performed by this particular class, as well as by their aptitude for social leadership in the particular form and manner which has become associated with each of these functions. Class structure is then the ranking of these families according to their collective social prestige. It thus corresponds ultimately to these differences of aptitude, or rather to the congealing of all such acquired prestige, into entrenched traditions and positions which then present the appearance of an established class, secured above and beyond the individual. At bottom, however, all such entrenched social positions, and the aggregate social stratification resulting from them, have been created or conquered through the behavior of individuals and families based on differences in their aptitudes (pp. 204–5). Among these aptitudes, a kind of "central factor" involving will power, energy, and leadership talent for a wide range of different functions, is perhaps particularly important (pp. 207–10).

Schumpeter's theory is thus clearly dependent on our psychological knowledge of aptitudes and motivations. He was well aware that the psychology and anthropology of his time were not adequate to carry this burden, but he felt that the main points of his analysis would be secure even if future research should show that heredity had no significant part in the transmission of aptitudes: established position, persistent prestige, and acquired training would still account for social stratification in terms of his theory (p. 209). Lacking adequate psychological data, Schumpeter fell back on common sense, his extensive knowledge of affairs, and on a brilliant analysis of the changing roles and membership of two social classes in Germany: the aristocracy from the early Middle Ages to the present, and the bourgeoisie, particularly the class of active businessmen, since the time of the Napoleonic wars.[6]

These matters cannot be possibly be discussed here, where we can try at most to get an impression of some of the bare bones of Schumpeter's theoretical argument. Suffice it to say that his historical insight and penetration are outstanding: most of us can learn more even from disagreeing with Schumpeter's judgments than from agreeing with those of a hundred mediocrities.

Many of Schumpeter's ideas are today a part of this or that particular research approach. We have a promising development of entrepreneurial history; a sociologist like the late Robert Lamb used the family approach in his study of the American political and business elite; theories of economic development are now more popular than they have been for a long time. What some of these specialized activities lack, Schumpeter had in abundance. His sociological essays have a unity of viewpoint, a power of abstraction, a breadth of learning, and a certain elegance of thought that might well inspire and benefit much of our work today. For while parts of his program have thus been accepted, his essays still deserve careful reading as a continuing challenge to contemporary historians, sociologists, as well as research workers and theorists in political and social science.

## IV

If it was suggested above that even Schumpeter's occasional wrongheadedness could be extremely stimulating and fruitful, it should be made explicit that the present volume contains evidence that Schumpeter sometimes could be very wrong indeed.

The last essay in the collection, "The Social Structure of Germany," was first published in 1929. It begins with a fascinating discussion of the relation of "national character" to social structure, and of the effects of changes in the latter on the former. Rarely has more been said on the theory of this topic more felicitously on a single page than by Schumpeter here (p. 215); it is to be hoped that anthropologists and others writing on national character will take a careful look at Schumpeter's suggestions.

From this theoretical start, the essay proceeds to analyze the social structure of Germany on the basis of the census of 1925. The result, viewed from the vantage point of hindsight, is a striking mixture of insights and misjudgments. Schumpeter saw everywhere social peace and moderation: "The sphere of agriculture . . . is socially at peace" (p. 219).

As for the German land-owning nobility, its economic difficulties were judged to be pressing, but its members had long failed to develop their political abilities, since their traditional roles had long been those of the soldier or the official, and had not included any significant leadership in their own right.

Industrial concentration was found to progress, but only very slowly. In addition, the continuing partial staffing of German industry with rural elements mitigates social problems and "stabilizes the social ship. It helps . . . to conserve existing states of mind, and it explains why . . . genuinely revolutionary ideas are held only by a negligible minority of our population" (p. 220). The artisans had found a niche in the industrial economy where they could make a living, "and they have learned accordingly to abandon the sharply anti-capitalistic attitude which they had held until the early 20th century" (p. 221). However, small merchants have a less favorable outlook; some proletarianization and radicalization of the lower middle classes must be expected in many instances (pp. 221–22), and the influence of the solid middle class with its traditional ethics of industry and thrift was bound to decline still further (pp. 221–22).

The large industrialists lacked number, prestige, and tradition to supply leadership in politics, or in cultural and social life. Since the aristocracy, as pointed out earlier, could not supply it either, "the Germany of today (1929) has no leading class at all" (p. 222).

In contrast to this failure of the upper classes, German industrial labor formed the largest and best organized group, as well as the strongest element of political power in the country. "Despite all antagonisms of culture, religion, and interest, labor is unmistakably coalescing into a single homogeneous mass. . . . And . . . the political weight of this mass must steadily increase. . . . What our workers are actually striving for

. . . is a lower middle class existence, secured through social policy. . . . [Thus social] pacification will come in the end" (p. 223).

The greatest increase among all the classes between 1882 and 1925 was that of the "intellectuals"—a term in which Schumpeter included clerical and white-collar personnel. He expected the gradual merging of all such groups into a single class whose social and political attitudes appeared as yet uncertain, but whose outlook was in any case likely to be that of the salaried expert: "The world of the future will be undoubtedly a world of bureaucracy" (p. 225).

As his conclusion from this survey, Schumpeter stressed "the very great and possibly still increasing stability of our social conditions. For any foreseeable time there must be an overwhelming majority opposed to any extreme course in whatever direction. . . . In no sense, in no field, in no direction are there any strong swings, surges or catastrophies likely to occur. A terribly frustrating situation for any white-hot will to shape political and social life—but it is certainly not a bad framework for other kinds of achievement" (p. 225).

One year later, North German peasants began to toss bombs into tax collectors' offices; unemployed youths started to flock to Nazi and Communist meetings; the National Socialists became the strongest party in the German Reichstag, and their brown-shirted storm troopers began parading everywhere. Three years after that, Hitler was dictator of Germany.

Had Schumpeter been unaware of what was happening almost before his eyes? Or had he asserted his faith in the statistical evidence for future moderation as a gesture to reassure himself or others? Had he never asked what an economic depression might do to the social structure he had described? Or, while somehow overlooking what was in front of him, had he yet uncovered some long-range forces that might render the German electorate for a long time resistant to Communist extremism, and potentially partial to the kind of moderate economic and political course that was to prove again successful under the Adenauer government after World War II?

We cannot ask him any more. We can only thank his publishers for having given us so much of his living thought in so slim a volume.

# Political Science / *Kurt Riezler*

H OW TO CONFRONT the two, the philosopher of history and the modern statesman? In actual life the philosopher of history and the statesman are not too willing to listen to each other—now less than ever, as ours is a time in which action tends to be thoughtless and thought inactive. Furthermore, we use both terms in a loose and flickering sense. Hence both the philosopher of history and the statesman are ambiguous animals.

Since it is dubious both what they are and should be, I shall take the liberty of a somewhat queer procedure. I shall first eliminate step by step a few types of both philosophers and statesmen—those who have nothing to say or had better not listen to each other—thus working my way upward to the real statesman and the real philosopher of history, intent on showing that they alone will be desirous and capable of listening to each other. They alone will have something worth while to say to each other, and thus by this very desire, capacity and worth may define each other mutually as the true philosopher and the real statesman.

The first I discard is the methodologist of scientific historiography whom many call nowadays philosopher of history, philosophy being nothing but the epistemology of science. This elimination raises no problem. He is a modest fellow and does not claim to be listened to by any statesman.

The second I discard is the politician proper. He is not quite so modest, though he has little to say to which any philosopher would listen, or should listen. I will try to identify him in a few words.

He is the puppet of history, not its maker except by default or accident. He merely plays a well known game, maneuvering from one short-lived smartness to the next, swimming now with this now with that current, to come to or to remain in power. He may be smart and yet equally stupid. If he is entrusted with the task of the statesman and called upon to shape the future of a nation he usually finds himself, after a time of clever maneuvering, caught or hopelessly entangled in the consequences of his own actions; even in the case of glamorous successes he may end up with the opposite of the aim which he or his nation intended

Kurt Riezler, "The Philosopher of History and the Modern Statesman," *Social Research*, XIII (September, 1946), 368–80. Reprinted by permission. Public lecture delivered at the meeting of the American Philosophical Association, Western Division, May 10, 1946, University of Chicago.

to pursue, or of the principles he proclaimed. His foreign policy will be
a manipulation of domestically expedient slogans, stereotypes, and emotions. Nations whose political leaders compete in that kind of smartness
will inevitably land together in a situation where forces that can be
unleashed, but once released no longer controlled, lead, blindly interacting, from war to war into deeper and deeper misery.

This kind of politician I discard; he may claim to be but he is not
the statesman. But since the statesman cannot come to or remain in
power without being also a clever politician, the skillful politician, after
some success on perishable paper, poses as statesman.

The next I must discard is a type of philosopher of history properly
to be called the metaphysician of history. He is as arrogant as the
methodologist is humble. He claims to be the only one to whom the
statesman should listen. Thus he is not so quickly discarded. His concern is with the meaning of the historical process as extended in time.
He interprets universal history as unity of a plot. He fancies that he
knows its meaning. He pretends to be able to declare it; he usurps the
throne of God and behaves as a divine observer outside history. Though
his respect for evidence is but small, he can be a forceful mind of great
speculative power and he may lay his hands on the thought of a century.

Though the great representatives of this philosophy of history belong
to the nineteenth century, the modern statesman will meet his power in
the mind of contemporary man. The historian may spurn his speculative
constructions, history itself may refute him—yet these constructions are
a response to a longing, deeply rooted in the uneasy soul of modern man.

Man, the ephemeral being, craves to think of the sweat and sorrow
of his few days as imbedded in a process that carries the past into
the future upwards toward a goal of ultimate meaning—by an inherent
necessity. As the power of religion fades and (in the mass society of our
own days) God and Providence evaporate behind a thin veil of words,
the metaphysician of history fills a void: his constructions of the historical
process become the raw material of the secularized religions we call
ideologies. Most of these modern ideologies are pseudo-scientific interpretations of universal history; man sees his present as a link in a chain of a
benevolent destiny which leads humanity, or at least his own nation as
the chosen representative of humanity, toward some ultimate promise.
The arrogance of a pretended knowledge is called upon to replace the
humble reference to an inscrutable will. And yet it can never play its
role in the soul of man—for two reasons: first, providence known is no
longer providence; second, the goodness and badness of man's actions
become functional—they depend on the pretended future, to which they

are thought to lead. The immediate relation of each moment to a god, the direct reference to an eternal judge, is discarded.

Despite these differences the ideology, like religion, is hope and belief; it protects, consoles, strengthens endurance and becomes a historical force of first magnitude and an instrument of power. Industrial man has conquered nature. She is no longer the power on which everyone's destiny hinges. This power is society. Society, however, is manmade. The same man who patiently bends to nature will not be so patient if, in an industrial society whose complexity he cannot grasp, he is to endure manmade poverty in a nature of potential plenty. Thus an ultimate promise and a law of history are called upon by victorious revolutions to delay the outbreak of man's impatience and thus to decrease the necessary amount, and to facilitate the task, of naked coercion by a secret police.

The modern statesman meets the power of such ideologies in many and complex ways—on the domestic scene, in the international field and maybe in his own soul. The original philosophies of history of great speculative minds have undergone a thorough change. The modern simplifiers and manipulators of mass movements have shaped and reshaped highly sophisticated theoretical bodies into systems of magic formulas of dubious meanings, to be waved as flags fitting the political purpose of the revolutionary movements. The philosopher of history himself would hardly recognize his original thought in the final product. Hegel would certainly scorn and spurn Marx, Marx the philosopher might even repudiate Marx the revolutionary leader, and each of the two Marxes might object to Lenin and Lenin to Stalin. History, however, cares but little; it shoves aside the real Hegel and the real Marx, without pity or respect, and upholds Stalin for a while at the top of the world.

In this process of simplification thought and action strangely intermingle. The revolutionary leader who forges an expedient instrument of power is usually the first victim of his own propaganda. Most propagandists are. To be efficient they indoctrinate first themselves. Even our propagandists do—and do not notice it.

The modern statesman of a still free society, trusting the power of reasonable discourse based on evidence, wonders at the tenacity of these mere constructions—even when they are not supported, as in the totalitarian states, by a joint monopoly of propaganda, violence and modern technology. Reasons and historical evidence to the contrary matter but little. Most of these constructions provide means and devices that can be used for explaining away any such evidence.

One of these devices is the "cunning of reason"—that *List der Vernunft* which accounts for all aberrations, detours or roundabout ways that the Weltgeist chooses to use; even the atomic bomb can be interpreted as *List der Vernunft*. In our own days the *List der Vernunft* has been replaced by the "period of transition." Though toiling humanity has lived since Adam's fall in a perpetual "period of transition" there appear, in the dubious constructions of the metaphysician of history, special periods of transition, connecting the phases in which the universal process is articulated. These transition periods are called upon to justify whatever acts, devices, and policies do not fit the scheme. These were "the in-evitable measures of transition" of the late Bucharin—until he himself fell victim to such an "inevitable measure." There is the secret police of the total state, which leads the bourgeois society into the stateless and policeless society of the future. The period of transition, an expedient excuse, both moral and intellectual, justifies the means and delays the promises; thus the revolutionary leader, unable to renounce those means or to fulfil those promises, goes on forever acting in a period of transition.

While the modern statesman in a still free society meets the power of a bygone philosophy of history in the ideologies of revolutionary move-ments and totalitarian states, he meets at home—in the most peaceful and complacent parts of his own society—another philosophy of history or its remnants, less visible, less noisy, but by no means less dangerous. It is but a specific kind of the philosophy of progress—the belief in an automatic progress as a law of the historical process as such, brought about not by man's actions and intentions but by a law of evolution—that "superficial notion" which in the words of T. S. Eliot "becomes in the popular mind a means of disowning the past." It leads to the strange but cheerful assumption that things after all cannot go wrong funda-mentally and ultimately.

This mostly half-conscious assumption cuts across the usual division of "reactionaries" and "progressives." It can be made by both. Disturb-ances are discarded as short-range events. It is taken for granted that the long-range trend is progressive. This belief may no longer be, or de-serve the honorable name of, a philosophy of history. It too has long ago forgotten its respectable ancestors and their arguments. What remains is hardly more than a broad generalization assuming that man's increas-ing power over nature implies an increasing power of reason over man —a wrong conclusion contradicted by more and more evidence, yet sug-gested by wishful thinking and subconsciously supported by the weight of economic theory in which, according to Adam Smith, "man is led by an invisible hand to promote an end which was not part of his in-tention." In an era and society to which economic life seemed to be the whole of life, the notion of a self-regulating process of the market under the ideal case of perfect competition was subconsciously generalized and transferred to the political process. It fitted and supported the smugness that takes the future of the society for granted, even if not part of any intentions, and served as excuse and mental background to that cheerful ease in which the ever smiling politician plays the political game this or that way, enjoying his smartness and entrusting the final outcome to an inherent law of progress.

I finally dismiss the metaphysician of history—despite his pretension. Though his relations to the statesman in concrete history are manifold and complex, he is not the kind of philosopher who deserve to be listened to by the real statesman. After all, philosophy is or should be concerned with reality and not with mere constructions, however lofty. I turn to the real philosopher of history, who is not a metaphysician of history, and to the real statesman, who is not a mere politician. But who are they? Where do they meet?

The statesman acts. He cannot escape deciding—he must either release or not release the atomic bomb. Even at its best his knowledge of the factors and forces working in the field is limited. Any decision opens one door and shuts another. Some of his decisions decide the future of his nation one way or the other. He acts. The deed once done cannot be undone. He cannot take it back. The bomb is released. The actions of others, the concatenation of events, probable or improbable, never entirely foreseen or foreseeable, take a hand, whirl his actions around and play with their consequences a cruel or benevolent game.

This is the fundamental situation of the acting man—here history is concrete. This situation, not the meaning of a universal process, constitutes history as history. It is its flesh and blood. In this situation, submitting to its inherent persuasive force, the statesman has a natural philosophy of history of his own. He may not be aware of it; he may rationalize it in terms of whatever philosophy he happens to have inherited, and in doing this he may be utterly inconsistent. The fundamental situation of acting as acting sways his heart, whatever his words may be. In this natural philosophy he looks at the future as not only unknown but still undecided. Much is pre-decided by the forces and factors working in the field—but they only limit the frame of action. Possibilities though limited are still open, even for the improbable. Their range is now wider, now narrower. There are moments when their range seems to narrow to zero and necessity sways the hour—such moments pass, the future is wide open again. The distribution of probabilities, their numerical values, change. This distribution is twofold—in the reality itself and in relation to his restricted knowledge.

At any rate, the present as the moment of decision separates a past that is decided from a future yet undecided—thus defining past and future as different modes of Being. This present, the moment of decision, marches on—mercilessly, without rest or respite, and carries with it and changes the wavering shadows which a waning memory throws on dimly glowing expectations. However great the impact of the past on the future, the future is still open; it is to be decided. A strong willed wisdom, grasping in a synoptic view the totality, the dynamic assessment of all the factors, can decide it—in coherent action from step to step, carefully refraining from unleashing those sinister social chain reactions in which the interplay of blind forces gets out of hand. The future has not yet any meaning derived from the historical process as a whole. Man—the present man—gives the meaning or fails to give the meaning: in the happiness or misery of man.

This is the natural philosophy of history of the acting statesman, as he is called upon not to interpret history but to make it. To this natural philosophy even the totalitarian statesman adheres in his heart, whatever the metaphysics of history that his lips profess. I stress this point: it may be that the "scientific" interpreter of history would do better to change his post of observation and exchange the usurped throne of an observer outside history for the soul of man inside history, lest the flesh and blood of life escape his eyes.

Now the real statesman and the politician part company. While the politician merrily plays his game from one short-lived smartness to another, trusting that he will find a way out of every mess in which he gets entangled, the real statesman is not allowed to be, like ordinary man, a short-range planner and a long-range dreamer. He is bent on shaping the future. He does not take it for granted. If he fails—there may be no future for his nation, or, under present conditions, even for mankind. He knows his ends, he has a goal, a hierarchy of purposes, long-term and short-term; he subordinates one to the other; he has a vision of both the possible and the desirable and looks at the one under the aspect of the other; he thinks the possibilities through to their end; he follows up his actions, keeping ready a possible answer for whatever their foreseeable consequence—trying to keep his hand on the events and their interaction, flexible at short range, rigid at long range, passionately reasonable, a knower of human nature, suspicious even of his own love and hate and of the many passions that blind the children of man. His eyes are cold and hard yet the flame burns in his heart as he opposes his specific virtue to the play that necessity and chance play with each other.

Who is, of what kind is, the philosopher of history to whom this statesman should listen? First it is he who listens to the statesman. He takes into account the fundamental situation of the acting statesman, which after all is only the situation of man, the finite being, writ large in the capital letters of history. He does not construct the unity of a plot or presuppose meanings to be derived from an ultimate end of a process in time. His meaning is here, present at any moment, in the happiness of miserable man, in the excellence of the peace we enjoy, in the deeds we do, the laws we give, the songs we sing, forever precarious. He worries as little as any man in action about the famous problem of freedom and determination; it is the problem of whether relatively to an all-knowing observer outside history the future is determined by a finite number of parameters which obey rules that have the mathematical form of linear differential equations of the second order—the specific system of determination which, applied to the succession of events in time, we call, or alone should call, "causality." History is what it is to man, and man's possible knowledge is limited. His problem is the inner structure of history, its "logos," the eternal interplay of its forces and factors as man, moving in a space that moves, acting and being acted on, carries the past into the future. As this philosopher of history is willing to listen to the statesman, the statesman will be willing to listen to him, as he surveys the enormous spectacle that history unfolds in space and time. Here man, the finite being, potentially the best of all animals and by far the worst, the history-made maker of history, in one its creator, its creatum, and its creandum, wrestles to give history a meaning, succeeds and fails. God is guiltless—the guilt is man's.

The play of births and deaths reaches from a half forgotten past through a confused present into an unknown future. Actualities emerge from the sea of possibilities, change, and sink. Societies, tribes, cities, realms, empires, nations strive and wane. Worlds in the world grow and decay. The gentle graciousness, the moans of sorrow, the shining deed, the dark misery, the smile of love—together they rise and fade away. The past curbs the future and releases it, begets and strangles it. Bodies of half completed worlds emerge and disappear. Many are choked in their youth, others dry up and ossify. Piles of debris cover the bones—only a few remain visible in the pale light of the historian. Thus this philosopher opposes to the metaphysician of history another picture, a pitiless one it may be, but one that at least is not in any moment contradicted by history itself, and is even able to stand the test of the atomic bomb without resorting to the cunning of reason.

It is a strange play; there is no audience. The actors themselves are its sole observers. No actor, not even a community of actors, stays through the play from beginning to end. Even any hero drops out after hardly more than half a scene. Most of us are poor actors, playing merely ourselves. There are no rehearsals, no script. We do not know our lines, though we have only a few to say. We must be satisfied if the two lines we improvise make sense to ourselves or to our nearest co-actors for some time or seem worth being remembered. It may not be a play at all, as it lacks the unity of a plot. If there is to be a meaning, the actors must provide it during the play. This is the core of their acting. Yet man, unable to do so or slighting this humble meaning, poses as a divine observer outside the play. The metaphysician of history pretends that every scene is what it is by virtue of its role in the play as a whole, whose meaning he knows and is going to proclaim. But any such interpretation of the plot as a whole and its meaning—the philosopher's insistence that there must be such a meaning of the whole which justifies the parts—is itself a product of history; the interpreter of history shapes his interpretation to fit the more or less ephemeral lines he wants to say.

This is a cruel picture. It does not, however, deprive history of meaning. It merely charges man with giving the meaning—to the present with respect to a foreseeable future. Thus it puts the statesman or the collective statesmanship of a nation before its ultimate task.

I come to the end. I return to the situation in which history as history is concrete—the situation of the acting man. It may be that the real statesman needs, though not any metaphysician of history, another kind of philosopher or his equivalent in his own soul—the knower of "the good" that guides his notion of the desirable and directs his quest for the right and wrong of his ends.

You find in some writings of a great man of ill repute—Machiavelli, who was not merely the technician of force we scorn—an occasional reference to the powers which jointly and interaction dominate the situation of man. He calls them necessità, fortuna, and virtù—necessity, luck, and virtue, though the latter word has not quite the connotations of our time. It has a more manly sense. Machiavelli follows an ancient tradition; the three in Greek are Ananke, Tyche, and Arete. We can formulate this specific virtue in terms of the ways in which the real statesman handles the two others and their interplay—how he recognizes, endures, stands, evades, slips by, or uses the power of necessità, how he gives fortuna a chance to help and no chance to thwart him, eagerly seizes its favor and firmly stands through its malignity. A description in these terms, however, though it may go pretty far, remains defective. This virtù may still be mere efficiency for power's sake.

But there is, obviously depedent on the same ancient tradition, another list of these "powers" that sway the destiny of man. Goethe, in a poem called "Urworte, orphisch," lists five, not three. Besides Ananke and Tyche appear—instead of Arete—Daimon, Eros, Elpis: the inner demon in man's soul, love, and hope. It is again not quite our meaning of love; it is nearer to Plato's Eros, the drive toward that idea of the good which is the ultimate source of all meanings. Now only can I complete the specific virtù of the real statesman. This virtù if defined as the capacity of wrestling with necessità and fortuna, would be blind though efficient; on the other side, it would be a mere dreaming and a powerless pity were it to be defined as the possession of mere love and hope, however sublime. This specific virtù of the statesman embraces both pairs; it refers the one to the other, end to means, knowledge to action, the desirable to the possible. Thus the ideal statesman strains himself to compel the play of necessity and chance to carry love and hope into the reality of a future.

Even the real statesman, however, may not succeed. Success is no reliable criterion. History is harder. The power of necessità and fortuna may be enough to crush the greatest skill of the greatest love.

Let me end with a quick glance at the particular situation of the modern statesman. My picture of the real statesman may seem unreal, beyond the fraility of man. It is an ideal. The ideal measures the performance. It is not arbitrary, however. It is what the logos of action in history requires. Since this ideal claims to be universal I did and could not formulate it in terms of any particular conditions such as ours. In the industrial society of our own age many seem to think of the historical process as nothing but the interaction of all social, economic, political, technological "trends." We make ample though rather loose use of this term. We believe in, rely upon, and like to comply with "trends." If, however, we condescend to take the soul of man as our post of observation we cannot help rediscovering behind and within these trends the living reality of action and decision. These trends drown in their averages the single action of any one of the many millions, and even the range of their divergences. To the statesman, who must make decisions, these trends are but material for recognizing, or guessing at, the element of necessità in the forces and factors whose interplay these trends reveal or conceal. To him those five eternal powers still stand—necessità is not alone. Many a belief in a trend is but a convenient excuse. Some of the most sinister trends of the past or coming decades are but the consequences of the blindness and stupidity of past actions and decisions. We shrug our shoulders and point to a trend. Yet the guilt is still man's.

I admit, however, that there are times in which the situation goes far beyond what any single man can do. If there was ever such a time it is ours. No single man can live up to the ideal picture of the statesman unless supported by the statesmanship of a whole nation. Look at the present scene: the aftermath of a total war, a half devastated world; shattered, dislocated or confused are minds, souls and bodies, the moral standards of both victors and vanquished, traditions, loyalities, hopes, ideas and interests; blind passions, held down but by hunger; a thick fog of old and new lies—this is the situation in which humanity gropes its way along the abyss of its technological advance, frightened yet still dreaming. But even this situation has not pre-decided the future. Man— in this case the equivalent of the statesman or the politician in the nation as a whole and thus in each of us in particular—man himself will decide it.

# Anthropology / *Margaret Mead*

T HE IDEA that periods of contact between hitherto isolated human societies have been periods of fruitful development is so old, so well accepted, that it is astonishing how often we have failed to use it as an analogy in discussing coöperation among different fields of human endeavor. Whether the advocates of "inter-disciplinary" research have felt it necessary to cast their arguments into a sterner pattern to match the self-conscious "purity" of those who wish to keep each discipline pure and uncorrupted by intellectual contact, only a specific inquiry could tell us. But it is evident, even to the casual ear, that "breaking down the barriers between disciplines" has usually been presented as a very arduous and, consequently, moral and exacting form of intellectual activity. From those who have attempted inter-disciplinary research, we hear report after report of hard going—how each group has held on to their own concepts and resisted the concepts of the others.

Even a summer holiday in Italy might be described in such unrewarding terms by a traveler who spoke only English—who, eyes to the ground, refused to eat fresh almonds unless they were pronounced in English, and by the Italian vendor who insisted that he would eat his own almonds himself unless they were designated in the exact lilt of the local dialect. But this is not the way lovers of foreign travel speak in describing how every cell in one's body feels different when one wakes in a strange land and eats a new kind of breakfast served with the accompanying excitement of a strange tongue in which the word for almond blends with the taste of almonds and with the quality of the sunlight on the Mediterranean.

Perhaps in a coöperative venture in which both "social sciences"—history and anthropology—are also often grouped together as "humanities," it may be possible to preserve enough of the concrete pleasures of the new and strange, that some of the grimmer aspects of inter-disciplinary coöperation—including the training table overtones of the phase "team work"—may be avoided in favor of the adventure of exploring each other's methods and delighting in each other's insights.[1]

Historians and anthropologists—in contrast to social scientists in other

Margaret Mead, "Anthropologist and Historian: Their Common Problems," *American Quarterly*, III (Spring, 1951), 3–13. Reprinted by permission. This paper was originally presented in part at the "Conference on American Civilization" held at Brown University, November 3 and 4, 1950, under the chairmanship of Dr. Edmund S. Morgan, at which the author was asked to discuss the contribution of cultural anthropology to historical studies.

fields—have a special relationship to their concrete materials, to the particular document or to the sequence of rites performed at a particular ceremony. For these concrete materials—whether they be the single copy of an obscure document from a remote historical period or the single record of the only initiation ceremony ever witnessed and recorded in a tribe which has since given up initiation, or whether they be one of a set of documents which differ among themselves or one of twenty records of initiation from the same tribe—are nevertheless irreplaceable, unique events from the details of which new insights may be drawn by succeeding, more sophisticated generations. Both historians and anthropologists are dependent upon that which occurs *in the natural course of human social life* for their materials, every facet of which becomes precious. This loving preservation of the actual detail contrasts with the single-minded emphasis upon abstractions and generalizations of the scientist who works with experiments that can be repeated and from whom it is required not that he "surrender to the material," but that he set up his hypotheses and so construct his experiments that they will provide him with data to prove or disprove them. The little phrase "the data shows" suggests a proper humility in the historian and anthropologist— and a state of incompetence in the experimenter.

From the necessities of their methods, both historians and anthropologists place a special value on the unique event in all its uniqueness. They know that it is the fine web of specific relationships, when something was done in relation to the occurrence of some other small act—a conversation, a letter, a resignation, a quarrel—which makes it possible for later historians, for other anthropologists, to ask, and to get answers to, new questions from old materials. The footnotes and interpolations and misspellings, which would be lost in reediting and rearranging materials, become invaluable sources. Similarly, the anthropologist may find that faces in the background of a photograph or moving picture provide a way of testing a hypothesis not fully developed in the field. So in the Balinese material,[2] psychiatrists who looked at the pictures were inclined to question the difference in the tone of voice of the mother who—lightheartedly—teased her child, and of the child who—heavyhearted—reacted against the same teasing by sulky withdrawal. A reexamination of films of the crowd scenes of two rituals—one of which embodied the parents' attitudes towards children (the *Sangijang Dance*) and the other the children's attitudes towards parents (the *Tjalonarang*)—showed a marked contrast in the faces of the children in the two crowds: relaxed, gay, and unanxious in the former; anxious and tense in the latter. If the abstractions had been drawn from the material and the "data" had then been thrown away, no such further exploration would have been possible.

This preoccupation with the actual data, which serves to unite historians and anthropologists, is less intelligible to those scientists who create their data by experiments as they need it, as critics they always seem to be asking why one didn't go somewhere else or study a different period, insensitive to the importance of learning what a particular culture or a particular period can provide—better than any other. It is only when historians and anthropologists become interested not only in what did happen and what does exist but also in the nature of social processes and in the regularities which may be found in them, that this gap between historical fidelity and experimental freedom can be bridged.

Traditionally, historians and anthropologists have been distinguished from one another by the materials which they have studied: the historian dealing with past periods and the anthropologist with primitive peoples. This distinction is fast becoming obsolete as both are turning their attention to contemporary problems of the great civilization of the world—including our own. There has also been a difference in the degree to which members of each discipline have been able to take the *whole* of a society into account. The early anthropologist dealt with part of the culture of a society, usually with a society which was already in process of rapid change: he attempted to reconstruct from the accounts of elderly informants such parts of the formal pattern as could be worked out without a detailed study of any living interacting group of human beings. The historian was limited by the nature of the documents which were available and by the current conventions of historiography which dictated the kind of constructs one could make from such documents. The units of both these traditional types of research were *items of behavior*, performed at an identified time and in an identified place by identified individuals; from them, patterns of "feudalism" or of "age societies" could be derived. In neither procedure was it possible to study living societies in which the units for analysis are not items of behavior, but instead *individuals* [and] *groups of individuals*.[3] The study of whole societies waited for field work in which the anthropologist would stop digging into the memories of old men and women and instead learn to speak the native language and record the living, changing, particular primitive community of his own time,[4] and research in which the historian would regard as part of his task the study of living institutions against the time depth provided both by the memory of older men and by available documentation.[5]

The discussions at the 1939 meetings of the American Historical Association suggested the growing preoccupation with groups which had been neglected by historians—the illiterate, the socially obscure, the peasant, the worker, the immigrant, and with sources, such as oral tradition, which had been overlooked in the past. The anthropologist was paralleling this new inclusiveness by adding observations of actual behavior to his former principal reliance on descriptive words. At the same time, both historian and anthropologist were looking for new types of connections which could be recognized when old sources were examined from a new point of view.[6]

So, both in anthropology and in history, we have been working steadily from a consideration of those parts of the society or those aspects of the culture, which our traditional methods made accessible, toward methods through which more of the whole could be included. For both disciplines this search has led to unorthodox uses of sources. The search has led also into the areas of the inarticulate, the unrecognized, the unformulated. Penetration of these new areas has been very much facilitated in anthropological studies, less so in historical studies proper, by the inclusion of findings from studies of human growth and learning and from clinical explorations of the unconscious.[7]

Anthropologists have begun to work toward theories of social change and so to compensate for their previous concentration on synchronic studies of single societies at one moment of time, and historians have begun to lay more emphasis upon the total social complex at a given period. In the past, anthropologists have compensated for the lack of a time dimension in their studies by spatial studies of the distribution of traits. The definition of the place of a given culture in a known "culture area"—the traits of which were also described—was, in effect, a way of holding "history constant,"[8] a way of saying that, as a member of a given culture area, the particular society may be assumed to have had access at some unspecified period to such a trait as the dog sled or pottery making. The enforced necessity of working without documents on the primitive level was carried over to some extent into early applications of anthropological methods to our society, notably in the Yankee City Series.[9]

Criticism of the lack of a complete time perspective in these earlier studies has sometimes been carried over into uncritical attacks on studies of contemporary American life which are not also historical treatises. It would be useful for anthropologists and historians together to clarify how cross-sectional studies, on the one hand, and studies of single developments through time, on the other, can be made so as not to violate their combined standards for the proper allowance for time-space dimensions. The present level of criticism both within and between the two disciplines tends to be either pejorative or meaningless, as studies are pronounced "too narrow" or "too broad," "too limited" or "too ambitious" without reference to criteria that have been agreed upon or are even identifiable. The more we try to work with *wholes*—with whole societies, with members of those societies seen as whole persons, and with whole periods—the more important it will be to find some way of deciding what whole should be taken into account in considering a given problem.

Within both disciplines, attempts to handle wholes—sychronically by historians and diachronically by anthropologists—and to relate structure, function, and change, have been given impetus by concepts of equilibrium and balance: in anthropology by the new approach of cybernetics; in economic history by Schumpeter's theory of "moving equilibrium."[10] This is perhaps the area where the use of models drawn from the natural sciences may be expected to provide the basis for cooperation among anthropologists and historians who are interested in systematizing problems of social change.

Another area where anthropologists' and historians' problems meet is that area, once known as "personality and culture," and currently referred to as "national character," because of the emphasis in such studies upon the contemporary cultures of great nation states. These present studies have little in common with earlier methods for the delineation of national character by reference to race or climate; instead they are ways of relating anthropological studies of culture, historical studies of consistencies within the same group of people over time, Freud's work on the formation of the individual character, and modern studies of child development and learning. In the Romanes lecture which he gave fifty years after Thomas H. Huxley's famous lecture on "Science and Ethics," Julian Huxley has pointed out that recent studies of the way learning takes place in childhood have provided us with the necessary links between man's biological nature and social ethics, so that man's highest aspirations as well as his most undisciplined and anti-social impulses can now be included within the natural order—rooted in the way human beings learn the patterns of their cultures.[11]

Briefly, these modern studies of national character are concomitant analyses of the character structure of individuals of different ages who embody a culture and of the child rearing, educational, and initiatory practices of the culture within which these individuals have been reared. By cross-checking these observations, we arrive at a diagrammatic statement of the particular process of character formation by which human beings—at birth capable of learning any human language and the rest of any human culture—come to learn a particular language and to embody their particular culture. In such a study, areas of experience are explored which are unverbalized or which are publicly disallowed, as well as those areas which are made explicit. We are thus carried one step further toward considering the whole, toward placing man-in-society with a long social history and man-as-a-mammal with a long biological history in one frame of reference.

National character studies, as these were developed during World War II, were wartime efforts to obtain rapid information about the expected behavior of enemies and allies. They were partial studies in that only a few adult informants were available, so that the behavior of a few adults, in interview situations, had to be analyzed in the light of reported, rather than observed, methods of infant care and education. This emergency method has now been developed, under the continued stress of need to understand peoples whose societies are inaccessible to direct observation, into a method that can be used to bridge the gap between the procedures of the historian and the cultural anthropologist. By working together on the understanding of the culture of societies which have greatly changed, so that there are only individual survivors and the culture can no longer be perpetuated (for example, the culture of Great Russia previous to the 1917 Revolution), or the members of which have dispersed into new environments in groups which still can be studied (for example, the culture of the Eastern European Jewish *shtetl* or small town), the special contribution of each discipline can actually become apparent to the other.

The crux of the methodological differences between historians and anthropologists can be summed up in the two words "document" and "informant." The historian uses written materials which have been created within the ordinary ongoing social process without reference to his inquiring intent, and he distrusts material as probably biased, when it has been written for the purpose for which he, himself uses it. In contrast, the anthropologist finds informants, whose place in their society he learns very carefully so that from these living human beings he can elicit materials on the culture, which traditionally he writes down, on the spot.

This contrast in method was summed up vividly by an experience in Bali with a visiting Dutch student of native law who had expressed an interest in the recent spread of a new dance form, called the *djanger*, which had recognizable European elements. We asked him whether he would like to see some *djanger texts*—meaning running observations in Balinese and in English and verbatim reports of conversations which had taken place at the meetings of the local *djanger* club. He was eager to do so, but then exclaimed in dismay: "These aren't texts! These are something that just happened."

Further light is thrown on the problem by the ill fate which met my attempt to regularize group research in contemporary cultures by having all the interviews with informants processed for group use, numbered and filed. When one of the group wrote an article in which he referred to this unpublished material by number, it was turned down by an anthropological editor on the ground that the article was based "only on unpublished material"—although it is acceptable anthropological practice to base published work on a statement of the order: "This material was collected during ten months' field work on the island of Borabora in 1910." Conversely, an historical editor asked me very severely on how many interviews with informants a certain statement was based. When I asked how many published documents would have been needed to authenticate it, he agreed that he would accept a minimum of one, providing there were no contradictory evidence. Finally, a young historian recently advised us to call our recorded interviews with carefully identified informants "unpublished memoirs."

In the course of cooperative work such as I shall suggest, most of these misunderstandings will disappear, if it is possible to push behind these disciplinary blind spots, so that an anthropologist can watch an historian criticize the usefulness of a *document*, weigh it, test it, compare it with "other evidence," and if an historian can watch an anthropologist record a series of interviews with an informant and weigh them, test them, and compare them with "other evidence." And they will disappear, I believe, in the exploration of what is meant by the term "other evidence"—which, aside from other documents, has remained largely inexplicit among historians as each one trusted to his growing "feeling for the period." This is an area in which anthropologists have become steadily more self-conscious; in their case, the "other evidence" can be handled systematically by reference to successive steps in the learning process or to the formal characteristics of some other facet of the culture.

For example, during the early days of our Balinese field work, we continually received accounts of "marriage by capture." This was definitely not in accord with such "other evidence" in Balinese culture as the almost complete absence of any physical fighting among children, the handling of quarrels by silence, and a break in all communication between the disputants, etc. Here historians, distrusting a document, and anthropologists, distrusting informants' reports, are still on the same ground—the item of information does not fit. We were able to solve this apparent incongruity when we found that "marriage by capture" was a carefully planned elopement in which it was necessary to simulate capture as a gesture of courtesy to the culturally preferred marriage which was being evaded, and that this was done with conscious theatricality. The theatricality of the Balinese could further be referred to in the way in which the climatic expression of emotional sequences was broken in

childhood by a mother whose only fully enacted sequences are of the-
atrical or simulated emotion.[12]

I would suggest that the most practical way for historians and anthropologists to learn from each other is in a situation in which they can
really experience each other's methods. Such a situation would be provided by work on a common problem located in a period for which both
living persons—as informants—and well-ordered documents were available, a problem so conceived that each facet would be systematically
referable to larger structural wholes.

Such a group working together might, for example, investigate a
small New England city between 1900–1914, studying its economic and
social development with particular reference to changes in job opportunity, shifts in ownership and decision-making, and in the way in which
the small city was integrated with the social and economic life of the
region, the nation, and the world. Older men and women could be used
as informants, actual changes in residence and communication within
the community could be mapped, the history of economic and social
change could be followed through local records. The pictures of the
past obtained by the different methods could be systematically compared,
and materials obtained by members of both disciplines could be referred
to the series of widening circles or wholes within which the study was
made.

In such a joint venture, historians would be responsible for maintaining the sense of trend, of movement over time, and for making it clear
to the anthropologists why they regarded it necessary to go back to the
Civil War in examining one sequence, back only to 1890 in examining
another, and why they were willing to label a sequence as new, or beginning in a certain year. At present it is exceedingly difficult for anthropologists to discover how the historian makes such selections, what in
fact are the criteria by which the historian decides that certain periods
provide the most relevant sequential or diachronic setting for his investigations. Instead of the young historian learning from his seniors until he
got a "feel" for the necessary data, he would be challenged by a "why"
from his contemporaries trained in a different discipline.

Meanwhile, the anthropologist, who would be responsible for the
adequacy and inclusiveness of the working model of the "whole community" and the "whole culture," would be equally and relevantly
pressed. Instead of carrying over in bits and pieces his knowledge that
kinship or ceremonials of crisis are something one ought to investigate,
he would have to show the relationship between the biological requirements of a human society (in which men and women with defined biological needs and potentialities must reproduce and nourish and train the
young) and the culture and specific social structure of that society.

Working together, historians and anthropologists would also become more sharply aware of the problems involved in surrendering their traditional devices for maintaining detachment—the historian by working with periods which are in the past,[13] the anthropologist by working with primitive peoples whose value systems are far removed from his own. Neither type of detachment is feasible for those working on contemporary societies.

Historians, after trying to obtain perspective on their material by permitting a sufficient amount of time to elapse, have often been much franker than other social scientists in recognizing that they belong to their own period and are writing for it. The interpretation itself has been treated as normative with a hope that it is tempered by a longer time perspective and the seasoned wisdom which comes from the knowledge of the follies men have committed, the depths to which men have fallen, and the heights to which they have risen again.

Anthropologists have taken a somewhat different course. We have explicitly demarcated an area of "applied anthropology" in which we are using our disciplined knowledge to affect the lives of identified people or groups. (A comparable area in the discipline of history would be the role of historians in policy formation, in international organizations, in the revision of textbooks for occupied countries, etc.) For this particular area we have adopted a code of professional ethics,[14] in which we assume responsibility for the foreseeable effects of our acts.

Studying and publishing upon our own civilization falls inevitably under the heading of applied science, because each pronouncement upon contemporary culture by historian, anthropologist, or any other student of society, will change that culture. One way of meeting this challenge is purposely to include the cultural membership of research workers in the research, orchestrating the research team by the inclusion of members of the culture being studied and members of at least two other cultures. It should be anticipated that in coöperative research on recently past periods, in which historians and anthropologists might work together for the express purpose of exploring each other's methods, this same procedure might be followed. In a study of American civilization of a given region between 1900 and 1914, a working team would include individuals who had matured in that city and at that period, younger students, and, in addition to American anthropologists and American historians, social scientists from at least one European society.

I myself have found the mere attempt to outline some of the possibilities of such collaboration so stimulating that it would seem reasonable that the experience of working on a common problem might prove rewarding to members of both disciplines.

# Psychology / *Frederick Wyatt*

*"The past is a work of art, free of*
*irrelevancies and loose ends."*
*Max Beerbohm*

## Alienation

Thε ʀ εʟᴀᴛɪᴏɴ s ʜɪ ᴘ of psychology and history has been scanty
for such a long time that the title line of this paper alone demands an explanation. Social change is certainly a subject historians and psychologists
have in common, although it is obvious, too, that they share in it neither
equally nor equitably. Each is dealing with human conduct. It should
not surprise us, therefore, if we found history and psychology not only
different, but, in important respects, also alike. The differences are clear
enough: the aim of the historian is to record behavior which has happened in the past, so that it must now be reconstructed from a variety
of records. Psychology treats the principles of behavior per se, which,
like the principles of other sciences, are usually conceived of as timeless.
Individual events in this scheme are relevant only as a case in point, in
that they demonstrate the universality of the principle, while each event
is for history an end in itself. Psychologists will argue that the difference
between history and psychology is in the *method* even if the two disciplines should overlap in subject matter. Psychology is an experimental
and quantitative science while history is merely descriptive. It will be
the aim of this paper to examine in greater detail what psychology and
history have in common, especially when the study of social change is
concerned; why the two disciplines have so little relationship at present;
and what the impact of method might be upon this state of alienation.

## Task and Problems of History

In this section I shall sketch out what present-day psychologists think
about history and historians. I am not concerned here with official statements of policy and sentiment which, in keeping with academic protocol,

Frederick Wyatt, "A Psychologist Looks at History," *Journal of Social Issues*, XVII
(no. 1, 1961), 66–77. Reprinted by permission.

are usually cordial. Any academically trained person will take history as a discipline for granted: it simply *is* and always has been. Ony when psychologists informally express sentiments derived from their professional orientation, will the difference become clear. At such an imaginary bull session psychologists will wonder why anybody should want to spend so much effort on finding out what happened in the past when no amount of investigation will make the past any less remote or any less uncertain. For the past which the historian is tracking down so laboriously is no more than a handful of dust, and the history which he writes of it is a composite of guesses held together by his own bias—an inventive conglomerate of equivocal cues. Things might have happened this way or that, but as history has failed to develop an exact methodology, there is no way of checking on it.

If this intimation of an attitude seems exaggerated, keep in mind that it represents a composite picture and not a survey of opinion. It should do no more than supply a tentative schema for the problems of communication between history and psychology. Withal, the psychological reader should have no difficulty in recognizing the elements which have been combined in this prototype. They refer to characteristic idiosyncrasies of psychology. First, the *stigma of the past.* For reasons which, by themselves, pose a neat problem for a sociology of ideas, psychologists are more prone than other social scientists to dismiss the past, including that of psychology. The pronounced bias of American psychology for the natural sciences (or what it worshipfully takes them to be, although they often are not) meets here with a kind of pragmatic fundamentalism. According to it, all important concerns are in, and of, the present. From this point of view, the historian's involvement with the past cannot but appear as dubious and futile.

Psychologists are even more outspoken about the *state of methodology* in history. There is no certainty in the reconstruction of the past. History is, therefore, in the end no more than a tissue of subjective impressions. Historical events are continuously described in different and conflicting ways by different historians. How can the results be taken seriously? History has no theory which could be confirmed by empirical test and no truly objective methodology which could do the confirming.

While based on a profound misunderstanding, this judgment of history is, on the face of it, not entirely incorrect either. Before the measure of history is taken it will be wise to examine the task and its premises. History has to work with immeasurably greater complexities than those to which psychology is accustomed. Her subject reaches from the actions and motives of the individual clear across to tradition and belief, social structure and institution, economics and culture. History is charged *a priori* with explaining how social action comes about. This involves not only the coalescence of innumerable lines of probable causation, but their waxing and waning, their unending emergence and absorption. Reflecting on history without prejudice, we find ourselves suddenly confronted with a paradox: in order to be appreciated in its natural complexity, human conduct apparently must first have receded into the past. With this limitation in mind, history in some fundamental respects seems to have a more realistic purview of human affairs than psychology or, for that matter, any of the other social sciences.

Compared with history, psychology is certainly dealing with much smaller segments, and with abstractions of behavior. They serve the purpose of psychology well, but also create a characteristic liability— namely, that of confusing the artifacts of inquiry with some ultimate kind of reality. The fact remains that psychology, even when it deals with conduct at large, must limit itself to specific strands of motivation, cognition, or interaction. Psychology usually operates within a short range of time. If time is essential, as in memory and learning experiments, or, on an even larger scale, in developmental studies, the focus is on a limited number of gradients of abilities or traits examined in relative isolation.

History works within a much broader scope of time. Even if it concentrates on a relatively short period—let us say, the Age of Jackson— its sights will be set on a much larger scope, both of time and of events. The administration of President Jackson lasted eight years; yet a recent book on it (Schlesinger, 1946) spans a much longer period in order to show what, in the historian's opinion, helped shape the events under study. Throughout a number of independent, though interacting, factors have to be considered, such as the relationship of finances to political organization, formal and informal—or class structure as related to changes in attitude and sentiment. Add to this the effects of leadership and the parts played by highly visible people in a period of transition, and the reflection that they, in turn, may have to be understood as the pawns of recondite social forces. All this and a great deal more needs to be reported and shown in its bearings in order to account for social change. True, a significant part of this is *interpretation*, pointing to connections, assigning meanings, proposing configurations of social causes and effects. The laws enacted by Congress for and against Jackson are facts; so are the messages of the President or the directives of the banks who opposed him; but, by themselves, they would no more make history than the assessment of traits makes a personality.

Professor William B. Willcox, in his comments on types of history-writing,[1] implied a gradient of complexity. First comes the spectacular history of wars and political events which defines change in the life of human communities largely in terms of the power to win armed conflicts.[2] The historian still has to explain the conduct of his princes and leaders as best he can. When he begins to place great in the center of history, a new dimension has accrued. In order to show the effect of individuals upon the shaping of events, the historian has to delve more deeply into their motives. The intricacies of the psychology of personality have thus been added to the historian's task. Before an individual can be credited with having taken charge of great events, he also must be shown in interaction with his milieu. If the resulting changes are attributed to his genius alone, he has probably been overrated; but the scope of history writing has been expanded by the inclusion of socio-psychological and sociological viewpoints. When historiography advances to the stage where it considers political events together with economic, social and cultural conditions as well as the persons who direct them, or are dragged along by them, it has reached what is its present standard of complexity. The expansion of history from the Great Spectacle and Great Man stage can be characterized as follows: an increasing number of factors, or dimensions, pertaining to other disciplines like economics, sociology, or psychology are introduced into the historian's record. Quite clearly, history does not always make equal and full use of them. It engages in specialized tasks like other disciplines, and then excludes other dimensions in order to pursue one in greater detail. Besides, history, like other disciplines, has been tardy in adopting techniques developed elsewhere (Langer, 1958).

To sum up: History deals with much more complex events than psychology. Many things feed into history, so that it has to cope with even more manifold interactions than psychology. Predicated on a longer time span, its inherent complexity grows in logarithmic proportion. History includes all imaginable kinds of human variables together with a variety of non-human ones (climate, natural catastrophes). By way of comparison, psychology is more concerned with principles: it aims at general rules, comprehending the unfolding adaptive changes in the behavior of any organism. Psychology admits the unique case, though rather grudgingly. Generally speaking, it is concerned with the predictable similarities of behavior while history consists entirely of unique cases. On the other hand, by isolating segments of behavior from their context, and abstracting them into entities, experimental psychology finds it increasingly difficult to reconstruct and comprehend the conduct of people in real life situations. When the professor of psychology walks from his lab to class in order to give his regular Monday lecture, it would take the greater portion of the Handbook of Experimental Psychology to account for all that is involved in this sample of behavior, and several aspects of it would still remain unexplained. It should not be overlooked, either, that even such a small instance of routine behavior will involve historical perspectives if anybody wanted to explain why it proceeds as observed, and not in some other way.

Could history be more accurate than it is? Oh yes, an historian might answer, if people would only take more care and leave appropriate records of their conduct. But the fullness of data is not the only problem. In modern times so much care is taken to retain things for posterity that it appears sometimes as if half the people were taking notes while the rest are making history. Yet, only a few years later the past is again much more indefinite than one would ever have thought. Take the history of the recent war as an example. The dates, the moves, the numbers are certain enough; so are the orders issued and the transcripts of conferences. What effected *this* turn of event or what caused *that* difference between intent and outcome still remains doubtful. Too many things of which nobody is aware go on in very large operations. On the other end of the scale, nobody else knows what passes in the mind of an individual; often he is not conscious of it either. One could well argue that the historan *knows* only of the facts in his grasp; those which might still be afield, but have eluded him so far, he can, at best, *suspect*.


## The Need for Reconstruction

The reason why history is not more accurate is, in the last analysis, inherent in the very task, the *reconstruction of the past*. Before standards of unequivocal certainty are demanded of history, it will be well to consider first whether such standards apply to it at all. There is no conceivable reason why an enterprise, which explicitly aims at reconstructing past events by inferring them from a range of unequal cues, should be judged by the same criteria as physics. The historian has the unique job of reporting the nexus of events to which (with the possible exception of the most recent past) he has no direct access (Russell, 1957; Wyatt, 1959). History affords no immediate observation; it is, strictly speaking, non-empirical. Nor can events in history be as neatly inferred by their physical consequence as the presence of sidereal bodies. Whenever such inferences are feasible, they are subject to stringent reservations and to an abiding uncertainty. It is much more an article of faith than a postulate of logic that the standards of quantifiable evidence apply unconditionally to psychology, or that the status of psychology as a science depends on their realization. How much less reason is there (apart from the conviction that it *is* that way because it *ought* to be) to judge history by standards derived from the study of an entirely heterogeneous subject. Briefly, the indigenous problems of history-writing lie in (1) the nature of its data; (2) the epistemological status of the past; (3) the manner of historical synthesis.

(1) The reconstruction of an event in the past obviously depends on somebody who first observed it and then left some sort of record of it. In addition, various kinds of tokens may have remained. Although they were not intended to convey any information about those who made them, nevertheless important conclusions can often be drawn from them. An observer is handicapped by his involvement in what he is observing. The closer he is to one of the centers from which action issues, the more likely is he to participate in aiding or in opposing it. Also, by being close to one fulcrum of change, the observer is necessarily removed from others. As the events of history tend to be multifarious and contrapuntal, it is easy to imagine how much *and* how little even a well-placed observer could have seen for himself, and how one-sided his judgment would have to be even if he is endowed with sterling objectivity. Professor Willcox cites several impressive examples for this most elementary problem of history-writing.

(2) What is the past? Only what somebody remembers of it, or what somebody else leaves to be remembered by others. If this sounds extreme, introspect for a moment what you imagine the past to be like. It turns out that most of us have an image of the past somewhat like that of a landscape, which becomes dim and recedes as we move away from it. It is something of a cognitive jolt[3] to realize that the past is utterly gone and does not continue in some faraway place where, with some luck, we could look it up. *Now* it consists only of what is left over of it— potsherds, ruins, artifacts—or what in more favorable instances is recorded of it in language. Any of these relics might contribute to conjectures of amazing scope; none by itself could with any stretch of the imagination be called "history." It is no more than a statement of fact to say that *the past* does not exist unless it is reconstructed (Wyatt, 1959).

Such reconstruction, however, is by its very nature never completed.[4] Ordinarily, we cannot know what jawbones, scrolls or diaries we may yet find. A statement in history is, therefore, correct only so long as it is not superseded by a more informed one. This applies to the uncovering of new data; but it applies also to the use of viewpoints and categories for the reconstruction of an age when they had not yet been conceived and when nobody could have understood them. It is therefore no paradox that we probably know more about many a celebrated event than any individual who was in the thick of it could have known.

(3) Historical synthesis, therefore, consists of the organization of data

into a coherent pattern. If the data are convincing, they will closely prescribe the pattern, although it must not be overlooked for a moment that even the most extensive array of facts needs to be given a *meaning* in order to become history. Thus, *interpretation* is an integral part of *reconstruction* (Wyatt and Willcox, 1959). As it depends on the data, on the concepts, and on the methods available at a given time (e.g., microscopic analysis, carbon dating, or psychoanalysis) and on the integrative faculties which the historian brings to his job, reconstruction is best viewed as an ongoing process rather than a completed state. History shares this condition with the psychological reconstruction of the individual past in psychoanalysis. What Freud said about the latter also applies to the former: both are interminable (Freud, 1952). The range of continuous self-emendation in history is, of course, extremely variable. Many facts of history have been established with a degree of probability that comes close to certainty, and many of our present views may undergo only minor changes in the future. This does not alter the principle; for we can in no way anticipate (and therefore not exclude) what new concepts might do to the views we hold now, how they might rearrange our data and what new vistas they might open up. History is most inchoate when its scope is large; but then it also seems to fulfill most its promise and indigenous function. For history administers one of the true powers of mind: man's present is certainly foisted upon him by all kinds of forces over which he has no control; but of his past he is really the maker.

## The Lesson of History

What psychologly could learn from history is already implied in the foregoing discussion. It would be useful for psychology from time to time to compare the complexity of its own endeavor with that of history. It should also be sobering for psychologists, intoxicated by the prospects of quantitative methodology, to contemplate the example of history in yet another sense: what historians raise from musty records usually tells us more about the human conditions than the most incisive experiment.

Because of the differences of scope and method between the two disciplines, psychologists have paid little attention to the fact that history, like literature, is an immense storehouse of data of human conduct. Unlike literature, however, it is a repository of observations of collective actions and large-scale change. I have discussed before the uncertainty which attends historical statements. In spite of these limitations, such statements afford a view of development, a configuration of events from beginning to end, which empirical observation in the social sciences can usually not provide. All the world's a stage, and history, with unequalled clarity, presents the complete play. This is also the great attraction in the psychological study of historical personalities. The data may be scanty and equivocal; yet the peculiar and frequently perverse logic of individual careers can hardly ever be studied so well, even under the most favorable clinical conditions (Wyatt, 1956). For this reason too, psychology should be more audacious in applying its viewpoints to history, as Weber has done with such provocative results in the case of sociology.

The most important lesson to be learned from history is identical with its own endeavor. Nothing in the field of human conduct can ultimately be meaningful unless it is put into a context of development which shows how the present emerged from the past. The anti-historicism[5] of present-day psychology is in this sense a major liability. It is a bad liability when it is defended by scientific dogmatism—a worse one still when psychologists have ceased even to be aware of it. The attitude toward history is part of the alienation of psychologists from the humanities at large. The resulting loss for psychology is obvious; it becomes ludicrous when ignorance pretends to be a virtue.

It seems almost tautological to say that *all* understanding is historical. In this elementary sense psychology, by being concerned with the antecedents of behavior, is historical too. It is perhaps a consequence of the methodical necessity of singling out and pursuing strands of experience and lines of conduct, that psychologists are so often found reluctant to face up to the contextual quality of any psychological event. Not that there has been a shortage of theories emphasizing the coherence of all human experiences in latitude (simultaneous events affecting each other) and in depth (the past affecting the present). Psychologists adopted them eagerly; but when the new ideas had to be fitted to the traditional canons of evidence, methodological considerations determined how much of the global viewpoint could be accommodated. The rest was dropped without questioning the benefits of the quantitative method. Were they certain to adapt a universal principle to the method?

There is finally the subject matter of history itself. Among others, it points to the continuity of cultural, psychological and social circumstances from the past to the present. If man does not live by bread alone, it is safe to assume that he is influenced in his conduct by more than the most immediate stimuli and the most obvious goals. Every psychological event refers back to a social condition which in turn receives its full meaning only from history. If, as psychologists, we aim to explain behavior or experience (Wyatt, 1958), it is hard to see how this can be accomplished without some knowledge of history, the none-too-silent partner of most of the events with which psychology is concerned.

## History, Psychology, and Social Change

Historians have, at various occasions, considered the application of the concepts of social science to *historical change*. The report of the Committee on Historiography (The Social Sciences, 1954) presents a lucid summary of recent thinking on this subject. In discussing *change and history* (pp. 106–127) the authors suggest that ". . . among the more important general factors of change in society are (1) a wide range of alternative opportunities; (2) a relative flexibility or looseness of structure in culture and social organization; and (3) lack of resistance because of the isolated character or gradualness of a change." (p. 116.)

Change, they continue, will then depend on how much the prospect of it appeals to those in power. It will also depend on how widely spread a latent fear of change is among the people at large. This in turn may have to do with the surplus energy available for experimenting with change, while all these factors must depend heavily on the physical environment and the biological state of the group which ponders change.

If we examine this analysis of change we cannot help noticing that it relies essentially on sociological, that is, group-and-institution oriented, concepts. Of 31 references to professional literature only two are psychological: one from the field of personality theory; the other from that of social psychology. Yet the determinants of change cited before obviously point to psychological problems, even though they were first stated in sociological terms. Rigidity, a key-concept of the chapter mentioned, certainly is a psychological concept; and the willingness for change, no less than the fear of it, can only refer to psychological events in individuals. If this is so, then it ought to be feasible to grasp the more forceful and persistent ones that register in many different minds when social change is taking place.

The question is, then, why psychology should have contributed so little to the bibliography of social change. It is tempting to refer to this restraint as *refusal* or *disdain*, but this not practical. When a science does not do what is wanted of it and what clearly pertains to its subject, we must conclude that it is not capable of dealing with the task at hand. The means may be lacking; or, more likely, the science has defined itself in such a way that it is not compatible with the task. Mediaeval medicine set out to achieve its aims largely by making deductions from certain philosophical and medical texts of inviolable authority. Unwilling to examine the etiology of diseases empirically, medicine could do little to cure them. Undoubtedly the absence of critical tools such as the microscope had much to do with that situation, as one could easily infer once the magnifying instrument had been introduced. Still more decisive for medicine's practical disability was the self-imposed restriction of its scope which prevailed far into the age of scientific discoveries. It may well be that the very orientation of contemporary psychology, especially in its representative academic purview, keeps it from concerning itself with *historical change*. Concepts are unavoidably complex. They do not lend themselves easily to measurement on some kind of scale, nor can they be readily visualized as a dependent variable. Some of the concepts of contemporary psychology obviously are more fit to describe social change than others. Not having been much concerned with the topic, psychology has had little opportunity to reflect on the problems of investigating it. The disaffection of psychology for social change has however, to do not only with a shortage of appropriate concepts and methods, but with the insistence in official psychology on the appurtenances of a scientific methodology *à tout prix*. Method in contemporary psychology often is an integral part of theory. It defines the scope of inquiry by prescribing what kind of data are acceptable and, in some instances, appears not only to express but to inform the theory.

An example may illustrate this point. One would think that the recent increase in childbirth and the size of families would rate a prominent place in the attention of psychologists. Propagation reaches from the biological roots of man to his most advanced social, economic, and political problems. It involves a wide variety of psychological events, individual and social, rational and emotional. The rate and timing of propagation seem to depend on the role of the sexes, the relationship of men and women to each other and to their culture, on the impact of their fantasies and insecurities, and, of course, on a vast array of unconscious dispositions. As far as I know, there are only very few studies on reproduction oriented toward a psychological point of view (Mischler, 1954). True, demographic research has not been concerned with individual motivation for reproduction. It is equally clear, however, that the large-scale statistical studies which have been the norm in this field do not explain the psychological determinants but, at best, only the social conditions of propagation. Moreover, the predictions of demographers have not proved to be correct during the recent increase in the birth rate. Yet this increase *must* have to do with processes of adjustment ranging from the psychological meaning of economic conditions for the individual to the impact of demands and expectations of the group upon him. On that plane the increase of the birth rate must derive from conscious decisions: from the division of labor in work and leisure; from subtle balances among self-regard, gratification, the admission and repression of instinctual needs; from the image the individual has of himself and of his sexual partner; from the management of realistic and neurotic anxieties; and from many other psychological conditions (Hoffman, 1960). In short, there is enough substance in the problems of reproduction for a dozen seminars in the major sections of psychology. The neglect of this area must have many causes, but at least it seems likely that the forbidding appearance of the problem, when approached in terms of the established methodology, has deterred psychologists. It is one thing to calculate what income or religious groups contribute to the steady growth of the population; another to understand a profound change in the style of life implying equally significant changes in the roles and images, the functions and identities of men and women. To investigate them would demand great flexibility of approach and a willingness to sacrifice the comforts of certainty to the goal of finding a plausible configuration for a complexity of interacting events. To be sure, the certainties of psychology have been somewhat more fictitious than is commonly admitted. At this point it would be more important to have a frame of reference than a controlled experiment.

In a previous section I have touched upon the relationship of psychological concepts to change. A certain predilection for static situations is obvious in contemporary psychology. The very principle of the experiment implies obliquely that the world stands still while it is being examined variable by variable. On the other hand, while the reproduction of life in terms of dependent and independent variables makes no assumptions one way or the other about time as the parameter of change, it does not exclude it either. In fact, change in time frequently is the dependent variable in learning experiments. Change is then usually conceived as a linear development of one or several variables which move in the same direction, such as the measure of abilities in a growth study; but *not* as the continued interaction of emergent forces in a broad stream of ongoing events as history, at its best, will present life.

This raises the question of a differential fitness of psychological concepts for comprehending social change. The discovery of a whole realm of pre- and praeter-rational motivation made it necessary for Freud to design not only a new terminology but a whole new system of psychological modalities and structures (Rapaport, 1960). Could it be that the language of psychology is somewhat obtuse with regard to the kind of change that manifests itself in society and history?[6] At this point no more can be done than stating the problem. We should also remind ourselves that it will not be solved by determined measurement. We might, on the other hand, gain for our purpose by studying the lessons of history.

## REFERENCES

FREUD, S. Analysis terminable and interminable. *Collected Works*, V. 316–57. Hogarth Press, London, 1952.

HOFFMAN, LOIS W. & WYATT, F. Social change and motivations for having larger families: some theoretical considerations. *Merrill-Palmer Quarterly*, 6, 1960, 235–44.

LANGER, WILLIAM L. The next assignment. *American Historical Review*, 1958, LXIII, 283–304.

MANDLER, G. & KESSEN, W. *The Language of Psychology*. John Wiley, N.Y., 1959.

MISCHLER, E. G. & WESTOFF, C. F. *A Proposal for Research on Social-Psychological Factors Affecting Fertility: Conceptions and Hypotheses*. Milbank Memorial Fund, 40 Wall St., N. Y. 5, N. Y., 1954.

RUSSELL, BERTRAND. *Understanding History*. Philosophic Library, N. Y., 1957.

SCHLIESINGER, ARTHUR M., JR. *The Age of Jackson*. Little, Brown & Co., Boston, 1946.

SIMPSON, LESLEY BYRD. *Many Mexicos*. University of California Press, Berkeley, 1959.

*The Social Sciences in Historical Study; a Report of the Committee on Historiography*. Social Science Research Council, N. Y., 1954.

RAPAPORT, DAVID. The Structure of Psychoanalytic Theory. *Psychol. Issues*, II, No. 2, 1960.

WYATT, F. A principle for the interpretation of phantasy. *Journal of Projective Techniques*, 22, 1958, 229–245.

——— Psychoanalytic biography. *Contemporary Psychology*, 1956, 1, 105–7.

——— The reconstruction of the individual and collective past. *Proceedings of the Fifth International Congress of Psycholgy*, Brussels, 1957. North Holland Publishing Co., Amsterdam, 1959. Pp. 161–2.

———, & Willcox, W. B. Sir Henry Clinton: A psychological exploration in history. *William and Mary Quarterly*, 1959, XVI, 3–26.

# Psychoanalysis / *Philip Rieff*

$\mathbf{F}$REUD WRITES: "We must look around for analogies."[1] He is certain he will find them, as have other men before him.

Social thought, like theology or physics or poetry, has always availed itself of analogy. All thought systems have used models to mediate between clusters of experience or events, showing them, by the connection located pivotally in the model, to be analogous. Indeed, analogy has been considered a necessary first step in all abstraction and law. Analogies may be a long way round to the truth, but "multiple failures have taught us the unwelcome lesson, that man can only arrive at . . . understanding . . . by a very circuitous route."

The great questions are "not accessible directly."[2] Rather, as Henry James taught the art of the novel, they must be approached by indirection, though perhaps not so indirectly as James himself found necessary. The way to knowledge is from one level of meaning to another, the one level mirroring the next. Nineteenth-century thought accepted the way more eagerly than many generations before it. Gierke assessed all medieval political thought as dependent upon the method of analogy and the model of macrocosm-microcosm.[3] It was not until the nineteenth century that the method and the model again rose to pre-eminence.[4]

In his dependence upon the method of analogy and the model of macrocosm-microcosm, Freud was a typical product of his century. Although his dependence is not explicit (as it was for the German organismic political philosophers, such as Bluntschli, and for natural philosophers such as Lotze and Fechner[5]), the analogical method is the key to the Freudian system, theoretic as well as therapeutic. It is the purpose of this paper to examine critically the basic theoretic construct of Freudianism: the analogy between the individual and the social and between the psychological and the historical.

## I

With Nietzsche, Freud proclaimed the master-science of the future to be not history but psychology. History became *mass* psychology. Thus, for the historical phenomena of religion, "the only really satisfactory

Philip Rieff, "History, Psychoanalysis, and the Social Sciences," *Ethics*, LXIII (January, 1953), 107–20. Reprinted by permission of the University of Chicago Press.

analogy," Freud thought, was to be found "in psychopathology, in the genesis of human neurosis; that is to say, in a discipline belonging to individual psychology, whereas religious phenomena must of course be regarded as a part of mass psychology."[6]

In the case of any historical phenomenon—any manifestation of mass psychology—Freud had "no difficulty in finding a full analogy to it in the mental life of an individual."[7] The analogy between individual and mass "is rather in the nature of an axiom."[8]

The axiom was applied to every kind of historical and individual experience. For example, the Freudian anthropology is totally dependent upon the analogy between taboo customs and compulsion neurosis. Summarizing the analogy, Freud listed the following correspondences: "1. In the lack of motivation of the commandments, 2. in their enforcement through an inner need, 3. in their capacity for displacement and in the danger of contagion from what is prohibited, 4. and in the causation of ceremonial actions and commandments which emancipate from the forbidden."[9]

A more subtle example of the analogical method was advanced in the psychoanalytic interpretation of the history of Judaism and Christianity. Between the "problem of the traumatic neurosis [the psychological event] and that of Jewish monotheism [the historical event]" there is a complete series of correspondences. Freud began with "the feature which one might term *latency*,"[10] and ended with a total analogy between traumatic neurosis and Jewish monotheism. Subjective psychological experience is analogous to objective social experience, as individual history is to race history.[11] "Thus we are prepared for the possibility that the solution of our problem [the development and stabilization of a certain belief system, e.g., Jewish monotheism] is to be sought in a special psychological situation."

The trauma is made dynamic by the latency period it must serve. "The phenomenon of the latency period in the history of the Jewish religion"[12] is explained as a repression of Mosaic doctrine at the time of the killing of Moses, the traumatic crime that was the origin point of Jewish society. Collective repression does not, any less than individual repression, "disappear without leaving a trace." It lives on as a potential in the inherited biological structure of man.

The cultural analogue of repression is "dormant tradition." Like repression on the individual level, that a "dormant tradition should exert such a powerful influence on the spiritual life of a peope [so as to fixate in latency the Mosaic religion and, in a sense, create the historical predestination of the Jews] is not a familiar conception."[13] Nevertheless,

Freud concluded, the theory of individual psychology could provide the necessary and sufficient explanation for the phenomena of social history—religion and, as we shall see later, art and politics.

The analogy between individual psychology and social history was developed into a definitive theory of religion and obsessional neurosis. Since *Totem and Taboo* (1912), Freud "had never doubted that religious phenomena are to be understood only on the model of the neurotic symptoms of the individual."[14] Obsessional neurosis is private religion, and religion is mass obsessional neurosis. The pious are simply the neurotics of another culture epoch. Penance was analogized to obsessional acts.[15] Freud reports that his insights into both the "origin of neurotic ceremonial" and into "the psychological processes" of religious ceremonial depended entirely upon the inferences his analogical method had enboldened him to draw about the latter from its resemblances to the former.[16]

Freud needed no other evidence, no study of the religious ceremonials (or other social processes) in themselves. The analogy was sufficient to draw the inference. Concrete historical documentation was superfluous. Psychoanalytic analogies were to comprehend all the traditional disciplines of the social sciences, as Freud himself proclaimed.[17] The first step toward knowledge is the instrumentation of the anthology. Christ and Hitler both become "father-images." The Freudian analogies permit uncontrolled shifts in the presentation of evidence and in its evaluation. Criteria remain unstated, or implicit, like the method itself.

Freud's analogical method often led him to artistic arbitrariness of criteria and to hidden shifts from one criterion to another, as intelligent critics and commentators have long pointed out. However, it is important to notice not only the construction of the basic Freudian analogy but also the evaluational position at the source of that construction as it has affected the social sciences. That evaluational position is basic to the dominant versions of contemporary social theory. Freudianism is only the most pervasive and influential of contemporary models and merits examination anew from that perspective. What Freudianism achieves by describing religion as mass obsessional neurosis and obsessional neurosis as private religion—and in the whole system of anthologies organizing the Freudian (and other psychologistic) social theories—is the devaluation of the social context within which given psychological processes (e.g., obsessionalism or identification) operate. A critical comparative analysis of the psychoanalytic devaluation of religion, art, and politics, and objective social processes in general, provides a basis for a systematic understanding of the psychological approach to social science.[18]

## II

In the Freudian analogical system, public, social events are only points at which private, psychological mechanisms reveal themselves. Thus, from Lasswell's political science to Koestler's vulgarization of Freudian theory in *Arrival and Departure,* public issues are dramatized private issues. Revolutionary ideologies—left and right—are treated as rationales for Oedipal conflicts.[19] This is the qualitative reading of Lasswell's famous equation for the study of politics: $p \{d\} r = P$. Finally, political action $(P)$ is a "displacement" $(d)$ and "rationalization" $(r)$ of private motives $(p)$.[20] What is definitive for the public and the social is the private and the psychological. The public and social is only the "manifest content." The "latent content" is the psychological mechanism which is masked by the manifest content. Psychologistic social theory is self-consciously dependent upon such a translation of the public into the private.

In Freudian thought, of whatever school, the meaning of social action is bifurcated onto two levels: (1) the determinative psychological mechanism and (2) its public reference, the manifest content of private experience. The second level is collapsed into the first. From a psychoanalytic point of view, since the psychological mechanism is the same on both levels, the psychological mechanism informs and defines the social process. The historical value context of social actions is assimilated to unconscious motivations. A nun telling her beads and a neurotic counting the buttons on his clothing are both viewed as engaged in obsessional actions. The cultural context of the nun's action is dismissed as superficial. The method of analogy allows the observer to understand the psychological mechanism informing the nun's and the neurotic's action as identical. It is in this sense that Freud interprets piety as neurosis.

The reading of the objective and social as the subjective and individual is Freud's particular version of the subjective idealism that was his Kantian heritage.[21] Kant's famous decision rerouted the approach to truth not through an analysis of objective reality but through an inquiry into the structure of cognitive experience. Man is not a passive observer of the cosmic spectacle. Only the matter of reality is given; its form is dictated by the mind. Reality is actively organized by a priori concepts contributed by the understanding, the "analogies of experience." Kant was certain that his critical philosophy had effected "a Copernican revolution."

Freud was equally certain that he had achieved a Copernican revolution and that his own construction of the idea of analogy was the principle of understanding. Freud's analogical discoveries were equally a destruction of metaphysics and a critique of knowledge as a preestablished harmony of nature and mind. Psychoanalysis, by its "view of the relation of the conscious ego to an overpowering unconscious, was a severe blow to human self-love." Freud "described this as the *psychological* blow to man's narcissism, and compared it with the *biological* blow delivered by the theory of descent and the earlier *cosmological* blow aimed at it by the discovery of Copernicus."[22]

Freud thought no knowledge was possible without analogy. Analogy was the bridge between the knower and the world. In Kant's words, only through analogy is that "context of experience" we call "nature" possible. For both Freud and Kant, the only possible knowledge is psychological knowledge. But psychological knowledge itself is analogical. Mind imposes analogy upon experience. There can be no experience outside the analogical forms of the mind, as there is no matter without form. Reality, apart from mind, can never be proved. Man is a piece of nature, not separate from nature.

But man must assume that his knowledge is more than the forms of his understanding. Since he can manipulate and predict nature, he must assume that his knowledge mirrors reality. This cannot be proved. But it is something which the mind cannot help but believe. Ultimately, both Freud and Kant could not deny that the principles of nature must be congruent to the principles of understanding. Nature is itself really analogical.

Kant had to admit the agreement between nature and the understanding, but only as a "transcendental deduction" a necessary assumption. Similarly, for Freud, (1) the objective world is a hierarchy of resemblances, and (2) (as disclosed by the Freudian theory of symbolism) the mind knows analogically. Freud, like Kant, could never prove that the analogical structure of objective reality existed apart from the analogical structure of the psyche. But he, too, was forced to make the "transcendental deduction." There were no plausible alternatives. Reality, distinct from man's vision of it, must still be analogical. "Reality will always remain 'unknowable'" if one expects something beyond its analogical structure.[23]

Having validated the analogical structure of objective reality, Freudianism could proceed to its central analogy (between the individual and society) and to the confident identification of the social as secondary elaborations of private psychological experience. But the identification does not withstand critical examination. Even if it is assumed that Paul's epilepsy definitively informs his conversion experience, all epileptics are not Pauls.[24] Paul was Saul before he became Paul. His Hellenized education, his struggle with the Judaizers, may have more to do with his revision of Christianity than his epilepsy. The road to Damascus was in that time, of that place. Paul's conversion experience can be understood only within the social context. Private psychological experience may implement the development of publicly relevant themes but it is history that imposes the connection.

Social situations refine heterogenous psychological materials in terms of their own dynamics. Freud's view was directly opposed to this. For example, psychoanalysis, or the "wound and bow" theorists strongly influenced by Freudianism (Edmund Wilson, Kenneth Burke, *et al.*), must treat art as a secondary elaboration of pathology. But to characterize the artist by the pathology of the man is to misunderstand the art. In Van Gogh's case, for example, what is most important is that a psychopath found solutions to problems bequeathed to him, *as an artist,* by an *aesthetic tradition.* Other artists, quite unpsychopathic, learned from Van Gogh. The Impressionist concentration on the problem of light had led to a devaluation of the object painted. Van Gogh, with his mad bas-relief vision of the object haloed by whirling light, showed that, given Impressionism as the objective style context, the objects the painter picks are in no sense indifferent. The Impressionists had come to a dead end: any object could be a vehicle for the portrayal of light and shadow. Breaking through the Impressionist impasse, Van Gogh reintroduced the dominance of the object but at the same time utilized Impressionism to formulate a new restriction and economy in its presentation. One might say that Van Gogh taught the world of art to see schizophrenically. But the objective vision he contributed to Western sensibility is the publicity relevant constellation within which his schizophrenia must be understood. His disease, qua disease, is irrelevant to an understanding of his art.

Private psychological mechanisms are necessarily incomplete explanations of the meaning of social action, or aesthetic creation and apprehension, unless they are placed within their objective contexts. History, not psychology, connects a given attitude or event and its psychological components. As Praz notes, it is quite secondary whether Bryon was really a psychopath or not. "Taste and fashion" provide "the genetic link." The critical focus must be the historical context within which Byron's personality dynamics were defined. Praz plainly moves from Crocean assumptions: history is the master-science, not psychology.[25]

Viewed psychoanalytically, neither Paul nor Van Gogh—nor Hitler, for that matter—is fully available as publicly relevant figures, as prophets or artists or politicians. This is at once the attraction and the ambiguity of the penetration of social science by psychoanalysis. Modern man is attracted precisely by the possibility of avoiding the public reference. Privatized in response to the overt horror and ubiquity of public life, modern man (to turn one of Harold Lasswell's finest insights) has sought out precisely those doctrines that are the intellectual modalities of privatization.

The examples of Velasquez or Rembrandt or Rubens would provide further tests of the modality of privatization, of which the Freudian method is both source and expression. Each artist can better be understood historically, as culture-revolutionaries against the Christian dualism of spirit and flesh. Following in the pagan traditions of the Renaissance, each, in his own style, broke up the segregation of spirituality and sensuality in Western painting. Freud's favorite artist-patient, Leonardo, had had a similar aim. But, because Freud collapses the artist into the patient, his book on Leonardo is a self-acknowledged failure as an analysis of the artist.[26] Freud understood Leonardo's art as an expression of his homosexuality. But what Freud, as a psychological determinist, did not acknowledge is that Leonardo's art is more importantly a revolt against Christian dualism.

In Leonardo's historical context, unlike Rubens', Christian dualism was still dominant. Leonardo's revolt needed to be covert. Both his pathological motivations (homosexuality) and his revolt against Christian dualism (the focus on the body) were legitimated by placing them within sanctioned religious subject matter. His great "St. John the Baptist" is assuredly the image of the mammalian man. When one looks at "St. John" in the Louvre, or at the figures in "The Last Supper," one understands, much more intensely than the reproductions in Freud's book allow, the insight of his description of Leonardo's male figures: "They are pretty boys of feminine tenderness with feminine forms; they do not cast down their eyes but gaze mysteriously triumphant, as if they knew of a great happy issue concerning which one must remain quiet; the familiar fascinating smile leads us to infer that it is a love secret."[27]

But Freud's insight, however true, has blocked others equally true, and thus equally necessary. His theoretical aim has been "to demonstrate the connection between the outer experiences" (Leonardo's art) and "inner experiences" (Leonardo's pathology).[28] After detailing the homosexual images in his painting and relating them to certain infantile fantasies and early biographical clues, Freud concludes that psychoanalysis has supplied "an understanding of [Leonardo's artistic] expressions and limitations." But this is precisely what the Freudian devaluation of the historical context fails to do. Leonardo's artistic expressions and limitations were primarily organized by his relation to a specific cultural configuration. His psychological motivations penetrated his revolt, but his revolt and the precise expressions of these motivations remain incomprehensible without an account of the historical situation.

Christian dualism presented no problem to Rubens. Living in an emancipated, bourgeois patrician culture, Rubens needed no covert resort to mask his adoration of the human body. To understand Ruben's frank paganism, compare his muscular, beautiful, athletic Christ, erotic, on the cross, to Rembrandt's thin, pale, beaten little Jew (cf. the Dresden "Christ at the Column"). In Rubens' orgiastic scenes and monumentally sensual bodies in motion, Christian dualism has given way to Greek eroticism. Only in a de-Christianized culture could such exuberant paganism become so popular. Rubens was an ambassador of his nation, a culture prince of his time.

Psychoanalysis could add little to the apprehension of Rubens' paintings by a study of his personality or by an analysis of the images in his painting. If Rubens' art is dominated by circular forms, as is commonly acknowledged, this need not be attributed to psychological motivations. An adequate explanation of the internal structure of Rubens' paintings can be made without recourse to psychological interpretation.

The circle is a closed form: in aesthetic terms, a device of limitation and control. All intense experience—the mystic's contemplation of God, the political drive toward power, or the aesthetic contemplation of physical beauty—needs to be controlled if it is not to break through the subject's intention and become demonic. As an artist, Rubens used a closed form to control his contemplation of physical beauty. He developed design values that controlled orgiastic movement. The compositional value of the circle reduced the possibility of demonic expression. Freud thought aesthetic forms, like intellectual systems, are essentially control devices, to integrate and limit the personality. Rubens, as painter, limited the sensual by closed visual designs. Freud, as intellectual, limited the sensual by the universal analogical designs of the mind and by the principle of balance within the sensual itself.

## III

Of course, Freud did not perceive the designs controlling his insight that performed the same function as aesthetic design. Whatever his own system-building achievements, he always subsumed intellectual efforts under private pathology, in his own case as in others. Philosophic systems are ultimately, he thought, expressions of paranoia.[29] The intent of this essay is to argue that the opposite may be true. Paranoia should be subsumed to philosophy. Neurosis should be subsumed to art, obsessionalism or epilepsy to religion, libidinal personality to politics. It is precisely art that may pick up a given neurosis—or religion that may pick up obsessionalism, or politics that may pick up a given personality type—and extend it beyond itself into the socially meaningful. By extending the psychological beyond itself into the social, the meaning of the psychological is totally changed.

Freud's favorite novel, *The Brothers Karamazov*, would be an absurdity instead of a great teaching on how men ought to live, if Alyosha's private psychological mechanisms informed his Christ-likeness. It is precisely for that reason that Dostoevski makes Alyosha a beautifully healthy, red-cheeked youth. Alyosha's Christ-likeness informs his psychology, not the reverse. Alyosha is not, any more than Prince Myshkin, the "constitutional Christ," as Nietzsche thought. This is the discovery toward which Dostoevski drives the un-Christian protagonists surrounding both characters. Alyosha (like the Prince) loves and wishes to marry. His imitation of Christ is, after all, this-worldly. And it is precisely the tension between the ordinary understanding of Prince Myshkin's sickness and the extraordinary context of it that gives *The Idiot* its extra-psychological—that is, moral—depth. The psychological level may be the most shallow, not the most deep.

"Depth psychology" may be easily a contradiction in terms. Individuals cannot be understood deeply. The deepest part of the individual may be his relation to society, his social self. Thus *The Idiot* is not a portrait of a sick individual, of an "unsocial" self. It is the portrait of a saint, in a society that does not recognize saints. The pathos of Myshkin is defined by his social relations. As it turns out, the Prince is the only "healthy" (i.e., for Dostoevski, moral) man in his society. This is the fact that is literally presented in the physical description of Alyosha. It is his brothers who are distorted and sick. And it is the others, not Prince Myshkin, who are really sick. Sickness, as Freud knew, is a social act. As a liberal, Freud saw the cause of sickness as a sick society. As a conservative, the great Janus mind of modern social thought of accepted society as the norm and made sickness a deviation from it. The contradiction was caused by his analogical elimination of historical processes.

Hegelianism constructed the precise opposite relation between the psychological and the historical. If Freud hinged meanings on the private psychological reference, Hegel hinged them on the public historical reference. Public contexts are autonomous and supreme as systems of social causation. Hegel decided that the world spirit has its own immanent purposes, to which private psychological constellations are secondary. The world spirit uses Napoleon's personality; Napoleon's personality does not use the world spirit. His own "mode of considering [personality]," Hegel concluded, in his attack on "these psychologists," "excludes the so-called 'psychological' view."[30]

Marx followed Hegel in his antipsychological orientation. Capitalism demands certain personality types; certain personality types do not first demand capitalism. It is impossible, in Marxist terms, to discover "capitalist personality types" in primitive society, as certain modern anthropologists, deeply influenced by one or another version of Freudianism, have done.[31] The capitalist personality is "personified capital." Marx would never have said capital was a "personification" of a certain character type. "Except as personified capital, the capitalist [as a personality] has no historical value, and no right to . . . historical existence."[32] As the stages of capitalist development evolve, so will the personality types involved in that objective process. Thus, an ascetic character structure is the psychological referent at one point, when abstinence is required by the objective process of capital accumulation. In later stages, "a conventional degree of prodigality" may be the demand placed upon the psychological material.

For both Hegel and Marx, psychological direction can be meaningful only when understood as a response elicited by the action-demand implicit in historical evolution. Hegelianism and Marxism can be understood as antonyms of Freudianism. For both, in contrast to Freudianism, "nature" may be held constant. Therefore, it is irrelevant as a motivational explanation of social processes. Freudianism, on the other hand, has regular recourse to the constant of "nature" as a grammar of social analysis. But the essence of social processes, according to Marx, is change. Freudianism, according to Marxism, is caught in the logical impasse of explaining change by constancy.

But Freud had a way out. In psychological terms, he insisted, there was no change. Society, as a psychological aggregate, was what it had always been. Freud the social theorist, so far as he depended upon Freud the natural scientist, showed the traditional positivist eagerness to eliminate the challenge of history by finding lawfulness in nature. As a positivist, Freud achieved a spatialization of time into an evolutionary sequence in which man, by virtue of his rational adaptability, is always at home. Individual history recapitulates racial history, and each historic stage is proper to man's genetic situation.

As a romantic conservative, however, Freud achieved a spatialization of time into cycles of recurrence bound by origins, in which man is also always at home by virtue of the repetition of his psychological problems and their solutions. The popularity of psychoanalysis, in an age frightened by its history, may be ascribed in some degree to the Freudian construction of nature-history. And in a Western world so profoundly concerned with its natural needs, the rejection of both Marxism and Christianity is due to an opposite construction, to their subordination of nature to history. Men, according to both Marxism and Christianity, live not in nature but in history. It is in this sense that Karl Mannheim understood both as utopian doctrines. (Indeed, Mannheim awarded Marxism the final honor of being the last utopianism of Western culture, before the sociogenetic analysis of sociology and psychoanalysis together closed off the future of illusions.)

If Hegel's subordination of nature made psychology irrelevant to social science, it was precisely the irrelevance of private psychological mechanisms as such that made social action more than any actor could possibly know. Social action is an expression not of subjective intention or drives but of the purposes of the evolving historical situation. The relation between personality and society was the relation between action-demand and the psychological response it elicits.

Marx went so far with Hegel. In terms of the relation of the freedom of man and the necessity of society, freedom is not the autonomous psychological structure of the individual asserting its claim against the direction of history. Rather, freedom is the action-demand of the historical situation, which is necessity.

Freedom cannot be located in some idea of supra-historical personality. By identifying freedom and personality as that action-demand implicit or explicit in a given social process, Marx could identify social change as at the same time opening up the possibility of psychological change. Socialism thus could mean, for Marx, a radical change in "human nature." Understood politically, the new society would mean the leap into freedom. Understood psychologically, it would mean the leap into full personality. Personality in the good society implies full, as well as true, consciousness. Previous societies have been characterized not only by fragmentary consciousness but also by false consciousness.

## IV

The polarity of Hegel and Marx, on the one hand, and Freud, on the other, is complicated by an important similarity in the formal structure of their thought. That similarity is best noted in the convergence of the Freudian concept of the unconscious and the Hegelian concept of the unawareness of the agents of the world spirit. Hegel's famous aphorism—that the owl of Minerva takes flight only at night—may be read profitably against Freud's assertions that all meaning is revealed in the night life and veiled in the waking life. And Freud's insistence on the primacy of the unconscious in human action may be read with Hegel's conclusion that it is "an unconscious impulse that occasion[s] the accomplishment of that for which the time [is] ripe."[33] All three—Hegel, Marx, and Freud

—were aware that history could proceed outside the consciousness of its actors. The actor need not be aware of the meaning of his action.

The idea of unconscious purposive action has a long history in the Western tradition. In Jewish prophecy, the historical actors may know nothing of Jahweh, but they are nevertheless under his leadership and are defined by what they mean to Irsael rather than by what they think Israel means to them. Israel may be a suffering servant without conscious intention. God chose Israel. Israel did not choose God. Even the Gentiles fulfill Jahweh's will, without—even against—their consciousness. Thus the prophets, in the great tradition of Hebrew prophecy, legitimated Israel's sufferings as punishments at the hands of the scourges of God.

In Christian tradition (for example, Bossuet), Israel was quite unaware that it was the bearer of the Christ. Thus, Western religious historiography operated on the assumption that there were certain objective demands upon which men were compelled to act, quite unconscious of the nature of their action.

Hegel only emptied the concept of objective demand and unconscious response of its specific Christian content; he kept the analytical structure intact. Now it was the "cunning of Reason" rather than God's will that used private psychological mechanisms in order to realize itself. Individual pathologies may drive men in apparently arbitrary directions, but in reality pathologies are selected out to serve the objective situation—Reason-History—the Ought toward which the Is assimilates itself.

As for Hegel, so for Freud, man does more than he knows. In contrast to Hegel, Freud thought that man is used not by the objective historical process but by the psychological. But Freud could not allow his theory of the unconscious to become a theory of individuation. At this point Freud may be partially reassimilated to Hegel. In order to establish the lawfulness and universality of the psychological process, he had to eliminate the contingent and individual and accidental as thoroughly as Hegel. The unconscious had to be collective if it were to register the law of psychic life. Freud's analogical assumptions allowed him to construct the unconscious as itself an objective process, free from the subjective intentions of its individual possessors. By virtue of his persistent analogy between the individual and the collective, Freud retained much of the tragic weight of objective social processes moving unconscious actors that one discovers in Hegel.[34]

There is another pervasive figure in modern social thought who held an illuminating anti-psychologistic view of historical dynamics. Max Weber's whole analysis of the role of personality in social causation rested on the Marxist separation between psychological and historical categories. In his remarkable discussion of ancient Judaism, Weber notices that the prophets are the most varied of personality types. But no matter how divergent psychologically, they converge into identity in their publicly relevant roles as prophets. All the prophets, however radically they differ psychologically, are defined as spokesmen for the messianic possibility.

Messianism, Weber concluded, could not be derived from private psychological mechanisms. There is no prophetic personality type. Prophecy cannot be understood psychologically, but only historically: as a publicly shared interpretive tradition, which has selected out and transformed the most varied psychological material and organized it into a common contribution. The prophets were not self-selected in terms of their personalities. Rather they were selected by the objective tradition of religious interpretation and by the social conflicts of their historical situation.

Given the covenant theology of the ancient Jews, the private psychological dynamics of the various prophets were irrelevant to their action as prophets. Prophets could act as such only within a certain objective frame of reference. If, theoretically, one should act differently, the social process would invoke the principle of fruitful misunderstanding to eliminate the psychological deviancy as a relevant social factor. Contemporaries have always tended to misunderstand deviants. The purpose of contemporaneous misunderstanding is to be a control device against the eruption of psychological factors as determinative in the social process.

The irony of history (enforced by contemporaneous misunderstanding) exhibited the regular disjunction between subjective intention or direction and objective function. This is Weber's concept of the decisive historical role of unintended consequences, as exemplified, in another case, by the fate of the Protestant ethnic.

Jewish prophetism also suffered the tragic fate of the unintended consequence. The irony of history forced these most unpolitical of personality types into critical political-action contexts. The prophets were passionately disinterested in politics. Their great passion was to stop religious syncretism. But in a historical situation characterized by the absence of separation between politics and religion, and in a permanent military crisis, the prophets—against their consciousness—could not help but be assigned to specific parties and to act influentially in politics. The historical "interaction" between the prophetic personality and the social situation in which he was involved was not simply a "reciprocal process," as contemporary social science's ameliorative vocabulary would have it.

## V

Influential theoreticians of contemporary social science like Talcott Parsons and Edward A. Shils have acknowledged Weber as well as Freud as their master. Plainly, however, they do not serve both masters. They owe more to Freud and less to Weber than they acknowledge. Marx is, of course, ignored.[35] And the fact that Weber saw psychology as a "natural science" and proposed to develop his *verstehen* sociology free from psychology is equally ignored by these eminent Weberians. Weber understood the problem of *verstehen* as a methodological construction of *it*'s not for *I*'s. For Weber, as for Hegel and Marx, the historical subsumed the psychological. The subsumption was irreversible.

For Freud, as for the dominant movements of contemporary social science, the psychological subsumed the social. Congruent with the meliorist intellectual tradition out of which it comes, contemporary social-science theory has tried to mediate between the two positions with a concept that is simultaneously its dominant value: "interaction." To confirm the classic meliorist value by rediscovering it as an analytical concept, social science has concluded that "neither the individual nor the group is adequate to comprise all the aspects of the life of man in society."[36] It is as if somehow all the aspects of social life are in a parliamentary situation and are of equal causal sovereignty.

The magic word in contemporary social science, as a perspective recent survey has noted, is "interaction." "If one wanted a single word to characterize the conception of man which governs the current activities of American social scientists, one might well select the term *interaction*."[37] A sanctioned alternative word is "reciprocal." The sanctioned vision of social action is as "complexes of the meaningfully oriented actions of persons reciprocally related to one another."[38]

But, within its ameliorative vocabulary, the social sciences have undergone their own "Copernican revolution." The social sciences' "present conceptualization of interactive man . . . directly reflects" Freud's "revolutionary reconceptualization." Freud's revolutionary influence has been toward "the re-emergence of the person" as the essential conceptual tool of the social sciences. The "individualizing tendency" initiated by the victory of Freudianism over Marxism among American intellectuals, "has been felt throughout the social sciences." With Freudianism as the decisive influence, the "personal reference" has become the dominant modality of social analysis.[39] Louis Wirth's summary dictum—"sociology deals first and foremost with psychological materials"—measures the basic reversal in social science's conceptual apparatus. The dictum once read:

"Sociology deals first and foremost with historical materials." And Marx and other philosophers of history were acknowledged as decisive influences. Now neither the discipline of philosophers nor that of historians provides the models with which social scientists identify themselves. As social scientists increasingly insist upon a prestigious self-image as natural scientists, they increasingly assimilate themselves to the self-image of psychologists and to the assumptions of given schools of psychology. It is important to notice that psychologists have traditionally insisted upon their status as natural scientists, while historians have traditionally denied an identification with the natural sciences.[40]

The assimilation of the social sciences to psychology as the master-science, instead of to history, is made complete when one moves from the problem of material to the problem of analysis. Not only is social data first and foremost psychological, but all knowledge of it must be purely nominal and subjective. It is normative, in the language of contemporary social science, to say: "The structure or system of [personal] interrelations *when seen collectively* constitutes the society which *may be regarded* as the bearer of culture."[41] History is mass psychology, and the knowledge of it pure psychologism. It is fortunate for contemporary social science that the structure of society has been discovered to be congruent with the psychological principle of "interaction," as Kant and Freud discovered the principle of nature congruent with the principle of understanding.

# Part III

# The Concepts

# Motivation / *Martin B. Duberman*

Most of the very large literature dealing with the concept of motivation, is highly technical and of little use to the historian. A great deal of motivational research is in allied fields, such as perception, learning, and personality structure.[1] Elements of motivational theory are discussed by Dr. Duberman in the analysis reprinted below. As he uses it, the concept of motivation leaps the disciplinary barrier of psychology and becomes involved with sociology and the study of group processes. This demonstrates, at once, the frailty of disciplinary barriers and the poverty of reductionism that equates historical and societal processes with interactionism on the psychological level.[2] Dr. A. L. Kroeber has said that if psychology were better organized and theoretically more productive, the organization of history also would be improved.[3] This may be true, but it is not the solution for all the problems of historical study.[4]

O UT OF THEIR heightened concern with the pressing question of Negro rights, a number of historians, especially the younger ones, have begun to take a new look at the abolitionists, men who in their own day were involved in a similar movement of social change. About both them and ourselves we are asking anew such questions as the proper role of agitation, the underlying motives of both reformers and resistants, and the useful limits of outside interference. From this questioning a general tendency has developed to view the abolitionists in a more favorable light than previously. As yet, however, it is a tendency only, and hostility to the abolitionists continues to be strong among historians.[1]

Perhaps one reason why no fuller re-evaluation has taken place is that historians have been made cautious by the fate of previous "revisionist" scholarship. We have seen how current preoccupations can prompt dubious historical re-evaluations. But this need not always be the case. Contemporary pressures, if recognized and contained, can prove fruitful

Martin B. Duberman, "The Abolitionists and Psychology," *Journal of Negro History*, XLVII (July, 1962), 183–91. Published by the Association for the Study of Negro Life and History, Inc. Reprinted by permission.

1. Dalbir Bindra, *Motivation: A Systematic Interpretation* (New York, 1959).
2. *Supra*, 7–8.
3. "An Anthropologist Looks at History," *op. cit.*, 287.
4. Popper, *op. cit., Open Society*, 290; *op. cit., Poverty of Historicism*, 142.

in stimulating the historical imagination. They may lead us to uncover (not invent) aspects of the past to which we were previously blind.

If historians need more courage in their re-consideration of the abolitionists, they also need more information. Particularly do they need to employ some of the insights and raise some of the questions which developments in related fields of knowledge have made possible. Recent trends in psychology seem especially pertinent, though historians have not attempted to evaluate and incorporate them. It is my hope in this paper to make some beginning in that direction.

It might be well to start by referring to one of psychology's older principles, the uniqueness of personality. Each individual, with his own genetic composition and his own life experience, will develop into a distinctive organism. There are, of course, certain universal processes common to the species—that cluster of basic drives and reflexes which are more or less "instinctive." There are also a variety of common responses conditioned by our membership in a particular group, be it family, class, church or nation. These similarities among human beings make possible the disciplines—such as sociology, anthropology and social psychology—which concern themselves with patterns of behavior, and demonstrate that no man is *sui generis*. But it does not follow from this that the qualities which are uniquely his are mere irrelevancies. As Gordon Allport has said, ". . . all of the animals in the world are psychologically less distinct from one another than one man is from other men."[2]

This is not to question, of course, the validity of attempts, whether they be by sociologists, psychologists or historians, to find meaningful similarities in the behavioral patterns of various human groups. The point is to make certain that such similarities genuinely exist, and further, to be aware that in describing them, we do not pretend to be saying *everything* about the individuals involved. Historians, it seems to me, are prone to ignore both cautions—their treatment of the abolitionists being the immediate case in point.

With barely a redeeming hint of uncertainty, many historians list a group of "similar traits" which are said to characterize all abolitionists: "impractical," "self-righteous," "fanatical," "humorless," "vituperative," and—if they are very modern in their terminology—"disturbed." The list varies, but usually only to include adjectives equally hostile and denunciatory. The stereotype of the "abolitionist personality," though fluid in details, is clear enough in its general outlines.

But did most abolitionists really share these personality traits? The fact is, we know much less about the individuals involved in the movement than has been implied. Some of the major figures, such as Joshua Leavitt, have never received biographical treatment; others—the Tappans,

Edmund Quincy, and Benjamin Lundy, for example—badly need modern appraisal. And the careers and personalities of the vast majority of significant secondary figures—people like Lydia Maria Child, Sidney Gay, Maria Weston Chapman, Henry B. Stanton, and Abby Kelley Foster— have been almost totally unexplored. Whence comes the confidence, then, that allows historians to talk of "the abolitionist personality," as if this had been microscopically examined and painstakingly reconstructed?

Certainly the evidence which we do have, does not support such confident theorizing. In order to adhere to this conceptual strait-jacket, it is necessary to ignore or discount much that conflicts with it—the modesty of Theodore Weld, the wit of James Russell Lowell, the tender humanity of Whittier, the worldly charm of Edmund Quincy. This does not mean that we need leap to the opposite extreme and claim all abolitionists were saints and seraphs. But if some of them were disagreeable or disturbed, we want, instead of a blanket indictment, to know which ones and in what ways; we want some recognition of the variety of human beings who entered the movement.

It seems to me that what too many historians have done is to take William Lloyd Garrison as a personality symbol for the entire movement (at the same time, ironically, that they deny him the commanding leadership which he was once assumed to have had). Latching on to some of the undeniably "neurotic" aspects of his personality (and bolstered, it should be said, by the eccentric psychographs of other abolitionists—a Gerrit Smith say, or a Stephen Foster), they equate these with the personality structures of all the abolitionists, and conclude that the movement was composed solely of "quacks." In doing so, they fail to do justice to the wide spectrum of personality involved; in fact, they do not even do justice to Garrison, for to speak exclusively of *his* oracular and abusive qualities is to ignore the considerable evidence of personal warmth and kindliness.

It may be that when we know more of other abolitionists, we may with equal certainty be able to single out qualities in them which seem palpable symptoms of "disturbance." But let the evidence at least precede the judgment. And let us also show a decent timidity in applying the label "neurotic." Psychiatrists, dealing with a multitude of evidence and bringing to it professional insights, demonstrate more caution in this regard than do untrained historians working with mere traces of personality. If the disposition to be hostile exists, "Neurosis" can almost always be established. Under the Freudian microscope, it would be a rare man indeed whose life showed no evidence of pathological behavior. (Think, for one, of the admirable William James, who, as his devoted biographer, Ralph Barton Perry, has shown, was subject to hypochondria,

hallucinations, and intense oscillations of mood.) I am not suggesting
that all men's lives, if sufficiently investigated, would show equally severe
evidence of disturbance. I mean only to warn that, given the double
jeopardy of a hostile commentator and the weight of a hostile historical
tradition, we must take special precaution not to be too easily convinced by
the "evidence" of neurosis in the abolitionists.

And even were we to establish the neurotic component of behavior,
the story would certainly not be complete. To know the pathological
elements in an individual's behavior is not to know everything about his
behavior. To say that Garrison, in his fantasy world, longed to be punished and thus deliberately courted martyrdom, or that Wendell Phillips,
alienated from the "new order," sought to work out his private grievances
against the industrial system by indirectly attacking it through slavery,
is hardly to exhaust the range of their possible motives. We know far too
little about why men do anything—let alone why they do something as
specific as joining a reform movement—to assert as confidently as historians have, the motives of whole groups of men. We may never know
enough about the human psyche to achieve a comprehensive analysis
of motivation; how much greater the difficulty when the subject is dead
and we are attempting the analysis on the basis of partial and fragmentary
remains.

Our best hope for increased understanding in this area—aside from
the artist's tool of intuition—is in the researches of psychology. But at
present there is no agreed-upon theory of motivation among psychologists.
Allport, however, summarizing current opinion, suggests that behavior
does not result solely from the need to reduce tension, but may also aim
(especially in a "healthy" person) at distant goals the achievement of
which can be gained only by maintaining tension.[3] Allport does not press
his views, realizing the complexity of the problems at issue. But his
hypotheses are at least suggestive as regards the abolitionists, for their
motives, rather than being solely the primitive ones of eliminating personal
tension (under the guise of ethical commitment), may also have included
a healthy willingness to bear tension (in the form of ostracism, personal
danger, and material sacrifice) in order to persevere in the pursuit of
long-range ideals.

Acceptance of these suggestions runs into the massive resistance of
neo-Freudian cynicism.[4] How old-fashioned, it will be said, to talk in
terms of "ideals" or "conscience," since these are only unconscious
rationalizations for "darker" drives which we are unable to face. How old-
fashioned, too, to talk as if men could exercise choice in their conduct,
since all our behavior is determined by our antecedents.

But the surprising fact is that such views are not old-fashioned. On the contrary, they have recently returned to favor in psychoanalytical circles.[5] Increasing dissatisfaction with the ability of behaviorist theory fully explain human action, has led to a re-consideration of the role of reason and the possibilities of purposive, deliberate behavior. The result is the influential new school of "ego psychology," which views man as endowed with a considerable margin of freedom and responsibility, and which has restored to the vocabulary such "old-fashioned" terminology as character, will power, and conscience. Moral earnestness, moreover, is no longer equated with self-deception. As Allport has said, the very mark of maturity "seems to be the range and extent of one's feeling of self-involvement in abstract ideals."[6] Some of these new emphases had been prefigured in the work of such philosophers as Sartre, who have long stressed social action as a sign of "authenticity" in man.

But although all of this makes a re-evaluation of the abolitionists possible, it does not make one necessary. Men may now be thought capable of impersonal devotion to ideals, but this does not mean that the abolitionists were such men. Maturity may now be defined as the ability to commit ourselves objectively to ethical values, but it does not follow that every man who makes such a commitment does so out of mature motives.

Yet at least some doubts should be raised in our minds as to whether we have been fair in regarding the abolitionists as psychologically homogeneous, and at that, homogeneous in the sense of being self-deceived. My own feeling goes beyond doubt, into conviction. I do not claim, to repeat, that because the abolitionists fought in a noble cause, their motives were necessarily noble—i.e., "pure" and "unselfish," unrelated in any way to their own inner turmoil or conflicts. A connection between inner problems and outer convictions probably always exists to some degree. But an individual's public involvement is never completely explained by discussing his private pathology. Yet it is just this that historians have frequently done, and to that degree, they have distorted and devalued the abolitionist commitment.

To provide a concrete example, by way of summary, consider the case of James Russell Lowell, whose biography I am writing, and about whom I can talk with more assurance than I might some other figure.

His history seems to me convincing proof that *some* people at least became abolitionists not primarily to escape from personal problems, but out of real commitment to certain ethical values—recognizing, as I have said, that the two are never wholly unrelated. Lowell's active life as a reformer came during the period of his greatest contentment—secure in a supremely happy marriage, and confident of his talents and his future. His contemporaries agree in describing him as a gay, witty warm man, without serious tensions or disabling anxieties. I have come across so little evidence of "pathology" in the Lowell of these years that when the standard picture of the abolitionist as a warped eccentric is applied to him, it becomes absurd.

And he *was* an abolitionist, though various arguments have been used to deny this. Lowell, it has been said, came to the movement late—and only at the instigation of his bride, Maria White, who was a confirmed reformer—he never fully committed himself to it, and he finally left the ranks in the early 1850's. There may be some justice to these charges, but on the whole the argument is not persuasive. Given Lowell's youth (he was born in 1819) he could not have joined the movement much earlier than he did (which was around 1840), and there is evidence that he was involved in the cause before he met Maria White. The main point is that for roughly ten years he was unquestionably a serious abolitionist, both as an active member of the Massachusetts Anti-Slavery Society, and as a frequent contributor to abolitionist periodicals. The reasons for his drifting out of the movement are complex, but turn largely on the fact that his wife's death in 1853 destroyed the structure of his life and left him apathetic to public issues. (Might not this give added weight to the argument that it takes a reasonably contented man to interest himself in the problems of others?)

Even when it is admitted that Lowell was an abolitionist, he is dismissed as not having been a "typical" one. But who was the typical abolitionist? Is the standard of measurement meant to be some outstanding individual—Garrison, say, or Theodore Weld—and is everyone else to be considered more or less of an abolitionist depending on how closely he approximated the personality structure of the model? But a man may be prominent in a movement without necessarily typifying it. And which of several leading—and very different—figures should be chosen as the model? The decision is likely to be arbitrary (even unconscious), varying with each historian.

Or is the standard of measurement meant to be some composite group of traits which accurately describe the large number of abolitionists, so that when any single individual fails to exhibit these traits, he may justifiably be dismissed as "the exception which proves the rule?"[7] This approach is more reasonable, but here again we run up against the old difficulty of drawing a genuinely valid group portrait. We know so little about the individual personalities and careers of the majority of abolitionists that it seems like putting the cart before the horse to even talk about a composite portrait. Certainly the one which is now commonly accepted ("impractical"; "self-righteous," etc.) fails adequately to describe many of the abolitionists about whom we do have information. I mean here not only Lowell, but a number of others. What I have seen in my researches into the papers of people like Edmund Quincy, Lydia Maria Child or Maria Weston Chapman (to name only a few of the more prominent), has created the strong suspicion in my mind that if their personalities were to be investigated in depth, they too would be found to deviate from the accepted portrait in so many significant ways as further to undermine its reliability.

A conceptual scheme may yet be devised which adequately describes the motives and actions of most of the abolitionists. But if so, it will not be of the primitive kind thus far suggested. There is no reason why historians cannot legitimately investigate group patterns, but to do so meaningfully, they must become skilled in the techniques of sociology and other related disciplines. This takes time and inclination, and the historian, busy with his special interests and orientated towards the particular, rarely has either. Unfortunately this does not always prevent him from trying his hand, though the result is frequently the elementary sort of categorizing used to describe the abolitionists.

Opinions will continue to differ as the best way of achieving desired social change. Our own generation's confrontation with segregation has made this clear. Many of us feel as strongly about the evil of that practice as the abolitionists did about the institution of slavery. Like them, too, we have scant faith in Southern voluntarism or the benevolent workings of time; patience and inactivity have not done their work. Naturally we would like to believe that our sense of urgency comes from concern for the Negro rather than from a need to escape from some private torment of our own. Because of this we are admittedly prone to credit our historical counterparts with equally good motives. Our wish to think well of them may account for our doing so. But as Erich Fromm has said, "the fact that an idea satisfies a wish does not mean necessarily that the idea is false."[8] There is much in the new psychology to encourage the belief that the idea is not false. At any rate, if we are to find out, we need less dogma, more research, and a chastening sense of wonder at the complexities of human nature.

# The
# Subconscious / *Frederick Wyatt and William B. Willcox*

Insofar as he is concerned with the unconscious, the historian is confronted by unfamiliar concepts and shadowy data that he is tempted to round out in terms of theory. The main problem is in the data of history, which are oriented toward overt behavior and conscious motivation and which, as a rule, blaze no broad highway to the subconscious. Rare, indeed, is the document which deals directly and explicitly with subconscious motivation. Letters, diaries, memoirs, and personal literature that reveal intimate facts useful in a psychoanalytical account generally do not survive to reach the historian. Henry Adams, for example, following the suicide of his wife destroyed his personal diaries—one of the few times an Adams did destroy documents. On the other hand, surviving fragments of the diaries of William Byrd II are a joy and challenge to the psychoanalytically oriented historian.

Writers, especially novelists, are easier to deal with in psychoanalytic terms because they sometimes leave behind in their imaginitive work images that the historian, using a Freudian framework, can exploit. With statesmen and soldiers the going is rougher, as in the case of Sir Henry Clinton. Dr. Wyatt, a psychologist, and Dr. Willcox, an historian, have indicated difficulties in probing the Clinton subconscious using a record that is incomplete. That their effort is only partially successful shows no lack of skill and energy, but attests that Clinton long ago effectively covered his tracks.

The manner in which Wyatt and Willcox have presented their findings, their frank avowal of the experimental character of the entire procedure and of the tentative character of their conclusions are very welcome. The moderation of their approach contrasts with what might be described as a tone of over-eager acceptance of the psychoanalytic theory as applied to history in the writings of William L. Langer[1] and Bruce Mazlish.[2] Hans Meyerhoff, too, has drawn an analogy between the historical and psychoanalytical processes—both, he says, are developmental —and, like all analogies, take us only so far.[3]

Frederick Wyatt and W. B. Willcox, "Sir Henry Clinton: A Psychological Exploration in History," William and Mary Quarterly, 3rd series, XVI (Jan., 1959), 3–26. Reprinted by permission.

1. "The Next Assignment" American Historical Review, LXIII (January, 1958), 283–304.
2. Psychoanalysis and History (Englewood Cliffs, 1963), 1–19.
3. "On Psychoanalysis and History," Psychoanalysis and the Psychoanalytic Review, XLIX (Summer, 1962), 3–19. Norman O. Brown, Life Against Death (Middletown,

*In addition to psychoanalytic concepts, there are other psychological techniques which help the historian to understand an emotional state. "It would be most helpful," wrote John A. Garraty, "if we could give the Rorschach test to Wilson, get Julius Caesar to look at the pictures of the T.A.T., or put Napoleon on a psychoanalyst's couch, but these things cannot be." Yet, he continues, other techniques can be used by the historian and the biographer. These include graphology, or the study of handwriting variables; content analysis in accordance with the theory that "the kind of words a person uses and the frequency with which he employs them are a reflection of his inner nature"; value analysis, whereby autobiographical and personal data can be objectively described and with reference to an underlying emotional pattern; and the quantitative measurement of tension.*[4]

I N RECENT YEARS historians have been experimenting more and more frequently with a psychological approach to their subject, just as psychologists have been extending their investigations into the realm of history.[1] Fruitful as these individual experiments have been, they have one major drawback: history and psychology are such exacting disciplines that few practitioners of the one can become more than amateurs in the other. The professional inevitably suspects the amateur's findings, for reasons that are much sounder than mere distrust of the interloper. If each discipline has in fact something to contribute to the other, a promising way to explore what it may be is by collaboration.

To the best of our knowledge collaboration has rarely been attempted. This paper describes such an attempt by a clinical psychologist and a historian, working on the personality of an eighteenth-century general. Our investigation is not yet complete, and probably will not be for some years; its substantive findings are still tentative and its methodology far from perfect. We are convinced, however, that it has already shown its value, not merely by elucidating our own particular problem but also by suggesting what teamwork may do to elucidate similar problems. For these reasons we are offering a progress report.

---

Conn., 1959), claims that "Psychoanalytical consciousness, as a higher stage in the general consciousness of mankind, may be likewise the fufillment of the historical consciousness, that ever widening and deepening search for origins." 19.

4. John A. Garraty, "The Application of Content Analysis to Biography and History" in Ithiel de Sola Pool, ed., *Trends in Content Analysis* (Urbana, 1959), 171–87.

*I*

For some years the historian has been working on the question of why the British frittered away the great military advantages that they had at the beginning of the War of American Independence. The reasons usually given do not constitute, in sum, an explanation cogent or complete enough to be satisfying. In such a situation the investigator's task is to look for supplementary factors that have hitherto been ignored or underemphasized, so as to establish an explanation that is more comprehensive, if also more complex, than its predecessors.

Research soon indicated that one such neglected factor was an internecine war within the British command in America. Generals and admirals were often as much absorbed in quarreling with one another as in fighting the enemy; their quarrels were for the most part due less to the structure of command, or to differences over strategy, than to personal friction. The result was a progressive breakdown of co-operation between the two services and within the army, so that by the spring of 1781 the commander in chief of the army, General Clinton, was at loggerheads simultaneously with his opposite number in the navy, Admiral Arbuthnot, and with his own principal subordinate, Lord Cornwallis. Although only the Clinton-Cornwallis controversy became notorious, it was merely the last in a long series that, taken together, was unquestionably a factor in Britain's defeat.

Sir Henry Clinton was party to almost all these quarrels. He served throughout the war, from the fall of 1775 to the spring of 1778, as second in command to Sir William Howe, and thereafter as comander in chief until he resigned in the spring of 1782. During these six and a half years he was constantly at odds with someone—his superior or subordinate in the army, one of his naval colleagues, the responsible minister in London —and sometimes with several people at once. His great moment was the capture of Charleston and its defending army in 1780, but he paid for victory by estrangement from Arbuthnot and Cornwallis. The latter, left to direct the war in the South, evolved a disastrous strategy of his own, moved northward into Virginia, and was bottled up at Yorktown. Soon afterward Clinton resigned and went home, to find himself the scapegoat for what he insisted had been his subordinate's folly. The war of pamphlets that ensued lasted until Cornwallis left for a new and successful career in India.[2] Clinton spent his remaining years in retirement, protesting futilely that he had not been to blame for losing the war. Perhaps he was right, but his inability to get on with his fellows certainly deserves some of the blame. His crucial role and prickly temperament make him the logical focus for investigating the war that the British commanders were waging among themselves

General Clinton left behind him a large chest full of personal papers, which eventually came to rest in the William L. Clements Library of the University of Michigan. They are of every conceivable sort—returns of troops, petitions for favors, official correspondence, private letters to and from his friends in England, and the journals, notes, and memoranda that he jotted down for his own eye. These manuscripts, which now fill more than two hundred fat volumes, range from the 1760's to the 1790's, but are largely concentrated on the years of his American career. Despite their profusion, however, they are almost silent about his private affairs. When he came to this country in middle age, in 1775, he suddenly developed a collector's instinct for everything that bore on his career *as distinct from* his personal life; but before 1775 he kept almost nothing that bore significantly on either one. Our information about the first forty-five years of his life is therefore woefully inadequate. We do not know where he was born, what his relations were with his parents and sisters, or what outside influences affected his adolescence and early manhood. We know that when he was in his late thirties he married a girl of twenty, who bore him five children before she died five years later; that he never remarried; and that he subsequently acquired a mistress and raised a family by her. But his wife and legitimate children are little more than names in the papers that have survived, and his illegitimate family he mentions only once. He guarded his privacy with great success against the prying eyes of the future. In consequence, the man as child, husband, father, and lover has almost disappeared.

We have a little evidence about his marriage, of the sort that so often fascinates and frustrates historians. It consists of two letters and a journey. The letters, written to him soon after his wife's death, indicate that his grief was more devastating than the mores of his circle condoned, and may well have been more than the normal and natural response of a devoted husband at any period. The journey, undertaken eighteen months later to Vienna and the Balkans, was bizarre enough to suggest that he was using it as an anodyne for his bereavement.[3] These slender clues point to his having had an unusually strong attachment to his wife. After her death, furthermore, he seems to have transferred the attachment to her family: her father became a second father to him (his own had died years before); her sisters took charge of his children, brought them up while he was in America, and were still living with them when he died. Father- and sisters-in-law apparently helped to fill a void created by the death of his wife.

Only conjecture is possible, however, because the documents are so uninformative about Clinton as a human being. He doubtless arranged that they should be, by judiciously discarding whatever touched on his emotional life. Such editing is likely to occur, in greater or less degree, in most collections of autobiographical material; when men reach years of discretion, they are likely to be as discreet as Clinton in what they save. Significant information about their childhood is equally seldom preserved, because even important historical figures, unless born to the purple, are not important as children. This pruning of the records, whether deliberate or accidental, hampers the biographer's search for the wellsprings of conduct. He lacks the data about childhood, upbringing, and later personal involvements that he needs the most if he is to trace a consistent development of character. Without such data he must rely on whatever he can discover about his subject's work and personal relations. Occasionally he finds seeming incongruities of behavior, which are particularly valuable; they are like fissures through which he may glimpse the substratus of personality. But he has no more than glimpses. He is reasoning backward from the known to the unknown, and his findings are perforce conjectual.

Although Clinton's papers have few direct references to his personal life, they contain an abundance of indirect references. In a period when British commanders were, by and large, a reticent lot, Sir Henry as a commander had no reticence at all. During his American service he discussed on paper—in letters to friends and in notes for himself—whatever he felt was relevant to his military career. Here he was singularly frank, and he apparently destroyed nothing. After the war he continued to write, storing up page after page of memoranda, often pathetically repetitive, to prove that he had no cause to reproach himself. From this mountain of manuscript emerges much more than he intended. His personal and his military life were two facets of the same thing, and in talking about the general he inevitably revealed the man.

The aim of the investigation seemed at the start relatively simple: to search through this wealth of material for an explanation of Sir Henry's character that would cover both his quarrels and his generalship. The historian, working on his own, began with the conventional assumption that Clinton's pattern of behavior was substantially what might be expected of a normal eighteenth-century officer of his background, training, and capacity. Some deviations from the norm were obvious. Personal relationships were peculiarly difficult for him; he was doubtless a trying colleague—aloof, sensitive, and petulant. His planning was peculiarly unsuccessful: as a subordinate he belabored his superiors with suggestions that were always sound, sometimes brilliant, and almost never accepted; as commander in chief his designs were equally good, if more cautious, but were rarely executed. It seemed likely, nevertheless, that these peculiarities could be accounted for without postulating unusual motives.

If he was difficult, most of his colleagues were equally so; his advice as a subordinate was perhaps too audacious, and the responsibility of command may have sobered him to the point where he dared not implement his strategy until he had more strength than he usually had. This line of reasoning led to the conclusion that he did what he could with the materials at hand, including his own personality, but that he simply did not measure up to the requirements for success.

The more the data were explored, the more inadequate the conclusion seemed. The paradoxes of Sir Henry's conduct deepened on acquaintance, and time after time raised the question, *Why?* The historian's techniques failed to provide the answer. This failure, which was the *raison d'être* of our joint inquiry, can be understood only by discussing in greater detail some aspects of Sir Henry's career, to make clear what questions baffled historical interpretation and what material was available for psychological reinterpretation.

The first aspect to be considered is Clinton's penchant for giving advice to his superiors. This trait appeared as soon as he arrived in America. General Howe, as commander in chief, escaped the barrage of suggestions only by getting rid of his subordinate, first to an outlying post and then on an expedition to the Carolinas. But Clinton returned for the New York campaign of 1776, and again plagued headquarters with proposals. Only one was accepted, according to him—the tactical masterpiece that became the Battle of Long Island. Soon Howe got rid of him again, on detached service and then on leave to England. When Clinton, now knighted, returned in July of 1777, he found the army about to embark for Pennsylvania just when Burgoyne was advancing from Canada. Sir Henry recognized the strategic folly in this separation of force, and urged instead a junction by way of the Hudson. He was persistent, Howe obdurate; after days of argument the two concluded that "by some cursed fatality we could never draw together."[4] So they drew apart for the last time. Howe moved to Philadelphia, his subordinate remained on Manhattan, and Burgoyne, unsupported, struggled south to Saratoga. The most that Clinton had accomplished, after three years of trying to influence the conduct of the war, had been one successful battle.

He was emotionally involved in the plans he put forward. Although they were sometimes elaborate, and revealed his almost pedantic zest for detail, they were well conceived and aggressive; and his confidence in them matched his skepticism about the plans of others, particularly those adopted by headquarters. The superior virtues of his own were so self-evident, to his mind, that he could not understand their rejection and felt wronged by it. He was therefore continually surprised, disgruntled, and anxious to escape from an intolerable position. His surprise, at least, is understandable. The repeated ignoring of his advice may have been due in part to the singularly tactless way in which he pressed it, but this explanation only raises a further question. In other respects he was not abnormally tactless; why was he in this?

The second aspect of his career to be considered is his relations with the navy. Here he showed the same inability to get his ideas accepted, but with the difference that he was dealing with his equals in the hierarchy of command. During his first independent expedition, to South Carolina in 1776, he shared responsibility with Commodore Sir Peter Parker; the two men never established communications, and after the venture had ended in fiasco they wrangled about it for years. Later, as commander in chief, Sir Henry had to work with a succession of naval colleagues: Lord Howe, Admiral Gambier, Commodore Collier, Admirals Arbuthnot, Rodney, and Graves. With Howe, Collier, and Rodney he collaborated smoothly and effectively, but for short periods of time. Gambier, whom he called an old woman, aroused him to the unusual step of requesting a successor from one of five naval officers he named. Instead, the government chose Arbuthnot, a devious and vacillating pomposity, who by the late summer of 1780 was so thoroughly at odds with Clinton that joint operations came virtually to a standstill. Sir Henry sent the Cabinet an ultimatum, backed by a threat to resign. One of his terms was Arbuthnot's removal, and this the government accepted (without stipulating who was to succeed or when); the other terms it ignored. But Clinton stayed on, grumbling and threatening, until Arbuthnot was finally called home some nine months later. This record shows a surprising number of failures in co-operation, and of an odd sort. Where Clinton might have been expected to cut his cloth to the modest measure of a Parker, Gambier, or Arbuthnot and do what he could to get on with the war, he tended to wrap himself in his annoyance and do nothing. What lay back of this retreat into inaction?

The quarrel with Arbuthnot raises a third significant aspect of Sir Henry's record: his vacillation about resigning. In 1777 he returned to America only at the urging of his friends; in 1778 he was as reluctant to become commander in chief as the government was to appoint him; seven months later he was trying to resign, and he went on trying intermittently for the next two years. In the autumn of 1780 the King at last permitted him to come home whenever he saw fit, and in 1781 he had ample cause to see fit: Arbuthnot hung onto the naval command until July; Lord Cornwallis upset his chief's plans by marching into Virginia and staying there; and the Cabinet brusquely expressed its preference for the Earl's strategy. Clinton had excuse to resign if ever man had. Yet he found one reason after another for not doing so. His reluctance to assume the command, then to retain it, was now matched by his reluctance to let it go. In the circumstances he had two sensible alternatives, to exercise the authority of his position or to give place to Cornwallis; but he took neither one.[5] Why not?

A fourth point of significance is that his planning changed its character when he became commander in chief. At moments he showed his old capacity to attack, but in general the fire went out of his strategy as soon as he was responsible for implementing it. Where his ideas had previously been sound and bold, they became sound and cautious; and some of his best designs were never put to the test. He showed a new consciousness of the difficulties in the way and his old skill at blaming inaction on others —on the admirals assigned him as colleagues, the government that withheld reinforcements or amended his plans, the subordinates who misconceived or flouted his intentions. The authority that he had craved when himself a subordinate oppressed him once it was in his grasp. He apparently lacked the self-confidence to use it or to give it up, and his generalship suffered in consequence. What caused this creeping paralysis of will?

The campaign of 1781 provides the most puzzling aspect, from the historian's viewpoint, of Clinton's entire career. In this instance alone his memoirs give a retrospective view of his conduct that is not merely at odds with the evidence, but is almost impossible to reconcile with a common-sense interpretation of the man. After he returned to England he misconceived the position he had been in during the campaign, falsified the tenor of his instructions, and tried to publicize his erroneous conclusions as the truth. In another kind of person such distortion might be dismissed as the technique of the big lie. But Clinton was not a liar. In all the rest of his career he adhered scrupulously to the evidence before him, reasoned meticulously from it, and held to his reasoning in retrospect; for all his bias he was never consciously deceitful. Only about this campaign did he try to confuse the record, and he apparently did so with righteous self-confidence. How can his conduct be explained?

These various aspects of Clinton's record indicate that his behavior was shot through with contradictions. At times he showed the skill and insight that circumstances required, and at times he did not; at times he was intent on serving his own self-interest, and at times seemed willfully to betray it. After the war he was thoroughly honest in describing all his campaigns except the last, and about that he lied. His conduct challenges the investigator to find some unifying pattern that will embrace and explain the contradictions.

Historians have long wrestled with such problems. To show how a man's actions meshed with those of his contemporaries to produce a certain result is for the most part relatively easy—and relatively superficial. The difficulty comes in probing below the actions for the motives. Here the historian becomes perforce a psychologist, and his psychological tools are those of common sense. He assumes from experience that people behave, for good or ill, substantially as they intend to behave; passion or self-seeking or stupidity may deflect them from a rational course and prepare their undoing, but by their own lights, however dim, they see their path and are to some degree aware of their motives. This assumption is psychologically inadequate, but for the historian's purposes it frequently serves well enough. The impersonal chain of cause and effect, combined with the avowed and conscious intent of the participants, explains the outcome sufficiently so that he has no need to uncover the hidden springs of conduct.

Avowed and conscious motives, nevertheless, are always complemented by unconscious motives. The historian cannot pretend, after the work of Freud, to understand fully a person's growth and conduct without exploring both kinds. He may not need full understanding, but he must decide whether he does. If he is studying the origins of the Wars of the Roses or of the American Revolution, for example, he may care almost nothing about the psychological idiosyncrasies of Henry VI or George III; if he is writing a biography of either monarch, he must care a great deal. In the latter case he is in difficulty. These two kings exemplify a group of historical figures who played important roles in ways that deviated, at various times and in varying degrees, from the accepted norms of their day, and who seem to have been unaware that the motives driving them were quite irrelevant to the goals of comon sense. The history of the arts is full of such figures (as witness Nietzsche, Van Gogh, and Nijinsky), and they are more common than might be supposed in political and military annals; Blücher, for example, suffered from delusions that would have staggered Clinton. All these men left their mark on their times, and they are baffling subjects for a psychology of common sense.

Yet their idiosyncrasies are part of the historian's data. If his investigation requires the fullest possible understanding of such a personality, he is perforce as much concerned with its irrational as with its seemingly rational aspect; the two are in all likelihood the two faces of a single psychological coin.[6] Labeling the irrational aspect erratic or confused, and letting it go at that, begs the question of why the person behaved as he did. To find an answer the historian needs different analytic tools from those of his own discipline. The search for such tools led to our joint experiment.

## II

Our purpose was to determine whether the historical data on Clinton would yield to diagnostic procedure and form a recognizable psychological pattern. A preliminary survey of the material convinced us that, if there was a pattern, it would be one of largely unconscious motivation: the incongruities of his behavior would be results less of a reasoned reaction to the forces of circumstance than of an inner conflict that impelled him to pursue what he was afraid of and to turn away from what he desired. Because his behavior was incongruous in a regular way, it suggested a neurotic disturbance of character as the real source of his difficulties. Our initial investigation of his career, in other words, led us to the tentative conclusion that a pattern existed, that he adhered to it consistently (or was constrained by it), and that its outline would grow clearer as our inquiry progressed.

The methods of clinical interpretation, it was obvious, would have to be adapted to a novel situation. As a rule these methods are part of the usual process of psychotherapy, which is designed for understanding the living, not the dead. The pattern of the subject's personality normally emerges from his interaction with the therapist, and the subtle, idiosyncratic communication between the two is of fundamental importance. With an historical figure, patently, no such communication is possible. The therapist has a thousand questions to ask, but the subject answers only in written words—his own or his contemporaries'—that have at best an accidental relevance to the questions. The psychological inferences, for example, that may be drawn from the combination of reticence and assertiveness in Clinton's writing are different in kind from those that may be drawn from a clinical conversation. Hence we had to expect that a great deal would be left unexplained, and that the sum of our hypotheses would amount to less than reconstruction of the entire man. This is merely to say, however, that our inquiry was limited by the nature of historical evidence.[7]

Such evidence is by its nature incomplete, and a complete reconstruction from it would be a contradiction in terms. The context of an event is an integral part of it, and history provides no full description of the event, still less of the context, but only clues from which to infer what the rounded event-in-context might have been. The clues are colored in the first instance by the subjectivity of whoever furnished them, and again by the subjectivity of whoever interprets them. Hence the basic historical datum, far from being Ranke's ideal event *wie es eigentlich gewesen*, is the incompletely and subjectively reconstructed event-in-context. Even this datum, furthermore, is meaningless in itself, and remains so until it is fitted into a larger pattern alongside other data. To say that an event points in a certain direction, or is part of a general trend, or reveals a particular quality in a person, is to make it meaningful by setting it in such a pattern. If event and pattern mesh, so that all that is known of one coheres with all that is known of the other, the interpretation that produces the meshing is plausible.

This is not to say that it is true in an absolute sense, for it is not necessarily exclusive or permanent. Not exclusive, because it may exist alongside another interpretation that is equally plausible, as when primary responsibility for the surrender at Yorktown is assigned either to the brilliance of Franco-American strategy or to British blundering. Not permanent, because it may be upset, as the conventional interpretation of Clinton was, by the appearance of new data that it will not cover. Historical research consists in re-examining old data as much as in hunting for new, and results not in definitive, verifiable conclusions but in a never-ending process of revision.

Such research, however, does produce knowledge of the past. The investigator comes in a real sense to *know* more about the events he is studying than any man of the time knew. The participant is rarely in a position to understand a constellation of related and often simultaneous events: if he chances to be an eyewitness of one or an actor in another, he is ignorant of a third that is equally important, and so cannot grasp the significance of the three in context. His conceptual basis, furthermore, is as narrow as his factual, because he has only such insights as his age and culture permit. Lastly, the future is hidden from him, and with it the end that alone gives meaning to a developing situation. The historian, unable to know all that the participant knew about that situation, can nevertheless understand it more fully because he sees it in perspective— its simultaneous parts in relation to one another, and the whole in relation to the ongoing stream of cause and effect. The outbreak of the War of Independence, for example, appeared to those who engineered it as primarily a revolt against an unreasonable government and its oppressive agents; not until much later could it be recognized as a conflict between developing colonial autonomy and Britain's clumsy attempt to put the empire on a reasonable footing. A million facts about that conflict we still do not know. But we do know more about its inner nature than contemporaries did.

These points may seem more abstract than relevant, but our inquiry illustrates them. We had the material for understanding Clinton's problems and personality more fully than he did; but the material, being the stuff of history, precluded rigorously scientific treatment. We could not verify, in a scientific sense, a conclusion drawn from one set of events in

Sir Henry's life by applying it to another set, because we knew the contexts of both so incompletely that precise correspondence could never be established; in most cases, furthermore, we had known of both sets before reaching the conclusion.[8] For verification, therefore, we substituted plausibility. Our initial assumption, that Clinton's conduct was psychologically consistent, led us to expect that a behavioral pattern would take shape as our data accumulated. In fact it did so, and against it we tested our conclusions to determine whether they were plausible.

This procedure is familiar in both our disciplines. The historian and the clinical psychologist assume that the people with whom they deal are basically consistent, although each defines consistency in his own terms. Each is looking for a pattern. The historian may conclude, for instance, that in the man he is studying ambition was the central and unifying force; the psychologist may conclude that in his patient a complex of conscious and unconscious aims has issued in disruptive (i.e., neurotic) conduct. Each uses the emerging pattern to test his conclusions. A single conclusion that fails to pass the test is presumably erroneous. If a number fail to pass, the conclusion itself is called into question. Even then the investigator does not ask whether he was wrong in assuming consistency; he asks whether he assumed the wrong *kind* of consistency. This is what happened in the historian's initial inquiry, and led us to shift the assumption from conscious to unconscious motivation. The latter proved more fruitful, and a pattern began to take form by which to test each tentative conclusion. If the conclusion did not fit, it was reserved for study when the pattern became clearer; if it did fit, it was accepted as plausible. Thus far we have had no persistent misfits, and feel reasonable confidence in the assumption, pattern, and conclusions.

Our methodology was based on data that were colored, as already mentioned, by the subjectivity of the original recorder and of the later investigator. The recorder was in most cases Sir Henry, and his prejudices interposed between us and the events of which he wrote. This in itself was no novelty; both of us were accustomed to evidence warped by the subject's personality. But in our case the historian had assembled, correlated, and to a considerable degree organized the evidence before our inquiry began. He had edited the memoirs and written the articles on which the psychologist was almost entirely dependent for his factual background.[9] When our discussion needed to be fed with further information, either the historian provided it from his research or we had to do without. Our reliance on his material meant that we were inevitably influenced by his interpretations. In so far as we accepted them, we were dealing with his views of Clinton's views of events, and were thus at two removes from the events themselves. We had to consider with some care the nature of this distortion.

In any investigation of individual conduct empathy is the investigator's road to understanding. He has, as a human being, preferences and prejudices that are as integral a part of himself as objective reason, and hence part of the empathic process by which he moves through the Looking Glass into another world—the world of a dead general or of a living patient. He must of course be conscious of his bias and keep a check on it, or it will lead him into fairyland. But his self-scrutiny is a negative requirement, a disciplining of the imaginative involvement that is the heart of his technique.

The more familiar we grew with Sir Henry, and the more our speculations about him began to fit together, the more important such self-scrutiny became. Our way of conducting it was by continually questioning and re-examining our premises, whether individual or joint, to see whether they squared with the evidence. The best way to make clear this procedure, which was scarcely formal enough to deserve the name of method, is to quote directly from the notes of our discussions.

*Wyatt:* Clinton was one of those, in Freud's phrase, "wrecked by success."[10] He saw himself as independent and forceful, but he had the greatest difficulty in living this role. His neurotic ambiguity came out in his continual, defiant advising when a subordinate, and in his wariness and even fear of action when he had sole responsibility.

*Willcox:* Aren't you taking over my pattern of his conduct?

*Wyatt:* The pattern as you presented it has certain psychological implications of which you were unaware. The trends that I observe, such as his ways of denying responsibility for his behavior, of shifting blame and guilt to others, emerge from the material itself. This seems to me proof that our interpretative pattern is sound. I wonder whether the pattern can be extended by saying that Clinton's neurotic fears led him to exhibit at one moment a timidity, at another a recklessness, that were equally unrelated to reality?

*Willcox:* I'm not agreed on recklessness. He was never reckless even in planning; his oscillation was rather between hypercaution and commonsense audacity.

*Wyatt:* No; it was between inability to act at all and plans of unreasonable grandeur—such as becoming generalissimo of all the forces on the continent, or dictating to the government the choice of an admiral.[11] Yet his self-confidence often seems to have been no more than an attempt to convince himself against an inner voice of detraction.

*Willcox:* Look at the record. When does he seem to you to have been really self-confident?

*Wyatt:* When, for example, he talks about knowing more than anyone else.[12]

*Willcox:* I'm convinced he never meant this.

*Wyatt:* Do we have any evidence? Is there any statement of his that
belies his opinion of himself or, I should perhaps say, the high expectations he had of himself?

This sort of colloquy, although it proves nothing in the scientific sense,
does provide safeguards against ungrounded speculations. We spent ten
evenings, over a period of eight months, in such discussions of the material, and in selecting and re-examining what seemed the most pertinent
parts; we spent as much time again in working out, separately and together, an interpretation that would meet the canons of our two disciplines. In the end we arrived at a theory of Clinton's personality that is,
we believe, contained in the data rather than in our own presuppositions.
The theory does not exclude others. On occasions when Sir Henry acted
like any normal general, a conventional explanation would admittedly
be as satisfactory as ours. But to explain his conduct as a whole (as theory
should, because the rational and irrational conduct issued from the same
person), ours seems preferable. It is consistent with the evidence, and
its various parts are consistent with one another; it accounts for behavior, as the final section will show, that can scarcely be accounted for
in any other way. Hence, although it is unprovable, it has a high degree
of plausibility.

### III

The crux of Clinton's personality, according to our theory, was an unconscious conflict over authority. This conflict affected both phases of
his American career. When he was intent on telling his superiors what
to do, he obviously craved power; he often implied, and occasionally said,
that he ought to have it because he knew better than anyone else how
to use it. As commander in chief, responsible only to the distant ministers
of the Crown, he was hesitant and unhappy about using his power; his
attitude suggests an unconscious conviction that he ought not to have it.
Unlike other restive subordinates who later became successful commanders in chief, such as Cornwallis, Clinton was no more effective in
one position than in the other.

He was dimly conscious of his ineffectiveness. For every failure he had
a multitude of excuses, which in sum do not explain. *Qui s'excuse s'accuse*
is a psychologically unproductive aphorism; it can be better rendered as
he who excuses himself reveals himself. What Clinton reveals, we believe.

is a pattern of conduct determined less by the actual situations confronting him than by his own inner conflict. Its terms cannot be precisely defined, but its causes and nature can be inferred from a combination of the historical data and present-day clinical experience.

Adjustment to authority is one of the most basic aspects of the individual's development. Although his adjustment is profoundly influenced by the mores of the society in which he is born and matures, and by his place in it, the major question is how he accepts authority as a child. The child is born under authority—the functional abstract of the parental love and power on which he depends for survival—and in due time grows out of it. But authority continues to mean to him what the parents mean: although his subsequent attitudes may be modified, covered up, even seemingly reversed, the early core of meaning fashioned in his relationship to parents and their surrogates perpetuates itself in his later life. As he grows up and progressively moves into the place once held by his parents, especially by his father, this core of meaning largely determines how he handles whatever portion of authority comes his way. If his childhood feelings for his father were more than commonly ambivalent—more charged with hostility and awe, and consequently with anxiety and guilt —he may be both eager *and* extremely reluctant to assume the paternal role of authority and power. In that case his unresolved conflict is likely to affect his behavior long after the father-and-son relationship is ended.

In Clinton's case we know almost nothing about his childhood and upbringing, but a great deal about his later life. We are therefore in the position of seeing the consequences and not the causes. We see him striving for authority when he does not have it, then unable to use it when he has it; and we seek the reasons for this paradox in a part of his life that is hidden. Present-day clinical studies also begin with adult symptoms, and attempt to uncover their causes in childhood. Even when the attempt fails to trace continuous lines of development between past and present, the established symptomatic pattern is sufficiently well understood so that its causes may be inferred with reasonable confidence. The gaps in our data compel us to employ just such inference.

But how reliable, it may be asked, are the results of inference? Granted that the paradoxes of Clinton's conduct *can* largely be explained by the assumption that he suffered from a conflict, unresolved since childhood, between craving and dreading to exercise authority, *should* they be so explained? Several reasons why they should not, immediately suggest themselves; if they are valid, our method produces no more than idle speculation.

The most sweeping but least important objection is that conduct may not have had the same psychological causes in the eighteenth century as today. We do not know that it had, but for the historian the assumption is axiomatic; if the wellsprings of human behavior did not remain constant through time, the past would be unintelligible to the present and no history could be written. A similar but more cogent objection is that Clinton's conduct may in fact have been sensible and appropriate, and may appear abnormal only because the data are misleading or we misinterpret them. Our answer is that occasional episodes may of course be distorted, but scarcely his entire career, the data are so abundant, and the picture of a personality that emerges from them is so clear and self-consistent, that the chance of mistaking the picture for a quite different one is negligible. A third objection is that attributing Clinton's many divergent traits to a single core conflict may be an oversimplification. Here again we have no categorical answer. But a considerable volume of clinical experience has established that repetitive peculiarities, such as those in Clinton's conduct, derive from a conflict over authority originating in childhood, and that the child's compulsive manner of dealing with this conflict produces the adult symptoms that Sir Henry showed. With a few minor exceptions that we cannot yet explain, but that do not subvert our theory, we can account for Clinton's behavior, by postulating one consistent syndrome of psychological causes and effects.[13] Hence we believe that our explanation is the most parsimonious as well as the most plausible.

The central point is that Clinton, although greedy for authority, was afraid of exercising it because it represented an area, the paternal, where a part of himself insisted he did not belong. Trespassing here produced a sense of guilt, with which he was threatened whenever he attempted to grasp the reins. Grasping and drawing back alternated throughout his career; the alternation was determined in part by external events, the favors and blows of fortune, and in part by the internal stimuli of his hopes or fears. His fears and sense of guilt did not reach his consciousness, except perhaps momentarily at the time of his wife's death; his conduct in general, as is common in such situations, both expressed his basic conflict and concealed the motives that engendered it. But fear and guilt seem to have become more dominant as his career progressed, until in the end he could not allow himself to succeed.

His relations with his associates reveal a pervasive strain of self-defeat. He was intent on transferring his own internal guilt to others, and his technique for doing so was compulsive and highly developed, an integral part of his character. The men with whom he had to work gave him, it is true, objective and abundant reason for complaint: Sir William Howe was stubborn and strategically myopic; Cornwallis, petulant and headstrong; Parker seems to have lived in an intellectual vacuum; and

Arbuthnot would have driven even a Marlborough to fury. The pattern of Clinton's quarrels, however, is largely unrelated to the character of any given opponent. He quarreled with a regularity that is almost predictable, and persisted long after victory if the quarrel had any chance of helping his reputation. In this respect his retirement was the climax of his career: he spent more than a decade in compiling his apologia, refighting every squabble as most old soldiers refight their campaigns, transferring all blame from himself to others, and lavishing such care on this labor of self-love that it was unfinished when he died. His absorption with controversy has an obvious psychological meaning, that he was driven to it by his own internal need more than by the external stimuli of cantankerous colleagues. Something within him was constantly preferring charges, which he had to fasten on the outside world in order to exonerate himself.

The same strain of self-defeat appears in his way of offering advice to his superiors. Because at bottom he doubted himself too much to be sure that he was right, he was driven to persuade those around him that he was. His methods of persuasion were extremely tactless, and the primary reason was that one part of him, the part that forbade him to wield "parental" authority, wanted persuasion to fail. If it had succeeded, he would have acquired a responsibility to which he felt unequal and, even worse, would have assumed a position to which his conscience told him he had no right. His failure to persuade protected him from these dangers. It also protected his high estimate of his plans, because they had not been tested, and allowed him to blame his superiors for whatever went wrong. His bitterness toward them, like his altercations with his other associates, was his means of externalizing and finding relief from his altercation wtih himself.

The same ambivalence appears in his planning as commander in chief. Because he longed to wield authority but distrusted his right to do so, his craving for command was at war with his fear that command was not for him. The craving led him to spin large offensive designs with a spider's pertinacity; the fear impeded their execution and prepared the way for shifting to a supine defensive. Thus his periods of inaction were responses to a psychological as much as to a military imperative. But he constantly labored to explain them on military grounds, and thereby raised his mountain of excuses. At moments, when his internal conflict was particularly intense, his need to excuse was so great that nothing else could stand in his way.

This brings us to the final aspect of his conduct that needs to be considered, his description of the campaign of 1781. If our data are correct, he reached retrospective conclusions about that campaign that were at odds with the evidence before him; he seems to have been a liar after the fact. The first step in our analysis is to establish his deception, the second to point out the difficulty—insuperable, in our opinion—of finding plausible conscious motives for it, and the third to show that he might well have had strong unconscious motives. Although we cannot prove that he was so motivated, our analysis provides a plausible answer where historical analysis does not, and is therefore a fitting conclusion to a brief for psychological interpretation.

The data are of two sorts, those on the actual campaign and those on Clinton's subsequent view of it; and the two must be considered in order. In June of 1781 Sir Henry was expecting to remain on the defensive during the summer. He believed, or at least professed afterward to have believed, that France had reached the end of her tether and was not planning to assist the Americans beyond the autumn, so that the British had only to avoid all risk of defeat in order to secure victory.[14] Sir Henry's immediate expectation was that he would be besieged in New York, and he consequently wanted Cornwallis to content himself with a small base on the Chesapeake and return the bulk of his force to Manhattan. Clinton had just received a letter from Lord George Germain, Secretary of State for the American Colonies, which made clear—with more force than tact —that the government favored Cornwallis's strategy of making Virginia the main theater of war, and hoped that no more troops would be withdrawn to New York; Clinton, however, was given latitude to use his judgment. This he did. He ignored the Cabinet's views, and continued until mid-August to ask Cornwallis for men. But the Earl found one reason after another for refusing the requests, and in consequence of his refusals, not of Clinton's policy, the Chesapeake army was at full strength when it was surrounded in September.

So much for the actual campaign; look now at Sir Henry's later view of it. Soon after he returned to England he made the claim that an order from London had forbidden him to withdraw a single man from Virginia and commanded him to support Cornwallis in force as soon as possible, and had thereby disrupted his entire plan. To back his claim he quoted the exact words of the order, contained in a letter from Germain, but did not precisely identify the letter. Sir Henry normally kept every communication from Lord George, and the Secretary's office kept copies. Both files of this correspondence are extant, and appear to be complete; one exactly duplicates the other. The words in question are simply not there. It cannot of course be proved that they were never written. But in the circumstances the conclusion is almost inescapable that Clinton fabricated them. In that case he did so after the campaign, not during it, because neither his papers nor his actions at the time give any hint that he knew of the order.

After Yorktown, in other words, he changed a general wish of the

Cabinet, which he had in fact ignored, into a specific command that he claims to have obeyed. In his memoirs he presents this command as the external factor that reversed his policy.[15] At the same time he describes his policy as it actually was, and seems unaware that it ran counter to his purported instructions. He nowhere hints, let alone says, that he was defying the Cabinet. Instead he implies that his continued attempts to get the troops back to New York were somehow consonant with a letter forbidding him to move a man from Virginia. He is saying two things at once, that he did and did not act as ordered; but his whole emphasis is on his unwilling obedience.[16] He has created in his own mind, that is, both a command that was never issued and the illusion that he followed it.

Was his fabrication intentional? If so, he broke with a rooted habit of accuracy that shows throughout his memoirs; they are full of long and scrupulously transcribed quotations from his correspondence, which attest his respect for the *ipissimum verbum* of written evidence.[17] He also broke with his rooted habit of caution, by circulating his falsehood among his friends and embodying it in the book he was preparing for the printer; if the book had even been published, Germain could readily have exposed him as a liar. Sir Henry seems to have been recklessly courting trouble, yet recklessness was no more in his make-up than forgery. Everything that is known of his character, in short, acquits him of a wilful effort to deceive. The only plausible alternative is that he believed what he wrote, which is another way of saying that he could not have had conscious motives for the fabrication.

Only unconscious motives remain. We are looking for them as they operated on Clinton's memory to distort his retrospective view. But they presumably grew out of his role in the campaign itself, and there the search must begin. In the summer of 1781 Clinton had two reasons for not wanting to fall in with Germain's suggested course: it would ruin his own defensive plans, and it would in effect transfer the command from himself to Cornwallis. But he was also, according to our interpretation, inherently reluctant to defy authority. Hence he was on the horns of a dilemma familiar to psychotherapists: if he did not do what he wanted, he would be pained by his failure to assert himself; if he did what he wanted, he would be pained by his insubordination. He actually chose the second alternative, and ignored the views of the government. There are some signs that he did so at a price, that a sense of guilt was aroused both by his conscious flouting of authority and by an unconscious fear that authority might be right. If so, he was a deeply troubled man before the external crisis burst on him in September.[18]

Once that crisis had ended at Yorktown, his internal conflict was accentuated by the pressures of the outside world. He was permitted to resign, and returned home under a cloud; Cornwallis and the government joined in attempting to saddle him with the blame. These factors were part of his background when he set out to describe, first for his friends and then for the general public, his last campaign as he thought had happened. He was under an external stress that might well have affected a less neurotic chronicler, but he reacted to it in a way peculiarly his own.

His unconscious motive must have been powerful, for it warped his memory and led him to throw caution to the winds. The motive, if plausible from our viewpoint, must also have been consonant with the psychological pattern we have outlined. The two possibilities that at once suggested themselves are his recurrent sense of guilt and his need to justify himself. He may have felt guilt during the actual campaign, as already mentioned. But his memoirs for once contain no excuses, and they give no other sign that guilt was predominant in retrospect. Look next at the urge for self-justification, a motive so closely allied to guilt that the two are frequently indistinguishable. In Clinton they had a common source in his conflict over authority, but somewhat different results: where guilt came out largely in excuses, self-justification tended to take more positive forms, such as his enthusiasm for his own plans, his interminable prolongation of controversies, and his sporadic boastfulness. Although the last may seem to have no kinship with his creating a fictitious command to do what in fact he had not done, there is a connection under the surface. His self-deception contained an inverted boast.

He invented not only the command, it must be remembered, but also his obedience to it. In this way, whether or not he assuaged guilt about his actual conduct, he achieved other psychological ends that were even more important to him. Ostensibly he said that Germain had ordered him to follow a specific course, and that he had done so; between the lines he said that the course had been mistaken (as witness Yorktown), that he had been right to resist it in so far as he had, and above all that authority, instead of permitting him to succeed, had once more blocked his plans, and by doing so had caused a disaster for which he was blameless. He thereby upheld the neurotic fiction by which he lived, that superior powers continually prevented him from exercising his true talents for command. The unconscious purpose of his falsification, in sort, was to bring him back to his familiar grievance system—to establish himself in his own eyes as, if not *sans peur*, at least *sans reproche*.

Although our theory does not provide a complete reconstruction of the man, it does provide a fuller one than the original theory that his motivation was essentially rational and purposeful. Assume that he himself was the chief source of his difficulties, that a coherent system of action below the conscious level produced what seem to be the paradoxes of his conduct, and the whole perspective changes. His behavior acquires a new consistency. Actions that had hitherto been obscure and baffling fall into place and make sense as parts of a pattern. If the various contradictions of his behavior had a single integrating cause—an unconscious psychic conflict over authority, which originated in childhood—his method of dealing with the conflict was what might be expected of the obsessive-compulsive personality. He tried to protect himself from anxiety and guilt, which the unsettled and unsettling nature of neurotic conflict constantly stirs up, by limiting his sphere of action and by defending interminably such actions as he took.

Our theory suggests plausible answers to the questions that originally baffled the historian. Why was Clinton's advice as a subordinate so consistently ignored? Because he did not really want to see it tried, and therefore did his best to present it in a way that would ensure rejection. Why was he able to work with some naval officers and not with others? Because the resolute ones, such as Lord Howe and Rodney, exuded authority and temporarily relieved him of his conflict, whereas the stubbornness and vacillation of an Arbuthnot or a Parker accentuated it. Why did Sir Henry seeks to resign for years, and then refuse to go? Because the struggle between his self-distrust and self-assertion reached a paralyzing climax on the eve of Yorktown. Why did the character of his strategy change when he became commander in chief? For much the same reason: acquiring sole responsibility intensified his self-distrust. Why did he falsify the record of his last campaign? Because his need to justify himself was stronger than his respect for evidence or regard for consequences. Some of these answers may turn out, on further investigation, to be less plausible than they seem. At this juncture we can only say that they look promising, and that we have not yet encountered the sort of dead end that blocked the historian's inquiry.

Whether our method is valid is for the reader to judge. If it is, its implications must be accepted along with it; and they are much more important than our small experiment. Clinton himself was a relatively minor figure. But his psychological kinsmen are legion, and some of them played crucial roles in history. The more their unconscious motives predominated in determining their conduct, the more difficult the problems that they pose for the historian. He is not equipped to venture into the unconscious, any more than the psychologist is equipped to collate and evaluate manuscripts. Each discipline has limits beyond which the professional, *qua* professional, cannot go; and these limits circumscribe his understanding. The central purpose of our report is to suggest that a team can pass the limits, explore new areas, and thereby gain more insight than either member could achieve on his own.

# Family Culture and
# Genealogy / *Howard K. Beale*

There is growing interest by historians in microunits, "those most primitive elements of history, people and families." According to Dr. Bernard Bailyn, "the closer one gets to those ultimate building blocks of history—the more one is immersed in a knowledge of specific lives and families—the farther he will find himself from the attractions of traditional formulas, and the more likely is he to see the unsuspected connections and relationships which lead to new and truer views." Professor Bailyn goes on to assert that "the lineage of families itself has suddenly been found to be greatly revealing, and genealogy has become if not a respectable study for historians at least a most respectable source.[1]

The traditional biography generally took into consideration ancestral and family background. It was not unusual for it to ascribe character traits to family and, beyond that, to ethnic background. More recently, there has been growing sensitivity by historians to cultural and family influences on the psychic development of the individual. A notable example of this is the first two chapters of Elting E. Morison's biography of Henry L. Stimson.[2] Robert Seager has made admirable use of family papers, those of the Gardiner family, in his important book, And Tyler Too.[3]

Genealogical materials are very relevant to the concept of family culture,[4] as are analyses of intra-family relationships, frequently in Freudian terms, and awareness of the role of family in creating a level of expectation for individual achievement. The later Professor Beale was probably unaware of the theoretical development of the concept of reference ancestry in relationship to individual motivation.[5] The substance of the concept is implied, however, in the article's conclusion.

The introduction to this volume has noted the relevance of genealogy to the study of mobility.

Howard K. Beale, "Theodore Roosevelt's Ancestry, A Study in Heredity," *New York Genealogical and Biographical Record*, LXXXV (October, 1954). Reprinted by permission. (Genealogical fan chart omitted.)

1. "The Beekmans of New York: Trade, Politics, and Families," *William and Mary Quarterly*, XIV (October, 1957), 598–608.
2. Elting E. Morison, *Turmoil and Tradition: A Study of the Life and Times of Henry L. Stimson* (Boston, 1960) 3–24.
3. (New York, 1963)
4. Lester J. Cappon, "Genealogy, Handmaid of History," *Special Publication of the National Genealogical Society*, no. 17.
5. "Reference ancestor" is considered in the editor's introduction to the concepts "status revolution and reference group theory."

T HE ANCESTRY of Theodore Roosevelt is interesting in itself as an example of the background of one recent American who stemmed from old colonial stock. Probably no one ancestor fixed his mark upon him, but the cumulative effect of certain ancestral qualities and thought habits is noteworthy. In the several branches of Roosevelt's family, ways of life, established through generations until they became family traditions, habituated these families to modes of living that came to be taken for granted. With these manners of life went family attitudes toward themselves and toward other people that were passed on to children and became as much a part of Theodore Roosevelt's inheritance as his Dutch name.

Many genealogists are concerned mainly with tracing down the male lines from the immigrant ancestor; sometimes they fail even to mention daughters, who do not carry forward the family name. The historian or biographer, on the other hand, is interested in women as well as men and in ancestors of currently unknown names as much as in those who originated the surname that one descendant has made distinguished. Whatever influence forebears and their ways of living and thinking do have is transmitted through women and bearers of obscure names as effectively as through male possessors of a well-known name.

Thus with Theodore Roosevelt, the genealogist has pursued the Roosevelt name to its obscure source and the record of Bullochs back to Scotland. Yet the first Roosevelt, about whom so much has been written, was only one out of 128 ancestors of Theodore in that original Roosevelt's generation. To the historian, the other 127 are as important as the bearer of the Roosevelt name. As closely related to Theodore as was the original Roosevelt were some, indeed, like Hendrick Van Dyck and David Schuyler, who bore names as distinguished as that of Roosevelt. The genealogist, however, has rarely connected them with Roosevelt at all. Even the famous Revolutionary Bulloch was still only one of sixteen people equally related to Theodore. When, instead of following the branching family tree from the first Roosevelt or the famous Bulloch down to all his descendants, the historian traces the lines back from Theodore to all his known ancestors, then the cumulative effect becomes much more significant than any one ancestor.

Theodore Roosevelt's forebears came early to this country and, like those of most Americans, included many simple folk who left little record. But the earliest extant American records of each ancestral family establish all of Theodore Roosevelt's forebears as colonial Americans and a number of them as seventeenth-century Americans. It is possible for the painstaking genealogist to list most of them in their diversity. The latest ancestor to arrive, Dr. John Irvine, is known to have been in Georgia in 1764, when he was Justice of the Peace, but earlier than he there were more than half a hundred other family names. The first appearance of a number of these may be briefly summarized.

Jean de la Montagne and Rachel de Forest landed in New Amsterdam from Leyden in the *Rensselaerwyck* on March 5, 1637. Abraham Isaacse Ver Planck and his wife, Maria Vinje, had a son born in New Amsterdam January 1, 1637 (Rec. v.24, p.39), and Cornelis Jacobsen Stille leased a farm on Manhattan Island Aug. 15, 1639 (Ibid. v.7, p.49). Hendrick Van Dyck and his wife Divertje Cornelise first came from Utrecht, Holland, in 1640 when he was ensign of militia in New Netherland. They returned more permanently in 1645 when he was sent out as *schout fiscal* (Rec. v.9, p.52). Claes Martensen van Rosenvelt had a son baptized Oct. 23, 1650, in the New York Dutch Church (BDC:I:28), is mentioned in the records of 1649, and may have been in America a decade earlier (New Netherland Register I, January 1911, pp.8–10; Charles B. Whittelsey, Roosevelt Genealogy, 1649–1902, pp.3–4). Cornelius Jansen Clopper had a business in New Amsterdam in 1652 (Edmund B. O'Callaghan, The Register of New Netherland, 1626–1674, p.176; David T. Valentine, Hist. of City of New York, 1853, pp.71–72). Resolved Waldron and his wife Rebecca Hendricks, daughter of Hendrick Koch, came to New Amsterdam in 1654 (NHR:84). Jan Peek sold two houses in Albany on April 14, 1655, and Volckie Jurriaense, who signed with her mark, was living there in 1657 (ERA:62,302,412 & PA:126). Also, the marriage of David Pieterse Schuyler was recorded on October 13th of the latter year. Jan Barentsen Kunst sailed to New Amsterdam on the *Gilded Beaver* in 1658, and Jan Louwe Bogert and Cornelia Evertse, arriving on the *Spotted Cow*, settled in Bedford (now a part of Brooklyn) in 1663 (DHNW:          :33 & NHR:4). In 1674, Wynant Gerritse Van der Poel, husband of Tryntje Melgers, was trading real estate and running a business in Albany (ERA:I:104).

Among his Pennsylvania forebears, Thomas Croasdale and his wife, Agnes Hathernthwaite, came to this country in 1682 in the ship *Welcome* with William Penn (Potts Fam. Colls., 1901, pp.442,445). Jan Luckens and Reynier Teisen disembarked from the *Concord* on Oct. 6, 1683, at Chester, Pennsylvania, and settled in Germantown, while David Potts, who served as a bondsman in Pennsylvania in 1692, was married in Bucks County in 1694 (Col. Fams. of Phila., v.1, p.689; Potts Fam. Hist. Colls., 1901, pp.441–43). Daniel Craig settled in Bucks County between 1720 and 1740, and Robert Barnhill petitioned the government concerning a road there in 1728 ("Land o' the Leal," Roosevelt's Ancestors in Bucks, 1902, p.1).

In the southern group, Edmund Bellinger appears frequently in the records of the Carolinas but first in 1674, when he settled on James Island in Charleston County, South Carolina (Bellinger, De Veaux, and Allied Fams. 1895, p.6). Archibald Stobo and Elizabeth Park arrived together in South Carolina in 1700, after an unsuccessful effort to settle in Panama, and Andre De Veaux was residing in the former colony as early as 1714 (Ibid.:49; Bulloch and Stobo Fams., 1892, p.32). John Stewart, Sr., grandfather of General Daniel Stewart, had landed in North Carolina and was living in Dorchester, South Carolina, by 1723 (Stewart, Elliott & Dunwody Fams., 1895, p.1). James Bulloch was in South Carolina at least by 1729, while the first record of Kenneth Baillie and his wife, Elizabeth Mackay, is found in Georgia in 1735 (Bulloch and Stobo Fams., 1892, pp.12–14; Gen. Recs. of the Baillies, 1923, p. 50).

Though his Roosevelt forebears and the Bullochs of Georgia are the ones usually described, Theodore Roosevelt stemmed from ancestors whose diversity of geographic location in America, national origin, religion, occupation, and economic status was striking. So far as is known he had no New England blood, though he chose both his wives from families that did have. His own progenitors, however, had settled in New York, New Jersey, Pennsylvania, Delaware, North Carolina, South Carolina, and Georgia. The first five Roosevelts in Theodore's line married Dutch wives quite consistently, and although Cornelius Jansen Clopper and Jan Kunst, of the first generation in America, were perhaps German in origin, their families had lived in Holland long enough to become thoroughly Hollandized. Theodore's paternal grandfather broke with the Dutch tradition and found his wife in Philadelphia. Margaret Barnhill brought to her grandson English blood of the Croasdales, the Dickinsons, and the Hathernthwaites; Welsh blood of the Pottses; Scotch-Irish blood of the Craigs, the Barnhills, and possibly of the McVaughs; and German blood of the Luckens and Teisens. Theodore's father, in turn, also married outside the Dutch strain so that, at most, Theodore was something less than one-fourth Dutch. From his mother he inherited a further variety of national origins. The Bullochs, the Baillies, the Douglasses, the Irvines, the Parks, the Stewarts, and the Stobos were Scotch, as were probably the Mackays. The Bellinger, Cartwright, and probably Fairchild ancestors were, on the other hand, English; Andre De Veaux was a French Huguenot, as were Jean de la Montagne and Rachel de Forest on his father's side.

In religious affiliation Theodore Roosevelt had an interesting background. He himself was reared a Presbyterian, though he later established a connection with the Dutch Reformed Church, in which numerous of his ancestors had worshiped. His father and mother and most of his

Scotch-Irish ancestors were Presbyterians, though some of his later Bulloch grandfathers were Episcopalians. The Van Hoesens were Lutherans and the de Forests French Protestants at Avesnes; Andre De Veaux attended the French Church in this country though his son abandoned it in favor of the Church of England. More interesting still, Theodore's Grandmother Roosevelt brought a long line of Quaker ancestry to the Roosevelt household. Her Luckens and Teisen ancestors had been Mennonites in Germany but became Friends before or soon after migrating to Pennsylvania, while her Croasdale, Hathernthwaite, McVaugh, and Potts forebears had been Friends whose names appeared in the annals of Friends' Meetings in America, as well as in England before their migration to this country (Bulloch and Stobo Fams., 1911, p. 15; Bellinger and De Veaux Fams., 1895, p.49; Baillie Fam., 1923, pp.47–50; J. W. De-Forest, The de Forests of Avesnes, 1900, pp. 18–20, 46–62; The Friend, XXX, p.229; Col. Fams. of Phila., v.1, pp.690, 744; PA:126; Potts Fam. Hist. Colls., 1901, pp.442–45, 451–52).

A surprising number of Roosevelt's ancestors are found in contemporary records. Not only are his parents, grandparents, and great-grandparents known, but thirteen out of the sixteen in the generation that witnessed the American Revolution were the sort of people that left records of themselves. Farther back, in the late seventeenth and early eighteenth century, forty-five per cent of the total number of his ancestors are found in records preserved by their contemporaries. Indeed, in the six generations back of Theodore, out of 126 ancestors only 34 are unknown, of four only the given name is preseved, about eight others only the surname is known, but eighty were important enough to appear in contemporary records; even in the seventh generation back, in the mid-seventeenth century, 38 of the 128 appear in the records, and eleven others are known by surname. Since the Southern ancestors came to this country later and left scantier records, it is this half of Theodore's forebears about whom little is known in the earlier generations.

Their occupations were varied. Melchior de Forest was a dyer in Avesnes, France, and he taught his skill to his son Jean and his grandson Jesse. After their flight from France, the de Forests set up as dyers of textiles in early seventeenth-century Luxembourg and Holland (Emily de Forest, A Walloon Fam. in Amer., 1914, v.1, pp.6, 10, 14–15). Resolved Waldron was a printer, Jan Kunst was a house carpenter and workman, Sioert Olferts was a mason and builder in New Amsterdam, and Joseph Yates a blacksmith in Albany, John Potts and his son Thomas were millwrights. Lucas Gerritse Wyngard was an Albany trader and Tryntje Melgers Van der Poel was a licensed midwife there.

Many tilled the soil. Some were land-owning small farmers while other had more extensive holdings. Claes Gerritse Van Schaack obtained a large grant of land in Rensselaerwyck, and his grandson Cornelius was a great landed proprietor near Albany (E. A. Collier, Hist. of Old Kinderhook, pp.61–62, 100 & 367; Dict. Amer. Biog. v.19, p. 213). In the South, several individuals were the sort of farmers that were designated "planters." Edmund Bellinger, with the title of landgrave, was one of the administrators of the Carolinas as well as a planter.

Professional men there were, too. Hendrick and Cornelis Van Dyck were "chirurgeons" in Albany and the former had a certificate showing four years of study there under Dr. Jacob D'Hinsse. Gysbert Van Imbroch and Jean de la Montagne were *meesters* or physicians in the early days of New Netherland and the latter had studied medicine at the University of Leyden. John Irvine was a physician who, after his exile in England, became the first vice-president and later president of the Georgia Medical Society. Archibald Stobo, who had acquired an A.M. degree at the University of Edinburgh in June 1697, and James Bulloch in mid-eighteenth-century Georgia were Presbyterian ministers. In the Revolutionary War generation, Archibald Bulloch was a Georgia lawyer and Peter Van Schaack a prominent New York lawyer who also practised in England and published books on New York law.

Ability in business early showed itself among these progenitors. In mid-seventeenth-century New Amsterdam, Cornelius Clopper, a blacksmith, strategically located where Long Island farmers had to pass his door, built up one of the most prosperous businesses in the city and his wife, Heyltje Pieters, managed it for years after his death (VM:1855: 517). Hendrick Van Dyck came to America as a government official but later dealt profitably in real estate and money lending, Jan Peek was an innkeeper, Jan Vinje a brewer, Isaac de Forest a tobacco dealer and brewer, and the first two Roosevelts were traders with the Indians and "millers." Thomas Potts was not only a merchant but, after his moving to New Jersey, owner of the Chelsea Iron Works, where he manufactured iron from mid-eighteenth century until his death in 1777. John Barnhill was first a farmer but later moved to Philadelphia where he was an innkeeper, and then during the American Revolution he turned to merchandising.

By the third generation in America the Roosevelts themselves had turned from fur trading to successful business ventures in their growing city. Thus the amassing of the family wealth began. Johannes Roosevelt was a manufacturer and entrepreneur who won for his linseed-oil factory a monopoly, made the metal chest in which the city kept its charter, owned and ran a tannery, a slaughterhouse, a chocolate factory, and a flour mill. With his brother Jacobus, who became Franklin Roosevelt's ancestor, he dealt extensively and profitably in real estate, whose value was rising with the growth of the city; they helped develop Beekman Swamp and at one time held a lease on Bowling Green. Theodore's great-grandfather, James I. Roosevelt, was a merchant with a hardware and glass business in Maiden Lane. He became a large-scale importer with European connections, specialized in glass and other building supplies, and in 1797 organized Roosevelt and Son, which later became an investment banking firm, one of America's oldest and most conservative business houses. His grandfather, Cornelius V. S. Roosevelt, was one of New York's important merchants and a founder and director of the Chemical National Bank. In 1876, his father, the elder Theodore, and uncle James A. Roosevelt sold the glass business and carried further the interests of Roosevelt and Son in floating investments, particularly in insurance companies and transportation. They managed it so well that the firm weathered the panic of 1873 without difficulty and survived to float bonds for James J. Hill's railroad ventures (William T. Cobb, The Strenuous Life: the Oyster Bay Roosevelts in Business and Finance, pp. 49–57).

Indeed, an important influence in Roosevelt's life was his forebears' long-established enjoyment of more than comfortable means and, in some cases, great wealth that created a sense of security, thus making possible participation in public affairs. In politics and in a society coming to be dominated by self-made men of colossal wealth, Theodore talked so constantly of himself as not wealthy that the actual facts are surprising.

In both early and later generations non-Roosevelt ancestors continued wealthy. For example, Kenneth Baillie owned a plantation called "Baillie's Island," near Sunbury in St. John's Parish, Georgia, and in his will, dated July 7, 1766, he provided, before the division of the rest of his estate, for the specific disposal of guns, pistols, a watch, a silver-hilted sword, buckles, furniture, silver plate, 150 pounds, his plantation, two city lots, twenty-two hundred acres of rice and timber land, five Negro slaves, and one Negro family. James Bulloch had title to plantations in South Carolina which he sold in 1762, acquired 450 acres in St. Matthew's Parish and two thousand acres in St. Mary's Parish, in Georgia, and divided his time between Mulberry Grove Plantation and a house in Savannah. James De Veaux was designated a "large land-owner" and was the proprietor of Wassaw Island and Shaftsbury Plantation on Argyle Island in the Sea Islands of Georgia. Theodore's grandfather, James S. Bulloch, possessed a plantation at Roswell, Georgia, valued in 1850 at six thousand dollars, a town house in Savannah, and stock in the company that sent the first steamship *Savannah* across the Atlantic. He was a director of this company and president of the Savannah branch of the United States Bank. With two others he supplied the capital for a factory built at Roswell in 1850.

Significant as this heritage of long-time affluence among other family connections may be for Theodore, it was his Roosevelt ancestors themselves who immediately contributed his means. At his death in 1840, his great-grandfather, James I. Roosevelt, willed to his four surviving children a fortune of several hundred thousand dollars. By 1855, the wealth of his grandfather, Cornelius, had grown to half a million dollars (the equivalent of $1,800,000 in 1950), which made him one of the wealthiest men in the city. When he died in 1871, Cornelius, with three million dollars (the equivalent of $13,500,000 in 1950), bequeathed each of his five sons enough to make them independently wealthy. Theodore's own father's estate, divided into four parts just seven years after grandfather Cornelius's death, gave Theodore as his fourth, some two hundred thousand dollars (the equivalent of $687,500 in 1950), and must, therefore, have been originally at least eight hundred thousand dollars (the equivalent of $2,750,000 in 1950), which even in the days of post-Civil War booming industry was no mean fortune. To protest, as Theodore always did, that the family was other than very wealthy was to carry modesty to the point of telling less than the whole story.

Theodore's ancestors also served their communities in military or civilian office. Archibald Bulloch (c.1730–1777) was elected a speaker of the Georgia Royal Assembly in 1772, president of the Georgia Provincial Congress in 1775 and 1776, member of the Continental Congress in 1775 and 1776, and was the first man in Georgia to read the Declaration of Independence. He was elected by the Provincial Congress as president and commander-in-chief of Georgia and served from June 20, 1776, to Feb. 5, 1777, when the state government was adopted (Biog. Cong. Dir., 1928, p. 758).

Few in the direct Roosevelt line served in a military capacity. During our various wars they were mostly business men and not soldiers, except for Jacobus Roosevelt, Theodore's great-great-grandfather, who served briefly as a private with the New York colonial troops. Indeed, when the Civil War broke out in 1861, Theodore's father, who was twenty-nine, the latter's brothers, and cousin James Roosevelt of Hyde Park, New York, were all of military age, yet not one of the five Roosevelt brothers or their Hyde Park cousin enlisted or was drafted. Instead, except for Theodore's father, who in a civilian capacity spent many months visiting Army camps on behalf of soldiers' families, they all devoted themselves to their own affairs and prospered in their business or legal practice while others fought the war.

On the other hand, one non-Roosevelt Dutch forebear and two French Walloon ancestors did see actual fighting. Jean de la Montagne led fifty soldiers and some sloops in June 1640 to strengthen the Dutch Fort Good Hope against the attacks of Englishmen at Hartford, Connecticut, and he later went down to the South River, as the Delaware was called, to get for the Dutch clear title to the lands around the Schuylkill. He also led an expedition of forty Dutch and thirty-five English against Indians on Staten Island and one of 120 men against other Indians, whom he annihilated, on Long Island (CDNY:I:186–87; HNN:I:266, 297, 299 &      :81). Ensign Hendrick Van Dyck led an unsuccessful attack in March 1642 against some Indians near Turtle Bay in the East River, and in the following year he was wounded and nearly killed while repelling an Indian attack on New Amsterdam itself. In 1649, Van Dyck was second in command of an expedition against Connecticut Indians beyond Stamford, during which the Dutch burned a village and its five hundred inhabitants in their huts (George W. Schuyler, Colonial New York, v.2, pp. 293–95, 298–305). In Theodore's paternal grandmother's direct ancestry, there were no soldiers, for many of that quarter of his ancestors were Quakers with conscientious scruples against war.

It was his mother's Southern ancestors who provided the fighters of whom Theodore was proud. Edmund Bellinger commanded the *Blake* in the Royal Navy in the 1690's, and Kenneth Baillie was an ensign, in 1735, in the Darien Georgia Company of Rangers. He rose to the rank of colonel in the Second Southern Colonial Regiment and, in 1740, went with Governor Oglethorpe on an expedition against the Spaniards, who captured him and sent him to Spain, whence he escaped to England and then returned to Georgia. James De Veaux was major in a colonial regiment in 1764 and rose to a colonelcy in 1775. Theodore's great-grandfather, James Bulloch, served as captain of Virginia State Garrison Troops, 1778–1781, and captain of Georgia state troops in 1787, while another great-grandfather, Daniel Stewart, fought as a Revolutionary soldier under Marion and Sumter and served as a brigadier general of cavalry in the War of 1812. During the Civil War, two of his mother's brothers, Irvine S. and James D. Bulloch, were in the Confederate Navy, where they had extended and interesting careers. Exiled in England after the war, these two naval uncles played heavily upon the imagination of a child who was to become a passionate devotee of the American Navy.

Civilian officeholders were more numerous than military men and were more scattered through the various lines of Theodore's ancestry. In the earliest generation, the newly arrived Jean de la Montagne took a really prominent place among the leaders of New Netherland. He was commissary of Fort Good Hope in 1641, member of a convention in

1653, and city surveyor in 1655. On numerous occasions he represented the colony as commissioner: to settle affairs on the Delaware River in 1648, to superintend the fortifying of New Amsterdam in 1654, and to recover Christians in the hands of the Esopus Indians in 1661, among others. From 1638 through 1646 he was the sole member of the Governor's Council; after that body was enlarged he still served on it, 1647–1656, holding a record of length of service in high office in Dutch days next only to that of Stuyvesant. As a councilor he won for himself a reputation for learning, careful deliberation, and administrative ability, and in the colony's troubles with the Indians he urged moderation and fairness (HNN:I:180, 266, 273, & II:21, 81, 310, 421).

Other forebears, too, held office, a few of whom may be briefly mentioned. Hendrick Van Dyck served the West India Company thirteen years in Holland and America—as ensign commandant, 1640–1645, and as *schout fiscal* from 1645 until Stuyvesant dismissed him in 1652. Resolved Waldron was an elder of the church and in 1665 became constable for the colony, in 1673 *schout* and *schepen*, and in 1683 assessor. Jan Louwe Bogert was a magistrate of Harlem, 1675–1676. In the early days of the other colonies his ancestors also held public positions. Jan Luckens in Germantown, Pennsylvania, was constable in 1691, burgess in 1694, sheriff in 1659, and bailiff in 1702 and 1704. Reynier Teisen sat in the Pennsylvania House of Burgesses four times in the 1690's and was chosen an elder by the Friends in 1725. David Potts represented Philadelphia County in the Provincial Legislature, 1728–1730, and was a trustee of the Abington Friends' Meeting. In the South, Edmund Bellinger was chosen landgrave of the Carolinas under what Theodore later termed "Locke's absurd Constitution," and he was appointed surveyor general in 1698 and receiver of land rents in 1700. Also, Kenneth Baillie served as a trustee for Sunbury, Georgia, and as assessor, collector, and surveyor for the county. James De Veaux sat as a judge of the General Court, as senior justice of the King's Court in Georgia, and as justice of the General Court of the Province. In his church he was a vestryman and a church commissioner, and in 1775 he represented the Sea Islands in the Provincial Congress of Georgia.

In a later day, Theodore's grandfather, James S. Bulloch, became deputy collector of the Port of Savannah and president of the Union Society. He was also active in politics. In 1846, after a wide sampling of county opinion, he wrote his congressman, Thomas Butler King, a Whig, approved his motto "Peace but prepare for War." Bulloch also supported Calhoun's handling of Great Britain. "Our Westernmen are too boisterous," wrote Theodore's grandfather. "The present crisis of our Foreign Relations require[s] cool heads and stout hearts indeed"

(James S. Bulloch to Thomas Butler King, Jan. 23, 1846, in King Mss., Univ. of N. Car., through courtesy of James Z. Rabun).

Theodore's father, of course, devoted much of his time to public activity and sat on various charitable boards, but most of it was unofficial in nature. Only twice did he hold minor public office: when he was a member of the New York State soldiers' allotment commission under Lincoln and when he was appointed presidential elector for Hayes. He was appointed to the collectorship of the Port of New York in Hayes's quarrel with the New York machine but failed to get confirmation by the Senate and never served.

Cumulatively then, the above recital makes it clear that Theodore's ancestry helps explain qualities he later displayed. His Americanism was partly based on his descent from families all of whom had been established in America by 1764 and most of them in the seventeenth century. His cosmopolitan outlook came in part from forebears who had settled in seven of the thirteen colonies, who had come from England, France, Germany, Holland, Protestant Ireland, and Scotland, and who religiously had included agnostics, members of the Dutch Reformed Church, French Protestants, Friends, Lutherans, Mennonites, Episcopalians, and Presbyterians. Some claim to kinship with ordinary folk was made possible by ancestors who had worked at trades as simple as that of midwife, baker, blacksmith, bricklayer, builder, cooper, carpenter, dyer, mason and millwright. Many of his ancestors had been humble farmers. Yet his ancestry also includes an unusual share of men of initiative and business acumen who had amassed great wealth and, more important, had acquired an habituation to cultivated and comfortable living. On his mother's side there are generations of great planters; on his father's, manufacturers of chocolate, leather goods, and linseed oil; a miller, an innkeeper, a fur trader, a land speculator, a slaughterhouse owner, a sugar refiner, money lenders, city real-estate dealers, merchants, bankers, and a steamship operator. These men had maintained mansions in New York and in Savannah, great plantation houses in Georgia, and fine country homes in Philadelphia and its environs. Grandmother Margaret Barnhill had brought her share of the accumulations of several generations of Philadelphians. His father was of the fifth generation of increasingly wealthy New York business men, and five generations of Bullochs had lived in comfortable plantation houses, with city dwellings for the social season.

A tradition of public service, especially conscientious performance of many small tasks for town, colony, or state, was also an important part of his inheritance. On his father's side, except in the early Dutch generations, his heritage was non-military, where not actually pacifist. On his mother's side, however, Southern forebears had often been soldiers or sailors and one had been commander-in-chief of Georgia's Revolutionary troops. There were physicians, lawyers, and two clergymen. His family had contributed church commissioners, vestrymen, and elders. In local government there had been a bailiff, a clerk of court, a collector of taxes, a constable, a county surveyor, a park commissioner, a justice of the peace, a road commissioner, and a town trustee. There had also been assessors, city magistrates, collectors of ports, district attorneys, mayors, *schout fiscals*, sheriffs, and numerous aldermen.

Before the Revolution, his ancestors served colonial governments as agent to the Indians, colonial commissioner, colonial secretary, ensign-commandant, receiver of land rents, solicitor general, and surveyor general. Several had been judges and colonial or state legislators, one, a state senator, and two, United States senators. A number had signed remonstrances and functioned on colonial committees at the time of the American Revolution. Several had been members and one a president of provincial congresses; two, members of governors' councils; one, a member of the Continental Congress; one, a landgrave of the Carolinas; one, a governor of Georgia; and one a minister to the Netherlands. From these, then, and especially from his remarkably public-spirited father, Theodore inherited the sense of *noblesse oblige* and a devotion to public service, which helps explain his early entry into public life and his lifetime concern over public questions. There is no reason to believe him aware of all the details of his family history, but as an American historian he could not fail to be impressed with the richness and diversity of an unusual heritage.

# Group Structure and Career-line Analysis / *Jack P. Greene*

The group, according to Louis Wirth, is a basic social science concept.[1] The historian, adds David M. Potter, is ill-prepared to cope with this concept because of the nature of his training.[2]

Social scientists also have difficulties with the group concept. Homans writes: "The trouble with generalization about large units of people is that we do not know enough to generalize well. The units are too complex, too many forces are operating for us to take account of, and we have as yet not developed adequate or reliable means of analyzing them." Accordingly, "limited general propositions about behavior" of groups are hard to formulate.[3]

Professor Charles A. Beard, in 1913, evolved a technique of career-line analysis. Since then career-line analysis has been utilized and further developed by David Donald, Richard Hofstadter, and George E. Mowry. It is employed by Dr. Ari Hoogenbloom in exploring the group structure of the civil service reformers.[4]

Something analogous to the questionnaire method used by the pollsters is involved in career-line analysis. The historian draws up a list of questions which he applies to the biographical data on individual members of the group. The answers can be correlated and, in some instances, can be treated statistically.[5]

However useful the career-line technique may be in the analysis of group structure, there are limits to its predictive role with respect to individual behavior. An individual may have all of the traits characteristic of the members of a group without his being a group member. Dr. Greene pointed out that there were Virginians with the "essential elements" of "wealth, family and education" who nevertheless were not part of the power group described. Plainly, the "capacity" to put these qualities to

"Foundation of Political Power in the Virginia House of Burgesses, 1720–1776," *William and Mary Quarterly*, (October, 1959), 485–506. Reprinted by permission.

1. "The Social Sciences," in Curti, op. cit., 40–5.

2. David M. Potter, "The Historian's Concern with the Problem of Large-Scale Community Formation," *Conference on the Social Sciences in Historical Study*, June, 1957. Mimeographed by the Hoover Institution on War, Revolution, and Peace.

3. G. C. Homans, *The Human Group* (New York, 1950), xii.

4. Ari Hoogenboom, *Outlawing the Spoils* (Bloomington, Indiana, 1962). For a critique of Hoogenboom and of aspects of the career-line method see H. J. Bass, *Mississippi Valley Historical Review*, XLVIII (March, 1962), 716.

5. Neale, "The Biographical Approach to History," op. cit., 196–8.

*use is not measurable by means of career-line analysis. Also, the latter cannot determine with certainty what particular line of action an individual of a given background will pursue when confronted by a specific issue.*[6]

Historians have devoted more attention to the Virginia House of Burgesses than to any other lower house in the continental colonies. They have treated its internal development, its part in royal government, its procedure, and its personnel. They have assessed its role in developing the leaders of the Revolutionary genration and tracd its part in the "struggle for liberty." Yet, no one has attempted to analyze the structure of power within the Burgesses in the half century before the American Revolution.

The first question to be asked in such an analysis is how was power distributed in the house? Was it spread more or less equally among all members, or was it generally concentrated in the hands of a few? The answer to this question lies in the committees where the work of the house was done and where the real decisions were made. The only way one can hope to determine the pattern of the distribution of power in the eighteenth-century house is by a qualitative analysis of committee posts— that is, by a study which takes into account not only the number of committee posts held by each member but also the varying degrees of importance of the committees themselves.[1]

I have undertaken such an analysis and used my findings as a yardstick to measure the influence or power of individual burgesses. The results indicate that relatively few members played significant roles in the proceedings of the house: of the 630 men who sat in that body between 1720 and 1776, some 520 can safely be eliminated from consideration, because only 110 members belonged at one time or another to the select few who dominated the proceedings of the house. Of these few, some, of course, were more powerful than others. In fact, the leaders as a whole may be divided into two groups, those of the first rank and those of the second. In any given session, the top level was composed of the speaker, who made appointments to all committees, and from two to perhaps seven

6. *Ibid.*, 195; Herbert Butterfield, "George III and the Namier School," *Encounter* (1957), 70–76; *George III and the Historians* (New York, 1959); review by Charles E. Cauthen of Ralph A. Wooster, *The Secession Conventions of the South* (Princeton, 1962) in *Mississippi Valley Historical Review* XLIX (September, 1962), 338.

or eight others, including, as a rule, the chairmen of the standing committees. Men of somewhat less importance, usually five to ten in number, constituted the second level. For example, in the 1736 session five men at the top level handled about a third of the committee assignments while seven others at the second level handled another fourth. Altogether these twelve burgesses—one-sixth of the total membership—occupied more than half of the committee seats. Until 1742 it was not uncommon for as many as one-third to one-half of the burgesses to serve on no committees at all; then, for reasons that are not now entirely clear, the size of the standing committees was enlarged and nearly three-fourths of the members were given assignments on these committees. Beginning in 1748, the speaker adopted the practice of giving each member at least one post on a standing committee, but this diffusion of assignments does not appear to have affected the structure of power in the house; in 1752 somewhat less than one-fifth of the members handled over half of the business of the house, with the six most powerful men occupying a fourth of the committee posts and eleven others holding another fourth. This pattern did not change significantly for the rest of the colonial period. It was modified slightly after 1766, when Peyton Randolph succeeded John Robinson as speaker. Randolph further increased the size of the standing committees and, more important, sprinkled the major assignments among a greater number of members, with the result that the number of men at both levels of power increased slightly.

These men of power provided the house with a certain continuity of leadership from 1720 until well after the Declaration of Independence. Some of them died, some retired, some were defeated at the polls, but never at any time was there any wholesale turnover in leadership. This continuity plus the lack of evidence of any major dissatisfaction with the leadership or of the existence of any group intent upon challenging it emphasizes the fact that organized political parties did not exist in colonial Virginia. There was often disagreement on specific issues, but, as St. George Tucker later suggested to William Wirt when the latter was preparing his biography of Patrick Henry, the disagreements were "only such as different men, coming from different parts of our extensive Country might well be expected to entertain." Tucker had never witnessed anything in the House of Burgesses "that bore the appearance of *party spirit*."[2]

The discovery of the fact that the House of Burgesses was dominated by the few rather than the many immediately raises some important questions about the leaders. What were their professional and economic interests, their social and family backgrounds and connections, their political experience and education, their national origins and religious affiliations, and their geographical distribution?

Most of these men were comparatively wealthy. Unfortunately, it is usually impossible to determine the extent of a man's wealth at any given time, but at least a general idea of the land and slave holdings of most of the 110 may be culled from existing wills, inventories, tithable and tax lists, and personal records. Information on land holdings is available for all but ten. Slightly less than three-fourths of them had large holdings —that is, holdings in excess of ten thousand acres. Seven of the 110, and perhaps three others, owned more than forty thousand acres; and the holdings of forty-six, certainly, and perhaps as many as sixty-four, exceeded ten thousand acres. A dozen possessed from one to five thousand acres. Only one man is thought to have owned fewer than five hundred acres. Records of slaveholdings are more difficult to find, but reasonably exact information is available for over half of the 110, and most of the others are known to have possessed some slaves. Quite naturally, the larger landowners—men like John Robinson, Charles and Landon Carter, Benjamin Harrison, and Archibald Cary—also owned the greater number of slaves. Eleven of those for whom records are available owned more than three hundred slaves—a staggering number for the times. Twenty-five possessed from fifty to three hundred slaves; twenty-two others had more than ten. Land and slaves were, of course, not the only assets of these burgesses. Livestock, plantation dwellings and outbuildings, farm equipment, and town houses must be added to their riches. Some men, like the Nelsons and Richard Adams, had large mercantile establishments; and a few dabbled in mining and manufacturing.

Most of the 110 leaders of the house were, of course, planters. Indeed at least ninety-one were directly involved in planting and raising tobacco, although a third of these engaged in planting only as a secondary occupation. The lawyers—most of whom were planters on the side—were the next most numerous professional or occupational group. Thirty-nine of the 110 were practicing lawyers, but they were far more significant than their number would indicate. The services of trained lawyers were invaluable to the house. They had precisely those talents required in framing legislation and carrying on the business of the Burgesses; and throughout the period under consideration, they were conspicuous by their presence at the top level of power. Of the four men who served as speaker, three—John Holloway, Sir John Randolph, and Peyton Randolph—were lawyers. Other occupational groups were less prominent. Of the thirteen men not accounted for above, ten were merchants, two were physicians, and one was a teacher.

Nearly all of the leaders of the house had secondary economic interests. It has already been pointed out that the majority of the lawyers were planters too. So also were the merchants, one of the physicians, and the teacher. Similarly, most of those who were primarily planters had other interests. Their most important secondary occupation was land speculation. Over two-fifths, and perhaps more, speculated in Western lands—a profitable avocation. A dozen participated in some form of mercantile activity. Three were engaged in mining; four were part-time surveyors; four were part-time soldiers; and one was a part-time teacher. Archibald Cary might even be classed a manufacturer, for one of his many secondary interests was an iron works.

Historians from the time of William Wirt to the present have considered family an important ingredient of political power in eighteenth-century Virginia. Bernard Bailyn has recently put forward the provocative thesis that a new ruling class emerged out of an immigration to Virginia that began in the late 1630's or early 1640's and continued through the 1660's. According to Bailyn, this ruling class supplanted the leaders of the earlier immigrants, secured more or less permanent control first of the county institutions and then of the House of Burgesses, and supplied much of the political leadership of the eighteenth century.[3] My own investigations of the family backgrounds of the Burgesses' leaders indicate that this thesis is only partly valid. Certainly, the generation that came to Virginia between 1635 and 1670 contributed more leaders than any other generation. Forty-nine of the 110 were descendents of that generation. Only seven derived from the pre-1635 immigrants. However, fifty others —nearly half of the leaders who dominated the Burgesses from 1720 to 1776—descended from the several generations that came to the colony after 1670.[4] This fact is significant, for it indicates that the earlier immigrants did not have a monopoly on political power or a very tight control over the House of Burgesses. In fact, families still comparatively new on the Virginia scene in 1720 supplied a significant proportion of the Burgesses' leadership during the fifty years preceding the Revolution. Nearly one-fifth of the 110 were drawn from families that arrived in Virginia between 1690 and 1720, and another tenth from those that came after 1720. Some of the newcomers, of course, found marriage into an established family a convenient avenue to social and political power, but many, like Speaker John Holloway, John Clayton, and James Power, acquired wealth, position, and political power without the advantages of connections with older families—an indication that social lines were still fluid and that political power was still attainable for the ambitious and gifted among the newly arrived.

It should not be inferred, however, that family connections were unimportant. Over half of the leaders were connected either through blood or marriage to one of the great eighteenth-century families, and only a conspicuous few reached the top level of power without such a connection. Indeed, certain families—notably the Randolphs, Carters, Beverleys, and Lees—supplied an unusually large proportion of the leaders of the house. Including descendants through both male and female lines, the Randolphs provided eleven, the Carters nine, the Beverleys eight, and the Lees six. The Blands, Burwells, and Corbins each furnished four, and the Blairs, Harrisons, Ludwells, and Nelsons three; these families were connected through marriage with other leading burgesses: six had marriage ties with the Carters, five with the Randolphs, and four with the Beverleys. Membership in, or alliance with, one of these families was certainly an important political asset, although, to keep the matter in proper perspective, from one-third to one-half of the leaders were not related to any of these families and not every member so related attained political power.

In religion and nationality the leaders were remarkably homogeneous. Of the 80 per cent ascertainable, all were Anglicans. It seems likely that those about whom information is not available were also Anglican, although it is entirely possible that several adhered to other Protestant faiths. In national origins the vast majority were English, and, if there were a few Scots, some Welsh, and even an occasional Irishman, still they all were Britons.

The educational level of the 110 leading burgesses appears to have been remarkably high. At least fifty had some education at the college or university level. Some forty attended the College of William and Mary, but others journeyed to England for at least a part of their formal schooling. Richard Henry Lee and Robert Munford studied at Wakefield Academy in Leeds; Charles and Landon Carter at Solomon Low's School, near London; Gabriel Jones at the Blue Coat School in Christ's Hospital, London; and four others at unknown schools in the British Isles. Ten others read law at the Inns of Court—for whatever that may or may not have been worth. A few matriculated at the universities; two at Oxford, another at Cambridge, and one, possibly two, at Edinburgh. Of those who had neither the benefits of an English education nor study at William and Mary, many, like Franics Lightfoot Lee, were taught at home by a private tutor. Others, like George Washington, got their education in parish schools conducted by local clergymen. No fewer than seventeen of those without university training successfully undertook the study of law; they proceeded either, like Edmund Pendleton and Paul Carrington, under the watchful eye of a practicing attorney or, like Patrick Henry, on their own. From the records at hand it is impossible to determine if the educational attainments of the leaders were higher than those of their fellow burgesses or just how much higher their educational level was than the general level in Virginia. In all likelihood, however, they were at least as well educated as any men in the colony.

The leaders' formal education was supplemented by practical experience at the county and parish levels. In fact, a record of active county and parish service was in the background of almost every burgess. The late Charles S. Sydnor, in his study of eighteenth-century Virginia politics, found that posts on the county courts, the parish vestry, and the county militia were important milestones on the pathway to political power.[5] My own investigation amply supports his findings. Either before or during their service in the house, well over four-fifths of the Burgesses' men of power between 1720 and 1776 served as gentlemen justices of the peace. Over half were vestrymen, and nearly two-fifths were officers of the county militia. A few had also been clerks, king's attorneys, sheriffs, surveyors, and coroners in the counties. Some had served as town officials; no fewer than five had been mayors of Williamsburg. Five others combined burgessing with the colony's attorney generalship. Each of these posts—military, judicial, civil, and ecclesiastical—gave the prospective burgess an opportunity to develop the sort of leadership that would prove useful in the house, to gain an intimate knowledge of his future constituents, and to learn something of the obligations and responsibilities of political office and political power.

An analysis of the geographical distribution of the leaders shows that no one section had a monopoly on political power within the house. Neither does there appear to have been any attempt by representatives from the older counties in the Tidewater to exclude from places of importance those burgesses who came from the newer areas. On the other hand, it appears that leadership and geographical origins were not unrelated, for leaders were rarely drawn from sections settled for less than a generation. During the period under consideration, more leaders came from the Tidewater, in particular from the region extending from the south side of the James River northward to the Rappahannock and from the western rim of Chesapeake Bay westward to the fall line, than from any other section; in fact, until 1730 most of the leaders were Tidewater men. However, from 1705 on, representatives from the Northern Neck, that area lying between the Rappahannock and Potomac Rivers and stretching westward to the mountains, played an increasingly important role in the affairs of the house and by 1730 equaled the Tidewater in supplying the house with leaders. In the 1730's, the counties around the fall line also began to contribute a significant number of leaders. This development was, after all, a logical one, especially since the social and economic patterns of the Tidewater were extended not only to the Northern Neck and the fall line area but also into the Piedmont,[6] and since family ties cut across geographical lines. From 1689 to the end of the colonial period, there appears to have been an almost continuous shift of the geographical center of power northward and westward, following the frontier by about a generation. Thus, the house did not draw leaders from the Piedmont until the later 1740's, nearly twenty-five years after the first settlement of that region. Similarly, although the occupation of the Shenandoah Valley and mountain area further west began in the 1740's, none of its representatives rose to positions of power until the late 1760's.

Why these particular 110 rose to positions of power rather than their colleagues is a question of fundamental importance. As individuals they exhibit most of the "qualifications" I have discussed. They were wealthy, derived part of their income from planting, were often related to the great Virginia families, were Anglicans, were of English (or at least of British) origin, had attained a high educational level for the time and place, were experienced in local politics, and came from areas settled for at least a generation. These were the tangibles upon which political power was based, although the lack of any one, two, or even three of these qualifications might not necessarily bar a man from a position of power. The more essential elements were wealth, family, and education; but even a generous helping of all three would not guarantee a position among the leaders of the house. Otherwise William Byrd III, Robert Wormeley Carter, Charles Carter, Jr., Richard Bland, Jr., and others would have been assured of such a place. In the long run the capacity to put these elements to effective use—call it political acumen, sagacity, the quality of political leadership—was probably decisive, although it is not susceptible of analysis in a study of this nature. But to secure the support of the electorate and the confidence of his colleagues and to exercise leadership in the Virginia House of Burgesses, 1720–76, a man had to have some measure of the tangible "qualifications" as well as the capacity to use them.

# Intergroup Conflict / *David Brion Davis*

*While emphasis of this volume is upon the concept rather than the area or the discipline as the core of a social science approach, historical studies of immigrant, ethnic, and minority groups invite social science analysis. Group relationships find their most dramatic expression in terms of conflict. Diverse interpretations of the sources of conflict are suggested in footnote 1 to Dr. Davis' article.*

*Oscar Handlin has attacked the close correspondence that some have found between racism and economic tensions and the conclusion that racism is a tool of an exploitative class.[1] Anti-Semitism, argued Handlin, was more prevalent among Populist agitators in the late nineteenth century than among the "exploiters" attacked by the Populists.[2] This conclusion has been questioned by Norman Pollack.[3]*

*In the article reprinted below, Davis is concerned with psychological mechanisms involved in the expression of group hostility. Among these are imagery and stereotyping, projection, guilt, incipient paranoia, and anxiety over status in a changing environment.[4]*

DURING THE SECOND quarter of the nineteenth century, when danger of foreign invasion appeared increasingly remote, American were told by various respected leaders that Freemasons had infiltrated the government and had seized control of the courts, that Mormons were undermining political and economic freedom in the West, and that Roman Catholic priests, receiving instructions from Rome, had made frightening progress in a plot to subject the nation to popish despotism. This fear of internal subversion was channeled into a number of powerful

David Brion Davis, "Some Themes of Counter-Subversion: An Analysis of Anti-Masonic, Anti-Catholic, and Anti-Mormon Literature," *Mississippi Valley Historical Review*, XLVII (September, 1960), 205–24. Reprinted by permission.

1. "Does Economics Explain Racism?" *Commentary*, VI (July, 1948), 79–85.
2. "American Views of the Jews at the Opening of the Twentieth Century," *Publications of the American Jewish Historical Society*, XL (June, 1951), 323–44.
3. "The Myth of Populist Anti-Semitism," *American Historical Review*, LXVIII (October, 1962), 76–80.
4. For a summary of the psychic forces involved in intergroup tensions see Selma Hirsh, *The Fears Men Live By* (New York, 1955).

counter movements which attracted wide public support. The literature produced by these movements evoked images of a great American enemy that closely resembled traditional European stereotypes of conspiracy and subversion. In Europe, however, the idea of subversion implied a threat to the established order—to the king, the church, or the ruling aristocracy—rather than to ideals or a way of life. If free Americans borrowed their images of subversion from frightened kings and uneasy aristocrats, these images had to be shaped and blended to fit American conditions. The movements would have to come from the people, and the themes of counter-subversion would be likely to reflect their fears, prejudices, hopes, and perhaps even unconscious desires.

There are obvious dangers in treating such reactions against imagined subversion as part of a single tendency or spirit of an age.[1] Anti-Catholicism was nourished by ethnic conflict and uneasiness over immigration in the expanding cities of the Northeast; anti-Mormonism arose largely from a contest for economic and political power between western settlers and a group that voluntarily withdrew from society and claimed the undivided allegiance of its members.[2] Anti-Masonry, on the other hand, was directed against a group thoroughly integrated in American society and did not reflect a clear division of economic, religious, or political interests.[3] Moreover, anti-Masonry gained power in the late 1820's and soon spent its energies as it became absorbed in national politics; anti-Catholicism reached its maximum force in national politics a full generation later;[4] anti-Mormonism, though increasing in intensity in the 1850's, became an important national issue only after the Civil War.[5] These movements seem even more widely separated when we note that Freemasonry was traditionally associated with anti-Catholicism and that Mormonism itself absorbed considerable anti-Masonic and anti-Catholic sentiment.[6]

Despite such obvious differences, there were certain similarities in these campaigns against subversion. All three gained widespread support in the northeastern states within the space of a generation; anti-Masonry and anti-Catholicism resulted in the sudden emergence of separate political parties; and in 1856 the new Republican party explicitly condemned the Mormons' most controversial institution. The movements of counter-subversion differed markedly in historical origin, but as the image of an un-American conspiracy took form in the nativist press, in sensational exposés, in the countless fantasies of treason and mysterious criminality, the lines separating Mason, Catholic, and Mormon became almost indistinguishable.

The similar pattern of Masonic, Catholic, and Mormon subversion was frequently noticed by alarmist writers. The *Anti-Masonic Review* informed its readers in 1829 that whether one looked at Jesuitism or Free-masonry, "the organization, the power, and the secret operation, are the same; except that Freemasonry is much the more secret and com-plicated of the two."[7] William Hogan, an ex-priest and vitriolic anti-Catholic, compared the menace of Catholicism with that of Mormonism.[8] And many later anti-Mormon writers agreed with Josias Strong that Brigham Young "out-popes the Roman" and described the Mormon hier-archy as being similar to the Catholic. It was probably not accidental that Samuel F. B. Morse analyzed the Catholic conspiracy in essentially the same terms his father had used in exposing the Society of the Illuminati, supposedly a radical branch of Freemasonry,[9] or that writers of sensa-tional fiction in the 1840's and 1850's depicted an atheistic and un-principled Catholic Church obviously modeled on Charles Brockden Brown's earlier fictional version of the Illuminati.[10]

If Masons, Catholics, and Mormons bore little resemblance to one another in actuality, as imagined enemies they merged into a nearly common stereotype. Behind specious professions of philanthropy or religious sentiment, nativists[11] discerned a group of unscrupulous leaders plotting to subvert the American social order. Though rank-and-file members were not individually evil, they were blinded and corrupted by a persuasive ideology that justified treason and gross immorality in the interest of the subversive group. Trapped in the meshes of a machine-like organization, deluded by a false sense of loyalty and moral obligation, these dupes followed orders like professional soldiers and labored un-knowingly to abolish free society, to enslave their fellow men, and to overthrow divine principles of law and justice. Should an occasional member free himself from bondage to superstition and fraudulent au-thority, he could still be disciplined by the threat of death or dreadful tortures. There were no limits to the ambitious designs of leaders equipped with such organizations. According to nativist prophets, they chose to subvert American society because control of America meant control of the world's destiny.

Some of these beliefs were common in earlier and later European interpretations of conspiracy. American images of Masonic, Catholic, and Mormon subversion were no doubt a compound of traditional myths concerning Jacobite agents, scheming Jesuits, and fanatical heretics, and of dark legends involving the Holy Vehm and Rosicrucians. What dis-tinguished the stereotypes of Mason, Catholic, and Mormon was the way in which they were seen to embody those traits that were precise antitheses of American ideals. The subversive group was essentially an inverted image of Jacksonian democracy and the cult of the common man; as such it not only challenged the dominant values but stimulated those suppressed needs and yearnings that are unfulfilled in a mobile, rootless, and individualistic society. It was therefore both frightening and fascinating.

It is well known that expansion and material progress in the Jacksonian era evoked a fervid optimism and that nationalists became intoxicated with visions of America's millennial glory. The simultaneous growth of prosperity and social democracy seemed to prove that Providence would bless a nation that allowed her citizens maximum liberty. When each individual was left free to pursue happiness in his own way, unhampered by the tyranny of custom or special privilege, justice and well-being would inevitably emerge. But if a doctrine of laissez-faire individualism seemed to promise material expansion and prosperity, it also raised disturbing problems. As one early anti-Mormon writer expressed it: What was to prevent liberty and popular sovereignty from sweeping away "the old landmarks of Christendom, and the glorious old common law of our fathers"? How was the individual to preserve a sense of continuity with the past, or identify himself with a given cause or tradition? What, indeed, was to insure a common loyalty and a fundamental unity among the people?

Such questions acquired a special urgency as economic growth intensified mobility, destroyed old ways of life, and transformed traditional symbols of status and prestige. Though most Americans took pride in their material progress, they also expressed a yearning for reassurance and security, for unity in some cause transcending individual self-interest. This need for meaningful group activity was filled in part by religious revivals, reform movements, and a proliferation of fraternal orders and associations. In politics Americans tended to assume the posture of what Marvin Meyers has termed "venturesome conservatives," mitigating their acquisitive impulses by an appeal for unity against extraneous forces that allegedly threatened a noble heritage of republican ideals. Without abandoning a belief in progress through laissez-faire individualism, the Jacksonians achieved a sense of unity and righteousness by styling themselves as restorers of tradition.[12] Perhaps no theme is so evident in the Jacksonian era as the strained attempt to provide America with a glorious heritage and a noble destiny. With only a loose and often ephemeral attachment to places and institutions, many Americans felt a compelling need to articulate their loyalties, to prove their faith, and to demonstrate their allegiance to certain ideals and institutions. By so doing they acquired a sense of self-identity and personal direction in an otherwise rootless and shifting environment.

But was abstract nationalism sufficient to reassure a nation strained by sectional conflict, divided by an increasing number of sects and

associations, and perplexed by the unexpected consequences of rapid
growth? One might desire to protect the Republic against her enemies,
to preserve the glorious traditions of the Founders, and to help insure
continued expansion and prosperity, but first it was necessary to discover
an enemy by distinguishing subversion from simple diversity. If Freemasons seemed to predominate in the economic and political life of a
given area, was one's joining them shrewd business judgment or a betrayal of republican tradition?[13] Should Maryland citizens heed the
warnings of anti-Masonic intinerants, or conclude that anti-Masonry was
itself a conspiracy hatched by scheming Yankees?[14] Were Roman Catholics plotting to destroy public schools and a free press, the twin guardians
of American democracy, or were they exercising democratic rights of
self-expression and self-protection?[15] Did equality of opportunity and
equality before the law mean that Americans should accept the land
claims of Mormons or tolerate as jurors men who "swear that they have
wrought miracles and supernatural cures"? Or should one agree with the
Reverend Finis Ewing that "the 'Mormons' are the common enemies
of mankind and ought to be destroyed"?[16]

Few men questioned traditional beliefs in freedom of conscience and
the right of association. Yet what was to prevent "all the errors and worn
out theories of the Old World, of schisms in the early Church, the
monkish age and the rationalistic period," from flourishing in such
salubrious air?"[17] Nativists often praised the work of benevolent societies,
but they were disturbed by the thought that monstrous conspiracies
might also "show kindness and patriotism, when it is necessary for their
better concealment; and oftentimes do much good for the sole purpose of
getting a better opportunity to do evil."[18] When confronted by so many
sects and associations, how was the patriot to distinguish the loyal from
the disloyal? It was clear that mere disagreement over theology or
economic policy was invalid as a test, since honest men disputed over the
significance of baptism or the wisdom of protective tariffs. But neither
could one rely on expressions of allegiance to common democratic principles, since subversives would cunningly profess to believe in freedom
and toleration of dissent as long as they remained a powerless minority.

As nativists studied this troubling question, they discovered that
most groups and denominations claimed only a partial loyalty from their
members, freely subordinating themselves to the higher and more abstract demands of the Constitution, Christianity, and American public
opinion. Morover, they openly exposed their objects and activities to
public scrutiny and exercised little discrimination in enlisting members.
Some groups, however, dominated a larger portion of their members'

lives, demanded unlimited allegiance as a condition of membership, and excluded certain activities from the gaze of a curious public.

Of all governments, said Richard Rush, ours was the one with most to fear from secret societies, since popular sovereignty by its very nature required perfect freedom of public inquiry and judgment.[19] In a virtuous republic why should anyone fear publicity or desire to conceal activities, unless those activities were somehow contrary to the public interest? When no one could be quite sure what the public interest was, and when no one could take for granted a secure and well-defined place in the social order, it was most difficult to acknowledge legitimate spheres of privacy. Most Americans of the Jacksonian era appeared willing to tolerate diversity and even eccentricity, but when they saw themselves excluded and even barred from witnessing certain proceedings, they imagined a "mystic power" conspiring to enslave them.

Readers might be amused by the first exposure of Masonic rituals, since they learned that pompous and dignified citizens, who had once impressed non-Masons with allusions to high degrees and elaborate ceremonies, had in actuality been forced to stand blindfolded and clad in ridiculous garb, with a long rope noosed around their necks. But genuine anti-Masons were not content with simple ridicule. Since intelligent and distinguished men had been members of the fraternity, "it must have in its interior something more than the usual revelations of its mysteries declare."[20] Surely leading citizens would not meet at night and undergo degrading and humiliating initiations just for the sake of novelty. The alleged murder of William Morgan raised an astonishing public furor because it supposedly revealed the inner secret of Freemasonry. Perverted by a false ideology, Masons had renounced all obligations to the general public, to the laws of the land, and even to the command of God. Hence they threatened not a particular party's program or a denomination's creed, but stood opposed to all justice, democracy, and religion.[21]

The distinguishing mark of Masonic, Catholic, and Mormon conspiracies was a secrecy that cloaked the members' unconditional loyalty to an autonomous body. Since the organizations had corrupted the private moral judgment of their members, Americans could not rely on the ordinary forces of progress to spread truth and enlightenment among their ranks. Yet the affairs of such organizations were not outside the jurisdiction of democratic government, for no body politic could be asked to tolerate a power that was designed to destroy it.[22] Once the true nature of subversive groups was thoroughly understood, the alternatives were as clear as life and death. How could democracy and Catholicism coexist when, as Edward Beecher warned, "The systems are diametrically opposed: one must and will exterminate the other"?[23] Because Freemasons had so deeply penetrated state and national governments, only drastic remedies could restore the nation to its democratic purity.[24] And later, Americans faced an "irrepressible conflict" with Mormonism, for it was said that either free institutions or Mormon despotism must ultimately annihilate the other.[25]

We may well ask why nativists magnified the division between unpopular minorities and the American public, so that Masons, Catholics, and Mormons seemed so menacing that they could not be accorded the usual rights and privileges of a free society. Obviously the literature of counter-subversion reflected concrete rivalries and conflicts of interests between competing groups, but it is important to note that the subversive bore no racial or ethnic stigma and was not even accused of inherent depravity.[26] Since group membership was a matter of intellectual and emotional loyalty, no *physical* barrier prevented a Mason, Catholic, or Mormon from apostatizing and joining the dominant in-group, providing always that he escaped assassination from his previous masters. This suggests that counter-subversion was more than a rationale for group rivalry and was related to the general problem of ideological unity and diversity in a free society. When a "system of delusion" insulated members of a group from the unifying and disciplining force of public opinion, there was no authority to command an allegiance to common principles. This was why oaths of loyalty assumed great importance for nativists. Though the ex-Catholic William Hogan stated repeatedly that Jesuit spies respected no oaths except those to the Church, he inconsistently told Masons and Odd Fellows that they could prevent infiltration by requiring new members to swear they were not Catholics.[27] It was precisely the absence of distinguishing outward traits that made the enemy so dangerous, and true loyalty so difficult to prove.

When the images of different enemies conform to a similar pattern, it is highly probable that this pattern reflects important tensions within a given culture. The themes of nativist literature suggest that its authors simplified problems of personal insecurity and adjustment to bewildering social change by trying to unite Americans of diverse political, religious, and economic interests against a common enemy. Just as revivalists sought to stimulate Christian fellowship by awakening men to the horrors of sin, so nativists used apocalyptic images to ignite human passions, destroy selfish indifference, and join patriots in a cohesive brotherhood. Such themes were only faintly secularized. When God saw his "lov'd Columbia" imperiled by the hideous monster of Freemasonry, He realized that only a martyr's blood could rouse the hearts of the people and save them from bondage to the Prince of Darkness. By having God will Morgan's death, this anti-Mason showed he was more concerned with national virtue and unity than with Freemasonry, which was only a providential instrument for testing republican strength.[28]

Similarly, for the anti-Catholic "this brilliant new world" was once "young and beautiful; it abounded in all the luxuries of nature; it promised all that was desirable to man." But the Roman Church, seeing "these irresistible temptations, thirsting with avarice and yearning for the reestablishment of her falling greatness, soon commenced pouring in among its unsuspecting people hoards of Jesuits and other friars." If Americans were to continue their narrow pursuit of self-interest, oblivious to the "Popish colleges, and nunneries, and monastic institutions," indifferent to manifold signs of corruption and decay, how could the nation expect "that the moral breezes of heaven should breathe upon her, and restore to her again that strong and healthy constitution, which her ancestors have left to her sons"?[29] The theme of an Adamic fall from paradise was horrifying, but it was used to inspire determined action and thus unity. If Methodists were "criminally indifferent" to the Mormon question, and if "avaricious merchants, soulless corporations, and a subsidized press" ignored Mormon iniquities, there was all the more reason that the *will of the people* must prevail."[30]

Without explicitly rejecting the philosophy of laissez-faire individualism, with its toleration of dissent and innovation, nativist literature conveyed a sense of common dedication to a noble cause and sacred tradition. Though the nation had begun with the blessings of God and with the noblest institutions known to man, the people had somehow become selfish and complacent, divided by petty disputes, and insensitive to signs of danger. In his sermons attacking such self-interest, such indifference to public concerns, and such a lack of devotion to common ideals and sentiments, the nativist revealed the true source of his anguish. Indeed, he seemed at times to recognize an almost beneficent side to subversive organizations, since they joined the nation in a glorious crusade and thus kept it from moral and social disintegration.

The exposure of subversion was a means of promoting unity, but it also served to clarify national values and provide the individual ego with a sense of high moral sanction and imputed righteousness. Nativists identified themselves repeatedly with a strangely incoherent tradition in which images of Pilgrims, Minute Men, Founding Fathers, and true Christians appeared in a confusing montage. Opposed to this heritage of stability and perfect integrity, to this society founded on the highest principles of divine and natural law, were organizations formed by the grossest frauds and impostures, and based on the wickedest impulses of human nature. Bitterly refuting Masonic claims to ancient tradition and Christian sanction, anti-Masons charged that the Order was of recent origin, that it was shaped by Jews, Jesuits, and French atheists as an engine for spreading infidelity, and that it was employed by kings and aristocrats to undermine republican institutions.[31] If the illustrious Franklin and Washington had been duped by Masonry, this only proved how treacherous was its appeal and how subtly persuasive were its pretensions.[32] Though the Catholic Church had an undeniable claim to tradition, nativists argued that it had originated in stupendous frauds and forgeries "in comparison with which the forgeries of Mormonism are completely thrown into the shade."[33] Yet anti-Mormons saw an even more sinister conspiracy based on the "shrewd cunning" of Joseph Smith, who convinced gullible souls that he conversed with angels and received direct revelations from the Lord.[34]

By empasizing the fraudulent character of their opponents' claims, nativists sought to establish the legitimacy and just authority of American institutions. Masonic rituals, Roman Catholic sacraments, and Mormon revelations were preposterous hoaxes used to delude naïve or superstitious minds; but public schools, a free press, and jury trials were eternally valid prerequisites for a free and virtuous society.

Moreover, the finest values of an enlightened nation stood out in bold relief when contrasted with the corrupting tendencies of subversive groups. Perversion of the sexual instinct seemed inevitably to accompany religious error.[35] Deprived of the tender affections of normal married love, shut off from the elevating sentiments of fatherhood, Catholic priests looked on women only as insensitive objects for the gratification of their frustrated desires.[36] In similar fashion polygamy struck at the heart of a morality based on the inspiring influence of woman's affections: "It renders man coarse, tyrannical, brutal, and heartless. It deals death to all sentiments of true manhood. It enslaves and ruins woman. It crucifies every God-given feeling of her nature."[37] Some anti-Mormons concluded that plural marriage could only have been established among foreigners who had never learned to respect women. But the more common explanation was that the false ideology of Mormonism had deadened the moral sense and liberated man's wild sexual impulse from the normal restraints of civilization. Such degradation of women and corruption of man served to highlight the importance of democratic marriage, a respect for women, and careful cultivation of the finer sensibilities.[38]

But if nativist literature was a medium for articulating common values and exhorting individuals to transcend self-interest and join in a dedicated union against evil, it also performed a more subtle function. Why, we may ask, did nativist literature dwell so persistently on themes of brutal sadism and sexual immorality? Why did its authors describe sin in such minute details, endowing even the worst offenses of their enemies with a certain fascinating appeal?

Freemasons, it was said, could commit any crime and indulge any passion when "upon the square," and Catholics and Mormons were even less inhibited by internal moral restraints. Nativists expressed horror over this freedom from conscience and conventional morality, but they could not conceal a throbbing note of envy. What was it like to be a member of a cohesive brotherhood that casually abrogated the laws of God and man, enforcing unity and obedience with dark and mysterious powers? As nativists speculated on this question, they projected their own fears and desires into a fantasy of licentious orgies and fearful punishments.

Such a projection of forbidden desires can be seen in the exaggeration of the stereotyped enemy's powers, which made him appear at times as a virtual superman. Catholic and Mormon leaders, never hindered by conscience or respect for traditional morality, were curiously superior to ordinary Americans in cunning, in exercising power over others, and especially in captivating gullible women.[39] It was an ancient theme of anti-Catholic literature that friars and priests were somehow more potent and sexually attractive than married laymen, and were thus astonishingly successful at seducing supposedly virtuous wives.[40] Americans were cautioned repeatedly that no priest recognized Protestant marriages as valid, and might consider any wife legitimate prey.[41] Furthermore, priests had access to the pornographic teachings of Dens and Liguori, sinister names that aroused the curiosity of anti-Catholics, and hence learned subtle techniques of seduction perfected over the centuries. Speaking with the authority of an ex-priest, William Hogan described the shocking result: "I have seen husbands unsuspiciously and hospitably entertaining the very priest who seduced their wives in the confessional, and was the parent of some of the children who sat at the same table with them, each of the wives unconscious of the other's guilt, and the husbands of both, not even suspecting them."[42] Such blatant immorality was horrifying, but everyone was apparently happy in this domestic scene, and we may suspect that the image was not entirely repugnant to husbands who, despite their respect for the Lord's Commandments, occasionally coveted their neighbors' wives.

The literature of counter-subversion could also embody the somewhat different projective fantasies of women. Ann Eliza Young dramatized her seduction by the Prophet Brigham, whose almost superhuman powers enchanted her and paralyzed her will. Though she submitted finally only because her parents were in danger of being ruined by the Church, she clearly indicated that it was an exciting privilege to be pursued by a

Great Man.[43] When Anti-Mormons claimed that Joseph Smith and other prominent Saints knew the mysteries of Animal Magnetism, or were endowed with the highest degree of "amativeness" in their phrenological makeup, this did not detract from their covert appeal.[44] In a ridiculous fantasy written by Maria Ward, such alluring qualities were extended even to Mormon women. Many bold-hearted girls could doubtless identify themselves with Anna Bradish, a fearless Amazon of a creature, who rode like a man, killed without compunction, and had no pity for weak women who failed to look out for themselves. Tall, elegant, and "intellectual," Anna was attractive enough to arouse the insatiable desires of Brigham Young, though she ultimately rejected him and renounced Mormonism.[45]

While nativists affirmed their faith in Protestant monogamy, they obviously took pleasure in imagining the variety of sexual experience supposedly available to their enemies. By picturing themselves exposed to similar temptations, they assumed they could know how priests and Mormons actually sinned.[46] Imagine, said innumerable anti-Catholic writers, a beautiful young woman kneeling before an ardent young priest in a deserted room. As she confesses, he leans over, looking into her eyes, until their heads are nearly touching. Day after day she reveals to him her innermost secrets, secrets she would not think of unveiling to her parents, her dearest friends, or even her suitor. By skillful questioning the priest fills her mind with immodest and even sensual ideas, "until this wretch has worked up her passions to a tension almost snapping, and then becomes his easy prey." How could any man resist such provocative temptations, and how could any girl's virtue withstand such a test?[47]

We should recall that this literature was written in a period of increasing anxiety and uncertainty over sexual values and the proper role of woman. As ministers and journalists pointed with alarm at the spread of prostitution, the incidence of divorce, and the lax and hypocritical morality of the growing cities, a discussion of licentious subversives offered a convenient means for the projection of guilt as well as desire. The sins of individuals, or of the nation as a whole, could be pushed off upon the shoulders of the enemy and there punished in righteous anger.[48]

Specific instances of such projection are not difficult to find. John C. Bennett, whom the Mormons expelled from the Church as a result of his flagrant sexual immorality, invented the fantasy of "The Mormon Seraglio" which persisted in later anti-Mormon writings. According to Bennett, the Mormons maintained secret orders of beautiful prostitutes who were mostly reserved for various officials of the Church. He claimed, moreover, that any wife refusing to accept polygamy might be forced to join the lowest order and thus become available to any Mormon who desired her.[49]

Another example of projection can be seen in the letters of a young lieutenant who stopped in Utah in 1854 on his way to California. Convinced that Mormon women could be easily seduced, the lieutenant wrote frankly of his amorous adventures with a married woman. "Everybody has got one," he wrote with obvious pride, "except the Colonel and Major. The Doctor had got three—mother and two daughters. The mother cooks for him and the daughters sleep with him." But though he described Utah as "a great country," the lieutenant waxed indignant over polygamy, which he condemned as self-righteously as any anti-Mormon minister: "To see one man openly parading half a dozen or more women to church . . . is the devil according to my ideas of morality virtue and decency."[50]

If the consciences of many Americans were troubled by the growth of red light districts in major cities, they could divert their attention to the "legalized brothels" called nunneries, for which no one was responsible but lecherous Catholic priests. If others were disturbed by the moral implications of divorce, they could point in horror at the Mormon elder who took his quota of wives all at once. The literature of counter-subversion could thus serve the double purpose of vicariously fulfilling repressed desires, and of releasing the tension and guilt arising from rapid social change and conflicting values.

Though the enemy's sexual freedom might at first seem enticing, it was always made repugnant in the end by associations with perversion or brutal cruelty. Both Catholics and Mormons were accused of practicing nearly every form of incest.[51] The persistent emphasis on this theme might indicate deep-rooted feelings of fear and guilt, but it also helped demonstrate, on a more objective level, the loathsome consequences of unrestrained lust. Sheer brutality and a delight in human suffering were supposed to be the even more horrible results of sexual depravity. Masons disemboweled or slit the throats of their victims; Catholics cut unborn infants from their mother's wombs and threw them to the dogs before their parents' eyes; Mormons raped and lashed recalcitrant women, or seared their mouths with red-hot irons.[52] This obsession with details of sadism, which reached pathological proportions in much of the literature, showed a furious determination to purge the enemy of every admirable quality. The imagined enemy might serve at first as an outlet for forbidden desires, but nativist authors escaped from guilt by finally making him an agent of unmitigated aggression. In such a role the subversive seemed to deserve both righteous anger and the most terrible punishments.

The nativist escape from guilt was more clearly revealed in the themes of confession and conversion. For most American Protestants the crucial step in anyone's life was a profession of true faith resulting from a genuine religious experience. Only when a man became conscious of his inner guilt, when he struggled against the temptations of Satan, could he prepare his soul for the infusion of the regenerative spirit. Those most deeply involved in sin often made the most dramatic conversions. It is not surprising that conversion to nativism followed the same pattern, since nativists sought unity and moral certainty in the regenerative spirit of nationalism. Men who had been associated in some way with un-American conspiracies were not only capable of spectacular confessions of guilt, but were best equipped to expose the insidious work of supposedly harmless organizations. Even those who lacked such an exciting history of corruption usually made some confession of guilt, though it might involve only a previous indifference to subversive groups. Like ardent Christians, nativists searched in their own experiences for the meaning of sin, delusion, awakening to truth, and liberation from spiritual bondage. These personal confessions proved that one had recognized and conquered evil, and also served as ritual cleansings preparatory to full acceptance in a group of dedicated patriots.

Anti-Masons were perhaps the ones most given to confessions of guilt and most alert to subtle distinctions of loyalty and disloyalty. Many leaders of this movement, expressing guilt over their own "shameful experience and knowledge" of Masonry, felt a compelling obligation to exhort their former associates to "come out, and be separate from masonic abominations."[53] Even when an anti-Mason could say with John Quincy Adams that "I am not, never was, and never shall be a Freemason," he would often admit that he had once admired the Order, or had even considered applying for admission.[54]

Since a willingness to sacrifice oneself was an unmistakable sign of loyalty and virtue, ex-Masons gloried in exaggerating the dangers they faced and the harm that their revelations supposedly inflicted on the enemy. In contrast to hardened Freemasons, who refused to answer questions in court concerning their fraternal associations, the seceders claimed to reveal the inmost secrets of the Order, and by so doing to risk property, reputation, and life.[55] Once the ex-Mason had dared to speak the truth, his character would surely be maligned, his motives impugned, and his life threatened. But, he declared, even if he shared the fate of the illustrious Morgan, he would die knowing that he had done his duty.

Such self-dramatization reached extravagant heights in the ranting confessions of many apostate Catholics and Mormons. Maria Monk and her various imitators told of shocking encounters with sin in its most sensational form, of bondage to vice and superstition, and of melodramatic escapes from popish despotism. A host of "ex-Mormon wives" described their gradual recognition of Mormon frauds and iniquities, the anguish and misery of plural marriage, and their breath-taking flights over deserts or mountains. The female apostate was especially vulnerable to vengeful retaliation, since she could easily be kidnapped by crafty priests and nuns, or dreadfully punished by Brigham Young's Destroying Angels.[56] At the very least, her reputation could be smirched by foul lies and insinuations. But her willingness to risk honor and life for the sake of her country and for the dignity of all womankind was eloquent proof of her redemption. What man could be assured of so noble a role?

The apostate's pose sometimes assumed paranoid dimensions. William Hogan warned that only the former could properly gauge the Catholic threat to American liberties and saw himself as providentially appointed to save his Protestant countrymen. "For twenty years," he wrote, "I have warned them of approaching danger, but their politicians were deaf, and their Protestant theologians remained religiously coiled up in fancied security, overrating their own powers and undervaluating that of Papists." Pursued by vengeful Jesuits, denounced and calumniated for alleged crimes, Hogan pictured himself single-handedly defending American freedom: "No one, before me, dared to encounter their scurrilous abuse. I resolved to silence them; and I have done so. The very mention of my name is a terror to them now." After surviving the worst of Catholic persecution, Hogan claimed to have at last aroused his countrymen and to have reduced the hierarchy to abject terror.[57]

As the nativist searched for participation in a noble cause, for unity in a group sanctioned by tradition and authority, he professed a belief in democracy and equal rights. Yet in his very zeal for freedom he curiously assumed many of the characteristics of the imagined enemy. By condemning the subversive's fanatical allegiance to an ideology, he affirmed a similarly uncritical acceptance of a different ideology; by attacking the subversive's intolerance of dissent, he worked to eliminate dissent and diversity of opinion; by censuring the subversive for alleged licentiousness, he engaged in sensual fantasies; by criticizing the subversive's loyalty to an organization, he sought to prove his unconditional loyalty to the established order. The nativist moved even farther in the direction of his enemies when he formed tightly-knit societies and parties which were often secret and which subordinated the individual to the single purpose of the group. Though the nativists generally agreed that the worst evil of subversives was their subordination of means to ends, they themselves recommended the most radical means to purge the nation of troublesome groups and to enforce unquestioned loyalty to the state.

In his image of an evil group conspiring against the nation's welfare, and in his vision of a glorious millennium that was to dawn after the enemy's defeat, the nativist found satisfaction for many desires. His own interests became legitimate and dignified by fusion with the national interest, and various opponents became loosely associated with the un-American conspiracy. Thus Freemasonry in New York State was linked in the nativist mind with economic and political interests that were thought to discriminate against certain groups and regions; southerners imagined a union of abolitionists and Catholics to promote unrest and rebellion among slaves; gentile businessmen in Utah merged anti-Mormonism with plans for exploiting mines and lands.

Then too the nativist could style himself as a restorer of the past, as a defender of a stable order against disturbing changes, and at the same time proclaim his faith in future progress. By focusing his attention on the imaginary threat of a secret conspiracy, he found an outlet for many irrational impulses, yet professed his loyalty to the ideals of equal rights and government by law. He paid lip service to the doctrine of laissez-faire individualism, but preached selfless dedication to a transcendent cause. The imposing threat of subversion justified a group loyalty and subordination of the individual that would otherwise have been unacceptable. In a rootless environment shaken by bewildering social change the nativist found unity and meaning by conspiring against imaginary conspiracies.

# Status Politics / *Richard Hofstadter*

Professor Hofstadter's article, reprinted below, amplifies the concept of status politics beyond the author's use of the term in an essay published some years ago.[1] Hofstadter asserts that his generation "was raised in the conviction that the basic motive power in political behavior is the economic interest of groups." The concept of status, he points out, embraces a wider range of human behavior than does simple economic explanation. Yet, so ramified is Hofstadter's development of this concept that in its complexity it subsumes other concepts related to cause.

This raises a problem already touched upon. Does social analysis require the reduction of concepts to nuclear elements? Are not some events explained more satisfactorily in terms of complex and composite concepts—like status, class, and frontier—that are expressive of interactionism among a variety of data? The fact that composite concepts such as frontier and class have been used imprecisely by Frederick Jackson Turner and Charles A. Beard need not invalidate the principle or idea of a composite concept whose meaning is carefully delineated and is more than the sum of integral conceptual parts.[2]

$A$ T THE TIME these essays appeared, many critics objected to an assumption that I believe underlies all of them—the assumption that the radical right is a response to certain underlying and continuing tensions in American society. It was held that the authors of these essays were being intellectually fancy and oversubtle. There was no need to go so far around the bend to find new explanations for these phenomena, critics complained, when the important explanations were obvious: the anxiety arising from the Korean stalemate, coming as it did right on the heels of the sacrifices of a major war; a series of startling revelations about Communist espionage; the long wartime and postwar inflation, the continuing high level of taxation, the frustration of the Republican Party shut out of the White House for twenty years. With all these things on tap to account for right-wing discontent, why invoke sociological forces whose relation to the issues seemed less direct?

Richard Hofstadter, "Pseudo-Conservatism Reprinted: A Postscript, 1962," in Daniel
Bell, ed. *The Radical Right* (New York, 1963), 81–86. Reprinted by permission.
1. Daniel Bell, ed., *New American Right* (New York, 1955).
2. *Supra*, 18–19.

Such criticism, I believe, was based upon a fundamental misconception of what these essays were trying to do. I can speak only for myself, but I doubt that any of the authors would deny that the Korean War was in the foreground of radical-right thinking, or that taxation had a good deal to do with its economic discontents. But the authors of these essays were curious about something in which their critics do not seem to have been interested—and that is the whole complex of forces that underlay the responses of the public to the frustrations of the 1950's. After all, not every wealthy American demanded the repeal of the income-tax amendment; not every Republican responded to the twenty-year period of Democratic ascendancy by branding the Democratic Party as treasonous; not every American who was wearied by the Korean stalemate called for all-out war at the risk of starting World War III—and, indeed, some Americans who expressed violent impatience over the conduct of the Korean War were those who were in fact benefiting from it economically. What puzzled us was how to account for the complex of forces in the structure of American society, in American traditions, that made it possible for men and women who were sharing the same experiences and the same disorders to call for drastically different types of remedies. After six or seven years of additional observation of the extreme right, it now seems more probable that our original approach was correct.

One aspect of my own essay that may be of enduring use and yet that now seems to require some modification is the concept of status politics. That there is a need for some such concept I have little doubt. My generation was raised in the conviction that the basic motive power in political behavior is the economic interest of groups. This is not the place to discuss at length the inadequacies of that view of the world, but it may be enough to say that we have learned to find it wanting as an account of much of the vital political behavior of our own time. However much importance we continue to attach to economic interests or imagined economic interests in political action, we are still confronted from time to time with a wide range of behavior for which the economic interpretation of politics seems to be inadequate or misleading or altogether irrelevant. It is to account for this range of behavior that we need a different conceptual framework, and I believe that the extreme right wing provides a pre-eminent example of such behavior.

However, it now seems doubtful that the term "status politics," which apparently was used for the first time in this essay, is an adequate term for what I had in mind. No doubt, social status is one of the things that is at stake in most political behavior, and here the right wing is no exception. But there are other matters involved, which I rather loosely assimilated to this term, that can easily be distinguished from status, strictly defined. The term "status" requires supplementation. If we were to speak of "cultural politics" we might supply part of what is missing. In our political life there have always been certain types of cultural issues, questions of faith and morals, tone and style, freedom and coercion, which become fighting issues. To choose but one example, prohibition was an issue of this kind during the twenties and early thirties. In the struggle over prohibition, economic interests played only the most marginal role; the issue mobilized religious and moral convictions, ethnic habits and hostilities, attitudes toward health and sexuality, and other personal preoccupations. There are always such issues at work in any body politic, but perhaps they are particularly acute and important in the United States because of our ethnic and religious heterogeneity. As I indicated in my essay, they loom larger during periods of prosperity, when economic conflicts are somewhat muted, then they do during periods of depression and economic discontent. Hard times mobilize economic group antagonisms; prosperity liberates the public for the expression of its more luxurious hostilities.

But this brings us to another aspect of the matter: at times politics becomes an arena into which the wildest fancies are projected, the most paranoid suspicions, the most absurd superstitions, the most bizarre apocalyptic fantasies. From time to time, movements arise that are founded upon the political exploitation of such fancies and fears, and while these movements can hardly aspire to animate more than a small minority of the population, they do exercise, especially in a democratic and populistically oriented political culture like our own, a certain leverage upon practical politics. Thus, today, despite the presence of issues of the utmost gravity and urgency, the American press and public have been impelled to discuss in all seriousness a right-wing movement whose leaders believe that President Eisenhower was a member of the "Communist conspiracy." It seems hardly extravagant to say that the true believers in a movement of this sort project into the arena of politics utterly irrelevant fantasies and disorders of a purely personal kind. Followers of a movement like the John Birch Society are in our world but not exactly of it. They intersect with it, they even have effects on it that could become grave, but the language they speak is a private language; they can compel the rest of us to listen to this language because they are just numerous enough, and because the structure of political influence is loose enough for them to apply a political leverage out of proportion to their numbers. They represent a kind of politics that is not exactly status politics or cultural politics, as I have defined them, but that might be called "projective politics." It involves the projection of interests and concerns, not only largely private but essentially pathological, into the public scene.

In action, of course, considerations of status and cultural role become intertwined with the content of projective politics, and what may be well worth making as an analytical distinction is not necessarily so clear in the world of political controversy. One of the reasons why the term "status" now seemed to me to be inadequate to suggest the full complex of realities that I had in mind is that several considerations are woven together in an unusually complex social fabric. One thing that has been at stake is the problem of an American identity, which has an especial poignance because of the heavy immigrant composition of our population and its great mobility. Many Americans still have problems about their Americanness and are still trying, psychologically speaking, to naturalize themselves. Ethnicity is in itself partly a status problem because American life does contain a status hierarchy in which ethnic background is important. Finally, because of the great mixture of religious and moral strains in our population, there is a constant argument over the social legitimacy of certain roles and values.

One of the facets of my own essay which I am disposed to regret is its excessive emphasis on what might be called the clinical side of the problem. Whether or not the psychological imputations it makes prove to be correct or not, I think a good deal more might have been said on purely behavioral and historical grounds to establish the destructive and "radical" character of pseudo-conservatism. The political character of this movement can be helpfully delineated by comparing it with true conservatism. The United States has not provided a receptive home for formal conservative thought or classically conservative modes of behavior. Lacking a formidable aristocratic tradition, this country has produced at best patricians rather than aristocrats, and the literature of American political experience shows how unhappy the patricians (for example, Henry Adams) have been in their American environment. Restless, mobile both geographically and socially, overwhelmingly middle-class in their aspirations, the American people have not given their loyalty to a national church or developed a traditionally oriented bar or clergy, or other institutions that have the character of national establishments. But it is revealing to observe the attitude of the extreme right wing toward those institutions that come closest here to reproducing the institutional apparatus of the aristocratic classes in other countries. Such conservative institutions as the better preparatory schools, the Ivy League colleges and universities, the Supreme Court, and the State Department—exactly those institutions that have been largely in the custodianship of the patrician or established elements in American society—have been the favorite objects of right-wing animosity.

And while the right-winger dislikes the social type that might be called conservative—a type represented by men like Dean Acheson, John Foster Dulles, Adlai Stevenson, and Harry L. Stimson—it also dislikes what might be called the practical conservatism of our time, as represented by the Eisenhower administration and by the eastern Dewey-Willkie-Eisenhower wing of the Republican Party. The Chicago *Tribune* expressed the dominant right-wing view some years ago when it lumped together "the nationalist, the Demi-Reps, the Truman Republicans, and the New Dealers, who . . . played footie-footie with the Communist for years." When the Democrats were finally ousted in the election of 1952, nothing less than a complete *bouleversement* in government would have satisfied the extreme right. Most of them were already highly suspicious of Eisenhower, and they felt they were justified when his administration neither uprooted the welfare reforms of the previous twenty years nor reversed the general strategy of American foreign policy. As the Chicago *Tribune* said of Eisenhower's 1955 State of the Union message, "Welfare statism and a tender if meddlesome solicitude for every fancied want of a once self-reliant citizenry were pyramided and compounded in this message."

Perhaps what is more to the point—though it is conjecture and not history—is that if Robert A. Taft had been nominated and elected in 1952, his administration might have been almost as disappointing to the hard core of the extreme right as Eisenhower's. The extreme right really suffers not from the policies of this or that administration, but from what America has become in the twentieth century. It suffers, moreover, from an implacable dislike and suspicion of all constituted authority. In part this is because, entertaining expectations that cannot be realized, it is bound to be dissatisfied with any regime. But still more decisive, in my opinion, is that the extreme right wing is constituted out of a public that simply cannot arrive at a psychological modus vivendi with authority, cannot reconcile itself to that combination of acceptance and criticism which the democratic process requires of the relationship between the leaders and the led. Being uncomfortable with the thought of any leadership that falls short of perfection, the extreme right is also incapable of analyzing the world with enough common sense to establish any adequate and realistic criterion for leadership. The right wing tolerates no compromises, accepts no half measures, understands no defeats. In this respect, it stands psychologically outside the frame of normal democratic politics, which is largely an affair of compromise. One of the most fundamental qualities, then, in the right-wing mentality of our time is its implicit utopianism. I can think of no more economical way of expressing its fundamental difference from the spirit of genuine conservatism.

If this essay were to be written today, there is one force in American life, hardly more than hinted at in my original formulation, that would now loom very large indeed, and that is fundamentalism. The little that we know from the press about the John Birch Society, the Christian Crusade of Dr. Fred Schwarz, and the activities of the Reverend Billy Hargis has served to remind us how much alive fundamentalism still is in the United States, and how firmly it has now fixed its attention on the fight against Communism, as it once concentrated on the fight against evolution. To understand the Manichaean style of thought, the apocalyptic tendencies, the love of mystification, the intolerance of compromise that are observable in the right-wing mind, we need to understand the history of fundamentalism as well as the contributions of depth psychology; and those who would understand it will do well to supplement their acquaintance with Rohrschach techniques or the construction of the F-scale with a rereading of the Book of Revelations. To the three sources of right-wing sentiment that are commonly enumerated—isolationism (or anti-Europeanism), ethnic prejudice, and old-fashioned "liberal" economics—one must add the fundamentalist revolt against modernity, and not by any means as a minor partner.

# Status Revolution and Reference Group Theory / *Richard B. Sherman*

Status revolution, involving "the changed pattern in the distribution of deference and power in society,"[1] triggers, especially among former holders of power and recipients of deference, status anxiety. The latter relates to reference group theory.

This process has been invoked by Professor David Donald in explaining support of the antislavery cause by those who suffered loss of status compared to newly-risen economic and social groups.[2] A similar explanation, in terms of reference group theory, informs Professor Hofstadter's account of the leadership of the progressive movement by men comparably situated.[3] That is, elements of the leadership of the abolitionist and progressive movements attempted to recoup power and prestige lost to competing groups.

What is reference group theory? It is defined by Professor Robert K. Merton as systematizing "the determinants and consequences of those processes of evaluation and self-appraisal in which the individual takes the values and standards of other individuals and groups as a comparative frame of reference."[4]

More recently, the definition of reference group has been extended to include group tradition and what Dr. Herbert Hyman described as a reference individual or ancestry against whose achievements the individual measures himself.[5] This ramification of the reference group concept is implicit in the work of Donald and Hofstadter, even before its theoretical explication by Hyman.

It has been suggested, with some justification, that reference group theory does not as yet exist; that it is really a central concept which embraces other concepts relating to perception, the social situation, and the social structure; that these other concepts enter into "the complex net-

Richard B. Sherman, "The Status Revolution and Massachusetts Progressive Leadership," Political Science Quarterly, LXXVIII (March, 1963), 59–65. Reprinted by permission.

1. Richard Hofstadter, The Age of Reform (New York, 1960), 135.
2. "Toward a Reconsideration of the Abolitionists," in Lincoln Reconsidered (New York, 1956).
3. The Age of Reform, 131–72.
4. Robert K. Merton, "Continuities in the Theory of Reference Groups and Social Structure," in Social Theory and Social Structure (Glencoe, 1957), 50–51.
5. "Reflections on Reference Groups," Public Opinion Quarterly, XXIV (Fall, 1960), 392.

work of concepts and empirically derived interrelationships which must be a part of reference group theory as theory."[6] Much of the criticism of reference group theory in historiography has been centered in the failure to recognize that, as Nelson pointed out, reference group is a composite concept, and that its components provide a more satisfactory and immediate explanation of causation than does the theory itself.[7] Dr. Sherman's critique of Hofstadter's use of the concept of status revolution has bearing upon supportive concepts such as reference group.

I N T H E *Age of Reform*, Richard Hofstadter has advanced a provocative thesis about the "status revolution" and the motivation of progressive leaders.[1] His analysis draws heavily upon two significant surveys of progressive leadership, one by Alfred D. Chandler, Jr. for 260 Progressive Party leaders throughout the United States and another by George E. Mowry for California.[2] Although there are some regional variations, the conclusions of both surveys are similar. Progressive leaders did not represent the population at large; rather they had some distinct and special characteristics. Thus progressive leaders were likely to be from urban, upper middle class backgrounds. They were generally rather young native-born Protestants of old Anglo-American stock. Many of them were college graduates. Most of them were either professional men, particularly lawyers or businessmen who represented neither the very largest nor the very smallest businesses. In New England especially they were likely to be managers of older established firms, not aggressive entrepreneurs. Hofstadter, for one, has used such summaries in presenting his notion of status anxiety as a major force in motivating men towards Progressivism, and his thesis certainly has been influential in recent revaluations of the Progressive Era. In the following analysis of Massachusetts a few reservations are suggested about the usefulness of the concept of the status revolution.

In general the Massachusetts Progressive Party leader resembles the "progressive profile" drawn by Mowry and Chandler. However, neither of these scholars has presented comparable surveys of other political leaders at that time, so there is no basis for knowing how special the characteristics of progressive leaders were other than the fact that they

6. Harold A. Nelson, "A Tentative Foundation for Reference Group Theory," *Sociology and Social Research*, XLIV (April, 1961), 280.

7. R. A. Skotheim, "A Note on Historical Method," *Journal of Southern History*, XXV (1959), 356–65.

clearly were not representative of the population at large. In my study of Massachusetts, Progressive Party leadership has been compared with that of the regular Republican and Democratic parties. The result suggests that the Progressive leader, particularly in comparison with his Republican counterpart, has essentially similar class characteristics.

In this analysis, fifty leaders of the Progressive Party in Massachusetts, including important party organizers, state committeemen, and candidates for important offices, were compared with Republican and Democratic leaders, for the period around 1912 and 1913, the years of greatest activity for the Bull Moosers.[3] It may be objected that the arbitrary division by party allegiance excludes some progressive Republicans who refused to bolt with Theodore Roosevelt in 1912, thus distorting the picture of the regular Republicans. However, as a matter of comparison note that Chandler's analysis is based upon Progressive Partly leaders, not progressives in general. Moreover, in practice there are few, if any, among the thirty-six Republicans whose record by 1912 would clearly place them in a progressive column. In fact the line between conservative and progressive was often far from distinct. For example, Congressman Augustus Peabody Gardner is one Massachusetts Republican whom some might consider a progressive because of his occasional insurgency. But it can be demonstrated, I believe, that Gardner's record was basically conservative.[4] Or a case could even be made for Senator Henry Cabot Lodge, the *bête noire* of many reformers, as a man who showed some progressive tendencies.[5] Fortunately the comparison by party affiliation avoids the necessity of making such subjective judgments and provides a clear-cut distinction.

The typical Massachusetts Progressive Party leader was fairly young. As of the end of 1912 the average age was 45.2 years, and a sizeable number of important men were in their early thirties. While Progressives came from all parts of the state, a leader was most likely to live in an eastern city. Only five of the fifty were foreign-born (including one born in Paris of American citizens). Of the native-born Americans, twenty-five were from Massachusetts, and nearly all the rest came from New England or the Northeast. British surnames abound, and many Progressive leaders traced their ancestry back to colonial America. Of thirty-five whose religious preference is known, twenty-nine were Protestant and six Catholic. The educational background is known for forty-seven of the group. Of these, thirty (63.8 per cent) attended college or some special training institution beyond secondary school, and sixteen studied at Harvard. Slightly over half of them were professionals, including sixteen lawyers and a few ministers, professors, and physicians. Businessmen of various kinds made up nearly all of the rest. Of these none was connected with the very large national corporations; most worked for or owned firms of medium size in which they played a prominent role. Some led family companies, but at least six were "self-made" men, rising from poor backgrounds. But no laborers, skilled or otherwise, and no routine white-collar workers were among the group. The Massachusetts Progressive Party leaders were relatively inexperienced in organized politics. Twenty-six of the fifty had no record of previous political activity at the time they joined the Roosevelt movement in 1912, and very few of the others had more than very limited experience in local or state politics.

Such a summary fits in reasonably well with the picture of the progressive presented by Chandler and Mowry, but it also bears very strong resemblance to the description of the regular Republican leader in Massachusetts. Republican leaders were slightly older than the Progressives, averaging 50.5 years at the end of 1912. All of the thirty-six Republicans studied were born in the United States, and twenty-five came from Massachusetts, a much higher proportion than among the Progressives. Most of them worked in the general vicinity of their birthplace, and more than a third came from the Boston area. Even more Republican leaders than Progressives had British surnames, and of those whose ancestry is known, seventeen traced their families back to the colonial era. Every one of the twenty-five for whom a religious preference is known was Protestant, with Episcopalian and Unitarian the most frequently listed denominations. Twenty-eight of the thirty-six (77.8 per cent, a higher figure than that for the Progressives) attended college or some post-secondary school. Of these, fourteen went to Harvard, four to Amherst and three to other Ivy League colleges, while eleven undertook graduate study of some kind. The professional pattern was also similar to that of the Progressives. Although none of the Republicans was drawn from teaching or medicine, the regular Republican leadership claimed twenty lawyers, seven manufacturers, four bankers, five journalists and a scattering of other occupations, including a few duplications where two professions were listed. The most obvious difference between the Progressive and Republican leaders was the degree of political experience. As a slightly older group in actual control of the dominant party in the state, the Republicans had considerably more experience in politics. All of them had been active before 1912, and two-thirds had engaged in state or local politics before 1901. But as for their class origins, the regular Republican leaders of Massachusetts, even more than the Progressives, came from Yankee, Protestant, well-placed backgrounds.

The leadership of the Democratic Party in Massachusetts was drawn from much more diverse backgrounds than that of either the Progressives or the Republicans, and it clearly reflected the nineteenth-century immigrant impact. But even it was remarkably well-placed in many ways. The Democratic leadership was distinctly younger than the Republican, averaging 44.2 years at the end of 1912. Of thirty-three whose birthplaces are known, all but one (from Prince Edward Island) was a native-born American, and twenty-seven came from Massachusetts, a much higher proportion than among the Progressive leaders.[6] The Boston area was heavily weighted, with fifteen born in the city and eight in the outskirts. Among eighteen Democrats whose parentage is known, nine had at least one parent who was born in Ireland. Of those whose ancestry is not known, many have surnames, of obviously Irish origin. However, seven of the Democrats descended from families dating from the colonial period, of whom six were of English and one was of French Huguenot extraction. Of twenty-eight whose religious preference is known, seventeen were Roman Catholic, ten Protestant, and one Jewish. The educational level of the Democratic leaders compared very favorably with that of the other two parties. Twenty-six of the thirty-four (76.5 per cent) attended college or some post-secondary school, a higher porportion than among the Progressives, and eighteen went on to graduate study. Of the college group, nine attended Harvard, three Boston College, two Dartmouth, and several went to various other colleges. Twenty-one of the group were lawyers, a somewhat higher proportion than among the Republicans and a much higher proportion than among the Progressives. One was a banker, six were businessmen (of whom two were manufacturers, one a merchant, and three in real estate), and six were journalists of some sort. Like the Republicans, most of the Democratic leaders had some political experience before 1912, although only twelve of the group were active before 1901, an item that could be explained by the fact that the Democrats were both younger and traditionally less successful in Massachusetts state politics than the Republicans.

This brief survey of the leaders of the Progressive, Republican and Democratic parties in Massachusetts indicates a considerable similarity between the first two, and a high level of educational and occupational attainment in the case of the third. For Massachusetts at least the leaders of *all three* parties were far from being anything like a reflection of the population at large as far as nativity, education, and occupation were concerned. Now this picture of Massachusetts leaders raises some questions about the explanation of progressives' motivation in terms of a status revolution. Hofstadter has written:

Men of this sort, who might be designated broadly as the Mugwump type, were Progressives not because of economic deprivations but primarily because they were victims of an upheaval in status that took place in the United States during the closing decades of the nineteenth and early years of the twentieth century. Progressivism, in short, was to a very considerable extent led by men who suffered from the events of their time not through a shrinkage in their means but through the changed pattern in the distribution of deference and power.[7]

Mowry has expressed similar views.[8] These conclusions are drawn in large measure from the fact that the typical progressive leader was a member of an older American, special status group. While there is considerable evidence that many progressives were from such a group, and Massachusetts is no exception, the conclusions about motivation do not necessarily follow from this fact. In the case of Massachusetts at least, it appears that political leadership in general, especially of the regular Republican, was well placed in society. At any rate the Progressive leaders by comparison no longer appear to have such distinct and special characteristics.

The Massachusetts Progressive leadership was actually less well educated than the Republican, and its ethnic composition was more diverse. To some extent the latter fact was a reflection of the deliberate effort of the Bull Moosers to provide candidates and leaders who would best attract the diverse elements of the state's population.[9] All but on of the top six or seven Progressive Party leaders were Harvard men whose social background typified the class described by Hofstadter. Nevertheless one important leader, James P. Magenis, was of Irish Catholic extraction, and the total Progressive picture was certainly more varied than the Republican. The most striking difference between the Progressive Party and the regular Republican leadership was not in class origins, but in degree of political experience. But this fact, after all, merely describes in part the formation of a new party in 1912 and suggests the importance of other elements besides class in awakening political interest at that time.

As most of the leaders of the regular Republicans came from backgrounds very similar to those of the Progressives, why did some men become Progressives, while others did not? If there was a status revolution, how do we explain the difference in reaction to it? Possibly the Massachusetts situation was a special case. Indeed one could well argue that the regular Republican leadership had shown a considerable amount of progressive conservatism in the past in terms of its legislative record.[10] Still, given the conditions of 1912, one would hardly label as progressive such men as Winthrup Murray Crane, Eben S. Draper, John W. Weeks, Samuel W. McCall, and many others holding similar views. This survey of the political leadership in Massachusetts does not, of course, prove that Progressive leaders were not concerned about apparent threats to their class status. I believe that some, at least, certainly were. But clearly we must be cautious in drawing conclusions from a class analysis of progressives alone, for in Massachusetts their status was not an independent variable. Much more needs to be learned about the individuals involved and the many factors that motivated such men before a more adequate explanation of progressive leadership can be made.

# Class / *Edward N. Saveth*

The article reprinted below aspires toward definition of a patrician class. Since there is no universally accepted definition of class, it uses theory and data to delineate some components of a patrician class model.

Fundamental to such a model are family and family history. Patrician types, ideal and real, derive from the data of family history that relate to time and place. Differences between patrician families and those of lower status are difficult to resolve because the second are not as well documented as the first. There is a further problem in the extent to which alterations in economic structure affect family and class structure.

Genealogical techniques, career-line inquiry, interactionism among members of a group, and the portrayal of life style are concepts involved in the study of patrician group structure. Once the nature of the group is ascertained and the extent to which it does or does not possess a unique identity is revealed, the problem is how does it function in relation to other structural elements in society. To what extent are its traditions unique and representative of a distinctive subculture? How much power does the class possess? To what extent does it represent an interest group? Is the patriciate united in pursuit of what might be described as class interests? Does reference group theory contribute to an explanation of patrician political behavior?

At present, when class is said by some sociologists to be of less importance as a societal force,[1] what is the significance of the rise of "men of family" to political prominence?[2]

A fascinating area of study is the evolution of the class concept in American historiography, beginning with Charles A. Beard's use of the term. Much of the material in this area, but not all, concerns the historiography of the American Constitution and the conceptions of class and group that inform the writings of Robert E. Brown, Forrest McDonald, Jackson T. Main, Lee Benson, E. James Ferguson, Stuart Bruchey, and others. Also relevant to the idea of class in American historiography is the work of Bernard Bailyn, Milton M. Klein, Roger Champagne, and Robert P. Sharkey. Very little of this writing is sociologically informed but there are interesting parallels between conclusions drawn by sociologists as to the role and function of class in a theoretical sense and those of historians who test their assumptions about class against the data of history.

Edward N. Saveth, "The American Patrician Class: A Field for Research," *American Quarterly*, XV (Summer Supplement, 1963), 235–52. Reprinted by permission.

1. Dennis Wrong, "Social Inequality Without Social Stratification," mimeo., *passim*.
2. See the interesting discussion in Robert E. Lane, *Political Life: Why People Get Involved in Politics* (New York, 1961), 220–34.

" "HISTORY RECEIVES its vocabulary, for the most part, from
the very subject matter of its study," remarked the late Marc Bloch. The
vocabulary, he added, lacked unity.[1] The word class, for example, had one
meaning for John Adams at the end of the eighteenth century and another
for his great-grandsons, Henry and Brooks, at the end of the nineteenth.
John Adams preferred "rank" to class. He thought of himself as belonging
to the "middle rank of people in society" and spoke of a patrician "rank"
which "exists in every nation under the sun and will exist forever."[2]
Thomas Jefferson noted the existence of "a Patrician order" in Virginia.[3]
Jefferson's and Adams' use of "rank" and "order" sustains Professor Briggs'
view that prior to the Industrial Revolution the word class was "used in
its neutral, 'classifying' sense, and its place supplied by the 'ranks,' 'orders' and 'degrees' of a more finely graded hierarchy of great subtlety and
discrimination."[4]

Following the Industrial Revolution, class became increasingly identified with conflict, a category for "the analysis of the dynamics of social
conflict and its structural roots." Recently, the tendency has been to treat
class as two analytically separable elements: class stratification harking
back to the eighteenth-century conception of rank and, secondly, class
action or conflict.[5]

Since history assigns many meanings to class, definition is the better
part of historical wisdom. Class theory, however, includes many definitions and the result, as Bloch observed, is to leave "every man for himself."[6] The historian, therefore, tends to write about class in the hope that
the outline of what he is discussing will flow from the narrative.[7] This approach avoids the bias inherent in schematization. To write about class
without struggling with definition, however, can lead to mistaken analyses
of the relationship between class and political action, the kind of analytical
errors for which Charles A. Beard and Howard K. Beale have been taken
to task.[8] What is required is interplay between class theory and the actual
situation, with the concept refined by the process.

Professor Robert A. Dahl's statement concerning the concept of power
is also true of class. "We are not likely to produce—certainly not for
some considerable time to come—anything like a consistent, coherent
'Theory. . . .' We are much more likely to produce a variety of theories
of limited scope, each of which employs some definition . . . that is useful
in the context of the particular piece of research or theory but different
in important respects from the definitions of other studies."[9]

An important clue to definition is Schumpeter's statement, echoed by
Parsons, that "the family, and not the physical person, is the true unit

of class theory."[10] This definition is applicable particularly to the patrician family that "has been established for at least one, and preferably two or three generations, as members of the upper class,"[11] that has a long tradition of literacy and a "moving sense of the overlap of history."[12]

Schumpeter's approach to class may be less meaningful when applied to the lower classes who have a shorter tradition of literacy, less of what Max Weber called "prestige of descent," and less of a sense of history and precedent. Only relatively recently have the Alfred Kazins and the James Baldwins been telling us how it really was in Brooklyn and Harlem.

Patrician personal literature—memoirs, autobiographies, letters, diaries and similar memorabilia—are plentiful throughout most of our history. On the other hand, family history which derives from these sources and which could advance us along the road to class definition, is an under-developed aspect of American historiography.

There are several reasons for this. If it is true, as many European observers noted, that the family unit was weaker here than in Europe, then the role played by family was less likely to impress itself upon the historian's consciousness.[13] Stress which American culture has placed upon the individual may have caused the historian to minimize or take for granted the extent to which family is important in providing means of access to education; to social, economic and political opportunity; to marriage; and to the various forms of status.[14]

Secondly, there is a tendency for the achieving individual to complicate further the historian's problem by minimizing, in public statements, the role of ancestry. Theodore Roosevelt, according to Howard K. Beale, consistently understated the wealth and accomplishment of his ancestors.[15] Indeed, in a society devoted to egalitarianism, pride of ancestry becomes for the patrician politician an aspect of covert culture that finds expression in privately printed and in manuscript genealogies; in personal and private papers; and in membership in ancestral and patriotic societies.[16]

Third, historians have tended to regard the field of family history as allied to genealogy. Those genealogists who interpret the concern of genealogy as limited to date of birth, date of death and the tracing of family relationship, deny the association.[17] On the other hand, most of the family history that has been written by genealogists, is by the standards of professional historiography, not a little amateurish and antiquarian. We have not as yet developed in America a Horace Round or an Anthony Richard Wagner, capable of blending successfully genealogy and history.[18] Lester J. Cappon concluded that the volumes which line the shelves of American genealogical societies, with their overtones of filiopietism, family pleading, and amateurism are not likely to interest grately the professional historian.[19]

In all fairness, however, no estimate has been made of this data provided the right questions are asked of it. The field of local history, for example, is a comparable intellectual desert, but Elkins and McKitrick have used the data of local history very effectively in seeking a new meaning for the Turner thesis. So have Curti and his associates.[20] Genealogy has the potential of a valuable tool for social analysis, as Joseph Schumpeter indicated decades ago.[21]

As a problem in historiography, family history is complicated by its not inconsiderable sprawl. In the preface of *The Cokers of Carolina: A Social Biography of a Family*, George Lee Simpson Jr. described both an "inherent problem" and an "inherent unfairness" in writing the history of a family over four generations. Caleb and Hannah Coker and their ten children, Simpson continued, have hundreds of descendants. "Clearly it is impossible to write in a single coherent volume of all those people who, whether they bore the Coker name or not, are members of the family."

Simpson concentrated on those "who bore the name of Coker and who identified themselves with the location where the family achieved recognition." He further limited himself to those Cokers who, "in the public eye and by common agreement," have been a part of a notable achievement, either as individuals or as a part of a persisting family unit bearing the name Coker.[22] Accordingly, it is the achieving individuals within the achieving family who become family history.

Bernard Bailyn is also troubled by the sprawl of family history and its nature "apart from the total of the unrelated careers of a number of people who happened to have the name. . . . In what way, that is, did the family have meaning in itself? What historical importance is there to the fact that these individuals, as opposed to any others, find places on the vast genealogical chart the author furnishes us within his text? What, in other words, can be said about the family as such that illuminates the lives of its members and the evolution of American society?" Bailyn suggests pruning the family tree except for those elements that determine the family life style, that contribute to comprehension of its "permanent identity," that establish the core of its "inner continuity," that are the "symbols of family permanence within the flux of births and deaths and passing careers."[23]

Family style, however, does not go on forever. Brooks and Henry Adams believed that three generations was the limit of familial adjustment and that, in the case of the Adams family, the world was too much for the fourth generation.[24] Alphonso Taft, father of William Howard and grandfather of Robert A. Taft, reminded a gathering of approximately one thousand Tafts who collected at Uxbridge, Massachusetts on August 12, 1874 that "brilliant political careers have not been characteristic of the Tafts in the past." He added, however, it was not safe to say what the future held in store because even as there was a tide in the affairs of men, there was a tide as well in the destinies of families.[25] The tide took its time in the case of the Tafts as it did with the Churchills who, like the Cecils (disguised as Salisburys, Cranbornes, and Balfours), for centuries, accomplished nothing except to remain on their estates.[26]

Insofar as a component of definition of the patrician class is the patrician family, a "working model" of the patrician family, both in its internal structure and external relations, is needed. Professor Bridenbaugh has identified the history of the American family as a priority in American historiography[27] and the following variables have been suggested as foundation for such a history: the family's "internal structure (the interrelated roles of father, son, daughter, mother, uncle and other kin), its relationship to the culture and society of which it is a part (the effects of industrialism, urban living, wider educational opportunities, the 'emancipation' of women, and similar elements), and the processes through which changes in internal structure are affected by, and in turn affect, its external relationships."[28]

To this list of variables should be added, in the case of the patrician family, the figure of the patriarch whose role, Talcott Parsons[29] and Daniel Bell[30] suggest, is conditioned by different stages in the evolution of capitalism. The patriarchal family is strongest under the conditions of agrarian, mercantile, and the early stages of industrial capitalism—all of which rely heavily upon family capital and family mangement. The position of the patriarch as head of family is strengthened by his role as chief of enterprise.

From patrician personal literature centered upon the middle decades of the nineteenth century, it is possible to limn the patriarch as a real type.[31] The patriarch makes his fortune and then establishes roots in the community. He builds a big house—big enough, as the first Nicholas Longworth explained, to accommodate "all the Longworths in the nation."[32] Master of the big house, the patriarch tended to be jealous of his brood and of his authority. The patriarch is the first Wade Hampton writing to an acquaintance: "I thank you for your friendly effort to procure me a landed estate for my Sons in the Western Country but must decline it for the present. . . . I do not wish my children at too great a distance from me."[33] The patriarch is James Lides, the South Carolina planter, who permitted his daughter to marry Caleb Coker, the rising young businessman from Society Hill, only after Coker promised that he would not take her West.[34] In the West, the hold of the patriarch did not loosen. Lawson Clay, trained in the law, wanted to move away from Huntsville, Alabama, "to some place where my services professional would be required" but he could not "gain the consent of any member of the family." The latter, said Lawson, "wish me to return to Huntsville and finish an existence, miserable in dependence and satiety." Despite efforts to be "on 'my own hook' unpropped by father," Lawson stayed on in the latter's large household which included many relatives in addition to the nuclear family.[35]

In Cincinnati, noted Clara Longworth de Cambrun, "a model son-in-law, according to the Longworth pattern, [was] content to spend more time in Ohio than in New York, and one who showed an affectionate veneration for his wife's parents. . . ." It was, she continued, a curious "clan" life, as it was lived under their father's roof. "He had invented an extremely simple plan in regard to accounts and allowances, 'hating to be pestered for money,' as he said. Daily, a liberal sum was placed in the open drawer of his desk, accompanied by the verbal recommendation: 'let every one take what he wants or what he needs, and don't bother me.'"[36]

A great deal more research is needed to establish the patriarch as a real type on a less tentative basis than the above, which is more outline than definitive portrayal. Even more uncertain is the status of the patriarch under the later stages of industrial and on into the era of finance and managerial capitalism. It is apparent that the business fate of the Coker family of South Carolina was typical of many other families as the needs of enterprise for money and managerial skill transcended what the family could provide. The result was separation between family structure and business. When Charles Coker died in 1931, the board of directors of the family-founded Sonoco enterprises was composed entirely of members of the Coker family. A quarter of a century later, nonfamily outnumbered family board members, two to one.[37]

What happens to the patriarchal status under industrial, finance and managerial capitalism is better established in theory than in fact. Talcott Parsons,[38] A. A. Berle,[39] and Daniel Bell[40] have discussed the waning of family capitalism and Bell, particularly, has emphasized the relationship between this phenomenon and the weakening of family structure. However, additional research is needed to determine the extent to which multimillionaire oilman J. Paul Getty is a representative mid-twentieth-century patriarch. He was divorced five times; his four sons by different wives are all but lost in the structure of the far-flung Getty business empire. Said one of the half brothers, "we don't keep up. Years and years go by when I see none of them, although recently we have been meeting about twice a year—once at the annual meeting of the family trust."[41]

While the Getty family pattern appears to sustain the thesis that the weakening of family structure is a concomitant of giant enterprise to which family is only remotely related, the Kennedy family experience demonstrates that there are factors beyond business which serve as basis for family cohesion.[42]

The patriarchal role may have altered since John Hay married Clara Stone in 1874 and Amasa, Hay's rich and patriarchal father-in-law, gave Hay a fine residence in Cleveland and a place in the business.[43] It seems logical to assume that there has been a change in the patriarchal role. But so little is known about the process of transformation that it is hard to say what it was, how it came about if, in fact, it has come about. Is Joseph P. Kennedy less of a patriarch than was Nicholas Longworth? What of the continuation of family influence in large, publicly-owned corporations such as Du Pont? What of managerial dynasties or continuities like the Sarnoffs in Radio Corporation of America?[44]

There is every indication that there are additional variables, beyond the economic factors stressed by Parsons and Bell, which condition family structure. The scope of these, however, is not likely to be revealed prior to intensive research into family history.[45] Only a history of the American family could comprehend these variables and provide basis for an accurate typology of the patriarch at various stages in American history as well as a contribution to class theory.

Family history is particularly relevant to that aspect of class which Max Weber called the "life-style." An important component of the latter is an inherited pattern of family culture—a rare emphasis in historiography and an important one that finds expression in Elting E. Morison's biography of Henry L. Stimson.[46] The current social science emphasis upon "achievement"[47] has no counterpart in historical studies of families which have been prominent in successive generations. Most family histories, those that are something more than puffed-up genealogical trees, revolve around the records of a business enterprise and the enterprise rather than family structure, or the aptitude that made possible the continuity of the enterprise, is stressed.[48] We have had political dynasties, now as in the past, but histories of political families such as W. E. Smith's *Francis Preston Blair Family in Politics* are by no means plentiful. Still more uncommon is the tracing of professional or artistic talent over the generations.

The facts of material inheritance, to say nothing of their implication for family culture, are barely known. In England, the continuity of aristocracy has been ascribed less to family feeling and blood ties than to the perpetuation of "the family estate, which provided the family not only with its revenue and residence, but with its sense of identity from generation to generation. . . ."[49] In America, inheritance was of no less significance. Professor Habakkuk has indicated that the role of inheritance has been little studied in this country. He ascribed this to the absence of a backlog of materials.[50] Perhaps a more accurate statement of the problem in its American context is not the lack of materials—but that the materials have been neither systematized nor used widely in historical and sociological treatises.[51] Legal history has failed to "tell of the shaping force exercised by law from outside it, by what people wanted, by the functional needs of other institutions, and by the mindless weight of circumstances,"[52] The reverse is also true. So admirable a study as Edmund S. Morgan's *The Puritan Family* places slight stress upon legal factors and inheritance.[53]

Primogeniture, an aspect of inheritance with manifold implications for family structure, lacks a full-scale treatment. Joel Barlow asserted that "the simple destruction of these two laws, of *entailment* and *primogeniture,* if you add to them the *freedom* of the press, will ensure the continuance of liberty in any country where it is once established."[54] However, the last significant study of primogeniture and entail was by Richard B. Morris more than thirty years ago.[55] At about the same time Charles R. Keim wrote of the "Influence of Primogeniture and Entail in the Development of Virginia."[56] More recently, knowledge of entail in Virginia has been extended by brief treatment in an article by Dr. Bailyn.[57] However, so significant an observation as that by Professor Morris that on the eve of the American Revolution there was a revival of entail in Massachusetts, has not been followed up.[58] It would be interesting to examine the background against which Thomas Cheseborough, in 1756, advised Ezra Stiles, perhaps facetiously and perhaps not, never to divide or alienate any land or other estate but leave it to the eldest son: "'tis not good to be upon a Level or Under the Foot of every Scoundrel." This scheme was to be kept quiet even as others were to be encouraged "to Divide their Estate."[59]

It is well known that in the last two decades of the eighteenth century, state legislation was enacted prohibiting entail and primogeniture. However, only in Virginia has the background of the legislation been explored.[60] Certain questions remain unanswered. Did legislation by the various states against primogeniture and entail apply only to cases of intestacy? What legal sanctions were there against individuals who wanted to concentrate the bulk of their property as a legacy to a single heir? What were the popular sanctions against such practices and how did they evolve?[61] What of the beneficiaries of partible inheritance who elected to leave an estate undivided that it might function better as an economic unit?[62]

Inheritance is an important factor determining family position within a class over the generations. Movement into and out of the patrician class has been more observed than analyzed largely because the elements that determine the patrician life style are difficult to isolate.[63] Using methods of genealogy and family history, it is possible to trace the status of individual families over successive generations. However, what did Schumpeter mean when he spoke of "the mobility of a whole social class?" Schumpeter himself insisted that any estimate of class mobility would be less "science" than "party slogan." He then went on to frame, virtually without proof, his own account of the ascendancy of European families as "uniformly along the lines of the American saying: 'Three generations from shirtsleeves to shirtsleeves.' "[64]

The "American saying" was a "slogan" put forth by Oliver Wendell Holmes Sr. who, in 1861, spoke of three generations as marking the duration of powerful New England families.[65] There remains a continuing tendency on the part of historians to write of mobility in terms of "slogans."[66]

Difficulties with respect to the ascertainment of "whole class" mobility[67] return the analyst to the individual family,[68] "the relative position of families within a class," and the discovery of what there is about family "life" and "spirit" which causes one family to adjust and go forward and another to decline.[69] In many respects, a model for this kind of investigation is William T. Whitney's account of the rivalry between the Derby and Crowinshield families for priority in Salem.[70] Yet, generalization about the movement of a "whole class" on the basis of what is known about a few families, involves a problem in sampling no easier to resolve in the case of the American patriciate than with respect to the status of the English gentry in the seventeenth century.[71]

Virtually all that is known about class is on the local and community levels, the domain of the community sociologists. Professor W. L. Warner and his associates identified a patrician class in Newburyport which was described as an "upper-upper class" within a pattern of stratification which included five other classes. The upper-upper class was identified as a precipitate of the economic activities of previous generations and prevailed in the older sections of the country, along the Atlantic seaboard and in the South.[72]

To mention the Warner system of community stratification is to invite a large body of criticism of it by historians and sociologists.[73] The historian sees the Warner approach as lacking in depth and rarely transcending what the late C. Wright Mills described as "that dull pudding called sketching in the historical background."[74] One of the best of the community studies is Robert A. Dahl's account of New Haven, a chapter of which deals with the period 1784–1842 when "public office was almost the exclusive prerogative of the patrician families." Yet, in his discussion Dahl shows scant awareness of newer understandings by historians of the nature of power in colonial America and its relationship to class structure and "patrician control."[75]

Understanding of the patrician class could be increased by integrating munity sociology and local history. Eric Lampard has pointed to the need for a blend of historical and social science techniques within an ecological framework.[76] Studies by Merle Curti and his associates and by Stanley Elkins and Eric McKitrick working together have advanced local history beyond mere narrative to engage it with such questions as mobility, social role, decision-making, group formation, and elite function.[77] The effect of this kind of an approach is not only to contribute a time dimension to community sociology, but to endow class with historical continuity.[78]

While discussions and analyses of class enter into numerous community studies, on the national level class is virtually undefined.[79] Efforts to depict a national elite by Mills[80] and Hunter[81] have met with sharp critical attack. Equally vulnerable is the attempt by E. Digby Baltzell to go beyond his rather good study of the Philadelphia upper class and in the direction of identifying a "national aristocracy." According to Baltzell, the communications revolution, the nationalization of business and the attendance by scions of prominent families at far-from-home New England boarding schools and Ivy League colleges where they allegedly meet marriage partners of the same life style but from different communities, has disrupted the local roots of aristocracy.[82] Unfortunately, however competent Mr. Baltzell's treatment of the Philadelphia scene, his assumptions nationally are unproven. They seem particularly vulnerable in the light of changes that have taken place in the admissions policies of the Ivy League colleges.[83]

With the patrician class difficult to define and identify nationally, the kind of research problem formulated by Dr. Pumphrey with reference to England has no American counterpart. Pumphrey sought to determine the extent to which industrialists penetrated the British peerage.[84] This problem, if it could be stated in terms of the American scene, would shed light upon mobility between old families and new wealth. But what is the American equivalent of an English peer?

The late Marc Bloch defined nobility as a class having legal status with its social privileges and hereditary succession receiving legal recognition.[85] However, at the time when the legal privileges of the nobility of most European nations were being defined constitutionally, the United States Constitution banned the class altogether.[86] Not only is there no

American establishment to sustain the American patriciate, but there is also no vestigial establishment which would give this class even a derivative basis.[87]

A third aspect of class, not unrelated to its economic basis and to the expression of a particular life style, is the political: "class oriented toward acquisition of 'social' power . . . toward influencing a communal action. . . ."[88] Among the concerns of research into the political role of the patriciate is the extent to which inherited ideas of responsibility and service, of what Edmund Burke called the gentle uses of power, developed in the course of centuries by the English aristocracy and the American patriciate, are incorporated into political action.[89] There is also the question, posed by Professor Hesseltine, as to the extent to which a political tradition is class-oriented and how much of its is diffused across class lines.[90]

Implied in political action is the concept of power. Social scientists disagree as to whether power in American society is concentrated in an elite or diffuse throughout the structure of society.[91] Historians have expressed different viewpoints concerning the nature and exercise of power in colonial society. Becker,[92] Sydnor[93] and Labaree[94] see power as concentrated in an elite composed of the great colonial families whose political actions were said to be expressive of a unified class interest. Another point of view regards interest group rather than class as the focus of power.[95] Interest group, in so far as it transcends class lines and is a basis of divergence within the class framework, encourages a conception of power that is more fragmented than concentrated. Dr. Klein's account of family politics in colonial New York, for example is of alliances cemented and broken; of shifting configurations of power within the framework of the patrician stratum.[96] The class concept, having become operational in terms of interest and conflict, breaks up into tangents of individual and family action.

How is group interest ascertained? Charles A. Beard's use of the technique of economic biography is generally credited with having established the rudiments of career line analysis. This is, essentially, a biographical approach to history in which certain questions are posed with reference to the individuals involved in a particular group. The answers are the basis upon which individuals are grouped and group attributes are correlated with political action so that a relationship between them becomes apparent.[97] I use correlate rather than cause because career line analysis, since it cannot comprehend all possible variables as well as for other reasons, has methodological limitations restricting it as a form of proof to correlation rather than cause.[98] How causation itself can be established is far from clear.[99]

Use of the technique of career analysis by David Donald, Richard Hofstadter, Alfred D. Chandler Jr., George E. Mowry, Ari Hoogenboom, among others, has illumined aspects of patrician political behavior.[100] However, career line analysis, correlating biographical factors with political action, does not explain how one leads to the other. One explanation of patrician political behavior is in terms of reference group theory which "aims to systematize the determinants and consequences of those processes of evaluation and self-appraisal in which the individual takes the values or standards of other individuals and groups as a comparative frame of reference."[101]

Using reference group theory as an explanation of motivation Professor Donald and Professor Hofstadter asserted that a certain amount of anxiety over status with reference to competing groups in the population led men of old family background into the abolitionist and, at a later date, into reformist political movements in an effort to recoup lost power and prestige. Recently, the reference group concept has been amplified to include not only a contemporary competing group but individuals and groups in the past, such as ancestry, for example, whose achievement must be equaled or exceeded.[102]

My own researches into the the history of the American patriciate tend to support Herbert H. Hyman's conception of the role of ancestry as reference group, apparent particularly in the careers of Henry Cabot Lodge, Theodore Roosevelt, Henry Adams, Brooks Adams, and Charles Francis Adams, Jr.[103]

Other explanations are advanced of patrician political behavior. Dr. Berthoff accounted for the prominence of the man of family in contemporary American political life in terms of the reintegration of "society somewhat as it was before 1815" in which the Roosevelts, Tafts and Rockefellers (he might have added Kennedy, Morgenthau, Steers, Stevenson, Wallace, Wadsworth, Scranton, Plimpton, Dilworth, Byrd, Saltonstall, and Stimson) not only accept responsibility of their class to lead the common voter but are in turn accepted by him, it is evident that we once again have an established upper class with privileges and duties roughly equivalent to those of the eighteenth-century gentry." Thus far in my own researches I have found little to sustain this aspect of Mr. Berthoff's "conservative hypothesis."[104]

Nor would I agree with Mr. Lipset's attempt to compress the patrician political tradition within the framework of the Republican party.[105] This thesis would be reasonable, if not altogether valid, applied to the politics of the 1890s when Republicanism qua Republicanism had a real meaning for Roosevelt, Lodge and the neo-Federalists. However, C. Vann Woodward has shown that even during this period the Virginia Populists were inclined to entrust leadership of their movement to Virginia's old families.[106]

There is no simple definition of the patrician class. It is possible, however, to present a model of what such definition involves. The model includes family history with stress upon the factors, material and cultural, which make for family continuity; the structuring of real types of the patrician family centered in factors related to the family's internal structure and external relationships. The development in history of these attributes contributes to a general description of the patrician class as "rank."

To comprehend class as cause involves awareness of group structure and component factors. The latter enter into career line analysis and, when correlated with action, contribute to ascertaining the group interest. Reference group theory, advanced as suggestive of motive underlying the expression of patrician group interest, has been attacked sharply in recent years and it is my impression that the assumptions of reference group theory, even as modified by Dr. Hyman, have marked limitations as explanation of patrician political behavior.

Even career line analysis, which takes less for granted about motivation than does reference group theory, is a device that must be used discreetly and with reference to the reservations expressed in Mr. Butterfield's critique of Sir Lewis Namier.[107] That is to say, there is more to history than its relationship with theory which has been stressed in this article. Theory and analysis are subsumed by the flow of historical narrative and this includes unique factors, which may be alien to an analytical framework but are very much part of the history of the American patrician class.

# Mobility / *Oscar and Mary Handlin*

The problem of why it is so difficult for the historian to deal with
mobility has been touched upon by Catherine S. Crary. According to
Dr. Crary: "it is a tedious, uncertain and often well-nigh impossible task
to trace the life threads of obscure immigrants who never achieved the
notice of history or even of family, and to weigh their economic and social
improvement in sufficient numbers to establish a measurable pattern of
success in a given period. Even were the records readily available, the
measurement of self-advancement is complex, subtle and elusive, for the
touchstone should include far more than acres and pounds accumulated;
it should take into account the richer but intangible legacies of educational and other opportunities afforded the children."[1]

The following selection by Oscar and Mary Handlin deals with the
nature of mobility in the United States and the problems involved in
studying it. Omitted from this discussion is reference to the role played
by ethnic factors in social mobility, a point that Oscar and Mary Handlin
have been concerned with elsewhere.[2]

AMERICANS JUDGED the voluntary association, as they judged
the state, by the criterion of the ends to be served. Just as the coercive
power of government was contained within procedures and limits defined
in the light of the goals of the society, so the activities of any groups were
circumscribed by the general acceptability of their purpose.

The conception of the proper end of social action at any given point
in history must be inferred from scattered utterances and fragmentary
measures; for a whole view was rarely formulated and expressed except
in such vague terms as "furtherance of the general welfare." Yet an un-

Oscar and Mary Handlin, *The Dimensions of Liberty* (Cambridge: Harvard University Press), Copyright 1961 by The President and Fellows of Harvard University.
VII, "Power and the Wealth of Men."

1. "The Humble Immigrant and the American Dream: Some Case Histories, 1746–
1776." *Mississippi Valley Historical Review*, XLVI (June, 1959), 48. For ramifications of
the concept of mobility see Richard F. Curtis, "Conceptual Problems in Social Mobility
Research," *Sociology and Social Research*, XLV (July, 1961), 387–95.
2. "Ethnic Factors in Social Mobility," *Explorations in Entrepreneurial History*,
IX (October, 1956), 1–7.

derlying consciousness of common purpose did exist and was kept alive by many elements in the American situation.[1]

In actuality, the population included a variety of disparate types. Planters and slaves, factory owners and farmers, miners and merchants formed distinct strata in the society; and the lines that separated them, while less rigid at some times than at others, were always there. The motives that moved these men as individuals and the interests that swayed them as groups were by no means always identical and were often contradictory. Since none was in a position arbitrarily to impose its will upon all the others, it remained necessary to formulate, explain, and justify particular objectives in terms of general goals attractive to the whole society.

Among the wide range of ends toward which Americans have been permissive, one has stood preeminent in the consistency of its general acceptance. The use of coercive power by the polity or of influence by association has most readily been recognized as valid when it tended to increase the wealth of the whole society, however that was defined. Other values have generally been subordinated to, or interpreted in terms of, this one.

Perhaps because settlement in the New World was long precarious, and dependent upon promotional activity that could only be sustained through the continuing proof of productivity, Americans were sensitive to the pressure of proving their ability to create wealth. Even the Puritans, dedicated as they were to the goal of exemplifying holiness on earth, early came to interpret prosperity as a measure of their ability to please God. Steps that added to the total store of goods were desirable as evidence of divine favor toward the community, just as the individual's acquisition of riches was a sign of his progress toward salvation.[2]

Later, the persistence of frontier conditions, the apparent abundance of the continent thrown open to the advance of thousands of new families, and the growing conviction that the material universe was utterly malleable in the hands of man confirmed the tendency to interpret social goals in terms of the creation of wealth. Still later, the successive thrusts of immigrant populations into the land of opportunity, the new horizons revealed by industrialization and science, and the confidence engendered by seemingly limitless expansion further strengthened the tendency. The release of energy toward productive ends has thus been a constant factor in terms of which Americans have interpreted their freedom. They were willing to consent to the acts of governments and associations which promised to increase the store of resources, for the well-being of each individual seemed to turn upon doing so.[3]

The growth of wealth was at first viewed absolutely and measured by the total of goods available to the whole society. So long as the community was whole, integrated, and homogeneous, the overriding consideration among its members was the extent of its common possessions, for the welfare of each was bound in with the welfare of all.[4]

As the community began to fall into fragments soon after settlement, the conception of wealth tended to become individualized. By the mid-eighteenth century, welfare came to be viewed in personal rather than social terms. The element of selfish calculation had never been absent from decisions on the numerous issues that divided men; but it had earlier been subordinate to, or at least couched in terms of, the larger good. Now each person was more likely to form his judgments in terms of a prosperity abstracted from that of the group of which he was a part. The change was an aspect of a general process which by the time of the Great Awakening also redefined virtue in an individual rather than in a communal context and by the second half of the century altered the ways of regarding property, weakening the emphasis upon its social use, and strengthening that upon the personal right to it.[5]

The idea of the commonwealth, of a state with an interest which transcended those of its component members, endured on into the nineteenth century, although it corresponded less than ever before to a social order in which diverse elements contended with one another. The gradual adjustments to the pressures of the real divisions within the country in time wore away the commonwealth conception; and thereafter the wealth of the nation was regarded as the sum of the wealth of the particular individuals aggregated in it.[6]

In the economy of the nineteenth century each man struggled toward the attainment of his own good, in the faith that a self-regulating competitive mechanism would assure the service of the good of all. But that faith itself required evidence; it was sustained by the widespread diffusion of the output of the productive system and by the opportunities open to men to make what they could of their talents, capital, and willingness to run risks. Whatever formal terms might measure the total yield or gross national product, the individual's standard of judgment remained the extent to which rewards were accessible to him. Without any overarching conception of the community as a whole, he now determined whether power was used to advance his liberty or not by the degree to which it widened or narrowed his opportunities.[7]

Hence the significance of social mobility in American history. The possession of a stake in society or of an opportunity to acquire one was the pivot upon which the representative republican polity turned, for it supplied assurance that men would consent to be governed. In the long argument over the nature of the American state that extended from the constitutional debates of the 1780's to the controversy between John Adams and John Taylor in 1814, the element that permitted an accommodation of opposing views was the belief that wealth would "be considerably distributed, to sustain a democratick republick."[8]

In the early nineteenth century, free land and free enterprise kept the goods produced by the society within the reach of all. Daniel Webster celebrated the virtues of an order that made every competent man a landed yeoman; and Edward Everett, pointing to the fluidity of business, explained, "the wheel of fortune is in constant operation, and the poor in one generation furnish the rich of the next."[9]

By the end of the century that conviction was more difficult to maintain. The apearance of great concentrations of wealth in the hands of a few was not so troubling as was the development of a depressed group of hopeless laborers. "In proportion as the working men feel the impassibility of the gulf that separates them from the rich class, they tend to become discontented and disaffected; and . . . the chances of the average poor man to acquire wealth becomes smaller, thus putting him among the protestants against the existing situation." Beneath the expressed fears of proletarians, foreigners, Negroes, anarchists, Populists, "agitators," and Wobblies was the perception that the number of men was growing who might not consent to be governed.[10]

The expressed creed of the society continued to affirm the possibility of individual achievement through self-enrichment. Americans accepted the assurance of Russell Conwell "that the opportunity to get rich . . . is within the reach of almost every man"; and that there was "not a poor person in the United States who was not made poor by his own shortcomings." The belief was necessary, for the underlying premise of the conception that power might properly be used to increase the wealth of the community was the assumption that wealth so maximized would be accessible to all. This was the basic meaning of the American idea of equality of oportunity.[11]

It is not at all clear, however, whether the idea that the opportunity to get rich was available to all, conformed to reality and to what extent it did so. It may be posited as a working hypothesis that most of the difficulties in defining liberty that arose in the purely political sphere in the United States were eased by the underlying fluidity of the social structure which in turn was derived from a relatively high rate of social mobility. Proof is not yet available. Plausible as these statements seem, the evidence to validate or refute them has not yet been collected or analyzed.

The history of social mobility has heretofore received no study whatever. Historians have taken for granted the fluidity of American society and have often ascribed to it a uniqueness as compared with other societies; but they have done so on the basis of general impressions rather than of systematically organized data. The sociologists who have more usually dealt with this question have not treated it across any extended time interval and their conclusions have therefore necessarily been limited.

Recent contemporary investigations have suggested that the extent and rate of American mobility have popularly been exaggerated, and have also cast doubt on the degree of difference that obtained between the United States and other countries. All societies have permitted some reshuffling among their members; and structural economic and social changes in the last two centuries have everywhere accelerated the rate.[12] Without more knowledge in chronological depth than we now possess it is hard to draw meaningful inferences from these suggestions. They could, conceivably, indicate either that mobility in the United States was more rapid in earlier periods and has now slackened or that there never was a consequential deviation by this country from the pattern of development in other societies.

There is a third line of approach to the problem. The failure to perceive significant differences between the situation in the United States and that in Europe or Asia may be the product of inadequacies in current sociological conceptions and methods of measurement. The conclusions of many generations of observers cannot simply be written off as biased or ignorant. The vast array of political and social materials which suggest that society was more fluid in America than elsewhere must be accounted for. Either there was a persistent distortion in the angle of vision of all these observers; or the contemporary sociological data is faulty; or the present mode of examining and assessing the phenomena thrown together as social mobility is deceptive; or the fluidity of a society is independent of the rate of social mobility, the capacity of some individuals to move from one rank to another being but slightly affected by the rigidity of the lines among them. All these possibilities need exploration.[13]

The poor quality of available historical information impedes the study of the general course of American social mobility. The uncertainty of registration data, the inability to trace individuals from census to census, and a complex of factors related to the migration of the population make it impossible reliably to trace either the career lines of large groups of individuals or significant intergenerational changes. A sustained effort is needed to compensate for the absence of governmental data by finding information on family employments over relatively long periods.[14]

However useful such investigations will prove, other lines of analysis will also be pursued. It may be a mistake to study social mobility in the gross as if it were a uniform process in which all movements from one occupational or status level to another were of equal importance. In the last two hundred years rapid economic change in every society has produced a high degree of spatial and occupational movement. Industrialization and urbanization have everywhere created a demand for factory and white-collar labor which could only be satisfied by recruitment from new sources. Yet not all such shifts of population had the same meaning. Peasants who moved to a city to become proletarians were certainly mobile socially. Their children who filled the large number of clerical and sales positions created by economic development would also register as mobile by the usual measurements. One could therefore expect everywhere to find large shifts from rural to urban, from "manual" to "nonmanual" callings.

But the consequences for the structure of society varied strikingly from place to place. Such intergenerational mobility may very well have been as characteristic of Japan in the first quarter of the twentieth century as of the United States. But the one society was far more stratified than the other.

Furthermore, social mobility, as many students have measured it, is not the only significant index of change in status. An apprentice who completed his term in 1820 might still be practicing his handicraft in 1860, yet have suffered a genuine decline in status through the operation of external economic forces. Conversely, the auto worker or coal miner climbed rapidly between 1930 and 1960, without a change in occupation.

What is necessary is not only a study of mobility as a general phenomenon, but also an examination of particular aspects of the relation between occupations, opportunity, and wealth, on the one hand, and the political and cultural components of power and freedom, on the other. Such an approach will add more useful insights into the degree of fluidity in American society to supplement those derived from broad comprehensive analyses of occupational shifts.

These relations may be examined both through studies of particular communities and through the systematic analysis of the general factors that influenced the structure of society. The wide variety of urban types in the United States, the relative recency of settlement in many places, and the great size of some cities complicate the tasks of analysis and render hazardous generalizations based upon the experience of particular communities. It will be profitable to examine a number of representative examples of varying sizes, tracing them through the initial phases of their growth until they displayed some degree of stability. Within these cities one could investigate concretely the operations of the economic, social, and cultural determinants of status. It will often be advantageous to select for study, places for which data from contemporary surveys can be compared with that drawn from historical sources.[15]

There will remain a wide variety of materials that will yield only to more comprehensive treatment independently of the framework of the individual community. These may be ordered through an investigation of the forces and institutional determinants that tended to ease or retard the ability of individuals to move a significant distance from one social level to another. The role of the government, the character of the educational system, the distribution of property, and the complexity of the social order were all relevant, although the precise nature of the relation involved is by no means clear.

The ability to move about the country freely satisfied one of the conditions of social mobility. The relative emptiness of the continent for a long time, the early breakdown of residence requirements, the rapid pace of expansion, and the frequent shifts in the location of industry encouraged fluidity in settlement. In addition, the weakness of communal ties and individual rootlessness permitted men to shift their families about to where opportunities were most attractive. The ease with which the population was constantly being redistributed acquired its significance from the social context. The process of migration offered the occasion for a reshuffling of status, for new beginnings outside inherited institutions. It opened to some the possibility of rising and exposed others to the danger of falling.

The factors that shaped the social context were complex. Efforts by the state to restrict access to the occupation of an individual's choice were never important in the United States. In the seventeenth century such restrictions were usual in the Europe from which the colonists migrated; and they survived across the Atlantic on into the nineteenth century. Yet in the United States attempts to limit the admission to any calling through government licensing generally failed entirely or succeeded only under very special circumstances. Neither provincial nor municipal controls were firm enough to put any branch of commerce out of the reach of ambitious entrepreneurs although special monopolies, as in the fur trade, were feasible for short periods. Efforts to license the handicrafts were as futile as those to restrain trade. With the decay of communal conceptions of wealth and property and later with the disappearance of the Commonwealth idea, the very basis for such state action collapsed, not to be restored until licensing was to be reinterpreted as a form of police regulation. The trend toward liberality was, no doubt, related to the developing attitudes toward monopolies and to the peculiar evolution of the professions. In any case, the failure to establish and maintain a rigid system of licensing in practice generally removed a potential drag upon social mobility in the United States.[16]

The development of the American educational system in the long run positively accelerated social mobility. The schools imparted to their students a set of values that were goads in the struggle for success; they supplied an alternative, of ever-growing importance, to the intergenerational or family succession to certain occupations.[17] Yet their precise role was by no means clear.

The connection between the schools and social mobility did not arise from their ability to equip the student with the specific skills of desirable careers. It was true that a mercantile society, and, even more so, an industrial one, required the services of men and women who could read and write, calculate, read blueprints, and follow the instructions necessary to operate complex machines. The preparation of the hands and minds needed for such tasks did not, itself, stimulate mobility. Indeed, it is more than likely that people trained for such particular jobs would be drawn from, and would remain in, the social strata already close to them.

The relation of the school to social mobility was more complex. The first significant changes in educational patterns in the colonies came in the late seventeenth century with the decay of apprenticeship. The old forms of craft training continued to decline thereafter in the context of radical shifts in the character of family and community organization.[18] Neither then nor later did the organized school system assume the task of instruction in particular vocational skills. On into the nineteenth century the grammar and primary schools, the academies and high schools, and the colleges explicitly disavowed the intention of preparing youths for specific jobs as apprenticeship had done. Vocational education tended to develop outside the formal educational arrangements; and when it did intrude into the recognized curriculum, it took a subordinate position of low esteem and applied primarily to the less desirable types of jobs. In callings that ranked high, such as medicine, law, and business, apprenticeship—even when it followed a college education—remained the predominant mode of preparation until almost the end of the ninteenth century.[19]

It is possible that the connection of the schools with social mobility lay in their ability to provide the student with generalized skills and attitudes which did not ready him for any specific employment, but did enable him to move from one to another, capitalizing upon opportunities as they turned up. The fact that the educational system was long only loosely articulated and never rigidly controlled by a central authority enabled individuals to enter it at varying points in their careers, to find second chances and to recoup from mistakes or wrong decisions. This is an attractive hypothesis. But it would have to be sustained both by an analysis of curricula and by an examination of sample career lines to discover a link between crucial moves and what had happened in the schools.[20]

Or, alternatively, it may be that the connection with social mobility lay not in what the schools did, but in who their students were. The educational system moved only slowly to accommodate a substantial percentage of all children. Until the twentieth century, whatever channels of advancement they opened up were available only to limited segments of the population. It is difficult as yet to estimate their influence upon social mobility. Only by understanding the factors involved in the recruitment of the student body can one judge whether the educational apparatus was itself important in creating access to good positions, or whether it simply seemed important because the types of students who used it moved into careers they would have taken up in any case. Did the high school of the 1890's, for instance, increase the career chances of the boys who graduated from it, or were only such likely to attend as were already assured advancement by strategic family or ethnic connections? Such questions are intimately related to the problems raised by the desire of various groups, from time to time, to use the schools as devices of exclusion, beyond the normal degree of selectivity in such institutions.[21]

In examining these alternative hypotheses it will be useful to focus upon those critical periods when the schools, at one level or another, opened their doors to new social groups. The rapid spread of colleges in the mid-eighteenth century and in the first quarter of the nineteenth century, the development of public elementary education toward mid-century, and the broadened clientele of the high schools after 1918, offer strategic opportunities for assessing the effects of education as a factor influencing the rate of social mobility.[22]

The effects of changes in education were bound in with the economic context in which they occurred. It has been all too easy to assume a relation between the lack of rigid stratification and the widespread diffusion of property among all but the very underprivileged in the United States. More important is the task of defining that relation precisely.

There has, for instance, been a long and largely fruitless controversy among historians over the safety-valve theory. Some, particularly the followers of Frederick Jackson Turner, have ascribed to the availability of empty land and to the liberal federal and state land systems a determining influence upon the mobility of labor which, in turn, eased discontent and inhibited the development of vigorous protest movements. Others have denied that the connection existed and have emphasized the relative paucity of the number of industrial workers who became farmers and the relative insignificance of the land given away through homesteading.[23]

Both positions are tenable, although neither is adequate. Neither takes account of the full range of influences that dispersed property among various sectors of the American population. The availability of land was but one of these. Alienated under political conditions which prevented the concentration of holdings and the collective enterprises that appeared on other frontiers, the open acres of the West supplied an outlet for the kinds of farmers and artisans who in eighteenth- and nineteenth-century Europe were depressed into the ranks of the industrial proletariat.[24]

The dominant patterns of inheritance also tended to disperse landed wealth. Primogeniture and entail had all but disappeared even before revolutionary legislation wiped them out; such practices were not as important in an empty continent where labor was scarce, as they had been in England. More consequential, the most prevalent practices in the bequeathal of estates preserved the individual holdings at a viable size. There was no parallel here to the process of morcellation that complicated the lives of German and Irish peasants. Despite unfavorable economic conditions, farming continued to open opportunities to those who wished to enter it. Even the development of tenantry late in the nineteenth century was sometimes a means of stimulating mobility.[25]

The expansion of the productive system also encouraged the diffusion of other forms of property among those groups which sought to advance through various types of entrepreneurial activity. The recent diffusion among many elements in the population of holding of investment securities, although not as widespread as is sometimes supposed, gave a stake in the economy to ever-broader sections of the population. That tendency was related to the development of capital markets and of stock speculation and to the evolution of the corporation. It may also reflect the effects of life insurance practice. More important still, it may have depended for a long time upon the inability of rigid institutions to reduce the amount available by laying a dead hand upon property. The holdings of churches, schools, and charities were relatively small and fluid as long as they depended primarily upon voluntary contributions to finance their expenditures. It remains to be seen when the recent growth of the capital in the hands of such bodies will appreciably alter the situation.[26]

The widespread diffusion of property has given a great many Americans access to disposable capital. The proportion who were potential entrepreneurs was unusually large in comparison with other societies. Recent interpretations which minimize the differences between the United States and Europe are not altogether convincing for they focus primarily on the derivation of big business leadership in a rather unusual period. The recent development of a corps of managers, not owners of the capital they use, may well have created an exceptional situation, not representative of American experience in the past.[27]

More to the point in any effort to understand the relation of business to social mobility would be a serious examination of the patterns of petty trade and retailing, especially in the nineteenth century. Small-town trade, even after it became vulnerable to competition from the chain store and the mail-order house, long offered a means to advancement through the independent employment of capital. The westward movement which generated new towns at each shift of the line of settlement also expanded the chances for enterprise. The effects upon retailing of the growth of metropolitan markets may have contracted those opportunities somewhat in the twentieth century, but they have hardly disappeared entirely. When we know more about the factors which enabled some Americans to move into the ranks of the independent proprietors while others remained bookkeepers, clerks, or salesmen, we shall better understand what is too often vaguely referred to as the middle classes.[28]

It is more difficult to make even preliminary judgments about the mobility of men in the industrial labor force. For a long time there was a great gap between the skilled and the unskilled. It is likely that those among the latter who sought to move upward found fewer opportunities in step-by-step promotion within the plant than in somehow breaking away from it to strike out on their own as contractors or businessmen or as politicians or labor organizers. More recently the development of industrial unions, along with closed shop and seniority practices, may have altered that situation, but to what extent remains to be measured.[29]

Some of these phenomena become more comprehensible in the light of the historic changes in the structure of the American family. In other societies, the character of the household, marriage patterns, and the relations of parents to children vitally affected the transmission of property, the definition of goals, and the degree of social mobility. None of these connections has been explored for the United States. The facile generalizations about the family as "a property institution dominated by middle class standards" are almost meaningless. And such schematic interpretations as usually describe the evolution of the "nuclear family" reveal little about the actual phasing and import of the changes in it. One could not now say with assurance, for instance, when marriage became the product of an autonomous decision of the partners, among which social groups, or in what regions. Yet this was certainly a crucial element in determining the rate of social mobility.[30]

One approach toward understanding these problems is through an examination of the ethnic elements in social mobility. The heterogeneous groups that constituted American society were drawn from dissimilar cultural backgrounds and displayed dissimilar attitudes toward the employment of capital, the value of savings, the use of windfalls, the assumption of risks, and the objectives of life. They exhibited also different patterns of consumption, of social control, and of kinship behavior. Such factors created variant patterns of expectation that shaped the motivation and the capacity for performance of the individuals who grew up within them. In addition, the members of these groups possessed connections and enjoyed prestige or suffered from discrimination to varying degrees. There were significant differences in their ability to locate themselves in desirable occupations.

Internal migration often juxtaposed in a single community groups derived from diverse backgrounds, each marked with its own cultural traits. Differences in the rate of social mobility among them may offer significant clues to the determinants of the pace of movement. Cities just behind the frontier line—Pittsburgh or Cincinnati in the 1830's, San Francisco or St. Louis in 1850's, Cleveland in the 1880's—were distinguished by peculiar combinations of restraint and opportunity. There Yankees and Southerners, Irishmen and Germans, each in the particularity of his own heritage, competed for the prizes of advancement. Who gained, and how much, was a measure of the qualities that counted.[31]

The rewards were genuine and within reach of many who strove for them. This was the tenor of the vast literature of success evoked by the experience of the American economy. Each period gave the theme its own variations. Cotton Mather extolled Sir William Phips who earned gold and godliness too; Ben Franklin praised the shrewdly calculating tradesman; Horatio Alger traced the rise from rags to riches through pluck and luck; and Frank Norris described the elemental struggle of the fittest to survive. How far the myth conformed to reality we shall know better when we understand the relation of the political, social, and educational systems to the diffusion of property. But, whatever the reality, the myth expressed a deeply held faith that the power to seek wealth was open to all and furthered the liberty of all.[32]

The consistent failure of occasional efforts to restrict the movement of individuals from one social level to another confirmed the belief that the rewards of the economic order were available to all Americans. The operations of potent forces kept American society fluid and frustrated all such attempts.

Although the number of *rentiers* in the United States was probably larger than has commonly been supposed, they never acquired the coherence of an organized group and were rarely able to transmit their incomes intact from one generation to another. The law did not favor institutional devices that tended in that direction; and the dominant factors in an expanding economy, generally prone to inflation, were hostile.

Nor did an aristocratic landed gentry develop in the American colonies despite the English background and despite the experience of colonial settlement elsewhere. The fragile beginnings of such a group in the plantation South and along the Hudson and Connecticut rivers in the North had no capacity for sustained growth. The putative American gentry proved incapable of maintaining their situation for more than one or two generations. The factors which rendered them unstable and deprived them of control cannot be ascribed simply to the Revolution. More complex elements were involved—the nature of the labor force that discouraged all large-scale agricultural enterprise, the difficulty of institutionalizing landed property, and the absence of a stable community, at the apex of which the squire could locate himself.[33]

A far more complex effort to acquire elite status absorbed the energies of the various occupational groups which struggled for recognition as professions. By the opening of the eighteenth century there was a widening distinction between the conditions of lawyers, physicians, ministers, and professors in America and their counterparts in England. In 1699, for example, the Attorney-General of New York was a man "bred to a trade and neither to learning nor to the law." As the number of practitioners grew in the New World, there were occasional attempts to emulate the mother country by restricting the admission of newcomers. Nevertheless, access to these callings remained relatively free, a condition no doubt connected with their loss of unique status in the community which exposed them to the general American hostility to restrictive privilege.[34]

The struggle for the definition of professional status continued through the nineteenth century in a variety of spheres. An adjustment was not ultimately arrived at until early in the twentieth century, and only at the expense of a radical modification of the very conception of what a profession was. The license was then restored as a selective device; it was, however, no longer a grant of privilege, but rather a mode of police regulation that extended to a multitude of skills, to those of barbers and electricians as well as physicians and lawyers.

Through this long history the heirs of traditional professions, like law and medicine, faced complex problems. They had to beat off the competition from such purveyors of rival services as midwives, apothecaries, and accountants. They had to demonstrate the great effectiveness of their own skills over the self-help of patent medicines and legal handbooks. At the same time, the steady increase in population led to a rising demand for professional aid.

These circumstances dictated the strategy of the struggle for position. Any increase in the numbers of doctors or lawyers diluted the privileges of the entrenched practitioners. Two alternatives were open to those who wished to preserve or add to those privileges—either to limit the new entries by excluding outsiders or to define, and achieve recognition for, stratified categories of practice that would protect a select inner group while opening the general field to competition. In either case, the result was a subtle change in the very conception of what the profession was.

There were few institutional means of attaining these goals. The authority of tradition was not binding; and the members of occupational groups that sought elite status displayed a significantly ambiguous attitude toward the state. They desired the support of government in excluding outsiders, yet resisted as an intrusion any suggestion of government regulation. Instead, they insisted that codes of ethics which they could promulgate themselves would be adequate to take care of any public interest that might be involved. Hence the importance, in their view, of a prescribed course of education which not only transmitted skills but also selected eligible novices and developed in them an *esprit de corps*. In effect, the practitioners sought to become a self-contained and self-perpetuating body of men with effective control over an important avenue of upward social mobility.

No profession wholly succeeded in making such a place for itself, although medicine came closest to doing so. That calling offers a very useful field for the examination of these forces, both because of the high position it acquired and because of its relation to government and education. From the Revolution to the last two decades of the nineteenth century there was a steady loosening of professional controls. There was, correspondingly, ever greater freedom to take up the art of healing, although proper antecedents and social position were still important in achieving eminence. From 1880 to 1940 the tendency toward relative ease of entry was reversed. Legal and educational regulations grew tighter and admission to the ranks of the physicians grew steadily more restrictive. After 1940, some of the exclusionary tendencies all but disappeared, without, however, a relaxation of professional standards. Medical, like engineering schools, could no longer discriminate against applicants on

the basis of religious or ethnic antecedents in the face of the acute shortage of qualified practitioners and of the social disapproval of such manifestations of bias.

A careful study of the various phases of this development in terms
broad enough to take in all the elements that influenced the recruitment
of doctors and the status of the medical profession would show the importance of the influence the physicians commanded through their connections with the university, the government, and powerful social groups,
and through the unique aura of their role as healers.[35] No other profession was able to establish the same degree of control, although some
attained partial, qualified success. The lawyers were never able to achieve
a limitation in the total number of practitioners; but they evolved a significant equivalent through internal stratification. Teachers, although
generally conceded professional status and esteem, exercised only slight
control over entry to their calling. By way of contrast, the notary or
conveyancer who had a position of genuine importance in Europe lost it
completely in the United States. Finally, a large number of callings which
have sought recognition have as yet only partially been conceded it—
morticians, realtors, accountants, and businessmen.[36]

The process of defining the professions was animated by a sustained
effort to restrict freedom of access to a strategic group of occupations
and to limit social mobility. Whatever success that effort had was conditioned by the necessity for transforming the concept of a profession into
a form justifiable by the criteria of the whole society, that is, into a
medium for maintaining standards to protect the public. The result was
always to leave some liberty for movement into the occupation.

The most striking attempt to create a truly oligarchic restrictive elite
met with complete failure. Between 1880 and 1930 an inchoate and ill-
defined but nevertheless significant movement sought to establish a
grouping, based upon birth as well as upon wealth, that would somehow
exercise the kind of social and political leadership ascribed to European
aristocracy. Historians who have paid any attention to it at all, have
been disposed to treat the effort to define "society" as the eccentric whim
of eccentric ladies eager for prestige. Yet the movement had a significant,
even though unrealized, potential. It arose in response to shifts in the
locus of wealth and power in the wake of massive industrialization. It
was related to the control of great fortunes; it developed an ideology
and a program; it exerted a profound influence upon American society,
law, and culture; it briefly entered politics; and it posed subtle questions
about the premises of American democracy and freedom.[37]

The effort failed. The political institutions proved resistant; the social underpinnings were shaky; and wealth could not be channeled into the hands only of those who thought it their due. Above all, those who aspired to be aristocrats misunderstood the role of leadership in a free society. The elite in the United States was not monolithic, but fragmented. Since the population was heterogeneous and was occupied in a variety of uncoordinated activities and associations, no single line of assent organized the whole people as a following. Leaders secured the support of particular segments with which they had institutional relations, but even they could count on their followings only within the terms of those limited relations. Respect and loyalty earned in politics, religion, or business did not of itself carry over into other spheres.[38]

The paths toward status and riches remained open—not to the same width for all men at all times, but enough to keep alive the faith that the goods of society were widely available. Power directed toward the goal of increasing wealth received the consent of the people because it promised to expand their liberty.

The persistence of social mobility had weighty consequences for the nation as well as for its citizens. It may be hypothesized that talent, free to express itself, moved where it was needed and leveled the barriers that impeded economic development in traditional or caste-bound societies. The stimulus to self-realization and autonomy destroyed the restraints of habit and inertia and encouraged spontaneity and originality. Despite the heavy personal strains that mobility sometimes entailed, these were among the most precious rewards of freedom.[39]

# Social Structure / *Sigmund Diamond*

Perhaps the broadest concept of any considered in this volume is social structure, the "sum total of the relationships which exist between the members of the group with each other and with the group itself."[1] In the selection reprinted below, the author's analysis of social structure centers on certain concepts, status and mobility among them, that are part of social structure as a composite concept. Needless to say, not all aspects of group relationship are capable of being revealed by the investigator, especially the historian, who is at the mercy of the surviving documentation. However, another analysis of Virginia's social structure in the seventeenth century, by Dr. Bernard Bailyn, employs similar and different concepts with the result that a dissimilar, if not a contradictory, pattern of Virginia's social structure in the seventeenth century emerges.[2]

F AD AND FASHION play their roles in the world of scholarship as elsewhere, and often products of the intellect may assume the quaint air of artifacts for no better reason than that, with the passage of time, they are made obsolete by the appearance of new, if not necessarily better, models. But in scholarship, if not in manufacturing, novelty is a virtue that has limits; and even old ideas and interests may be resurrected if they demonstrate the existence of problems or give promise of solving problems for which more recent ideas have proved inadequate. So it is that historical sociology, though conceded to be one of the roots from which the discipline itself emerged, has, in this country at least, suffered from the competition of more stylish fashions. And so it is, too, that there is increasing evidence today that historical sociology, so long an outmoded form of inquiry, is once again commending itself as an important subject of research. What follows is, frankly, an attempt to aid in the rehabilitation of historical sociology, not by exhortation, but, it is hoped, by a per-

"From Organization to Society: Virginia in the Seventeenth Century," *The American Journal of Sociology*, LXIII (March, 1958), 457–75. Reprinted by permission, copyright the University of Chicago.

1. Fairchild, ed., op. cit., *Dictionary of Sociology*, 293.
2. "Politics and Social Structure in Virginia," James M. Smith, ed., *Seventeenth Century America* (Chapel Hill, 1959). Note the critique of a phase of Bailyn's analysis in the article by Jack P. Greene, reprinted above.

suasive demonstration that questions of considerable importance for sociological theory may be raised when problems are examined in historical perspective. Our interest in this essay is in the utilization of certain aspects of the history of Virginia in the early seventeenth century to suggest significant questions concerning the creation of new statuses and the circumstances under which the character of an organization may be so altered as to be transmuted into something which is not, properly speaking, an organization at all but a society.

## I

It must be conceded at the outset that the group we have selected for study was pathetically small. In 1607, when the Virginia Company established a settlement at Jamestown, its population numbered 105; and in 1624, when the crown revoked the charter of the Company, the population of Virginia amounted to just over 1,200, despite the fact that the Company had sent more than 5,000 emigrants during that seventeen-year period.[1] But, just as a limited duration of time is no necessary detriment to a study of this kind, because there are periods of history when the rate of change is accelerated, so, too, the limited size of the group affords no accurate measure of the importance of the enterprise. Judged in terms of its outcome, its importance is self-evident. But, judged even in terms of the criteria of importance imposed by contemporaries, the verdict must be the same. The articles on the Virginia settlement in the *Kölnische Zeitung* and the *Mercure françoise;* the running series of reports from the Venetian ambassadors in London to the Doge and Senate; the letters from Jesuit priests in England to the Propaganda Fide in Rome and the newsletters from Venice and Antwerp in the Vatican archives; the continuing stream of dispatches from the Spanish ambassadors to King Philip III, pressing him to attack Jamestown, advising him of the latest decisions of the Virginia Company, and relating their efforts to recruit English spies; and the existence in the royal archives at Simancas of a discreption of the layout of Jamestown and the earliest known map of the town, the work of an Irish spy in the service of Spain[2]—all this is eloquent testimony of the position of Virginia in the international relations of the seventeenth century and of the concern felt in the capitals of Europe in the Virginia Company's undertaking. Nor was the expression of this concern merely verbal. In August, 1613, when the population of Virginia barely exceeded 200, the settlement at Jamestown had a decidedly cosmopolitan cast, for it contained eighteen prisoners—fifteen Frenchmen, including two Jesuits and several members of the nobility; a Spanish spy, Don Diego de

Molina; a renegade Englishman in the pay of Spain; and an Indian princess, Pocahontas.[3]

At the May Day, 1699, exercises at the College of William and Mary, one of the student orators—who must have been a sophomore—explained:

Methinks we see already that happy time when we shall surpass the Asiaticians in civility, the Jews in religion, the Greeks in philosophy, the Egyptians in geometry, the Phoenicians in arithmetic, and the Chaldeans in astrology. O happy Virginia.[4]

We may be intrigued by the ingenuousness of the student, but we are interested in the statement as evidence of the fact that in 1699—and for some time earlier—Virginia was a society and Virginians were nothing if not ebullient about its prospects. For it had not always been so.

At its inception—and for a number of years thereafter—it had been a formal organization, and if the joyous outburst of the student reflects its character at a later date, its earlier character is better revealed by the instructions given by the Virginia Company to Sir Thomas Gates on the eve of his departure for Jamestown in May, 1609:

You must devide yo$^r$ people into tennes twenties & so upwards, to every necessary worke a competent nomber, over every one of w$^{ch}$ you must appointe some man of Care & still in that worke to oversee them and to take dayly accounte of their laboures, and you must ordayne y$^t$ every overseer of such a nomber of workemen Deliver once a weeke an accounte of the wholle comitted to his Charge . . . you shall doe best to lett them eate together at reasonable howers in some publique place beinge messed by six or five to a messe, in w$^{ch}$ you must see there bee equality and sufficient that so they may come and retourne to their worke without any delay and have no cause to complain of measure or to excuse their idleness uppon y$^e$ dressinge or want of diet. You may well allowe them three howers in a somers day and two in the winter, and shall call them together by Ringinge of a Bell and by the same warne them againe to worke.[5]

And, if in later years "O happy Virginia" could be a spontaneous outcry of its citizens, it could not have been earlier. Testifying in 1625 about conditions under the administration of Sir Thomas Dale in 1614–16, Mrs. Perry, one of the fortunates who survived more than a few years in the first quarter-century of Virginia's history, revealed that

in the time of Sr: Thomas Dales Government An leyden and June Wright and other women were appoynted to make shirts for the Colony servants and had six nelds full of silke threed allowed for making of a shirte, w$^{ch}$ yf they did not p'forme, They had noe allowance of Dyott, and because theire threed naught and would not sewe, they tooke owt a ravell of y$^e$ lower p$^{te}$ of y$^e$ shirte to make an end of y$^e$ worke, and others y$^t$ had threed of thiere owne made it up w$^{th}$ that, Soe the shirts of those w$^{ch}$ had raveled owt proved shorter then the next, for w$^{ch}$ fact the said An leyden and June Wright were whipt, And An leyden beinge then w$^{th}$ childe (the same night thereof miscarried).[6]

Our first inquiry, then, must be into the characteristics of the original settlement at Jamestown—characteristics which changed so markedly during the course of the next quarter-century.

Virginia was not established as a colony to take its place among the territories governed by the British crown; it was not a state, and properly speaking, it was not a political unit at all: it was property, the property of the Virginia Company of London, and it was established to return a profit to the stockholders of that company. Under the political and economic conditions of seventeenth-century England, speculators in overseas expansion could count on no support from the government except verbal encouragement and some legal protection—and sometimes precious little of these. Under the circumstances, therefore, colonization had to be undertaken as a private business venture, and the first charge imposed on the property was the return on the shareholder's investment. Traditionally, this episode has been dealt with primarily in terms of the motivation of participants—did they come to establish religious freedom, to seek a haven for the politically persecuted, or to found a "First Republic"?—and it is true that those who joined the Virginia enterprise did so for many reasons. Some, like Richard Norwood, were footloose and fancy-free after having completed their apprenticeships. Robert Evelin wrote his mother that he was "going to the sea, a long and dangerous voyage with other men, to make me to be able to pay my debts, and to restore my decayed estate again . . . and I beseech you, if I do die, that you would be good unto my poor wife and children, which God knows, I shall leave very poor and very mean, if my friends be not good unto them." In its promotional literature the Virginia Company took advantage of this broad spectrum of motives and cast its net wide to snare the purses and bodies of all sorts and conditions of persons in support of a venture in which

> . . . profite doth with pleasure joyne,
>     and bids each chearefull heart,
> To this high praysed enterprise,
>     performe a Christian part.[7]

But, from the point of view of the managers of the enterprise, recruitment was perceived less as a problem of motivation than of achieving an organizational form through which the resources and energies of the participants could be mobilized. The basic objectives of the promoters in establishing a plantation in Virginia are quite clear: to exploit the mineral resources which they were certain were there; to search for that elusive will-o'-the-wisp—a water route to the Pacific through North America—and to monopolize whatever local trade existed and whatever oriental trade would be developed with the opening-up of the northwest passage.

The organizational form adopted for the venture was not created by the promoters; the roots of the joint-stock company, though it was still subject to considerable experimentation, lay deeply imbedded in English history. Nor were the proprietors themselves totally without experience in the establishment of plantations or unaware of the experience of others. Sir Thomas Smythe, a leader of the Virginia enterprise, was one of the merchant princes of London, a governor of the East India Company, the Muscovy Company, and many others. And they had before them the experience—which was, as we shall see, not entirely an unmixed blessing—of the colonizing effort of Sir Walter Raleigh and Sir Humphrey Gilbert, of the trading posts established by the great commercial companies, of Spain and Portugal, and of the founding of plantations in Ireland.[8]

What they established was a business organization; and, though the form of that organization was changed at various times during the Company's history, those changes were at all times dictated by the need to make the business pay, which, in the words of Sir Edwin Sandys, one of the two great leaders of the Company, was "that whereon all men's eyes were fixed."[9] It problems were those of any business organization. It sold shares, begged contributions, and organized lotteries to raise the necessary funds; it was concerned to recruit a proper labor force; it had to cope with the problem of adequate supervision and administration so as to maintain its authority; and it engaged in a full-scale advertising campaign to sell to potential adventurers and planters the glories of a land where the "horses are also more beautiful, and fuller of courage. And such is the extraordinarie fertility of that Soyle, that the Does of their Deere yeelde Two Fawnes at a birth, and sometimes three." And it was confronted with the petty harassments of cajoling those whose good will was needed for the success of the organization. "Talking with the King," wrote the Earl of Southampton to Sir Robert Cecil, "by chance I told him of the Virginia Squirrils which they say will fly, whereof there are now divers brought into England, and hee presently and very earnestly asked me if none of them was provided for him. . . . I would not have troubled you with this but that you know so well how he is affected by these toyes."[10]

But though the Company's plans were eminently rational, its grand design suffered from a fatal flaw: reality was far different from what the Company expected. Its model had been the East India Company, and its dream had been to reproduce the Spanish looting of a continent; but conditions in Virginia were not those of India or Mexico and Peru. "It was the Spaniards good hap," wrote Captain John Smith later in the history of the Virginia Company.

to happen in those parts where were infinite numbers of people, whoe had manured the ground with that providence that it afforded victuall at all times; and time had brought them to that perfection they had the use of gold and silver, and the most of such commodities as their countries affoorded; so that what the Spaniard got was only the spoile and pillage of those countries people, and not the labours of their owne hands. But had those fruitful Countries been as Salvage, as barbarous, as ill-peopled, as little planted laboured and manured, as Virginia; their proper labours, it is likely would have produced as small profit as ours. . . .

But we chanced in a land, even as God made it. . . . Which ere wee could bring to recompence our paines, defray our charges, and satisfie our adventurers; wee were to discover the country, subdue the people, bring them to be tractable civil and industrious, and teach them trades that the fruits of their labours might make us recompense, or plant such colonies of our owne that must first make provision how to live of themselves ere they can bring to perfection the commodities of the countrie.[11]

But though the error in conception made by the leaders of the Virginia Company was, from their viewpoint, a grievous one, it is also thoroughly understandable. It is true that the late sixteenth and early seventeenth century was a period of rapid expansion in the organization of trading companies; no less than thirty-four were chartered during that time. But the significant point is that the Virginia Company was the eighteenth to be founded, and, of the previous seventeen, whose experience could be taken as models, all dealt with countries within the European seas, with settled communities along the African coast, or with the advanced societies of Asia. For them, the problem was to exploit the already existing labor force of a settled society.[12] For the Virginia Company, the problem —and it is in this that the crucial difference lies—was to recruit a labor force.

It must be understood, therefore, that, in conformity with its objectives and organizational form, the establishment planted by the Virginia Company at Jamestown was a private estate, which, in the absence of an amenable local labor force, was worked on the basis of imported labor. Basic policies were laid down in London by the General Court of the Company, the body of those who had purchased the £12 10s. shares or who had been admitted for favors in the Company's behalf; the management and direction of affairs were intrusted to agents of the shareholders; and the supervision of those whose labor in Virginia was necessary for the attainment of the Company's objectives was placed in the hands of officials appointed in London.

Under the circumstances there were many potent inducements to English investors to purchase the Company's £12 10s. shares, a price, incidentally, which was the Company's estimate of the cost of transporting a settler to Virginia. Under the charter of 1606 they were guaranteed that after a five-year period, during which the settlers in Virginia would be supported by a stream of supplies sent at Company expense, the profits gained through trade and the discovery of minerals would be divided among the investors in proportion to the number of shares they held, and grants of land would be made to them on the same basis. But what were to be the inducements to become the labor force of a company trading post?

It should be noted at once that the English imitated the Spaniards in attempting to mobilize native labor. For the Company the key to the integration of the Indians into the labor force was in the ease with which, it was anticipated, they could be converted to Christianity and thereby won over as well to the secular values of Europeans. To them would accrue spiritual benefits; the Company, already blessed with those, would receive something more substantial. As a certain "Maister Captaine Chester" put it:

> The land full rich, the people easilie wonne,
> Whose gaines shalbe the knowledge of our faith
> And ours such ritches as the country hath.[13]

But though the Company succeeded for a time in exacting some tribute from the local tribal chiefs in the form of goods and weekly labor services, the Indians proved unwilling to accept the Company's spiritual and secular offerings. Long before the Indian uprising of 1622 gave an excuse to the settlers to engage in a campaign of extermination, it was clear that the Virginia Company would be forced to import its own labor force.[14]

Between 1607 and 1609, when its charter was changed, the Virginia Company sent over 300 persons to Jamestown. They were a disparate crew of adventurers and roughnecks, imbued with the hope that after a short period in Virginia they would return home with their fortunes in their purses. The social composition of the original labor force, the tasks they were expected to perform, and the nature of the settlement they were expected to establish can all be inferred from the passenger lists of the first expedition and the three subsequent supplies that were sent out by the Company before its charter was modified in 1609. The original expedition numbered 105 persons, of whom we have the names of 67. Of these 67, 29 were listed as gentlemen and 6 were named to the local council; the rest were listed by occupation—1 preacher, 4 carpenters, 12 laborers, 1 surgeon, 1 blacksmith, 1 sailor, 1 barber, 2 bricklayers, 1 mason, 1 tailor, 1 drummer, and 4 boys—and 2 were unidentified. In the three succeeding supplies, the rather high proportion of gentlemen was not substantially reduced, nor did the range of occupations alter significantly. Seventy-three of the 120 persons in the first supply of 1608 can be identified. In this group, gentlemen exceeded laborers 28 to 21. The remainder was made up of an odd assortment of craftsmen, including jewelers, refiners, and goldsmiths—bespeaking the expectations of the Company—apothecaries, tailors, blacksmiths, and—mute testimony to the fact that gentlemen must be gentlemen whether in the wilds of Virginia or a London drawing room—a perfumer. In brief, the two most striking characteristics of this original labor force are the presence of so high a proportion of gentlemen and the absence of any occupations indicative of an intention to establish a settled agriculural community.[15]

From the point of view of the promoters of the Virginia enterprise, these men were not citizens of a colony; they were the occupants of a status in—to use an anachronistic term—the Company's table of organization and the status was that of workman. Such other qualities or attributes that they possessed might have been of importance when they were in London, Norwich, or Bristol, but what counted in Virginia was that they should accept the directions of their superiors and that they should be willing to work.

Even under the best of circumstances, the problem of maintaining discipline and authority would have been crucial to the success of the Company. But these were hardly the best of circumstances, for the very social composition of the original labor force intensified what in any case would have been a grievously difficult problem. In the long intervals between the arrival of supplies under the direction of the Company's admiral, Christopher Newport, conditions in Jamestown bordered on anarchy; men were beaten by their officers, plots were hatched to escape the country, and insubordination was rampant. The Company's administrative methods, characterized by the utmost laxness, could not cope with the situation. "I likewise as occation moved me," wrote President Wingfield, discussing the supplies in Virginia, "spent them in trade or by guift amongst the Indians. So likewise did Captain Newport take of them . . . what he thought good, without any noate of his hand mentioning the certainty; and disposed of them as was fitt for him. Of these likewise I could make no accompt." Nor did the high percentage of aristocrats help matters. Unused to the heavy work of axing timber, they cursed so much at their blisters that the president of the council ordered that at the end of the day's work a can of cold water be poured down the sleeve of each offender for every curse he had uttered. To Captain John Smith, the problem was the presence of too many gentlemen: "For some small numbr of adventurous Gentlemen . . . nothing were more requisite; but to have more to wait and play than worke, or more commanders and officers than industrious labourers was not so necessarie. For in Virginia, a plaine Souldier that can use a Pickaxe and spade, is better than five Knights."[16]

Clearly, even if the mortality figures had been less gruesome than they were—in July, 1609, between 80 and 100 were alive of the 320 who had been sent since 1607[17]—qualitative considerations alone would have dictated a change in the composition of the labor force. For the Company the situation was brought to a head with the realization that there were to be no quick returns from metals and trade and that profits would have to be made through the exploitation of agricultural resources.

Never did the Company rely fundamentally on the recruitment of involuntary labor, but so desperate were its labor requirements and so necessary was it to keep the good will of those authorities who favored the transportation of undesirables that it felt compelled to resort to forced labor.

As early as 1609, a letter from Lisbon revealed that the Portuguese were transporting fifteen hundred children over the age of ten to the East Indies and suggested that the same be done in the case of Virginia. Shortly thereafter the Privy Council notified the mayor of London that the plagues of the city were due mainly to the presence of so many poor persons and recommended that a fund be raised, with the help of the commercial companies, to send as many of these as possible to Virginia. The Virginia Company promptly gave an estimate of the expenses involved and of the terms that would be offered to the emigrants; but, though a large sum of money was raised, no persons were actually transported at that time. In 1617, however, the City of London raised £500 to pay the cost of shipping one hundred children to Virginia, where they were to be apprenticed until the age of twenty-one, thereafter to be the fee-simple owners of fifty acres of land each. So delighted were the Company and the Virginia planters that they continued the practice, but it is evident that not all the children were equally pleased by the future arranged for them. In January, 1620, Sandys wrote to Sir Robert Naunton, the king's principal secretary, that "it falleth out that among those children, sundry being ill-disposed, and fitter for any remote place than for this Citie, declared their unwillingness to goe to Virginia: of whom the Citie is especially desirous to be disburdened; and in Virginia under severe Masters they may be brought to goodness." Since the City could not deliver and the Company could not transport "theis persons against their wills," Sandys appealed to the Privy Council for the necessary authority. It was quickly given. Exact figures cannot be determined, but, before the demise of the Company in 1624, additional shipments of children had been delivered to Virginia, and it is evident that several hundred must have been involved.[18]

Concerning the shipment of convicts and rogues and vagabonds the information is scanty. Some convicts were certainly in Virginia before 1624, though we do not know how many; but the Virginia Company was antagonistic to the importation of such persons, and, in any case, convict-dumping on a large scale did not become a characteristic of the colonial scene until the second half of the seventeenth century.[19] So, too, was the Company antagonistic to the importation of rogues, possibly because, unlike the case of the London children, it was forced to assume the cost of transportation. It engaged in the practice under pressure from King James I. For one group of fifty boys sent out in 1619, the Company expected to receive £500 in tobacco from the planters to whom they were indentured; but as late as October, 1622, it had received only £275.15.6, and Governor Yeardley was told that the planters "should be caused to make satisfaccon for the 224[ll]4:6:w[ch] is remayninge due unto the Companie this yeare in good leafe Tobacco." That still others were sent is certain; the Court Book of Bridewell Hospital records that in 1620 Ellen Boulter was "brought in by the Marshall for a Vagrant, that will not be ruled by her father or her friends," to be kept at her father's charges to go to Virginia.[20]

But throughout its history the Company was dependent upon the recruitment of voluntary labor, and especially was this true when it realized that profits would have to be made from agricultural staples and not minerals. The change in objective not only emphasized the necessity of recruiting a large labor supply but required that it be qualitatively different from the earlier one, for now that the glitter of gold was vanishing the Company needed not soldiers of fortune but sober workmen who would be able to extract from the land the food supplies necessary for their own support and the staples whose export would produce profit for the shareholders.[21] But what could the Company offer as sufficient inducement to motivate large numbers of persons to come to Virginia, especially when—as the evidence indicates—enthusiasm for emigration from England was confined to the wealthy, who themselves were hardly likely to exchange the comforts of life in England for the dangers of life in Virginia?[22] The difficulties the Company faced in this respect were exacerbated by the whispering campaign started by settlers who had already returned from Virginia. "Some few of those unruly youths sent thither," said a Virginia Company broadside in 1609, (being of most leaued and bad condition) and such as no ground can hold for want of good direction there, were suffered by stealth to get aboard the ships returning thence, and are come for England againe, giving out in all places where they come (to colour their owne misbehaviours, and the cause of their returne with some pretence) most vile and scandalous reports, both of the Country itselfe, and the Cariage of the business there.[23]

The Company now determined to be discriminating in the selection of settlers:

And for that former experience hath to clearly taught, how muche and manie waies it hurtheth to suffer Parents to disburden themselves of lascivious sonnes, masters of bad servants and wives of ill husbands, and so to dogge the business with such an idle crue, as did thrust themselves in the last voiage, that will rather starve for hunger, than lay their hands to labor.[24]

It was conceded that some "base and disordered men" might inveigle themselves into the body of settlers, but they could not do too much harm, for, as the Reverend William Crashaw said on the departure of Governor de la Warr to Virginia, "the basest and worst men trained up in a severe discipline, sharp laws, a hard life, and much labor, do prove good members of a Commonwealth. . . . The very excrements, of a full and swelling state . . . wanting pleasures, and subject to some pinching miseries," will become "good and worthie instruments."[25]

Clearly, if prospective settlers in Virginia faced "severe discipline, sharp lawes, a hard life, and much labour," substantial concessions would have to be offered to induce them to emigrate. The status the Company was asking them to accept was that of servant, employee of the Company, but it was one thing to create a position and quite another to get men to fill it. Since perpetual servitude was obviously no inducement, the Company was required to limit the period of service and to make other concessions. Every settler over the age of ten, whether he paid his own way or was shipped at Company expense, was promised one share of stock in the Company, with potential dividends from the profits of trade and a land grant to be made at the time of the first division after seven years. Every "extraordinarie" man—such as "Divines, Governors, Ministers of State and Justice, Knights, Gentlemen, Physitions" or such as were "of worth for special services"—was given additional shares according to the value of his person. The Company expected, in return for assuming all the costs of maintaining the plantation and providing supplies to the emigrants, that each settler would work at tasks assigned him under the direction of Company-appointed officers. For a period of seven years, all supplies were to be distributed through the Company store, all exports were to be shipped through the Company magazine, and all land was to be held by the Company.[26] In effect, the Company created the status of landowner in order to induce persons to accept the status of non-landowners; it was asking emigrants to accept the present burdens of membership in a lower status in anticipation of the future benefits they would receive upon promotion to a higher status. From the point of view of the structure of an organization, this was simply automatic progression —promotion to a higher position in the table of organization after a limited tenure in a lower position. From the point of view of a society, however, this was a guaranty of social mobility, and, as we shall see, it seriously compromised the Company's ability to secure its organizational objectives.

That the Company expected the combination of limited servitude and potential landownership to solve its labor problem is quite clear; sufficient numbers of workmen would be induced to emigrate to Virginia and, having arrived, would be motivated to do the work that was essential to the Company's success. Virginia planter and London adventurer were to be united in a single relationship. Do not discourage the planters, the London stockholders were admonished, "in growing religious, nor in gathering riches, two especiall bonds (whether severed or cojoined) to keepe them in obedience, the one for conscience sake, the other for fear of losing what they have gotten." How the planter's concern for his own interests was to benefit the Company was quite clear. "The Planters," wrote Alderman Johnson, "will be in such hope to have their owne shares and habitations in those lands, which they have so husbanded, that it will cause contending and emulation among them, which shall bring foorth the most profitable and beneficiall fruites for their ioynt stock."[27]

But land for the settlers and profits for the stockholders were affairs of the future, and both were dependent upon the skill and speed with which the planters could be molded into an efficient labor force. It was of the utmost importance, therefore, that the Company establish its authority in Virginia and maintain discipline, and for the achievement of these purposes the Company was not content to rely simply on the self-discipline it hoped would be the by-product of the effort to obtain profits. The first step was taken with the issuance of the new charter of 1609. During its first three years in Virginia, the Company felt, "experience of error in the equality of Governors, and some out-rages, and follies committed by them, had a little shaken so tender a body." To avoid the evils of divided authority, "we did resolve and obtain, to renew our Letters Pattents, and to procure to ourselves, such ample and large priviledges and powers by which we were at liberty to reforme and correct those already discovered, and to prevent such as in the future might threaten us . . . under the conduct of one able and absolute Governor."[28] But changes in the formal structure of authority were not sufficient.

Religion, too, was counted upon to do its part in maintaining order. Doctrinal conflict was minimized from the start by the ban on Catholics, but what really distinguishes the role of religion under the Virginia Company was its conscious utilization for disciplinary purposes. No less an authority on colonization than Richard Hakluyt had pointed to the advisability of taking along "one or two preachers that God may be honoured, the people instructed, mutinies better avoided, and obedience the better used."[29] The Company was quick to take the hint. Religion was used to screen prospective planters before their arrival in Virginia, and it was used to discipline them after their arrival. "We have thought it convenient to pronounce," stated the Company in a broadside of 1609, "that . . . we will receive no man that cannot bring or render some good testimony of his religion to God."[30] And during the time that Sir Thomas Dale's code of laws was sovereign in Virginia—from May, 1610, to April, 1619—the settlers were marched to church twice each day to pray for relief from dissension and for the showering of blessings upon the shareholders:

> O Lord . . . defend us from the delusion of the devil, the malice of the heathen, the invasions of our enemies, & mutinies & dissentions of our own people. . . . Thou has moved . . . the hearts of so many of our nation to assist . . . with meanes and provision, and with their holy praires . . . and for that portion of their substance which they willingly offer for thy honour & service in this action, recompence it to them and theirs, and reward it seven fold into their bosomes, with better blessinges.[31]

In a society of ranks and orders, deference is owed to certain persons by virtue of their social position, and the Company attempted to maximize the potentiality for discipline in such an arrangement by appointing to leading posts in Virginia those persons to whom obedience was due because of their high status. Insofar as it was possible, the Company selected only persons of high birth to be governor; when it was not possible, as in the case of Governor Yeardley, it quickly, and it seems surreptitiously, secured for him a knighthood.[32] And at all times the governors were urged to surround themselves with the pomp and circumstance of high office, the better to impress the governed. "You shall for the more regard and respect of yo.r place," read the Company's instructions to Sir Thomas Gates,

> to beget reverence to yo.r authority, and to refresh their mindes that obey the gravity of those lawes under w.ch they were borne at yo.r discrecon use such

formes and Ensignes of government as by our letters Pattents wee are enabled
to grant unto you, as also the attendance of a guarde uppon your pson.[33]

Ultimately, however, the Company relied upon a military regimen and
upon the imposition of force to obtain labor discipline. Governor de la
Warr had been instructed that his men were to be divided into groups and
placed under the charge of officers "to be exercised and trayned up in
Martiall manner and warlike Discipline."[34] Settlers were forbidden to return to England without permission, and their letters were sealed and
sent first to the Company in London before being forwarded.[35] But the
full code of military discipline was not worked out until the arrival in
Jamestown of Captain Thomas Dale, marshal of the colony, who had been
granted a leave of absence from his post in the Netherlands army at the
behest of the Company. Dale supplemented the usual list of religious
offenses and crimes against the state and the person with a series of enactments designed to protect the Company's interests. Slander against the
Company, its officers, or any of its publications; unauthorized trading with
the Indians; escaping to the Indians; theft; the killing of any domestic
animal without consent; false accounting by any keeper of supplies—all
were punishable by service in the galleys or death. Failure to keep
regular hours of work subjected the offender to the pain of being forced
to lie neck and heels together all night for the first offense, whipping
for the second, and one year's service in the galleys for the third.[36]

Moreover, Dale created a military rank for every person in Virginia
and specified the duties of each in such a way as to provide us with important clues into the nature of labor discipline and what was expected
to provide the motivation to work.

> Because we are not onely to exercise the duty of a Souldier, but that of the
> husbandman, and that in time of the vacancie of our watch and ward wee are
> not to live idly, therefore the Captaine . . . shall . . . demand . . . what service,
> worke, and businesse he hath in charge, from the Governor . . . in which
> worke the Captaine himselfe shall do exceeding worthily to take paines and
> labour, that his Souldiers seeing his industry and carefulnesse, may with more
> cheerfulnesse love him, and bee incouraged to the performance of the like.

Of the corporal:

> His duty is to provide that none of his Squadron, be absent, when the
> drumme shall call to any labour, or worke, or at what time soever they shall be
> commanded thereunto for the service of the Collonie, in the performance of
> which said workes he is to be an example of the rest of his Squadron by his
> owne labouring therein . . . that thereby giving incoraging to his superior of-
> ficers he may be held by them worthy of a higher place.

Of the private soldier:

> He shall continue at his worke until the drumme beat, and . . . be conducted into the church to heare divine service, after which he may repayre to his house or lodging to prepare for his dinner, and to repose him until the drumme beate shall call him forth againe in the afternoone . . . the Generall having understanding of his promptitude and dilligence may conferre upon him, and call him into place of preferment and commaund.[37]

What is so striking about Dale's Code is the way in which it stripped from people all attributes save the one that really counted in the relationship which the Company sought to impose on them—their status in the organization. Behavior was expected to conform to a set of prescriptions the major characteristic of which was that the rights and obligations of persons depended on their position within the organization. In this respect, the contrast between Dale's Code and the first set of laws the settlers were able to enact for themselves at the General Assembly of 1619 is startling. For then, considerations other than status within an organization were fundamental:

> All persons whatsoever upon the Sabaoth days shall frequente divine service and sermons both forenoon and afternoone. . . . And everyone that shall transgresse this lawe shall forfeicte three shillinges a time to the use of the churche. . . . But if a servant in this case shall wilfully neglecte his Mr's commande he shall suffer bodily punishment.

Or consider the following petition drafted by the Assembly:

> . . . that the antient Planters . . . suche as before Sir T. Dales' depart were come hither . . . maye have their second, third and more divisions successively in as lardge and free manner as any other Planter. Also that they wilbe pleased to allowe to the male children, of them and of all others begotten in Virginia, being the onely hope of a posterity, a single share a piece.[38]

For the planters in Virginia, considerations of length of residence and of varying degrees of freedom now affected the rights and obligations of persons. No longer could relations be determined exclusively by the positions persons held within a single system—the organization of the Company. By 1619 Virginia was becoming a society, in which behavior was in some way determined by the totality of positions each person held in a network of sometimes complementary, sometimes contradictory, relationships. The key to this transformation from organization to society lies in the concessions the Company was forced to offer to induce persons to accept positions in the organizational relationship; for those concessions so multiplied the number of statuses and so altered the status of persons that a system of relationships was created where only one had existed before.

The fact is that the reforms the Company instituted in 1609 were not sufficient either to swell the supply of labor migrating to Virginia or to motivate the planters who were there to work with the will the Company expected. The Company had hoped that by its reforms it would be able to obtain not "idle and wicked persons; such as shame, or fear compels into this action [but] fit and industrious [persons], honest sufficient Artificers."[39] Yet so unproductive were they that as late as 1616 John Rolfe could indicate to Sir Robert Rich that what had been was still the Company's most serious problem. Our greatest want, he wrote, is "good and sufficient men as well of birth and quality to command, soldiers to marche, discover and defend the country from invasion, artificers, labourers, and husbandmen."[40] And so dissatisfied had the settlers become with their situation that, in a letter smuggled to the Spanish ambassador in London with the connivance of English sailors, Don Diego de Molina, the prisoner in Jamestown, reported that "a good many have gone to the Indians . . . and others have gone out to sea . . . and those who remain do so by force and are anxious to see a fleet come from Spain to release them from this misery."[41] The hope that Don Diego attributed to the colonists was, no doubt, the wish of a patriotic Spaniard; but it is nevertheless true that some settlers did flee to the Indians, that the Company did succeed in obtaining authority to deport to Virginia those settlers who had escaped back to England, and that Coles and Kitchins, who had been Don Diego's guards, were executed in 1614 for organizing a plot to escape to Florida.[42]

Nor did the concessions granted to superior colonists in 1614, including a kind of modified right to private property and some relief from the obligation to work on the Company lands, suffice to solve the labor problem.[43] For the simple fact was, as Captain John Smith wrote, that "no man will go from hence to have less liberty there then here."[44] The Company, determined in 1619 to make a final effort to create of Virginia the profitable investment it had always hoped it would be, took his advice to heart. Though it was faced with declining financial resources, with internal bickering, and with increasing evidence that the king was losing patience with its meager achievement, the Company decided to pin its hopes on a quick return. The key to profits, it felt, lay in raising the value of the Company lands through increasing population and in diversifying products through the importation of labor skilled in many trades. The success of the effort, obviously, rested upon the strength of the additional inducements that could be offered to both investors and potential emigrants.[45]

As always, one of the principal devices used by the Company to attract labor and to increase productivity was that of easing the terms on which land could be acquired. The effect of the reform was to create within the Company a new group of statuses differentiated from one another in terms of the amount of property attached to each or the length of time required to obtain land on the part of those who were not yet entitled to it:

1. "Ancient planters" who had come to Virginia at their own cost before 1616 received 100 acres per share in perpetuity rent-free.

2. "Ancient planters" who had come to Virginia at Company expense received 100 acres at an annual rent of 2s. after the completion of their seven-year period of servitude on the Company's land.

3. All persons who came to Virginia after 1616 at their own expense received 50 acres at an annual rent of 1s.

4. All persons who came to Virginia after 1616 at Company expense were to receive 50 acres after having worked on the Company's land for seven years, during which time half their produce belonged to the Company and half to themselves.

5. All tradesmen received a house and 4 acres of land so long as they plied their trades.

6. All persons who paid for the transportation of emigrants received 50 acres per person.

7. Company officers not only were entitled to their regular land grants but were supported by the labor of tenants-at-halves on large tracts of land reserved by the Company for that purpose.[46]

8. Indentured servants, whose transportation was paid by the Company or by private associations of investors and who were then sold to planters on their arrival in Virginia, were entitled to "freedom dues"—including a land grant—on the expiration of their servitude.[47]

Nor was this all. Determined to improve the moral of the colonists and, eventually, to relieve the Company of the burdensome cost of transporting labor from England, Sandys also began in 1620 to ship women to Virginia to become wives of the planters. There had been marriages in Virginia before, of course, but the supply of single women, restricted to the few female servants of married couples, was far smaller than the demand. Now, however, the Company organized the shipment of women on a business basis, forming a separate joint-stock company for the purpose. Though the women were, in any case, to be paid for by the planters at the rate of 120 pounds of the best leaf tobacco per person and though the Company conceded that it was dubious as to its authority to control marriages—"for the libertie of Mariadge we dare not infrindg"—it nevertheless discriminated between classes of planters in the bestowal of the women. "And though we are desirous that mariadge be free according to the law of nature," the Company wrote to the Governor and Council of Virginia, "yett would we not have these maids deceived and married to servants, but only to such freemen or tenants as have meanes to maintaine them."[48]

Finally, in a radical departure from previous policy, the Company limited the scope of martial law and ordered Governor Yeardley to convene an assembly of elected representatives from each district in Virginia. The Company did not intend to diminish its own authority, for the Governor was given the right to veto all enactments of the Assembly, and the General Court of the Company in London retained the right to disallow its decisions. Rather was it the Company's hope that the degree of acceptance of its program would be increased if it had the added sanction of approval by representatives of the planters themselves.[49]

In a sense, the Company's reforms succeeded too well. Lured by the new prospects in Virginia, about 4,800 emigrants departed from England between November, 1619, and February, 1625, nearly twice as many as had gone during the entire period from 1607 to 1619.[50] But, while the Company's propaganda could refer blandly to "each man having the shares of Land due to him" and to "the laudable forme of Justice and government,"[51] actual conditions in Virginia were quite different. Goodman Jackson "much marviled that you would send me a servant to the Companie," young Richard Freethorne wrote to his parents:

> He saith I had beene better knocked on the head, and Indeede so I fynde it now to my great greefe and miserie, and saith, that if you love me you will redeeme me suddenlie, for wch I doe Intreate and begg. . . . I thought no head had beene able to hold so much water as hath and doth daylie flow from mine eyes. . . . But this is Certaine I never felt the wante of ffather and mother till now, but now dear freinds full well I knowe and rue it although it were too late before I knew it.

"To write of all crosses and miseries wᶜʰ have befallen us at this tyme we are not able," said Samuel Sharp. "So the truth is," Edward Hill wrote to his brother, "we lyve in the fearfulest age that ever Christians lived in."[52]

Though Company policy was not responsible for all the suffering endured by the settlers, it was responsible for intensifying their sense of deprivation by having promised too much. "My Master Atkins hath sould me," Henry Brigg wrote to his brother, Thomas:

> If you remember he tould me that for my Diett the worst day in the weeke should be better then the Sonday, & also he swore unto you that I should never serve any man but himselfe: And he also tould us that there they paled out their groundes from Deare & Hoggs. But in stead of them we pale out oʳ Enemyes.

"If the Company would allow to each man a pound of butter and a pounde of Chese weekely," wrote a planter to Sir John Worsenholme,

they would find more comfort therin then by all the Deere, Fish & Fowle is so talked of in England of w^ch I can assure yo^u yo^r poore servants have nott had since their cominge into the Contrey so much as the sent.

"I am pswaded," George Thorp wrote to John Smyth of Nibley,

that more doe die of the disease of theire minde then of theire body by having this country victualls over-praised unto them in England & by not knowing, they shall drinke water here.[53]

No doubt the chasm between expectation and reality contributed to the planters' alienation from the organizational relationship into which they had been lured by the Company's promises. But that relationship was affected even more by the development of a network of relations that followed inevitably from the inducements to get men into the Company.

At one time in Virginia, the single relationship that existed between persons rested upon the positions they occupied in the Company's table of organization. As a result of the efforts may by the Company to get persons to accept that relationship, however, each person in Virginia had become the occupant of several statuses, for now there were rich and poor in Virginia, landowners and renters, masters and servants, old residents and newcomers, married and single, men and women; and the simultaneous possession of these statuses involved the holder in a network of relationships, some congruent and some incompatible, with his organizational relationship.

Once the men in Virginia had been bachelors who lived in Company-provided barracks. Now they lived in private houses with their families, and, though the Company attempted to make use of the new relationship by penalizing each "Master of a family" for certain crimes committed by those under his authority[54]—hoping thereby that the master would use his authority to suppress crime—it can hardly be doubted that its action involved the head of the family in a conflict of loyalties.

Once all persons had been equal before Company law, and penalties had been inflicted solely in accordance with the nature of the offense. Now, the General Assembly found that "persones of qualitie" were "not fitt to undergoe corporall punishment."[55]

Once length of residence was irrelevant in determining the obligations of persons to the Company. Now, however, it was enacted that all "y^e olde planters, y^t were heere before, or cam in at y^e laste cominge of Sr. Tho: Gates they and theire posteritie shalbe exempted from theire psonall service to yᵉ warres, and any publique charge (Churche dewties excepted)."⁵⁶

Once Virginians had been governed administratively through a chain of command originating in the Company's General Court. Now an authentic political system existed, and the members of the Assembly demanded the same right to disallow orders of the General Court that the Court had with respect to the Assembly.

Once all land had been owned by the Company. Now much of it was owned by private persons, and even more had been promised to them, and the opportunities for the creation of private fortunes involved the planters in a new relationship with the Company. No longer was the planter willing to have his tobacco exported through the Company at a fixed price, when as a free landowner, he might strike his own bargain with the purchaser. No longer was the planter willing, at a time when labor meant profit, for the Company to commandeer his servants. Even officers of the Company, expected to administer its program in Virginia, saw the chance to subvert it to their own purposes; "The servants you allow them, or such as they hire," Captain John Smith told the Company, "they plant on their private Lands, not upon that belongeth to their office, which crop alwaies exceeds yours." Indeed, it became increasingly difficult to get planters to accept Company positions:

> Sʳ George is taken up with his private. . . . Capt. Hamor is miserablie poore and necessities will inforce him to shift. . . . Capt: Mathews intends wholie his Cropp, and will rather hazard the payment of forfeictures, then performe our Injunctions. . . . Mʳ Blanie is now married in Virginia, and when he hath discharged your trust in the Magazine wilbee a Planter amongst us. . . . And I would you could persuade some of qualities and worth to come out.⁵⁷

The increase in private wealth tended to subordinate status in the Company to status in a different relationship among the planters. The muster roll of early 1625 shows 48 families bearing various titles of distinction, most of which had been earned in Virginia. They alone held 266 of the appproximately 487 white servants in Virginia, 20 of the 23 Negro servants, and 1 of the 2 Indian servants.⁵⁸ These were the families at the apex of Virginia society, determined to uphold their rights as over against other persons and sometimes going beyond their rights. Acting through the General Assembly, they insisted upon scrupulous enforcement of contracts of servitude, forbade servants to trade with the Indians, and, so as not to lose their labor, regulated the right of their servants to marry. Nor, as the chronic complaints bear witness, were they loath to keep their servants beyond the required time.⁵⁹ That aspect of the rela-

tionship between master and servant was eloquently revealed in a petition
to the Governor by Jane Dickenson in 1624:

[She] most humblie sheweth that whereas her late husband Ralph Dickenson Came ov$^r$ into this Country fower Yeares since, obliged to Nicholas Hide
deceased for y$^e$ tearme of seaven yeares, hee only to have for himselfe & yo$^r$
petitioner y$^e$ one halfe of his labors, her said husband being slaine in the bloudy
Masacre, & her selfe Caried away w$^{th}$ the Cruell salvages, amongst them Enduring much misery for teen monthes. At the Expiration it pleased God so to
dispose the hartes of the Indians, y$^t$ for a small ransome yo$^r$ petitioner w$^{th}$
divers others should be realeased, In Consideration that Doctor Potts laid out
two pounds of beades for her releasement, hee alleageth yo$^r$ petitioner is linked
to his servitude w$^{th}$ a towefold Chaine the one for her late husbandes obligation
& thother for her ransome, of both w$^{ch}$ shee hopeth that in Conscience shee
ought to be discharged, of y$^e$ first by her widdowhood, of the second by the law
of nations, Considering shee hath already served teen monthes, two much for
two pound of beades.
The pmises notw$^{th}$standing D$^r$ Pott refuseth to sett yo$^r$ peticioner at liberty,
threatning to make her serve him the uttermost day, unless she pcure him
150$^{li}$ waight of Tobacco, she therefore most humbly desireth, that you$^u$ wilbe
pleased to take w$^t$ Course shalbe thought just for her releasement fro' his servitude, Considering that it much differeth not from her slavery w$^{th}$ the Indians.[60]

But that was only one aspect of the relationship. Conditions in Virginia
were now more fluid than they had been, and persons of low estate might
also rise. Secretary of State John Pory wrote Sir Dudley Carleton that
"our cowekeeper here of James citty on Sundays goes accowtered all in
freshe flaminge silke; and a wife of one that in England had professed the
black arte, not of a scholler, but of a collier of Croydon, wears her rought
bever hatt with a faire perle hat band." The Company was opposed to
such unseemly displays of wealth on the part of persons of low estate,[61]
but it could not prevent them.

The ultimate stage in the transition of Virginia from organization to
society was reached when the settlers came to feel that the new relationships in which they were now involved were of greater importance than
the Company relationship, when their statuses outside the organization
came largely to dictate their behavior. For at that point they were no
longer willing to accept the legitimacy of their organizational superiors.
William Weldon warned Sir Edwin Sandys that the planters who now had
land were grumbling at Company policy:

I acquainted them w$^{th}$ my restraint of plantinge Tobacco w$^{ch}$ is a thinge so
distastefull to them that they will w$^{th}$ no patience indure to heare of it bitterly
Complayninge that they have noe other meanes to furnish themselves with
aparell for the insuinge yere but are likely as they say (and for aught I Can
see) to be starved if they be debarred of it.[62]

From general discontent it was but a short step to ridicule of Company officials and outright refusal to accept a Company assignment. Wrote planter William Capps to John Ferrar:

> The old smoker our (I know not how to terme him but) Governor, so good so careful mild, Religious, iust, honest that I protest I thinke God hath sent him in mercie for good to us, he undergoeth all your cares & ours and I feare not but god will bless him in all his pceedinges but who must be th'Instrument to make all this whole againe? Why Capps: all voyces can sett him forth about the business: But who must pay him his hyre? The Contrey is poore and the Companie is poore and Cappes is poore already, & poorer he will be if he follow this course.

Like other men, planter Capps believed that "Charity first beginnes at home," and he divorced his own interest from that of the Company:

> I will forsweare ever bending my mind for publique good, and betake me to my own profit with some halfe a score men of my owne and lie rootinge in the earthe like a hog, and reckon Tobacco ad unguem by hundreths, and quarters.[63]

That the Company could no longer expect to command obedience was clear, for even its officers in Virginia perceived themselves as having a set of interests distinct from those of their London superiors and turned their backs to their authority. "Such is the disposicon of those who glorie in their wisdomse," wrote George Sandys, the treasurer in Virginia, to his brother, Sir Miles,

that they will rather Justifye and proceed in their Errors than to suffer a supposed disgrace by reforming them. . . . Who clere themselves by the wrongings of others; objecting unto us their Instructions, whereof manie are infeasible and the most inconvenient, for to say the truth they know nothing of Virginia.

"Such an Antipathy is there between theyr vast Comands and o$^r$ grumbling Obedience," Sir Francis Wyatt wrote to his father:

> Mingling matters of honor and profit often overthrow both. They expect great retournes to pay the Companies debt. . . . For me I have not a third part of my men to inable me to either. . . . I often wish little M$^r$ Farrar here, that to his zeale he would add knowledge of this Contrey.[64]

In 1607 there had been no "Contrey," only the Virginia Company. It was the Company's fate to have created a country and to have destroyed itself in the process. More than a century later, James Otis wrote bitterly: "Those who judge of the reciprocal rights that subsist between a supreme and subordinate state of dominion, by no higher rules than are applied to a corporation of button-makers, will never have a very comprehensive view of them."[65] His comment was intended as an observation on contemporary political affairs, but we can detect in it a verdict on the past as well.

The Company had been faced with the problems of motivating its members to work for the ends which it was created to achieve and, at the same time, of maintaining the discipline that was essential for its organizational integrity. The solution it adopted for the first problem made it impossible to solve the second; and the burden of achieving order and discipline now became the responsibility not of an organization but of a society.

Among the papers in the Sackville collection is a document entitled "A Form of Policy for Virginia," written when it was already apparent that the Company had failed. The proposal was never adopted, but it is significant nonetheless, for, as Professor Fernand Braudel reminds us,

victorious events come about as a result of many possibilities, often contradictory, among which life finally has made its choice. For one possibility which actually is realized innumerable others have been drowned. These are the ones which have left little trace for the historians. And yet it is necessary to give them their place because the losing movements are forces which have at every moment affected the final outcome.[66]

The significance of the document, drafted as a royal proclamation, lies in its awareness of the problems of motivation and order, in its realization that they could no longer be solved by instructions handed down through a chain of command, and in its conscious application of particular social inventions to solve them:

Wee . . . knowinge that the perfection and happinesse of a commonwealth, lyeth . . . first and principally in the government, consisting in the mutuall duties of commandeing and obeyeing, next in the possessing thinges plentifully, necessarie for the life of man, doe professe that . . . we intend wholely the good of our subjects . . . end eavouring to cause both England and Virginea, to endowe each other with their benefittes that thereby layeing aside force and our coactive power, we may by our justice and bountie marrye and combinde those our provinces to us and our soveraigntye in naturall love and obedience.

The problem of order was solved by the meticulous enumeration of every social status that was to exist in Virginia, with a specification of the rights and obligations that inhered in each. The problem of motivation was solved by the granting of both economic rewards and social privileges to each status and by the opportunity given to move from one to another:

The meanest servant that goeth (God soe blessing him and his endeavours, that hee can purchase and [an] estate in England or compasse to carrie over or drawe over with him of his friends and adherences the number of 300 men) he may become a lord patriot which is the greatest place the commonwealth canne beare.

The problem of consensus was solved through devices to enhance the mutual affection of persons in these statuses:

To the end that love may be mayntayned, and that theise degrees may not estrange the upper orders from the lower, we wish that the heires and eldest sonnes of the upper orders may marrie with the daughters of the lower orders. . . . And that the daughters of the upper orders being heires may marrye with the sonnes of the lower orders, makeing choice of the most vertuous . . . that all degrees may bee thereby bound togeather in the bonds of love that none may be scorned but the scorner. To this end alsoe, although we would not have you imitate the Irish in their wilde and barbarous maners, yet we will commend one custome of theires unto you, which is that the poorer sort sueing to gett the nurseing of the children of the lordes and gentrie, and breedeinge upp in their minorities as their owne, this breedinge . . . doth begett anoether nature in them to love their foster children and brethren, as if they were naturally bread of the same parentes.

Written in the margin of the document, by whom we do not know, is a lengthy commentary. Concerning the importance of status and order, the following is written: "This maintenance of theire degrees will immoveably fix the frame of the collonie." Concerning the importance of mobility and motivation, the following is written: "Soe framinge the government that it shall give all men both liberty and meanes of riseinge to the greatest places and honours therein, whereby they will receave such content that they will all strive to maintaine it in the same forme we shall now settle it."[67]

Shakespeare had written:

> Take but degree away, untune that string
> And hark, what discord follows.

The author of the document agreed. He rested his hopes for stability on the attachment of each person to a position in which recognized rights and responsibilities inhered. What he did not realize is what may be learned from the history of the Virginia Company—that each man is attached to many positions, that each position involves him in a separate relationship that imposes its own necessities, and that his behavior is the product of all the positions he holds and, because he has a memory, of all the positions he once held.

*II*

The generalizations that emerge from our study are of two kinds: those directly tied to the events of the time and place that we have analyzed and those of a more abstract kind that derive from the analysis of these historical particulars but can be stated in such a way as to be of more general applicability.

There seems little room for doubt about some of the conclusions we have drawn: that the character of seventeenth-century North American society was shaped decisively by the fact that, in contrast to the situation in Latin America, the creation of the society was accomplished through the recruitment of a voluntary labor force; that higher statuses in that society were created as a result of the need to induce persons to accept positions in lower statuses; and that the behavior of persons in that society was determined not only by opportunities for advancement, as Whiggish interpreters of our history would have us believe, but, as well, by the fact that these opportunities were less than people had been led to expect.

With respect to more general hypotheses, it may be suggested that the mechanism by which the change from organization to society was accomplished lay in the very effort to apply the blueprint that was intended to govern the relations between persons, for this so multiplied the number of statuses persons held, and therefore the relationships in which they were involved, as to alter their behavior in a decisive fashion.

The testing of these hypotheses, of course, would involve the examination of still other consciously selected historical situations for the purpose of comparison—the experience of the British in establishing other colonies in North America and in coping with a totally different problem in India, of the French in Canada and the Spanish in South America, of the reasons for the difference between the blueprint in accordance with which utopian communities were planned and the outcome of their establishment, and the like. Herein lies the design for a research in historical sociology.

# Leadership / *Henry Steele Commager*

*It is by now redundant to assert that individual concepts have multiple meanings. This, of course, is true of leadership. One can appreciate the despair of a sociologist who, in classifying studies of leadership, grouped them as such "only because those reporting such studies call it leadership."[1]*

*While there is no universally accepted formulation of the concept of leadership,[2] the term is studied generally with reference to the traits of the leader and in terms of the "situational-interactional approach."[3] Commager's study of leadership incorporates both these understandings without attempting to pattern itself upon any of the more elaborately structured theoretical formulations of leadership.[4] Indeed, one of the remarkable features of Commager's brilliant essay is that it makes leadership in the eighteenth century comprehensible without overt reference to the large social science literature on this subject.*

WITH HIS customary insight Tocqueville observed back in the 1830's that leadership was more difficult in a democracy than elsewhere, and more difficult therefore in the New World than in the Old. In the Old World leadership was already given: it was attached to birth, rank, position; in the New World it had to be achieved by trial and error, and as there were no fixed standards the chances for error were limitless. In the Old World there was no problem at all of formal leadership: it was all arranged by birth and inheritance—the kings, the princes, the aristocracy; in the New World there was no such thing as formal leader-

Henry S. Commager, "Leadership in Eighteenth-Century America and Today." Reprinted by permission from *Daedalus* (The Journal of the American Academy of Arts and Sciences), Fall, 1961, 652–673. Also in Stephen R. Graubard and Gerald Holton, eds., *Excellence and Leadership in a Democracy* (New York: Columbia University Press, 1962). Reprinted by permission.

1. Leon Festinger in Calvin P. Stone, ed., *Annual Review of Psychology* (Stanford, 1955), 187–216.
2. Donald W. Olmsted, *Social Groups, Roles, and Leadership: An Introduction to the Concepts* (East Lansing, Michigan, 1961), 39.
3. K. F. Janda, "Towards the Explication of the Concept of Leadership in Terms of the Concept of Power," *Human Relations*, XIII (November, 1960), 345–63.
4. John W. Thibaut and Harold H. Kelley, *The Social Psychology of Groups* (New York, 1959), 290.

ship—it had to be won each time, and each time the rules of the contest might change.

Yet who can doubt that in the last quarter of the eighteenth century it was the New World—not democracy by our standards but certainly democracy by European—that provided the most impressive spectacle of leadership, rather than the nations of the Old World? Who can doubt, for example, that in the crisis of 1774–1783 the American colonies and States enjoyed far more competent leadership than the British Empire?

The situation is too familiar to rehearse. In the last quarter of the century the new United States—a nation with a white population of less than three million, without a single major city, and wholly lacking in those institutions of organized society or civilization so familiar in Europe—boasted a galaxy of leaders who were quite literally incomparable: Franklin, Washington, Jefferson, Hamilton, John Adams, Samuel Adams, John Jay, James Wilson, George Mason, Benjamin Rush, James Madison, and a dozen others scarcely less distinguished.

What explains this remarkable outpouring of political leadership, this fertility in the production of statesmen—a fertility unmatched since that day? Was it an historical accident? Was it a peculiar response to the time or the place, or to a combination of the two? Or was it a product of conditions and attitudes that were cultivated and directed to calculated ends, and that can be if not recreated at least paralleled in our time?

There is of course an element of mystery, if not of fortuity, in the outbreak of genius at any time. How, after all, explain the flowering of the little Athens of Pericles and Sophocles and Phidias; the Florence of Michelangelo and Raphael and Machiavelli; the England of Hakluyt and Shakespeare and Francis Bacon; the Copenhagen of Hans Anderson and Thorwaldsen and Kierkegaard; the Vienna of Haydn and Mozart and Beethoven? We do not know with any certainty, yet clearly it would be absurd to ascribe these and comparable outbursts of genius, or of talent, to chance. There must be some principle that explains why the climate of fifth-century Athens was favorable to literature and philosophy, why the climate of fifteenth-century Florence encouraged art and architecture, why the climate of sixteenth-century England encouraged the discovery of new worlds of geography, science, and philosophy; why the climate of eighteeth-century Salzburg and Vienna grew musicians. And there must be some principle that explains why the little frontier colony of Virginia, with a white population less than that of present-day Syracuse or Dayton, without a single city or a major university or a proper school system or a press, produced in one generation Washington, Jefferson, Mason, Wythe, Madison, and Marshall. It is not enough to say that statesmanship was the specialty of Virginia as art was the specialty of Florence and music of Vienna. We want to know why.

The first consideration is elementary and practical. Eighteenth-century America offered extraordinarily few opportunities for the unfolding of talent. Almost the only opportunities it did offer were in the public arena. American society was pastoral and undifferentiated; American economy, rural and parochial; American life, singularly uninstitutionalized. In the Old World the young man of talent—certainly if he belonged to the upper classes—could take his choice, as it were, among the institutions which invited or even competed for his services; nor was he in fact limited to the institutions of his own country but could operate almost anywhere. The New World had few of these institutions, and those which did exist, in a kind of elementary fashion, offered few temptations; and while some colonials—Benjamin West and John Singleton Copley come to mind —could move to the mother country, the overwhelming majority could not. What Henry James later wrote of Hawthorne's America, was far more true of and more pertinent to the America of Thomas Jefferson and John Adams. Like Hawthorne, they looked out upon a "negative spectacle"— how fortunate that they did not know this:[1]

No State, in the European sense of the word, and indeed barely a national name. No sovereign, no court, no personal loyalty, no aristocracy, no church, no clergy, no army, no diplomatic service, no country houses, nor parsonages, nor thatched cottages, nor ivied ruins, no cathedrals, nor abbeys, nor little Norman churches; no great Universities, nor public schools . . . no literature, no novels, no museums, no pictures, no political society, no sporting class.

If these things were left out, said James, everything was left out. Yet the spectacle that greeted a Jefferson or an Adams was even more negative, even more barren, for one might add: no capital, no cities, no manu-factures, no newspapers, no journals, no libraries, no professions (except, somewhat feebly, the law and the clergy), no Society. In England, or France, or the Empire, a young man of talent could go into the Church; these was no Church in America, with a capital C, and religion had lost much of its appeal. In the Old World the young man could enter the army or the navy; the new America had neither. He could become a scholar and attach himself to an ancient university, or a man of letters, or an academician. In America these and similar activities were avocations.

Not only did the New World offer few opportunities for the display of talent except in the public arena; it presented few temptations to distract talent from preoccupation with public concerns. There was no quick way to wealth and no likelihood of piling up great riches: nothing is more eloquent of the simplicity of American life than Washington's casting

about to borrow a few hundred dollars to take him to the Inauguration, or
Secretary of the Treasury Hamilton's requests for a loan of twenty dollars
or so. There were no fields for military glory or adventure; the challenge
to adventure was there, but with no promise of reward, and soldiers who
had served their country well ended their days in penury, while officers who
naïvely hoped to enjoy membership in the Society of the Cincinnati were
regarded as models of depravity to be compared only with an Alcibiades
or a Caligula. Society offered no distractions—indeed there was no Society
in the Old World sense of the term, for that was a function of cities, of
courts, of a class system. In the Old World young men of talent might
become courtiers or adventurers, but it is almost as difficult to imagine a
Madame Du Barry, a Lady Hamilton, or a Madame de Staël in eighteenth-
century America as a Chesterfield, a Struensee, or a Casanova. It is relevant to recall Jefferson's warning[2] that young men who went abroad to
study would surely sink into debauchery, or John Adams's feeling of out-
rage at the avuncular gallantries of the aged Benjamin Franklin; it is relevant to note that Benjamin Thompson and Aaron Burr, who were adventurers and gallants, found Europe more congenial to their talents than
America.

Such talents as there was, then, had no effective outlet except in public
channels. But how did it happen that there was so much talent? And how
did it happen—it is a question Henry Adams never ceased asking himself
—that American society of the eighteenth century was prepared to encourage and use such talent as was available, whereas the America of a
century later was not.

Here again, we do well to begin with a practical consideration. Not only
were the opportunities for leadership and for distinction almost wholly
in the public arena, but the opportunities in the public arena were
numerous, urgent, and inviting. Has any one generation of less than a
million adult men ever been called upon to do more than the generation
of Washington and Adams and Jefferson in these creative years? They had
to win independence; set up state governments; write a constitution; win
the transmontane West and defend it against Indians and against formidable foreign powers; create a nation and all those institutions, political
and cultural, that go into the making of a nation. There is nothing like
war for bringing out courage; there is nothing like emergency for bringing
out ingenuity; there is nothing like challenge for bringing out character.
This is Arnold Toynbee's argument of challenge and response; it is the
moral put in simpler form by Lowell's once familiar poem, "The Present
Crisis":

> New occasions teach new duties; time makes ancient good uncouth,
> They must upward still, and onward, who would keep abreast of Truth.

In the last quarter of the eighteenth century Americans were exposed to new occasions as well as to new duties. They found themselves not only required to perform heroic deeds, but challenged to do so by the special circumstances of their being. No one can read their public papers or their private correspondence (and how the two are alike!) without realizing that these men saw themselves as characters in history, and that they were weighed down (or perhaps buoyed up) by a special sense of responsibility. A hundred quotations propose themselves, but the best is the most familiar: Washington's moving admonition to the States in his "Circular Letter" of June 1783:[3]

This is the time of their political probation, this is the moment when the eyes of the whole World are turned upon them, this is the moment to establish or ruin their national Character forever. . . . For according to the system of Policy the States shall adopt at this moment, they will stand or fall, and by their confirmation or lapse, it is yet to be decided whether the Revolution must ultimately be considered as a blessing or a curse: a blessing or a curse, not to the present age alone, for with our fate will the destiny of unborn Millions be involved.

The Founding Fathers—even the term is not improper—were quite aware that the American people were the first to break away from a mother country, the first to set up as a nation, to try the experiment of self-government, to write constitutions, and to fashion a new colonial system. They thought of themselves not as actors on some provincial stage but as characters in the greatest drama of all history. Thus Jefferson's comment that "Americans undertook to make a communication of grandeur and freedom" to the peoples of the entire world. Thus Tom Paine's conclusion that "we have it in our power to begin the world over again. A situation similar to the present hath not happened since the days of Noah until now. The birthday of a new world is at hand."[4] Thus Ethan Allen's assurance that "it is in our power to make the world happy, to teach mankind the art of being so, to exhibit on the theatre of the universe, a character hitherto unknown . . . to have a new creation entrusted to our hands."

And now we come to the heart of the matter. What was it that impelled so many Americans, from the seacoast of Maine to the frontiers of Georgia, from tidewater Virginia to the backwoods of Pennsylvania, into service to the commonwealth? What was it that made that service on the whole so spontaneous and so harmonious, so that eighteenth-century America presents a spectacle of consensus and cooperation without parallel in modern history? What was it that seemed to give the same character, the same animus, the same style even, to almost every public man—an aristocratic soldier like Washington, a Puritan like John Adams, a Scots immigrant like James Wilson, a West Indian emigrant like Alexander Hamilton, a scholar-statesman like Jefferson and Madison, a scientist like Benjamin Rush, so that their philosophies, their conduct, and even their letters are almost indistinguishable from their public papers? We have greatly busied ourselves with identifying the authorship of the disputed numbers of the *Federalist Papers;* we have not sufficiently remarked how astonishing it is that there should be a dispute: imagine a dispute over the authorship of contributions to a volume by Eisenhower, Stevenson, and Truman!

When we study our history in a vacuum, or in isolation, as we so commonly do, we exaggerate differences and minimize similarities. Contrast the American Revolution with the English Revolution of the seventeenth century, or the French from 1789 to 1815, or the many revolutions in the states of Latin America: what emerges most sharply is the harmonious quality that pervades the American. We pivot history on the contest between Jefferson and Hamilton, but their similarities are more profound and pervasive than their differences. We have made much of the differences between Jefferson and John Adams, but the two men cherished the same philosophy of history and even of man, worked happily together on the Declaration of Independence and on state constitutions, and in their long and fascinating correspondence rarely wandered off common ground. How much alike, too, are the constitutions of the States and that of the United States; how similar their Bills of Rights; how almost monotonously familiar are the arguments over the ratification of the Federal Constitution in the various conventions, how superficial the criticisms, how insignificant the proposed amendments; how interchangeable the two factions or parties before and after ratification! Of this whole generation of statesmen and public figures, we can say that the things that divided them were inconsequential, and the things that united them were fundamental.

It is not merely that they were all children of the Enlightenment, consciously or unconsciously: so, for that matter, were Lord Shelburne and Diderot and Casanova. It is more to the point that they were all part of what we may call the American Enlightenment—an Enlightenment that differed strikingly from the French and English versions in that (unlike these) it found support in experience as well as in philosophy, vindicated itself by reference to environment and circumstances, as well as to imagination and logic. That, I suppose is the underlying reason why John Adams was not really a misanthrope, despite his natural inclinations in that direction; why Washington was not really a Tory, despite his natural predisposition to be so; why Hamilton was such a failure as an aristocrat or an oligarch.

But there were other common denominators for the Americans of this generation besides the ideas of the Enlightenment and the realities of an environment, or a Providence, which "by all its dispensations proves that it delights in the happiness of man here and his greater happiness hereafter";[5] there were other common denominators that operated to encourage service to the commonwealth. There was, for example, the growing secularism, or deism, of society generally and of the upper classes (if we can use such a term for America) in particular. It is suggestive that whereas in the seventeenth century the best brains tended to go into the church, after Jonathan Edwards few first-rate minds were content with theological speculations, and the clergymen who are most familiar to us are remembered for other than contributions to theology: the politically minded Jonathan Mayhew, for example, or the brave John Peter Muhlenberg, or the egregious Manasseh Cutler, or the omniscient William Bentley. But it is not merely that men of talent no longer gravitated instinctively into the ministry; it is rather that deism supplanted piety and that virtue came to be judged by classical rather than Biblical standards. The passion that had earlier gone into the service of God was transferred into service to the commonwealth, and the expectation of personal immortality was transformed (is it possible to say sublimated?) into concern for historical immortality and for the welfare of posterity.

The confession of obligation to posterity can, of course, be merely a rhetorical flourish—doubtless it was in Jefferson's grandiose reference to "our descendants to the thousandth and thousandth generation." But no one who immerses himself in the writings of the men of that Revolutionary generation can doubt that it was genuine and pervasive. Remember Tom Paine's plea for independence: "'Tis not the concern of a day, a year, or an age; *posterity* are virtually involved in the contest, and will be more or less affected to the end of time." Or John Adams' moving letter to his beloved Abigail when he had signed the Declaration, "Through all the gloom I can see the rays of ravishing light and glory. *Posterity* will triumph in that day's transaction, even although we should rue it, which I trust in God we shall not."[6] Benjamin Rush recalled that "I was animated constantly by a belief that I was acting for the benefit of the whole world, and of future ages, by assisting in the formation of new means of political order and general happiness."[7]

No one appealed more frequently to posterity than Washington; nowhere is that appeal more moving than in the Newburgh address: "You will, by the dignity of your Conduct, afford occasion for Posterity to say, when speaking of the glorious example you have exhibited to Mankind, 'had this day been wanting the World had never seen the last stage of perfection to which human nature is capable of attaining.'"[8] Were the echoes of this in Churchill's mind when he spoke of "their finest hour"? And here is Washington's friend, Arthur St. Clair, accepting the governorship of the Northwest Territory in 1788: "I am truly sensible of the Importance of the Trust" and aware "how much depends on the due execution of it—to you Gentlemen over whom it is to be immediately exercised, to your Posterity! perhaps to the whole Community of America."[9] Or listen to George Mason's admonition to his children in his will: "If either their own inclinations or the necessity of the times should engage them in public affairs, I charge them . . . never to let the motives of private interest or of ambition induce them to betray nor the fear of danger or of death deter them from asserting the liberty of the country and endeavoring to transmit to their posterity those sacred rights in which they themselves were born."[10] Finally, here is Jefferson on the eve of death—and beyond mere rhetoric—to his friend James Madison, "It has been a great solace to me to believe that you are engaged in vindicating to posterity the course we have pursued, of preserving to them, in all their purity, the blessings of self-government which we had assisted in acquiring for them."[11]

A fourth common denominator of the minds of the late eighteenth-century Americans was education, formal and informal. It is customary now to disparage eighteenth-century education, to equate the colleges of that day with the better high schools of our own day, and to recall how few Americans were exposed to the advantages of formal education. Yet the products of the eighteenth-century educational machinery seemed to think more deeply (certainly in the political realm; and to write more clearly (in any realm) than the products of the far more elaborate educational systems of our own time. But again what is most interesting is that almost all the public men of that generation appear to have absorbed the same maxims of conduct, to have studied the same texts, to have subscribed to the same philosophical precepts. All of them knew Plutarch and Thucydides and Tacitus; all knew (at first hand or merely as the common sense of the matter) John Locke and Bolingbroke and Hume and Montesquieu. Almost every one of them might have said, with the Rev. Jonathan Mayhew, "Having been initiated in youth in the doctrines of civil liberty, as they are taught in such men as Plato, Demosthenes, Cicero, and other persons among the ancients, and such as Sidney and Milton, Locke and Hoadley among the moderns, I liked them; they seemed rational."[12] Almost everyone might have provided in his will, as Josiah Quincy did, that "I leave to my son, when he shall have reached the age of fifteen, the Works of Algernon Sidney, John Locke, Bacon, Gordon's Tacitus and *Cato's Letters*. May the spirit of liberty rest upon him."[13] How familiar the *Maxims of Civil Conduct*, which the youthful Washington learned; how familiar the long excerpts that went into Jeffer-

son's *Commonplace Book,* or that made up the substance of so much of
John Adams's *Defence of the Constitutions,* and *Discourses on Davila.*
Adams—as representative a figure as you can find in this generation—took
for granted the duty of the academies to inculcate virtue and the love of
liberty, and saw to it that the education which he arranged for his son
did just that. Thus the youthful *Dissertation on the Canon and the Feudal
Law* concluded with the appeal that "the colleges join their harmony in
the same delightful concert. Let every declamation turn upon the beauty
of liberty and virtue, and the deformity and turpitude and malignity of
slavery and vice. Let the public disputations become researches into the
grounds and nature and ends of government, and the means of preserving
the good and demolishing the evil. Let the dialogues and all the exercises
become the instruments of impressing on the tender mind . . . the ideas of
Right and the sensations of freedom."[14]

It is unnecessary to elaborate on what is so familiar. What is important
are the lessons that this generation drew from its study of the classics of
Greek and Roman literature and of the literature of English liberty. It
learned (the predisposition was there, of course) that the same rules of
morality operated at all times, in all places, and in all societies; that the
affairs of men were controlled by undeviating "laws of Nature and Nature's God," laws which neither God nor Nature could alter; and that
there was, in the words of Washington, "an indissoluble union between
virtue and happiness, between duty and advantage, between the genuine
maxim of an honest and magnanimous policy and the solid rewards of
public prosperity and felicity." And they learned that the first duty of the
good citizen was service to the commonwealth. "Every man in a republic,"
said Benjamin Rush, "is public property. His time and talents, his youth,
his manhood, his old age, nay more, life, all, belong to his country." And
Elbridge Gerry (something of an expert on the matter of public service)
observed that "it is the duty of every citizen though he may have but one
day to live, to devote that day to the service of his country."[15]

This was what philosophy admonished; this was what history taught.

History—almost inseparable from literature and philosophy—is a
fifth common denominator of the American mind, or character, in this
generation, a fifth influence beckoning or persuading men into the public
service.

Few aspects of American intellectual history are more astonishing—
perhaps we should say puzzling—than the contrast between political and
historical writing in the last quarter of the eighteenth century. For the
generation that gave us, indisputably, the most eloquent and profound
political treatises in our literature—the *Farmer's Letters,* the *Summary*

*View,* the Declaration of Independence, the Virginia Bill of Rights, the Virginia statute of Religious Freedom, the Constitution, the *Federalist Papers,* Washington's "Circular Letter," his Inaugural and Farewell Addresses come to mind—gave us not a single work of formal history that anyone but an expert can remember or that anyone, even an expert, can read except as an act of duty or of piety. Hutchinson's *Massachusetts Bay* is pedestrian; Gordon's *American Revolution* is plagiarized from the *Annual Register,* and so, too, much of Ramsay's sprightlier *American Revolution;* the Rev. Jeremy Belknap is interesting chiefly to antiquarians and local historians; Ebenezer Hazard was a collector; Noah Webster a dilettante; Mercy Warren lively but unreliable and amateurish; John Marshall's ponderous five volumes on Washington (much of it cribbed from other books) is universally unread. Only the grotesque Parson Weems wrote histories that survive, and everyone agrees that he was not an historian, that he really belongs in the Romantic era, and that his books are fiction anyway.

Yet no other American generation has been so deeply immersed in or preoccupied with history. Indeed, we might say with considerable justice that the Founding Fathers thought history too serious a business to be left to the historians. It was the concern of all, but especially of statesmen— just the view that Winston Churchill took all his life. If we want to read the historical writing of this generation, then, we turn to the writings, public and private, of John Adams, Jefferson, Madison, Franklin, Hamilton, Washington, Rush, Wilson, and others. And the great historical treatises are not the formal histories, rather such books as the *Defence of the Constitution,* or *Notes on Virginia,* or the *Federalist Papers,* or Wilson's *Lectures on the Constitution,* while commentary and interpretation of history run like a broad stream through the correspondence of most of the leading statesmen.

The evidence here is overwhelming: see, for example, the continuous rain of references to the experience of the ancient world in the debates in the Federal Convention and the State ratifying conventions, and the preoccupation with ancient history—and some more modern—in the *Federalist Papers.* All John Adams's major writings were historical, and so was much of what John Dickinson, James Wilson, and Madison wrote as well.[16]

But the view of history entertained by the philosophers of the Enlightenment was very different from that which had been accepted in the past, or which was to be embraced by the future. It completely repudiated the antiquarianism of the Annalists of the seventeenth century; it would have repudiated, just as convulsively, the narrative and romantic history of the nineteenth century and the scientific history of the nineteenth and twentieth centuries, which addresses itself to what actually happened.

Certainly what happened did not interest the historian-philosophers of the Enlightenment.[17] "Other historians relate facts to inform us of facts," wrote Diderot to Voltaire. "You relate them to excite in our hearts an intense hatred of lying, ignorance, hypocrisy, superstition, tyranny."[18] The tribute to Voltaire was just: "Confound details," that historian had said, and the reason was, clearly enough, that details tended to confound the historian. The same point of view is reflected in the statesmen of the New World when they turned their attention to history. "The sacred rights of mankind are not to be rummaged for among old parchments or musty records," wrote the youthful Hamilton. "They are written as with a sunbeam in the whole volume of human nature by the hand of Divinity itself."[19]

Particular facts, then, were of no interest or importance; only general facts. Details were insignificant and trivial; only general truths commanded attention. When Lessing reviewed Voltaire's *Essay on Manners* (a characteristic eighteenth-century title), he observed that "to know man in particular . . . is to know fools and scoundrels. The case is quite different with the study of Man in general. Here he exhibits greatness and his divine origin."[20] That is what the American statesmen-philosophers were interested in, man in general. "When in the course of human events," Jefferson began his great Declaration, and it is a breathtaking phrase. It is "the laws of Nature and Nature's God" that entitle the American people to "assume among the powers of the earth an equal station." The truths that justify this claim to equality are "self-evident" and apply to "all men" and to "any form of Government."[21]

So American statesmen, when they turned to the past, drew with equal confidence on the histories of Athens and Sparta, of Carthage and Rome, of the Swiss cantons or the low countries, of Anglo-Saxon England or Stuart England; it was all one. They had in fact no sense of place, as they had no sense of time; they repeated with Samuel Johnson (whom they otherwise detested):

> Let observation with extensive view
> Survey mankind from China to Peru;
> Remark each anxious toil, each eager strife,
> And watch the busy scenes of crowded life
>        —*Vanity of Human Wishes*

The laws of nature were everlastingly the same, and so, too, the laws of history, for the same laws that regulated the movement of the stars in the heavens regulated the movements of politics and economy on earth—the anxious toil, the eager strife, the busy scenes of crowded life.

And just as evolution was unsuspected in the natural order, so it was excluded from the historical. Progress, if it existed, was cyclical, or it was a happy parallel to the movement of the sun from the east to the west: it was as simple as that. The Enlightenment was not really interested in the past at all; in its sight a thousand years were as one, and if the thousand years did not yield a moral lesson, they were as nothing. The historians of the Enlightenment were like Diogenes; they went about the past with a lantern, looking for truth. They knew truth when they saw it, and brought it forth into the light, but they had no interest in what was not truth.

This is one reason they had so little interest in individuals, but only in the individual as a type, and they were always putting contemporaries into some historical niche. Washington was Cincinnatus, and Greene was Fabian, and Burr was Cataline, and Franklin was Solon, and so it went. It is no accident that the American Enlightenment did not produce a single biography of any value: Marshall's *Washington* was not really of any value, and Weems's *Washington* was not a product of the Enlightenment at all.

History, then, in the era of the Enlightenment, in America as in the Old World, addressed itself to great public questions, to broad general issues, to profound moral problems, and left the details to the pedants and the antiquarians. The historians of that day wrote on Man, not men; on the spirit of the laws rather than on specific laws; they gave lectures on the study of history, or commentaries on the Constitution, or provided a *Defence of the Constitutions,* or *Notes on Virginia.* When they submitted "facts to a candid world," they did so only as illustrations of a general principle, and it did not so much matter if the facts failed to illustrate the principle, for the principle was valid anyway.[22] The best of histories—the American in any event—were all designed to prove something: *Notes on Virginia* to prove the superiority of the American environment over the European; *Defence of the Constitutions* to prove the superiority of the Massachusetts Constitution to the kind of constitution celebrated by Turgot; the *Federalist Papers* to prove the adequacy of the new Federal Constitution; the *Rights of Man* to prove the necessity of revolution in Great Britain, and so forth. Thus, history was utilitarian, but only in a highly moral sense. It took the place of the Bible, and drove home truths which heretofore had depended for authority on the Scriptures.

But if human nature was always the same, and if history was regulated by the laws of nature, what hope was there that man and nature would be different in America? What reason was there to suppose that the

New World could escape the fate of the Old? That was a hard nut to crack. In a sense, it was the secular version of the familiar conflict between predestination and free will. Was there any room for the exercise of free will in American history? What a question to ask, in this New World whose very existence was a monument to the exercise of free will, in this new nation which had come into existence through a mighty effort of free will! What a question to ask of a people who were not only prepared to new-make the world, but were actually engaged in doing so!

History was not inexorable, nor was Man's Fate. History, rightly read, presented a spectacle of virtue as of vice, of weal as of woe, of triumph as of failure. The outcome depended on what man did with nature and nature's laws. More specifically, it depended on three things: the natural environment, the political and social institutions, and the character of the men who served—or betrayed—the commonwealth.

Environment was important, far more important in the New World than in the Old, where it had been tamed and brought under control. All Americans were by nature (as they still are) environmentalists, for in America environment triumphed over inheritance. It is the awareness of this that explains the almost convulsive reaction of so many Americans to the Raynal-Buffon theories of degeneracy in the New World. Those theories were not actually extreme, and Raynal at least apologized handsomely enough for his errors, but Jefferson and Franklin and others found them unforgivable.[23] For, to attack nature in America was to destroy the promise of American life. The expectations of future glory so confidently entertained by Washington and Jefferson and Paine and their colleagues were based in considerable part on the American environment. Nor was that environment a simple matter; it operated in two distinct ways to assure both America's escape from the evils that had afflicted the Old World and the promise of future well-being: both can be read luminously in the public papers of Washington and Jefferson. First was the sheer physical bounty of the New World—soil, forests, water, sheer size—"land enough for . . . the thousandth and thousandth generation." Second was isolation from the Old World; as Jefferson put it, we were "*kindly* separated by Nature from the exterminating havoc of one quarter of the globe; too high-minded to endure the depredations of the others." The isolation was not only physical but social, political, and moral as well.

Here, then, was something really new in history: for the first time a numerous and virtuous people were vouchsafed an ideal environment and were freed from the tyrannies, the superstitions, the injustices, the vices, the miseries that had for centuries made a shambles of the history of the Old World. But a rich and spacious environment was not enough. It proved, to be sure, that "by all its dispensations Providence delighted in the happines of mans," but—if we may shift to Washington (and why not, as the Founding Fathers are philosophically interchangeable?)—"there is still an option left to the United States . . . it is in their choice and depends upon their conduct whether they will be respectable and prosperous, or contemptible and miserable as a Nation." In short, everything depended on what Americans did with their environment. Everything depended on the institutions they established, the constitutions they wrote, the laws they enacted. Everything depended on the health and the virtue of society. Everything depended on the integrity and devotion of its leaders. Here is where history, properly read, was really useful. For history was the great school of virtue.

As early as 1749 Benjamin Franklin drew up a series of Proposals relating to the Education of the Youth of Pennsylvania. History occupied a central position in that scheme of education. Among many other things it would:[24]

. . . give occasion to expatiate on the Advantage of Civil Orders and Constitutions; how Men and their Properties are protected by Joining in Societies and establishing Government; their Industry encouraged and rewarded; Arts invented, and Life made more comfortable. The Advantages of *Liberty*, Mischiefs of Licentiousness, Benefits arising from good Laws and from a due Execution of Justice, etc. Thus may the first principles of sound Politicks be fix'd in the Minds of Youth.

And Franklin added that in a proper system of education,

The idea of what is true Merit should also be presented to Youth, explained and impressed on their Minds, as consisting in an Inclination joined with an Ability to serve Mankind, one's Country, Friends and Family.

Jefferson, too, thought that history occupied a central position in any scheme of education, because it taught the young the dangers of tyranny and the virtues of freedom. "History, by apprizing them of the past," he wrote, "will enable them to judge of the future; it will avail them of the experience of other times and other nations; it will qualify them as judges of the actions and designs of men; it will enable them to know ambition under every disguise it may assume; and knowing it, to defeat its views."[25]

This, after all, was but the common sense of the matter. Everyone agreed with Bolingbroke that history was philosophy teaching by example. Everyone read in Hume that,[26]

History tends to strengthen the Sentiments of Virtue by the Variety of Views in which it exhibits the Conduct of divine Providence. . . . A regard to divine Providence heightens our Satisfaction in reading History, and tends to throw an agreeable Light upon the most gloomy and disgusting parts of it.

Though the Americans did not know him, they would have agreed with the fascinating Dr. Zimmermann of Berne and Hannover, who ransacked ancient history to discover "examples . . . that shine as patterns to posterity," and that[27] "awaken in every noble mind an irrefragable sense of the duties we owe to our country; and the preservation of the history of these examples is nothing more than the propagation of that national pride founded on real advantages," and who concluded that confidence and self-esteem, based on familiarity with the historical past, "gives us the power to exalt ourselves above the weakness of human nature, to exert our talents in praiseworthy enterprises, never to yield to the spirit of slavery, never to be slaves to vice, to obey the dictates of our conscience, to smile under misfortune, and to rely upon seeing better days."

The historical-philosopher with whom Americans were most familiar (after Bolingbroke, in any event) was the extraordinary Dr. Priestly, clergyman, scientist, statesman, and historian. All knew his *Lectures on History* (they had gone through many editions before Priestly came to the United States), lectures prefixed by an "Essay on a Course of Liberal Education for Civil Life" and addressed to that lively young Benjamin Vaughan who later career was a monument to their value. Priestly's American friends could read in these lectures that history serves to amuse the imagination and interest the passions, that it improves the understanding, and that it tends to strengthen the sentiments of virtue.[28]

The chorus was harmonious; too, it was overwhelming; there were no discordant notes—none of any importance. History taught (that was its business) that man was master of his fate, that virtue could triumph over vice and reason over folly, and that the surest road to immortality was service to the commonwealth. The men whom history celebrated (it was the theme of the historians, the poets, the dramatists) were those who devoted their talents to their fellow men. That whole generations drew strength,

. . . not merely from twice-told arguments—how fair and noble a thing it is to show courage in battle—but from the busy spectacle of our great city's life as we see her, and remembering that all this greatness she owes to men with the fighter's daring, the wise man's understanding of his duty, and the good man's self-discipline in its performance—to men who, if they failed in any ordeal, disclaimed to deprive the city of their services, but sacrificed their lives as the best offerings on her behalf.

And they knew, too, that "the whole earth is the sepulchre of famous men; and their story is graven not only on stone over the native earth, but lives on far away, without visible symbol, woven into the stuff of other men's lives."[29]

That was the immortality they sought, and it was the immortality they found; it is impossible to doubt the sincerity of their detestation of the adventurers or soldiers who solaced themselves with private rather than public gain, as it is impossible to doubt their own genuine desire for retirement to their farms or their studies.

These then, were some of the circumstances, pressures, and considerations that help to explain the phenomenon of public leadership in eighteenth-century America. Talent was to be found everywhere, but in America it was directed, inevitably, into public channels. The zeal for service was to be found everywhere, but in America it could be satisfied on the public stage: who can believe that a Hamilton, a Gallatin, or a Wilson would have found scope for their talents in the countries of their birth? The philosophy of the Enlightenment flourished everywhere in the Western world, but in America it was given a chance to operate in the political and social as well as the moral and cultural realms, and that without the necessity of violence or revolution.

Eighteenth-century Americans assumed that history was philosophy teaching by example, and went far to prove it by modeling themselves on the examples they supposed—sometimes mistakenly—to be history. We no longer subscribe with any confidence to Bolingbroke's dictum, and even if we did we would be unable to agree on the selection or the interpretation of the examples. If we find history in general unusable in a direct or practical way, what of the experience of the Founding Fathers can we use in our search for leadership?

We know that all those who cry Lord, Lord, shall not enter into the Kingdom of Heaven, and we cannot take refuge in admonitions. Nor can we hope to lift ourselves by our moral bootstraps by an ostentatious search for values: our problem is not to define our values, but to realize them. Let us inquire rather what part of the eighteenth-century experience that provided our country with such distinguished leadership is or can be made relevant to our needs today.

First, we noted that in eighteenth-century America public careers were almost the only careers that were open to great talent. Today openings—indeed invitations—are innumerable, and talent finds more glittering rewards in private than in public enterprise. Can we do anything to tilt the balance back to public enterprise?

Certainly we can, if we will, do something to restore the balance in the purely material realm; in a society where prestige is associated with material status, that is not unimportant. We can and should pay salaries that do not impose too heavy a sacrifice upon those who enter public life. We can use the instrument of taxation to encourage education, literature, the arts and sciences, and to reduce the financial rewards of private enterprise. We have not sufficiently explored these possibilities.

Second, we can and should protect our public servants from some of the more ostentatious penalties that are now associated with public enterprise; we might even give them the same protection and immunity that is enjoyed by those who are engaged in private business. Not only is public service poorly paid: it is exceedingly vulnerable. Horace Greeley observed during the campaign of 1872 that he did not know whether he was running for the Presidency or the penitentiary; a good many politicians, not Presidential candidates alone, must have felt that way during recent campaigns: the "twenty years of treason" campaign comes to mind. The civil servant, even with tenure, is at all times fair game: fair game for demagogues making political capital; for Congressional committees which allow themselves a degree of irresponsibility unparalleled in Britain or Canada; for security investigators whose work—witness the Service and Condon cases—is never done; for journalists who yield nothing to these investigators in their contempt for privacy and for decency. If we are to encourage able men to enter public life, we may have to curb the self-indulgence, vanity, and sadism which now operate to keep so many people out of it.

Third, can we do anything to encourage a livelier awareness of posterity and our responsibility to it? Perhaps the situation here is desperate; after all a people who were really concerned for posterity would not produce so much of it! Yet here too something might be done by deliberate policy. Remember Pericles' boast in the great Funeral Oration:

Ours is no work-a-day city only. No other provides so many recreations for the spirit—contests and sacrifices all the year round, and beauty in our public buildings to cheer the heart and delight the eyes day by day.

It is but natural, Pericles added, "that all of us shall work to spend ourselves in her service."

We can, if we will, emulate the Athenians who built so splendidly that their citizens "drew strength from the busy spectacle of our great city's life" and that posterity, too, could delight in its beauty and its glory. We can do this by the deliberate support of those monuments and memorials which are designed at once to remind us of our responsibility to posterity and to remind posterity of its obligation to us. Instead of turning the hearts of our great cities into scabrous parking lots—as Boston is doing even now—we can use public and private money to build parks, squares, fountains, galleries, libraries, theatres, operas—whatever will keep constantly before the eyes of the young of future generations a sense of the

greatness of the city and of the spirit of those who built her. A society
that wastes its affluence in self-indulgence cannot expect to excite in the
young a passion to spend themselves in the service of the commonwealth.

Fourth, what role for education?

Eighteenth-century education with its emphasis on the classics and on
history was designed to instil in the young an avid sense of duty and of
civic virtue. The Fathers, we remember, were brought up on Plutarch
and Cicero, and read Locke and Montesquieu and *Cato's Letters*. They
saw history as a morality play whose acts unfolded in ceaseless progression, and themselves as cast in the roles of Solon or Aristides or Brutus or
Cincinnatus. Often they consciously displayed the antique virtues which
they associated with these Plutarchian characters.

It is an understatement that education and history no longer fulfil
these traditional functions. Can they be persuaded to do so?

Certainly not in any calculated way; to "use" history to inculcate particular principles, even good ones, is a dangerous business. But at a time
when the history of Greece and Rome and even of England have all but
disappeared from the school curricula, and when history itself is giving
way to civics, or current affairs, or "world problems," it is relevant to recall
that the men who fought the Revolution and wrote the Constitutions and
the Bills of Rights were brought up on the histories of Greece and Rome
and England. At a time when narrative history has given way to "problems" and when the celebration of heroes is regarded as a vestigial rem-
nant of Victorianism or a subtle attack upon the behavioral sciences, it is
relevant to observe that, if we deny young people the wonder and excitement of historical narration and of heroes, we cannot expect them to
respond passionately to the moral crises of our own time.

The eighteenth century, which vouchsafed us the most distinguished
leadership that any nation has enjoyed in modern times, can, then, furnish
us, if not with models and directives, at least with illustrations and guides.
Our eighteenth-century experience suggests that leadership is not fortui-
tous, that both formal policies and informal attitudes influence its appearance and its character, and that considerations of material rewards, prestige, opportunity, philosophy, and education are all involved in the
formulation of such policies and attitudes.

# Power / *Anthony F. Upton*

The introduction to this volume asserts that the relationship among concepts is uncertain and the role of the concept in theory building is unresolved. Some concepts appear to be related more closely than others. It is difficult, for example, to dissociate leadership from power.[1]

There is a considerable historical literature centered around the concept of power, which involves not only leadership but elite, mobility, and other concepts that relate to social structure. Dr. Jack P. Greene has used quantitative and career line analysis in studying power in the Virginia House of Burgesses.[2] William A. Reavis has written of power and elite mobility in Maryland.[3] Bailyn, Labaree, Diamond, Sydnor, and Klein, among others, have made important contributions to our knowledge of the nature of political power in the colonial period.[4] Professor J. R. Pole has analyzed power in Virginia in the early national period with reference to voting behavior.[5] A somewhat similar analysis has been made by Richard McCormick for the states of New York and North Carolina.[6] John Morton Blum's The Republican Roosevelt is an important study of the personal aspects of power.[7]

Power, in the writing of most of the historians named above, emerges as diffused rather than concentrated, as fragmented rather than the monopoly of an elite. Thus, Milton M. Klein views the power structure of colonial New York as less monolithic than Carl Becker, at an earlier date, believed it to be. Klein does not deny that politics in New York were controlled by a few families whose wealth and power derived from land and commerce, but he stresses the rivalries among individuals and families in pursuit of private interests—rivalries that were to some extent disruptive of class solidarity. As the eighteenth century yielded to the

Anthony F. Upton, "The Road to Power in Virginia in the Early Nineteenth Century," The Virginia Magazine of History and Biography, LXII (July, 1954), 259–80. Reprinted by permission of the Virginia Historical Society.

1. Janda, op. cit. See also William B. Hesseltine, *The Confederate Leaders in the New South* (Baton Rouge, 1950).

2. Jack P. Greene, "Foundations of Political Power in the Virginia House of Burgesses, 1720–1776," William and Mary Quarterly (October, 1959), 485–93.

3. William A. Reavis, "Maryland Gentry and Social Mobility, 1637–1676," William and Mary Quarterly, XIV (July, 1957), 418–28.

4. Sigmund Diamond, "From Organization to Society: Virginia in the Seventeenth Century," American Journal of Sociology, LXXXIII (March, 1958), 457–75. Bernard Bailyn, "Political Experience and Enlightenment Ideas," American Historical Review, LXVII (January, 1962), 341–42. Complete references are in Saveth, "Class," supra.

5. J. R. Pole, "Representation and Authority in Virginia from the Revolution to Reform," Journal of Southern History, XXIV (February, 1958).

6. "Suffrage Classes and Party Alignments: A Study in Voter Behavior," Mississippi Valley Historical Review, XLVI (December, 1959), 397–410.

7. (Cambridge, 1954).

nineteenth century, the sources of power became increasingly diversified.[8]

Historiography in recent years has tended to sustain that view of power, to which the bulk of the sociologists subscribe, as derivative from diverse sources and expressive of multiple interests. This is opposed to the theory of power elite advanced by the late C. Wright Mills and Floyd Hunter.[9]

It is unfortunate that the historical record does not reveal more about the nature of power. If rule and authority in the colonial period rested upon the dignity of the ruler and the deference of the ruled, then what is dignity and what is deference, and how are both revealed in interpersonal relationships? Data about the subtleties and niceties of power frequently do not come through in the historical record. In the article reprinted below, use of the papers of the Clopton and Campbell families enabled the author to view at close range typical techniques employed in the acquisition and, to some extent, the exercise of power in Virginia.

I N 1 8 0 0 A N E W G E N E R A T I O N of politicians was coming to maturity in Virginia. They were men who had been too young to participate in the Revolution and whose political experience was confined within the framework of the Virginia constitution of 1776 and the Constitution of the United States. These men were the heirs of the statesmen from Virginia who had so largely made the Republic and guided its early years. Their introduction to serious politics came, as it would have forty years earlier, when they sought the votes of their neighbors for public office.

Members of the House of Delegates, the State Senate, and the United States House of Representatives were alone subject to popular election.[1] On a convenient court day in April a poll was held in each county, which was presided over by the sheriff, or after 1817, by commissioners appointed by the justices of the peace. The candidates and the presiding officer sat on a platform either inside or outside the courthouse, and the voters came up and voted orally for the man of their choice in the presence of all the local notables and a large crowd of spectators. Refreshments were usually provided by the candidates and unless feelings ran too high, or drink flowed too freely, the occasion was a festive one. Only

8. "Democracy and Politics in Colonial New York," New York History, XL (July, 1959), 221–46; Carl Becker, The History of Political Parties in the Province of New York, 1760–1776 (Madison, 1909).
9. Robert A. Dahl, "A Critique of the Ruling Elite Model," American Political Science Review, LII (1958). Additional references are in n. 91, Saveth, "Class," supra.

white property owners might vote. In the case of the State Senators and the Congressmen, where the electoral districts comprised three or more counties, each held a separate poll, often on a different day so that the candidates might attend all of them, and the several sheriffs met later to add up the returns.

Before there could be an election there had to be candidates, and the choosing of candidates was a delicate business. The first factor to be considered was the incumbent of the office in question, and it may be said as a general rule, to which there must of course be exceptions, that he had a recognized right to continue in office if he so desired. The sitting member would often simply write to his friends and ask them to let it be known on court day, that he would be a candidate again,[2] or alternatively that he would not.[3]

This last was most important, since matters were held up until the wishes of the sitting member were known. In 1806, when "several influential Republicans" wanted to put a Mr. Harvie forward for John Clopton's seat in Congress, Clopton was asked whether he was resigning, as he had often hinted. Otherwise Mr. Harvie could not be brought to consent, and his friends were "anxious to begin the business of electioneering."[4]

The man who already held the seat had rights which it would have been both bad manners and bad tactics to ignore. John Randolph of Roanoke thought that his candidate should not even be whispered until the previous member was informed, it would have been "highly indelicate."[5] Once it was known that the incumbent would not stand again, the field was open to competition. Selecting a candidate was not easy, and the question of party politics played a minor part, for Virginia was a one party state in this period and Federalists were simply excluded. Most contests were between Republicans, not even between Republicans from different wings of the party, but between men who professed the same political views.

The ideal was to avoid a contest. In 1823 the Richmond *Enquirer* was taking pride in the fact that fourteen, or two-thirds of the Virginia seats in Congress, were uncontested.[6] In an election address written by David Campbell for a State Senate election in 1816 he says that the voters might be surprised that there were "two Republican candidates," but the members of the General Assembly from the district had met "to choose a candidate and named him [Campbell]." At that time there had been no objections, it was only later that his opponent, General Francis Preston, had declared himself. At Montgomery County Court Preston had suggested that they should ask some gentlemen "to say which of us should decline," but since Campbell felt that he was the official candidate, he would not give up his right. By this sort of gentlemen's agreement among

the leading men of the district, with the sitting members playing a prominent role, it was very often possible to avoid a contest.

However, if the local families were hostile for one reason or another,
or if they were too numerous for the available places, or too ambitious to
be able to compromise, then there would be a fight for places which would
begin before the candidates declared themselves openly and might last
until the last freeholder had voted. In such cases, the candidate had to
wage war on two fronts, fighting openly before the voters and privately
among the men of power and influence in the district.

The intensity of the campaigning depended on the nature of the opposition, but in general the candidate had to put in a few public appear-
ances and be present on the day of the poll. As early as 1785 Joseph Jones,
uncle of James Monroe, gave it as his opinion that it would be indispensable for Monroe to appear in person, at least for a few days before
the election, and on the actual day.[7] In 1830 John Clopton, Jr., wrote that
his proposed successor "has stated that he cannot mingle with the people,
or attend elections—and unless he attends the elections—I do not think
he could be elected."[8] This represented the bare minimum of campaigning, something more was usual.

Three techniques were commonly used in the public solicitation of
votes. First, to issue a printed address either as a circular, or published in
a newspaper, secondly, to deliver public speeches, often in open debate
with the opponents and most commonly on court days, and thirdly, to
make a personal canvass of the voters. When Judge Spencer Roane was
advising his son William how to conduct his election, he wrote:

Judge Brockenbrough will have published in the *Enquirer* and *Argus* of tomorrow a simple notification that you are a candidate. These papers will get to the
Bowling Green before Monday. I send also, 200 *short* printed addresses to the
Freeholders. It was written by Brockenbrough, and corrected and approved by
me. No doubt it will please you. Some of these may be stuck up in all public
places in the district; and the rest distributed in the form of letters, through
the district. Being addressed to the Freeholders generally, they will be thereby
gratified, while by endorsing them to influential characters, that will be a mark
of attention to them which will also please. . . . You had better go to Caroline
Court if possible, and where ever you go address the people in a short speech.
But if you do not go, make the proper arrangements, and perhaps an apology.[9]

There is no mention of personal canvassing in this letter, but John
Randolph used to ride around his district personally soliciting votes. "To
ask an humble voter for his support was galling to nature; but he must
do it."[10] It seems to have been considered better to leave it to friends.
In his election address previously mentioned, David Campbell accused
his opponent of paying agents to ride over the area soliciting votes, and

described them as descending in showers on the freeholders.[11] He obviously thought that such a practice would discredit the opponent.

A well established candidate could afford to disdain such devices. John Tyler wrote to his agent who wished him to come down and campaign, "my course is before them, and I have served them for three years, I should hope, therefore, that a personal canvass might be dispensed with."[12] Necessity was the criterion by which a candidate and his friends decided to campaign more or less vigorously.

Since all the candidates were usually Republicans, it is not always clear what issues the candidates fought over. Generally the contestants seem to have descended to personalities. Most of David Campbell's address was devoted to an elaborate defense against his opponent's charge that he had been instrumental in leasing a local salt works to outsiders, a most damaging accusation to judge by the vehemence of his denial.[13] John Clopton, Jr., was defeated for the House of Delegates in 1812 by an opponent who, as his father wrote, "urged against you the circumstance of your being a lawyer,"[14] but he does not unfortunately enlarge upon the subject of what was wrong in being a lawyer. Occasionally a straight political issue arose. John Taylor wrote to James Monroe: "In the senatorial district of Essex, King and Queen and King William, John H. Upshaw, allied to the powerful Roane interest, was turned out by a republican of inferior talents and connexions, but supposed to be less violent."[15] By this he meant not in favor of the war of 1812.

But the general unimportance of political issues can be seen in a letter of advice which John Clopton wrote to his son, who was standing for the House of Delegates. There were three candidates for two seats and since Clopton did not have an electoral alliance with either of the other candidates he preferred his friends to split their second vote. His father told him "not to side with either of them yourself," and if his friends pressed him which of the others to support "tell them that it is left entirely to themselves." Then the question of political opinions came up. "As to your political sentiments, let them never be suppressed when fit occasion requires, but always be expressed without reference to either of your competitors."[16]

Letters and campaign literature give the impression that it was enough to assert that the candidate was a Republican of irreproachable orthodoxy and if possible, that the opponent was not. This most damaging of accusations was used against David Campbell in 1816,[17] and John Clopton suggested that his son, who had been defeated, should strike back by calling his rival a Federalist.[18] This was rather mean, since the man was an old supporter of the Clopton family, and they knew very well that such a charge was groundless.

In many respects it was the private gathering of influential support which was the more important side of the campaign. It was usual for each of the leading men in the county to have a connection or interest, and the key to political success was the joining of these connections and interests into a sufficiently powerful coalition. One observer remarked that elections are "the ordeals by which you can test your friends and find out your enemies,"[19] and this testing of friends was the great business which most occupied the candidates.

The sitting member had an interest already formed, and this accounts for his very strong position, for if he did not need it himself, he could probably transfer it to anyone he chose. John Clopton, Sr., had a well organised connection in his district. This he had built since his first entry into Congress in 1796, and he was proud of it.[20] Looking through his letters, one finds about six or seven men in the district with whom he corresponded regularly, giving them news of developments at Washington, and receiving from them warnings about the manoeuvers of his opponents.[21] Clopton could then request them to thwart these moves by correcting malicious rumors, and usually his letters ended with some formula requesting the recipient to convey the contents to his friends and neighbors, or even read it out loud on court day. His son too had to do his share of keeping up his father's position in the district.[22]

The system of interests presupposes that a few men in any area were sufficiently influential to be able to sway the opinion of the district on the strength of their own declared preferences. It suggests that the humbler voters could be relied upon to follow the lead of their more powerful neighbors to some predictable extent, for the constant reference to a candidates' friends cannot mean all the people who would vote for him; it must indicate a few who could sway the votes of others.[23]

Thus, when it was a question of organizing opposition to a candidate, one of the first questions to be asked was who his active friends were.[24] Some of these men of influence were credited with being very powerful so that one or two were supposed to be able to carry the votes of whole counties. When Thomas Preston died in 1812, a man of great importance in the southern Valley region, it was said that his death might give that area to the Federalists.[25] Again, Major Richard Claiborne wrote to Governor James Monroe that in his county, "the personal influence of a few old Residents" was so strong that the people simply followed their lead "by habit or premeditation and perhaps not just reasoning."[26]

In the electoral districts comprising several counties, it was especially important to have powerful friends, for the people who did not live in the candidate's home county "were of course ignorant of the Candidate[s] from whom they had to make their choice."[27] When David Campbell was organising his campaign for the State Senate in 1816, he was fortunate in having relatives and friends in one of the counties where he was unknown. He set high hopes on these, reckoning that "if Mr. Russell can go over and personate me—and Uncle Fleener and Mungle will give their assistance, I will get all the votes in that county," and although another friend, Major Bowen, could not for some reason come out in open support, Campbell had the assurance that "all his relations are for me."[28]

The gathering of support in this manner was obviously a very personal process, and the reasons that led men to align themselves on one side or the other were probably equally personal. The ideal still was to avoid a contest. It was important for a strong candidate to declare himself in good time, for this would deter potential rivals from standing,[29] or one could try what flattery and ingratiation would do to bring an influential figure to give his support or defer making a bid for office himself at an unfortunate time.[30]

It follows that it is impossible to analyze the structure of an interest; the forces that held it together can only be surmised. The politicians in their letters simply state that some men are friends and others are not, the reasons for this were presumably well known to their correspondents. There is nothing at all to show why the lesser men followed the lead of the greater. The ordinary voter leaves no record of the motives that swayed his vote. One can imagine that he might be reluctant to offend a powerful neighbor, who might be a justice, with wide powers over the daily life of the county, or a lawyer who would be a useful friend to have, or a creditor.

Even the humblest voter was quite likely to have a personal relationship with the candidates. The voter was after all a property owner and by no means belonged to the lowest strata of society. He belonged in fact to a very select and exclusive group. The number of votes cast varies, a figure of 824[31] in Frederick County in 1824 is rather high. The general trend was for fewer persons to attend the poll as time went by. Westmoreland County, which in colonial times generally cast over three hundred votes was averaging only about one hundred in the twenties.[32] "In 19 elections held in nine counties from 1786 through 1800, the average number of voters was 299."[33]

In an election for the House of Delegates, the candidate would thus have only two or three hundred voters to consider, and in a district election three or four times that number. Therefore, the votes of the candidate's own family and relatives and of his friends and their relatives could be quite a substantial factor. When a man had finished his negotiations he knew fairly accurately what his chances were. But of course he could miscalculate. This would call for a deep analysis of the causes of failure.

The sad truth was that often the promises of friends proved worthless. John Campbell commiserated with his brother: "The conduct of some of the Delegates who thought proper to promise you their support has I have no doubt been as mean and as base as it could have been."[34] Sometimes a man was the victim of a trick. An opponent of John Clopton, Jr., who had been a supporter in previous elections, had on the strength of this got Clopton's friends to give their second votes to him. His own friends, however, threw away their votes on a third candidate.[35]

One would like to be able to cast a balance between the value of the candidate's open campaign and his private negotiations. If on the one hand it might seem that the public campaign was in the nature of a circus to put the voters in a good humor and get them to attend the poll, it is clear that there would not have been so much effort spent in printing addresses, stumping the district, and canvassing the voters if the election had really been tied up beforehand by private treaty. The candidate had to combine the two and without using one would probably have had little success with the other alone.

The ambitious man was unlikely to be finally satisfied with the offices which were in the gift of the voters. Once a man had got into the General Assembly he might hope to attain one of the range of higher offices which were subject to election by that body. These ranged from the Governor of Virginia, United States Senator, or General of Militia, through the hierarchy of judicial offices, the Privy Council down to the humbler posts like the clerkship of the House. The General Assembly was of course primarily legislature, but the objects of its legislation were in general of an extremely local and petty nature. In consequence the business of making appointments was far more exciting and interesting.

In general, competition was keen and lively. It is true that in 1811 there was apathy over the election of a new governor, but probably only because it was known that Monroe was a candidate, and it was hardly worth opposing him.[36] Even the choice of a sergeant at arms, who after all was really little more than a doorkeeper, brought forward six candidates and was the cause of an intense canvassing campaign among the members.[37]

Offices for which there was less competition included those of the judges. A good lawyer could make better money as an advocate than he could as a judge, and this caused at times a real dearth of suitable candidates. In 1811 there were only three candidates for one judicial vacancy and John Campbell wrote: "I have never felt more difficulty on a subject in my life—The above mentioned gentlemen were the only persons who would accept of the appointment—The characters of Johnson and Preston you know—Smith is a dunce. Now who would you have chosen? . . . I acknowledge that I chose between evils."[38]

The best sort of recommendation to public office was a good record of service: "If Colonel Preston wishes to be popular he must let himself down and come into the Assembly and like the great Monroe show a disposition to be useful to his country . . . you see nothing of flattery or manoeuvre about him . . . he is popular because he is useful."[39] For the higher offices it was expected that the aspirants would have shown some ability which would entitle them to consideration. One reason why James Pleasants was not elected United States Senator in 1824 was alleged to be that, "he has been the pet child of the state long enough without ever having done anything in the way of intellectual exertions to entitle him to such high claims on the public confidence."[40] A record of sound public service was a good recommendation, and failure to be reasonably competent could ruin a career. But one did not have to be as popular or as able as Monroe to be elected; the efforts of friends could make up for a great deal.

John Campbell once set out the conditions needed for election as a Chancery Judge. "If he were known in the legislature he could be appointed. Or if he were known intimately to some of the men of talents in the legislature I believe his chance would be a very good one . . . the members from the part of the country where Edward is known will vote for him. The Russell, Scott, and Lee members will vote for him. But you know that their representatives have no weight with the legislature."[41] In addition to such qualities as this it was useful to do a little tactful negotiation with members who were likely to be favorably disposed. John Clopton, Sr., told his son how this should be done: "If you can find a convenient opportunity with some of the members with whom you are best acquainted, (not the members from New Kent) bring up the subject of councillors and introduce such a sort of conversation as may lead to enquiry into their opinion of the law—and discover whether they think a member of Congress is eligeable. Suggest to them that you believe (as you may after receiving this) that if I were to be appointed in lieu of one of the others, who will be voted out, I would be willing to accept it."[42]

This procedure was rather like the business of angling for support in popular elections. The biggest single bloc of votes in the General Assembly was that of the western members. They were bound together by common interests and by their minority position. As they converged on Richmond from the mountains, pouring down "like the Goths and the Vandals"[43] they had a good chance to become acquainted and to exchange views. They could not be ignored by the easterners. Often they held a balance of power as in 1826 when their votes put John Tyler into the United States Senate instead of John Randolph.[44] Their power was recognized by others. When a big expansion of the militia was contemplated in 1814, it was asserted that: "Some pains must be taken to make it popular, to select all the Generals from this side of the mountains won't do."[45]

In 1821 David Campbell was trying to get his brother onto the Privy Council, where he had previously served many years. He discovered that as a result of this former service, it would not be difficult. David and his friends conferred and decided that if they could get the western members to give their support on the first ballot there would be no doubt of the issue. Accordingly two members from Washington County were approached and they undertook to get their fellow westerners to support Campbell's brother. However, the plan nearly went astray for it was discovered that one of the members from Washington County, Peter Mayo, was himself intending to stand for the Privy Council. David had to bluff them out of it: "My coolness and apparent indifference made Mayo and his friends believe John was much stronger than he really was . . . and they were deterred from asserting themselves."[46]

But even in the General Assembly, this sort of negotiation could not be relied upon to guarantee success. There had to be a public debate and this might upset things. Making a good nominating speech was worthwhile, but it was not invariably successful. John Campbell wished to bring forward the name of a friend of the family as major general of the militia.

"I said everything, I am satisfied, in his praise that any man could say with truth and perhaps more too . . . but all in vain.—The House thought proper to prefer old General Smith of Frederick who I am told is so deaf that he could not hear the sound of a cannon 100 yards."[47] In this instance Campbell showed himself either too inexperienced or too honest. A friend suggested that he withdraw his candidate and nominate the existing Brigadier as major general. He would almost certainly be elected. Then the original candidate could be proposed for the vacant place of brigadier, which would be better than nothing. Campbell refused this advice on the grounds that the Brigadier was too old and besides "had turned Methodist."[48]

The elements of success in the competition for higher office seem to have been good reputation, powerful friends, and skillful backstage bargaining. This process had its funny side. John Campbell once wrote: "This session may well be called the celebrated Session of Appointments. Such manuvering and intriguing you have no idea of . . . I shall keep you laughing a week if I ever live to see you again."[49]

Such a system did not work perfectly and some bad choices were made. They were particularly unlucky with their treasurers. John Preston was exposed in 1820 after he had extracted $152,594.65 from the public funds. This was quick work in three years out of an annual budget of only $500,000. He had got $50,000 from the literary fund alone, and the Privy Council, which was supposed to guard against that sort of thing, seems to have been somewhat negligent.[50] After that it is not surprising that there was some difficulty in finding a successor, as many persons who were nominated declined to stand for the vacant office. So by default Jerman Baker was elected.[51] He was rather unambitious for after eight years, when he committed suicide, his defalcations were variously estimated from twenty thousand dollars to forty thousand dollars.[52]

There were other defects to such a system; David Campbell thought that no state in the Union was so subservient to wealth and family as Virginia.[53] He was particularly annoyed by the election of a notorious drunkard to one post because he was the brother of James Madison. The members of the General Assembly very naturally elected their relatives and friends; and since there were over two hundred members by 1829, and all had relatives and friends, a certain amount of bargaining and intrigue was inevitable. At least the intense competition did something to give the advantage to men who had some distinction or reputation.

The Governor and his Privy Council could make a few appointments, although much of their power in this respect was nominal. The General Assembly was apt to keep a jealous eye on such rights as the executive still retained. W. C. Gooch remarked bitterly on this and declared of the legislature, "they love power and particularly power of this sort."[54] This tight control was not always unjustified. In 1808 the General Assembly, under the prodding of the western members, had investigated the Richmond Armory, whose managers were appointed by the executive. They were proved to have sold state property for their private profit and manufactured defective war material. Eventually the Governor himself was implicated. In this instance the General Assembly took the appointment of the manager into its own hands.[55]

In time of war the executive got much wider powers of appointment, particularly to the militia, and one member of the Privy Council expressed the gratifying situation which arose. "Everybody wants appointments and we poor councillors who afforded so much amusement to the Legislature a few weeks since are now hugged to death with affection . . . when we enter the legislature all seats are given to us in a moment. We scratch now in our turn."[56] But these were rare moments. The Privy Council was a poor sort of life for an ambitious man. It involved hard work, residence in Richmond even during the intolerable summer heat, and the irritating awareness that all the real power belonged to the General Assembly. It is not surprising that the chief attraction was the wages. Few men of distinction stayed on it for any length of time.

It would present an incomplete picture to describe the means of obtaining office if nothing were said of the sort of men who were elected or sought to be elected. They were mostly obscure men and to make a comprehensive study of what they were would be an immense task. However, by examining the notices in the *Biographical Directory of the American Congress,* one can obtain some idea of the type of men who became the personnel of Virginia politics, although this method has obvious limitations. Classified by occupations, they fall into three main groups. The first have no recorded means of livelihood but the ownership of a plantation, the second are lawyers, and the third are those who seem to have combined legal practice with ownership of land. Of course to stand for office every man would have to own some land or town property. Outside the main categories are a few doctors, surveyors, merchants, and soldiers.

The highest rank of political leadership is represented by the men who became United States Senators. In the period from 1789 to 1830 there were twenty-four such men, ten of whom also became Governor of Virginia. They had all received a college education except four. Of these, one was privately educated, one received a legal training, and the education of the other two is not recorded. Throughout the forty years the Senators were overwhelmingly lawyers by profession but usually also owners of large estates.

Probably the figures on the members of the House of Representatives are of more interest; there are far more of them, and they are much more representative of the average politician. Over the same forty years a marked change occurred in the composition of this group. In the decade from 1789 to 1800, 37.7 percent of the Representatives were lawyers, 11.4 percent lawyers and landowners, and 37.7 per cent were planters. In the decade from 1820 to 1830, the lawyers had increased to 45.6 percent, the lawyers and landowners to 17.3 percent, and the planters had declined to 10.8 percent. The members of other professions, though always a small minority, show a steady increase in the period. Thus the most marked trend is the decline of the political position of the planter and the rise of the lawyer, so that by the last decade the legal element among the politicians had risen to almost 63 percent of the whole.

This tendency need cause no surprise. The abolition of the laws of primogeniture and entail after the Revolution, combined with an almost continuous depression in the agriculture of the state were having a most damaging effect on the planter class that had supplied the leaders of Virginia in the eighteenth century. The rise of the legal profession to a position of leadership, even in the General Assembly was noted and deplored

by John Randolph, one of the last of the great aristocrats in Virginia politics. He wrote towards the end of his life: "I should as soon expect to see
the Nelsons, and Pages, and Byrds, and Fairfaxes, living in their palaces,
and driving their coaches and sixes; or the good old Virginia gentlemen
in the assembly, drinking their twenty and forty bowls of rack punches,
and madeira, and claret, in lieu of a knot of deputy sheriffs and hack
attorneys, each with his cruet of whiskey before him, and puddle of
tobacco-spittle between his legs."[57]

There is of course nostalgic exaggeration in this passage, but essentially the figures bear him out. Randolph knew what he was talking about,
and as one who most nearly resembled the vanished figures of colonial
days and tried to keep on their traditions, he naturally regretted the
change. However he was also oversimplifying what was happening. Not
all lawyers were "hack attorneys." In one of his essays, William Wirt,
himself a distinguished lawyer wrote: "Men of talents in this country my
dear S——, have been generally bred to the profession of the law: . . .
I have met with few persons of exalted intellect, whose powers have
been directed to any other pursuit. The bar, in America, is the road to
honour."[58]

All the lawyers did not concentrate their whole efforts on the profession. Henry A. Wise considered it essential to give his main effort to
farming, "to assist my quota of fees,"[59] and his biographer wrote: "His
life was that of the lawyer and planter combined, so common in the
country at that time. 'Such a lawyer,' as said a distinguished jurist of our
day, 'lived upon his farm, which he cultivated, and attended the courts,
without any strict devotion to business in his office.' "[60]

To conclude this point one can cite a letter written in 1811, which
suggests the normal course of the young Virginia gentleman after he left
the College of William and Mary. "He resolved to take the station in society which fame had prepared for him and display his talents at the
bar. Not indeed that he had any strong passion for the practice of the
law; but then it was genteel, and was besides the highroad to the House of
Delegates and Congress."[61]

It appears that the change from planter to lawyer as the main ruling
class was not so drastic as it might at first seem. The planter was not being
driven out by the lawyer; he was becoming a lawyer himself, and this
seems to have been regarded as the natural profession for the sons of
gentlemen.

Another approach to the subject of the personnel of politics is to try to
discover the attitude of the politician to his public service. Particularly it
is important to know how far this attitude was disinterested. There was a
degree of obvious attraction in entering public life, the prestige, power,

and esteem which it usually confers. But the politician might also be thinking of his private interests, and hoping to promote these through a political career.

When Jefferson was anxious to persuade William Wirt to enter Congress he did not at first mention financial inducements. He wrote: "The object of this letter, then, is to propose to you to come into Congress. That is the great commanding theatre of the nation. . . With your reputation, talents and correct views, used with the necessary prudence, you will, at once, be placed at the head of the republican body in the House of Representatives."[62] Thus the prospect of gaining power and influence, and rendering public service were the points most stressed.

In general there was no obvious financial advantage in entering politics: quite the contrary, a financial loss was regarded as inevitable. Charles Fenton Mercer would not enter politics until he believed "his fortune sufficient to secure his independence," and even then it proved insufficient, for his notes say: "He had entered public life with an ample fortune; he left it encumbered with debts which made his retirement an act of justice to his creditors."[63] John Clopton, Jr., reckoned as one reason for retiring that it would enable him, "to devote my exertions to the practice of the law and redeem myself from the pecuniary consequences of former negligeance."[64] When the politician had been a planter he had been able to attend the legislature in winter and look after his plantation in summer, but as Clopton found, the peak season in the courts tended to coincide with legislative sessions. In the end he had to abandon public life. He wrote the following resolution in his day book:

> I returned home from Richmond on Wednesday the 24th of February having previously declined public life from a consciousness that my private business was in great confusion and much behind hand from that negligeance which attention to public duty had superimposed and knowing that I am now in debt I feel the necessity of an effort to render the practice of Law profitable. . . . Whereas I declined public life in consequence of the great difficulties (amounting almost to an impossibility thereby thrown in the way of a due and proper attention to my private affairs, and feeling the necessity in my retirement, of an undivided attention to business, and a devoted and holy renunciation of the debasing follies of man,
> Resolved therefore that from and after this the last day of my public life, I will not at any time, or in any manner, play at any game of chance, nor will I ever drink any ardent or other intoxicating liquor except in case of sickness.[65]

One begins to see why public life was such a strain on the pocket. In the letter to Wirt, previously mentioned, Jefferson had to admit: "I will not say that public life is the line for making a fortune; but it furnishes a decent and honorable support, and places one's children on good ground for public favor."[66]

Wirt, who had a profitable practice, was not impressed by the prospect and replied that he could not accept as he had "a wife and children entirely unprovided for. They subsist on the running profits of my practice."[67] Indeed it was ten years before Wirt could be persuaded to take the post of Attorney General of the United States, and then he complained of the salary, only three thousand dollars, but since he could at the same time practice in the Supreme Court, where the fees are good,[68] he put up with it. However, Wirt was a parvenu, son of a Swiss emigrant tavern keeper, and always kept a sharp eye on the financial aspects of affairs.

Entry into public life was commonly regarded at the time as a sacrifice from a material viewpoint. But there are reasons for believing that for those who tried to find them, there were compensations. John Randolph at the end of his life, accepted the post of Ambassador to Russia from President Andrew Jackson. His estate, which was large, was also burdened with debt. "The receipt of salary and outfit," William B. Green remarked, "enabled him to pay all his debts and purchase the 'Bushy Forest' estate." Powhatan Bouldin, who knew him well, enlarged upon the point. "It was well known to his constituents that until he received this appointment he was exceedingly hard pressed for the means to meet his engagements. . . . The presumption, therefore, is strong that he accepted the appointment for the pay."[69]

Senator William Cabell Bruce, a more recent biographer, denies this charge,[70] but it is incontestable that Randolph was very generously rewarded for his brief and unfinished service, and that he had been in financial trouble.

When John Clopton, Sr., feared defeat, he wrote to his son, "There is an uncertainty of my being elected to Congress again should I be a candidate." He wanted a seat on the Privy Council as a sort of insurance which would enable the family to move to Richmond and "better means of yours and your brother's getting your professions and the girls their education"; he added that "the wages of a councillor" would be very useful.[71] When he was in Congress, Clopton found that it put him in a strong position. Thus in 1813 he heard of a vacancy for the post of principal assessor before it was generally known and was able to arrange that his son should get the place.[72]

If someone remarks that obviously these people were not in politics for their health, there is an example of someone who very nearly was. John Campbell wrote to his brother in 1811: "I have heard with much pain that you have not recovered your health yet. Would a session in the legislature be of benefit to you?"[73] The activities of the Campbell family bear study. They lived near Abingdon in the far southwest of Virginia, where David was clerk of the county court. Besides he was a businessman and a dealer in military land warrants. The rest of the family seem to have been lawyers and had spread into Tennessee and South Carolina. David Campbell was the political chief of his district, and the family as a whole made a very effective unit.

Second member of the family was David's brother John, and their rising fortunes really began with the entry of John into the House of Delegates in 1810. There began a long correspondence between the two and the first letter set the tone.

Dear Brother, The day before yesterday I received your letter in which you mentioned that an appointment in the executive council would be a suitable place for Brother Edward.

I am sorry that I did not receive the information of this sooner, I never heard Edward's opinion on this subject[74] and I did not know that such an appointment would be accepted by him—if I had known this at the commencement of the session I am satisfied by making his merits known, he could have been appointed. Today the election took place.[75]

However, John did not waste too much time making up for this initial slip. During his second session in the House of Delegates he secured a place on the Privy Council and prepared "to regulate his little business,"[76] for he was a lawyer. Once established himself, John set about providing for other members of the family. In January 1812 he was busy planning to make a cousin deputy marshal,[77] but the main business was to get David a commission in the army, for the war with Britain was about to begin. This involved seeking the aid of all the family friends and eventually succeeded, for David was appointed major and sent off to the Canadian border.[78] In July 1812 the Privy Council was preparing to survey part of the state line, and John wrote to ask whether Uncle Russell or brother Edward would like to be a surveyor. But since they could not clear more than one hundred dollars from it, the idea was dropped.[79]

David Campbell served through two campaigns in Canada and then his health brought him back in the beginning of 1814. He stopped in Washington on the way and did not waste his time, but started calling on the great men there and getting himself known. He told John, "No part of my life has been better spent for I do think that knowledge of this sort is almost essential to a public man."[80] On his return, John Campbell set about getting his brother elected a brigadier of the Virginia militia, which was being expanded. After some very intensive lobbying in the General Assembly, this was accomplished, only the coming of peace made it an empty triumph.[81]

By this time John knew everyone at Richmond of importance, and was able to assure his father that his lawsuit was in no danger for he had the "honor of being on terms of the most perfect intimacy" with the judges in the Court of Appeals.[82] About this time, the Campbell family quarrelled with their powerful neighbors the Prestons, and this caused David to be defeated when he stood for the State Senate in 1816. Worse followed, for the Prestons practically captured the government of the state when General James P. Preston was elected Governor of Virginia, and his brother treasurer.

This seemed to limit John's usefulness. He wrote: "The government is now in the hands of a family . . . a more odious and disgusting aristocracy never existed."[83] He talked without enthusiasm of returning to legal practice, but David had given him better advice to get some office which would support him comfortably before he left the council.[84] Once more the family resources were mobilized, people were written to and at length, President Monroe promised that John "should certainly be provided for."[85] After staying long enough to be able to offer to get James Campbell a post as principal assessor, John Campbell went to Alabama Territory, where he had been given some position and sat in the first constituent assembly of the territory and had hopes of becoming the first Secretary of State of Alabama, but failing in this he returned to Virginia.

Before long David Campbell, in the State Senate, had got John back on the Privy Council,[86] and he resumed his former course in June 1821. In the next two or three years, certain junior members of the family failed to live up to expectations. Arthur Campbell actually declined the office of deputy sheriff and John was astonished. "Was it offered to him? and could he have obtained it and was there anything to be made by it? If these questions could have been answered affirmatively I am astonished beyond measure. What in God's name are his calculations on the future!"[87] In the same letter, referring to a neighbor who was in the House of Delegates, John remarked that he had no business there, "he will never make money by it."

Edward Campbell was the black sheep of the family. At least four attempts were made either to get him into Congress or have him appointed a Chancery Judge, but he seems to have lacked ambition. In 1827 the family made every effort "to bring Edward out" but in vain.[88] The most significant development of these years was a growing friendship between David and John Campbell and General Andrew Jackson. The Campbells did not campaign for Jackson in 1824, but by 1827 David was busy swinging his county over to support the General.[89] John particularly seems to have caught the fancy of Jackson, and when the General won the election of 1828, there were high hopes of getting a job.

"Some of my Tennessee friends have been talking to Genl. Jackson on the subject,"[90] John reported, and he thought that he could have any place he wanted in reason. He was thinking of something like Secretary of Legation. He went on to tell his brother that other friends were "taking steps in relation to this matter by writing to their friends in Congress. You could write to Judge White and others." Having been a prominent Jackson supporter, John felt it would look bad if he openly solicited a job, almost as though he had been expecting some reward for his services, however, he added, "If you can throw in any aid in a delicate way, I would be glad if you would do so."

Finally, the post of Treasurer of the United States was offered to him, rather above his expectations. After a desperate search for securities, which the family put up, he and David went up to Washington to take possession. John Campbell had arrived at last and seemed well content with the prospect of three thousand dollars a year.[91]

It would be foolish to deduce from the history of the Campbell family that all the Virginian politicians of the day were quite so hard-headed in their attitude to their public service. What it does show is that to those who tried, there was money to be made in politics, and in fact it was possible to make a fair living as a professional politician. The extent to which this mercenary attitude had spread is a matter of speculation. William Wirt, whose own view was, to put it mildly, realistic, wrote in 1803 that Virginia "wants one most important source of solid grandeur; and that, too, the animating soul of a republic. I mean, public spirit. . . . There seems to me to be but one object throughout the state; *to grow rich*: a passion which is visible, not only in the walks of private life, but which has crept into and poisoned every public body in the state."[92] There was at least some substance to his statement.

The Cloptons, the Campbells, and John Randolph were not averse to receiving the due reward of their public services in hard cash. This is not to suggest that they were dishonest or corrupt in seeking office; they were all able and competent men, but one cannot escape the probability that the increasing prospects of making money out of politics and the possibility of making a career of it, must have affected the sort of people who sought office and their conduct of public affairs. A political career was tending to be less a public service, rewarded by public esteem and rendered gratuitously, or even at a loss, from a sense of social privilege and class duty, and more a useful way of earning a living for the politician and his family.

Charles Henry Ambler, a prominent authority on the politics of Virginia, regretted her adherence to Jackson in 1828. Her leaders he said, "began to play the political game as it had never been played before in the Old Dominion. They had thus fallen easy victims to the spoils system and to its methods. To their own and the great detriment of those who came after them, Virginia has followed . . . the lead of New York ever since."[93] It would seem that he overestimated the innocence of Virginia and did some injustice to New York. It does not appear from the story of the Campbells that Virginia had much to learn about the spoils system. The only new factor was that prior to 1824, a line of Virginia presidents made it possible for Virginians to get what they wanted in an easy and dignified manner. Under Jackson they had to fight and bargain for places, which was much less gentlemanly, but was in essence the same thing.

The Clopton and Campbell families, on whose papers this study chiefly rests, were not of the first importance in Virginia, neither were they insignificant. Their experiences were quite typical in all probability and suggest that the roads to power in Virginia during the three opening decades of the nineteenth century were outwardly the same as they had been fifty years earlier.

A recent work by Charles S. Sydnor[94] has shown that in the eighteenth century a few families in each Virginia county filled all the offices of local government and exercised an absolute power in their counties undisturbed by any outside forces. The representatives of these autonomous counties carried on the general government of Virginia on a quasi-federal basis in the legislature. By 1830 the county structure was unchanged, it had survived the Revolution intact; each was still controlled by a few families free from outside interference.

If these could agree together, power was shared, if they could not there were contests. Only rarely did outside forces, in the shape of national party issues disturb the traditional pattern of local politics. When they were assembled at Richmond in the legislature, the county leaders shared out the higher offices among themselves, electing their relatives and friends to posts they did not want themselves. As it had been in colonial times, there was little formal democracy in the process, it was rather aristocratic or perhaps oligarchical.

Two aspects of political life in Virginia had changed since the Revolution. Independence and the adoption of the federal Constitution had opened up new ranges of lucrative offices, which provided a material reward for the successful politician and which had not existed before the Revolution. Secondly, the rule of the great landowners was passing in Virginia. The Carters, Byrds, Fairfaxes, and Randolphs no longer dominated as they once had. Their sons had either moved west to new lands or turned to the law or business enterprise to prop up a ruined agriculture. But they still monopolized public life. Politics was still the preserve of gentlemen, but it might seem that in the process of change, some of the finer qualities which had made the Virginia planters such able leaders of the Revolution and the early Republic were being lost.

# Voting Behavior / *Lee Benson*

*Voting is interpreted by some social scientists as "not just as a ra-*
*ther unique kind of act in a democratic system but as one that brought*
*to a head a special kind of decision that persons are expected to make*
*in any number of contexts, such as committees and the economic*
*market place as well as elections. The integrative quality of the decisional*
*approach is most apparent at this level."[1] Richard P. McCormick is not*
*the only historian to suggest that the voter must enter into the traditional*
*accounts of American political history and that "studies of his behavior*
*hold some promise of adding a new dimension to our perception of the*
*nature of our democracy."[2] In the following selection, Dr. Lee Benson*
*evolves a theory of American voting behavior.*

T HERE IS OCCASIONS and causes why and wherefore in all things,"
Shakespeare assures us. Historians find it easier to accept that proposition in general than to apply it in particular. Human motives are so complex that even when we are able to reconstruct human behavior, we are
not necessarily able to reconstruct the "why and wherefore." Specifically,
to identify who in New York in 1844 voted for whom does not necessarily
enable us to explain why they did. But it does give us valuable clues. Put
another way, systematic classification of voters on the basis of attributes
such as membership in socioeconomic, ethnocultural, or religious groups
stimulates *questions* that may lead to credible explanations. The working
assumption of this study is that the question comes first, the "word"
comes later.

The study's research design has thus far been based on elementary
logic. Once historians know what happened and where and when it happened, it seems reasonable to believe that they are in a better position to
detect who caused it to happen. Going on to take another leaf from Sher-

Reprinted from *The Concept of Jacksonian Democracy: New York as a Test Case*, by
   Lee Benson, by permission of Princeton University Press, 270–287. Copyright 1961,
   Princeton University Press.
   1. Charlesworth, ed., "Limits of Behavioralism," op. cit., 23.
   2. "Suffrage Classes and Party Alignments: A Study in Voter Behavior," *Mississippi
Valley Historical Review*, XLVI (December, 1959), 397–410.

lock Holmes's book, we can say that once historians know *who* did something, they are in a better position to reconstruct motives.

For example, it is highly improbable that we must invoke Chance to explain these phenomena: 1) In New York, in 1844, "immigrants" voted overwhelmingly for one party, whereas "natives" tended to divide much more evenly. 2) The New British and New non-British displayed almost completely opposite voting patterns. 3) Catholics voted overwhelmingly Democratic, Protestants tended to divide evenly. 4) "Puritans" and "non-puritans" voted in significantly different ways. 5) Urban and rural voters tended to vote alike. 6) With certain exceptions, no significant relationships between voting behavior and economic class (or occupation) can be detected. But if Chance did not produce these phenomena, what did?

Transforming factual descriptions of who voted for whom into a series of questions constitutes, I believe, a crucial stage in research design and practice. It forces us to think concretely about why Protestant Irish and Catholic Irish citizens, for example, ranged themselves in opposite sides of the political barricades. Concrete questions of that order are more conducive to fruitful research than inherently vague speculations concerning the partisan behavior of otherwise undifferentiated men.

A well-grounded and well-developed theory of voting behavior, combined with concrete questions about group affiliations over time and place, would make it easier to interpret the 1844 New York results. Unfortunately, no such theory exists at present. True, from Plato's time to the present, we can find "sporadic disquisitions on the meaning, method and motivation of voting." And empirical studies have advanced almost countless hypotheses about the determinants of voting behavior. But as Samuel J. Eldersveld puts it, to date all such efforts "fall far short of integrated theory construction"[1]—a conclusion peculiarly applicable to American political historiography.

One response to the lack of a credible theory of American voting behavior might be to ignore it. Dispensing with attempts to develop a general orientation to voting, we might concentrate exclusively upon digging up empirical data relevant to the particular problems that attract us. Or we might concentrate exclusively upon theory construction before proceeding to empirical research.

In the present study I have rejected the notion that historians must choose between "integrated theory construction" and no theory. I have, instead, attempted both to develop some crude theoretical generalizations and to exploit clues provided by empirical identification of who in New York voted for whom.

## A. Some Crude Generalizations About American Voting Behavior

Other than Frederick J. Turner's frontier-section version and Charles A. Beard's class version of economic determinism,[2] the historical literature provides no set of interrelated principles to guide researchers attempting to organize the data of American voting behavior. One major reason for the popularity of the Turner and Beard theses is, I believe, that they give a semblance of order to what otherwise seems a bewildering multiplicity of unrelated "facts." No doubt the two theses have serious logical and empirical defects. But at least both men attempted to rescue American historians from metaphysical notions about the country's "divine democratic mission," or the "peculiar political genius of the Teutonic race," as well as from the intellectually sterile position of seeing the past as "merely chaos floating into chaos."[3]

It now seems clear, however, that credible interpretations of American voting behavior cannot rely upon either the Turnerian or the Beardian versions of economic determinism—a conclusion that in no way denies that their *search* for an overall theory entitles them to a high place in the American historical pantheon.

It also seems accurate to observe that American historians are now adrift on the sea of intellectual uncertainty from which Turner and Beard once seemed to rescue them. Fortunately, two books have recently appeared that may help us to attack the difficult problems of integrated theory construction. In a sense, what I attempt to do in this chapter is to consolidate and extend the complementary theses presented by Richard Hofstadter in *The American Political Tradition* (1948) and Louis Hartz in *The Liberal Tradition in America* (1955).

### 1. IDENTIFYING AREAS OF AMERICAN POLITICAL AGREEMENT

As is true of most significant innovations, after Hofstadter showed the way, we can discover earlier statements that resembled his thesis. But to stress precursors misses the point. Unlike earlier, vague statements, his book explicitly called for and gave strong impetus to a fundamental reorientation of American historiography. Breaking free from the Turnerian and Beardian frames of reference that focused upon political conflict, Hofstadter focused upon the "common climate of American opinion."

It is generally recognized that American politics has involved, among other things, a series of conflicts between special interests . . . and that it has not shown, at least until recently, many signs of a struggle between the propertied and unpropertied classes. What has not been sufficiently recognized is the consequence for political thought. The fierceness of the political struggles has often been misleading; for the range of vision embraced by the primary contestants in the major parties has always been bounded by the horizons of property and enterprise. However much at odds on specific issues, the major political traditions have shared a belief in the rights of property, the philosophy of economic individualism, the value of competition; they have accepted the economic virtues of capitalist culture as necessary qualities of man. . . . The sanctity of private property, the right of the individual to dispose of and invest it, the value of opportunity, and the natural evolution of self-interest and self-assertion, within broad legal limits, into a beneficent social order have been staple tenets of the central faith in American political ideologies. . . .[4]

Hofstadter's thesis is consonant with ideological clashes deriving from different conceptions of the proper balance of agriculture, commerce, and industry in a liberal capitalist society. Also consonant with it are clashes over the division of profits, or over the best way to develop and preserve a liberal capitalist society. That the slave segment played an important role in the American economy until the Civil War does not affect the essential validity of the thesis. Southerners were sometimes carried away by flights of rhetorical fancy when they discussed their "peculiar institution," but racist doctrines enabled most southerners to accept the shared beliefs of liberal capitalism. The rubric "peculiar institution" testifies to the exceptional nature of slavery and the extent to which it was regarded as outside the mainstream of American society.

Hofstadter simultaneously enlarged and sharpened our vision by giving new, substantive meaning to the old concept of American uniqueness. He saw that one of its major components was that throughout most of our national history, no significant group has challenged the *legitimacy* of a capitalist system of *political economy*. And Louis Hartz in effect extended the concept by focusing attention upon another major component of American uniqueness: wide agreement on the fundamentals of *political theory*.

The title of Hartz's book summarizes his thesis—the liberal tradition is *the* American political tradition.[5] In his reading, liberalism means the classic theories of John Locke unencumbered by "all sorts of modern social reform connotations." In that sense, "Locke dominates American political thought, as no thinker anywhere dominates the thought of a nation. He is a massive national cliché." And although Hartz nowhere explicitly defined liberalism in the "classic Lockian sense," he would presumably agree with George Sabine that "instead of law enjoining the common good of a society, Locke set up a body of innate, indefeasible, individual rights which limit the competence of the community and prevent interference with the liberty and property of private persons."[6]

As the critical determinants of American history and politics, Hartz emphasized two closely related factors: "the absence of feudalism and the presence of the liberal idea." He organized his book around a famous Tocqueville dictum: "The great advantage of the Americans is, that they have arrived at a state of democracy without having to endure a democratic revolution; and that they are born equal, instead of becoming so." Repeated frequently throughout the Hartz book, the phrase, "born equal," expressed the idea that Americans never experienced subjection to the "canon and feudal law."

Statements of an innovating, broad-ranging thesis almost inevitably sacrifice precision for impact. Thus, in my opinion, Hartz followed Tocqueville too closely and exaggerated the extent to which feudalism and the canon law have been absent, the liberal idea present, men born equal, and democracy has prevailed in American history. By the 1840's, however, as I tried to suggest earlier, the nation had essentially completed the transformation from a liberal aristocratic republic to a populistic democracy. And long before, America could accurately be described as a politically liberal society, in the "classic Lockian sense." After 1789, men differed strenuously on whether government should represent property or people; but restoration of a political system based on monarchy or hereditary nobility was unthinkable—and practically unthought of.

Although Hartz and Hofstadter concentrated upon different aspects of American political theory and experience, both have forcefully directed the attention of historians to the broad and deep areas of fundamental agreement that make the country relatively unique. In effect, they have viewed American history as the record of a liberal capitalist society, relatively unscarred by "feudal tenures, centralized and arbitrary government, a national church, a privilege-ridden economy, and hereditary stratification."[7] As I reformulate it, the combined Hofstadter-Hartz thesis holds that in the United States, broad and deep agreement has existed upon the very issues which elsewhere have provided the fundamental bases of political conflict, namely, form of government, relations between church and state, and system of political economy. Of course, there has always been some disagreement on fundamentals, particularly on church and state relations. But compared to elsewhere, disagreement in this country has been relatively narrow in scope and limited in intensity.

This does not mean that there have been no significant, profoundly experienced American political conflicts. Quite the contrary. Reversing Von Clausewitz, I am saying that politics essentially is war carried on by other means—even if men fight over nothing more fundamental than the expression of different ideas about how to achieve the same objectives. And, apart from short-lived insurrections such as the Shays' and Whiskey rebellions, the Civil War demonstrates that on at least one occasion

American political conflicts grew so intense as to require resolution by armed force.

Given the specific conditions of American historical development and the existence of a federal system of government,[8] rather than deduce that agreement on fundamentals will necessarily produce harmony, it seems more logical to deduce that agreement on fundamentals will permit almost every kind of social conflict, tension, and difference to find political expression. An almost endless list of such conflicts, tensions, and differences virtually compiles itself when we consider that the United States is relatively unique in the following *combination* of characteristics:

A country of continental proportions, it contains vast amounts and varieties of natural resources; it has been settled at considerably different times and in considerably different ways by an unequalled number of intermingled religious and ethnic groups from an unequalled number of different cultures; most of its inhabitants have been physically and socially mobile to an unparalleled degree; with certain exceptions at times and places, most of its inhabitants have had equal legal rights and opportunities to become "successful," and have been stimulated to do so by the strongest cultural imperatives.

In an extremely heterogeneous society whose members tend to have high personal levels of aspiration, with a federal government system and agreement on political fundamentals, it seems logical to predict that a wide variety of factors will significantly determine voting behavior and that political parties will function essentially as decentralized aggregates of state and locally based organizations. The prediction assumes that deep, sustained cleavages over political fundamentals would lessen the possibility that many factors operate to influence voting behavior; the absence of such cleavages would increase the possibility.

The theory may be summarized in propositional form: the wider the area of agreement on political fundamentals, the more hetrogeneous the society (or community), the larger the proportion of its members who have high levels of personal aspirations, and the less centralized the constitutional system, then the greater the number and variety of factors that operate as determinants of voting behavior.

Applied specifically to the United States, this proposition leads us to claim that all American history is reflected in past and present voting behavior. As a result, because it requires us to enlarge the range of data that we consider, I regard the theory derived from the Hofstadter-Hartz thesis as better designed than its predecessors to orient research in American political historiography. The theory does not focus attention exclusively or primarily upon disagreements arising from the simultaneous existence of different "stages of society" or clashing economic interests.

Rather, it assumes that in the United States, unlike other countries, almost every social conflict, tension, and disagreement may function potentially as a significant determinant of voting behavior.

If the assumption is granted, we can then deduce that a comprehensive theory of American voting behavior must satisfy the following requirements: 1) It should be consonant with the agreement on political fundamentals stressed by Hofstadter and Hartz. 2) It should not only identify but classify the kinds of determinants that have influenced American voting behavior. 3) It should specify the conditions under which certain determinants are likely to exert more rather than less influence upon voting behavior. 4) It should identify the kinds of voters most likely to be influenced by certain determinants under specified conditions.

I cannot even pretend to offer such a theory. In this book I try to do little more than make a start upon the problem, by trying to develop a compressed, crude, and incomplete classification system in which voting determinants can be more or less systematically ordered. Such a guide to research can, I hope, help to generate empirical propositions and thereby contribute to a general theory of American voting behavior.

## 2. WHY BOTHER WITH CLASSIFICATION SYSTEMS?

Historians who are skeptical of the value of scientific procedures when applied to refractory human beings in nonlaboratory or non-experimental situations, may ask Why bother with devising an abstract classification system? Why not concentrate upon finding out the actual determinants of voting behavior in specific situations?

In my opinion, a clear, logical system of categories helps to alert historians to the *possible* determinants of human behavior in specific situations. It is axiomatic that before decisions are made about the relative importance of any determinant, the range of determinants that may have operated in a given election should be considered. The record demonstrates that the axiom has not always been recognized. For example, I believe that lack of a comprehensive classification system has significantly contributed to the long dominance of economic determinism in American political historiography.

If we look only for "economic factors," we are likely either to find *only* economic factors or *no* economic factors at work. Collecting only certain limited types of economic data, we ignore the possibility that other determinants may have modified or counterbalanced the impact of economic factors. It seems reasonable to assume, therefore, that a comprehensive classification system can serve to guide us, and help to guard us, against such errors of omission.[9]

A set of comprehensive, clearly-defined categories serves as more than a check list. By providing a framework for ordering data in some systematic and logical fashion, it brings into focus relationships among empirical data that are not readily apparent.[10] Thus insights derived from seeing how one determinant influences voting behavior can illumine other determinants that have much the same effect. Conversely, recognizing the uniformities that link a number of determinants points up sharper distinctions among them and leads to fuller understanding of how they individually influence behavior.

No doubt a "gift" for historical research, a sense of the "human condition," and saturation in source materials enable some scholars who ignore "scientific procedures" to detect causal relationships hidden from others who faithfully use them. Genius makes its own rules, however, and I do not maintain that *all* historians need the aid of a formal classification system. But, particularly during the early stages of research, when assailed by impressions of multitudinous economic, political, intellectual, cultural, and social "forces" at work, it is likely that most historians see the world of human motivation as William James imagined that external sensory impressions seem to a baby: "one great blooming, buzzing confusion. . . ."[11] In seeking to find order and value among "minute particulars," all historians, whether they are aware of it or not, use some general principles of classification. Henry James says that the artist, searching for "hard latent *value*," should sniff "round the mass as instinctively and unerringly as a dog suspicious of some buried bone."[12] Perhaps. But the argument here is that most historians would find it helpful to combine the intuitive and the directed approaches.

## B. A Tentative Classification System for American Voting Behavior

At this early stage of development, the main function of the theory sketched above may be to widen the frames of reference of American historians. Two quotations from editorials by Horace Greeley transform the vagueness of "a wide range of factors" into a more concrete, vivid image of Americans behaving politically. The first quotation calls attention to a subtle process by which group voting patterns, originally shaped by a "political" issue (defined later), tend to be perpetuated after the resolution, or disappearance, of the conflict:

In Connecticut a good deal of sectarian bitterness exists and thousands of Episcopalians, Methodists, Universalists, etc., who would be Whigs almost anywhere else, usually vote Loco-Foco [Democratic] in Connecticut, primarily from hostility to the "Standing Order of Orthodox Congregationalists," who formerly were favored by law in Connecticut [disestablishment took place in 1818], who are still by far the most numerous denomination there, and who are somehow mixed up in the popular sentiments of the other sects with the Whig party; so that while an "Orthodox" citizen votes as *Political considerations* [italics added] impel him to do, a citizen of another church or no church is strongly drawn toward the support of the opposite party by considerations which have properly nothing to do with Politics. This side-current may not always be perceptible even to those drawn by it, but it is none the less potent for that; and we believe that not less than an eighth of the votes cast against the Whig party are influenced by variance of religious creed from the church with which the Whig party is in that State popularly identified.[13]

Systematically analyzed, the process described by Greeley falls into three stages. During the first stage, an issue (here church-state relations) generates intense conflicts until it is resolved by some government action, or until the issue ceases to command attention and disappears from the political arena. In the second stage, antagonisms aroused by the original conflict remain acute and influence voting behavior through the formation of what sociologists call "negative reference groups." That is, certain voters continue to range themselves against each other, even though the original political conflict is no longer an active issue (for example, Connecticut Episcopalians "vote against" Congregationalists after as well as before disestablishment). In the final stage, sufficient time elapses so that neither the original conflict nor the subsequent political antagonisms stemming from it are perceptible to contemporaries. Nevertheless, both factors continue to influence voting behavior in the form of *political roles* traditionally played by members of certain groups (for example, Connecticut Episcopalians vote Democratic because members of that group "always have").

A consideration not mentioned by Greeley deserves emphasis. During any one of the three stages described above, the emergence of another political issue that is related to the original conflict, or that pits the same antagonists against each other, reinforces established group voting patterns and makes them more visible to contemporaries. And, though not as directly, much the same results are produced by antagonisms originating outside the political sphere (for example, Episcopalian and Congregational denominational rivalries).

The next quotation is from an editorial by Greeley which also observed that voting behavior was determined by factors other than views on politicoeconomic issues. If a "real" political issue, such as the tariff, were forcefully presented to the workers in any machine shop or shoe factory in the Union, Greeley insisted, three fourths would vote Whig:

But the very shop wherein fifteen of twenty workmen would be with us on the Tariff issue fairly made and fully considered, will often give a majority *against* us in the absence of such discussion. Jones hates the Whigs, because Esq. Simpson is a leading Whig, and feels too big to speak to common people. Marks has been trained to believe that the Whigs were Tories in the Revolution and starved his father in the Jersey prisonship; so he is bound to hit them again at each election. Smithers is for a Tariff himself, but his father before him was a Democrat, and he isn't going to turn his coat. Smolker don't object to anything his Whig shop mates propose; but he is a Foreigner and thinks the Whigs hate foreigners, so he feels bound to go against them. Pitkin is a heretic in religion and most of the leading Whigs he knows are Orthodox; and he can't stand Orthodoxy anyhow you can fix it. And so, for one or another of a hundred reasons, *equally frivolous or irrelevant* [italics added] voters are piled up against us not for anything we as a party affirm or propose, but because of considerations as foreign from the real issues of the canvass as is the subjugation of Japan.[14]

### I. THREE CATEGORIES OF VOTING DETERMINANTS

In the quotation above, Greeley emphasized men's conscious motives. But, as the earlier quotation shows, he recognized that voting determinants operating on less conscious levels are no less potent. For our present purposes, the accuracy of Greeley's specific observation is immaterial. But his editorials illustrate how we can classify the determinants of American voting behavior under three main headings or categories. In time, I believe they can be developed to form an inclusive classification system; and dependent upon the specific elections and groups analyzed, we can devise subcategories for each of these three main categories:

1) *Pursuit of political goals by individuals or groups.* For example, the disestablishment of the "Standing Order of Orthodox Congregationalists" in Connecticut; the establishment of a protective tariff.

2. *Individual or group fulfillment of political roles.* For example, "Smithers is for a Tariff himself, but his father before him was a Democrat, and he isn't going to turn his coat"; Connecticut Episcopalians continuing long after 1818 to vote against the "Congregational Party."

3) *Negative or positive orientation to reference individuals or groups.* For example, "Jones hates the Whigs because Esq. Simpson is a leading Whig, and feels too big to speak to common people"; "Marks has been trained to believe that the Whigs were Tories in the Revolution and starved his father in the Jersey prisonship; so he is bound to hit them again at each Election." (The quotation would have exemplified positive orientation had it read: "Jones *likes* the Whigs because Esq. Simpson is an admirable man and he is a leading Whig.")

As is true of any classification, these categories are doubtless easier to distinguish analytically than empirically. But surely significant differences exist and can be recognized among these three types of alleged behavior: a) Connecticut Episcopalians voting before 1818 to abolish a State Congregational Church; b) men voting Democratic because their fathers voted Democratic and they weren't going to "turn their coats"; c) voting Democratic because they substituted the Whigs for the Tories who had maltreated their fathers.

A. PURSUIT OF POLITICAL GOALS. If, for our present purposes, we assume that Greeley accurately observed voting patterns, then a clear-cut political issue originally determined the voting behavior of Connecticut Episcopalians. They used political means to get the state to take "political action" which they regarded as beneficial to them, or to the community at large, or to both. Political actions are broadly defined here to include actions taken by any state agency in respect to laws, policies, rulings, government personnel, and government structure. Sometimes voters' choices (including no choices) are determined by their opinions of party positions on specified political actions, or a general, more vaguely-defined program of action; at other times, they are determined by the belief that the candidates of one party will carry our desired political actions either more effectively or more faithfully than will the candidates of another party. Whether the desired political actions represent grand "disinterested" measures, petty "selfish favors," or appointment of members of a particular group to a particular office, all behavior determined by such considerations is assigned to the category, "pursuit of political goals." Concrete examples may clarify the discussion and indicate how subdivisions can help differentiate voting behavior within the same main category.

According to this classification system, passage of a high tariff law and appointment or election of an Irish Catholic to high office are both defined as political goals. Desire for a high tariff exemplifies an economic goal, desire for appointment of an Irish Catholic exemplifies a status goal (that is, attainment of a political objective that would give members of certain groups greater power to command respect or deference from other members of the community or society). Though their motives differ significantly, men who pursue either one of those goals are seeking to get the state to take some action, or are approving some action the state has taken. In other words, their common desire for state action determines and links the behavior of men who pursue the different kinds of economic and status goals described above. (Of course, men can also pursue "nonpolitical" economic and status goals, that is, goals that do not require state action.)

For our present purposes, it is irrelevant whether voters are consciously aware that they are seeking political goals or whether historians can empirically distinguish among degrees of conscious awareness. The point is that, logically at least, a category can be created to encompass all voting behavior designed to produce specified state actions. By definition, therefore, voting behavior determined by other considerations is assigned to one of our remaining two categories.

B. FULFILLMENT OF POLITICAL ROLES. As the Greeley quotations pungently suggest, men knew and used the concept of social role long before social scientists invented the term. In this context, brief definition and exposition convey its central premise and indicate its usefulness to a theory of American voting behavior: "The ways of behaving which are expected of any individual who occupies a certain position constitute the [social] *role* . . . associated with that position."[15]

Individuals occupy many positions, however, and the great majority of them do not usually carry expectations of prescribed *partisan* political behavior (for example, males, husbands, adults). Moreover, role definitions vary, at least in the United States, and positions expected to produce certain ways of behaving politically at one time and place do not necessarily carry the same expectations at other times and places. In short, occupancy of a certain position constitutes a "political role" only when it is associated with clearly defined and recognized ways of behavior. Such roles, I contend, are unlikely to be deduced theoretically by analysts and must be discovered empirically.

In Greeley's description, Smithers' father was a Democrat in an era when sons were expected to vote for their fathers' parties. Thus, despite his agreement with the Whigs on a "real" political issue (tariff), he voted Democratic. Otherwise he would have regarded himself and have been regarded by others as "turn[ing] his coat," that is, not fulfilling his political role. It is worth noting that Smithers could conceivably have favored a protective tariff strongly enough to disregard the pressures exerted upon him by his political role. That he did not do so indicates, therefore, the relative importance he attached to his political role and to his political goal.

Establishing the category "fulfillment of political roles" makes it easier to discover in voting behavior essential similarities which might otherwise appear disparate. Men may vote in a particular fashion because they are their fathers' sons, because they are members of certain ethnic, religious or socioeconomic groups, because they reside in certain areas or political units, because they belong to and are loyal to a certain political party. Whatever the surface differences, at least two significant uniformities characterize the voting behavior that fulfills political roles. It is determined primarily by membership in a certain group or occupancy of a certain position and by adherence to tradition or habit rather than by a desire to have the state take certain actions or follow a less precisely defined general course of action.

Inconveniently for a fool-proof classification of voting behavior, men's motives in real life are less neatly compartmented and less easily distinguished than we should like. But lines of demarcation are universal problems for analysts. Whatever phenomena or objects are classified, whatever kind of system is used, borderline cases always cause trouble and blurring always occurs as one moves away from the extremes. Though historians can never dispense with judgment in classifying determinants of voting behavior, the argument here is that agreement is not always impossible. For example, significant differences clearly distinguish these phenomena: 1) Connecticut Episcopalians using political means to rid themselves of politically-established disabilities; 2) the same men voting for one party because their group has traditionally done so.

In both of these hypothetical cases, membership in a religious group determined how men voted. But in the first case, to attain their objective some specific state action was necessary. In the second it was not; they may well have voted for the traditional party of their group even though they preferred the program of the opposing party and thought its candidates were better qualified. Thus it seems reasonable and possible to differentiate between the pursuit of political goals and the fulfillment of political roles.

C. ORIENTATION TO REFERENCE GROUPS AND INIVIDUALS. Like the type of voting behavior assigned to the category "fulfillment of political roles," the type assigned to our third category is not primarily determined by a desire for specific state action. But it differs from the second type of behavior in a crucial respect: it designates men who behave according to patterns set by *groups to which they do not belong, or by certain individuals whose patterns influence them in determining their own.* The difference between those two categories is perhaps best suggested by quoting Robert K. Merton on the difference between "social role" and "reference group" theories:

That men act in a social frame of reference yielded by the groups of which they are a part is a notion undoubtedly ancient and probably sound. Were this alone the concern of reference group theory, it would merely be a new term for an old focus in sociology, which has always been centered on the group determination of behavior. There is, however, the further fact that men frequently orient themselves to groups *other than their own* in shaping their behavior and evaluations. . . .

In general, then, reference group theory aims to systematize the determinants and consequences of those processes of evaluation and self-appraisal in which the individual takes the values or standards of other individuals and groups as a comparative frame of reference.[16]

Unlike Smithers, whose vote was determined by his political role, Marks voted Democratic because he identified the Whigs with the Tries and wanted "to hit them [Tories] again at each Election." In Merton's terms, the Tories represented for Marks a negative reference group. Thus his behavior fundamentally resembles that of Jones who voted against the Whigs because he idetnified them with the arrogant Esquire Simpson whom *he* wanted "to hit again at each Election." But we surely are justified in saying that the behavior of Smithers, Marks, and Jones differed from that of Connecticut Episcopalians who voted to achieve disestablishment, or from that of iron manufacturers in Essex County, New York, who, we have seen, voted to secure a high protective tariff.

In an attempt to distinguish between such varied types of voting behavior, some political analysts have classified men as acting rationally and irrationally. In my opinion, such categories have value connotations that make them necessarily subjective and drastically limit their usefulness. That contemporaries and later historians have sometimes stigmatized men's behavior as irrational because it was designed to achieve objectives that *they* regarded as undesirable is not news. And that historians with different frames of reference frequently disagree about the rationality of exactly the same behavior is not news either. Why then employ categories more likely to compound than to reduce confusion?

The system suggested here makes two assumptions that may help us to overcome subjective influences: 1) Men try to act so as to maximize their satisfactions. 2) Different men achieve maximum satisfaction in different ways. These assumptions, of course, tell us nothing about the kinds of men who find maximum satisfaction in specified types of behavior, nor why they do and other men do not. That is not the point. The point is that from these assumptions it logically follows that equally rational men may find maximum satisfaction in widely different or directly contradictory behaviors.

Judged by the criterion of maximum satisfaction, for example, it may have been as rational for Marks to hit the Whig-Tories and Jones to lash out at the arrogant Esquire Simpson as for iron manufacturers to vote Whig in order to secure a high tariff. *The different objectives to be achieved, rather than the degree of rationality displayed,* is what intrinsically differentiates those two tpyes of behavior. And, I maintain, historians are more likely to agree about the different objectives men want to achieve than they are about the "rationality" of men's different objectives.

To act either in agreement with or in opposition to the pattern established by some other individual or some group other than their own is the objective of men whose voting behavior is assigned to this third category. By definition, therefore, the question of what determines the behavior of the reference groups or individuals is irrelevant; the relevant point is that they help to determine the voting behavior either of men who belong to other groups or of other individuals.

D. COMBINATIONS OF DETERMINANTS. It is worth repeating that the three main categories sketched above are more easily established analytically than demonstrated empirically. It is also worth noting that I do not regard monistic explanations of voting behavior as credible, whether the "single factor" is ascribed to all men or to specific individuals and groups. "No man," Coleridge observed, "does anything from a single motive." Thus the problem of interpreting voting behavior at a given time and place is always to decide which *combination of determinants* influenced voters identified by some attribute, or set of attributes. Under certain conditions, and in certain cases, it may be possible to give particularly heavy weight to one determinant or factor. But such assessments are not monistic. They recognize that other determinants contribute to the same result, although to a lesser degree.

# Public Opinion / *Dexter Perkins*

Before the emergence of public opinion as a field of social science inquiry, historians were aware of its influence. Ellis Paxson Oberholtzer's work contains numerous references to "men said" and the public attitude. These were estimated by Oberholtzer sometimes with reference to actual sources, especially those sources which suited his own biases, and sometimes with no reference at all.[1]

More meaningful historical studies of public opinion include Allan Nevins, American Press Opinion, Washington to Coolidge;[2] Joseph E. Wisan, The Cuban Crisis as Reflected in the New York Press;[3] Marcus Wilkinson, Public Opinion and the Spanish American War;[4] Dwight L. Dumond, Southern Editorials on Secession.[5]

In contrast to the materials used in traditional historical studies of public opinion—accounts of "American Attitudes toward . . . as Reflected in . . ." that are for the most part based upon newspaper and periodical sources—the pollster's materials are living people. The focal point of the poll is the questionnaire, based upon sampling theory geared to such variables as age, sex, occupation, and group adherence. Dr. Robert Kann has indicated how an historical study of opinion can be structured in the manner of a contemporary opinion study. Substituted for the questionnaire is "planned observation of group action or conclusive nonaction as found in or deduced from historical records."[6]

The historian is aware of the pollster's limitations, which have a direct bearing upon the use to which materials from polls can be put. Polls can go awry because of biased samples, ambiguous phrasing of questions, or casual attitudes of interviewers. The pollster is also aware of these problems and of the need to introduce into questionnaires a greater number of variables, and more probing in depth. There should be less concern with short-range and immediate issues, and a greater emphasis upon developmental trends. The latter would permit a future historian to deal with related rather than unrelated findings; with evolution in public opinion, and with the factors that induced change.

Dexter Perkins, "Was Roosevelt Wrong," The Virginia Quarterly Review, XXX (Summer, 1954), 355–72. Reprinted by permission, The Virginia Quarterly Review, The University of Virginia.

1. A History of the United States Since the Civil War (5 vols., New York, 1917–1937).
2. (Boston, 1928.)
3. (New York, 1932.)
4. (Baton Rouge, 1932.)
5. (New York, 1931.)
6. "Public Opinion Research: A Contribution to Historical Method," Political Science Quarterly, 73 (September, 1958), 374–96, esp. 381.

Finally, *polls must question more deeply than they now do to bridge the gap between attitude and action.*[7]

*In the following selection, Professor Dexter Perkins uses data from polls to illuminate a controversial historical problem.*

REVISIONISM MAY BE defined as an after-the-event interpretation of American participation in war, with the accent on the errors and blunders that provoked the struggle and on the folly of the whole enterprise. If we accept this definition, we shall certainly agree that there has been plenty of revisionism in the course of our history. The war of 1812 has sometimes been judged to have been futile and sometimes described as a war of intended conquest. The Mexican War has come in for harsh treatment as a war of unnecessary aggression. James G. Randall, one of the foremost students of the Civil War period, suggests that a less passionate view of the sectional problem might have made the conflict avoidable. Again and again it has been stated by reputable historians that William McKinley might have prevented the war of 1898 had he stressed in his message to Congress the very large concessions that had been made by Spain. The First World War was brilliantly represented by Walter Millis as the product of a blundering diplomacy and of economic pressures not entirely creditable. And since 1945 we have had a crop of historians, headed by so eminent a member of his historical generation as Charles A. Beard, attempting to show that the maddest folly of all was our entry into the conflict that ended less than a decade ago. Clearly, revisionism is an American habit; though, in saying this, I do not mean to imply that it is unknown in other lands.

The roots of the revisionist tendency are worth speculating about. Such a point of view, I take it, is particularly apt to find expression in a country where peace is highly treasured and where the glorification of war is relatively uncommon. Just as many Americans easily put away the hates and resentment of war at the end of the struggle and display a tendency towards reconciliation with the vanquished, so they tend to forget the passions that animated them and drove them into the conflict, and to view what at the time seemed reasonable and natural as something that with a little more forbearance or wisdom could have been avoided. And there are other factors that reinforce this point of view. Wars are apt to end in

7. Paul. F. Lazarsfeld, "Obligation of the 1954 Pollster to the 1984 Historian," *Public Opinion Quarterly*, XIV (Winter, 1950–1), 617–38.

disillusionment. After the glorious hopes of the years 1917 and 1918 came the clash of national selfishnesses at Versailles, and a distraught and threatened world. In 1945 the defeat of Hitler and Japan was soon seen to have left grave problems ahead. In the East, the American defense of China and the hopes of a strong democratic nation in the Orient ended in the victory of the Chinese Reds. And in Europe, though the peril from the ambitions of Hitler was exorcised, the United States found itself face to face with a new totalitarianism, far-ranging in its ambitions like the old. In such a situation it was natural to forget the menace that had been defeated, and to ask whether there might not have been a better solution to the problems that ended with the capitulation ceremonies at Rheims and on the deck of the *Missouri*.

After every large-scale war, moreover, there is a reaction against that strong executive leadership which is almost inevitably associated with periods of crisis in the life of the nation. This was true in 1920; and it was true after 1945. During the conflict the personality of Mr. Roosevelt loomed large, and almost immune from attack. But under the surface there was hostility, and this was to take the form of criticism of his war policies. Sometimes this criticism came, as in the case of Frederic R. Sanborn in his "Design for War," from one who had a strong animus against the New Deal, and who approached the record of the administration in the field of foreign policy with this animus. Sometimes, on the other hand, as in the case of Charles A. Beard, it came from one who regarded the Roosevelt diplomacy as jeopardizing and perhaps wrecking far-reaching programs of internal reform. In these two cases, and in virtually every other, strong emotions entered into the account. It has been a satisfaction to the revisionists to tear down the President; and there has always been—and it was inevitable that there should be—a reading public to fall in with this point of view, either from personal dislike of Roosevelt or from partisan feeling.

Revisionism, then, has roots in the very nature of the case. But, if we analyze it coolly, what shall we think of it? This is the question I propose to examine in this essay.

It seems to me fair to say at the outset that it is impossible to avoid the conclusion that revisionism is essentially history by hypothesis. It suggests—indeed in some instances it almost claims—that the world would have been a better place, or that at any rate the present position of the United States would have been happier, if this country had not intervened in the Second World War. Such a proposition can be put forward, but it cannot be established like a theorem in geometry. We cannot go back to 1939 or 1941 and re-enact the events of those stirring and tumultuous years. In a sense, we are bound by the past.

None the less, it seems worth while, even though we are in the realm of speculation rather than scientific history, to state the revisionist point of view. First, with regard to Germany, the point of view is advanced that the United States was in no essential danger from Adolf Hitler, that he demonstrated no very great interest in the American continents, that he desired until almost the day of Pearl Harbor to keep out of trouble with the United States, that there is no reliable evidence that he meditated an assault upon the New World. It is possible for the revisionist to go further. The ambitions of Hitler, it would be maintained, would have been checked and contained within limits by the presence of the great totalitarian state to the East. The two colossi would act each as a restraint on the other. It needed not the intervention of the American government to preserve the safety of the New World. As to Asia, the argument runs somewhat differently. Less emphasis is placed on the question of national security and more on a certain interpretation of national interest. The United States, we are told, had only a meager interest in China; its trade and investments there were insignificant, and were likely to remain so. They were distinctly inferior to our trade and investments in Japan. The shift in the balance of the Far East that might come about through a Japanese victory over Great Britain was no real concern of the United States. As to the Philippines, they might have been left alone had we stayed out of the war, or conversely, they were not worth the sacrifice involved in maintaining our connection with them. Such are the assumptions, implied, if not always expressed, in the revisionist view of the problem of the Orient.

Now some of the assertions in this rationale are unchallengeable. It is true that Hitler desired to avoid a clash with the United States until just before Pearl Harbor. It is true that the economic interests of the United States in China were inferior to our interests in Japan. These are facts, and must be accepted as facts. But there still remain a good many questions about the revisionist assumptions. For example, was there in 1940 and 1941 no danger of the destruction of British naval power, and would that destruction have had no unhappy consequences for the United States? Granted that the documents show great reluctance on the part of the Fuehrer to challenge the United States, would this reluctance have outlasted the fall of Great Britain? Granted that the Kremlin might have exercised a restraining influence on the Germans, is it certain that the two powers might not have come to an understanding as they did in 1939, and had at other periods in the past? Just how comfortable a world would it have been if the psychopathic leader of Germany had emerged from the Second World War astride a large part of the Continent, with the resources of German science at his command? There are questions, too, that can be asked about the Orient. Did the United States have no responsibility for the Philippines, and would the islands have been safe for long if the Japanese had dominated the Far East? Could the United States divest itself of all concern for China, abandoning a policy of nearly forty years duration and a deep-seated American tradition? Was the destruction of British power in this part of the world a matter of no concern to this country? Could the defeat of Britain in the East be separated from the fate of Britain in the world at large? These are extremely large questions, and it is a bold man who will brush them aside as inconsequential or trivial, or who will reply to them with complete dogmatism. Indeed, it is because they raise so many problems cutting to the root of our feelings, as well as our opinions, that they arouse so much controversy. Nor is there any likelihood that we can ever arrive at a complete consensus with regard to them.

We must, I think, seek a somewhat narrower frame of reference if we are to answer the revisionists with facts, and not with speculations. One of the ways to answer them, and one particularly worth pursuing with regard to the war in Europe, is to analyze the policy of the Roosevelt administration in its relation to public sentiment.

Foreign policy, in the last analysis, depends, not upon some logical formula, but upon the opinion of the nation. No account of American diplomacy in 1940 and 1941 can pretend to authority which does not take into account the tides of sentiment which must always influence, and perhaps control, the course of government. It is not to be maintained that a President has no freedom of action whatsoever; he can, I think, accelerate or retard a popular trend. But he does not act independently of it; the whole history of American diplomacy attests the close relationship between the point of view of the masses and executive action. A peacefully-minded President like McKinley was driven to war with Spain; a President who set great store by increasing the physical power of the nation, like Theodore Roosevelt, was limited and confined in his action; and Franklin Roosevelt himself, when, in the quarantine speech of October, 1937, he sought to rouse the American people against aggression, was compelled to admit failure, and to trim his sails to the popular breeze. These things are of the essence; to fail to observe them is to fail to interpret the past in the true historical spirit.

Let us apply these conceptions to the period 1939 to 1941. It will hardly be denied that from the very beginning of the war public sentiment was definitely against Germany. Indeed, even before the invasion of Poland, the public opinion polls show a strong partiality for the democratic nations. As early as January, 1939, when asked the question whether we should do everything possible to help England and France in case of war, 69 per cent of the persons polled answered in the affirmative, and the same question in October produced a percentage of 62 per cent on the same side. No doubt this sentiment did not extend to the point of actual participation in the war, but it furnished a firm foundation for the action of the President in calling Congress in special session, and in asking of it the repeal of the arms embargo on shipments of war in the interest of the Allies. The measure to this effect was introduced in the Congress towards the end of September; and it was thoroughly debated. There are several things to be said in connection with its passage. The first is that after its introduction there was a consistent majority of around 60 per cent in the polls in favor of passage. The second is that, though there was a strong partisan flavor to the debate, the defections when they came were more numerous on the Republican than on the Democratic side. It is true that, without the leadership of the President, the repeal could not have been enacted. But also it did not fly in the face of public sentiment (so far as that can be measured), but on the contrary reflected it.

With the fall of France there took place a deep and significant development in public opinion. This change the revisionists usually do not mention. They prefer to treat of American policy as if it were formed in a vacuum without regard to the moving forces that have so much to do with the final decisions. Yet the evidences are ample that in June of 1940 the American people were deeply moved. Take, for example, the action of the Republican nominating convention. There were several outstanding professional politicians in the running in 1940, Senator Taft, Senator Vandenberg, Thomas E. Dewey. Each one of these men represented a policy of caution so far as Europe was concerned. Yet what did the convention do? It turned to a relatively unknown figure, to a novice in politics who had, however, more than once declared himself as advocating extensive assistance to the democracies. The choice of Wendell Willkie as the Republican candidate for the Presidency is a fact the importance of which cannot be denied. It is worth while calling attention to other like phenomena. One of these is the overwhelming majorities by which the Congress appropriated largely increased sums for the armed forces, not only for the navy but for the army and the air force as well. Perhaps the American people, or the representatives of the American people, ought not to have been perturbed at what was happening in Europe. But the fact is that they were perturbed. They were perturbed in a big way. And the votes in the legislative halls demonstrate that fact.

Or take another example. The movement for a conscription law in time of peace developed rapidly after June of 1940. It developed with very little assistance from the White House. It cut across party lines. And it resulted in a legislative enactment which reflected the excitement of the public mind. How can we interpret the measure otherwise? Was there not a substantial body of opinion in the United States that feared a German victory?

Another important factor to be noted is the formation in June of 1940 of the Committee to Defend America by Aiding the Allies. It is highly significant that this movement arose at all. It is doubly significant that it found a leader in a Kansan Republican such as William Allen White. It is trebly significant that, once initiated, it spread like wild-fire, and that by September there were more than 650 chapters in the United States. And it is also to be noted that in New York there soon came into being a more advanced group, the so-called Century Group, which advocated war if necessary to check the aggressions of Germany.

And it is further to be observed that out of the Committee to Defend America came an agitation for what was eventually to be the bases-destroyer deal of September 2, 1940. This deal, by the way, was approved by 62 per cent of the persons polled on August 17, 1940, two weeks before it was actually consummated.

Let us go further. The next important step forward in American policy was the lend-lease enactment of the winter of 1941. This measure, it would appear from the polls, was based on a very distinct evolution of public sentiment. In July of 1940, 59 per cent of the persons polled preferred to keep out rather than to help England at the risk of war, and 36 per cent took the contrary view. In October the percentages were exactly reversed: they were 36 to 59. By January of 1941 68 per cent of those interviewed thought it more important to assist Great Britain than to keep out of war. And the lend-lease enactment, when presented to the Congress, passed the Lower House by the impressive vote of 317 to 71 and the Senate by 60 to 31. As in the legislation of 1939, though the vote again had a partisan flavor, there were more defections from the Republicans in favor of the measure than of Democrats against it. And there is something more to be added to the account in this instance. By the winter of 1941 the America Firsters had appeared upon the scene. A counter-propaganda was now being organized against the administration. Yet this new group, despite its vigorous efforts, failed signally to rally majority opinion. And Senator Taft, who represented the most thoughtful opposition to the administration, himself proposed a measure of assistance to Great Britain.

I shall treat a little later of the various measures requiring no legislative sanction which the President took in the course of the year 1941. But it is important to observe that throughout the period there was a strong public sentiment that believed that it was more important to defeat Germany than to keep out of war. This view was held, according to the polls, by 62 per cent of those interrogated in May of 1941 and by 68 per cent in December of 1941. As early as April, 1941, 68 per cent of the pollees believed it important to enter the war if British defeat was certain.

We should next examine the legislation of the fall of 1941. By this time the Congress was ready to authorize the arming of American merchant ships, and this by a heavy vote. The measure was passed by 259 to 138 in the House and the Senate amended it and passed it by 50 to 37. Congress was ready, more reluctantly, to repeal those provisions of the neutrality acts which excluded American vessels from the so-called war zones. It was moving in the direction of fuller and fuller engagement against Hitler. We shall never know, of course, what the next step would have been had not that step been taken by Germany. It was the dictator of the Reich who declared war on the United States, not the American national legislature that declared war on the Fuehrer and his minions. But in the period between 1939 and 1941 it seems safe to say that the foreign policy of the Roosevelt administration was in accord with the majority public opinion of the nation. It seems incontestable that the President was acting on assumptions which majority opinion accepted, and pursuing a course of action which majority opinion approved.

This circumstance is naturally either ignored or obscured in the revisionist literature. And what makes it easier to forget is the undeniable fact that Franklin Roosevelt was unhappily sometimes given to equivocation and shifty conversation. Very early, it is true, as early as the quarantine speech of October, 1937, he sounded the alarm against the totalitarians. Very often he stated his conviction that their continued progress presented a threat to the United States. On occasion he took his courage in his hands as, when at Charlottesville in June of 1940, in an election year, he came out frankly in favor of aid to the democracies, or in the declaration of unlimited emergency in the address of May 27, 1941. There is little doubt that he deemed the defeat of Hitler more important than the avoidance of war (as did many other Americans, as we have seen). Yet he was often less than frank in his approach, and the emphasis he laid on his devotion to peace was often excessive. He shocked even his ardent admirer, Robert Sherwood, in the election of 1940. His presentation of the case for lend-lease does not at all times suggest candor; indeed, the very phrase seems a bit of cajolery. With regard to the question of convoy, in the spring of 1941, he was clever and, though verbally correct, hardly wholly open in his approach to the problem. In the famous episode of the *Greer* (an attack by a German submarine on a vessel which was reporting its position to a British destroyer), he misrepresented the facts, or spoke without full knowledge of them. All this it is only right to admit. Yet we must not exaggerate the importance of these considerations. The country knew where it was going with regard to Germany. It accepted lend-lease as desirable. Of the patrolling of the ocean lanes which followed, the President spoke candidly in the speech of May 27, 1941. There was nothing clandestine about the occupation of Greenland or Iceland. The pattern in the fall of 1941 would most probably not have been much altered if Roosevelt had been more scrupulous with regard to the *Greer*. In the last analysis we come back to the essential fact that Roosevelt represented and expressed in action the mood of the country with regard to Germany.

The question is, I believe, more difficult when we come to examine American policy towards Japan. We can say with some assurance that the denunciation of the treaty of commerce of 1911, undertaken by the administration in July of 1939 as an indication of American displeasure with Japanese policy, was distinctly well received. Indeed, if the State Department had not acted, the legislature might have. We can also say that in August of 1939 there was an overwhelming feeling against sending war materials to Nippon. When in September of 1940, an embargo on the export of scrap iron was imposed, 59 per cent of the persons polled on this issue approved the step that had been taken. And in 1941 the number of persons who believed that some check should be put on Japan even at the risk of war rose from 51 per cent to 70 per cent between July and September, and stood at 69 per cent at the time of Pearl Harbor.

But we have fewer indications of the direction of public sentiment in the action of Congress, and no actual votes on which to base our estimate of how the representatives of the American people felt with regard to the important problem of our course of action in the Orient. We must, I think, speak less confidently on this question of public opinion than in the case of Germany. We must turn rather to an analysis of the policy of the administration, and to revisionist criticism of that policy.

First of all, let us look at some of the uncontroverted facts. We know that there were militarist elements in Japan. We know that as early as 1934 Japan proclaimed its doctrine of a Greater East Asia in the famous Amau statement. We know that in the same year it upset the naval arrangements made at Washington and London. We know that it set up a special régime in North China in 1935. We know that it became involved in a war with China in 1937. This, of course, was only prelude. The outbreak of the European conflict in Europe, and the collapse of France, offered to the sponsors of further aggressive action a great opportunity. The occupation of Northern Indo-China followed. In the summer of 1940, the impetuous and aggressive Matsuoka came to the Foreign Office. On September 27, 1940, there was signed a tripartite pact with Japan, which bound Nippon to come to the assistance of the Axis powers if they were attacked by a power then at peace with them. In other words, the Tokyo government sought to confine and limit American policy. In April of 1941 came a neutrality pact with Russia which freed the hands of the Japanese militarists for a policy of advance towards the South. In July came the occupation of the rest of Indo-China. The occupation of *northern* Indo-China made some sense from the point of view of blocking the supply route to the Chinese Nationalists. The occupation of *southern* Indo-China made no sense, except as the prelude to further acts of aggression. And in due course the aggression came.

Admittedly, this is only one side of the story. The question to be examined is, did these acts take place partly as a result of American provocation? Was it possible for a wiser and more prudent diplomacy to have avoided the rift that occurred in December, 1941? Revisionist criticism of our Oriental policy has been expressed in a variety of ways. In its most extreme form, it suggests that the President and his advisers actually plotted war with Japan. In its less extreme form, it directs its shafts at a variety of actions, of which I shall examine the most important. They are the conversations with the British as to the defense of the Far East, the commitments made to China, the severance of commercial relations, the failure to accept the proposals of Prince Konoye for direct conversations with the President, and the breakdown of the modus vivendi proposal of November, 1941. I shall examine each of these briefly, but let us first turn to the accusation that American policy was directed towards producing and not avoiding an armed conflict in the Orient.

It seems quite impossible to accept this view on the basis of the documentation. During the greater part of 1940 and 1941, it was certainly not the objective of the Roosevelt administration to bring about a clash in the Far East. On the contrary such a clash was regarded as likely to produce the greatest embarrassment in connection with the program of aid to Britain. The military and naval advisers of the President were opposed to it, and said so again and again. Even on the eve of Pearl Harbor this was the case. In addition, Secretary Hull was opposed to it. Ever the apostle of caution, he made his point of view quite clear almost up to the end. And as for the President, it is worth pointing out that on the occasion of the Japanese occupation of southern Indo-China he came forward with a proposal for the neutralization of that territory in the interests of peace, and that in August he frankly stated it to be his purpose to "baby the Japanese along." That he feared Japanese aggression is likely, almost certain; that he desired it is something that cannot be proved.

But let us look at the various specific actions which have awakened criticism on the part of the revisionists. In the first place I cannot see that staff conversations with the British were open to any objections whatsoever. If the object of the Roosevelt administration was to limit Japanese

aggression in the Far East, then it seems wholly rational to take precautions against such aggression, and surely it could reasonably be expected that such precautions would serve as a deterrent rather than as
an incitement to action. It is, in my judgment, rather distorted thinking
that regards such action as provocation. This is precisely the point of view
of the Kremlin today with regard to the North Atlantic treaty and the
European defense pact, or, to take another example, very like the contention of the Germans when they invaded Belgium in 1914. Because the
British had engaged in military conversations with the Belgians looking
to the possible violation of the neutrality treaty of 1839, it was claimed by
apologists for Germany that the violation of neutrality was defensible.
Where is the possible justification for such reasoning?

There is more to be said with regard to the breaking off, by the
United States, of commercial and financial relations with Japan on the
heels of the Japanese occupation of southern Indo-China in the summer
of 1941. Undoubtedly this created an extraordinarily difficult situation for
the government in Tokyo. Undoubtedly the cutting off of the oil supply
from the United States gave great additional force to the arguments of
the militarists. Undoubtedly, in the absence of a far-reaching diplomatic
arrangement, it presented a strong reason for "bursting out" of the circle,
and going to war. If the administration put faith in this measure of economic coercion as a substitute for physical resistance, its faith was to turn
out to be groundless. For myself, I have for a long time believed that
economic coercion against a strong and determined power is more likely
to produce war than to prevent it. But there are circumstances that ought
to be mentioned in favor of the action of the administration. It is to be
emphasized that the severance of commercial and financial relations resulted not in a breach of the negotiations with Japan but in a resumption
of those negotiations. It is to be remembered that Prince Konoye's proposal for a personal conference with the President came after and not
before the President's action. American policy by no means put an end
to the efforts of those substantial elements in Japan who feared a clash
with this country and who were laboring to prevent it. It must be pointed
out, also, that the alternative was by no means a pleasant one. At a time
when we were deeply engaged in the Atlantic, when we were being more
and more deeply committed with regard to the war in Europe, when our
domestic supply of oil might have to be substantially curtailed, the continuation of our exports to the Far East to assist Japan in possible projects
of aggression was a very difficult policy to follow. It may even be that it
would have proven to be totally impracticable from a political point of
view.

We come in the third place to the efforts of Premier Konoye to
establish direct contact with President Roosevelt. It is well known that

Ambassador Grew believed at that time, and that he has more than once stated since, that a good deal was to be hoped from such a meeting. And it is by no means clear why, if the objective were the postponement of a crisis, the experiment should not have been tried. Secretary Hull brought to this problem, as it seems to me, a rigidity of mind which may properly be criticized. In insisting on a previous definition of the issues before the meeting was held, he was instrumental in preventing it. While we cannot know what the result of such a meeting would have been, we are entitled, I think, to wish that it had been held. All the more is this true since it would appear likely that Prince Konoye was sincere in the effort which he made to avoid war.

But there is another side to the matter. We cannot be absolutely sure of Konoye's good faith. We can be still less sure of the willingness of the Tokyo militarists to support him in the far-reaching concessions that would have been necessary. And in the final analysis we cannot be sure of the ability of the American government to make concessions on its own part.

And here we come, as it seems to me, to the crux of the matter. It was the American policy in China that created an impassable barrier in our negotiations with Japan. It is necessary to examine that policy. From one angle of vision the patience of the American government in dealing with the China incident seems quite remarkable. There was a good deal to complain of from 1935 onward, certainly from 1937 onward, if one were to think in terms of sympathy for an aggressed people and in terms of the traditional policy of the United States with regard to this populous nation. The Roosevelt administration moved very slowly in its opposition to Japan. It made its first loan to Chiang Kai-shek in the fall of 1938. It denounced the commercial treaty of 1911 with Nippon only in the summer of 1939. And it embarked upon a policy of really substantial aid to China only contemporaneously with the signing of the tripartite pact in the fall of 1940. Its increasing assistance to Chiang is intelligible on the ground that to keep the Japanese bogged down in China was one means of checking or preventing their aggressive action elsewhere.

The fact remains, however, that it was the Chinese question which was the great and central stumbling block in the long negotiations that took place in 1941. Though the Japanese had entered into an alliance with the Axis powers, it seems not unlikely that, in 1941, as the issue of peace or war defined itself more clearly, they would have been willing to construe away their obligations under that alliance had they been able to come to terms with the United States on the Chinese problem. But by 1941 the American government was so far committed to the cause of Chiang that it really had very little freedom of maneuver. The various Japanese proposals for a settlement of the China incident would have involved a betrayal of the Chinese Nationalist leader. The proposal for a coalition government, a government of the Nationalists and the puppet régime of Wang Ching-wei, could hardly have been accepted. The proposal that America put pressure on Chiang to negotiate, and cut off aid to him if he refused, was by this time equally impracticable. And the question of the withdrawal of the Japanese troops in China presented insuperable difficulties. True it is that in October of 1941 the idea of a total withdrawal seems to have been presented to Mr. Welles by Mr. Wakatsuki, Admiral Nomura's associate in the negotiations. But the idea was emphatically rejected by the militarists in Tokyo, and perhaps there was never a time when they would have agreed to any proposal that at the same time would have been acceptable to Chungking. The American government had been brought, by its policy of association with the Chinese Nationalists, to the point where understanding with Japan was practically impossible.

This fact is dramatically illustrated by the negotiations over the *modus vivendi* in November, 1941. At this time, as is well known, proposals were brought forward for the maintenance of the *status quo,* and a gradual restoration of more normal relations through the lifting of the commercial restrictions, and through the withdrawal of the Japanese from southern Indo-China. At first it seemed as if there were a possibility of working out some such proposal. But the Chinese objected most violently, and Secretary Hull dropped the idea. In the face of Chinese pressure, and of the possible popular indignation which such a policy of concession might produce, and acting either under the orders or at least with the assent of the President, he backed down. We must not exaggerate the importance of this. There is no certainty that the *modus vivendi* would have been acceptable to Tokyo, and, judging by the Japanese proposals of November 20, there is indeed some reason to think otherwise. But the fact remains that our close association with Chiang was a fundamental factor in making the breach with Japan irreparable. And it seems fair to say in addition that our hopes with regard to Nationalist China were at all times, in 1941 as later, very far removed from political reality.

Let us not, however, jump to absolute conclusions with regard to questions that, in the nature of the case, ought not to be a matter of dogmatic judgment. If there was a party in Japan, and a substantial one, which feared war with the United States and earnestly sought for accommodation, there was also a party which regarded the course of events in Europe as a heaven-sent opportunity for national self-aggrandizement. That this party might in any case have prevailed, whatever the character of American policy, does not seem by any means unlikely. It is significant that in July of 1941 the fall of Matsuoka brought no change in policy in the

Far East, and that the so-called moderate, Admiral Toyoda, gave the orders for the crucial and revealing occupation of southern Indo-China in the summer of 1941.

Let us not forget, either, that after all it was the Japanese who struck. The ruthless act of aggression at Pearl Harbor was no necessary consequence of the breakdown of negotiations with the United States. If new oil supplies were needed, they were, of course, to be secured by an attack on the Dutch East Indies, not by an attack on Hawaii. Though there were strategic arguments for including America in any war-like move, there were strong political reasons for not doing so. No greater miscalculation has perhaps ever been made than that made by the militarists at Tokyo in December, 1941. By their own act, they unified American opinion and made their own defeat inevitable. It will always remain doubtful when the decisive involvement would have come for the United States had the bombs not dropped on Pearl Harbor on the 7th of December of 1941.

What, in conclusion, shall we say of revisionist history? There is a sense in which it is stimulating to the historian, and useful to historical science, to have the presuppositions, the conventional presuppositions, of the so-called orthodox interpreters of our foreign policy, subjected to criticism. There is surely some reason to believe that the candid examination of the views of these critics will, in the long run, result in a more accurate and more objective view of the great events of the prewar years and in a better balanced judgment of President Roosevelt himself.

But there is another side of the question which, of course, must be recognized. It is fair to say that virtually all revisionist history (like some orthodox history) is written with a *parti pris*. It is hardly possible to speak of it as dictated by a pure and disinterested search for truth. It is, on the contrary, shot through with passion and prejudice, with passion and prejudice that may spring from comprehensible or even good motives, but which are passion and prejudice none the less. It also rests upon hypotheses which, in the nature of the case, cannot be demonstrated, and assumptions that will, it is fair to say, never be generally, or perhaps even widely, accepted. As to its practical effects, there are no signs that the isolationism of the present era has important political effects, so far as foreign policy is concerned. Conceivably, it provides some reinforcement for partisan Republicanism. But even here it seems considerably less effective than the unscrupulous campaign of Senator McCarthy and his colleagues to represent the previous administration as one saturated with Communists. The urgency of present issues may make revisionism less of a force in our time than it was two decades ago. As to this, we shall have to see what the future unfolds.

# Image / *Rush Welter*

*Perhaps the most popular social science concept to be taken over by historians, especially those close to the American Studies movement, is image. This concept has been defined by Merrill D. Peterson as a "composite representation [of] ideas and ideals; policies and sentiments" associated with a man or movement. "The image is highly complex, never uniform and never stationary. It is a mixed product of memory and hope, fact and myth, love and hate, of the politician's strategy, the patriot's veneration, and the scholar's quest." An image is neither true nor false, but reflects and illuminates "evolving culture" which, within limits, it has the power to shape.[1]*

*That some images are received better than others is the result of congruence between the needs structure of society and the societal image as it was propagandized. Mr. Welter has dealt with both the needs structure and the image, in the article reprinted below.*

"IN EUROPE," Alexis de Tocqueville wrote in the second volume of *Democracy in America*, "people talk a great deal of the wilds of America, but the Americans themselves never think about them; they are insensible to the wonders of inanimate nature and they may be said not to perceive the mighty forests that surround them till they fall beneath the hatchet. Their eyes are fixed upon another sight: the American people views its own march across these wilds, draining swamps, turning the course of rivers, peopling solitudes, and subduing nature. This magnificent image of themselves does not meet the gaze of the Americans at intervals only; it may be said to haunt every one of them in his least as well as in his most important actions and to be always flitting before his mind."[1]

The French observer's description of American attitudes, antedating the homestead agitation and independent of the imagery of the yeoman farmer that supported it, admonishes us that we have not yet fully understood the image of the frontier West as a primary element of American social thought.[2] Indeed Tocqueville's statement is doubly significant, be-

Rush Welter, "The Frontier West as Image of American Society: Conservative Attitudes before the Civil War," *Mississippi Valley Historical Review* (March, 1960), 593–614. Reprinted by permission.

1. Merrill D. Peterson, *The Jefferson Image in the American Mind* (New York, 1960), VII.

cause it represents the opinions of ordinary men of affairs rather than literary figures, and because it is heavily influenced by the perspectives of conservative eastern spokesmen for American institutions, whom he mainly interviewed. On the one hand, the very emphasis it places on the difference between European images of a wild continent and American preoccupation with material conquest warns us that the predominantly literary antithesis between Nature and Civilization in the West that Henry Nash Smith has traced in *Virgin Land* may not have influenced the American people as much as their novels and some of their congressional rhetoric may suggest. On the other hand the statement also indicates that even during the early 1830's avowed conservatives in the East identified themselves with their emigrant countrymen's achievements in the West. If so, their sympathy with trans-Appalachian exploits reversed a tendency exemplified in several decades of eastern thought—echoed, as Smith points out, by many of the literary figures of the Middle Period—to fear and hence to deprecate the influence and prospects of the West in the growth of the American nation. Within two generations after the founding of the republic, that is, eastern conservatives were apparently ready to embrace a West they had begun by rejecting.

It is the purpose of this essay to explore in some detail this shift in conservative perspective, which had large consequences for American social thought. It was probably to be expected that spokesmen for the democracy of the Middle Period should have adopted the frontier West (and the frontier westerner) as an image of their hopes. It was less to be expected, and for that reason more significant, that self-conscious eastern conservatives should also have done so. By adopting new perspectives on western settlement, indeed, conservatives helped to define the terms in which the whole nation was to see itself.

The most obvious and at the same time the most useful starting point for an analysis of shifting conservative opinion of the West is the disapproval of western religious mores that eastern commentators, and especially spokesmen for New England orthodoxy, expressed near the turn of the century. Indeed Timothy Dwight, Congregational clergyman and for twenty-one years president of Yale College, has become famous for the harshness of his criticism of the early settlers of Vermont, whom he took to be typical of a wider class of frontiersmen. On the one hand he believed that they were "too idle; too talkative; too passionate; too prodigal; and too shiftless; to acquire either property or character," and he complained that they were "impatient of the restraints of law, religion, and morality," not to mention likely to grumble at taxes, "by which Rulers, Ministers, and School-masters, are supported." On the other hand he also believed that the New England virtues might yet flourish among the departed children of Connecticut and Massachusetts. But the very fact that he expressed hope for Vermont amounted by implication to a perpetual condemnation of other regions that were to be settled by immigrants alien to New England ways; and (for that matter) his experience even of Vermont offered slight encouragement. "Intelligence and piety flourished under the fostering care of those, who founded Connecticut [he wrote]. They are growing up in Vermont, in spite of their founders."[3]

A generation or so later three equally orthodox commentators were hardly more enthusiastic over the prospects of religion in the West. In 1828 an anonymous writer observed in the *Quarterly Journal of the American Education Society* that more schools and colleges and a better educated ministry were needed in the West "to dispel ignorance, check vice, and create a pure public opinion, favorable to sound morals and true religion."[4] In December, 1834, a western missionary addressed himself, in the columns of the *Quarterly Christian Spectator,* to the same problem. The West is not hopelessly lost, he explained, but it is susceptible to ignorant doctrinal innovations as well as outright heresy, and it requires the intervention of a trained ministry, which the East must in the first instance supply.[5] Eighteen months later the *Biblical Repertory and Theological Review,* discussing the qualifications for such a western ministry, made clear that in addition to heresy the West was troubled with dangerous forms of heterodoxy, which thanks to the influx of immigrants from many different lands threatened ultimately to destroy the republic. "It is evident [this essayist wrote] that we cannot be a mixed people and prosper. The permanency of our civil and religious institutions, and the happiness of all, demands that this mass of heterogeneous and discordant materials, be formed into one consistent and harmonious whole."[6] Neither the sense of urgency nor the apprehensions that gave rise to it were restricted to New England.

Yet despite the eastern prejudices that obviously colored such evaluations of the West, the content of the attitudes expressed by eastern critics had begun to shift. Nor was the shift merely a reflection of the obvious wish to do something about the West while there was still time. It was, for example, neither missionary zeal nor infectious fear alone, but apprehension partly lost in admiration, that led the missionary author to say in the *Quarterly Christian Spectator* that the immense extent, the unequalled fertility, and the future overwhelming influence of the west, are trite subjects. Every school-boy is by this time familiar with topics which have formed so large a part, not only of the epistolary eloquence and anniversary declamation of those who live there, and who may be viewed as interested; but of the more sober statements of judicious and unprejudiced observers.[7] Even eastern critics were compelled to admit (in the words of the *Quarterly Journal of the American Education Society*) that "Before the present generation shall have passed off the stage, the 'star of empire' will have taken 'its way westward,' and the consequence will be either a blessing or a curse, just in the degree that virtuous or vicious principles prevail among the people"; or to concede, with the *Biblical Repertory*, that "every thing is springing up and growing into maturity with a rapidity unparalleled in the history of the world."[8] If the hectic pace of western development stimulated orthodox fears, it also introduced something closely akin to pride into eastern contemplation of the frontier challenge.

The extent to which fear might turn into wonder was even more dramatically revealed in Lyman Beecher's *Plea for the West* in 1835. Like so many missionaries before him, Beecher had gone West to perpetuate orthodox New England belief, and the substance of his book was an appeal for funds in support of Lane Theological Seminary in in Cincinnati, while its chief mode of argument was an appeal to anti-Catholic prejudice. Nevertheless the volume opened with a tribute to the power and future prospects of the West that matched anything its most ardent sons had yet delivered. It is plain, Beecher wrote, "that the religious and political destiny of our nation is to be decided in the West. There is the territory, and there soon will be the population, the wealth, and the political power. The Atlantic commerce and manufactures may confer always some peculiar advantage on the East. But the West is destined to be the great central power of the nation, and under heaven, must affect powerfully the cause of free institutions and the liberty of the world." Moreover, Beecher was at least half convinced of the approach of the Christian millennium, which he thought the prosperity of American institutions would insure if Protestantism kept pace with the westward expansion of the country. Hence he came, almost inevitably, to associate the millennium itself with the American West. "The West," his apostrophe continued, "is a young empire of mind, and power, and wealth, and free institutions, rushing up to a giant manhood, with a rapidity and a power never before witnessed below the sun. And if she carries with her the elements of her preservation, the experiment will be glorious—the joy of the nation—the joy of the whole earth, as she rises in the majesty of her intelligence and benevolence, and enterprise, for the emancipation of the world."[9] A *Plea for the West* was striking evidence of the power of the West to move an essentially conservative imagination.

Nor was this exaggerated image of the West the property only of those who believed with Beecher in the advent of the millennium. The *Christian Review* acknowledged the appearance of a second edition of

the book by disavowing Beecher's millennial expectations, pointing to
evils abroad in the land that must prevent it from regenerating mankind.
Yet the Baptist quarterly's objection hardly diminished the luster of its
own vision of the West, for it quoted the whole of Beecher's millennial
exhortation (including the paragraphs above) with evident appreciation.[10] Moreover, in 1836 even a Boston Unitarian critical of western
mores was moved despite the rationality of his faith to adopt a view of
the West very much like Beecher's evangelical vision. Reviewing Mann
Butler's *History of the Commonwealth of Kentucky* and James Hall's
*Sketches of History, Life, and Manners in the West* for the *North American Review*, the Reverend James Freeman Clarke praised the western
character but objected to its excesses and its laxity. As Henry Nash
Smith points out, here was evidence that even a young and relatively
radical minister could not escape prejudices inherited from early New
England leaders. But there was also evidence of something else, for
although Clarke observed that "Religious restraint is needed, moral
principle is needed, wise guidance is needed" to discipline western
character, he concluded his paragraph and his review by invoking an
image of western perfectionism. "A deep reverence for truth [he said],
a profound respect for law, a ready submission to right, a loyal allegiance
to duty, these will make the western character as perfect as humanity
can ever hope to become."[11]

Clarke's reflections, like those of other religious commentators, indicated that even under the best of circumstances the new West would
continue to seem a burden upon eastern virtues; neither New England
nor the East as a whole would surrender its traditional religious authority
easily or gracefully, and any aberration in the West would produce
renewed concern over its safety and its morals. Yet his views also document the process of conversion that had undermined traditional eastern
fears of the West. On the one hand, conservative apprehension over the
heterodox West had stimulated ministers and other spokesmen for
eastern orthodoxy to adopt the West as a special field for missionary
endeavor. On the other hand, and although the missionaries went to
impart the true faith, the magnitude of their responsibilities came to be
matched in the eyes of eastern commentators by the magnitude of their
opportunities. In spite of eastern prejudice, and to some extent because
of it, the West conquered the imaginations of many of its most likely
detractors.

More significantly still, the very terms in which religious commentators were wont to critize western mores gradually became points of
approbation of the region. That is, whereas it had once seemed a reproach
to the pioneers that they fled the settled East, abandoning its traditions

and careless of its institutions, their migration came in time to seem a measure of their achievement, and beyond that a mark of their country's future greatness. This process of redefinition is already apparent in Clarke's tribute to the potential western character as well as in Beecher's exaggerated hopes; it reached a climax some twenty years later in the *North American Review* for January, 1855, the Reverend Charles W. Upham described the whole peopling of the American continent as an act of social and political "regeneration" of which no man knew the outcome. Dealing primarily with the future of the West in the struggle between proslavery and antislavery forces, Upham went on to associate the fate of liberty in the world with its fate in the western territories. "It is obvious [he said] that no issue can possibly arise, more important in its bearings upon the future of America or of mankind, than that which determines the character of the people who are to occupy the region just described and the institutions of government and society to be established there. It cannot but decide the destinies of the continent, and the last great experiment of humanity."[12] If fear over the influence of the West motivated the eastern commentator, it took form nevertheless in a remarkable expression of belief in the West as embodying the mission of America.

Upham spoke for more than the ministry, however, for he had given up his pulpit in 1844 for reasons of ill health only to enter politics in 1848, and he was now a Whig congressman from Massachusetts. In other words, while his views marked a reversal of traditional religious prejudices against the West, they also reflected a reorientation of eastern political perspective. The shift of eastern attitudes toward the West as a force in American politics is as striking as the shift in religious perspective.

The political grounds of apprehension were already clear at the time of the Constitutional Convention. In his famous pronouncement, made during debate on provision for the admission of new states into the Union, Gouverneur Morris observed that "The Busy haunts of men not the remote wilderness, was the proper school of political Talents. If the Western people get the power into their hands they will ruin the Atlantic interests. The Back members are always most averse to the best measures." Subsequently Elbridge Gerry made much the same point, and even George Mason, speaking in behalf of the equal rights of states not yet founded, conceded that "If it were possible by just means to prevent emigrations to the Western Country, it might be good policy," only to explain, "But go the people will as they find it for their interest, and the best policy is to treat them with that equality which will make them friends not enemies."[13] In political terms the West seemed a problem even when it did not present an overt threat to the East.

As Mason's argument suggests, one cause of eastern apprehension in 1787 was a feeling that Spain might either detach the trans-Appalachian settlements from the United States or cause them to involve the new nation in hazardous diplomatic controversies over the navigation of the Mississippi. In 1803, therefore, the acquisition of Louisiana should have seemed a sound political and diplomatic measure; but it elicited instead an opposition reminiscent of Morris and Gerry. During the debate that followed President Jefferson's message recommending the Louisiana Purchase to Congress, for instance, both Representative Roger Griswold of Connecticut and Representative Thomas Griffin of Virginia were struck with the political imbalance that the new territory would ultimately create. By the same token, Senator Samuel White of Delaware would not be reconciled to the purchase even if an attempt were made to contain the frontier population by establishing a permanent Indian reserve on the west bank of the Mississippi, for any prohibition on settlement would be useless, while the inevitable dispersion of population would be ruinous to national interests.[14] Indeed Fisher Ames, commenting privately at the time, expressed a prevalent conservative view in his celebrated epitaph for the republic: "Our country is too big for union, too sordid for patriotism, too democratic for liberty."[15]

During the course of his travels, meanwhile, Timothy Dwight had found no more reason to suppose that western politics would prove acceptable than to trust western morals. In a new society, he pointed out, political influence "is chiefly gained by those, who directly seek it: and these in almost all instances are the ardent and bustling. Such men make bold pretensions to qualities, which they do not possess; clamour every where about liberty, and rights; are patriots of course, and jealous of the encroachments of those in power; thrum over, incessantly, the importance of public economy; stigmatize every just and honourable public expenditure, arraign the integrity of those, whose wisdom is undisputed, and the wisdom of those, whose integrity cannot be questioned; and profess, universally, the very principles, and feelings, of him, with whom they are conversing." Yet in an equally invidious characterization of the "class of men" who "have already straggled onward from New England, as well as from other parts of the Union, to Louisiana," Dwight strikingly reversed the political argument against emigration. Restless idlers constantly threaten the stability of free institutions, he said, and even New England's institutions have not been able to prevent their "noxious disposition" to be unruly. "In mercy, therefore, to the sober, industrious, and well-disposed, inhabitants," he concluded his harangue, "Providence has opened in the vast Western wilderness a retreat, sufficiently alluring to draw them away from the land of their nativity. We have many troubles even now: but we should have many more, if this body of foresters had remained at home."[16]

The full significance of Dwight's political reflections lay in the future, when his bitterly critical characterization of the western democrat would give away to a positive national identification with precisely the traits Dwight had condemned. Yet his conception of a western safety-value for eastern political institutions already served to present the new West in a perspective that threatened to undermine conservative fears. Dwight did not temper his prejudices, which operated indiscriminately to cloud his political as well as his religious judgment of the West, but in restating the role of the West he also restated its significance for the East. Already, under impeccable auspices, a process of conservative redefinition was in progress.

One of the ways in which that redefinition went on during succeeding decades was a practice that eastern commentators adopted of speaking about the the West as a testing-ground for, rather than simply as a threat to, established republican institutions. Reviewing Timothy Flint's *Recollections of the Last Ten Years, Passed in Occasional Residences and Journeyings in the Valley of the Mississippi* for the *North American Review* in 1826, for example, James Flint observed that the new West "presents a fruitful theme of anxious contemplation and prophetic conjecture to the statesman and philanthropist," both as the "destined theatre" of events to come and as the scene of the "future trial" of the principles of free government and religious toleration adopted by the federal constitution.[17] In conceding that a political experiment was in progress, of course, Flint acknowledged the possibility of a good as well as an evil outcome. By 1829, indeed, the *American Quarterly Review* was ready to say, in a review of the same author's *Condensed Geography and History of the Western States*, that the extension of republican institutions to the West had been an unqualified success. "The friends of civil liberty [it remarked] cannot but rejoice at the successful results of these experiments, tried as they have been in the wilderness, and under the most disadvantageous circumstances; for, if the elements of discord exist in our country at all, we should naturally look for them in new settlements, where people of opposing politics and various opinions, assemble from every quarter, and enjoy an equal voice in public affairs."[18]

This was, perhaps, too optimistic and too urbane a view of western political institutions to be wholly acceptable to eastern conservatives during the 1830's, and the text suggests that the anonymous reviewer may have been both a westerner and a democrat. Nevertheless the sense that the United States was successfully engaged in a great republican experiment also affected unmistakably conservative writers, and it opened the way to a significant restatement of Timothy Dwight's safety-valve theory. For Dwight, the only political virtue the West possessed was that it drew off trouble-makers from the East. But for Edward Everett, reviewing Flint's *Condensed Geography and History* for the *North American Review*, it was something else. While what he wrote was intended to say no more than that the westward movement of population demonstrated the liberality of American political institutions, he also implied that a continuing reciprocal relationship existed between western expansion and eastern freedom. "The young men [he said], who have emigrated from the Atlantic coast to the West, did not, like the emigrants from Ireland and the Palatinate, leave potato-fare and six pence a day behind them. On the contrary, they left a country of high wages and hearty diet. If emigration be the safety-valve of states, ours is calculated to open at a very low pressure; in others, the governments have loaded it with additional weights, threatening the most disastrous explosions."[19]

We shall consider the social and economic implications of Everett's statement in another place. What is important here is that the West has in its own right begun to take on positive political qualities that neither Dwight nor James Flint visualized; nor was Everett's doctrine the ultimate judgment of western influence. For within a dozen years at least one conservative easterner found himself acknowledging the republican habits of the West in terms that insisted upon westerners' shortcomings yet credited them at the same time with unique political virtues. In 1842, in reviewing Caroline Kirkland's *Forest Life* for the *North American Review*, Cornelius C. Felton of Harvard College observed that a "bold but not over-educated population" was growing up in the West, "with none of the restraints which fetter the characters of the working classes in other countries."

No feudal feeling [he continued] tempers the natural overflowings of passion, and restrains the growth of individual humors. The sentiment of loyalty to any thing except a political party, does not exist to bind them in respectful obedience to a head and representative of the sovereignty of the nation. Each man is himself a sovereign by indefeasible right, and has no idea that another is his better in any one respect. Manners are, therefore, of the most unrestrained sort, and one accustomed to the conventions, and deferences, and distinctions, that have grown up even in our republican cities, is apt to find himself annoyed and embarrassed, when he gets into a circle of these tree-destroying sovereigns. But there are compensations for these things. There is more activity and stir in one of these new communities than in the ancient towns. Public affairs more engross the minds of men, and are more discussed, within doors and without. Poetry and art,—music, sculpture and painting,—the last new novel, to-morrow evening's concert, last evening's "Lowell Lecture," are things unheard of; but political disquisitions, not always of the wisest, stump speeches, the affairs of the town, county, or state, and the pretensions of rival candidates, are vehemently argued.

After a visit to the West, one cannot but be struck with the comparative apathy of the New England people. We look with wonder on communities of men who attend to their own business, and seem to care but little who is made President of the United States, or even County Commissioner.[20]

Henry Nash Smith paraphrases this passage, inadequately I believe, as an instance of the "covert class bias" of easterners trained to the theocratic prejudices of New England.[21] It has this quality, indeed; but what has happened is that the emotional context has shifted, until traditional fears have metamorphosed into a tacit recognition (however reluctant) that the West embodies American political institutions in their most characteristic form. Neither the principles nor the aberrations of Jacksonian Democracy have prevented the development of an image of western politics as peculiarly American.

Indeed in cataloguing the qualities of the Old Northwest for the readers of *Hunt's Merchants' Magazine* in 1840, James H. Lanman had already remarked that "A widely-diffused, deeply-stamped spirit of equality and republicanism extends throughout the whole social frame of the northwest"; and in subsequent essays on western topics he invoked the independent yeoman of the West as the surest guardian of republican institutions.[22] Lanman was obviously a western booster, and not everyone was ready as yet to adopt the region with the enthusiasm he displayed, but in political terms his view of the West amounted to a complete inversion of early fears in which conservatives as well as innovators, easterners as well as westerners, might join. Far from threatening eastern political institutions, the West promised to guarantee their continuing prosperity.

Obviously Lanman's statement drew heavily upon the pastoral tradition of the self-sufficient farmer that is identified in American thought with the agrarian theory embraced by Thomas Jefferson. (For that matter, even Felton's review of *Forest Life* owed something to this tradition.) By the same token, it represented a significant modification of the social and economic as well as the political judgments of an earlier generation of conservative spokesmen. Although some aspects of this shift in attitudes have already become apparent during our discussion of religious and political estimates of the West, the change in social perspective is worthy of separate treatment here.

When traditional religious and political values were at stake, eastern commentators like Timothy Dwight saw little that was good in the westward movement. In their reflections on the character of the people

who took up land in the West and on the social situation in which they
found themselves, however, such conservatives betrayed a grudging admiration for men and social institutions they would not otherwise have
respected. Their relative tolerance in this respect helped to prepare the
way for an idealization of the man of the West as the American hero and
of western society as the model of our social aspirations.

Dwight's ambivalence toward the westward movement as a social
phenomenon is apparent in his identification of early emigrants from
New England as those who "have met with difficulties at home" or who,
"having large families, and small farms, are induced, for the sake of
settling their children comfortably, to seek for new and cheaper lands,"
together with a number of "the discontented, the enterprizing, the ambitious, and the covetous." Even the adjectives are mixed, while the image
of a society attractive to those who have met with difficulties at home is
far less invidious than his comparable political image of restless idlers
and potential trouble-makers straggling westward. Moreover, although
he described the West as a means for drawing off socially undesirable
individuals, Dwight also suggested that the acquisition of property makes
the second type of settler, the "planter," actually civilized.[23] In such
pronouncements he was far from abandoning his fears of the religious
and political hazards implicit in frontier expansion, but he imputed to
the West a degree of economic opportunity, and a formative influence
on human character, that made it seem in spite of its handicaps a promising vehicle for the social institutions of the East.

Other contemporaries who were no more enthusiastic than Dwight
over the political prospects of the West also betrayed odd social sympathies when they sought to elaborate upon their hostility to further
expansion. During debate over the Louisiana Purchase, for example,
Senator White argued heatedly that a perpetual Indian reserve on the
right bank of the Mississippi was impossible because of the "adventurous,
roving, and enterprising temper of our people." For that matter even the
most dogmatic social critic of the West was hard put to state the case
against western expansion in unambiguous terms. During the same debate
Representative Griffin announced that he feared all of the consequences
of the acquisition of Louisiana, without exception: "he feared the effects
of the vast extent of our empire; he feared the effects of the increased
value of labor, the decrease in the value of lands, and the influence of
climate upon our citizens who should migrate thither."[24] Griffin did not
mean to praise western prospects, but the social and economic premises
on which he based his condemnation threatened the very core of his
argument.

This mixed perspective on western society continued to affect a later generation of conservative spokesmen for eastern interests. During his discussion of the obstacles that geographical dispersion placed in the way of intellectual and moral progress, for example, James Flint pointed out that the West "is an interesting country, as it will long continue to offer a wide field for the emigrating and enterprising population of the older states, and as the great receptacle of the shoals of foreigners, good and bad, that yearly cross the seas to seek, under the tutelar genius of American liberty, an asylum from the oppression, the poverty, or the justice of their native country."[25] Even the *Biblical Repertory* described the problem that a mixed population would cause the United States in terms that glorified as well as criticized the westerners' challenge to the East. "The people of the west [it said], viewed as individuals, resemble the inhabitants of almost every clime; but taken as a whole, they are unlike every people under heaven. They have come hither from the four quarters of the globe, with manners and habits and genius and temperament, as different as the nations from which they severally sprung. Every thing is new, just coming into existence."[26] In such phrases eastern critics of western character succeeded both in reiterating a whole complex of conservative fears and in paying reluctant tribute to the country and its people.

Such judgments as these, however, reflected a clear sense of the differences between West and East, which necessitated missionary efforts. Nevertheless other spokesmen for the East had already begun to depict the settlement of the West as an extension or an illustration of national character and institutions. This sense of identification was implicit in Edward Everett's portrait of the West as a republican safety-valve, and it became explicit in the *American Quarterly Review*, which expressed high praise in 1829 for traits that men like Dwight had criticized.[27] A generation later, moreover, during the course of a critique of western educational institutions written for the *Biblical Repository and Classical Review*, the missionary president of Wabash College asserted that "All who have become acquainted with American society, have observed that its most marked feature, is restless activity. Enterprise is more characteristic of us than a high civilization; a passion for the glitter and parade of wealth, more than a tendency to substantial, unostentatious investments and solid comforts. It has now become a universal statement and opinion, that a spirit of adventure and advancement, as also an actual forward and ascending movement, are no where in the country more apparent than in the Valley of the Mississippi. This ardor and progress, as is always the fact in new countries, respect the physical more than the intellectual; fortunes and honors more than facilities of knowledge and achievements of mind. All education is in a depressed condition."[28]

If there were still flaws visible in the western character, they now seemed to reflect national rather than merely regional traits—and (the article hastened to add) they did not interfere significantly with the progress of civilization in the West.

The aspect of western life that appealed most unambiguously to eastern commentators during this period, however, was the great material advantage that western society and western resources offered easterners who wished to migrate, which elicited in turn the most vigorous statements of national identification with the region. Moreover, this was no mere safety-valve doctrine such as Timothy Dwight and Edward Everett had expressed, for it made the West the focus of the American enterprise rather than simply a refuge from eastern poverty or a security against eastern political disturbances. During congressional debate on western land policy in 1830, for example, Representative Tristam Burges of Rhode Island clearly aligned himself against western interests in supporting distribution of the proceeds from land sales and in opposing a graduation proposal, yet he also appealed to an image of the West as the very definition of our social system. "In what other country," he asked,

is freehold and inheritance so acquired as it is in the United States? Young men in the old States, who "work out" from sixteen to twenty-one, and whose fathers receive one-half their wages for their clothing, their home, and subsistence while not employed, can then go to the West, purchase a farm, and, with labor and economy, they are, in a few years, independent and prosperous. Many, many have followed that course—they now find themselves well off in the world and members in the first rank of flourishing and highly cultivated communities. What would fathers, in any part of Europe, not willingly lay down in exchange, could they purchase such establishments for their sons?[29]

In 1844, furthermore, William H. Seward identified both our economic and our social institutions with the influence of the frontier West, when he told the Phi Beta Kappa Society of Union College that "A rapid increase of population in newly explored districts maintains labor at higher prices, the interest of money at high rates, and science and skill in higher estimation, here than elsewhere. From these causes, as well as from the reverence of weary, down-trodden men, to our free institutions, we derive a perpetual influx of emigrants from Europe, with talent and capital in just proportion."[30] Indeed Seward's words not only attributed American advantages to the West but also praised the immigrants whom it attracted, and thus inverted the judgments that both James Flint and the *Biblical Repertory* had applied to western settlement.

Obviously the major point of social and economic identification between East and West was the economic and social opportunity that western lands seemed to offer to every worthy citizen—a calculation of western advantages that led in time to the Homestead Act. The role that western spokesmen played, and the images they employed, in securing passage of a homestead law are familiar to us. It is equally significant, if less apparent, that with the growth of a favorable image of the West, eastern critics of homestead legislation were as likely to defend their views in essentially pro-western terms as to reiterate traditional fears of the region. The alternative perspectives were clearly demonstrated during the first major congressional debate on the homestead bill in 1852. Representative Josiah Sutherland of New York, a die-hard critic of liberal land legislation, undertook a bitter attack on the effect of free lands in raising the wages of eastern labor and hence the costs of manufacturing. In effect, the major vice he saw in the West was the social and economic promises it held out to eastern democrats. By contrast Representative Thomas J. D. Fuller of Maine, also an opponent of homestead legislation, defended the status quo as a great engine of progress. "Our present land system," he declared,

operates like a great balance-wheel upon our political institutions. It regulates the value of real property; it controls the wages of labor; and so long as one day's work will purchase an acre of productive land, and secure a certain and sure title, directly from the Government—eastern manufacturers can never control the wages of labor. . . . As our population increases and becomes more dense, they will emigrate to this broad domain, occupy and cultivate the soil, establish schools and churches, and form settlements, and thereby avoid those evils incident to a more dense and thickly-settled country. . . . I trust, sir, that our public domain may be long so held, and that our children, and our children's children, may always have the privilege of resorting to it for settlement and support, and at an unvarying price, with a certainty of title, until the almost countless acres of our unoccupied domain shall be covered with a virtuous, industrious, and happy people.[31]

Here, indeed, was a compelling image of the nation's future, which attracted those who might with good reason have continued to oppose the further extension of western settlement. Their anguish and their perspective were both well expressed by Senator John P. Hale of New Hampshire during debate over a proposal to cede additional lands to the state of Wisconsin in order to compensate for those in the original cession she had been prevented from exploiting. The senator observed that his state had never benefited from the public lands but he supported the measure anyway, remarking that "I know the lands will go West, and, what is worse, you will take our children, too; our young men and young women. You will take those who till the soil; those who give character to the State will go West, and carry our means with them.

When we grant to the West, we grant to our own kindred, our own sons and brothers, who will leave the sterile and hard soil of the East to people the fertile valleys of the West; and so far as I am concerned my blessing shall go with them. . . . That is an inevitable destiny and a fixed fact *per se,* and I am not disposed to oppose it or cavil at the result."[32] If Hale's statement echoed the attitudes toward the West that eastern spokesmen had expressed half a century earlier, the terms had been reversed. He not only conceded economic advantages to the region but also saw in it, in spite of eastern consequences, the greater fulfillment of his own people.

By such paths were conservative eastern prejudices against the West and its inhabitants converted into approbation and even identification with the region—in religion, in politics, in economic and social affairs. The process of conversion was twofold. On the one hand conservative attitudes simply shifted, until traditional apprehensions virtually disappeared, to be supplanted by recognition of the obvious achievements and prospects of the region. On the other hand, the very grounds of apprehension often metamorphosed into grounds of approbation: later generations of conservative commentators saw positive virtues in western institutional developments and traits of character that had once antagonized fearful easterners. Significantly, the *New Englander* suggested in 1846 that western expansion would encourage the spread of Puritan ideals because, in a new settlement, men are "thrown upon their own resources, and compelled to think and act; and hence, by the same law of necessity . . . forced to read, observe, and resort to all available sources for information."[33]

We may account for these developments in several ways. Obviously, one's perspective on the West was more than likely to be shaped by sectional political interests. Hence a shift of sectional interests would tend to alter prejudices once expressed toward the West by eastern spokesmen. Indeed the political history of the Middle Period has very generally been written in terms of shifting sectional relationships to the West and shifting alliances for the exploitation of western resources and the disposition of the public lands. Yet the evolution of a characteristically optimistic evaluation of the frontier West was by no means a product wholly of such realignments. For one thing, many of the crucial sectional issues in American politics were not resolved in eastern minds until the 1850's, yet the image of the West as a special property of American civilization was already well on the way to being established by then, and it affected opponents as well as advocates of measures sponsored by western interests. Furthermore, even when easterners sympathized with western aspirations, their political situation gave them little reason to accept the West in the exaggerated terms that its own spokesmen were wont to use. Not all of them did, of course; but a sufficient number of representatives of what may be characterized as traditionally reluctant eastern interests had long since adopted a view of the region that owed more to the imagination than to sober conjecture.

In part, of course, the shift reflected the triumphs of Jacksonian Democracy, for however Andrew Jackson happened to win election he made the whole nation conscious of the West, and he attracted votes even in New England. On the one hand, he undoubtedly appealed to eastern partisans who had little or no interest in the West or in its future, yet who were brought via their commitments to the man or to his party to value western qualities and attitudes that they had originally been taught to condemn. On the other hand, to the extent that Jackson stood for new ways to political success, eastern conservatives could hardly avoid catering to a self-consciously "western" population—as William Henry Harrison's log-cabin candidacy in 1840 clearly indicates. But though these circumstances may help to explain the evolution of a favorable image of the West in eastern democratic eyes, they are inadequate so far as many eastern conservatives are concerned: if they illuminate Democratic ideology they do not explain why, even before 1830, Whigs should also have begun to adopt a new perspective on the region.

Finally, the actual experience of two generations of western expansion and western travel undoubtedly influenced a number of eastern observers to feel more charitable toward western institutions and western innovations than had their immediate ancestors. But like other explanations this does not account for the enthusiasm with which sober eastern commentators came to portray the history and prospects of the land across the mountains. Experience may have taught them to be charitable (although it does not seem to have had the same effect on foreign travelers), but of itself it could not have persuaded them to be so optimistic. Somehow the West—the area of close settlement as well as the pioneer fringe, the urban future as well as the agricultural beginnings —enlisted powerful ideological commitments that were more lasting than political advantage, more powerful than the data of experience.

In other words the revision of conservative opinion of the West was more than a simple response to contemporary realities. It seems plausible to suggest, in fact, that far from being a mere datum in religion or politics or economics, the West served as a means of dramatizing fundamental conservative convictions. During the early years of the republic, when most institutions were unsettled and the future seemed clouded, apprehension predominated in conservative evaluations of the region, which already seemed likely to determine the course of our history. During later years, when the future of the republic appeared more promising, conservatives looked forward with greater confidence to the West's role in American life. The effect was to define the West in the light of eastern needs; to shape its image according to eastern concerns.

If we accept this interpretation of eastern attitudes we recognize that what conservatives imagined was as significant as the act of imagining itself. Originally conservative spokesmen were apprehensive lest westward migration undermine the orthodox, republican, middle-class customs of the eastern seaboard. As time passed they came more and more to hope for the triumph of just these institutions on the frontier. Beyond this, however, they also tended to impute to the West a unique power and an extraordinary responsibility for such a triumph, until in some instances they portrayed the region as a virtual utopia. At their hands, that is, the West ultimately became more than a vehicle for eastern institutions; it embodied the lasting hopes of the American nation.

Above all it amounted to an economic and social utopia within the reach of every man. Significantly, even commentators who were thoroughly skeptical of the religious and political prospects of the West, for example Timothy Dwight, represented the region as an unmixed economic blessing to the American people. Even more significantly, the original safety-valve doctrine—the belief that western emigration might protect the East against heterodoxy or radicalism or poverty—metamorphosed into a positive identification of American hopes with unexploited land and resources in the West. Conservative writers ended by describing a perfected liberal society in which economic vice and economic virtue would receive their appropriate rewards; and even Timothy Dwight had been confident that in such a society economic opportunity would lead men toward moral and political stability.

In these terms the West was an invention of the conservative imagination that may well have served important partisan purposes. For it is plausible to argue that by appealing to the economic promise implicit in western settlement conservative spokesmen helped to divert democratic discontent in the East into harmless channels. Yet there is little reason to suppose that the conservative image of the West as middle-class utopia was deliberately adopted in order to achieve this effect. The chronology is wrong (conservative elaborations of the safety-valve doctrine antedated the social unrest of the 1830's), and conservative enthusiasm over the political and religious prospects of the West, which should have accompanied any deliberate remaking of the western image for partisan purposes, lagged behind the economic estimate. Rather, the conservatives' West would seem to have been an invention that reflected their deepest beliefs. It was not a product of experience alone, not simply a reflection of contemporary politics, but above all a vivid statement of commitment to the status quo in an era marked by drastic social change.

Yet it also corresponded in some degree to the reality, which almost everyone in the United States shared vicariously if not in practice. If there had been no West, that is, it would have been necessary for conservatives to invent it. Invent it they did, but with a sufficient degree of concreteness to make plausible their maturing hopes. As a result their social theory, far from being discarded as irrelevant, helped to shape the popular definition of American institutions according to their model of a western utopia. Their fears were not convincing, in a society of optimists. Their hopes were.

# Type / *Gabriel Kolko*

The concept of type has been treated in its developmental aspects in the introduction to this volume. Perhaps the business and economic historians have made most use of type in their concern with the entrepreneur and entrepreneurship.[1] A danger in use of the type concept in historiography is the tendency to include material supportive of the type and to disregard other data. The article by Kolko is important for its critique of Max Weber's development of the ideal type. The best discussions, to my knowledge, of the theoretical implications of the ideal type are by Arthur Spiethoff and in the introduction to Spiethoff by Frederic C. Lane and Jelle C. Riemersma.[2]

In addition to real and ideal types, Arnold Toynbee has called attention to the usefulness of fictional types in historical description. There are, wrote Toynbee, "three different methods of viewing and presenting the objects of our thought, and, among them, the phenomena of human life. The first is the ascertainment and recording of 'facts'; the second is the elucidation, through a comparative study of the facts ascertained, of general 'laws'; the third is the artistic re-creation of the facts in the form of 'fiction.'"

Toynbee states further that "all histories . . . cannot entirely dispense with the fictional element. The mere selection, arrangement and presentation of facts is a technique belonging to the field of fiction." Moreover, which technique the historian elects to use is conditioned by "suitability for dealing with 'data' of different quantities. The ascertainment and record of particular facts is all that is possible in a field of study where the data happen to be few. The elucidation and formation of laws is both possible and necessary where the data are too numerous to tabulate but not too numerous to survey. The form of artistic creation and expression called fiction is the only technique that can be employed or is worth employing where the data are innumerable."

Toynbee concludes: "With . . . rare exceptions students of human life in the field of personal relations are confronted with innumerable examples of universally familiar experiences. The very idea of an exhaustive recording of them is an absurdity. Any formulation of their 'laws' would be intolerably platitudinous or intolerably crude. In such circumstances, the data cannot be significantly expressed in some nota-

Gabriel Kolko, "Max Weber on America: Theory and Evidence," *History and Theory* I (1961), 243–60. Reprinted by permission.

1. Fritz Redlich, "The Business Leader in Theory and Reality," *The American Journal of Economics and Sociology*, VIII (April, 1949), 223–37.

2. Frederic C. Lane and Jelle C. Riemersma, eds., *Enterprise and Secular Change* (Homewood, Illinois, 1953), 431–63.

tion which gives an intuition of the infinite terms; and such a notation is fiction."[3]

A sense of interplay between real, ideal, and fictional types has a place in historical description and social analysis. On the other hand, pure theory is inadequate, in itself, to delineate this role which must be developed non-dogmatically with reference to a specific historical situation.

M AX WEBER, in his discussions of methodology in the social sciences, formulated the concept of "ideal-types" in a manner which suggests that evidence is often not of primary concern to the historian. We are asked to create substantive concepts which in their conceptual purity may not be empirically verifiable. A conventional hypothesis, in contrast to an ideal-type, must be tested, and we must have or discover means for its proof or disproof; if the hypothesis does not refer to ultimately verifiable, concrete, or experiential phenomena, basic communication is undermined, and virtually anything may be asserted or believed. The ideal-type, we are told, "is formed by the one-sided *accentuation* of one or more points of view and by the synthesis of a great many diffuse, discrete, more or less present and occasionally absent *concrete individual* phenomena, which are arranged according to those one-sidedly emphasized viewpoints into a unified *analytical construct*. In its conceptual purity, this mental construct cannot be found empirically anywhere in reality. It is *utopia*." The ideal-type "is not a *description* of reality but it aims to give unambiguous means of expression to such a description."[1] In the social structure the ideal-type creates a normative standard for action from which we can deductively analyze "factors of deviation from a conceptually pure type of rational action."[2]

Weber effectively utilized the ideal-type in his religious sociology by showing what he alleged to be the causal importance of Calvinism in the development of Western capitalism. And, using Calvinism as the comparative standard, Weber in his studies of Hindu, Jewish, and Chinese religion attempted to show why the absence of economic rationalization and development in the East illustrated the causal significance of Calvinism in the West.

Here I shall attempt to show that Weber's ideal-typology of the causal importance of Calvinism in the development of Western capitalism suffers

3. This is a development of the references in footnotes 31, 72 and 73 of the article, "The American Patrician Class: A Field for Research," reprinted in this volume.

from serious methodological ambiguities, and that Weber's substantive historical treatment of American colonial economic history illustrates the fundamental inadequacy of the ideal-typology and of his specific theory of the Protestant Ethic as a tool of historical analysis. When one examines Weber's substantive theory as a hypothesis and by conventional canons of proof it becomes indefensible.

Most of the criticisms of Weber's Protestant Ethic have been written primarily in terms of its European relevance of his one-sided interpretation of Calvinist doctrine to suit his conceptually pure, if exaggerated, model. But it is worth noting that perhaps his most important single proof, colonial America, has been largely ignored by Weber scholars. This is unfortunate, since Weber viewed America as "the field of [capitalism's] highest development." He wrote the second half of *The Protestant Ethic and the Spirit of Capitalism* in 1905, immediately after a tour of the United States which had a profound impact on him, and part of his research was done in the libraries of Haverford College and Columbia University.[3] Throughout *The Protestant Ethic* Weber continually referred to colonial American history to sustain his thesis, and thereby advanced large-scale generalizations on early American development.

Weber saw no medieval antecedents or complicating institutional heritage to mitigate the impact of the Protestant Ethic on American economic development. "Without doubt, in the country of Benjamin Franklin's birth (Massachusetts), the spirit of capitalism . . . was present before the capitalistic order. . . . In this case the causal relation is certainly the reverse of that suggested by the materialistic standpoint."[4] In parts I and V, I shall examine whether Weber fully understood the economic implications of Puritan doctrine and the dimensions of Franklin's ideas and personality, because to Weber, as to Werner Sombart, Franklin was without equal as the personification of the capitalist spirit.

Weber quite erroneously contrasted the economic development of the New England colonies to that of the non-Calvinist Southern colonies, where he claimed that "capitalism remained far less developed . . . in spite of the fact that these latter were founded by large capitalists for business motives, while the New England colonies were founded by preachers and seminary graduates with the help of small bourgeois, craftsmen and yeomen, for religious reasons."[5] In part II, I shall examine the extent to which the two regions differed on such matters as usury and a variety of economic controls Weber assumed conducive to capital accumulation, and whether economic realities, beyond those necessitated by climate, differed between Calvinist and non-Calvinist settlements. In the same context, in part III, I shall inquire whether the similarities in economic development in the Northern and Southern colonies suggest causal determinants, such as the frontier and common problems faced by all seeking to create a society in a wilderness, which were substantially more important than religious ideologies. In part IV, I shall examine whether the larger conditions of American life permitted the development of routine enterprise and a systematic, predictable trade (which Weber thought reflected the impact of Calvinism on economic life).

I conclude in my final section (VI) that the economic structure which emerged in colonial America, including New England, reflected the larger political and geographical realities which Weber did not even begin to appreciate, and that these factors tended to create a political capitalism in which economic success was determined far more by political and social connections than by any special religious motivations. Ultimately, we shall see, Weber's description of America was based more on deductions from a rigid thesis than a valid understanding of American history.

## I

Weber assumed that Calvinism provided an impetus for systematic economic behavior and laid the foundation for modern capitalism. This doctrinal stimulus purportedly found its expression in institutional changes and the creation of the necessary conditions for rationalized capitalism, but nowhere in Weber is there a consideration of the extent to which Calvinist or Puritan doctrine provided a hindrance to continuous rationalized economic behavior and capital accumulation. In its total context, however, Puritanism in America was both a help and a hindrance to systematic economic behavior, and this hindrance was not only a matter of specific regulations on economic activities, but of questions involving "the glory of God and one's own duty."[6]

It was, according to the Puritans, the obligation of man to follow a calling and to conscientiously cultivate his vineyard. The Covenant of Grace which God contracted with the faithful made salvation possible, but this involved more than simple faith, since it included the obligation of external behavior and works as well. The pattern of such behavior must not be understood as being merely economically oriented, although it was that too. Signs of salvation were reflected not in the actual achievements of material signs of grace, as Weber suggested, but in man's continuous efforts and intentions to fulfill the Covenant.[7] One thing which the Puritan oligarchy unequivocally condemned in economic activity was the notion, which Weber erroneously associated with Puritanism, that "Labour must . . . be performed as if it were an *absolute end in itself*."[8] To the Puritans, however, excessive concern with wealth resulted in vanity, the neglect of the public good, the undermining of scholarship, and, above all, a challenge to the dominance of the spiritual oligarchy in God's Commonwealth. "Neither riches nor poverty . . . but a meane between both," declared Thomas Morton.[9]

Weber not only misunderstood the demands of Puritan doctrine on economic behavior, but he was never conscious of the immediate economic and doctrinal tensions within the Puritan Commonwealth, between those desiring to live strictly by the prescriptions of Puritan ethics and those willing to deviate from them. Weber assumed that the attitude to economic behavior held by the merchants could be deduced from the doctrines which he believed they held. The result was a failure to appreciate the conflict between ideas and economic reality. The Puritan oligarchy, drawn heavily from the traditionally anti-business minor English gentry, saw the tension between religion and wealth. In Perry Miller's summary phrase: "At every point, economic life set up conflicts with ideology."[10]

This conflict found its first expression when the large majority of the merchants supported the Antinomian heresy of Ann Hutchinson, the wife of a merchant, just a few years after the founding of the Massachusetts colony. The Antinomian belief in faith and revelation as the sufficient assurance of election undermined the orthodox belief in probable grace manifested in an indispensable combination of faith and works, which Weber believed to be essential to systematic economic behavior. Although exile soon stamped out the leadership of the heresy, older Boston merchants remained ready to support the initiative of the newer merchants in the political conflicts with the Puritan oligarchy.[11]

Adherence to less rigorous theology marked another breach with Puritan doctrines, and the children of Calvinists tended to be assimilated into the larger merchant world where status was determined more by accumulated wealth than theological niceties. Intermarriage took place among the families of Boston merchants and in the process religion was a secondary consideration. This pattern was not only dominant in Massachusetts, where the conflict between Calvinism and the merchants was the greatest, but in other areas with large Calvinist communities. In South Carolina, the large Huguenot settlement experienced an "absorption into the Anglican church [which] was indirectly coercive, rapid and thorough."[12] In New York very few pure denominational lines remained by 1750.

In Massachusetts the connection between Puritan religion and economic interest might well be seen in the light of considerations which Weber ignored. The power of the oligarchy lasted only so long as the merchant class was unable to organize its latent power and political influence; until then, social unity could be maintained by the binding power of Puritan doctrine. This was only for a very brief period. The Puritans themselves thought it lasted, in something like its ideal state, for a decade. The Puritan religion could thus be viewed as ideology; not sustained by concrete class and economic interest, it proved a weak prop upon which to build a new political structure. Had the alliance between the religious conceptions of the Puritans and the merchant class been as real as Weber assumed it to be, the conflict might not have occurred so quickly. If the failure of Puritanism to maintain itself without larger class support tells against Weber, so does the converse; we find the merchants ready to turn to theologies capable of neutralizing or counteracting the alleged doctrinal superiority of the Puritan elite. When heresy failed to succeed, assimiliation to less restrictive denominations served the purpose.

## II

Because of the multiple economic aspects of Puritanism, most of which Weber did not appreciate, the Puritan oligarchy attempted to create a state not unlike that which Weber described as the goal in China during the domination of the literati—a commonwealth that "had the character of a religious and utilitarian welfare-state, a character which is in line with so many other typical traits of patrimonial bureaucratic structures bearing theocratic stamps."[13] It is a state of this character, rather than one basing its economic policy on pro-merchant beliefs, that might serve as a useful model as we turn to consider some exigent problems of the colonial economy.

On such matters as economic control, usury, and just price there was little difference between the colonies. The general need to prevent starvation placed certain limits on economic freedom, and the pervasive acceptance of much essentially mercantilist practice made active government intervention inevitable. In Massachusetts, contrary to what one might infer from the Calvinist position as presented in *The Protestant Ethic*, the Puritan oligarchy strictly regulated the conditions upon which usury might be practiced, and these conditions virtually eliminated any predictable chance for repayment. If a potential poor borrower could not repay a loan he was to be the object of charity and not commerce, and charity was as much a Christian obligation as was business. More important, if a debtor was unable to execute his obligation, the good Christian was to excuse the debt and refuse to take pledges of goods necessary to the daily life at the debtor. Although the merchants ignored the economic prescriptions of the Calvinist divines, they undoubtedly received no comfort from the assertion that they were acting against the laws of

Christianity. The attitude toward usury in Massachusetts, in any event, merely confirms the criticisms of H. M. Robertson that Weber did not understand the entire Calvinist position on usury.[14]

The Southern colonies, no less than the Northern, attempted to control prices and prevent profiteering, and like the Northern colonies generally failed. Massachusetts, obeying necessity as much as following medieval precedent and religious conviction, fixed prices from 1633, but failure to maintain effective control forced it to decentralize much of the responsibility to the towns after 1641. Virginia, from its inception, established limits on profits, as did the Council of New Netherland after 1653. Boston controlled the import and export of wheat and the price of bread until the post-revolutionary period, and Charleston, South Carolina, maintained extensive control over the quality, price, and marketing of food until then as well. New York also regulated the price of basic foodstuffs for a significant period.[15] It was assumed as a matter of course in the colonial period that one of the purposes of the state was to prevent the ruthless exploitation of the public's immediate and basic needs, or at least to make an effort in that direction. Survival in a frontier situation often made public control indispensable, and in Massachusetts Puritan concepts of just price merely reinforced the trend.

According to Weber, asceticism aids capital accumulation, and asceticism was a characteristic Puritan virtue—"the English, Dutch, and American Puritans were characterized by the exact opposite of the joy of living."[16] Yet in South Carolina the characteristic French *joie de vivre* was by no means absent from the large settlement of Huguenots, right from the beginning of their establishment in the latter part of the seventeenth century. In New York and Philadelphia as well, the merchant community, regardless of denomination, soon fell into a modish and socially exclusive pattern of life and consumption which diverted potential capital into non-productive activities, into the attempt to consolidate status on a level corresponding with their economic power. In Boston the pattern was no different.[17] Sumptuary legislation, established in Virginia as well as Massachusetts, broke down functionally several decades after its introduction.

The utilization of barter as the primary means of exchange in the West India trade created a situation in which New England not only failed to represent ascetic virtue, but spread moral ruin, or at least one of its preconditions, wherever it might. Rum and molasses became the basic staples of the crucial West India trade, and the ability of the New England merchant to exchange his produce, fish, wood, and goods for West Indian rum was contingent on the decidedly unascetic customs of the farmers, mechanics, and fishermen throughout the colonies. By 1720, the major

New England manufacture was rum, about one-seventh of which was transported to Africa for the slave trade.[18] Some went to the Indians in the fur trade, but the bulk of it remained in the colonies or was sent up the Maine and Canadian coast in exchange for fish. "Throughout all the colonies drunkenness was a prevailing vice, as it was in England," writes James Truslow Adams, "and nearly every event, such as house raisings, harvestings, christenings, college commencements, funerals and even the ordination of ministers, was frequently made the occasion of scandalous intemperance."[19]

## III

For the American Colonies, the difference between the Puritan North, where, on account of ascetic compulsion to save, capital in search of investment was always available, from the conditions in the South has already been clearly brought out by Doyle. . . .
The existence of iron-works (1643), weaving for the market (1659), and also the high development of the handicrafts in New England in the first generation after the foundation of the colonies are, from a purely economic viewpoint, astounding. They are in striking contrast to the conditions in the South, as well as in the non-Calvinistic Rhode Island with its complete freedom of conscience. . . . It can in fact hardly be doubted that the compulsion continually to reinvest savings, which the Puritan curtailment of consumption exercised, played a part.[20]

While these assertions may buttress Weber's thesis, they are incomplete or invalid historically. The stimulus to self-sufficiency existed in all colonies, not merely in Calvinist Massachusetts, and it was expected that, given the shortage of capital which was a problem in all the colonies, the colonial governments or towns would stimulate the creation of industries and crafts. In this respect Virginia was no different from Massachusetts. Discussions of religious ethics are extraneous to an accounting for the events that actually occurred. Indeed, insofar as Rhode Island, Virginia, and Maryland wished to foster social unity and avoid the religious conflict and bigotry characteristic of Massachusetts, they were in a more advantageous, rational economic position.

From its inception, the London Company had diverse motives for founding a colony in Virginia. Politically the settlement was to strengthen English power in the hemisphere *vis-à-vis* Spain and Portugal. Profits were to be limited, religious conflict avoided, and industry as well as agriculture fostered.[21] Small local mills and industries sprang up throughout the colonies as demand warranted and state and local bounties and grants made the means available.[22] Virginia's first brick kiln was set up in 1611, its first glass plant in 1621, and Virginia claimed the first two glass plants in America. Massachusetts' first glass works stopped operations in 1670 "for lack of capital."[23] In 1640, the Puritan oligarchy suggested the consideration of "what course may be taken for teaching the boys and girls in all towns the spinning of yarn," but in 1646 Virginia actually opened two public flax houses in Jamestown to teach the art of linen making, and in 1666 ordered each county to do the same. Maryland also founded such schools, and although it did lag behind Virginia, Massachusetts eventually followed suit.[24] Bounty laws and acts to maintain craft quality and stimulate production were common in all colonies but most effective in Pennsylvania, which later became the leading manufacturing colony.[25] Weber's citation of Massachusetts' weaving for the market is a misleading example. Its repeated measures in the 1640's and 1650's to create self-sufficiency and build the industry failed despite an ample supply of raw materials. Cloth production was for home use, of poor, isolated farmers wherever they might be.[26]

Success in early colonial manufacturing was due to tangible factors to which religious concepts cannot be said to have made much difference. The iron industry developed where the resources were most abundant and, as in the case of Pennsylvania, where the high cost of transportation for agricultural goods stimulated diversification.[27] The textile industry later developed in New England for similar reasons: water power, ports, proper humidity for production, and a surplus labor supply.[28]

The impression given by Weber was that the iron industry began in New England and centered there because of an initially religiously-motivated class of dynamic entrepreneurs. The assertion that an ironworks existed in Massachusetts in 1643 is, by itself, a meaningless fact. One of the reasons Virginia was founded was to supply iron to England, and in late 1621 a complete iron mill was finished at Falling Creek. In March 1622, when the mill was about to begin production, the entire population was massacred by Indians and most of the machinery thrown in the river.[29] The first Massachusetts iron mill began with substantial state bounties and considerable *English* capital, which eventually grew to £15,000, but by 1652 it was so overwhelmed with debts that its production thereafter was sporadic.[30] When the colonial iron industry is established, it is in precisely the place where anyone committed to a belief in the nexus between Calvinism and industrial enterprise would expect not to find it. In 1715, Maryland was the largest colonial iron producer, but Pennsylvania became the leader in the field by 1750. Throughout the colonial period, however, Virginia and Maryland were far more important producers than New England, and in 1775 the colonies produced one-seventh of the world's output.[31]

## IV

To Weber the essential quality of capitalism was its rationality, and it was the role of Puritanism in evoking a systematic "supramundane orientation" of works as a sign of probable salvation which made modern rational capitalism possible. Such an attitude toward the world was indispensable, and its expression would be found in predictable trade based on peaceful profits from exchange and freedom of mobility, trade, and occupational choice—"sober, strict legality and the harnessed rational energy of routine enterprise."[32] Man's salvation was in large measure in his own hands.

Rather than having "a horror of illegal, political, colonial, booty, and monopoly types of capitalism" and unpredictable economic chances, the American merchant lived with this form of commerce throughout the colonial period. These circumstances were quite beyond his control and had nothing to do with his own attitude toward the situation, to which he rather unreflectively accomodated himself. If one were to characterize succinctly the colonial economy, one would say that it lacked most, if not all, of the prerequisites for the creation of a rational capitalism in Weber's terms. And, as we shall see, the merchants lived with these conditions, thrived on them for at least a century, and eventually developed a vested interest in continuing certain of their political aspects.

Given the crucial importance of the West India trade to the merchants as a means of acquiring the credits for their English debts, it was inevitable that unpredictability characterize American commerce. A shipload of goods sent to one destination often found the market glutted, or no return cargo, and might have to wander throughout the Indies in search of a suitable exchange. Since, after 1700, the discretion of making a bargain was generally left to the ship's captain, the merchant was always unsure of the results. Combined with this insecurity was frequent unreliability among factors and the bills of credit of West Indian planters. Frequent colonial wars increased the danger of losses in the hands of privateers. In addition, there was the general unpredictability in the quality of goods one might receive from a West Indian planter or American merchant when ordering goods sight unseen.[33]

Far more important in creating uncertain and illegal economic conditions was the conscious mercantilist policy of Great Britain from 1660 on. Although no concerted attempt was made to enforce mercantile restrictions until 1763, the colonal merchants nevertheless were compelled to conduct the better part of their trade in a technically illegal fashion. This might take the simple form of false bills of lading to avoid taxation, or running goods ashore illegally. It might also involve privateering, direct trading with European nations or, in wartime, lucrative trade with the Dutch, French, and Spanish enemies of England. This illicit trade resulted in "debauched public sentiment and corrupt official practice," declared no less loyal a son of New England than Weeden.[34] According to Schlesinger: "Smuggling was almost exclusively a practice of merchants of the commercial provinces [New England]."[35]

Because of the desire to facilitate smuggling, and because it was necessary to have the cooperation of the official authorities to build illegal slitting mills or produce beaver hats, it was vital for colonial merchants to "dissuade" the proper authorities from performing their duties effectively. The means utilized were all illegal, some more than others. Many of the colonial governors had their own investments in illegal operations and were naturally sympathetic to the merchants. In several instances governors were bought out, and others were too dependent on colonial legislatures for their incomes, or without means of enforcement, to protest effectively. When unfriendly, governors were generally isolated. As a matter of procedure, however, most of the vice-admiralty was controlled by the smuggling merchants, and many of the best lawyers were retained to represent the merchants. The result was that most illegal slitting mills and similar establishments were freely built and never reported by the governors to the Board of Trade in London.[36]

In his discussion of China, Weber declared that "wealth, and especially landed wealth, was not primarily a matter of rational profit-making."[37] Much of this land was acquired through the political accumulation of capital, which purportedly characterized the Chinese economy as a whole and represented a diversion of capital which might otherwise have been spent in rational economic activity. Given the traditional status of land in England, the general lack of other transferable property within the colonies, and the unpredictabiliy of trade, currency, and investments, it is not surprising that much of the capital within the colonies soon found its way into land-holdings and, eventually, land speculation. In this respect, and often in the means of acquiring land, there was little difference in principle between colonial Massachusetts, South Carolina, or China.

Exact economic calculation, according to Weber, was possible only with free labor, and since this was a precondition of rational capitalism he expected the Puritans to naturally favor it. He held that "the early history of the North American Colonies is dominated by the sharp contrast of the adventurers, who wanted to set up plantations with the labour of indentured servants, and live as feudal lords, and the specifically middle-class outlook of the Puritans."[38]

The New England Puritan, however, merely conformed to the accepted colonial principles for securing and utilizing labor, and apparently nothing in Puritan doctrine changed that fact. At least half of the total white population in the Thirteen Colonies arrived as indentured labor, and Massachusetts received its fair share. Indentured servants entering the colonies because of their criminal records were generally received in the South and Pennsylvania, but those voluntarily emigrating were distributed throughout the colonies. Massachusetts established laws governing indentured servants from the inception of the colony, strictly enforced their obligations to their masters, and fixed the length of their service at seven years, which was the general average in the early colonial period. When the supply lagged, bounties were offered. In 1710, the Massachusetts Legislature offered 40 shillings a head to any ship captain bringing in male servants between the ages of eight to twenty-five. Prisoners captured by the English in their wars were often sent to the colonies, and part of the labor force of Massachusetts' first iron-mill consisted of captured Scottish soldiers.[39]

The first Negro was brought to Virginia in 1619 by the Dutch, but slavery assumed no real importance in Virginia, and did not even become legally enforceable, until the end of the century and the rise of the West Indies trade. It was never the plan of the Virginia "adventurers" to establish slavery, and until the middle of the seventeenth century indentured servants automatically became landed freeholders. In 1700, sixty percent of Virginia's free whites had neither slaves nor indentured servants. When slavery did grow in the South, the Southern Calvinists showed no hesitancy in owning them, and more "Cavaliers" descended from English merchants than from any other group.[40]

## V

Weber saw in Benjamin Franklin's ideas the quintessence of the Protestant Ethic. Franklin's *Advice to a Young Tradesman* was considered, as Weber's wife tells it, as "the characteristic document of the capitalist spirit," and Weber quoted it at great length in *The Protestant Ethic*. "That it is the spirit of capitalism which here speaks in characteristic fashion, no one will doubt, however little we may wish to claim that everything which could be understood as pertaining to that spirit is contained in it."[41] And: "the *summum bonum* of this ethic, the earning of more and more money, combined with the strict avoidance of all spontaneous enjoyment of life, is above all completely devoid of any eudaemonistic, not to say hedonistic, admixture."[42]

After reading Franklin's *Autobiography* Weber saw in the man the personal fulfillment of the influence of the Protestant Ethic as well. In an important sense Franklin was the fulfillment of what is most characteristic of the typical bourgeois, but the reasons for this were hardly appreciated by Weber. Seeing economic action as a consistent reflection of doctrinal beliefs and influence, Weber was unaware of the element of paradox, conflict, and hypocrisy in the typical American bourgeois. Franklin, in reality, was much more like the Chinese mandarin who purportedly made capitalism impossible than Weber's stereotyped Puritan ascetic.

Franklin's economic ideology was much more involved than Weber presented it or could have known after a brief and selective reading of his more popular works. Influenced by the Physiocrats in his later life, Franklin accepted free trade, saw agriculture as the source of all productive wealth, and on this basis viewed manufacturers, merchants, professionals, and mechanics as little more than useless in the economic process. As far as he was concerned, "there seem to be but three ways for a nation to acquire wealth. The first was by *war,* as the Romans did, in plundering their conquered neighbours. This is *robbery.* The second by *commerce,* which is generally *cheating.* The third by *agriculture,* the only *honest way.*"[43] Franklin believed in interest, however, and in this respect differed from most Physiocrats.

Franklin accepted most of the vices of man and himself by no means refrained from them any more than he refrained from the vices of economic life. Upon travelling to London at the age of twenty to learn the printing trade, Franklin did not save his money like a true Puritan but rather spent evenings at such notably unascetic activities as theaters, sports, drink, and women. He returned to America with an illegitimate son who eventually fathered another who in turn did the same. In Philadelphia Franklin set to work determined to make something of himself, living a well scheduled life which included only eight hours a day for work. Franklin was a wise promoter, however, and his newspaper tried many things, from discussions of hypothetical adultery to Poor Richard's Almanac, to increase circulation.[44]

Franklin was never a prude and never became one. He retired from business at what is still the ripe young age of forty-two in order to escape "the little cares and fatigues of business."[45] His letter on how to choose a mistress is relevant to his asceticism, and while serving as American ambassador to France, Franklin in his old age left his wife at home and carried on several amorous affairs. In addition to women, Franklin indulged in good food and excellent wine. According to Weber, however, "transition to a pure, hygienically oriented utilitarianism had already taken place in Franklin, who took approximately the ethical standpoint of modern physicians, who understand by chastity the restriction of sexual intercourse to the amount desirable for health."[46]

Franklin not only appreciated the value of good health and food, but also the value of political connections in achieving wealth (Poor Richard had nothing to say on the matter, which is one reason why he, unlike Franklin, never became rich). He used his position in the political caucus of the Junto and wrote a tract advocating the "Necessity of a Paper Currency," in order to get the contract to print money, and eventually much of Pennsylvania's printing work, for his own firm. Franklin was the public printer of Pennsylvania until 1764, and it is commonly agreed that his advocacy of paper money was motivated to an important extent by that fact.[47] His political influence was too great to stop at mere printing contracts, for Franklin became involved with some of his Philadelphia associates in an attempt to form two new colonies on an enormous tract of 1,200,000 acres they obtained in the West on the basis of a flimsy and probably illegal purchase from Indians. Franklin's task was to convince the royal government to authorize the project, a matter to which he actively but unsuccessfully gave his efforts in 1766–67.[48]

## VI

In China, wrote Weber, a class of prebends accumulated land and property through the unpredictable exploitation of political offices. Modern industrial capitalism cannot grow in such a politically irrational environment, and *The Religion of China* was devoted to the question of why the Chinese social structure never created the rational political conditions essential to capitalism. Weber believed the answer could be found by examining Chinese religious ethos.[49]

In the American colonial period we can discern a pattern of development in which the role of political capitalism, as in China, is decisive in the economic process. The relationship of the state to the economy, and the impossibility of pursuing economic action without regard to it, was made inevitable by English mercantilist practice, by the insufficiency of private capital, and by precedent.[50] The basic political history of Massachusetts in the seventeenth century is centered around the struggle between the Puritan oligarchy and merchants who wished to control the state for their own interests. The control or bribery of the imperial bureaucracy, itself filled with men seeking their own fortunes, was necessary from the moment the attempt to implement mercantilist controls occurred. The everyday lives of the merchants were unpredictable, and circumstances and lack of knowledge hindered rationalization and predictability in economic life. In early American economic development the advantages of political capitalism were exploited by the merchants and large landowners within each colonial government at the same time that the imperial government was ignored or opposed within the larger mercantilist system when it failed to work to their benefit and profit. In this context the existence of the Protestant or any other ethic was immaterial.

As long as promising economic opportunities could be exploited within the framework of mercantilist restrictions, the merchants could be satisfied. The result was illegality and corresponding unpredictability, but the merchants simply adjusted to this fact. Only when England wished to end illegality, a basic conflict between the merchants and the imperial system arose. Until that time the merchants supported or opposed policies and actions only to benefit themselves.[51] The closing of the trans-Appalachian lands by the Quebec Act of 1774 aided the belief by many merchants that the direct control of the state was a necessary precondition for the exploitation of existing economic opportunities. The revolution was not a measure against the role of the state in the economy, at least insofar as the revolutionary merchants were concerned, but an attempt by merchants and land speculators fully to utilize the state for their own economic operations.

In the immediate post-revolutionary period the internal class discord between frontier debtors and coastal planters and merchants crystallized a conflict which had begun in the colonial period. The state, especially in New England, became a prize not only because of the economic advantages it actually and potentially afforded, but to preserve the power of the economic elite against democratic encroachments and to enforce its debt claims.[52] But it is the utilization of the state for its economic advantages that interests us here. And it was land which became the primary object of the efforts of Boston merchants and Virginia planters.

The utilization of political contacts to acquire desirable economic goals was, of course, nothing new prior to the revolutionary period. Indeed, political office or personal political contacts were among the comparatively sure ways to economic success for ambitious governors and merchants alike. When the Massachusetts Legislature began the legal distribution of land for primarily speculative purposes in the 1720's, it was the town merchants with influential political connections who acquired it. In addition, "the chartered trading companies had by 1750 come to be regarded purely as semi-political 'vested interests.'"[53] In the colonial period, however, the legal definition of the charter was vague, and served primarily as a political guarantee of economic monopoly or special privilege—an instrument of political capitalism such as that obtained by the Chinese prebend. The revolution only served to intensify the importance of political and personal contacts in obtaining land and government privileges. It was a conventional and accepted manner of getting what one desired, and on this question there was no difference between the Massachusetts and Virginia planters.[54]

Most American historians concerned with colonial history, especially that of the seventeenth century would question the priority of causal factors in Weber's explanation. Even ignoring the disparity between religious concepts and economic behavior, and the impossibility of predicting economic development by deduction from theologically-grounded attitudes, we are left with Weber's misunderstanding of the nature of Puritanism and his sharp exaggeration of its differences with Anglicanism as a means of social control and economic stimulus. Weber ignored the impact of the frontier in creating the major preconditions of economic activity in all sections. He also ignored the degree to which geographic and climatic circumstances generally explain the important differences between the regions which were to develop in the eighteenth century—by which time theology was in rapid flux throughout the colonies and had become far less powerful in New England. In this context, Weber's utilization of the Protestant Ethic as the explanation of American colonial history is a classic example of the dictum that correlation is often confused with causation.

Some of the implications of this study for historical theory in general may be worth noting. I have attempted to disprove the causal role of the Protestant Ethic in its early American context, primarily by an appraisal of historical facts that can be independently established but were ignored by Weber or unknown to him. Weber's theory is not disproven by pitting other theories against his, thus leaving us with a multiplicity of conflicting historical interpretations, but by an attempt to solve the debate, so to speak, empirically. If our specific historical facts are valid, historical theories which ignore them can be refuted as mere substitutes for historical enquiry, often quite easily. This is a different business, in principle at least, from attempting the disproof of the validity of one kind of historical explanation out of arbitrary preference for another.

My attempt to refute Weber's arguments does not imply a desire to impugn the objectivity or validity of contingent historical hypotheses, those based to a much greater extent on established historical facts than Weber's theory was. The multiplicity of such hypotheses and the controversies over their merit, relative to one another or to concepts like those employed by Weber, lend superficial support to the relativist's claim of the "subjectivity" of historical knowledge. In fact, however, they often lead to new hypotheses and concepts of a higher degree of independent validity. Ironically perhaps, refutation of the Protestant Ethic, as Weber understood it, also leads to a validation of the concept of political capitalism, which Weber limited to China, as a central element in any analysis of early American history.

As an ideal-typology, as an analytical construct rather than a hypothesis contingent on facts, the concept of the Protestant Ethic in America may perhaps be defended. But the question remains to what extent a useful fiction in the form of an ideal-typology is any more fruitful in the social sciences than a hypothesis that is verifiable.

# Role / *Thomas C. Cochran*

Role has been defined as the anticipated behavior pattern when an individual is confronted by a specific situation. Roles generally derive from status: an individual of a given status has numerous roles consistent with age, sex, occupation, and position in the community.[1] Social role is "an understanding shared more or less fully by the members of a group as to what a given position entails for individuals who occupy it."[2] According to Professor Cochran, "a nineteenth-century railroad president would behave in certain general ways not necessarily expected of a politician or a college president."

In the following selection, the individual and social roles of railroad executives were delineated through an analysis of their correspondence between 1845 and 1890. Professor Cochran's preoccupation with role is auxiliary to an attempt to define "norms of thought and attitude" for a particular group. For the present, Professor Cochran sees these norms as "impressionistic and loosely defined" and he makes their clarification contingent upon "more mature social hypotheses than now exist, and analysis of the actions corresponding to statements of opinion."[3]

IN THE BROAD view, a particular social role is a product of the types of personality common in the society interacting with the physical and cultural setting. The fertility of western farming land, the low ratio of population to resources, and the existence of certain metropolitan centers were all physical determinants of the types of role possible for American railroad executives. Similarly, the forms of government in the United States, our major cultural traditions, and the habits of an expanding economy also shaped the roles. Since no significant work has been carried on to establish nineteenth-century American personality types these must remain relatively unknown influences save as some suggestions of common patterns arise from the evidence used in this study. These background

Reprinted by permission of the publishers from Thomas C. Cochran, *Railroad Leaders,* *1845–1890,* Cambridge, Mass.: Harvard University Press. Copyright, 1953, by The President and Fellows of Harvard College.

1. Francis E. Merrill, *Society and Culture* (Englewood Cliffs, 1962), 170–74.
2. Leland H. Jenks, "The Role Structure of Entrepreneurial Personality," *Change and the Entrepreneur* (Cambridge, Mass., 1949), 136.
3. Thomas Cochran, *Railroad Leaders* (Cambridge, Mass., 1953), 13–15; Karl Mannheim, *Essays on the Sociology of Culture* (London, 1956), 26, 29.

elements will not be continuously emphasized here, but they underlie the following discussion of the specific mechanics of role determination.

Outstandingly important among the immediate pressures shaping the executive role was the character of personal relations in the large corporation. As we have continually emphasized, the consistency of top-executive attitudes appears to have arisen largely from the fact that there was a small and relatively homogeneous prescribing group made up of the chief officers and directors of the companies. While the public, the government, and the customers were also groups whose opinions might count, and hence were to be conciliated by proper words, the expectations of these outsiders formed railroad policy only if they won the approval of the director group. Furthermore, such outsiders did not police the avenues to personal success inside the company. Within the relatively small prescribing group the views of a still smaller number of important general entrepreneurs from similar social strata in Boston, New York, and Philadelphia appear to have set the tone. A letter from a railroad officer in Chicago to a shipper in Lincoln, Nebraska, therefore, would tend to be phrased in accordance with the executive social role as seen on State, Wall, or Chestnut Street. There were relatively few differences of opinion in the letters on methods of business, on subjects, that is, where the role was well defined. Or, to put it another way, the ideas and attitudes of the railroad elite as projected through their conceptions of the executive role were fairly uniform, and they were largely the attitudes arising from the conditioning of large-scale finance.

## The Role as Seen by the General Entrepreneurs

Therefore, while in point of numbers the prescribing group was largely composed of other top officers, and of directors who were not very active in the affairs of the road, it is often covenient and accurate enough to think of the pressure exerted by the group in terms of the ideas of the important general entrepreneurs, the men like Corning, Forbes, Griswold, Osborn, the Vanderbilts, and Villard. While the characteristics that follow have emerged from written evidence, often from the words of the big financiers themselves, it would be possible to deduce many of them in answer to the question: what should the manager or director write in order to promote the interests of the general entrepreneur?

In a role conceived by men of the topmost business and social elite it is not surprising that deference toward superiors was a *sine qua non*. But this principle was not peculiar to nineteenth-century railroad companies; it is probably basic to all business hierarchies. "The typical operating executive, no matter how high his position," state the authors of a recent publication of the Harvard Business School, "is likely to be extremely sensitive to anyone who happens to be senior to him."[1] This was the glue that helped to hold the role material together, accounted for striking uniformities, and gave the role force as a means of social control.

In a majority of the letters cited in this study the writer was dependent for his job on the good will of certain general entrepreneurs. And the power of the general entrepreneurs themselves usually depended on some collective approval by their peers. The similarities in opinion are most striking in matters involving finance, for example, because here it was essential that the leader be regarded as sound by big investors in general.[2]

With the representatives of large investing interests setting the role, it is not surprising that "the company" was identified with the major stockholders rather than with the employees, and that policy was supposed to be based on the welfare of the company measured in terms of earnings.[3] It also follows logically, as well as from the evidence, that strict regard for property rights and respect for stockholders somewhat in the ratio of the size of their holdings and general wealth were essential elements in the role.

A characteristic of the executive role, so obvious that it is easy to overlook, was reliance on reason and logic. His associates expected the executive to act rationally and explain his actions logically. No artistic temperament, or what John Murray Forbes referred to as a "queer, vague vein about the blood," was wanted in these men of topmost business responsibility. There was a premium on exact, terse expression. "Facility of pen or tongue," wrote Forbes, "is a great misfortune unless to a lecturer or a patent lawyer."[4] In a period given to fanciful and ornate writing, the lean and pointed phraseology of these business letters is striking. Compare, for example, James F. Joy: "These are times when bold action is the only safe action and in this daring action the Southern Company have shown themselves wise," with the famous William Ellery Channing's roughly contemporaneous observation: "There are periods when the principles of experience need to be modified, when hope and trust and instinct claim a share with prudence in the guidance of affairs, when, in truth, to *dare* is the highest wisdom."[5] Although about 40 per cent of the writers had attended college, and most of them came from prosperous families of the areas in which learning was most highly regarded, there are few allusions to literature, art, or scholarly writing.

The general entrepreneurs also expected a manager to have a number of traits or attitudes that might be summed up as "good business qualities." He should have experience and prudence, yet be prepared upon occasion to execute a bold stroke. He should put daily emphasis on exact and orderly routines. While he was not to forget that competition was a natural law, nor expect progress or efficiency in individuals without the spur of competitive struggle, he should not apply this doctrine too vigorously to relations between railroad companies, where coöperation rather than competition was often the life of trade. He should regard profit as the primary justification for administrative action, regardless of other motives entering into its inception. In so far as honesty was the best policy, the executive should be truthful and dependable, but he should also recognize that the conventions of business imposed limitations on frankness in dealing with competitors. Above all, the executive should keep his personal sentiments and emotions out of his work, and decide all questions on the basis of how they would affect the long-run welfare and stability of the company. "Your first duty and mine also," wrote President Watrous of the New Haven, "is to the property with which we are respectively connected and we have no duty or right, even, to sacrifice that for anything or anybody."[6] The executive could use fairly wide latitude in selecting the means of performing his duty to the company, provided the practices were not of a type disapproved by the general entrepreneurs (were within their concept of the role), or regarded as dangerous by the legal counselors.

## Variables in the Role

The occasional conflicts between the views of the general entrepreneur and the professional executive appear to have been the result of differences in situation more than in principle. And the role of the professional executive was, of course, to seek ways of minimizing or avoiding such clashes. Many of these arose from new, unprescribed functions or relationships peculiar to railroads or to large companies, and others from the executive's need for maintaining the morale of his subordinates.

A conflict of the former type arose in regard to the private interests of managers. There was, in 1845, no conventional answer to the problem of how investment by an executive in subsidiary ventures affected his devotion to the financial welfare of the railroad company. In the early years, lack of definition in the role favored a wide latitude on the part of the executive to invest in special companies for constructing the road, or selling it land, materials, and equipment. This leeway was a carry-over from an age of small owner-managed enterprises, and was also perpetuated by the fact that in the early days the large railroad stockholders were likely to be interested in the auxiliary companies as well, so that the general entrepreneurs thought more as men active on both sides of the fence and less as absentee investors in the railroad alone. But as time went on and railroad ownership became further separated from activity in auxiliary enterprises, the danger to the interests of the railroad company inherent in such divided loyalties on the part of management became further apparent, and sanctions against managerial "side lines" appeared in the role. By 1885 the Perkins letter to a fellow executive stating that "the smallest kind of interest in a coal mine would be objectionable" probably represented a general attitude on the better-managed roads.[7]

Another difference in interpretation of the proper executive role was in attitudes toward expansion. The professional manager wanted to keep a step ahead of his competitors in both equipment and occupation of new territory, whereas the general entrepreneur thought more in terms of the availability of capital and good rates of return. Or, to put it another way, as one went downward in the hierarchy, managers increasingly saw themselves as engaged in competitive struggles for which they needed all available resources, whereas on the often interlocking boards of directors harmony and community of interest with competitors might seem the more profitable or safer approach. But the managerial conception of role sometimes dominated and directors were persuaded to build or control strategic branches in order to improve their long-run competitive position, even when short-run returns seemed unlikely and conservative financiers would have preferred to do nothing.

In still another way the personal ambitions of managers were held in check: they were not permitted to be dynasts. The inheritance of jobs connected with ownership such as the Vanderbilt posts in their railroad system were looked upon as normal aspects of the system of private property, but the appointment of the relatives of professional executives to managerial posts was frowned upon.

In his daily running of the railroad the top executive's relations were mainly with underlings. They constituted a group, less vital to his career than the general entrepreneurs, but one whose expectations undoubtedly influenced his thought and actions. Probably because of such sanctions from below, the executive language and attitude were in many ways democratic, in spite of insistence on strict obedience. But as the corporation grew bigger the chief executive found it necessary to protect his time by becoming somewhat aloof from the lower ranks. This led to formalized channels for communication, and he came to know the views of underlings mainly from a few subordinate officers. Along with this bureaucratization of communication and command, however, went recognition of the probability that fairly wide latitude for local managers in determining their own roles increased efficiency.

The common belief in unalterable economic laws such as those governing supply and demand and competition helped to reconcile the views of the subordinates with those of the prescribing group at the top. Both groups recognized that humanitarian or personal feelings would be sacrificed to efficiency, that the manager who exercised objective business judgment was reliable and predictable.

## Role in External Relations

Since the railroad was under social and political pressure from its earliest days, ideas soon developed on how managers should conduct the external relations of their companies. Believing that the public lacked understanding of railroad problems, in doubtful cases executives and directors favored secrecy. They thought that relatively little would be gained by granting public favors at the expense of revenue. In their role as business executives they should judge requests for aid from schools, churches, and similar institutions strictly in terms of the effect on the welfare of the company. To repeat Brooks's statement: "Our mission is not that of aiding institutions of learning or religion because they commend themselves to our personal judgment . . . We can properly help . . . when it is clearly for the advantage of our stockholders to do so."[8]

Executives were expected to be particularly wary in dealing with politicians, but the executive role was not precisely defined. There was no uniform philosophy regarding the degree to which railroads were "affected with public interest." Clarke, Ledyard, and Perkins, for example, used "private" enterprise as something distinct from the big corporation, as for example Ledyard's statement: "Private enterprise could not manage many of our corporations, and would not if it could."[9] But none of them attempted to define an intermediate or semipublic position for the railroad. Regardless of any public obligations that might adhere to the railroad because of corporateness, bigness, or function, entrepreneurs generally held to the premise that what business did was economic and developed the country while government action was usually negative and parasitical. This belief gave executives the feeling of having virtue on their side. As Leland Jenks has put it, the railroad leader "considered himself as an agent of civilization, an embodiment of collective enterprise."[10]

Many instances have been noted in which the influencing of political action by the railroad, or the disregard of laws pending their testing by the courts, were regarded as the proper and justifiable course. For example, Forbes took at a tolerant view of Oakes Ames's bribery of Congressmen in the Credit Mobilier scandal: "The Road was better built—

quicker and did work better than such a plan promised or would have been accomplished under any but so strong and energetic a head as Ames." Forbes added: "I have always tried to avert blame from him for the mistake he made."[11] In this, as in similar cases, the good material end justified the questionable means.

Social role, both as a framework for initially estimating executive qualifications and as a control over conduct, probably either excluded from appointment or inhibited the development of any men likely to favor wide departures from conventional ways. While it may seem unnecessary to point out that among these sixty-one railroad leaders there were no socialists, religious zealots, militant atheists, exponents of free love, utopian dreamers, artists, poets, or outstanding philanthropists, the fact, nevertheless, indicates the selective character of the role. Even Harris, who appears the most deviant of the executives, confirmed his unorthodoxy within relatively narrow limits. The politicians among these men were routine and distinguished for little beyond able, hardheaded manipulation. Forbes might be classed as a scholar, although he did not so consider himself; and Henry Villard could, by broad definition, be called a literary man. But both were relatively orthodox in their political, social, and economic views.

## Directions of Change in the Role

The tendency toward orthodoxy illustrates one facet of the relative stability in the executive role throughout these forty-five years of railroad history. As emphasized in the first chapter, in the long view of economic development this whole period will probably be seen as one of rapid expansion under much the same conditions of technology and finance. Because of the apparent lack of change in major qualities, it seems worth while to summarize the alterations that did occur in the role.

As noted in this chapter, important modifications arose from an increasingly precise definition of fiduciary obligations to the stockholders. In 1850 it was all right for the executive to be on both sides of many bargains, to sell his own goods to the company at what the traffic would bear. By 1875 such practices were seriously questioned by leaders like Forbes, and by 1885 they were specifically condemned, even in minor forms, by Perkins and other presidents.

As companies grew larger, the role of top manager in routine administration became more formalized. The old days of the small company when any assistant superintendent might confer with the president had to give way to communication through prescribed channels. Along with this increasing routinization, however, went stronger assurances of a policy of promotion from the ranks. As the organization grew larger and more stable, the expectation that an executive would have a career within a single company became a normal part of the role. While these changes were gradual and continuous, problems of administration were a particular subject for thought and writing in the period after 1873.

Conduct in relation to public authorities was another part of the role that grew in complexity through force of circumstances. Keeping within the law was easy when there were few laws, and steadily more difficult as state and federal regulations multiplied in the seventies and eighties. The rise of a public demand for regulations also put a new emphasis on successful public and political relations. In so far as some of the earliest executives of the period had been active politicians, these elements were always present in individual roles. The post-Civil War change was that ability to conduct such relations came to be required of most top executives.

## Notes on Role Behavior

In addition to supplying material on the ideas that characterized the executive role, the letters also provide some information regarding entrepreneurial behavior, clues to the reason why railroad companies acted as they did. Since remarks in letters are not adequate by themselves for a study of the activities of management, such findings should be regarded mainly as clues for future research.

From the letters it appears that except for some geographically limited eastern areas, competitive strategy was the greatest incentive for expansion. And extensions into new farming areas, to occupy the country ahead of competitors, had to be justified by expectations of future rather than present traffic. The long-run welfare and survival of the heavily capitalized enterprise had to be the primary concern in such policy-making. Often the needs of the expanding economy made the risk of inaction as great as the risk of further investment. In these and countless other cases the alternatives were not one anticipated rate of profit as against another, but the probability of some eventual profit as against long-run loss. Seldom in such a large complex structure as a railroad could estimates of return on investment be closer than "good," "handsome," or some other vague term.

Both professional executives and general entrepreneurs probably made most of their personal profit from sources other than dividends on the stock of the major railroad company. They seem, therefore, to have been primarily interested in stability and strength for the main corporation, through whose existence they made profits on subsidiary roads and other enterprises. In no instance does the correspondence suggest the possibility of a quick profit for the railroad stockholders as a group. Such conclusions support the general ideas of railroad finance elaborated by Ripley, Cleveland and Powell, and Riegel. Perhaps because the roads in this group were relatively prosperous and well managed, however, and because commentators usually select the worst examples to illustrate bad practice, finance seems more orderly and honest than in the conventional historic picture. Some of the abuses complained of by Josephson in *The Robber Barons* are seen in the Northern Pacific and Villard papers.[12] But the behavior appears in these records to emerge from the situation of building ahead of traffic in an area of high construction costs more than from what would then have been regarded as unethical practices by J. Pierpont Morgan or Henry Villard.

While the slogan for rate-making, "what the traffic will bear," sounds similar to "maximization of profit," in operation the letters indicate differences. Since high fixed costs necessitated a large volume of business, the general attitude of freight agents appears to have been to try to hold trade by secretly cutting rates. So complex was the rate structure that there was always the possibility that some business would be bid for at less than marginal cost. Even where the road had a relative monopoly of carriage, desire to build traffic in the area introduced a long-run or indefinite time factor into ideas of proper return. Other deterrents to immediate maximization of gains in such monopolized areas were fear of further regulation and encouragement to potential competitors.

While there was no public philosophy for the conduct of managers of large semimonopolistic firms, there were generally held sanctions after the 1860's against large profits for railroads. The evidence suggests that such public attitudes led railroad executives to seek safe and conservative profits rather than to exploit their markets to the utmost. But even without this external pressure there was a tendency for professional managers to want to invest earnings above the traditional or anticipated rate in ways that might insure the long-run market position of the enterprise, rather than needlessly swell the income of the stockholders. And long-run maintenance of a position might differ in financial results from maximization of profit over any finite time period.

Protection of the market position of a heavily capitalized enterprise led to an early development of intercompany agreements regarding rates, and ultimately to extensive pooling of traffic. The letters give some additional insight into the mechanics of such operations, and the difficulty of maintaining agreements that had no legal force. The railroad executive believed that the Interstate Commerce Act should have legalized pooling rather than prohibited it.

The irregularities in the rate structure caused by competitive pressures at certain points or by the bargaining power of big shippers were a steady source of antirailroad feeling among the less favored customers. To meet this ill will by a uniform rate structure was regarded by the managers as both uneconomic and practically impossible. The only recourse seemed to be a mixture of "educational" public relations and protective lobbying against regulatory legislation. By the seventies railroad executives had a mature understanding of both techniques. The letters show that the rise of professional public-relations men, which is often regarded as a product of the twentieth century, occurred in this industry during the last half of the nineteenth.

Finally, the letters suggest that much of the behavior of railroad executives objected to by contemporary moralists was simply the carrying out on a large scale of the aims and cultural beliefs of American business society. The letters also demonstrate that occasionally it was the "small" local man in the West who defrauded the capitalists in the East rather than the conventionally accepted reverse pattern.

## Some Implications of Social Role

The constellation of social roles that shaped corporate business attitudes and conduct in the United States can be seen as a way of life differing from that of other industrial societies. A culture less deeply patterned by feudal or other traditions may serve as an explanation of the peculiar strength in the United States of the business folkways and mores, which came in themselves to represent a structure as distinct as feudalism or some theocratic system. Like other cultural systems it had its discrepancies between doctrine and practice, such as the conflict between the "natural law" of competition and the real practice of coöperation. But in the business way of life, at least, praticality rather than introspection was the final test. Theoretical conflicts in social or economic doctrines were treated lightly by these men of action. Perkins, for example, who would "found a school for the study of political science to harden men's hearts," also wrote: "The struggle for existence and the survival of the fittest is a pretty theory,—but it is also a law of nature that even the fittest must live as they go along."[13] Harris probably spoke for the majority in saying: "There is so much to be done in connection with Railroad transactions that is characterized by unreason that we can hardly expect to establish the 'philosophy' of any arrangement."[14]

But granting that in spite of the lack of formal philosophy the evidence establishes certain uniformities, a major question is: how does viewing this segment of business society from the standpoint of these role patterns of the railroad executive suggest new interpretations for American history?

To begin with, social role can replace many inexact implications and dubious guesses as to the character or motivation of railroad leaders that appear in the histories of this period with more definite hypotheses. The role characteristics indicated provide an explanation for various attitudes and a scheme for their logical arrangement which can be elaborated and amended by additional evidence. Refusal to aid a young boy who, through his own carelessness, had lost both legs in a railroad accident, for example, is now seen not as unusual callousness on the part of the president of the Michigan Central, but as normal action in accordance with the sanctions of the social role regarding the conservation of the stockholders' money. Similarly, the strong sanctions for executive conduct in accord with the assumed laws of supply and demand explain much of what would seem today to be shortsighted personnel or labor policy.

As would be expected in a culture oriented toward physical achievement, those parts of the role that were directly functional for economic ends were rather closely defined, while those that had to do with nonbusiness matters were but loosely indicated. Ideas on religion, politics, and learning, or various personal enthusiasms and prejudices, such as belief in the value of more public education or distrust of Indians, had no definite place in the executive role. It could be argued that leeway in such matters illustrated lack of any theories directly connecting the particular belief with company welfare. And it could be further surmised that if the view held so departed from the normal as to threaten interference with business it would meet negative sanctions. This supposition is supported by the fact that while nonbusiness ideas varied they did so only within relatively narrow limits. A warmer than average humanitarianism in some men or a little more religious or political enthusiasm in others seem to have been the chief departures from the average, and when these deviations projected into business roles they were checked by the prescribing group.

This last idea suggests the force of business roles in shaping other goals and sanctions in American culture. Unfortunately, the evidence collected for this study is, by its business origin, weak as a guide to nonbusiness elements. To see the projections of business roles on other social relations the material analyzed here should be tested against family and personal letters.

Like the Hindu Ragas, general role systems are subject to endless variation or subdivision. Each different situation and each different individual tend to modify the role in spite of the unifying force of the prescribing group. The difference in role interpretation that has been noted between boards of directors and distant operating managers not only explains battles over rates and traffic between local representatives of roads with harmonious ownership interests, but also suggests such leeway in other branches of corporate business.[15]

This leeway principle or tolerance for personal interpretation permitted innovation. Such an explanation of change based on deviation in performing roles is a "field theory." New types of conduct are seen as arising from the reaction of the individual character to a particular situation. For example, Perkins's contributions to the theories of railroad management came from a particular man, with the partially unique conditioning that is the lot of every individual, coming in contact with the problems of the big corporation, and suggesting modifications in the executive role such as greater responsibility for branch managers, and sharper functional lines between top executives.

But in spite of this room for innovation and conflict in role behavior, the relatively tight control of railroad affairs on a nationwide basis in accordance with the attitudes of the prescribing groups of eastern financiers is a highly significant feature of American economic or social development. It explains, for instance, some of the mechanics of social control and cultural continuity that prevented frontier customs and behavior from being wholly products of their local environment. It also indicates the complexity of cultural change both in the United States and in other nations. Shifts in opinion regarding proper business practices in Dubuque, Iowa, for example, might be transmitted from Boston financial circles. And on the other hand, exploitation of new business opportunities on the upper Mississippi might be impeded by the fact that the social role of the railroad managers involved was not immediately responsive to local conditions.[16]

By its very nature a uniform and well-understood role offers resistance to any change in condition. And presumably the rigidity should be to some degree proportional to the precision of the role and the sanctioning force of the prescribing group. Thus a role set by a closed and conventional group in Boston could explain "cultural lag" not only in the West but in Boston itself. And the assumption that the executive roles in large corporations were particularly clear would serve to explain the widely held belief that big corporations were slower than small enterprises in adapting their policies to new conditions. It may also be true that corporate leaders, like politicians in power, felt the great social and economic responsibilities of their position and sought more than most men to conform to the expectations of their "constituents." Orthodox failure could be attributed to forces beyond the control of the entrepreneur, but un-orthodoxy and failure was a combination highly detrimental to an executive reputation.

It seems probable that knowledge of one type of social role will lead to readier definition of allied ones, until, let us say, the business social roles at various stages of American culture are tolerably well understood. This, in turn, should not only illuminate the past connections between physical development and concomitant ideas and attitudes, but should also suggest possible forecasts regarding future interaction.

# Microanalysis / *Benjamin W. Labaree*

As if he were addressing himself to the opening paragraph of Dr. Benjamin Labaree's article on Newburyport, Professor David M. Potter suggested: "a microcosm is just as cosmic as a macrocosm. Moreover, relationships between the factors in a microcosm are just as subtle and the generalizations involved in stating these relationships are just as broad as the generalizations concerning the relation between factors in a situation of larger scale."[1]

In a critique of Mr. Labaree's article, Dr. Bayrd Still has asked whether "the behavioral pattern of the smaller cities differed from that of the larger ones in the Revolutionary crisis, and to what extent the smaller cities were satellites of the larger ones in this connection." Dr. Still also points to other difficulties in comparing microcosm and macrocosm. There is need in comparative study for consistency of definition. Are the elements Labaree included in his merchant or leadership category the same as those Professor Carl Bridenbaugh included in describing some of the larger colonial cities? "If so, does this account for the fact that Mr. Labaree finds only 40 percent of Newburyport's population in the 'middling' group whereas Mr. Bridenbaugh finds two-thirds of the population of the larger cities in this category? Or does this lack of consistency spring from an essential difference in the relative size or occupational patterns of the two communities?"

It would be helpful, too, added Dr. Still "if Mr. Labaree would give us a further breakdown of his leadership group to show, for example, the number and activity of the lawyers, in view of what other students of the period have shown concerning the influence of practitioners of the law in the 1760's, especially in such communities as New York City."[2]

Although the transition from microcosm to macrocosm is by no means easy, other aspects of the microcosmic approach are of importance in historiography. Assuming the diversity of New England Puritanism, Professor Edmund S. Morgan has proposed to study "the history of early New England localities, town by town and church by church . . . Such a study would require a thorough examination of the records of a large number of towns—records of town meetings, proprietors' meetings, and tax lists, records of births, marriages, and deaths, of baptisms . . . Information would be compiled on every known individual in a town . . .

Benjamin W. Labaree, "Newburyport," in "Local History Contributions and Techniques in the Study of Two Colonial Cities," *Bulletin of the American Association for State and Local History*, II (February, 1959). Reprinted by permission.

1. "Explicit Data and Implicit Assumptions in Historical Study," *op. cit.*, 191.
2. *Bulletin of the American Association for State and Local History*, II (February, 1959), 246–49.

With such information from towns all over New England and for several
periods we might test our current assumptions . . ."[3]

   Aspects of the article reprinted below are developed more fully in
Dr. Labaree's volume Patriots and Partisans: The Merchants of Newburyport, 1764–1815.[4]



RECENTLY SCHOLARS have encouraged the study of local history
as a means of deepening our understanding of national developments.
Research on this level, they point out, leads to a more intimate knowledge of events which on a broader plane may be obscured in complexity.
In some cases a fresh interpretation may result; at the least the study of
a single locality provides admirable grounds for testing the validity of
general statements. The materials available to the local historian enable
him to reach beyond the recording of events toward a greater understanding of individual and group behavior. By utilizing such documents as
deeds, wills, and tax lists, in addition to town records and resolutions, I
have in effect reconstructed on paper the town of Newburyport, Massachusetts, during the American Revolution. The results of this project may
point the way to certain conclusions about class, caste, and power in a
New England town at a period especially marked by turbulence and
change.

   The town of Newburyport separated from its parent Newbury in 1764
at the request of those inhabitants who, residing by the Merrimack
River, had long since turned to maritime pursuits quite incompatible
with the old settlement's agricultural past. The act of incorporation
created a town whose 647 acres were devoted almost exclusively to the
houses, shops, and streets of an urban center. In the years just prior to
the war Newburyport's population averaged around three thousand inhabitants, of whom about six hundred were adult males. The examination
of deeds and other documents reveals the trades of more than three-
fourths of these men, who seemed to be of three fairly distinct occupational groups. Some fifty individuals, styling themselves merchants, along
with a similar number of shipmasters, formed the nucleus of one group,
whose membership included shipyard and distillery owners, the more
prosperous shopkeepers, and the few doctors, lawyers, and other pro-

   3. "New England Puritanism: Another Approach," William and Mary Quarterly,
XVIII (April, 1961), 237.
   4. (Cambridge, Mass., 1962).

fessional men of the town. This merchant group, as we shall call them for the sake of brevity, totaled no more than 150 men, or about 25 per cent of the adult male population. Next came the artisans, with occupations ranging from such domestic pursuits as cordwainer and tailor to the maritime skills of the shipwright, caulker, and mastmaker. Two hundred and thirty-five inhabitants of Newburyport, nearly 40 per cent of the adult male total, earned their living by one or another skilled trade. The remaining adult men, some 215 in all, were either identified as laborers, truckmen, or common seamen, or were men whose existence was disclosed only by the presence of their names on the town's tax rolls.

Of these three groups the merchants enjoyed almost complete domination of town affairs. Each year they placed three or four of their own on the five-man board of selectmen. The assessors, wardens, and other key officials almost invariably were drawn from this class, and during the growing crisis with Great Britain these merchants held firm control of the committees which drew up resolutions, made policy decisions, and enforced the various non-importation agreements. For example, of the thirty-five members comprising the Committee of Safety and Correspondence in September 1774, all but seven were merchants.

Since all of these officials were crosen by town meeting, it is reasonable to assume that by examining this institution the foundations for the merchant class's domination will be revealed. Fortunately, enough evidence in the case of Newburyport town meeting has survived to provide a clear picture of the electorate in the years before the Revolution. A valuation list for the year 1768 shows which citizens owned property ratable at £20, the minimum requirement for voting in town affairs. A tax collector's book, along with an incomplete valuation list, yields similar data for 1771. Computations on the flyleaf of the book, incidentally, show that the collector followed the rule that anyone paying taxes amounting to two-thirds of the assessment on each poll qualified as a voter. The most valuable of these documents is one entitled "A List of Voters Agreeable to the Tax of 1773." We have, then, data concerning the franchise for three different colonial years.

Averaging all the figures for the years 1768, 1711, and 1773 minimizes the effect of possible error for any one year and provides a broader basis on which to generalize. Among the pertinent facts concerning Newburyport's electorate in this six-year period are the following: first, 59 per cent of all males could vote in town affairs; second, 36 per cent of those voters were merchants, 43 per cent were artisans, and 21 per cent were of the laboring group. These figures suggest several conclusions concerning town-meeting democracy, or the lack of it, in colonial Newburyport, but the significant fact for our purpose is that only just over a third of the voters were merchants; at no time did they comprise a numerical majority of those qualified to vote in town meeting. Any attempt to explain how they enjoyed such complete political control must therefore reach beyond a simple analysis of the electorate into a study of the merchants' position in the community at large.

Clearly the mercantile group dominated Newburyport's economic life. Carpenters, caulkers, and riggers found employment in their shipyards; many of the town's youth went to sea on their vessels; others found work on their docks and in their warehouses. Some forty shops supplied the housewives with goods from nearby Haverhill and far-away London. Merchants brought timber from New Hampshire and molasses from the West Indies, and manufactured them into shingles and rum for export. Through ownership of wharf and shop the mercantile group controlled the economy of Newburyport.

Economic supremacy was accompanied by social leadership. It was most often a merchant's voice which issued the call to a vacant pulpit, and when the old Puritan foundations no longer satisfied, several gentlemen, i.e., merchants, established an Episcopal church. The school committee consisted almost entirely of merchants, as did the many groups visiting the educational institutions on inspection tours. Prestige organizations such as the Masons and the Marine Society, the latter restricted to masters of ocean-going vessels, brought other social distinctions to the merchant class. Even the right to protect the town from fire and invasion seems to have been a near-monopoly of the mercantile group.

The merchants enjoyed other advantages as well. For one thing, they led a broader, more cosmopolitan life. They read extensively from the periodicals of the time; they traveled almost as often to the West Indies and England as to Boston and Philadelphia, and, when at home, they corresponded with men in all parts of the British Empire. These gentlemen were as a result well informed on world affairs, which bettered their understanding of their fast-changing, revolutionary generation. Because of their greater wealth and less formal workweek, moreover, the merchants could more easily than artisans accept the time-consuming responsibilities of office-holding. Perhaps most significant was the fact that these merchants were men long used to command. Not only the active shipmasters, but also many of the merchants who had but recently retired to more sedentary careers, spoke with a quarter-deck authority which by the traditions and laws of the sea few mariners dared challenge. Since many of the artisans and laborers had shipped before the mast in their youth, and others continued to do so, it is little wonder that they listened when the same voices commanded their attention in town meeting.

But is it enough to explain the merchants' dominant position solely in terms of economic and social supremacy? The answer is probably no, for their leadership was of course subject to annual recall by the majority of town meeting. When the Boston merchants abandoned their aggressive policies toward Great Britain, they soon lost control of town meeting to Sam Adams. And a similar fate nearly befell the merchants of Salem and Marblehead. Only through the pursuit of a popular program could the mercantile group maintain its hold on the affairs of the town. An examination of several events during the period before the outbreak of war shows just how responsive those Newburyport leaders were to the will of the majority.

When Boston reacted to the Townshend duties late in 1767 by inviting neighboring towns to participate in a non-consumption agreement, Newburyport chose a committee of four merchants, two jurists, and a shipyard owner to draft a reply. The town had previously shown its colors in the Stamp Act crisis by labeling that measure a step toward the enslavement of America. Somewhat surprising, then, is the fact that the committee submitted, and the town adopted, a resolution rejecting Boston's proposal. It is natural to suspect that the merchants railroaded this conservative measure through town meeting for their own ends against the will of the artisans. In fact, however, all the evidence points otherwise, that the artisans and laborers opposed non-importation. The reason was this: Newburyport's principal industry was the construction of ships, many of which were bought in England and paid for by British manufactured goods. To cease importation of these commodities would sharply cut back ship production and throw a large number of artisans and laborers out of work. The merchants themselves favored non-importation. Less than a month later, twenty-four of the town's leading firms endorsed a private non-importation agreement with their Boston and Salem counterparts, and among the subscribers were the four merchants who had drawn up the town's resolution rejecting the more formal plan. The Newburyporters were cautious enough, however, to exclude from their boycott those goods which were imported in payment for locally constructed ships, which reservation did not seem to bother the Boston and Salem merchants, since they had made several exceptions of their own. Not until September 1769 did a Newburyport town meeting finally endorse the policy of non-importation, temporarily bringing to a close this double standard between public resolution and private practice.

A similar dichotomy occurred a few years later, in May 1774. A group of Newburyport merchants, having just received news of the Coercive Acts, proposed that the seaports of Massachusetts withdraw from the sea all their vessels but those engaged in coastwise trade until the disputes between Great Britain and the colonies should be satis-

factorily settled. This action, taken quite independently of a similar proposal adopted in Boston town meeting, surprised and impressed Sam
Adams very much. But a proposal by the town's merchants in an informal
gathering was a different matter from a resolution of action endorsed
by town meeting. When it received an invitation in early June to join
in Boston's "Solemn League and Covenant," Newburyport contented itself
with patriotic words instead of deeds. But in mid-summer a special
town meeting called by petition of twenty-one merchants and traders
did vote unanimously to stand by the actions of the impending Continental Congress, "even if it be to the Cessation of all Trade."

In September the town chose a committee of five men, all of the mercantile class, to draw up instructions to the newly-elected representative
in General Court. Four of these men had served on the committee of
1768 which had rejected the original nonimportation agreement, while the
fifth was the son of a former committee member. This time the committee
submitted, and the town unanimously adopted, a resolution which en-
joined the representative from taking any action which would in the least
imply a submission to the Coercive Acts. "We design not madly to brave
our own destruction," the resolution said, "and we do not thirst for the
Blood of others, but reason and Religion demand of us that we guard
our invaluable Rights at the Risque of both." The town had traveled far
along the road to revolution in the decade since its incorporation, guided
each step of the way by the leadership of its mercantile group.

During the critical war-time years the merchants of Newburyport
tightened their domination of town affairs. Political control in this
period meant more than a free rein over the town's war effort. Independence posed a new problem—the establishment of some sort of stable
government to replace the old provincial structure of colonial days—
and the mercantile group was in a good position to make its opinions
felt on the state level as well as in the town. The merchants whole-
heartedly supported their fellow townsman, Theophilus Parsons, as he
led the opposition to the proposed state constitution of 1778 through
his pamphlet *The Essex Result*. When a special convention was called
to draw up a new constitution in the following year, men from the merchant group comprised the entire Newburyport delegation. Equally important, this class also controlled the three-man committee to whom town
meeting referred the completed document for study. Endorsement by
this group assured the constitution's unanimous adoption by over three
hundred freemen of the town, with no evidence of opposition from
those who were to be disfranchised by the new frame of government.

With the establishment of stable government and of peace with
Great Britain, some of the older merchants retired to private life. But

their withdrawal did not result in any loss of political influence by the mercantile group as a whole. Their position in town meeting remained virtually unchanged. Average figures for the years 1784 and 1786 show that more than one-third of the freemen were still without franchise. Merchants constituted about 38 per cent of the town meeting, while the artisans increased their share to nearly 47 per cent, entirely at the expense of the laborers, who dropped off to less than 16 per cent of the electorate. Joined by a few new faces, the old group of merchants still dominated both the annual boards of selectmen and the delegations to General Court, relying as before on their ability to satisfy the will of the majority to continue them in office. They were thus in a strong position to lead the town in its most important decision of the post-war decade—ratification of the federal constitution.

Evidence indicates that until early in 1787 most of the Newburyport merchants had no clear concept of the kind of government they thought best for uniting the thirteen states. Under their direction the town had instructed its representatives in the winter of 1777–78 to vote for ratification of the Articles of Confederation. When in 1785 the Massachusetts legislature requested its delegates to suggest a convention for the revision of the Articles, Rufus King, then a resident of Newburyport, was among those who refused to comply. The states were not ready for such a sweeping action, the opponents of revision said. In the following year another Newburyporter, Tristram Dalton, was among those men chosen to represent Massachusetts in the Annapolis convention but whose distrust of Virginia was so strong as to prevent them from even attending.

The constitution proposed in 1787, however, quickly won the support of Newburyport's merchant group, and it's delegation to the state's ratifying convention consisted of four staunch federalists. The town conspicuously failed to include one of its former representatives who was clearly opposed to ratification. In the words of the young anti-federalist, John Quincy Adams, the town was "very unanimous" for the proposed constitution. Both Rufus King and Theophilus Parsons played significant roles in the convention, especially in the back-room politics which finally persuaded Hancock to declare for the constitution.

Having done its best to assure political stability on the national level, the merchant group of Newburyport once again retired to private pursuits and local problems. Its world had undergone many changes in the twenty-five years since the town's incorporation. For many the war and the subsequent depression brought economic ruin; for others the post-war situation meant new opportunities. By 1790 new merchants had taken the places of the older generation—on the board of selectmen, in General Court, and, in some cases, in the High Street mansions. But the traditions of merchant-class rule lived long after the passing of those men of New-buryport's revolutionary generation.

At the beginning of this paper it was suggested that the study of local history often brings fresh insight into historical problems; in other cases graphic examples illustrating hard-to-prove interpretations are provided. I should like to conclude by demonstrating these points from our examination of Newburyport, first making it clear that I do not regard Newburyport as an average town. Rather, I rely on this study simply as a springboard to a better understanding of a most complex era in our history.

One of the most controversial problems facing the historian of the American Revolution has been to determine the degree of democracy found in the colonies. In his recent study *Middle Class Democracy and the Revolution in Massachusetts*, Professor Robert E. Brown has maintained that "as far as Massachusetts is concerned, colonial society and the American Revolution must be interpreted in terms of something very close to a complete democracy with the exception of British restraints" (p. 60). Brown bases this statement on the well-documented evidence that most adult males in Massachusetts could vote, and upon it rest the two major points of his reinterpretation of the revolution in Massachusetts. First, he maintains that "after the passage of the Stamp Act, there was simply no question that democracy was in the saddle in Massachusetts" (p. 223), and second, he holds that "the ingredients for internal revolution were conspicuously absent in the Bay Colony" (p. 119).

The assumption is that political democracy automatically existed wherever the franchise was held by a substantial majority of citizens. The situation in Newburyport suggests a fallacy in this reasoning: society in colonial Massachusetts was something less than democratic, and without a high degree of social and economic equality true political democracy does not easily flourish. For no matter how many men held the franchise, they consistently used their power to elect leaders whose economic and social status was far above average. Furthermore, to maintain that the revolution in Massachusetts was in the hands of democrats overlooks the fact that most of its leaders hailed from the major eastern seaports, communities in which by Brown's own figures less than 60 per cent of the adult males could vote.

Walter Bagehot once coined the phrase "the habit of deference" to describe the yeoman's attitude toward the squirarchy of eighteenth-century England. How much stronger this "habit of deference" must have been when placed within the maritime context of a New England seaport! The analogy which immediately comes to mind to illustrate this relationship between a minority group of merchants and the majority of citizens in town meeting assembled is that of the typical college faculty.

Technically, of course, both junior and senior faculty members have but one vote each. It is the latter group, however, though outnumbered, which usually controls the important committees and policy-making machinery. Senior professors generally rule on the strength of their over-all position in the academic community. New England town meeting probably fell short of a pure democracy for somewhat similar reasons.

Historians of an older generation, notably Samuel Eliot Morison, Arthur M. Schlesinger, Sr., and Charles M. Andrews, fully realized the significant relationship in colonial America between social position and political rule. It is clear from the Newburyport example that actual political leadership—the holding of office and the determination of policy —remained almost entirely in the hands of a select minority group based on social and economic status.

This study of Newburyport suggests that other interpretations of the Revolution and the Confederation should be subjected to re-examination. It may pay us well to follow Edmund Morgan's recent advice to give closer attention to local institutions in our attempt to understand the era of the American Revolution.

# Turner Thesis: Predictive Model / *Stanley Elkins and Eric McKitrick*

*"Frederick Jackson Turner," wrote the authors of the selection re-printed below, "has stated the undeniable fact—that an organic connec-tion exists between American democracy and the American frontier. The insight is his. But Turner never offered a conceptual framework by which it might be tested. We are proposing such a model; it involves the establishment of new communities. Its variables are a period of problem-solving and a homogeneous population whose key factor is the lack of a structure of leadership."*

*What is a predictive model? It represents a postulated statement on the basis of which predictions are made. If these predictions are accurate, the model is validated.[1] The predictive model created by the authors by-passes much of the traditional criticism of Turner insofar as it affirms Turner's conclusions despite the fact that the foundations of Turner's theories have been weakened by the impact of a large body of criticism. This model has not been applied in the comparative studies of other frontiers, such as those of Canada, Australia and New Zealand.[2] Such application would provide further tests of its validity, which Turner him-self would have welcomed.*

I T WOULD BE difficult today, now that sixty years have passed, to revive the sense of intellectual ardor with which Frederick Jackson Turner's paper on the American frontier was greeted so soon after its first inauspicious reading.[1] So full of promise did the remarkable theory then appear, so charged with import, that its present status as an aca-demic curiosity seems to symbolize some profound intervening disillusion-

Stanley Elkins and Eric McKitrick, "A Meaning for Turner's Frontier Part I: Democracy in the Old Northwest," *Political Science Quarterly*, LXIX (September, 1954), 321–53. Reprinted by permission.

1. Marshall Walker, *The Nature of Scientific Thought* (Englewood Cliffs, 1963), 3–5, 147.

2. A. L. Burt, "If Turner Had Looked at Canada, Australia, and New Zealand When He Wrote About the West," in Walker D.Wyman and Clifton B. Kroeber, ed. *The Frontier in Perspective* (Madison, 1957), 59–77; Paul F. Sharp, "Three Fron-tiers: Some Comparative Studies of Canadian, American and Australian Settlement," *Pacific Historical Review* XXIV (November, 1955) 3, 69–77.

ment. A crucial motif of American spiritual experience seemed at one time to have found its fittest expression in Turner's inspired essay, and with his ceremonial "closing" of our frontier in 1893 a generation of publicists began finding the terms, products of convictions already deeply felt, whereby great stretches of American history might at last be given meaning. Persistent echoes of these convictions are heard even today.[2] And yet by now nearly every attempt to impose conceptual structure upon the lyricism of Turner and his followers has been abandoned. Intuition and cool reason appear to have succeeded in baffling each other.

It needs little prompting to recall the "frontier thesis," with its message that the presence of cheap land and an ever-receding frontier "explain" American development; its arguments, indeed, could be assorted under three rough headings. Turner's first claim for American culture was one of "uniqueness"; in mutiny against the Johns Hopkins "germ theorists" of the 1880s and their genealogical accounts of American political institutions traced back to England, back even to the gloomy forests of central Europe, Turner felt that these institutions and their character were to be accounted for most plausibly in terms purely American. Next, he produced a metaphor: the open frontier with its easily available land was a "safety valve" for underprivileged Easterners, its promise serving as a minimizer of urban unrest. The third claim, an extension of the first, was a report, again metaphoric, of the origins of true democracy. As settlers pushed out beyond the mountains, ties with the East and with Europe were steadily weakened, ancestral memories grew dim, and a "shearing-off" process took place: "layers" of civilization were removed until the pioneer stood in native worth, self-reliant, individualistic, a democrat of Jacksonian model. "American democracy was born of no theorist's dream; it was not carried in the *Susan Constant* to Virginia nor in the *Mayflower* to Plymouth. It came out of the American forest, and it gained new strength each time it touched a new frontier."[3]

A new phalanx of critics has now demolished the Turner conception. His vagueness, his abstraction, his hopeless imprecision, his poverty of concrete example, have each been held up to the scientific eye. Turner, in all but ignoring the English origins of our institutions, gains nothing but misunderstanding by his "ungracious exclusion of Locke and Milton."[4] The "safety valve," moreover, is at best a misleading poetic figure. How could the Eastern worker, poverty-stricken and ignorant of agriculture, think seriously of so staggering a project as removing to the West? The new Western farmer was most typically a recent Eastern farmer who had emigrated with at least a little money in his pocket, and the cities themselves, ironically indeed, eventually came to serve as safety valves for all farmers embittered with the agrarian life. But the deadliest criticisms of all are reserved for the Turneresque vision of the frontier's role in the birth of American democracy. Turner's state of nature, his shearing-off of civilized corruption, hints at a pastoral anarchy neither realized nor remotely desired by the bands of settlers in their wilderness outposts. The first efforts of these pioneers were to set up and to stabilize those very political institutions, parallel in as many ways as might be, which they had left behind them in the East. A kind of primitive geopolitics is brusquely challenged by a riddle which Turner could not have answered: why the *American forest*—why didn't democracy come out of other "forests"—why not the Siberian frontier?[5] The few remaining defenders of Frederick Jackson Turner have been able to produce very little in the way of rejoinder.

And yet, though conviction now burns so low, it remains to be noted that even the unkindest of Turner's critics have conceded, with a kind of bedeviled monotony, that *some* relation most likely does exist between our history and our frontier. The fact thus stands that, in this direction at least, no advance has yet been made beyond Turner's own dazzling abstraction. The problem is still there, its vitality unextinguished. It is no further resolved than ever.

If we examine with suspicion the body of critical work, we discover an interesting paradox. Turner and his teachings have been approached with deadly seriousness on their own terms—no other—and handled with what turns out to be *textual* criticism: a method which is illuminating but whose value for the analysis and correction of theoretical material is acutely limited.[6] The result has been to demonstrate the absurdities of Turner's internal logic—which is an undoubted contribution to perspective. Yet it should still be recognized that no concrete attempt to restate Turner's idea has ever actually been undertaken. Now might there not, after all, be a way of rescuing Turner? Is it possible to ask the great question itself in a form permitting a concrete answer?

Turner's critics may be allowed the most sweeping of concessions. Nearly everything[7] could be sacrificed—everything, that is, except the one thing that matters: the development of political democracy as a habit and the American as a unique political creature. This was the supreme fact which overwhelmed Tocqueville in the 1830s; every American still knows in his heart that the frontier had something to do with it. "What?" is, of course, the crucial question. It has always been difficult to ask it, if only because it has never seemed very important to discover a working, functional definition of "political democracy." "Democracy" is alluded to, invoked, celebrated, its collapse predicted daily. Democracy, in our traditions, has rich connections with the yeoman farmer (involving, as it were, "grass roots" and freedom from the urban banker); it is at once individualistic and coöperative, equalitarian and fraternal; hand in hand with stout self-reliance goes the civic exercise of universal suffrage. For most of our daily purposes democracy is a synonym for all that is virtuous in our social traditions and on the public scene.

Yet it still appears that we need a *working* definition of political democracy. It should in some way account for concepts central to most traditional notions, but it should also be functional, in the sense that its terms may be tested. Its focus should undoubtedly be upon participation —participation by large numbers of people in decisions which affect their lives. But it should be real, not ceremonial, participation. The extent of the suffrage would not be its most dependable measure, any more than the casting of one man's vote is the quickest way of influencing a political decision. Awareness of the community's affairs should have something to do with it, but only to the extent that individuals themselves feel capable of interfering in those affairs. Would this be to the community's best interest? Often, but not always; yet here we are not required to think of democracy as a community virtue. Some have, indeed, called it a national vice.

Suppose that political democracy be regarded as a manipulative attitude toward government, shared by large numbers of people. Let it be thought of as a wide participation in public affairs, a diffusion of leadership, a widespread sense of personal competence to make a difference. Under what conditions have such things typically occurred? When have the energies of the people been most engaged? What pushes a man into public activity? It appears that nothing accomplishes this more quickly than the formation of a settlement.

Our national experience, indeed, furnishes us much material for a hypothesis. Political democracy evolves most quickly during the initial stages of setting up a new community; it is seen most dramatically while the process of organization and the solving of basic problems are still crucial; it is observed to best advantage when this flow of basic problems is met by a homogeneous population. Now "homogeneity" should here involve two parallel sorts of facts: not only a similar level of social and economic status and aspirations among the people, but most particularly a lack of, or failure of, a traditional, ready-made structure of leadership in the community. A simple test of the effectiveness of structured leadership is its ability to command acceptance and respect.[8]

With a heavy flow of community problems, in short, and without such a structure of natural leadership, democracy presents itself much less as a bright possibility than as a brutal necessity. The very incomprehensibility of alternatives has always made it most unlikely that an American should see this. But Tocqueville saw it instantly. "In aristocratic societies," he wrote, "men do not need to combine in order to act, because they are strongly held together."

Among democratic nations, on the contrary, all the citizens are independent and feeble; they can hardly do anything by themselves and none of them can oblige his fellow men to lend him their assistance. They all, therefore, fall into a state of incapacity, if they do not learn voluntarily to help each other.[9]

Before turning to history for a trial of this so simple yet interesting idea, let us set it in yet another dimension by examining a series of extremely important findings in contemporary sociology. Robert K. Merton has conducted a study, whose results are soon to be made public, of social behavior in public housing communities.[10] A theory of political democracy which would meet all our criteria may be derived from Mr. Merton's work; there is little that we shall say from a historical viewpoint which has not already, in a present-day setting, been thoroughly documented by him.

He and his associates have observed two public housing projects, one being designated as "Craftown" and the other as "Hilltown." Craftown, located in southern New Jersey, administered by the Federal Public Housing Authority, and set up originally to house warworkers, was much the more active and interesting of the two. The key to the activity there was a "time of troubles" in the initial stages of the community's existence. The people who settled in Craftown ("homogeneous" in the sense that a majority were employed in nearby shipyards and defense plants) were immediately faced by a staggering series of problems of a fundamental sort, affecting the entire community. These bore on law and order, government, public health, housing, education, religion, municipal services, transportation, and markets. Slovenly construction had resulted in leaky roofs, flooded cellars, and warped floors. There were no schools, no churches, no electricity, no community hall, no grocery stores. Bus service was irregular and the nearest depot was a mile away. There were no hard-surfaced roads or sidewalks and much of the area was flooded during the rainy season. There was a wave of vandalism and no organization for its suppression. There was an epidemic of poliomyelitis. There were no municipal services of any kind; the environing township did not want to assume the cost of such services and by legislative action Craftown was gerrymandered into an independent township—which meant that it had to set up its own institutions for government and for the maintenance of law and order.

Craftown did have a ready-made structure, as it were, of leadership; its affairs were under the administration of a federal bureau, the Federal Public Housing Authority, and handled by a resident manager and staff.

Under stable conditions such a structure would have been adequate for most of the community's basic concerns. Yet the problems in Craftown were so overwhelming, so immediate, so pressing, that the residents could not afford to wait upon the government for action. They were therefore forced to behave in that same pattern which so fascinated Tocqueville: they were driven to "the forming of associations." Mass meetings, committees and subcommittees were organized, a township board was set up, officials of great variety were elected; a volunteer police force, fire department, and local court were established, with residents serving as constables, firemen and judges. A coöperative store soon came into existence. An ambulance squad, a nursery and child care center, and a great variety of organizations devoted to community needs made their appearance during this critical period. Pressures brought upon the bus company and the government agencies resulted in the improvement of transportation, the paving of streets, repair of houses, drainage of swamps, and the erection of buildings for education, worship and other functions of the community.

This experience resulted in an extraordinary level of public participation by people who for the most part had never had previous political experience; and it produced a political life charged with the utmost energy. Many jobs were created by the crisis—by the flow of problems— and they had to be handled by someone; many roles were created, someone had to fill them. The key was necessity. Persons who had previously never needed to be concerned with politics[11] now found themselves developing a familiarity with institutions, acquiring a sense of personal competence to manipulate them, to make things happen, to make a difference. Thus the coin of necessity had its other side: there were compensations for the individual. With many offices to be filled, large numbers of people found themselves contending for them; the prestige connected with officeholding, the sense of energy and power involved in decision-making, became for the first time a possibility, a reality, an exploitable form of self-expression.[12]

Now Hilltown, in contrast to Craftown, may be regarded as something of a control case. Many factors present in Craftown were present here— but a crucial one was missing. Hilltown, like Craftown, was a public housing project in an industrial area; it too was managed by the Federal Public Housing Authority; its population was likewise characterized by "homogeneity"—insofar as that involved a similar level of social and economic status among the residents. What Hilltown did not experience was a "time of troubles." Unlike Craftown, it was well planned and operated, it was not faced with a failure of municipal services, it was not confronted by lack of transportation, stores, electricity, or facilities for education and religion. The residents, to be sure, had their individual problems—occasional badly fitting doors and the like—but they were not of a community nature, not of a sort that made community organization seem indispensable. Widespread public participation in community affairs was never needed there, and it never took place. Sporadic efforts toward the establishment of a council, the election of officers, and the setting up of community activities aroused little interest and met with failure. The original structure of leadership—the federal agency and its local office —proved quite adequate for the handling of Hilltown's concerns, it was never seriously challenged, and it required no supplementation by resident activity.[13] "Democracy", in short, was unnecessary there.

One more reference to the Craftown episode should be made, in order to note two interesting subsidiary consequences of this problem-solving experience, this wide participation, this sense of individual competence spread among such great numbers. One was a close supervision of the officialdom which the Craftowners themselves had created—and a lesser degree of respect for it[14] than had apparently been the case in their previous communities. The other was a body of shared "traditions," with a common vocabulary, rich with meaning, whereby the experience might be relived and reshared. Although the level of activity was never as high in later times as it was in the beginning—the problems by then had been solved—the intensity of the "time of troubles" served to link the "pioneers" and the later-comers together by a kind of verbal bond. Talking about it was important: once this experience had been undergone, it was not lost. In such a usable fund of tradition, resources for meeting a new crisis, should one appear, would remain always available.[15]

How might such a contemporary model square with the pioneer frontier? No sorcery of forest or prairie could materialize the democrat, yet it should be safe to guess that the periods of wholesale migration to the West forced a setting in which such an experience as that just outlined had to be enacted a thousand times over: an experience crucial in the careers of millions of Americans. Frederick Jackson Turner has stated the undeniable fact—that an organic connection exists between American democracy and the American frontier. The insight is his. But Turner never offered a conceptual framework by which it might be tested. We are proposing such a model; it involves the establishment of new communities. Its variables are a period of problem-solving and a homogeneous population whose key factor is the lack of a structure of leadership. We shall test these terms in various ways by the examination of three frontiers, each of which should illustrate a special dimension of the argument. They are the Old Northwest, the Southwest frontier of Alabama and Mississippi, and the Puritan frontier of Massachusetts Bay.

2

"The frontier", to Turner and his followers, as well as to most others, seemed almost automatically to mean the Old Northwest—the "valley of democracy"—whose settlement took place during the first third of the nineteenth century. To discover why the connection should be made so naturally, let us select this region, with its key states Ohio, Indiana, and Illinois, as the first frontier to be observed.

The chronicles of these states abound with reminiscences of the pioneer; close upon them in the county histories came haphazard statistics which proudly mark progress from howling wilderness to fat countryside and prosperous burgs. Between these points come many a crisis, many a relished success. We should consider not the solitary drifters, the Daniel Boones, but the thousand isolated communities each of which in its own way must have undergone its "time of troubles." There, the basic problems of organization were intimately connected with matters of life and death. They were problems to be met only by the united forces of the community. Think of the basic question of housing itself, and how its solution was elevated by necessity, throughout the Old Northwest, to the status of institution and legend: the cabin-raising.[16] The clearing of the forest and the manner in which this was accomplished gave an idiom to our politics: the logrolling.[17] Defense against the Indians required that the experience of the Marietta settlers, forced to raise their own militia in the 1790s, be repeated elsewhere many times over at least until after the War of 1812.[18] And there was the question of law and order: the traveler Elias Fordham, stopping one night in 1818 at a cabin near Paoli, Indiana, found himself in the midst of preparations by the citizenry for apprehending a gang of brigands. How often must such a scene—the formation of *ad hoc* constabularies, the administration of emergency justice—have been enacted in those days?[19]

Close behind such supreme needs came that of educating the young, which claimed an early order of concern throughout the Northwest. Traveling instructors were often employed to go from house to house; later, when the children could pass through the forest without danger, they might gather for a time at one of the settlers' houses until community labor could be assembled to put up a school.[20] The demand for religion was little less urgent; first came the circuit rider to a house or barn designated for worship; denominational differences might then have to be submerged in the erection of a common chapel until each sect could build its own meeting house.[21] Even problems of public health, with no hospitals and few doctors, had to be solved occasionally under heroic circumstances. When cholera struck Jacksonville, Illinois, in 1833, the cabinetmaker John Henry boarded thirteen persons at his house for three weeks, supervised a crew of assistants in the building of coffins for each of the fifty-five dead, personally visited each house of sickness, took fifty-three corpses to the burying ground, and, assisted by two farmers, a blacksmith, a shoemaker, a brickmaker and a carpenter, dug the graves and interred the dead—a series of functions quite above the line of normal business.[22]

Now as these communities toiled through the process of stabilizing their affairs, what effect must such an experience have had upon the individuals themselves, exposed as they were to the sudden necessity of making great numbers of basic and vital decisions, private and public? With thousands of ambitious men, predominantly young men[23] looking for careers, pouring into vast unsettled tracts, setting up new communities, and being met with all the complex hazards of such an adventure, the scope and variety of new political experience was surely tremendous. A staggering number of public roles was thrust forward during such an enterprise, far too many to wait upon the appearance of seasoned leaders. With the organization of each wilderness county and pioneer township, the roster of offices to be filled and operated was naturally a perfect blank (how long had it been since this was so in Philadelphia?); somebody, willing or unwilling, must be found to fill each one.

Whether farmers, lawyers, merchants, artisans, or even men of means, the "leading citizens" in county after county were typically men of no previous political experience.[24] For example, there was Morgan County, Illinois. Its first settler was Seymour Kellogg, who brought his wife and seven children from New York State, was made a commissioner at the first election and shortly afterward became justice of the peace. Murray McConnel, who read law on his farm at odd hours and became Jacksonville's first lawyer, was forthwith sent to the legislature (though unwillingly) and later served the community in various other capacities. Jacksonville's first cabinetmaker, the aforementioned John Henry (scarcely literate), was drawn into politics immediately, and before his career was over had been an assemblyman, state senator and member of Congress, not to say superintendent of the local insane asylum and patron of learning to the Female Academy. The first printer there was Josiah Lucas, who had arrived from Maryland ("without friends") and established a paper with local support. Championing Henry Clay, he was shortly in a maelstrom of politics, and the experience thus gained netted him a postmastership to the House of Representatives and "many offices both civil and military," culminating in a minister's post in Europe.[25]

Variations on this typical pattern are to be found in county after county in the Old Northwest.[26]

What we exhibit here are the elements of a simple syllogism; the first settlers anywhere, no matter who they were or how scanty their prior political experience, were the men who had to be the first officeholders. This meant that the pioneers, in the very process of establishing and organizing their settlements, were faced with a burden of decision-making disproportionate to that exacted of the later-comers. The political lore, the manipulative skills, which must have been acquired in that process should somehow be kept in the foreground when judging the ferocious vitality, the extravagant energy, of early political life in the Old Northwest.

Inasmuch as many new political roles were being created by the needs of this new society, both necessity and opportunities for political careers might more and more be seen reflected in the long lists of candidates and high level of participation. In Hamilton County, Ohio, there was an election of delegates to the constitutional convention of 1802, and for ten openings there were ninety-four candidates—twenty-six of them receiving from 121 to 1,635 votes apiece.[27] The personal canvass, the practice of hawking one's political appeal from door to door, not generally assumed to have entered American politics until the Jacksonian era, was familiar in the Northwest well before 1824. A cabin-dweller's effusion in the *Illinois Intelligencer* of July 1, 1818, describes how hosts of candidates, at the approach of an election, would descend upon him with whisky, trinkets for the children, compliments, and grand promises.

> But what most rarely does my good wife please,
> Is that the snot nos'd baby gets a buss![28]

"And every body", wrote Baynard Rush Hall of Indiana's New Purchase, "expected at some time to be a candidate for something; or that his uncle would be; or his cousin, or his cousin's wife's cousin's friend would be; so that every body and every body's relations, and every body's relation's friends, were for ever electioneering." Even boys verging on manhood were "feared, petted, courted and cajoled."[29] Such arts of cajolery could be appropriate and necessary only to a society in which officials were watched far more closely and respected far less than was the magistrate of Boston or the justice of the peace in Fairfax County, Virginia. Hall, an Easterner of refinement, reflected with deep distaste that if "eternal vigilance" were the price of liberty it was well paid in the New Purchase, the "sovereign people" there being "the most uncompromising task masters": "Our officers all, from Governor down to a deputy constable's deputy and fence-viewer's clerk's first assistant, were in the direct gift of the people. We even elected magistrates, clerks of court, and the judges presiding and associate!"[30]

Thus the extraordinary animation with which the people of Craftown flung themselves into political activity may be seen richly paralleled in the life of the Old Northwest. Every militia muster, every cabin-raising, scow-launching, shooting match, and logrolling was in itself a political assembly where leading figures of the neighborhood made speeches, read certificates, and contended for votes. Sometimes at logrollings rival candidates would take charge of opposing sections of workers, fitness for office having much to do with whose group disposed of its logs first. The enterprising farmer understood, it is said, that this political energy could be exploited at its height about a month before election time, and tried to schedule his logrolling accordingly.[31]

Our concept of political democracy, it may be remembered, involved a homogeneous population. Can it be asserted that these early Northwest communities were characterized by such a population? There is striking evidence that both attributes of "homogeneity" a similar level of aspiration and status, and conditions rendering impossible a prior structure of leadership—were widely present here, just as they were in Craftown. A leading symptom of this may be found in the land arrangements. Beverly Bond has made calculations, based on lists of lands advertised for delinquent taxes, as to typical holdings in the Northwest about 1812, and concludes that the "average farm" at that time was probably less than 250 acres.[32] Though such tentative statistics are embarrassing in themselves, the limiting conditions which make them plausible are clear enough—uniform conditions not only permitting but forcing a reduced scale of holdings. Much has been made of large engrossments of land by speculators in the Northwest Territory, yet before the admission of Ohio in 1803, and many years before that of Indiana and Illinois, it was apparent to all that the day of the great land magnate was at an end. His operations were doomed by the very techniques of settlement and by the measures taken by the settlers themselves to thwart his designs.

Despite large quantities of government land on the market, much of which was bought by speculators, the attraction of choice locations led regularly to settlement in advance of purchase—squatting, in short—especially when sales were delayed, as they often were. Thousands of such petty *faits accomplis* all over the Northwest frontier could hardly be reversed,[33] no matter how powerful the petitioners, and the terms of sale, reflected in a series of land laws ever more generous,[34] were but one indication of such a state of things. An even more formidable token of doom to the great absentee holder was revealed in the tax rates levied on unimproved land by the early legislatures. While all these future states were still under one territorial assembly, that body at its first session passed a law taxing three grades of land—a law which was only the first of several, each more severe than its predecessor, consecrated to the mission of breaking up large unimproved tracts held by nonresidents. Increasing powers were given to local sheriffs presiding over the sales of delinquent holdings.[35] This meant that in practice the large speculator, forced as he was to pay cash for these tracts, must effect relatively quick turnovers in a buyer's market: there was really plenty of land to be had and the costs of holding it for a rise were becoming higher year by year.[36] For the rest, with labor costs uniformly high and with a population whose average resources, either in land or in liquid wealth, must initially be moderate, the great farm on the Southern model could never be a widespread reality. What this particularly indicates is that a land-holding élite —with all the traditional functions, social and political, that such an élite would certainly exercise—was rendered quite out of the question. The leadership of *this* society would have to be recruited on manifestly different terms.

Who was it, then, that organized the pressure for these land acts; who goaded the federal Congress into passing them; who connived in the legislature; who wrote the tax laws? Who indeed but the frontier politician who kissed the "snot nos'd baby" in that lonely cabin? He well understood how his majorities depended upon the zeal with which he and his friends could manipulate the government on their constituents' behalf. Their problems were concrete; the guaranteeing of preëmption rights was an urgency of the topmost order; this was the primary stimulus which forced the tax laws, the universal suffrage clauses in the state constitutions, and the Congressional land legislation. The "sovereign people" of the Old Northwest was a "most uncompromsing task master" to its servants. Symbolic of the future was the case of William Henry Harrison, to whom fell the unhappy office of mediating, so to speak, between "the people" and the Northwest's greatest land speculator, John Cleves Symmes. Harrison, as territorial delegate to Congress, was successful in bringing about the Land Act of 1800 in the interests of the settlers but a dismal failure in his efforts to get justice for Symmes, his father-in-law, whose vast holdings in Ohio were crumbling away in an avalanche of claims and judgments. The unfortunate Symmes was no match for a thousand ruthless frontier manipulators.[37] The democracy of the Northwest would be that of the squatter, the frontier business man, and, no doubt, that of the *small* speculator.

Granted that a structure of *landed* political leadership was impossible, might not a different species of élite appear, say an élite of lawyers? It is true that admission to the bar in the early days was a virtual guarantee of political advancement. But the stability of any such structure must be certified by some recognized assurance of self-perpetuation. The very recruitment patterns, the conditions under which political preferment had to be gained and held in the Northwest, should make us think twice before considering the great majority of lawyers in politics there as constituting such a structure. Every lawyer was literally on his own. It was the desperate need for wits and talent on the frontier that gave him his chance, a chance renewed by the community as long as he continued to deliver. Here the roles of patron and client are reversed; it is difficult for a "ruling class" to establish and guarantee tenure under such conditions. Murray McConnel, the self-made lawyer of Jacksonville, was once warned that his politically ambitious young clerk—Stephen Douglas —was using him as a steppingstone. "No matter," he replied, "his ambition will probably prove of more worth to the nation than all our modesty."[38] This was about the only kind of laying on of hands possible in the Northwest: the embodiment of success, of frontier virtue, was the self-made man.

What we have done so far is to discover a kind of "primitive" level of the frontier experience, a level at which a vast flow of problems forced a high degree of participation in the making of decisions, an acute pitch of political awareness among the settlers. The traditions of the pioneers remind us that this experience was not lost. An egalitarian tone was set, and ceremonial observances by which the experience was reinvoked and reshared made their way into the social habits of the people. Stephen Douglas, for one, understood its obligations, and by stopping at Geneva on one of his county canvasses to assist at a logrolling he was performing a symbolic act.[39]

Now another frontier was being developed at this same period in the Southwest, the frontier of Alabama and Mississippi, where scenes more or less similar were enacted. Yet we are unable to speak of "democracy" there with quite the same lack of ambiguity as we may with the Northwest. One reason for this is that throughout the Northwest the "problem-solving" experience did not generally stop with the taming of the savages and the establishment of law and order, but was continued, and indeed more or less perpetuated, on another level.

This second level of experience may be called that of town life. Let us remember that our focus has been fixed upon the *community* character of political democracy, involving a setting in which the people are close enough together to make common efforts possible, and a social texture thick enough to make it not only feasible but crucial to organize for a variety of objects. It is true enough that the basis of most such settlements was rural agriculture. But it is undoubtedly true as well that the ease with which the basic agrarian experience flowed into that of commercial small-urban enterprise was much greater and more natural in the Northwest than in the Southwest. The primitive, "agrarian" level of democracy is the one from which we have drawn democracy's folklore, a folklore still appropriate enough for our ceremonial. But it has been chronically difficult for our serious thought to go very far beyond it. The very vision of "grass roots democracy," with its herbivorous overtones, is it-self a reproach to an urban culture to which it no longer seems to apply.[40]

Yet we should not feel that there is actually any paradox. Indeed, there are formidable reasons for concluding that the development of American small-town enterprise (and by extension, of urban capitalism) is most centrally—organically—connected with that of American political democracy.[41]

Watching the organization of the Old Northwest, county by county, we are struck by something which is not duplicated on our Southern frontier: the appearance of teeming numbers of *small towns*. By this we mean, not the post-office hamlet with its fifty souls, but rather the market center which had two hundred or more people and was struggling to become bigger. It was a development quite automatic and logical in the Northwest. Cheap land and dear labor set fatal limits on wide-scale land engrossment for purposes other than speculation (and we have already seen the limits set on speculation), so that, for agriculture, subsistence and market farming, rather than extensive raising of staples, would largely be the rule in the '30s and '40s. It was toward the town that an increasingly market-conscious population was orienting itself, not toward the plantation, nor to the cosmopolitan port city, nor yet to the cross-roads courthouse. Large amounts of money, if and when made in the Northwest, had to come from commerce, from industrial activity, and from real estate whose value depended greatly on its nearness to or loca-tion in a town. It was unquestionably the town from which the tone of life in Ohio, Indiana, and Illinois came to be taken, rather than from the agriculture in which an undoubted majority of the population was engaged. It is no exaggeration to say that there were five to six times as many such towns per capita here as in Alabama or Mississippi.[42]

The town, becoming the natural focus of exchange for goods and services in the Northwest, must thus inexorably be the focus of politics as well; this fact on the very face of it would mean a faster tempo of political life than on the rural countryside. Things were less simple in the town; the organizational needs were more involved; there were more functions to perform, more offices to fill. But what was is that so energized the Northwest town, what sustained this tempo, what made its democracy *real?* It was the fact that every town was a promotion.

The bright young man of talent and enterprise in the Northwest—unlike his opposite number in Alabama—naturally gravitated to the town; it was there that his future lay; roles in politics or business were enacted from there rather than from rural strongholds. In the Northwest the typical success story of the young man with wits or money, or both, does not show him accumulating baronial acres for the cultivation of profitable staple crops. Instead, if it shows him buying up choice lands —and oftener than not it does—it is with quite different designs in view, designs centering on the development of town sites. It was estimated that during the boom years 1835, 1836, and 1837 over 500 towns were laid out in Illinois alone.[43] The energetic Wesley Park, first settler at Auburn, Indiana, besides filling many local offices, besides using his cabin as hotel, jail, church, and courthouse, had as a matter of course personally platted the town. He had done so, as had all Northwest town planners, to increase the value of his real estate and future business prospects.[44] But there was an essential difference in type between this petty-urban speculator and the speculator who engrossed vast cotton lands and held them for a price rise. The distinction was between the monopolist and the promoter.[45]

It was the promotion which gave the tone to the entire life of the town, and most particularly to its politics, which meant that the placation and "cajolery" so displeasing to Baynard Rush Hall in the New Purchase would become, so to speak, universal in the town. Everyone understood that success must depend upon the town's prosperity, that it must be advertised, its virtues broadcast. The town must grow—it was vital to get people there and keep them there. Capital must be attracted—it was of the essence to allure the man with money.

The result was, naturally, a torrent of problems centering in the advancement of business. It was important for the town to obtain for itself the location of the county seat. Here the promoter donated land and made large promises to the county commissioners; in Mississippi the commissioners typically had to *buy* the land for courthouse site.[46] The population must be increased, for this meant automatic benefits, more customers; in the cotton country it might mean greater competition and a drop in cotton prices. Capital must be brought in; expansion of plant was easier and less risky in an Indiana town than it would be on an Alabama cotton plantation. The town must be made attractive; it must be a suitable place to live in; it must have stable government; lapses of law and order would be a reflection upon its peace. Schools and seminaries must be established (no general public school system would exist in Alabama or

Mississippi until after the Civil War);[47] roads, bridges, canals and banks were crucial for the nourishment of the town's enterprise. Civic services, churches, facilities of every sort, were urgently demanded. And the keynote, the watchword, the trumpet call, must be Opportunity.

Without a ready-made structure of leadership, how would such a myriad of problems be met and who would meet them? "In no country in the world," wrote Tocqueville, "has the principle of association been more successfully used, or more unsparingly applied to a multitude of different objects, than in America."[48] How familiarly do the county chronicles dwell upon mass meetings for worthy objects, upon committees for the advancement of this or that; how appropriate that John Henry and Murray McConnel should trouble themselves for the Jacksonville Lunatic Asylum, for the College, for the Female Academy. Here was a society in which the setting up of institutions was a common experience; indeed, Tocqueville thought that the typical American addressed him "as if he were addressing a meeting," and would infallibly say, "Gentlemen."[49] Everything on the balance line between politics and civic consciousness was directly related to the prosperity of the town's citizens. There was an acute general awareness of this. For instance, the business prospects of a town were much enhanced by its becoming the county seat, and a perennial feature in the history of each Northwest state was the "county seat war" in which entire communities took part. The efforts of towns to make the legislature locate or relocate the seat in their favor typically occasioned great lengths of maneuvering and often actual violence. Scarcely a county in all of Indiana failed to see one or more such "wars."[50]

The very factor of success—an accelerating population—created new enterprises and new opportunities in the Northwest town: an index might be found in the sheer numbers of small business men there in contrast to those in the Southwest.[51] It also created new problems, all of which meant that talent was at the highest premium. Consider the variety of roles, commercial and political, to be filled. There would be a role for the man with money looking for a place to invest it, a role for the business man with a heavy stake in the community (the natural organizer, the booster); there would be one for the early settler-business man who knew the scene and who knew everyone (he would be the mediator of interests, the grand master placator.) And a role would exist for the bright young lawyer who could make connections, who could manipulate the legislature: he must get a charter for the bank, a charter for the bank, a charter for the academy; he must press for the county seat, the highway, the canal. Directly to his rear would be the entire town, pressing *him*. This dependence for success upon growth and development, this need for aggressive political representation, forced the community to seize upon whatever talent it could find and watch it closely. Those who rose in politics must continue to placate; the relation between economic welfare and politics was direct and continuing. Such a society would reward its adroitest politicians, not so much with awe and veneration[52] (their activities were too much a matter of general concern), but by reelecting them to office: they were too badly needed to be dispensed with. Responsibility, here, meant the art of returning home with whatever a politically sensitive electorate might demand.

There is no better illustration of this complexity of political life on the local level, this intimate connection between business and politics, this variety of demand, diffusion of power, and diffusion of pressure than in the promotion of the internal improvement systems of the 1830s. Enthusiasm for improvements found expression all over the country, but the energy of the Northwest states was unmatched for subtle haggling, deep maneuvering, and grandiose objects. The "System" in each of them was like a tract of jungle, lush, overgrown, unplanned, extravagant, magnificent. In Ohio a public works program involving roads and canals at an estimated cost of $8,577,300 was coupled in 1837 with a general law for state aid in credit and subscriptions to private improvement schemes, an act variously known as the "Loan Law," the "General Improvement Law," and the "Plunder Law." The most relentless pressures from all counties lay behind the fashioning of the bill.[53] The Indiana system, even more spectacular, was in 1836 embodied in a mammoth law of forty-four sections which provided for a network of roads, canals and railroads, omitting virtually no community in the state. It reflected the grand aggregate of many local pressures; the entire movement was of local rather than metropolitan origin,[54] and the interested assemblymen were involved in endless deals and logrollings.[55] The growth of the Illinois Internal Improvement Act of 1837, an imperial scheme of canals and railroads, was the result of a monster bargain. It was kindled by illuminations, bonfires and conventions of the citizenry everywhere, it was energized by the hopes of real estate speculators up and down the state, complicated by the rivalries of Springfield, Alton, Vandalia, and Jacksonville over the location of the capital, and compounded by prodigious scheming and haggling in the legislature. Two master Illinois politicians, Stephen Douglas and Abraham Lincoln, were in the very midst of it.[56]

Nothing of any resemblance to this occurred in Alabama or Mississippi, though they too were seized by the internal improvements enthusiasm of the 1830s. Allowing for the probability that the river systems of these states to some extent relieved the need for wide-scale transportation schemes, it is at the same time true that political machinery there was not organized in such a way that local pressures could be anticipated and reacted to with the sensitivity so characteristic in the Northwest. Little or nothing was done there.[57]

Now what was it in the Northwest that made these activities so classically democratic? It was dependence on the favor of large numbers of people in market communities where manipulation was a daily habit, dependence on a favor which must be constantly renewed. This was the process by which the "equal rights" attitude, so symbolic of the Jacksonian period, was developed: room for the aggressive young man on the make. This was the setting in which intolerance of cultural and religious differences could not be permitted to interfere with the promotion: the organizer must be free to boast of schools and churches for all.[58] And this fundamental tolerance,[59] this built-in attitude of placation, had its other side. The booster would adjust to his neighbors but would adjust to no one who tried to limit *his* activities; he would instruct his representatives but would not tolerate their instructing *him*. The balance was a delicate one and easily upset by the vicissitudes of business.

Under such conditions a prior structure of leadership, a self-perpetuating planter oligarchy, an aristocracy of money and birth, would simply have melted away. A burgeoning capitalism recognizes no prior structures, is impatient of élites, tolerates few restraints. Expressed in classical theory this is *laissez faire;* acted out on the Illinois frontier it meant unfettered opportunity for all, careers open to talent, and a gleeful willingness to manipulate the government, starting at the local level, in any and all ways that might advance business. The principle whereby a small-town culture such as this accomplished its political needs was typically not that of *noblesse oblige,* but of the bargain. The agents were numerous, the demands constant, the haggling intense. The parallel, then, cannot be that of an élite holding sway, but rather of tradesman maintaining a clientele.[60]

It is possible to compress virtually everything we have said about political democracy in the Old Northwest into the experience of a single county in Ohio. Let Stark County, organized in 1890, furnish that profile. There, the "primitive" level of pioneer democracy, forcing upon the settlers the burden of organizing communities and fashioning institutions, was to be seen in every township. There, the lack of seasoned leadership in Sandy township did not absolve the Hewitts, the Downings, the Van Meters, from serving as constables, sheriffs, justices of the peace, or from organizing themselves against the Indians. Nor was it possible to be fastidious in Plain township, where the uncouth Henry Friday, a paroled Hessian soldier, was the only man available for constable. (Once during a plague of locusts he had a locust pie made, "which he ate.") Rudy Bair, whose wife once threw firebrands at the wolves to protect her baby, was the first settler in Paris township; he was the first justice of the peace, a delegate to Ohio's constitutional convention, and a member of the first legislature.[61] The very profusion of public roles during the first few years should give a key to the energy of the people who would shortly organize Canton, Massillon, Alliance, and Louisville. The very first election in Lawrence township involved the naming of two justices of the peace, a clerk, a school examiner, three trustees, two overseers of the poor, two fence viewers, two appraisers of property, three supervisors, two constables, and a lister of taxables. This, multiplied by the number of townships (there were fourteen in Stark County by 1816) and added to the county officers,[62] is in striking contrast to the relatively simple organization of the Mississippi county court.

Stark County did have one landed baron, Bezaleel Wells, who had all the attributes which would seem to make for influence, leadership and power. Wells's career there, however, so similar in some respects to that of John Cleves Symmes, may typify the vulnerability of the great speculator to the aggressions of small operators in the early Northwest. Brought up in surroundings of refinement, Bezaleel Wells had become a staunch Federalist in the 1790s and had excellent political connections which included Arthur St. Clair and George Washington. His own public activity in Ohio included service as judge of probate, prothonotary to the Court of Common Pleas, clerk to the court of general quarter sessions of the peace of Jefferson County, member of the Ohio constitutional convention, and state senator. Having realized substantial profits from purchases of over 15,000 acres in the Steubenville area, he shifted his activities in 1805 to the present Canton township, undoubtedly with foreknowledge of the Indian treaty of Fort Industry. Though the tax laws and the Harrison Land Act had meanwhile made largescale operations less feasible than they had been at Steubenville, his holdings of 6,500 acres in Osnaburg, Plain, and Canton townships still put him in a class by himself.

Since competition had become greatly enlarged, with new towns being platted everywhere, it was clear to Wells that at Canton he must become a promoter. His inducements for attracting settlers were of the most royal sort: wide streets were laid out, whole blocks were donated for schools and churches, and special terms were offered for the purchase of town lots. He even sponsored a horse race at the south end of town to stimulate interest in sales. He made princely offers to the county commissioners to induce them to fix the county seat at Canton; sizable gifts of land and proceeds of sales were to be turned over to the county should Canton be chosen. The seat was, in fact, located there in 1808, but the artful commissioners—themselves small business men and petty speculators—seized upon the vague and contradictory wording of the proposals to exploit Wells in the most callous fashion. They accused him of fraud; by means of court action and merciless pressure they finally made him disgorge 150 unsold lots and a choice courthouse location. Meanwhile Wells, attempting to set up another town in Wayne County, was forced to liquidate the venture when his town failed to be chosen as county seat, and after the disastrous fray with the Stark commissioners his name virtually disappears from Canton history. By 1829 we see Bezaleel Wells —the only man in Stark County's early annals who might possibly have qualified, by virtue of wealth, experience, and extent of landholdings, for anything like a position of privilege—taking the pauper's oath in a debtor's prison. He had failed as a placator.[63]

What of the "secondary" level of democracy in Stark County, that of small-town enterprise? The county's first eleven permanent towns were established between 1805 and 1816—an average of one a year—which was different from the way it was in Alabama: there, even by 1850, only twenty-eight towns of over 200 inhabitants could be found in the whole state.[64] For the success of any of these eleven towns the factor of growth was crucial, and the promoter's art was at a premium. It involved the immediate setting up of services; schoolhouses were built before there were children enough to fill them. It called for toleration, since business always came before religious particularism; it called for placation, and, especially, for the instinct of manipulation; James Leeper's failure to donate lots for churches and schools cost Osnaburg the county seat.[65] The initial problems of settlement were thus carried over into those of promotion, and roles for the politician and manipulator went hand in hand with roles for the business man and promoter.

That these roles, both commercial and political, were not only profuse but interchangeable is seen in the careers of Canton's earliest leading citizens. One result of Bezaleel Wells' disappearance from Canton's town life "was the growth of a democratic, self-reliant, enterprising group of town leaders, who took matters into their own hands." Among the foremost of these, as might be expected, was the chief man on the board of commissioners which had ravished Wells of his holdings, the tavernkeeper Samuel Coulter. Besides entertaining the public, Coulter practiced law, speculated in land, was one of the first trustees of the Farmers' Bank, and served as Judge of the Court of Common Pleas. William Fogle, who kept a general store, was also a county commissioner and later became trustee, director and cashier of the Farmers' Bank, from which he resigned in 1816 to accept the county treasurership. John Shorb, Canton's first storekeeper, became the Bank's first president, was instrumental in founding the first Catholic church, and was highly active in public affairs at large. James Lathrop, a young Connecticut Yankee brimming with talent and ambition, having been admitted to the bar the year of his arrival, plunged instantly into public life, organizing Canton's first library, becoming its librarian, and leading the movement for an Academy. Lathrop was appointed receiver for the Bank when it failed in 1818; he helped get the town incorporated in 1822 and became the first town president; he was elected county auditor the same year and went to the legislature two years later, serving several terms and heading the committe which wrote Ohio's first compulsory school tax law. His name is preserved in Canton legend. The hatter, George Stidger, arriving from Baltimore in 1807, organized and commanded his own company in the war of 1812 and rose to the rank of general Upon his return, having accumulated considerable real estate before the war, he built a tin and copper shop, set up a tanyard, and ultimately amassed a veritable chain system of such enterprises. He served as Judge of the Court of Common Pleas.[66]

These were the men who headed Canton's "first families". They and their descendants became the only "aristocracy" that Canton could ever have.

# Party: Comparative Model / *William Nisbet Chambers*

*In the selection reprinted below, Professor Chambers has attempted to define political party in the context of the materials of American history. This definition is a model in whose context the political parties of this and other nations are compared. The discussion, incidentally, summarizes many of the recent contributions by historians to an understanding of early American political behavior.*

*It should be noted that an earlier model, although it was not identified as such, was structured by American historians in the late nineteenth century who used the comparative method to demonstrate the alleged Teutonic origins of American institutions. This episode in American historiography demonstrated the extent to which a structural device can reenforce preconceptions and lead to distortion.[1]*

A CCORDING TO much conventional historiography, modern political parties arose first in Great Britain and later in America. A more accurate view would assert the contrary—that parties in the proper sense appeared first in the United States with the Federalists and Jeffersonian Republicans of the 1790s, and in Great Britain only some decades later with the Whig-Liberal and Tory-Conservative formations of the 1830s, and 1840s. The dates themselves are not of great moment; it is rather the issue of when, how, or under what conditions modern parties emerged that is significant. It is an argument of this essay that much about the nature and role of party can be learned from an historical analysis of the origins of party in America. A further argument can further clarify such understanding. The American case is at once "special" and indicative of certain key aspects of party development in general.

The term "proper sense," of course, suggests some conceptual or theoretical distinction between parties and other formations. The point here is that it is of primary importance for the historian or political scientist who is concerned with party development or action to distinguish in a con-

William Nisbet Chambers, "Party Development and Party Action: The American Origins," *History and Theory*, III (1963), 91–120. Reprinted by permission.

1. Saveth, *American Historians*, op. cit., 13–64.

scious, analytical manner between pre-party political formations or fractions on the one hand, and parties on the other. If this distinction is carefully made, much else follows, including clarification which opens the way to historical explanation of the early development of party in the United States, and ultimately of the origin of parties generally. Thus, party is explored here as a modern political phenomenon and indeed as an aspect of political modernization in general. Finally, party is also understood as being associated with some form of *mass* politics, whether actively "democratic" or passively "plebiscitarian".[1] Democracy is construed summarily as popular representation, popular participation or initiative, and popular choice.

The focus of inquiry is on the American experience and literature, against a limited comparison with the English background. Throughout, emphasis is on certain key notions—structure and function, as central defining aspects of party action; and ideology, as a crucial but not sole defining characteristic of party behavior.

## I

Studies of party development in the United States, as well as general histories of America and studies of party history in general, surprisingly seldom fix a conception of party sharply.

One may, of course, apply "party" quite loosely. The term has been used in effect to mean any considerable aggregate of men who exhibit parallel action in politics, or, alternatively, any set of men who share similar beliefs, perspectives, or attitudes concerning government or policy. The first usage implies a kind of rough structural conception: the second an equally rough ideological distinction. Such notions turn out to be the unexamined conceptions of much conventional historiography. Thus, in England, a list of parties may include Court and Country (a demarcation of geography and interest), or Royalists and Parliament Men or Whigs and Tories (loose cleavages of persuasion or outlook), whether they involve divisions in Lords and Commons only, divisions in the population, or both.[2] In America, such conceptions have encompassed Court and Country in the colonies, Patriots and Loyalists in the Revolutionary War of 1775–1783, or above all Federalists and Anti-Federalists in the conflict over the proposed Constitution in 1787–1789. As distinguished a scholar as Charles A. Beard tends thus loosely to use the term "party." He consequently draws clear, dramatic lines of continuity between the pro- and -anti-Constitution forces of the 1780s on the one hand, and the Federalists and Republicans of the 1790s on the others.[3]

Several difficulties attend such usage. Conceptually, it provides no differentiation between transient, formless aggregates or alliances such as the so-called Federalists and Anti-Federalists of 1787–1789, and the more durable social formations we call parties today; and it offers no differentiation between parties, interest groups, bodies of opinion, and factions. Empirically, for the American case, such usage fits ill with the fact that the contest over ratification was actually a pluralistic sprawl of innumerable forces in thirteen state arenas rather than a clean dualistic national (much less party) conflict, or with the fact that the Federalists and Republicans of the 1790s were not in truth mere continuations-in-metamorphosis of elements involved in the ratification question.[4] Finally, loose notions of party slur over problems which are important for analytical history and political science. They encourage evasion of distinctions between party and non-party politics, and leave unexposed questions which are basic to a theory of modern party politics.

To be sure, nearer approaches to a conception of party may be found in the historical treatments. One approach is to mark party as *organization*. This concept is contained in the monumental work of Ostrogorski as it refers to both Great Britain and the United States, and it is quite explicit in the valuable historical summary by Robinson, who stresses for America in the 1790s the existence of two "party organizations" whose "activity" rather than beliefs were of "primary importance." Finally, it is stressed in a comparative analysis by the political scientist Avery Leiserson.[5] Difficulties attend this approach also. Conceptually, it does not distinguish parties from organized interest groups or organized factions; and indeed Leiserson argues that it is probably not important to separate parties from factions. Empirically, for the American instance at least, there is a fatal flaw. The Federalists and Republicans of the 1790s may certainly be thought of as parties before they were organizations, if indeed the Federalists ever accomplished organization in any strict sense.[6] Furthermore, though in Britain organization follows more closely upon origins, Liberals and Conservatives stood as effective parties before they had achieved much in the way of organization.

A third approach to party, derived from Beard and his school of neo-Madisonian interpretation, is emphasized and reiterated by Wilfred E. Binkley in the currently leading (and most substantial) treatise in American party history.[7] He views parties, at least major or majority-bent parties, as broad *combinations* of interest groups—the "grand coalitions" of semi-sophisticated historical writing and popular commentary. This is certainly a useful conception with considerable analytical "bite," yet it too is attended by many difficulties and inadequacies. First, Binkley's conception does not distinguish parties from extended factions, which may also embrace a plurality of interest groups—and, one may add, a plurality of bodies of opinion. Second, his approach does not clarify any conceptual distinction between transient combinations on the one hand and parties as somehow more durable formations on the other. Third, the notion of party as combination of interest groups tends implicitly to locate parties in the public and in the electorate—"party-in-the-electorate," in Key's phrase[8]—thereby slurring over important questions of intra-party relationships and behavior. Fourth, particularly as Binkley employs it, the concept emphasizes the role of economic group interest at the expense of other important aspects of party behavior and politics, particularly ideology or general perspectives, *élan*, leadership, innovation, and organization. Fifth, in consequence, the tendency in combination analysis is toward a tacit model of party action as a set of mechanical reflex-responses to the pressures of interest groups in the party coalition.

Indeed, Binkley himself treats some of these problems. On the structural side, he explicitly allows for resolving "differences" among "the several social groups attracted by common interests into an unplanned [party] association," through "the familiar practice of finding the formula that ends debate." He does not, however, make it clear *who* "finds" the ultimate party formulas of agreement, or *how*, though the task is implicitly treated (sometimes at least) as a leadership function. On the ideological side, he speaks of the Federalist coalition of 1787–1789 becoming "the first of our several national political parties" *when* it "coalesced into a permanent combination [and] developed a consistent ideology" in the 1790s. He thus at least implies ideas of durability and distinctively partisan perspectives. He also juggles notions of "a cherished tradition, a passionate faith, and sometimes a crusading spirit" within parties.[9] Nevertheless it is difficult to see just where this party mind-stuff or ideology lodges in Binkley's framework of party as a congeries of economic interest groups.

More cogent suggestions as to the nature of party may be found in two European observers who share a concern for theory, Max Weber and Maurice Duverger. In Weber we find a stress on the relationship between leaders on the one hand and a party following on the other. Distinguishing between "politically active and politically passive elements," he argues that "a relatively small number of men [who] are primarily interested in political life . . . [will] provide themselves with a following through free recruitment." The result is that "active leadership and their freely-recruited following are the necessary elements in the life of any party." The "structure of parties varies," however, from "the purely personal followings" of "the 'parties' of the medieval cities, such as those of the Guelphs and Ghibellines," to highly developed relationships in "the most modern form of party organizations." Without elaborating the suggestive notions of structure, and of leader-follower relationships as that structure, Weber proceeds to his well-known and useful typology: parties of aristocracy, parties of notables, and parties of politicians. These last he sees as "the children of democracy, of mass franchise, of the necessity to woo and organize the masses"—in short, of the need to mobilize a following.[10] Unfortunately, however, Weber does not go on to provide a finished concept of party operating in a political system.

In discussing the genesis of parties, Duverger suggests a recurring pattern which sheds light on the nature of parties. The mode of genesis, he maintains, at least for what he thinks of as "cadre" parties, is "the creation of parliamentary groups", followed by "the appearance of electoral committees", and then by "the establishment of a permanent connection between these two elements". Thus, given "parliamentary groups and electoral committees . . . it is enough that some permanent coordination be established between them and that regular connections unite them for us to find ourselves faced with a true political party." In fact it is not "enough"; a great many problems remain; but at least we are on the way. As parties develop, Duverger notes, and "as a result of an impulse from the centre," electoral committees are created in areas where the party previously had none.[11] This conclusion is drawn largely from an overview of experience in Great Britain, and the American story, as we shall see, is somewhat different. Yet Duverger's point is suggestive, and he himself admits other patterns.

Even so, however, a sense of puzzlement or confusion must persist, for Duverger's concept of party also remains incomplete. Puzzlement is likely to lodge even more strongly in the mind of the serious student who ranges the vast uneven quarry of the literature on American parties. If he wants to make effective use of the material, and certainly if he wants to undertake any measure of comparative or historical explanation, he must feel a need for greater conceptual clarity and firmness. As a means to such ends, it will be useful to review some of the data of politics in the American states in the 1770s and 1780s, and in the new American nation in the 1790s. In particular it should be fruitful to compare patterns of faction politics in the first period with party politics in the second.

## II

With only one clear exception, early American state politics was non-party politics. This was true, as noted above, even in the contest (or contests) over ratification in 1787, and it remained true in the initial "national" elections for President and Congress in 1788–1789,[12] when for the first time a potential national electoral arena existed. In the states themselves, politics was a kaleidoscopic flux of interest groupings and opinion aggregates, of free-style individual action, of shifting alignments between notable-leaders, groups, unstable factions, juntos, caucuses, and cliques.

The configurations of the political hurly-burly varied from state to state. So also, as Luetscher pointed out long ago, did the methods of politics, whether in nominations, elections, legislative behavior, or propaganda.[13] Only sophisticated Pennsylvania, with its continuing rivalry between organized Constitutionalists and Republicans (the titles referred to state issues) brewed a state party system. Yet even in Pennsylvania the alignments of leaders and interests between and within the parties were often nearly invisible to any but the practiced eye.[14] In New York, sometimes marked as a state with parties, politics actually continued with the old gruel of personal-family cliques and satellite factions inherited from colonial times. Clintonians were dominant from about 1777 to 1789 against the Delanceys or Schuylerite, Livingstonian, and (ultimately triumphant) Hamiltonian rivals. Methods were sophisticated enough to foreshadow Tammany Hall, but principals like George Clinton or agents like Alexander Hamilton remained the foci of political formations.[15] These formations showed many similarities to the old Whig "connexions" of eighteenth-century England, depending as they did on the leadership and patronage of notables, important personages, or magnates, and resting as they did on intricate webs of personal ties. Indeed, Edmund Burke would have found them familiar.[16]

Despite variations, and with the exception of Pennsylvania, this early American state politics may be described most generally as *faction politics* —with the variations lying in personal cliques, the planter-élite "Fifty Families" junto in Maryland, the caucuses of Massachusetts, and the like.

Analysis of these early formations affords some important distinctions. Generally, a *faction* appeared as a portion of an electorate, political élite, or legislature, whose adherents were engaged in parallel action or co-ordination of some consistency but of limited durability, in conflict with other portions. Innumerable such loose factions characterized the early American scene. A *clique* was a portion whose relationships depended upon a commanding individual, a family, or a close coterie of personal associates; generally, the death or retirement of the focal individual led to the extinction of a clique. A *junto*, as the term was commonly used, meant a portion which operated as a small, often secret dominant group at a seat of government, whether state, county, or town; this variety of formation was most commonly found in the Southern states. A *caucus* was generally the coordinating nucleus group of a large faction. None of these formations took on the stature of a party, and such formations were not generally thought of as parties by contemporaries. It is in this sense of its hinging on factions rather than parties that we may speak of early American politics as "faction politics," using the term "faction" to include lesser but similar formations such as cliques, juntos, and caucuses. Except where factions were unusually broad in their range, we might speak of "connexion politics." It is with such patterns of political operation,[17] and their implications, that we shall later contrast party politics.

Faction politics in America in the 1770s and 1780s was, broadly speaking, premodern. Like English politics in the eighteenth century, it depended heavily on personalities and personal connections, and often on the deference of plain men to "notabilistic" leaders. Again like English politics, it was disorderly, subject to abrupt changes, and semi-invisible—often, for example, the factional ties of candidates or government officials were unknown to the public, or changed without notice from election to election or between elections; and few factions showed much durability. While political methods were frequently sophisticated, they were also highly variable and subject to change according to the impulses of leaders of the moment. Policy-making was, like much policy-making in eighteenth-century England, heavily influenced by shifting factional or bloc combinations in the legislatures, by clique or junto domination, by the plurality of group pressures or opinions at the moment, and by individual caprice. In short, early American faction politics lacked the degrees of order, visible continuity and relative clarity of political formations or positions, and stable rationalization of political methods, which may be counted among the characteristics of modern party politics. Compared with English politics of the same era,[18] however, it was less hierarchical, aristocratic, or élitist, and in this sense may be viewed as a transitional form.

Such politics also offered differential advantages to persons or groups who stood high on the scale of property, position, and power. Government was broadly republican and a substantial potential electorate existed despite property and tax qualifications. The extreme looseness, semi-invisibility, and confusion of informal politics, however, tended to limit effective popular influence, to the advantage of "well-placed" interests.

## III

Although the Constitution of 1787 provided a national electoral arena, obstacles to the formation of national parties remained. The pluralism of American society and early politics—regional dissimilarities, the variety of economic undertakings, the multiplicity of groups and religious sects, varying perspectives across the country—all stood in the way. Individuals resisted being herded, many citizens feared what George Washington called "the baneful effects of the spirit of party generally,"[19] and state leaders and populations clung to special local identities and interests against national "consolidation."

The earliest impetus for party formation came from the new center of national government. Furthermore, as Joseph Charles has argued effectively, party origins sprang from cleavage over significant national issues affecting the shape the new nation would take and over general ideological outlooks, together with critical questions of world politics and foreign policy.[20] Controversies which began at the national capital were carried to the country, and provided the reference points for party development.

The first representative leader in polarizing proto-party forces was Hamilton, whose political style is thus critically relevant. In a new, almost unstructured situation, he stepped forward as a bold advocate determined to create policy innovation, and his controversial five-point program for capitalist development was far more than a mere reflex to established views of business interest groups. To innovation Hamilton added a driving, shrewd talent for political management—in the executive branch, in the Senate and House of Representatives, in caucuses, with notable leaders across the country, and with the public. The effects of Hamilton's initial leadership told first on Congressional behavior. From his post as President Washintgon's Secretary of the Treasury, he worked to establish ties between the separated executive and legislative branches. In doing so, he gathered an entourage of sympathizers in the cabinet and of caucusing followers in Congress, who came soon to constitute a distinct capital faction. In the process he was able to rely on the prestige of Washington's name and generally on Washington's support. By the sessions of 1790 and 1791, the scattered and individualistic activity that had marked the first session in 1789 began to show signs of co-ordination and policy coherence.[21]

Before long, Hamilton's leadership (and politics in general) also became embroiled in world issues. The French Revolution was at first widely hailed in America; but regicide, the rise of the Jacobins, radical republicanism, and the Terror, followed by France's declaration of war on Great Britain in February, 1793, divided Americans sharply. A lush pamphlet and periodical literature sprang up. Men took sides emotionally as Anglomen (stigmatized by opponents as "Monocrats") or Gallomen (stigmatized in turn as "Jacobins"). Thus issues of domestic interests and outlook were supplemented by ideological reactions to European events and the result was a further consolidation of political forces.

In time, a series of steps led from the Hamiltonian capital *faction* to a national Federalist *party*. The process may be sumarized under four headings.

First, linkages of association, parallel action, and finally co-ordination were extended from the capital into the states, counties, and towns. Correspondents, personal friends, natural sympathizers, business associates, the many individuals whom Hamilton as Secretary of the Treasury had been able to oblige—all were sounded. Active response came particularly from local notables such as former military officers, mercantile magnates in New York, Congregational divines in New England, and many planter-nabobs in the South. National leaders gave cues to local leaders and to lesser party spokesmen and sponsors in the localities, and such men came to form the working vertebrae of the party. Many of them stood as prototypes of a new breed of party politicians, or party "cadre." In short, a firm and distinctive Federalist structure was in the process of forming and of finding a following.

Second, national leaders and local leaders or cadre collaborated to develop increasingly standardized ways of performing certain key political functions. These ranged from managing and conecting (between branches) in government, to nominating candidates, electioneering and mobilizing voters, and shaping opinion in the states and localities. A national factional or party paper under John Fenno, the *Gazette of the United States,* disseminated Federalist perspectives, and local sheets followed its lead.

Third, a substantial combination of interests and opinions was enlisted in the Federalist following. Domestic merchants, exporters, shippers and shipbuilders, holders of public securities, bankers, investors and financiers generally, struggling manufacturers, certain great planters, dependent business and professional men—all could see concrete advantages in Federalist policies. Yet the Federalist combination came also to include many wage-earners, particularly in shipbuilding, and farmers producing commercial and particularly export crops; and thus, contrary to the conception of much of the older historiography, the Federalists possessed a significant mass base—although their Achilles heel remained an insensitivity to the concerns of agriculture as a whole.[22] The interests of all these groups were not necessarily identical, however, and Hamilton and other leaders in developing policy inevitably performed a function of political brokerage, devising at least tacit formulas of agreement among the varied groups.

Fourth, the emerging Federalist force developed distinctive attitudes and unifying faiths and loyalties—in short, the beginnings of a partisan ideology. At the outset, the charisma of Washington was a key ingredient, and Hamilton remarked years later that "he [Washington] was an *Aegis very essential to me.*"[23] Other items became integral to the Federalist persuasion, such as a stress on "respectability," a concern for national capitalist growth and stability, an emphasis on a national government which was strong and "energetic," an élitist tone. In the backwash of revolutionary Jacobinism, Federalists also saw themselves as a bulwark against a threatening world-revolutionary spirit, of sanity against madness, of order against chaos. Thus ties of interest were supplemented by shared outlooks and symbolism. Indeed, it was the development of the emotional *élan* of ideology, more than any other element, which marked the transition of the Federalists from faction to party.

The upshot of all these developments was a new kind of national linkage. It was far more than a "connexion," in the old sense of a shifting set of personal, familial, or clique relationships. It was rather a stable "connection," in the modern spelling and meaning, a structure of men across the nation who not only shared interests, but who were coming together into co-ordinated rationalized patterns of action around a set of national leaders, on the basis of shared social, economic, political, or moral perspectives. It was, or became by sometime around 1793 or 1794, a modern party in the proper sense—that is to say, a political formation which exhibited *all* of the characteristics which an empirically and theoretically viable conceptual scheme might identify as belonging to party. It marked a progress from faction politics to party politics.

Two observations may be made concerning this development. First, although the Federalist party was in part a combination of groups, it was also *more* than a combination of groups as Beard or Binkley construe the term, in that it was an articulated, semi-independent structure of stable relationships between leaders, cadre, and following, built by the purposeful energies of men, who gave it more in action than they took in reflex reaction to group impulses. Second, the party did not exhibit any significant degree of organization in the strict sense. If we insist on seeing party as organization, as Robinson or Leiserson do, we will have very little to say about America's first national party.

Opposition to the Federalists was soon forthcoming. It also took form at the capital, where James Madison in the House of Representatives played initial antagonist to Hamilton's protagonist—contrary again to much of the conventional historiography, which lists Jefferson as the founder of the Republican party.[24] From the outset, however, the Republican opposition moved in accord with popular stirrings of interest and opinion.

Dissent in the states, counties, and towns was directed at Hamilton's economic program, but it also turned to issues of foreign policy and world-political ideology. After Washington's proclamation of neutrality towards warring France and England in 1793, for example, an opposition voice in the western reaches of Pensylvania cried out that "the cause of France is the cause of man, and neutrality is desertion."[25] In 1794 John Taylor of Virginia published a fat polemical pamphlet, A Definition of Parties, or the Political Effects of the Paper System Considered, which gave focus to the domestic and world-political strains of opposition. In 1795 widespread protest against the treaty the Federalist John Jay had negotiated with Great Britain drew divisions over issues of world politics even more sharply. Meanwhile, gaining momentum in 1793 and 1794, several local political associations had sprung up across the country. Called variously Democratic or Republican Societies, they were remarkable for the number of intellectuals in their membership and leadership though, as Eugene Link has shown, they drew on a number of elements in the population.[26] They were also remarkably modern, in that they were open, voluntary assemblages of individual men, and in the degree of formal organization they achieved under democratically adopted constitutions. Their approach originally was largely in terms of ideology, discussion of political philosophy and issues, and propaganda; but they also doled out blessings or censure on members of Congress and endorsed candidates for elections. They began to disappear after Washington, in the wake of the Whisky Insurrection of 1794, denounced them as "self-created societies," presumably all disruptive of public order. Yet, flourishing as they did from Vermont to South Carolina and Kentucky, they were significant while they lasted. The varied voices of dissent and their institutionalization in the Societies indicate the degree to which the Republican opposition was indigenous in nature, and of local and popular origin, rather than simply a product of mobilization by leaders at the center of government. Such coruscations did not, however, make a party. Rather, they constituted a potential following for a potential party.

The Republican party found its structure in linkages between the Congressional faction Madison was drawing together at the capital and the groundwork of national opposition. No bold, creative antagonist, Madison began slowly though industriously in the session of 1790 and moved painfully ahead in succeeding sessions, relying particularly on the Virginia men and increasingly on certain members from Pennsylvania. In particular John Beckley of Virginia, Clerk of the House, worked behind the scenes and began to exhibit talents as a national cadre politician that would have been admired by later Van Burens, Hannas, Cannons, or Farleys.[27] From their base in Congress, Republican leaders reached out to the countryside. Like the Federalists before them, they gradually established connections in states and localities; encouraged the development of local leaders and cadre; labored to co-ordinate the choice of candidates, election activities, and propaganda; secured a general following; and worked up a significant group combination. National leaders made fruitful connections with the Clintonians in New York and with remnants of the old state-Constitutionalists in Pennsylvania, but elsewhere their local elements were generally newly built. With the founding of the *National Gazette* under the poet-polemicist Philip Freneau in 1791, and an alignment of satellite papers, they established a loose information office which gave impetus to distinctively Republican attitudes and *élan*.

The Republican forces were slower in effecting a clearly party-like structure than the Federalists, however—and again, it was an issue with intensely emotional, symbolic, and ideological overtones that brought them to full party status. It is probably not proper to speak of a stable Republican *party* nationally earlier than the Jay Treaty controversy of 1795 and Congressional debate of 1796,[28] the assumption by Jefferson of effective party leadership in the latter year, and the intensification of cleavages in political perspectives which contention over the treaty engendered.

As they shaped a party formation, the Republicans exhibited distinctive characteristics in their general attitude toward relations between leaders and followers, and in the character of their party structure. Unlike the tone of the Federalists, which was broadly élitist, the tone of the Republicans was broadly democratic. To Federalist leaders, the purposes of party were to amass and stabilize support in the public and electorate for policies the leaders had already adopted. Their party was overwhelmingly a "party of notables," in Weber's term, despite their significant mass base. Republican leaders, who were in effect evolving a formation which marked a transitional stage between a "party of notables" and a "party of politicians," generally believed that the relationship between leaders and mass following should include responsiveness or responsibility to the wishes and opinions of the following, and that policy should in some degree be shaped accordingly. Thus the Republican ideology embraced a considerable notion of intra-party democracy, in which party following might play a somewhat less "passive" and more "active" role than Weber's abstract formulation suggests. The matter is put aptly if too simply by Robinson, when he speaks of Federalists approaching elections as merely "a test upon [their] policies," while Republicans viewed elections as "a guide to the desires of public opinion."[29] In short, we may conceptualize the Federalists as operating in terms of *plebiscitarian* ideology and action, while the Republicans moved in terms of *democratic* ideology and action. It is thus possible to speak of the Republicans not only as a modern party, but as a *"popular"* party, in the sense of a party grounded in and sensitive to a broad and durable base in the population or electorate. Despite recurring counter-tendencies to oligarchy noted by Michels,[30] this is the form that many modern parties have taken in nation after nation in the last century and a half. Others, however, have pursued the plebiscitarian path.[31]

Furthermore, as compared with the Federalists, Republican development was not only more popular but more complex. The indigenous opposition movement developed sometimes ahead of, and at least partially independently of, the Madisonian capital faction. This was notably the case with the Democratic or Republican Societies. Some writers have leapt to the conclusion that these associations were integral, organized local units in a national Republican party; actually, however, there was no structural connection between the Madisonian capital faction on the one hand and the Societies on the other. Rather, as Noble E. Cunningham argues persuasively, the associations acted as pressure groups,[32] with a primarily ideological approach. The significance of indigenous Republican sentiment and the Democratic-Republican groups is that they provided pre-existing enclaves of support at the periphery to which Madisonians at the center could reach out. Contrary to Duverger's suggestion that parties of the "cadre" type are typically generated from the center "out," as the Federalists were, they may also emerge in part from the periphery "in," as the Republicans did, in a very complex pattern indeed.

Finally, the Republican party came to include some organization in the strict sense, as a continuing rationalized division of labor and co-ordination of functions toward shared goals. Indeed, figures like Beckley and Freneau or his press-successor Benjamin Franklin Bache show an obvious kinship with Disraeli's later Taper or Tadpole, who tied up votes or swam in the muddy waters of opinion in Great Britain in the 1830s and 1840s.[33] Organization was spotty, however, and its full development remains a phenomenon of later mature parties of politicians with an enlarged mass electorate to mobilize.

In the development of both the Federalist and the Republican parties, ideology played a catalytic role. As it appeared in this development, it was partial rather than total, consistent with a basic national consensus, and somewhat amorphous—though not so loose as the flaccid ideological outlooks of later American parties have often become. It was also limited in that its "factual assertions about society," to use Birnbaum's terms, were never presented in a form that was wholly comprehensive or even "systematic," and neither were its "evaluations of the distribution of power"— and this circumscribed range of ideology has been typical of the American experience. Yet a sense of identity and direction, patterns of commitment, at least a loose world-view, what Washington called "the spirit of party generally," and consequent cohesion and *élan*, were all essential ingredients in the consolidation of durable linkages of Federalist and Republican party structure and action, and all may be thought of as ideological components. Ideology as it appeared in American party development, furthermore, was more than merely a rationalization of interests, a shadowy variable dependent on economic or other self-oriented group concerns, or a figment of the psyche to satisfy inward personal needs. It was rather a positive force which shaped perceptions (or misperceptions) of political reality. It thereby generated faiths and loyalties which might have remained dormant, and prompted effective political action.[34]

The establishment of parties brought a significant degree of order to American politics. Parties operated as continuing bonds between the decision-making processes of government on the one hand, and individuals and groups in the public and electorate on the other. Distinguishable party positions were put forth, and Congressional behavior was increasingly bipolarized on partisan lines at the expense of dwindling numbers of center-individualists.[35] Candidates for office ran as Federalists or Republicans, thereby providing voters with a reasonably clear two-way choice. More and more voters identified with party symbols and party ideology. Thus, in the emergence of two-party politics and rivalry, pluralism was harnessed to some degree, the effects of state-by-state fragmentation in politics were reduced, and political methods were increasingly rationalized, standardized, and modernized.

Party politics also reduced the differential advantages in power that had fallen to well-placed individuals and groups. Farmers, small traders, artisans, members of low-status religious groups, many intellectuals, reformers, even aliens found in the Jeffersonian Republican party a representative of their interests, perspectives, opinions, and rights, as against the demands of larger property, ascribed position, high respectability, and established influence. The existence of the two parties in competition provided a meaningful option between Federalist and Republican perspectives, policies, and leaders; and voters quickly learned to make use of the choice the parties put before them. Thus, in an open political system, the first modern political parties brought such important gains in democracy as representation, substantial participation, and choice.[36] In a few short years, the new American nation—decades before its British ancestors—had moved well into a new world-era of politics.

## IV

Some analytical generalizations based on the formative years of American experience may now be offered, as a step toward a model of party. First some generalized comparative distinctions between factions and parties are in order. While both have appeared as formations in the conflict of politics, performing functions or activities such as leadership recruitment, contesting for power or office, the conduct of government, or representation of some sort, significant differences as well as resemblances are to be found between them. Historically, the differences have been matters of degree rather than total dichotomies of quality, but they are sufficient to sustain some important conceptual distinctions.

Factions have often developed as chance, almost unconscious, *natural* "growths," or "conexions" of men with parallel interests. Parties, by contrast, as more complex formations, appear as *artifacts*, "built" by purposeful effort. It is misleading to speak, as Binkley does in his subtitle, of a "Natural History" of parties. Structurally factions have been unstable, generally of short life or life-expectancy, irregular; while parties historically have exhibited greater stability, durability, longevity, and so are clearer to identify. A faction, for example, may easily coalesce for one election or issue only and then disappear. Parties typically continue or expect to continue from election to election or from issue to issue.[37]

Factions also have not typically offered *stable* procedures for performing certain essential political functions. In American and British history, these have come to include nominating; campaigning or electioneering; formulating opinion; group brokerage, managing in government; and establishing connections between branches or agencies of government. Unlike factions, parties have generally undertaken or offered to undertake these functions in a regularized, standardized, continuing fashion. It has been said, only half-flippantly, that the purpose of party is "to elect."[38] In a free society, and in an ultimate sense even in a non-democratic "plebiscitarian" society, if a party is to elect and re-elect its candidates, it must perform the other functions noted here.

Factions have usually generated little in the way of distinct and durable ideological perspectives, while parties have generally evolved substantial sets of perspectives. Exceptions may surely be found among factions—in the Royalists and Parliament Men of seventeenth-century England, for example—but more often than not factions do not develop significant identifying symbolisms. In a plural party system, symbolisms or perspectives become durable "we"-"they" perspectives. Partisans see "our" outlooks or positions on issues as "right," and "theirs" as "wrong"; and it thereby becomes important that "we" gain power and not "they." Perhaps, when ideology has reached a stage of flaccid formalism, it is really important only that power and its perquisites be "ours" and not "theirs"; and yet even so party spirit remains among the great cements of politics. As a party acquires a history, it canonizes heroes, develops traditional symbols, exalts present leaders, and relates all this symbolism in some kind of ideology, whether vivid and meaningful or blurred and muddled. Thus, while ideology is not in itself party, it is a critical characteristic *of* party.

Factions have typically scored low and parties high in range and density of following. While factions *may* develop as combinations of a broad range of groups and opinion aggregates, they generally have not done so, whereas parties generally have. There are obvious exceptions, however, and this cannot be a defining, but only a contingent, characteristic of party. Again, factions have not generally achieved or even sought to achieve a high density of following. Parties, on the other hand, have generally done so or sought to do so.

All four of these differences between faction and party were apparent in the emergence of party politics out of faction politics in early America. Furthermore, as we have seen, the transition was significant for the shape of politics. A concept or analytical-historical model of party in terms of structure, function, and ideology may now be formally stated.

A *party* proper or *modern party* may be conceived as a social structure which operates within the political arena, and which is directed toward exercising the power, filling the available offices, and shaping the general policies of government. The structure[39] is distinctive in that it exhibits four defining characteristics and one contingent characteristic:

1) *There is a comparatively stable or durable leader-following relationship; that is, a relationship among party leaders, cadre, and officials-in-government on the one hand; and with a following, or adherents or identifiers, on the other.*

This definiens places stress on Weber's notion of leader-R-following,[40] adding emphasis on *stability* or *durability* as an aspect of structure. "Adherent" indicates individuals who are strongly attached to and may be counted on to support the party, while intensity of attachment declines as we move through "identifiers" to what may be called occasional voters. Structure itself may include *organization* in the strict sense, that is, organization$_1$ a group of persons (particularly cadre and officials) who have an interest separable from other interests in maintaining and perpetuating the party structure, and who thus undertake and conduct organization$_2$, a continuing, regularized pattern of division of labor and coordination of tasks to maintain party structure and perform party functions, which pattern tends to become institutionalized and formalized.

2) *There is communication and co-ordination of activity (short of, or including, organization proper), between central leaders, cadre, and officials, and local cadre or lesser actives.*

This characteristic does not entail any particular *form* of articulation or organization; thus a given party may be more or less élitist or hierarchical, more or less cohesive or disciplined, and exhibit more or less intra-party democracy.

Strictly speaking, in what may be called after Duverger "cadre" parties, *"the* party" consists of leaders, cadre, officials, and actives who make decisions for the party, conduct party affairs, and appeal to the public as representatives of the party, while adherents or identifiers constitute the following. Where parties have formal membership like the Labor party in Great Britain and stand as what Duverger calls "mass" parties, members may be included in *"the* party," while persons who may vote for the party but are not formal members may be thought of as a following. Even so, the leaders whom Duverger refers to as the *"Inner Circle"*[41] will constitute the core of the party for most practical or functional purposes.

3) *There exist, or are offered as an undertaking, regular procedures for performing functions linking the public or electorate and the governmental decision-making process, thus—*
   a) *nominating, campaigning or electioneering, opinion-formulating;*
   b) *group-brokerage, managing in government, connecting (branches or agencies of government).*

This definiens, which stresses party-as-function, is dependent on the concept of structure, but the latter is in turn clarified by the concept of function. Thus, in terms of actual behavior, those who constitute *"the* party" are those who perform the function of party among the public or electorate. It follows from this functional definiens as well as from the statement of structure that a party is not its leaders *and* following, but rather its structure of leaders, cadre, officials, and actives (or Inner Circle and *active* members), who in turn mobilize a following. If we employ Goldman's or Key's term *"party*-in-the-electorate"[42] without considerable care, we may seem to allude in circular fashion to a party as an aggregate mobilizing that same aggregate, and we are perilously close to the loose notions of party as any aggregate of men engaged in parallel political action or sharing similar political outlooks.

4) *There exists in the party and is shared in the following a set of in-group perspectives, or faiths, loyalties, and commitments, which constitute an ideology.*

This definiens emphasizes the role of ideology as an essential element in party, without however defining party solely as any body of men who may share an ideological view. Perspectives may extend from minimal loyalties and attitudes through emotive symbolism, hagiography, and traditional adherence, to ideological or programmatic commitment. In plural party systems, party perspectives or commitments may be more or less clear and contrasting, thereby providing a greater or less degree of voter choice between parties, or inter-party democracy.

5) *There is attached to the party structure a comparatively durable combination of interests or opinion-aggregates, which the cadre may count on as a power-base.*

In open systems and particularly in two-party systems in multi-group societies, and in certain instances or stages of one-party systems, there is a tendency toward both substantial *range* in interests and aggregates of opinion in the party, and significant *density* (number of persons involved: potential number of persons) in the power-base. Range and density may be promoted through what Binkley calls *formulas of agreement* in the conflict of interests and opinions, by means of brokerage in some situations; or by program mobilization (through opinion-formulation), charismatic leadership, or brokerage in other situations.

These five characteristics, when present in significant degree, may be taken as criteria of party proper. Major parties in modern, mass politics— the American Federalists and Republicans of the 1790s are early instances —may be thought of as exhibiting all of the characteristics of the model in marked degree; minor parties, or closed or élitist ruling parties in one-party systems, may exhibit them in different degrees, or for Item 5—the key criterion for Binkley[43]—sometimes hardly at all. Factions or similar formations on the other hand will exhibit few if any of the five characteristics in significant degree, and certainly not all of them to a high degree. This was true of "connexions" and factions in England in the eighteenth century, as well as of factions, cliques, juntos, or caucuses in America before the 1790s. It also appears to be the case that no political formation in Great Britain exhibited the four or five characteristics of party in high degree before the emergence of the Whig-Liberal and Tory-Conservative parties in the nineteenth century. Thus again it may be argued that the advent of the Federalist and Republican parties marked a new phase of political development, which carried the United States significantly beyond the politics of its mother nation.

## V

The remarkably early development of political parties in America is worth exploring, particularly as it may illuminate relationships between social structure, national political culture, and ideology on the one hand, and party origins on the other. It is true that the first parties in America survived through only three decades, and that by 1819 or 1820 Federalists and Republicans had ceased to exist as effective structures in the national political arena. Yet their advent reveals most of the generic aspects of American party development, and the successor Democratic and Whig parties of the 1830s trod paths that had already been marked.

American party action, as Weber has noted, "brought the plebiscitarian principle to an especially early and an especially pure expression." It is, however, superficial to argue as Weber does: "That the plebiscitarian 'machine' has developed so early in America is due to the fact that there, and there alone, the executive—this is what mattered—the chief of office-patronage, was a President elected by plebiscite."[44] Patronage and presidency are indeed relevant, but hardly sufficient to explain the early American development. A more general comparative approach should prove more fruitful. It will focus here on a central type of factor or cause in the American situation as contrasted with the British situation; it will then relate this central point to contrasting sets of proximate social conditions, types of factors, or causes. The approach here will thus aim at a kind of immediate or relative historical explanation, partly in terms of a succession of events ("continuous series"), partly in terms of modest, middle-range generalizations (theory). At a later stage, a broader explanation of the rise of parties in modern politics will be offered.[45] Throughout, the assumption is that the problem can best be dealt with by some comparison of American and British development, although the focus remains on the former. Ultimately, of course, such a comparative approach should be deepened, and broadened to include still other societies.[46]

The central point of contrast is the presence in England and the absence in America of a feudal background, and the obverse of this fact —the flowering in America of a "liberal tradition," in a broadly "liberal society," in a highly favorable "material setting." The issue has been argued effectively by Louis Hartz, and the terms are used here basically as he uses them. His analysis, although it deals at once with "the absence of feudalism and the presence of the liberal idea" in America, is basically a single-factor analysis—"in terms of European history itself the abstraction of the feudal force implies the natural development of liberalism, so that for all practical purposes we are dealing with a single factor." The liberal idea or liberal tradition in a non-feudal, atomistic-individualistic, or loosely Lockian sense, is taken as the "significant historical variable" in, among other things, "the early triumph of American democracy" in general.[47]

In the eighteenth century in England, politics operated within a social structure and political cuture inherited from a feudal past with its established, fixed estates. Even in the long period of the slow decline of feudalism, a relatively rigid structure of ranks, classes, or established interests emerged. Thus, in the eighteenth and early nineteenth centuries, political representation was effectively representation of such fixed entities, "natural" and/or "virtual," rather than representation of individual voters in geographical districts, or of the open pressures of diverse interest groups in the modern pattern. Thus, organic representation was largely built into the system, as it involved the decision points of Crown, Lords, and Commons. Furthermore, as another part of the feudal heritage, politics was substantially a game for aristocrats, magnates, notable leaders, and their agents. There had developed over the centuries patterns of deference to or reliance on such leadership which, among other consequences, retarded the development of popular initiative or participation in politics.[48] Moreover, the suffrage was severely limited, up to and even after the bourgeois Reform Bill of 1832.

In the New World, history and its impact on social structure and political culture were different. Social distinctions, "nabobs," pseudo-aristocrats, notables there were in the American colonies and early American states. Habits of deference to such figures of eminence were part of the colonial heritage, along with distinctions between rich and poor or "high" and "low," indentures, and slavery. Nonetheless, most Americans were freeholding farmers; opportunity was broadly open in a new continent; and a high degree of individual freedom and social mobility existed. A liberal ethos readily developed which saw the units of society as free, atomistic, assertive individuals. This ethos took on more and more strongly equalitarian overtones in an ideology or developing political culture of "irrational Lockianism," in Hartz's terms, or perhaps "the Jeffersonian dream." The social impact of the Revolution, "the Spirit of '76," and the liberal decade which followed, were to emphasize and strengthen all of these tendencies, and to speed a process of dissolution of social distinctions and deference patterns, a process which was to culminate in the equalitarian democracy of the Jacksonian era. From the outset, political representation was of necessity representation of individuals choosing more or less freely in geographical districts. There was no Crown, no Establishment, no Lords and therefore no Commons linked in organic relationships—for if a society consists of free individuals and boasts no First and Second Estates, it can hardly have a Third.[49] Finally, the national Constitution of 1787, far from being merely a stratagem of a privileged élite, provided an intricately limited but for the times remarkably democratic frame of government.[50]

All of these matters of fact and faith entailed certain consequences in America which would hardly be expected in the British experience. By giving free play to fluidity, differentiation, and complexity of interests in a developing society, they produced in the first instance an *open, unstructured, complex conflict of interests and opinions as the standard stuff of politics*—the lush, almost uncontrolled pluralism so characteristic of American life.[51] Add to such phenomena the lack of an organic representation built into the political system as in Great Britain, and a second consequence follows in the American context *if* any group of men was to win power and get the business of governing done; that is, *a need for some mode of political action which would serve as a means of representing, combining, and mobilizing the individuals and variety of interests and opinions in the society.* Third, given this fluid, open situation, it remained only for *men with political vision, ambition, and talent to come forward to meet the need and seize the obvious opportunity.* Such men soon emerged as party leaders, exploring the paths to modern popular parties, building party structures. Furthermore, such men building early American parties in the late eighteenth and early nineteenth centuries did not have to batter down obstacles of the sort they would have faced in Great Britain in the same period—the undergrowth of fixed orders, fixed patterns of organic representation, fixed ways of doing things. Another consequence of the liberal and Revolutionary tradition in America was the development of *a consensus which provided the formal and effective freedom in which parties could take shape, speak out, act, and develop.* Despite early attitudes inimical to the idea of party and of opposition, the American atmosphere was probably considerably freer and more open to party action than that of Great Britain in the same era.

In its more general hypothetical form, the argument here is: where social structure and ideology provide certain types of social and political conditions (an open, pluralistic or atomistic politics characterized by complex conflicts of interest, concomitant needs and opportunities will arise for certain types of political functions and activities (action to represent, combine, and mobilize pluralities of free individuals and interests in order to exercise governmental power); and in the absence of significant obstacles (such as limiting patterns of social and political structure, limitations on freedom of political expression and action, or others), these opportunities will attract men with the requisite political ambition and skills, with the consequent development of the indicated modes of political action, which become modern political party action. In terms of this *general* proposition, and in contrast with the English context, the *particular* conditions of the American field in the late eighteenth century seemed both to require and to invite party building and party leadership.[52]

Further aspects of contrast between Great Britain and the United States are relevant. Lacking an Establishment—the Crown, the nobility and the peerage, the Church, their prerogatives and power, their overtones of prestige—the American political system lacked an established center for "court politics." There was no national power-institution of majesty, or array of pomp and circumstance, around which interests, factions, or cliques could seek influence almost without regard to the populace or electorate, and thereby find almost invisible corridors to success in the game of who gets what, when and how. It is significant that, when American advocates of "high-toned" government proposed such panoplies, they were frustrated by what contemporaries called the "republican genius" of the people, or what we may call the democratic aspects of the developing national ideology. To this may be added for the United States the relative absence or steady decline of deference patterns through which aristocrats or notables could count on almost automatic followings, without dependence on free public opinion or a free electorate. The consequence in an increasingly equalitarian, republican political system was *a peculiarly democratic or plebiscitarian imperative, which was the necessity, if individuals or groups were to satisfy their ambitions or interests through politics, to appeal to public opinion and to the electorate for support.* This was the path even the élitist, notabilistic Federalists had to walk, if they were not to lose their objectives.

The American situation and ideology also produced the earliest instances of mass suffrage in the modern world. Tax or property qualifications there were at the outset, but their effect had been greatly overstressed by older historians. More recent research and conclusions are well expressed by Edmund S. Morgan in his summary of the states after the Revolution—"the vast majority of white Americans could probably meet the property qualifications required of them."[53] The right of suffrage was not always used, yet near the end of the party-building decade of the 1790s voting reached something like 25 per cent or more of all white adult males for important elections. (The exercise of suffrage rose still further, with liberalizations of legal qualifications and the *hoi-polloi* thrust of the Jacksonian era, to 56 per cent of white adult males in Jackson's first election in 1828, and reached a peak of 78 per cent in the "Log Cabin" campaign of 1840 which capped the Jackson period.) The data are striking,[54] particularly if they are contrasted with the limited suffrage of Great Britain, and with the fact that the long agitation for the first Reform Bill finally won suffrage in 1832 for only a few hundred thousand rate payers. Furthermore, democratic attitudes—in the sense of political equalitarianism, notions of popular participation and a popular voice in politics beyond elections, and representative government—became more and more central to American political culture. (These attitudes also began to develop early and were, as Marcus Cunliffe has argued perceptively,[55] by no means just the product of the Age of Equalitarianism which Tocqueville observed, although once again they reached new, *hoi-polloi* heights in the Jacksonian thrust of the 1830s.) The contrast between Great Britain and the United States is once again striking and important. Those who would succeed in American politics *found it necessary—in the face of mass suffrage and general political participation —to deal with, mobilize, and shape into a power-base broad elements of a mass electorate and public.* The task called in effect for party-like structure—for an array of leaders, cadre, and actives who could undertake sustained appeals to public opinion and employ effective campaigning techniques, and for the performance of basic party functions.

The general hypothetical statement of this portion of the argument is: where social structure, ideology, and related socio-political conditions fail to provide, or preclude, some form of closed or limited politics with special accesses to influence (for example, through "court politics," or in an Establishment, or through other closed élites), and preclude or restrict reliance upon established patterns of deference as sources of power (as in the nearly unchallenged sway of aristocrats or notables, or of other élites of ascribed social status), and where such conditions produce mass suffrage or regular patterns of mass participation which must be reckoned with in the distribution of power (such as the American electorate in the 1790s or American mass-participative attitudes), means to power will be sought by politically active elements through mobilization of mass public opinion or a mass electorate, with the consequent development of the most efficient available means (modern political party action). In particular, where such phenomena are conditioned by the incidence of active, "democratic" consciousness and expression of interests, opinion, and ideology within the public or electorate, the development of modern parties is likely to occur most rapidly, and to move toward parties of the popular or "democratic" rather than the merely "plebiscitarian" type. Of the four statements of types of factors stressed above, factors of the first two types (inhibitive of modern party development) were strongly apparent in the English situation in the late eighteenth century, and absent or declining in the American experience; conversely, factors of the second two types (facilitating party development) were of major significance for the American experience in the 1790s and after, and of no or limited significance in English politics until much later. Once again, given the *general* propositions, the *particular* conditions of American life appear as especially favorable to party development.

Taken as a whole, the items set forth in this discussion constitute a proximate explanation for the early rise of parties in America, in terms first of an inter-related sequence of conditions and events, and second of two related middle-range generalizations or theoretical formulations. Methodologically, the theory as it is related to American experience as against the contrasting background of English experience is mono-

factorial or univariant in its foundations, in that the central variant isolated
is the absence or a feudal past in the United States as contrasted with
Great Britain, stressed by Hartz,[56] with all of the ramifications of this fact.
Insofar as mono-factorial analysis may be questioned, or univariant comparison may be difficult to verify, the explanation may be vulnerable. On
the other hand, the theory is multi-factorial or multivariant in its statement of types of social conditions, aspects of political culture, or ideology,
as these conditions may impinge upon structure and behavior in politics.
Insofar as multivariant comparative analyses are arguable, the explanation
may again be vulnerable. Yet the two lines of analysis might be thought of
as substantiating one another in this instance at least, with the first
approach linking many variables into a pattern, while the second specifies
in effect consequences or deductions from the larger proposition, which
are more readily subject to confirmation or disconfirmation.

Further testing of this relative explanation in American and English
history is, of course, in order. It may be reiterated also that the theory
itself might be tested more fully if comparisons with still other nations
were undertaken, such as France or Germany on the one hand and
Canada or Australia on the other.


## VI

A more general explanation of the genesis of modern parties may now be
offered, as a hypothesis extrapolated from American as contrasted with
British experience—a generalization of possible interest to both historians
and political scientists, with applications to the present as well as the past.

Parties proper are, apparently, the products of certain types of social-
structure conditions and ideological configurations which have come to
characterize political modernization as it has taken place in western
societies. The relevant social conditions appear to be those which are
related to the absence or dissolution of closed, traditionalistic, and hierarchical social structures and modes of conducting politics. The relevant
ideologies appear to be those which point to mass or democratic involvement or participation in the political process. In short, parties proper
appear to be products of the process of modernization and the emergence
of mass or democratic politics, and of democratic or plebiscitarian ideologies—and at the same time to be themselves steps toward political
modernization. If the hypothesis is valid, one would expect to find stable
parties *if* and *only if*, or *when* but *only when*, the indicated types of social-
structural conditions and ideological configurations are present in a
society in some significant degree.

Near the center of the argument is the matter of ideology itself. The ideological perspectives which characterized Federalists and Republicans in America in the 1790s were only *particular* ideologies in Mannheim's terms, and as such they were of course conflicting in some measure and representative of the outlooks and interests of particular individuals or groups in the society.[57] Yet each party's ideology was also related to a more general or *total* ideology, or to what we might call, again in Mannheim's terms, a Lockian liberal-democratic "utopia" in the process of becoming the standard American ideology, and one which stressed the roles of a broad public and a broad electorate in politics. It would of course have been shocking to Hamilton and other "High Federalists" to hear themselves called Lockians, and they were not Lockians in any full sense. Nonetheless, they found it necessary in the American context to construct a political formation and espouse a party ideology which allowed room for popular involvement in politics, although their élitist attitudes led them to perceive such involvement mainly in the mode we have called "plebiscitarian." To Jefferson and his colleagues the Lockian liberal-democratic utopia seemed, as Jefferson himself put it, "the common sense of the subject." The Republicans developed their party structure accordingly and adopted the Lockian ideology with certain adjustments to the immediate American scene as their party ideology, in a form which was fully "democratic." Thus both the Federalist and the Republican particular ideologies partook of the more general developing American total ideology, the first by way of somewhat grudging concession and the second by whole-hearted acceptance.

The working-out of the general hypothesis of party genesis is seen in its earliest and simplest form in the American case. In England the actual phenomena of genesis were bound to be vastly more complex, if the hypothesis is accurate, and to extend through a far longer period of time and through a far more intricate set of transitional stages. In England it took a long, halting process of evolution to break down the feudal past and eighteenth-century patterns of hierarchy, corporatism, virtual representation, "connexions," deference, and the like, and also a tortuous passage through various mixed or intermediate modes of politics, before modern parties stood clearly in the ascendancy. In short, in accord with the explanatory hypothesis, circumstances should be expected to alter cases in their timing, development, and form, but not in their ultimate general result. One of the values of the hypothesis should be heuristic, as it suggests questions of difference as well as of similarity.

Even so, Great Britain in the nineteenth century moved more and more toward patterns of party action which had been explored earlier in the American experience, and certain party practices were thought of, often contemptuously, as "American" methods.[58] Similarly, at least loose parallels to the American party innovation may be discerned in Canada and Australia, with British adaptations, or in the development of parties of the cadre type on the European continent.

However, as Weber has correctly noted, the "structure of parties varies."[59] At least two broad types of later party development may be noted, which differ from the American experience in specific conditions of origin and in resulting specific forms of structure and action. One is represented by the Socialist, Social Democrat, or Labor parties of continental Europe or Great Britain, with variations in later Communist or Fascist developments—in short, the emergence of parties which Duverger has described as departing from the American "cadre" form to assume structure which he calls "mass," "cell," or "militia."[60] By and large such parties at least began as tools for militant social-reformist, social-revolutionary, or social-reactionary purposes, which were expressed in total or near-total rather than particular ideologies or utopias. A second broad type of party development is represented by the new mass nationalist formations in "backward" or "emerging" areas in Asia or Africa—militant parties which have generally been created by alienated intellectuals and others to bring their peoples to nationhood and their new nations up to a par with the already modern nations abroad. Such parties also have had their particular structures and their distinctive ideologies or utopias of modernization, which again, in their utopian beginnings at least, have tended more toward the total than the particular type and also toward extreme intensities of ideological emphasis. These parties have grown not out of indigenous processes of modernizations, but rather—in a reversal of western modes—have been created as broad adaptations of alien party prototypes to bring about just such modernization, again on western models.[61]

Yet, in all these instances of party development, certain common elements which were part of the American experience reappear. All of the instances of party genesis noted here were associated with processes of modernization, or with mimetic ideologies of modernization and consequent mimetic party structures, and all were also associated with mass politics, or patterns of mass mobilization or participation. Thus, these general types of factors stand as the apparently irreducible conditions for modern parties, even where the parties assume varying forms of structure or are shaped as reconstructions of foreign models. Some of the European mass parties have approached the problems of mass politics in a manner which is broadly democratic, as cadre parties of the American type generally have, while others such as the Communist or various Fascist formations have been clearly plebiscitarian, with significant consequences in structure and behavior especially when power is attained. In underdeveloped areas, patterns of society and the political backwardness of the masses have not so far been conducive to full democratic development. Thus the new parties of the emerging nations have frequently been mass-mobilizing but not significantly oriented to popular initiative or broad popular participation, and have been keyed to a new structural and ideological élitism of paternal "guidance" by leaders. In consequence, they have tended to be plebiscitarian. Indeed, it follows from the analysis offered here that such parties could not be expected to emerge as fully popular or democratic parties until modernization, social-structural conditions, and ideology in the new nations provided the necessary foundations —and not automatically even them. It would be naive and Procrustean to expect othewise.[62] However, whether plebiscitarian or democratic, structures of both the broad types distinguished here have performed or offered to perform the central functions of party in mass politics.

In short, the American case as it developed in the eighteenth century stands as only one instance of the general hypothesis of party development, an instance with a strongly democratic bent. For actual historical parties in other situations important differences must be distinguished in purpose, political role, structure, ideological outlook, leadership, organization, style—and the whole general hypothesis is of course subject to review. Yet, basic generic elements discernible in American development appear to remain relevant to the development of parties generally, as instances, in a variety of particular contexts, of party viewed as structure, ideology, and function.

# National Character / *David M. Potter*

An incomplete bibliography of national character, published in 1960, lists 988 studies, most of them in English, French, and German.[1] This does not include tangential references to national character by historians who note the existence of national character but do not define the concept.

The most common approach to national character has been in terms of distinguishing traits. These were said to add up to national character, although there was no universal agreement as to which traits should be included. Indeed, it is not unusual for one scholar or commentator to select a particular trait as characteristic of a people, and another scholar to select its opposite.[2] Basic traits are not generally distinguished from ephemeral traits; nor are traits invariably labeled as racially, culturally, or environmentally determined. In American historiography of the late nineteenth century, "race" was an important determinant of national character. But "race" was seldom rendered explicit.[3]

War and its aftermath have been a stimulus to studies of national character.[4] In a period of engagement with enemies, it is important for a people to know who they are and how they differ from their antagonists. Following the First World War, books by Madison Grant, Lothrop Stoddard, and Clinton Stoddard Burr, written in the racist motif, had a large sale. Less widely circulated were the anthropological studies by Franz Boas, which challenged the racial determination of culture and even the physiological criteria whereby one "race" is presumed to be distinguished from another.

In the 1930s clarification and separation of such concepts as race and culture caused the pendulum to swing the other way. Racial determinism was recognized for the nonsense that it was and the impermanent nature of national character was stressed. American involvement in the second World War caused differences once again to become important. These, however, were no longer based upon crude racist formulations but were framed in terms of the interaction of

David M. Potter, "American Women and the American Character," *Stetson University Bulletin*, LXII (January, 1962). Reprinted by permission.

1. H. C. J. Duijker and N. H. Frijda, *National Character and National Stereotypes* (New York, 1960).

2. Lee Coleman, "What Is American: A Study of Alleged American Traits," *Social Forces*, XIX (May, 1941), 492–99.

3. Saveth, *American Historians and European Immigrants, passim.*

4. Arvid Brodersen, review of Duijker, *National Character op. cit.*, in *Social Research*, XXVIII (Winter, 1961), 506–507.

*culture and personality. Behavioral scientists—anthropologists, pyschologists, and psychoanalysts—were in the foreground.*

*To the concepts of Margaret Mead, Geoffrey Gorer, David Riesman, and others, Dr. Potter has contributed the element of historical depth. The last chapter of Potter's People of Plenty is a synthesis of behavioral theory and historical data.*

*In the selection reprinted below, Dr. Potter is critical of descriptions of the national character that are based upon analysis of a segment of the population, however large.*

THERE IS an old riddle which children used to ask one another concerning two Indians. One was a big Indian, the other was a little Indian, and they were sitting on a fence. The little Indian, the riddle tells us, was the big Indian's son, but the big Indian, was not the little Indian's father. How, asks the riddle, can this be?

Boys and girls for a long time have found that this riddle succeeds very well in mystifying many people. And the fact that it does presents another puzzle as to why the riddle is hard to answer. If we were to state the question in more general terms: there are two human beings, one adult and one child; the child is the son of the adult, but the adult is not the father of the child, probably no one would have much difficulty in recognizing that the adult is the mother. Why then do the Indians on a fence perplex us? If we examine the structure of the riddle, I think we will find that it contains two devices which inhibit our recognition that the big Indian is a female. First, the two Indians are described as being in a very specific situation—they are sitting on a fence. But women, at least in our culture, do not usually sit on fences; if the two Indians had been roasting some ears of corn, or mending their teepee, how much easier the riddle would have been. Second, we are perhaps especially prone to think of Indians as masculine. If the riddle had said two South Sea Islanders, or perhaps, two Circassians, the possibility of their being female might occur to us much more easily.

But most of all, the riddle owes its baffling effect to the fact that our social generalization is mostly in masculine terms. If we said that the little Indian is the big Indian's daughter, but that the big Indian is not the little Indian's mother, the possibility that the big Indian is the father would come to mind readily enough. For in our culture, men are still in a general category, while women are in a special category. When we speak of mankind, we mean men and women collectively, but when we speak of womenkind, we mean the ladies, God bless them. The word humanity is itself derived from *homo,* that is man, and the species is *Homo sapiens.* Neuter nouns or general nouns which are ambiguous as to sex—nouns like infant, baby, child, sibling, adolescent, adult, spouse, parent, citizen, person, individual, etc.—all take masculine pronouns. In our culture, a woman, at marriage takes her husband's name. Though born a Cabot, if she marries Joe Doaks, Mrs. Joe Doaks she becomes and Mrs. Doaks she remains, usually for the rest of her life.

This masculine orientation is to be expected, of course, in a society which is traditionally and culturally male-dominated—in what we call a patriarchal rather than a matriarchal society. Even women themselves have connived at maintaining the notion of masculine ascendancy, and in the rather numerous concrete situations in which they actually dominate their men, they often dissimulate their control by pretending to be weak, dependent, or "flighty." In such a situation one must expect that men will be regarded as the normative figures in the society, and that, in popular thought at least, the qualities of the masculine component in the society will pass for the qualities of the society as a whole.

If this habit were confined to popular thought, it would hardly be worth examining. But it also sometimes creeps into academic and scholarly thought, which ought to have more rigor, and when it does so, it can sometimes distort our picture of society. Thus a writer may sometimes make observations on the traits or values of American men, and then may generalize these as the traits or values of the American people. If he did this deliberately, on the theory that since male values dominate the society, they must therefore be American values, we would have to concede that he is aware of what he is doing, even though we might question his results. But when he does so unconsciously, his method may easily lead him to assume first that since American men are dominant, the characteristics of American men are the characteristics of the American people, and that since women are people, the characteristics of the American people are the characteristics of American women, or in short, that the characteristics of American men are the characteristics of American women.

To avoid this trap, when one meets with a social generalization it is frequently worthwhile to ask concretely, Does it apply to women, or only to the masculine component in the population? Does the statement that Prussians are domineering mean that Prussian women are domineering, or only Prussian men? Does the statement that Americans are individualistic mean American women as well as American men? The question seems worth asking, for it appears more than possible that many of our social generalizations which are stated sweepingly to cover the entire society are in fact based on the masculine population, and that if we took the feminine population into account, the generalization might have to be qualified, or might even run in an entirely different direction.

A notable example of this can perhaps be found in Frederick Jackson Turner's famous frontier hypothesis, stated so brilliantly at Chicago almost seventy years ago. The gist of Turner's argument was, of course, that the frontier had been a basic influence in shaping the character of the American people. Primarily, as he saw it, the frontier provided economic opportunity in the form of free land. When this free land was suddenly conferred upon a people who had previously been held in dependence by the land monopolies of the Old World, it made the American economically independent and this independence made him more individualistic and more egalitarian in his attitudes. Also, the necessity for subduing the wilderness by his own personal exertions, in a situation where he could not call upon doctors, dentists, policemen, lawyers, contractors, well-drillers, repairmen, soil analysts, and other specialists to aid him, made him more self-reliant.

Not even Turner's harshest critics deny that there was much truth in observations, but many of them have pointed to his lack of precision, and it is fair to question to what extent Turner's generalizations applied to all frontier people, or to what extent they applied restrictively to frontier men. Sometimes it becomes clear that the life-process which he identifies with the frontier was primarily though not wholly an experience shared by men rather than by women. There is one famous passage, for instance, which begins, "The wilderness masters the colonist." Now *colonist* is a neuter noun, and could apply to a female colonist. But the passage continues to say that the wilderness, finding the colonist "European in dress, industry, modes of travel, and thought, . . . takes him from the railroad car and puts him in a birch canoe (this sounds progressively less as if it could be a woman). It strips off the garments of civilization and arrays him in the hunting shirt and the moccasin." Soon, this colonist hears the call of the wild almost as clearly as Jack London's dog, and when he does, "he shouts the war cry and takes the scalp in orthodox Indian fashion."[1] Here, at least, the pioneer in question is hardly a woman.

Certainly it is true that the frontier offered economic opportunity, and certainly, also, frontier women shared in some of the social consequences which flowed from the fact that this opportunity was available to their men. But is it not true, in cold fact, that the opportunities offered by the West were opportunities for men and not, in any direct sense, opportunities for women? The free acres of the West were valuable to those who could clear, and break, and plow and harvest them. But clearing and breaking, plowing and harvesting were men's work, in which women rarely participated. The nuggets of gold in the streambeds of California in 1849 represented opportunity to those who could prospect for them. But the life of the prospector and the sourdough was not a woman's life, and the opportunities were not women's opportunities. Similarly, the grass-covered plateau of the Great Plains represented economic opportunity for those who could use it as an open range for the holding and grazing of Longhorn cattle. But the individuals who could do this were men; the Cattle Kingdom was a man's world. Thus, when Turner says that "so long as free land exists, the opportunity for a competency exists," he means, in effect, an opportunity for males.

Again, it may bear repeating, there is no question here that the frontier influenced women as well as men. It had its Molly Pitcher and its Jemima Boone, as well as its Davy Crockett and its Kit Carson. It left its stamp upon the pioneer women as well as the pioneer men. But when Turner states that it furnished "a new field of opportunity, a gate of escape from the bondage of the past," one must ask, exactly what was the nature of women's participation in this opportunity? Before this question can be analyzed, it is perhaps necessary to recognize that women's place in our society is invariably complicated by the fact that they have, as men do not, a dual status. Almost every woman shares the status of the men in her family—her father or her husband—and if this is a privileged position, she is a recipient of some of the privilege. This is an affiliated status, but if her men gain, she gains with them. Thus, if her family became landowners on the frontier, she participated in their advancement, and no one can deny that free land was, in this indirect sense, opportunity for her also. But woman also has a personal status, which is a sex status, as a female. As a female, on the frontier, women were especially dependent upon having a man in the family, for there was no division of labor there, as there was in settled communities, and most of the tasks of the frontier—the hunting, the wood-chopping, the plowing—could hardly be performed by women, though many of them of course, rose to these tasks in time of emergency. In fact, the frontier was brutally harsh for females, and it furnished its own verdict on its differential impact upon the sexes. "This country," said the frontier aphorism, "is all right for men and dogs, but it's hell on women and horses."

If we accept Turner's own assumption that economic opportunity is what matters, and that the frontier was significant as the context within which economic opportunity occurred, then we must observe that for

American women, as individuals, opportunity began pretty much where the frontier left off. For opportunity lay in access to independent employment, and the empolyments of the frontier were not primarily accessible to women. But in the growing cities, opportunities for female employment began to proliferate. Where the work of the frontier called for the strong back and the powerful muscles of a primeval man, the work of the city —clerical work, secretarial work, the tending of machines—has called for the supple fingers and the ready adaptability of a young woman, and it was in this environment, for the first time in America, that women found, on any scale worth mentioning, access to independent earning power. Once a woman possessed access to such earning power, whether she used it or not, the historic basis for her traditional subordination had been swept away. The male monopoly upon jobs was broken, and the breaking of this monopoly was no less significant for American women than the breaking of the landlord's monopoly upon fertile soil had been for American pioneer men. As a symbol, the typewriter evokes fewer emotions than the plow, but like the plow, it played a vital part in the fulfillment of the American promise of opportunity and independence. The wilderness may have been the frontier for American men, and the cabin in the clearing the symbol of their independence, but the city was the frontier for American women and the business office was what gave them economic independence and the opportunity to follow a course of their own.

Another social generalization which is often stated as if it applied to all Americans, men and women alike, is that our society has experienced a vast transformation in the occupational activities of its people, and that we have passed from the independent, self-directed work, of the kind done by a land-owning farmer, to the regimented, externally-directed activity of the employee who labors for pay. In 1850, 63% of the gainfully employed workers in the United States were engaged in agriculture, and a high proportion of these were land-owning farmers—perhaps as nearly independent as people can be. In the past the farmer, more than most of his fellows, was in a position to plan, decide, and act for himself—to maintain his own values without regard for the approval or disapproval of his fellow man, to work at his own pace, to set his own routine. But today, as the census figures show, the American who labors is no longer self-employed. In 1958, it was estimated that 50,000,000 people gainfully employed in the United States received salaries or wages, while only 8,000,000 were self-employed, which means that in general the American worker does not work for himself. He works under direction in an office or a factory. He does not decide what to do, when

to do it, or for what purpose, but he waits for instructions which come
to him through channels. Even the junior executive, despite his prestige
is no more a self-employed man than the factory worker, and if we may
believe *The Organization Man* he is in fact considerably less independent
after hours. With these ideas in mind, we speak in broad terms about the
disappearance of the old forms of autonomous, self-directed activity.

Yet none of this applies in any sense to women, except for women
who are employees, and although female employment has increased
steadily to a point where nearly one-third of all women are employed it
is still true that two out of three American women are not employees, but
find their occupation chiefly in the maintaining of homes and the rearing
of children. Millions of housewives continue to exercise personal choice
and decision not only in arranging their own time-table and routine but
also in deciding what food the family shall have and how it shall be
prepared, what articles of purchase shall have the highest priority on the
family budget, and, in short, how the home shall be operated. Despite
strong tendencies toward conformity in American life, it is clear that
American women exercise a very wide latitude of decision in these
matters, and everyone knows that there are great variations between the
regimes in various American homes. Indeed it seems fairly evident that
the housewife of today, with the wide range of consumer goods available
for purchase and the wide variety of mechanical devices to free her from
drudgery, has a far broader set of alternatives for her household procedure than the farm wife of two or three generations ago.[2] Moreover
there are now great numbers of women working independently in their
own homes, who a generation ago would have been working very much
under direction as domestic servants in the homes of other women. If
we based our social generalizations upon the experience of women
rather than that of men, we might drop the familiar observation about
the decreasing independence of Americans in their occupational pursuits.
Instead we might emphasize that in the largest single occupational
group in the country—the group which cooks and rears children and
keeps house—there is a far greater measure of independent and self-
directed work than there was in the past.

Closely connected to this question of the disappearance of the independent worker is another commonplace generalization, namely that
the American people have become the victims of extreme specialization.
Everyone is familar with the burden of this lament: American industry
has forced the craftsman to abandon his craft, and with it the satisfaction
of creative labor, and has reduced him to operating a machine or to
performing a single operation on the assembly-line as if he were a
machine himself. Further, the complaint continues, modern conditions

provide fewer and fewer opportunities for a worker to be an all-round person of varied skills and resources, as the American farmer used to be, and instead conditions make of him a diminished person, a narrow specialist hardly fit for anything save his narrow specialty.

Despite the exaggerated and somewhat hackneyed character of this outcry, it contains an important element of truth as regards the work of American male workers. But this generalization, too, is in fact applicable largely to the male component in the population rather than to the American people as a whole. For the American housewife is not a specialist, and in fact her modern role requires that she be far more versatile than her grandmother was, despite the greater skill of the grandmother in cooking, sewing, and other household crafts. A good housewife today must not only serve food to please the family palate, but must also know about calories, vitamins, and the principles of a balanced diet. She must also be an economist, both in her knowledge of the quality of the products offered to her and in her ability to do the impossible with a budget. She must not only maintain a confortable home, but must also possess enough skill in interior decoration to assure that her own menage will not seem dowdy or unappealing by comparison with the latest interiors shown in Hollywood films. She must not only rear children, but must also have mastered enough child psychology to be able to spare the rod and still not spoil the child. She must not only get the children ready for school, but must also, in many cases, act as a kind of transportation manager, participating in an elaborate car pool to convey them to and fro. In addition to all this, society now enjoins her not to rely upon the marriage to hold her husband, but to keep her personality and her appearance so attractive that he will have no incentive to stray. Whatever else she may be, she is certainly not a specialist, and even if she fails to meet all these varied demands upon her, her mere effort to do so would remove her from the category of specialist. If we based our social generalizations upon women rather than upon men, we might quite justifiably affirm that the modern age is an age of diversified activity rather than an age of specialization.

The profound differences between the patterns of men's work and women's work are seldom understood by most men, and perhaps even by most women. In terms of the time-tables of life, however, the contrasts are almost startling. For instance, man usually beings work in the early twenties, labors at precisely timed intervals for eight hours a day and five days a week, until he is sixty-five, when his life as a worker may be cut off with brutal abruptness and he is left idle. Woman, also usually begins work in the early twenties, perhaps in an office on the same time-table as a man, but after a very few years she becomes a wife, whose work is keeping house, and mother whose work is rearing children. As such she labors often for from fifty-one to fifty-six hours a week, and she does not have the alternation of work and leisure which help to lend variety and pace to the life of her husband. Her work-load will continue to be heavier than her husband's until the children are older, after which it will gradually diminish, and she may ultimately re-enter employment. But most women do not; they continue to keep house.[3] And as long as a woman does keep house, either as a wife or as a widow, she never experiences the traumatic, sudden transition from daily work as the focus of life to enforced idleness—the transition which we call retirement.

Another far-reaching consequence of the difference between man's work and woman's work is forcibly expressed in a recent public interest advertisement in *Harper's Magazine* by Frank R. Neu, entitled "We May Be Sitting Ourselves to Death." Neu presents some very impressive data about the poor physical fitness of a large percentage of American men, and about the deleterious effects of the sedentary life of Mr. Joe Citizen as an office worker whose principal exercise is to go around a golf course on an electric cart on the week-end. Then Mr. Neu says:

Let's consider Jill, Joe's wife, for a moment. Chances are, on the basis of current statistics, Jill will outlive Joe by anywhere from five to 25 years. Medical science is not sure yet whether this is because Jill has different hormones from Joe or whether it is a result of the different roles which Joe and Jill fulfill in our society.

The average suburban Jill is likely to be a home-maker responsible for rearing two or more children. It is safe to assume that any woman with this responsibility is going to get a lot of daily exercise no matter how many gadgets she has to help her do the housework. A homemaker does a lot of walking each day merely to push the buttons and start the machines that wash the clothes, cook the meals, and remove the dust. And she also does a good deal of bending each day to pick up after Joe and the junior members of the family. All in all, Jill is likely to get much more exercise than Joe. This may have a significant relationship to Jill's outliving Joe, who no longer hikes the dusty trail to bring home the buffalo meat and hides to feed and clothe his family.[4]

In the light of differences so great that they may radically alter the duration of life, it is again evident that a serious fallacy results when generalizations derived from the experience of American men are applied indiscriminately to the American people in such a way as to exclude the experience of American women.

As a further illustration of the readiness with which one can fall into a fallacy in this way, let me suggest one more generalization about

Americans which has been widely popular in recent years. This is the proposition, formulated by David Riesman in *The Lonely Crowd*, that the American has been transformed, in the past century, from an inner-directed individual to an other-directed individual. A century or so ago, the argument runs, the American learned certain values from his elders, in his youth. He internalized these values, as matters of principle, so that, in Riesman's phrase, they served as a kind of gyroscope to hold him on his course, and he stood by them throughout his life whether they were popular or unpopular. When these values were involved, he did not hesitate to go against the crowd. Thus he was inner-directed. But today, says Riesman, in a universe of rapidly changing circumstances, where the good will of our associates is more important to our success than it ever was to the nineteenth century farmer, the American no longer internalizes his values in the old way. Instead, he responds very perceptively, very sensitively, to the values of others, and adjusts his course to meet their expectations. Indeed their expectations are a kind of radar-screen for his guidance. Thus he is other-directed, or to use an older and less precise term, he is much more a conformist.

Riesman does not discuss whether his thesis about "the changing American character" is applicable to American women, as well as to American men.[5] But we are entitled to ask, does he really believe that American women were so inner-directed as his analysis would suggest? Perhaps yes, if you believe that women have been more steadfast than men in defending the values on which the security of the home is based. But on the other hand, woman, historically, was a dependent person, and as a dependent person, she developed a most perceptive sensitivity to the expectations of others and a responsiveness in adapting herself to the moods and interests of others. She has always had a radar screen. If women are quicker to conform to the expectations of a group of other women than men are to a group of other men, and if we should say that this has been true in the past, what it would mean is that women have been other-directed all along, and that when Riesman says Americans are becoming other-directed, what he means is that American men are becoming other-directed. As women gain more economic and social independence, it might be supposed in terms of Riesman's own analysis, that more than half of the American people are becoming less other-directed rather than more so. With the gradual disappearance of the so-called "clinging vine" type, who dared not call her soul her own, this is, in fact, apparently just what is happening.

If many of the generalizations which apply to American men, and which purport to apply to Americans generally, do not actually apply to

American women, anyone who attempts to study the American character is forced to ask: to what extent has the impact of American historical
experience been the same for both sexes, and to what extent has it
been dissimilar? Viewed in these terms, the answer would probably have
to be a balanced one. Certainly the main values that have prevailed in
American society—the belief in individualism, the belief in equality,
the belief in progress, have shaped the thought of American women as
well as of American men, and American women are no doubt more
committed to individualism, and to equality, and to progress, than
women in many other societies. But on the other hand, some of the major
forces that have been at work in American history have impinged upon
men and upon women in differential ways. For instance, as I have already
suggested, the frontier placed a premium upon qualities of brute strength
and of habituation to physical danger which women did not possess in
the same degree as men, either for biological or for cultural reasons. The
result has been a differential historical experience for American men and
American women which must be analyzed if there is any basis to be
found for asserting that there are differences in the character types of
the two sexes.

What then, we might ask, have been the principal transformations
that history has brought in the lives of American women? Surprisingly
enough, this is largely an unexplored field, but there are certain answers
which appear more or less self-evident.

One of these is that our society has, during the last century and a
half, found ways to do most of its heavy work without the use of human
brawn and muscle. Water-power, steam power, electric power, jet power,
and the power of internal combustion have largely eliminated the need
for brute strength and great physical stamina in most forms of work.
This transformation has emancipated men in a revolutionary degree, but
it has even more strikingly emancipated women, for women are physi-
ologically smaller than men, and they lack the muscular strength and
physical endurance of men. As the factor of hard labor in human work
is reduced and the factor of skill is enhanced, therefore, women have
found that inequality in ability to meet the requirements of work is
greatly diminished. This basic fact, by itself, has probably done more
than anything else to promote the equality of women.

But if this is the most fundamental effect of the mechanization of
work, mechanization has also had a number of other sweeping consequences. One of these is that it has destroyed the subsistence farm as a unit
of American life, and the disappearance of the subsistence farm, in turn,
has had the most far-reaching implications.

To appreciate this, we must remember what life was like on the sub-

sistence farm. The only division of labor that existed in this unit was
the primitive division between men and women. The men constructed
the dwelling, planted and cultivated the crops, raised the cattle and hogs
and poultry, sheared the sheep, and chopped wood for the stoves and
the fireplaces. In short the man was the producer—the producer of food,
of fuel, of the raw materials for clothing. The farm wife, in turn, not
only cooked, kept house, and cared for the children, as modern wives still
do, but she also performed certain other tasks. She used ashes to make
her own soap, she put up vast quantities of preserved food, she spun
fibers into cloth, and made cloth into clothing. In economic terms, she and
her daughters were processors. Together, they worked in a small, close-
knit community, in which all lived very much together.

It hardly needs saying what happened to this typical unit of life in
an earlier America. The use of machinery, the increased specialization of
labor, and the development of an economy of exchange superseded it,
and rendered it almost obsolete. Today a limited number of farmers with
machines raise enough food for the entire population. Men go out to work
instead of working on their own place, with their own sons, and their reward is not a harvest but a weekly wage or a monthly salary. Instead of
"making a living" they make an income. All this is obvious, and oft-
repeated. But what are the implications for the American woman?

Some embittered critics have retorted that modern woman, no longer
a processor of goods, has lost her economic function, and that she re-
tains only a biological function as mate and mother and a social function
in the family. This loss of function, they would say, accounts for the
frustration and sense of futility which seems to plague modern woman
even more than it does modern man. But if we take a hard look at this
argument, clearly it will not stand up. What has happened is that women
have acquired a new role, in a new division of labor. With her husband
away from the home, held by the compulsions of the clock, it falls to her,
first of all, to use the family's income to take care of the family's needs.
In short, while her husband has changed from a producer to an earner,
she has changed from a processor to a consumer in a society where consumption is an increasingly important economic function.

The responsibilities of the consumer are no mean task. To handle
them successfully, a person must be something of a dietitian, a judge
of the quality of many goods, a successful planner, a skillful decorator,
and a budget manager. The business of converting a monthly sum of
money into a physical basis for a pleasant life involves a real art, and it
might be counted as a major activity even if there were not children
to rear and meals to prepare. But the increased specialization of the work
of men at offices and factories away—frequently far away—from the

home has also shifted certain cultural duties and certain community tasks
in ever-greater measure to women.

In the Old World, upper-class men, claiming leisure as the principal
advantage of their status, have made themselves the custodians of culture
and the leaders in the cultural life of their communities. In America,
upper-class men, primarily businessmen, working more compulsively and
for longer hours than any other class, have resigned their cultural responsibilities to women and then have gone on to disparage literature
and the arts because these pursuits, in the hands of females, began to
seem feminine. Women have shouldered the responsibility, have borne
the condescension with which their cultural activities were often treated,
have provided the entire teaching force for the elementary schools, and
most of the force for the secondary schools, and have done far more than
their share to keep community life alive. This is another of the results,
impinging in a differential way upon women, of the great social transformation of the last two centuries.

So far as we have examined them, all of these changes would seem
to operate somewhat to the advantage of women, to have an emancipating effect, and to diminish her traditional subordination. No longer
handicapped by a labor system in which biceps are at a premium, she
has moved into the realms of employment, and has even preempted the
typewriter and the teacher's desk as her own. If she has exercised a
choice, which she never had before, and has decided to remain in her
home, she has encountered a new economic role as a consumer rather
than as a processor, with a broad range of activities, and with a new
social role in keeping up the vigor of the community activities. In either
case, the orbit of her activities is far wider than what used to be regarded
as women's sphere, and it has been wide enough in fact to lead some
optimistic observers to speak of the equality of women as if it were something which had reached some kind of absolute fulfillment and complete-
ness about the time of the ratification of the woman's suffrage amendment in 1920.

Yet before we conclude our story with the ending that they all lived
happily ever after, it is necessary to face up to the fact that women have
not found all these changes quite as emancipating as they were expected
to be. Indeed, much of the serious literature about American women is
pessimistic in tone, and makes the disatisfactions and the sexual frustration of modern American women its principal theme. Great stress is laid
upon the fundamental dilemma that sexual fulfillment seems to depend
upon one set of psychological attitudes—attitudes of submissiveness and
passivity—while the fulfillment of equality seems to depend upon an

opposite set—attitudes of competitiveness and self-assertion. At its grim-
mest level, this literature stresses the contention of Sigmund Freud that
women instinctively envy the maleness of a man and reject their own
sex. There is no doubt that these psychoanalytic views are important and
that attention to questions of the sex life of an individual is basic, but a
very respectable argument can be and has been made that what women
envy about men is not their maleness in purely sexual terms but their
dominance in the society and their immunity from the dilemmas which
the needs of sexual and biological fulfillment on one hand and of personal fulfillment on the other pose for women.[6] The inescapable fact that
males can have offspring without either bearing them or rearing them
means that the values of family life and of personal achievement can be
complementary for men, where they are conflicting values for women.

This one immutable and timeless fact, more than anything else, seems
to stand forever in the way of the complete and absolute equality of
men and women. Political and legal emancipation and even the complete
equality of women in social relations and in occupational opportunities
could not remove this handicap. So long as it remains, therefore, no one
who finds a measure of inequality still remaining will have to look for an
explanation in social terms. But it is legitimate to ask whether this is the
only remaining barrier to emancipation, or whether other factors also
serve to maintain adverse differentials against woman, even in modern
America, where she seems to be more nearly equal than she has been in
any other time or place, except perhaps in certain matriarchal tribes.

There are, perhaps, two aspects of woman's role as housekeeper and as
consumer which also contribute, in a new way historically, to work against
the prevailing tendencies toward a fuller equality. These aspects have,
in a subtle way, caused society to devalue the modern activities of women
as compared with those of men, and thus may even have contributed to
bring about a new sort of subordination.

One of these is the advent of the money economy, in which income
is the index of achievement, and the housewife is the only worker who
does not get paid. On the farm home, in the days of the subsistence
economy, neither she nor her husband got paid, at least not very much,
and they were economic partners in the enterprise of making a living.
But today, the lowliest and most trivial job which pays a wage counts
as employment while the most demanding and vital tasks which lack the
sanction of pecuniary remuneration do not so count. A recent, and in fact
very able book entitled *Women Who Work* deals, just as you would expect, not with women who work, but with women who get paid for their
work. Sociologists regard it as an axiom that the amount of income is as

important as any other criterion in measuring social status today, and in one sense, a woman's status may reflect the income of her husband, but in another sense it should be a corollary of the axiom that if income is esteemed, lack of income is followed by lack of esteem, and even by lack of self-esteem. If it needed proving, Komarovsky has shown that the American housewife tends to disparage herself as well as her work, as both being unworthy because they do not receive recognition in terms of cash income.[7]

If woman does not command respect as an earner, she is also likely to incur a certain subtle lack of respect for herself in her role as a consumer. For there is a strong tendency in some phases of American advertising to regard the consumer as someone who may be flattered or may be bullied, but who need not be treated as a mature person. Insofar as the consumer is an object of condescension, someone to be managed rather than someone to be consulted, someone on whom the will of the advertiser is to be imposed by psychological manipulation, and insofar as consumers are primarily women, it means that women become the objects of more than their share of the low esteem in which the consumer is held, and more than their share of the stultifying efforts to play upon human yearnings for prestige and popularity or upon human psychological insecurities. Anyone who recalls the recent publications about the rate at which the blinking of women's eyes increases when they view the display of goods in a supermarket, and the extent to which this display causes them to spend impulsively, rather than according to need, will recognize that the role of the consumer has not enhanced the dignity of women.[8] This aspect was very clearly and wittily recognized by Sylvia Wright in an article in *Harpers* in 1955, in which she dealt ironically with the assertion which we sometimes hear, that America has become a woman's world.

Whatever it is (she wrote) I'll thank you to stop saying it's mine. If it were a woman's world, people wouldn't yammer at me so much. They're always telling me to do, be, or make something. . . .

The one thing they don't want me to be is me. "A few drops of Abano Bath Oil" they say, "and you're not you . . . you're Somebody New lolling in perfumed luxury." But I'm not allowed to loll long. The next minute I have to spring out in order to be Fire and Ice, swathed in satin, not a thing to do but look stark, and wait for a man to pounce. Turn the page, I've got to make sure it's Johnson's cotton buds with which I swab the baby. A few pages later, the baby gets into the act yelling for fullweight diapers. . . .

I'm supposed to use a lot of make-up to keep my husband's love, but I must avoid make-up clog. I'm supposed to be gay, spontaneous and outgoing, but I mustn't get "expression lines" [Expression lines are to wrinkles as morticians are to undertakers]. . . .

In the old days, I only had to have a natural aptitude for cooking, cleaning, bringing up children, entertaining, teaching Sunday School and tatting. . . .
Now I also have to reconstitute knocked-down furniture and build on porches.[9]

If a woman as a consumer in a world of producers and as an un-because, at the very time when efforts to exploit her as a female began to abate, the efforts to exploit her as a consumer began to increase. And at the time when the intrinsic value of her work was gaining in dignity as compared with that of the male, the superficial value as measured in terms of money income was diminishing. The essential strength of her position has increased, but the combined effect of the manipulation by the media and the emphasis upon monetary earning as a standard for the valuation of work has threatened her with a new kind of subordination, imposed by the system of values which she herself accepts, rather than by masculine values imposed upon her against her will.

If a woman as a consumer in a world of producers and as an unpaid worker in a world of salaried employees has lost some of the ground she had gained by emancipation as a female in a world of males, even the emancipation itself has created some new problems for her. For instance, it has confronted her with a dilemma she never faced in the days when she was confined to her own feminine sphere. This is the dilemma that she is now expected to attain a competence in the realm of men's affairs but that she must never succeed in this realm too much. It is well for her to be intelligent, but not intelligent enough to make a young man feel inferior; well for her to find employment and enjoy it, but not enjoy it enough to be unwilling to give it up for the cradle and the sink; well for her to be able to look after herself but never to be so visibly able that it will inhibit the impulse of the right men to want to look after her; well for her to be ambitious, but never ambitious enough actually to put her personal objectives first. When a man marries, no one expects him to cease being a commuter and to become a farmer because it would be good for the children—though in fact it might. But when a woman marries, her occupation becomes an auxiliary activity.

Here we come back to the presence of a fundamental dualism which has made the so-called "emancipation" of women different from the emancipation of any other group in society. Other emancipated groups have sought to substitute a new condition in place of an old one and to obliterate the old, but except for few of the most militant women in a generation of crusading suffragettes, now almost extinct, women have never renounced the roles of wife and mother. The result has been that their objective was to reconcile a new condition with an old one, to hold in balance the principle of equality, which denies a difference, and the practice of wifehood and motherhood which recognizes a difference in the roles of men and women. The eternal presence of this dualism has not only caused a distressing amount of confusion and tension among women themselves; it has also caused confusion among their many volunteer critics. The result is that we encounter more wildly inconsistent generalizations about modern American women than about almost any other subject.

For example, modern woman, we are told, is gloriously free from the inferiority of the past, but she is miserable and insecure in her new freedom. She wields the purse strings of the nation and has become dominant over a world of increasingly less-masculine men who no longer trust themselves to buy a suit of clothes without their wife's approval. But also she does the routine work at typewriter and sink while the men still run the universe. Similarly, we are assured that the modern woman is an idle, parasitic, bridge-playing victim of technological unemployment in her own mechanized home, and also that she is the busy manager of a family and household and budget whose demands make the domestic chores of the past look easy by comparison. She escapes from reality into the wretched, petty little world of soap opera and neighborhood gossip, but she excels in her knowledge of public affairs and she became an effective guardian of literary and artistic values when her money-grubbing husband defaulted on this responsibility. She is rearing the best crop of children ever produced on this planet, by the most improved methods ever devised, while her over-protectiveness has bred "momism" and her unwillingness to stay at home has bred delinquency.

Clearly, we are still a long way from having arrived at any monotonous unanimity of opinion about the character of American women. Yet if we will focus carefully upon what we really know with some degree of assurance, we can perhaps begin the process of striking a balance. We certainly know, for instance, that many of the trends of American history have been operative for both men and women in somewhat the same way. The emphasis upon the right of the individual has operated to remove legal disabilities upon women, to open many avenues to gainful employment, to confer the suffrage, and so on. Even our divorce rate is an ironic tribute to the fact that the interests of the individual, and perhaps in a majority of cases the individual woman, are placed ahead of the protection of a social institution—namely the family. The rejection of authority in American life, which has made our child-rearing permissive and has weakened the quality of leadership in our politics, has also meant that the relation of husband and wife is more of a partnership and less of an autocracy in this age and in this country than at any other time or place in Western civilization. The competitive strain in American life has impelled American women as well as American men to strive hard for their goals, and to assert themselves in the strife —indeed European critics complain that they assert themselves far more strenuously than European women and entirely too much for the tranquility of society.

On the other hand, we also know that the experience of women remains in many ways a distinctive experience. Biologically, there are still the age-old facts that women are not as big as men and not as strong; that the sex act involves consequences for them which it does not involve for the male; that the awareness of these consequences conditions the psychological attitudes of women very deeply; and that motherhood is a biological function while fatherhood is, in a sense, a cultural phenomenon. Historically, there is the formidable truth that the transformations of modern life have impinged upon men and women in different ways. The avenues of employment opened to men are not the same as the avenues of employment opened to women. The revolution in our economy has deepened the division between work in the home and work outside the home by according the sanction of monetary reward to the one and denying it to the other—thus devaluing in a new way work which is distinctively woman's. The economic revolution, while converting most men from producers to earners, has converted most women from processors to consumers, and the exploitation of the consumer has, again, added a new devaluation to women's role. Society has given her the opportunity to fulfill her personal ambitions through the same career-activities as a man, but it cannot make her career aspirations and her family aspirations fit together as they do for a man. The result of all this is a certain tension between her old role and her new one. More of an individualist than women in traditional societies, she is by no means as whole-heartedly individualistic as the American male, and as a study at Berkeley recently showed, she still hesitates to claim individualism as a quality of her own.[10] If she enters the competitive race, she does so with an awareness that the top posts are still pretty much the monopoly of men, and with a certain limitation upon her competitive commitment. In short, she is constantly holding in balance her general opportunities as a person and her distinctive needs as a woman, and when we consider how badly these two go together in principle can we not say that she is maintaining the operative equilibrium between them with a remarkable degree of skill and of success?

The answer to my childish riddle was that the big Indian is the little Indian's mother. To say that she is a squaw is not to deny that she is an Indian—but it is to say that she is an Indian for whom the expectations of the masculine world of Indians, or of Americans, do not apply. It is to say that her qualities and traits, whether she is an Indian, or an American, will reflect the influence of the same sweeping forces which influence the world of men, but that it will reflect them with a difference. In this sense, what we say about the character of the American people should be said not in terms of half of the American population—even if it is the male half—but in terms of the character of the totality of the people. In this sense, also, attention to the historic character of American women is important not only as a specialty for female scholars or for men who happen to take an interest in feminism, but as a coordinate major part of the overall, comprehensive study of the American character as a whole. For the character of any nation is the composite of the character of its men and of its women and though these may be deeply similar in many ways, they are almost never entirely the same.

# Part IV

## Quantification and Machine Processes

# Econometrics / *Lance E. Davis, J. R. T. Hughes, and Stanley Reiter*

"Econometrics," asserts a textbook in the field, "is a way of studying history—a very systematic way. . . . The econometrician tries to piece together the fundamental aspects of economic behavior by looking at the interrelationships of the quantitative magnitudes generated historically, and then tries to extrapolate past behavior into the unknown future. . . . Even without the attempts at extrapolation, however, econometrics is interesting as a study of the past to show how quantitative magnitudes interacted at that time."[1]

In the selection reprinted below, the authors indicate various applications of econometrics to historical problems. If W. W. Rostow is correct in asserting that the growth concept is a meeting ground for historian and economist, the development of historical statistics and of techniques for their use has made the encounter that much easier.[2] Using such sources as Historical Statistics of the United States: Colonial Times to 1957[3] and Trends in the American Economy in the Nineteenth Century,[4] Professor Thomas Cochran has written an imaginative article challenging the familiar thesis that the Civil War accelerated the growth rate of the American economy.[5]

The conclusions of econometric research are, at best, probabilistic. Behavior is exceedingly complex and a "limited number of variables related together in fairly simple and elegant equations cannot explain the whole of such behavior."[6] Econometric research should be combined with the traditional materials of historiography, as the following brief survey suggests.

I F WE ARE successfully to relate our work with the main body of Economic History, we must be able to show the fundamental relationship between quantitative analysis and more conventional methods of eco-

Lance E. Davis, Jonathan R. T. Hughes, and Stanley Reiter, "Aspects of Quantitative Research in Economic History," *Journal of Economic History*, XX (December, 1960), 539–47. Reprinted by permission.

1. L. R. Klein, *A Textbook of Econometrics* (Evanston; 1956), 2.
2. W. W. Rostow, "Economics," 34, above.
3. (Washington, 1960)
4. (Princeton, 1960)
5. "Did the Civil War Retard Industrialization?" *Mississippi Valley Historical Review*, XLVIII (Sept., 1961), 197–210.
6. Klein, *Textbook, op. cit.*, 2.

nomic historians. The historian reconstructs events of the past, and with them attempts to understand the institutions and modes of behavior associated with those events. He seeks to construct a consistent story revealing the fundamental nature and meaning to us of the past, thus creating insight into the past and understanding of it—something considerably beyond a mere account of what probably happened. However, this story must be based upon, and be consistent with, the reconstructed events of the past, "what probably happened."

This view of historical study is a familiar one and, in fact, almost any working historian would accept it as a definition of his activities. What has this view to do with quantitative methods in economic history, and how does quantitative economic history differ from non-quantitative writing in economic history? The answer lies partly in the nature of the materials from which the reconstruction is to be made, and partly in the technique employed to analyze these materials. We may distinguish two broad classes of materials. First, each society generates its own accounts of, and commentaries upon, contemporary affairs, as well as its own histories of the past. This class of materials can be more or less explicitly labeled historical writings. Second, in the course of its characteristic processes each society generates a body of artifacts, debris left behind in time. The processes of economic life, for example, produce masses of receipts, books of account, legal documents, tax returns, and various kinds of rolls, lists, and records; and these materials can be used to reconstruct the past. Such a reconstruction is analogous to the process frequently employed by archeologists who utilize the surviving debris of an ancient city to provide materials for understanding the civilization that built it and lived there. Characteristically, this material consists of a mass of individual items, each of which contains a relatively insignificant piece of information. This collection, originally generated for purposes other than historical study, usually requires reorganization and analysis to enable the information contained to be brought to a form useful to the historian. This is, the information must be organized on some principle and made the basis of inferences about the past, a task familiar to the historian, but that also contains the essential elements of a statistical problem.

If we had at hand every item of the kind under consideration (for example, every warehouse receipt issued in New York State between 1870–1900), we would face the task of formulating meaningful questions with which to confront these data, and of organizing the data to bear on these questions. Thus we might be interested in the geographical distribution of warehouses, in the time-shape of business activities, in the commodity composition of consumption, or in the profitability of warehousing, and each question would require a different method of systemization and analysis. We must, therefore, first formulate a statistical-historical model in terms of which historical meaning can be given to the observations. Having formulated such a model, we are still confronted with a large collection of observations that must be statistically summarized and described. We shall have more to say later about the problems of data processing.

In fact, however, since we generally do not have the complete collection of all observations of a given land, but rather only a sample of the surviving ones, the study of the historical process is even more complicated. For in addition to the question of analysis and systemization, we must also decide, on the basis of the observations at hand, what the whole collection would reveal if we had access to complete information. This last is the problem of statistical inference.

In brief, the logical structure necessary to make historical reconstructions from the surviving debris of past economic life essentially involves ideas of history, economics, and statistics. The offspring of such an act of interdisciplinary miscegenation calls for a name worthy of it; at Purdue the resulting discipline has been labeled "Cliometrics."

## II

An examination of the literature of economic history indicates that, while the qualitative stream in the discipline has usually been the larger, there has been from earliest times a significant and respectable flow of quantitative work. The political arithmeticians—Graunt, King, and the like—as early as the seventeenth century were trying to infer from data an explanation of some aspects of economic history.[1] In 1851 William Newmarch produced his pathbreaking study on the circulation of bills of exchange—a study that, in statistical sophistication (given the knowledge of the time), is the equal of anything produced more recently.[2] At yet a later date, F. W. Taussig's *History of the Tariff*, and still later, the work of Arthur Cole (as represented both by his work on the evolution of the American foreign exchange market and with W. B. Smith, *Fluctuations in American Business 1790–1860*), were attempts to infer the state of the world of the past from quantitative information.[3] The National Bureau of Economic Research, although not much given to interpretation, has produced a vast amount of quantitative information that others could use, and the works of some of their authors (Kuznets, for example) certainly fall within the category of quantitative economic history.[4] More recently, excellent work combining economic theory and quantitative methods can be found in R. C. O. Matthew's *A Study in Trade Cycle*

*History* and in what is perhaps the most notable recent study of this kind, the paper by Conrad and Meyer on slavery in the ante bellum south.[5]

None the less, the total amount of work in the field is small. Why? Is it because quantitative work is unrewarding? We think not. The dearth of quantitative economic history can probably be traced to two factors: first, the extraordinary effort that has been necessary in the past to sift and classify quantitative information; and second, the relatively recent development of statistical theory and techniques capable of handling these problems. Let us examine each of these problems in turn.

### III

Recently developed computing equipment has opened to economic historians the possibility of performing prodigies of data-processing and statistical calculation. Where the archeologist can dig with spade and hard labor into the mounds of the past to unearth artifacts, the economic historian needs power shovels and bulldozers to move the mountains of paper records. The power shovels and bulldozers are now available to economic historians, but these developments in the analysis of data by machine processing methods have scarcely been applied to the more significant questions of economic history. We need to recognize that data-processing at last provides us an opportunity to study the kinds of problems that, because of the unwieldiness of the purely mechanical processes of computation, have long been cast aside.

There is nothing novel or revolutionary in the problems themselves. There have always been problems in which masses of data had to be "processed" by ones means or another; the early work on index numbers by Jevons and Sauerbeck are well-known examples of such large-scale computations. Another, and better, example of early data-processing is to be found in the work of one of our most illustrious predecessors, William Newmarch. His work is a particularly germane example of the nature of data-processing problems.

Newmarch's celebrated survey of the circulation of bills of exchange in Great Britain, one of the most brilliant contributions to the British monetary-policy debate of the mid-19th century (although not one which noticeably affected policy, interestingly enough), and subsequently, one of the pieces of historical evidence most often used in the study of 19th century monetary phenomena, appeared in 1851.[6] Anyone who has processed data will experience a distinct "shock of recognition" when he first reads Newmarch's paper. Newmarch obtained a sample "at hazard" of the total bill circulation. The sample size was 4,367 inland and foreign bills with a nominal value of £1,216,974. From each bill he took three pieces of information, or a total of 13,101 separate pieces of numerical information. On the basis of these data and the stamp-tax returns on bills of exchange for Great Britain and certain subdivisions Newmarch was able to compute an estimate of the total bill circulation. In his computation only three arithmetic operations were required once the initial classification and organization of the data had been done. Such a study by present-day computing standards would not be cumbersome. In "The First 1,945 British Steamships," for example, there were 13 initial observations per ship, or 25,285 separate pieces of numerical information on 1,945 punch cards.[7] Once on the cards, the actual computing (far more extensive than was Newmarch's) of tonnages, estimated speeds and the index of transport capacity was not a particularly tiresome job. But in Newmarch's case, one hundred years ago, 13,101 separate pieces of information to be classified, summed, averaged, and the results used to convert stamp-tax yields into aggregate value figures was an enormous undertaking. After explaining his ingenious methods to his audience, Newmarch noted that the final operations were "clearly a mere matter of calculation; but I confess that, if I had foreseen, before I undertook the task, the extent and severity of the labour it would impose, I am not at all certain that I should have ventured upon the inquiry."[8]

That data-processing on this scale was done so long ago with quill pens instead of electronic computers underscores our main point. It is only the absence of machinery which is novel in the Newmarch story, not the presence of a data-processing problem. Some kinds of historical problems are by nature data-processing problems. In the past they have too often (but perhaps understandably) been neglected simply because too much labor was involved. Today, with the purely mechanical computational problems much reduced, economic historians have the means to study these questions. In particular these new techniques will permit the opening of new sources that, while always in existence, have heretofore been largely closed to research because of the magnitude of the task involved. First, business records that hold many of the answers to questions concerning early 19th century American development can be made available to the study of broader questions than the history of a single business. While corporate letters, minutes, and like documents have long been utilized in business history, the labor involved in organizing sales slips, time cards and the like has frequently prevented their use in producing data on prices, output, investment, and employment that would be more useful to the economic historian. Second, largely unorganized government data existing in committee and bureau reports could be brought together in manageable shape. And third, even correspondence, long a bug-a-boo of historians, could, perhaps be better analyzed by data-processing techniques together with some form of content analysis. Both economics and economic history stand to gain enormously if this work is done and done wisely.

Our work at Purdue along these lines is, we hope, only the beginning of extensive data-processing work in Economic History. Since 1957 five data-processing studies in Economic History have been produced at Purdue. In all of our studies we have developed entirely new statistical series which are now readily available as "building blocks" for other economic historians to use in their studies. Our main results from these five papers may be briefly summarized.

In "Sources of Industrial Finance: The American Textile Industry, A Case Study," one hundred seventy-five observations on each of eight financial variables were brought together in a multiple regression model. The analysis of this data indicated that heretofore economic historians had tended to overstate the role of retained earnings in 19th century American corporate finance and understate the role of borrowed capital. In addition, the analysis indicated, as might be suspected, that the impotance of loans grew concomitantly with the development of the capital markets and that a firm's capital structure was responsive to short-term changes in the capital markets, output, and employment.[9]

In "Stock Ownership in the Early New England Textile Industry," data-processing techniques were used to systematize some 3,782 separate stock accounts (representing the equity holdings of at least 854 individuals and firms in eleven textile mills) to uncover the trends in stock ownership over the period 1829 to 1859. The analysis indicates, first, that while mercantile capital represented a large proportion of the investment, the transfer from merchantile to industrial capital appears to have been slower than has been generally assumed. Second, that there was a considerable degree of backward integration with textile merchants and mercantile firms contributing a significant block of capital. Third, that financial intermediaries made a substantial contribution to the finance of new industry. And fourth, that out-of-state and foreign investors made no significant investments.[10]

In "The First 1,945 British Steamships," the growth of the British steam merchant marine up to 1860 was chronicled and measured in detail, by type of propulsion and build. It was shown that not only was this development more rapid than had previously been thought, but that the transport capacity of the fleet grew more rapidly than did the tonnages to the extent that it could have played the powerful role in overseas earnings which had been asigned to it by contemporaries, and which had been heavily discounted by modern scholars.[11]

In "The New England Textile Mills and the Capital Markets: A Study of Industrial Borrowing 1840–1860," 2,385 industrial loans were systematized by machine techniques in order to provide some new information about the ante-bellum capital markets. The analysis produced a new series of interest rates independent of the frequently-cited Bigelow estimates. It seemed to indicate that a theory of a sectored money market better explains the term structure of rates than does the more classical Lutz-Hicks expectation theory, and it presents some new data of the relative importance of various types of lenders in the markets and the cyclic and secular changes in the composition of this lender group.[12]

Finally, in "A Dollar Sterling Exchange 1803–1895," data processing techniques permitted us to organize 2,789 bills of exchange and, from the bill prices, to deduce a series of pure exchange rates. In addition to this new series, the analysis indicates that exchange rate stability did not always characterize "the gold standard"; instead, it is only after 1875, when transportation, communications, and the money markets had evolved into near-modern form, that exchange stability became common. Finally, the paper casts further light on the development of the foreign exchange market and the rise of the major foreign exchange houses—a subject previously explored by Arthur Cole.[13]

## IV

We now turn our attention briefly to statistical inference. Broadly speaking, statistical inference refers to a body of techniques that permit the user to garner with some confidence a knowledge of certain characteristics of populations on the basis of observations from these populations. For example, Newmarch's estimate of the average value of all bills based on the average of the sample drawn is a statistical inference. In that case the unknown quantity (called a parameter) is the average of all bills. In the Hughes and Reiter paper on the first 1,945 steamships a more elaborate, but essentially similar, technique was employed to estimate the speed and carrying capacity of the ships from a knowledge of other related facts about them.

In other cases the unknown quantity of interest might be, for example, a measure of dispersion, or the largest observation in the population. Inference of this kind can achieve remarkable accuracy, more accuracy sometimes than that yielded by an attempt to count an entire population. This was the case in World War II when Allied estimates, based on the serial numbers of samples of German military equipment observed in battle, proved to be more accurate than the information supplied to the German government from production records, and, in addition, were available much sooner than the data derived from the latter source.[14] Further, there are techniques for the study of relationships among various observable quantities, ranging from simple regression analysis to highly elaborate statistical schemes for detecting the presence of association between one pair of variables in the presence of many other associations or influences. A simple multivariable regression model, for example, was used in the study of textile financing previously cited to sort out the effects on corporate finance of firm age and historic time.

Before closing this desperately brief discussion of statistical inference, we should point out that one ought not to have too narrow a concept of the phenomena subject to quantitative analysis. It is, of course, obvious that observations, given in the form of numerical quantities such as money amounts or physical units of output, are subject to quantitative analysis. However, the possibilities of quantification go much further than this. Any phenomena whose occurrence may be noted or counted is quantifiable, and, in addition, coding sometimes permits apparently non-quantitative phenomena to be quantified. This attitudes, opinions, and perceptions are studied with the aid of quantitative techniques by psychologists. Content analysis of written material provides another example of the usefulness of an extended notion of quantification. In our study of 19th century exchange rates we coded proper names, origins and points of payment of the bills. Thus "quantified," the mass of information could be handled and yielded us important evidence of the development of specialization in the exchange market.

## V

We are not suggesting in this paper that there is to be a "new" economic history which will render non-quantitative economic historians technologically unemployed. It should be obvious that we regard ideas from statistics and data-processing as natural aspects of problems of historical study. It should also be obvious that the historian's special knowledge and viewpoint is essential to the useful employment of quantitative methods. Our main point is that modern statistical techniques and computing equipment make possible the intensive exploitation of a vein of historical materials that was perforce only little worked in the past; and that if even a few economic historians would take the time to learn even a little of these new techniques, the 1960's could easily prove the most productive years in the history of the discipline. On the other hand, if the discipline chooses to remain completely in the literary tradition, we can see small hope for anything but a continual rehashing of the already existing sources and a continuation of the century-long cleavage between economics and economic history—a cleavage that should soon disappear if the economic historian is able to provide the economists with new data and new interpretations of the process of economic life.

# Sampling
# and Correlation / Merle Curti,
Judith Green,
and Roderick Nash

There are some historical problems which are mainly data-processing problems and which, before the rise of a method and a technology for dealing with them, were neglected.[1] Nineteenth-century historians such as George Bancroft and Henry Adams were aware of the importance of statistics in historical research. More recently, the Owsleys' use of unpublished census data as bases for their conclusions concerning the structure of southern society pointed to the need for other than traditional methods of data processing.[2]

In the work of Merle Curti and his associates machine processes have made possible computations too lengthy and too arduous to have been carried out by traditional means. The procedure involved "random sampling," whereby "each individual or element in the universe is assured an equal or independent chance of being included" and the derivation of correlations from data is coded on IBM cards. A correlation is an expression of a relationship between variables. Coding and machine processes make possible consideration of a great many variables and numerous correlations.

Not all historical data bearing upon the subject of American philanthropy lends itself to quantification, coding, and statistical relationship. In the article reprinted below, traditional historiographic methods supplement the machine.

Note the acknowledgment that "In every sense this project was a

Merle Curti, Judith Green, and Roderick Nash, "Anatomy of Giving: Millionaires in the Late 19th Century," American Quarterly, XV (Fall, 1963), 416–35. Reprinted by permission.

    In every sense, this project was a cooperative one. Dr. Margaret Wooster Curti helped to plan the project. Professor Irvin G. Wyllie offered helpful suggestions during the planning stage. Charles Strickland, a research assistant in the University of Wisconsin History of Philanthropy Project, gave valuable aid in planning the layouts and in collecting and coding biographical material. Professor and Mrs. Burton Fisher, while in no way responsible either for planning procedures or for interpretations, have given valuable criticisms and suggestions.

1. Davis, Hughes, and Reiter, "Econometrics," 450 above.
2. "The Economic Basis of Society in the Late Ante-Bellum South, *Journal of Southern History*, VI (February, 1940), 24–25; Barnes F. Lathrop, "History from the Census Returns," *Southwestern Historical Quarterly*, LI (April, 1948), 293–312; Ralph A. Wooster, *The Secession Conventions of the South* (Princeton, 1962).

*cooperative one," and the multiple author credits. This is more characteristic of studies in the social sciences than it is of history, where single authors prevail.*

THE PROLIFERATION of large-scale philanthropic institutions in twentieth-century America has encouraged, in the past few years, interest in the history of voluntary giving. Long before this writers, without benefit of either quantitative studies of American giving or of careful comparative analyses of philanthropic behavior in the United States and in other countries, maintained that generosity had been an important and indeed a distinguishing aspect of the national character.[1]

These generalizations, which rested on impressions, can be illustrated by representative examples. James Bryce, writing in 1888, declared that "in works of active benevolence, no country has surpassed, and perhaps none has equalled, the United States. Not only are the sums collected for all sorts of philanthropic purposes larger relatively to the wealth of America than in any European country, but the amount of personal effort devoted to them seems to a European visitor to exceed that he knows at home."[2] Informed observers and scholars have largely supported Bryce's judgment. In 1953 a leading authority on American history wrote that successful Americans "shared their money with others almost as freely as they made it, returning at least part of their substance to channels of social usefulness through munificent gifts and bequests. This philanthropic streak in the national character, an index of the pervasive spirit of neighborliness, appeared early and has in our own day reached fabulous proportions."[3] Some years later a scholar competent in the economic history of both Europe and America concluded that, despite the inadequacy of the statistical record, "the best data available indicate that philanthropic contributions in Western Europe, for all purposes—education, social work, religion, scientific research, and art—amount to less than one-half of one per cent of the annual national income, whereas in the United States they amount to some two per cent of the national income."[4]

While several studies lend support to the thesis of outstanding generosity on the part of Americans in the past,[5] we have nothing comparable to the elaborate and detailed quantification that marks the notable work of W. K. Jordan for British philanthropy in the Tudor and Stuart periods.[6] The work of F. Emerson Andrews, to be sure, is admirable in its statistical base and methodology, but it is largely confined to the recent period.[7] The extent to which the American reputation for generosity is valid over time has been one of the many inquiries that has concerned the University of Wisconsin Project on the History of American Philanthropy, defined as private and voluntary giving for public purposes.

Many other questions might and ought to be asked concerning the activities of American donors and the Wisconsin Project has tried to fill some of the gaps. What, for instance, are the fields that have received the most support from donors, and what trends are discernible over a period of time? How much philanthropy has been in the form of lifetime gifts rather than bequests? Are gifts and bequests more likely to be made by those with few or no dependents or survivors than by those with many? Was there any marked difference between men and women donors in the causes chosen for philanthropy? What part does religion, educational background, means of acquisition of fortune, and occupation play in philanthropic giving? On the assumption that philanthropy reflects social trends, can an analysis of American giving reveal any definite trends?

Widespread concern during the 1890s and early years of the twentieth century over the creation of million-dollar fortunes and the uses of great wealth resulted in the publication of several relevant articles and studies. This interest was reflected in and stimulated by the compilation of two nation-wide lists of millionaires. The more important appeared as a supplement of the *New York Tribune* and was the work of Roswell G. Horr, a financial editor of the paper.[8] The report listed 4,047 men and women reputed to be millionaires. The list was arranged state by state, city by city. The kind of economic activity thought to be the major factor in the creation of each fortune was indicated. The *Tribune's* financial editor claimed to have consulted 1,500 merchants, bankers, commercial agents, lawyers, surrogates of counties, trustees and other citizens all over the country in a position to know the facts. The concentration on major cities and on the Eastern section of the country may have resulted in some exaggeration of the proportion of millionaires in this region. The *New York Tribune's* commitment to protective tariffs may also have resulted in a slight bias in minimizing the importance of protected industries in the growth of great fortunes. Yet scholars who have studed the compilation believe that it was carefully and honestly done.[9] In 1902 the *New York World*, a staunch advocate of income and inheritance taxes and a vigorous opponent of protective tariffs, made a comparable list of millionaires for that year.[10]

These lists of millionaires were only one factor in explaining the increasing discussion of the origins and uses of great wealth around the turn of the century. As evinced by a rash of book and periodical publications many Americans were pondering the Spencerian concept of social Darwinism and the gospel of wealth as enunciated by Andrew Carnegie. The sharp debates over trusts, tariffs and income taxes, together with the growing strength of Populism, also accentuated the issue of the sources of great fortunes and the uses to which they were put. Moreover, a series of notable gifts for philanthropic purposes attracted a good deal of attention. These included Rockefeller's 1886 gift of $600,000 to resuscitate the defunct University of Chicago and Stanford's to the West Coast institution bearing that name; Armour's bequest of $100,000 for the establishment of a mission for poor Chicago youngsters, which was a start toward the technical institution bearing the family name; the Drexel endowment of a similar school in Philadelphia; and the donations for libraries associated with the names of Pratt, Newberry, and Crerar. Most spectacular of all benefactions were those of Andrew Carnegie for public libraries and other educational institutions. These implemented the thesis advanced in his famous essay, "The Gospel of Wealth," which first appeared in the *North American Review* for June 1889. Carnegie argued, in secular terms, for a vast extension of the ancient doctrine of stewardship. A man of wealth was obligated to society to spend all but a minimal part of his fortune for desirable social purposes which did not properly engage the public treasury and which did not undermine individual initiative and self-reliance.[11] In the context of all these things it was natural to raise questions concerning the reputation of millionaires for benevolence and to make the *New York Tribune* list a point of reference.

Within a few months after the appearance of this list the *Review of Reviews* published an article entitled "American Millionaires and their Public Gifts."[12] It was unsigned but may have been written by the editor, Dr. Albert Shaw, who was known to have been interested in the general problem. The author observed that it would be interesting if the millionaires enumerated by the *Tribune* could be separated into givers and nongivers and if, further, the list had included men worth less than a million dollars, many of whom were known to be generous contributors to philanthropic causes. In preparation for the article the writer had consulted knowledgeable men in several cities regarding the local reputation for benevolence of the millionaires listed. The New York contingent included 1,003 men and women, but the writer of the article found that this number was too large to classify. No estimates were available for Philadelphia, and the correspondent from Boston had a low opinion of that city's philanthropic habits. Although 200 millionaires were listed, there were no great benefactions: Henry Lee Higginson's support of the Boston Symphony Orchestra was an exception. Of eastern cities, Baltimore enjoyed an especially favorable record: half of its 55 millionaires were checked as generous. The correspondent in Cleveland noted that of 68 millionaires in that city 28 were considered "to a moderate extent at least, mindful of their public opportunities and duties."[13] Of the 67 millionaires listed for Cincinnati, 21 were checked as being comparatively liberal givers. At least 12 of Detroit's 42 millionaires enjoyed a reputation for benevolence. The St. Louis correspondent checked 10 out of 45 persons listed in his city. In St. Paul, nine of the 28 millionaires had a reputation for giving, James J. Hill being the best known, while in Minneapolis, 14 out of 44 were so regarded. The California respondent felt that the millionaires of his state were not reasonably mindful of their responsibilities despite the examples of James Lick, Darius O. Mills, Edwin Searles, and Serranus C. Hastings.

Desiring, perhaps, more complete data on the giving habits of men and women of wealth than the fragmentary and imprecise estimates revealed by the article in the *Review of Reviews*, George J. Hagar, a member of the staff of *Appleton's Annual Cyclopaedia*, began in 1893 to collect figures on gifts and bequests during the year for religious, charitable and educational purposes. He decided to exclude all gifts or bequests under $5,000 in money or material, all national, municipal and state appropriations, and all ordinary contributions to churches and missionary societies. "The result of the first year's quest," Hagar later wrote, "was such a grand tribute to the humanity of the American men and women" that he continued to make similar investigations through the year 1903. In that year Hagar summarized and commented on the figures he had collected, which he believed to prove "a stalwart unselfishness, a willingness of favored ones to promote the welfare of the less favored, and particularly a growing tendency on the part of men and women of large means to personally administer a fair share of their estates to aid the educational, religious and philanthropic activities of the country."[14] The following table shows in round numbers the amounts of gifts and bequests that were made or that became legally available. No claim was made for their completeness. In fact the compiler was certain that the total contributions in the eleven-year period must have been at least $250,000,000 more than his record indicated.

As one might expect, the figures reflected the general financial condition of the country. In 1896, when almost every business was depressed, the total contributed was the lowest in the record. In 1898 benevolence tended to meet the immediate demands of war relief, with the result that contributions to religious, charitable, and educational purposes dropped. The high water mark in 1901 was explained by the fact that in that year Carnegie's gifts aggregated more than $31,000,000, but even so more than $75,000,000 were contributed by other benefactors. In 1903, 19 persons

### Table I—Annual Contributions in Gifts and Bequests 1893–1903 according to Investigations of George J. Hagar of Appleton's Encyclopaedia

| Year | | Amount |
|------|------|------|
| 1893 | Over | $ 29,000,000 |
| 1894 | | 32,000,000 |
| 1895 | | 32,800,000 |
| 1896 | | 27,000,000 |
| 1897 | | 45,000,000 |
| 1898 | | 38,000,000 |
| 1899 | | 67,750,000 |
| 1900 | | 47,500,000 |
| 1901 | | 107,360,000 |
| 1902 | | 94,000,000 |
| 1903 | | 95,000,000 |
| Total | | $610,410,000 |

gave or bequeathed more than $65,000,000. Gifts and bequests ranging from $5,000 to $25,000 aggregated nearly $2,000,000, and those from $25,000 upward composed the sum of more than $87,000,000. Hagar added somewhat ambiguously that in the great majority of cases the money came, "not from those considered rich in the present meaning of the word, though the acknowledged wealthy contributed the bulk of the total."[15]

Suggestive as these contemporary reports are, the light thrown on the larger questions under discussion leaves much to be desired. To find out whether an application of quantitative methods would be helpful in further illuminating the problem of the alleged generosity of Americans of great wealth, the authors conducted two related investigations of philanthropic activities. Our emphasis, as the study proceeded, was on the allocation of gifts and bequests to particular philanthropic areas, but where possible we also assembled data on factors which may have influenced motivation. The period chosen was that between 1851 and 1913.

For our first project we undertook a detailed study of the philanthropic habits of a sample from the 1892 list of 4,047 reputed millionaires compiled by the *New York Tribune*. Our sample, chosen by using Tippet's Table of Random Numbers, included 124 names. By means of a careful numerical analysis of this sample we hoped to establish the patterns of philanthropy among a class which, as we have shown, enjoyed in some quarters the reputation of fulfilling voluntarily and privately the welfare functions which in many countries are the charge of religious and political institutions. All but one of our sample are deceased so it was possible, within the limits of available data, to survey their life-long giving habits. Our quantitative study affords, we feel, a more reliable indication of certain conditions in American philanthropy and trends than do prevailing impressions based merely on general surveys and biographies.

Our procedure was to collect personal and philanthropic data on the 124 subjects, record the coded data on IBM cards, and then tabulate and analyze the information with the aid of a mechanical sorter. Only a few in the sample bore such familiar names as Crerar, Widener, Fahnestock, and Frelinghuysen. But the wealth of many men and women in the sample often secured them a local reputation, so we were able to learn a good deal about them through correspondence with local libraries, historical societies, and surrogate courts. On our numerical analysis data sheets we recorded such biographical data as family background, education, religion, occupation or source of wealth, and philanthropic gifts and bequests amounting to more than $5000. These donations were assigned to eleven categories: social welfare and health, religion (including missionary activities), civic improvement, liberal arts education, vocational and technical education, libraries and adult education, research in natural sciences, research in social sciences and humanities, the arts, aid abroad, and movements for peace and international understanding. All gifts and bequests for each category were then lumped together for each individual.

We had hoped to ascertain fairly accurately at least the major amounts

### Table II—Recorded Gifts and Bequests above $250,000
### (New York Tribune *sample*)

| Name | Gift or Bequest | Field | Amount |
|---|---|---|---|
| Barber, Ohio, C., born 1841 | G | Vocational-Technical | $3,000,000 |
| | B | Education | 417,000 |
| Crerar, John R., 1827 | B | Libraries | 2,000,000 |
| | B | Religion | 750,000 |
| | B | Voc.-Tech. Ed./Civic | 300,000 |
| Drexel, Joseph, 1833– | G | Welfare | 600,000 |
| Fahnestock, Harris C., 1835– | B | Welfare | 505,000 |
| Phelan, James, 1824– | B | Art | 310,000 |
| | B | Welfare | 1,175,000 |
| Proctor, John C., 1822– | G | Welfare | 500,000 |
| | B | Welfare | 1,590,000 |
| | B | Civic | 300,000 |
| Ralston, William C., 1826– | G | Art | 300,000 |
| Rose, Chauncy, 1794– | | Voc.-Tech. Ed. | 350,000 |
| Thorn, John, 1811– | G | Civic/Welfare | 500,000 |
| Webb, William H., 1816– | G | Voc.-Tech. Ed. | 250,000 |
| | G | Welfare | 250,000 |
| Widener, Peter A. B., 1834– | G | Lib. Arts Ed. | 1,000,000 |
| | G | Voc.-Tech. Ed. | 6,000,000 |
| | G | Libraries | 1,000,000 |
| | B | Art | 2,500,000 |

donated by millionaires and to correlate type and magnitude of gifts with biographical variables. Three major problems, however, required us to limit our plan severely. First, despite sustained effort, virtually no data concerning the presence or absence of philanthropic activity was found for 68 of the 109 men and 15 women in the sample. Second, we had reason to believe that many donations were given anonymously. This prevented our making even the relatively simple distinction between "givers" and "non-givers" for the names in the sample. Finally, the records frequently did not specify amounts of gifts, particularly for repeated donations to the same institution; some donations were simply labeled "generous" or "liberal."[16] In other words it was, within our experience, impossible to discover records of lifetime giving comparable to the detailed and comprehensive ones which Professor W. K. Jordan found for his study of philanthropy in Tudor and Stuart England in accessible and carefully kept records at central depositories.

Records on bequests were the most reliable, but for 53 millionaires no testamentary information could be found at all. Consequently, attempts to analyze statistically dollar amounts even in the bequest category were effectively frustrated. Table III summarizes our over-all findings:

**Table III—Methods of Giving and Summary of Knowledge about the Sample of 124 Millionaires from the New York Tribune 1892 Listing.**

| Donors | Men | Women | Total |
|---|---|---|---|
| Gifts only | 15 | 2 | 17 |
| Gifts and Bequests | 23 | 1 | 24 |
| Bequests but no information on possible gifts | 5 | 1 | 6 |
| Gifts but no information on possible bequests | 8 | 1 | 9 |
|    Totals | 51 | 5 | 56 |
| Unknown | | | |
| Absence of bequests ascertained but no information on possible gifts | 24 | 1 | 25 |
| No information | 34 | 9 | 43 |
|    Totals | 58 | 10 | 68 |

We decided, therefore, to limit any conclusions to those 51 men and five women for whom we had some evidence of philanthropy and to consider in the main only the number and intent, not the sketchily reported dollar amounts of gifts and bequests.[17] The factors of anonymity and unspecific reporting are fairly constant among the categories of philanthropy, and we assumed that discrepancies in reporting donations to the various categories would roughly balance out among the 56 donors. This enabled us tentatively to establish correlations and non-correlations between biographical categories and philanthropic habits for the *New York Tribune* sample.

The most salient aspect of the patterns of recorded giving among the millionaires is their provincialism. *Virtually all giving was directed toward the local community.* With the exception of missionary activities there was little or no "world consciousness" among the donors, even those of foreign birth. Hospitals, museums and vocational schools might serve a small region, but the givers extended their horizons only for institutions of higher education. Nor did millionaires feel responsible for extending intellectual horizons into new fields. In strong contrast to our contemporary donors, those of the *Tribune* sample *gave virtually nothing directly to further research in either the social or natural sciences.* Funds given to vocational, technical, and liberal arts education may have had an indirect effect on the sciences and humanities, but the zest for research had not yet intrigued the American benefactor.

*Education in the broad sense rivaled health and welfare in the competition for the largest share of contributors' dollars.* Aid to liberal arts, technical and vocational education, libraries, adult education and the arts accounted for slightly over a third of the philanthropic categories chosen by the millionaires. Relief to the poor, sick and aged likewise took another third. Our evidence indicates that these funds usually were given to institutions rather than individuals, but many of the donors were reported to have made informal gifts to individuals which did not appear on the record. Religious organizations ranked next in the minds of contributors and received about a quarter of the donations. Less than a tenth went to civic improvement, chiefly to public buildings, monuments and parks.

On the whole, *the millionaires did not alter their lifelong philanthropic preferences when they included charitable and educational bequests in their wills.* Although our evidence shows some individual variations, the over-all allocations of gifts and bequests were virtually identical. Since it was impossible to determine the net worth of most of the estates, the relative weight of philanthropic and other bequests could not be reliably calculated in three out of four cases. But we found that while 54 per cent of the donors made some bequests, at least 30 per cent made none at all. It was impossible to find wills for the remainder. Table IV summarizes the allocations of gifts and bequests to

**Table IV[18]—Allocation of Gifts and Bequests in Relation to Philanthropic Categories**

| | Welfare | | Religion | | Civic | | Lib. Arts Ed. | | Voc.-Tech. Ed. | | Libraries | | Art | | Totals | |
|---|---|---|---|---|---|---|---|---|---|---|---|---|---|---|---|---|
| | No. | Per Cent | No. | Per Cent | No. | Per Cent | No. | Per Cent | No. | Per Cent | No. | Per Cent | No. | Per Cent | No. | Per Cent |
| Gifts only | 40 | 36 | 24 | 22 | 9 | 8 | 11 | 10 | 9 | 8 | 13 | 12 | 5 | 4 | 111 | 100 |
| Bequests only | 19 | 33 | 15 | 26 | 4 | 7 | 4 | 7 | 5 | 9 | 5 | 9 | 6 | 9 | 58 | 100 |

seven of the eleven philanthropic categories, the only ones which received attention from donors.

*Our figures suggest that women were more interested than men in donating to religious organizations and welfare activities.* They were also possibly less interested in vocational and technical education. But since there are only five women in our sample, we cannot draw any really significant conclusions about their habits of philanthropy. Table V may, however, be regarded as suggestive of a general tendency.

### Table V—Allocation of Gifts and Bequests in Relation to Sex (51 men, 5 women)

| | Welfare | | Religion | | Civic | | Lib. Arts Ed. | | Voc.-Tech. Ed. | | Libraries | | Art | | Totals[19] | |
|---|---|---|---|---|---|---|---|---|---|---|---|---|---|---|---|---|
| | No. | Per Cent | No. | Per Cent | No. | Per Cent | No. | Per Cent | No. | Per Cent | No. | Per Cent | No. | Per Cent | No. | Per Cent |
| 51 men | 41 | 3 | 27 | 21 | 11 | 8 | 12 | 11 | 12 | 8 | 17 | 12 | 10 | 8 | 131 | 100 |
| 5 women | 4 | 30 | 4 | 30 | 1 | 8 | 2 | 15 | — | – | 1 | 8 | 1 | 8 | 13 | 100 |

Ten of the givers were of foreign birth, but this had no discernible effect on their allocations to fields of philanthropic interest. Place of residence, on the other hand, seems to have had a slight influence on allocations. Those living in New England and the Middle Atlantic states tended somewhat to emphasize welfare and health, while those in the old Northwest were more interested in libraries. For the West we have a much smaller number of millionaires to work with, but they tended to fall below the average in welfare and above it in gifts to civic improvements and to liberal arts education. Table VI gives the breakdowns.

### Table VI—Allocation to Philanthropic Categories Compared with Residence (all gifts and bequests integrated for each individual)

| | Welfare | | Religion | | Civic | | Lib. Arts Ed. | | Voc.-Tech. Ed. | | Libraries | | Art | | Totals | |
|---|---|---|---|---|---|---|---|---|---|---|---|---|---|---|---|---|
| | No. | Per Cent | No. | Per Cent | No. | Per Cent | No. | Per Cent | No. | Per Cent | No. | Per Cent | No. | Per Cent. | No | Per Cent |
| New Eng. and Mid. Atlantic States (34 philanthropists) | 29 | 39 | 16 | 21 | 4 | 5 | 7 | 9 | 5 | 7 | 8 | 10 | 6 | 8 | 75 | 100 |
| Old N.W. and Middle West (16) | 13 | 28 | 10 | 22 | 4 | 9 | 3 | 7 | 5 | 11 | 8 | 17 | 3 | 7 | 46 | 100 |
| West Coast (5) | 3 | 15 | 4 | 20 | 4 | 20 | 3 | 15 | 2 | 10 | 2 | 10 | 2 | 10 | 20 | 100 |
| South | 1 | | 1 | | | | | | | | | | | | 3 | 100 |
| Totals | 46 | | 31 | | 12 | | 14 | | 12 | | 18 | | 11 | | 144 | |

It appears clear from our study *that residence did not greatly affect the propensity to give.* The proportion of millionaires definitely identified as donors was 44 per cent in both areas—Northeast and Middle West— for which we had a sizable number of millionaires. The very small number of millionaires in the South and Southwest that turned up in our sample was too small to make comparisons between donors and non-donors in these regions meaningful. We cannot be at all sure that "non-donors" including unknowns really gave nothing (unlikely), but if we assume that the amount and reliability of our data on individuals were fairly constant for all parts of the country (a fair assumption), then the closeness of these percentages indicates that the proportion of donors to non-donors was also constant even if we cannot establish definitely the numbers of these two classes.

Since the regilious affiliation of 70 millionaires in the sample of 124 could not be identified, no over-all conclusions could be drawn about the proportion of contributors in each group. Among those that could be identified, the 27 Protestants gave slightly more often than the average to religious activities. The six unaffiliated and "liberal" Protestants (Unitarians, Universalists and members of the Ethical Culture Society) ranked slightly lower in giving to religion and to technical and vocational education but gave more than the average for libraries. Tables VII and VIII present our findings.

### Table VII—The Religious Pattern of Givers and of Unknowns in the 124 Tribune Sample

| Religion | No. of Givers | No. of 124 | Percentage of Givers |
|---|---|---|---|
| Catholic | 2 | 3 | 67 |
| Jewish | 3 | 5 | 60 |
| No affiliation or Liberal | 6 | 7 | 86 |
| Unknown | 18 | 70 | 21 |
| Protestant | 27 | 39 | 44 |
| Total | 56 | 124 | 278 |

### Table VIII—Allocations to Categories Compared with Religion

| | Welfare | | Religion | | Civic | | Lib. Arts Ed. | | Voc.-Tech. Ed. | | Libraries | | Art | | Totals | |
|---|---|---|---|---|---|---|---|---|---|---|---|---|---|---|---|---|
| | No. | Per Cent | No. | Per Cent | No. | Per Cent | No. | Per Cent | No. | Per Cent | No. | Per Cent | No. | Per Cent | No. | Per Cent |
| 2 Catholics | 1 | 14 | 2 | 29 | 1 | 14 | 1 | 14 | 1 | 14 | | | 1 | 14 | 7 | 100 |
| 27 Protestants | 25 | 32 | 23 | 29 | 7 | 9 | 7 | 9 | 5 | 6 | 8 | 10 | 4 | 5 | 79 | 100 |
| 3 Jews | 3 | 43 | 2 | 29 | | | 1 | 14 | | | | | 1 | 14 | 7 | 100 |
| 6 no affiliation or Liberals | 3 | 28 | 2 | 18 | 1 | 9 | 1 | 9 | | | 3 | 28 | 1 | 9 | 11 | 100 |
| 18 unknown | 14 | 35 | 2 | 5 | 3 | 8 | 4 | 10 | 6 | 15 | 7 | 18 | 4 | 10 | 40 | 100 |
| Totals: | 46 | | 31 | | 12 | | 14 | | 12 | | 18 | | 11 | | 144 | |

To our surprise *no very meaningful relationships could be discovered between the number of dependents or survivors and propensity to donate.* Those without children, however, tended to give less frequently to welfare and health. Table IX summarizes our findings.

### Table IX—Dependents and Philanthropy

| | Welfare | | Religion | | Civic | | Lib. Arts Ed. | | Voc.-Tech. Ed. | | Libraries | | Art | | Totals | |
|---|---|---|---|---|---|---|---|---|---|---|---|---|---|---|---|---|
| | No. | Per Cent | No. | Per Cent | No. | Per Cent | No. | Per Cent | No. | Per Cent | No. | Per Cent | No. | Per Cent | No. | Per Cent |
| 80 percent (45) had children | 37 | 33 | 23 | 21 | 9 | 8 | 11 | 10 | 8 | 7 | 14 | 12 | 10 | 9 | 112 | 100 |
| 18 percent (10) had no children | 8 | 25 | 8 | 25 | 13 | 3 | 10 | 4 | 4 | 13 | 4 | 13 | 1 | 3 | 31 | 100 |
| 2 percent (1) family unknown | 1 | 10 | | | | | | | | | | | | | 1 | 100 |
| | | | | | | | | | | | | | | | 144 | |

The level of education attained by the millionaires seems to have had no regular or logical effect on their philanthropy, although no conclusions could be drawn with any confidence since the education of almost half could not be established. But on the basis of available data *those who had no more than secondary education seem to have done more for charitable, educational and other philanthropic causes than those with either elementary or higher education,* while the proportion of donors with elementary and with college educations (excluding graduate, professional and business schools) was approximately the same.

Among the donors, however, one notices that those with only elementary education apparently gave somewhat more often to liberal arts education and somewhat less to welfare and health. Those with secondary education tended in their giving to be more generous to libraries and less generous to religion. Those with higher education tended to emphasize religion and to slight vocational and technical education.

Only those with college and graduate professional school education omitted any categories in their choices of fields for philanthropy. No donors in either group gave to vocational and technical education. The graduate and professional school donors likewise did not give to liberal arts education or to art. Table X presents the over-all picture.

In our sample *neither sex, place of birth or residence, religion, family, or education had more than a slight relationship to the decision of millionaires to donate to philanthropic causes.* A composite millionaire contributor would be male, native-born, resident in the Northeast, Protes-

### Table X—Allocation to Categories Compared with Education

| Percent No. | Welfare No. | Per Cent | Religion No. | Per Cent | Civic No. | Per Cent | Lib. Arts Ed. No. | Per Cent | Voc.-Tech. Ed. No. | Per Cent | Libraries No. | Per Cent | Art No. | Per Cent | Totals No. | Per Cent |
|---|---|---|---|---|---|---|---|---|---|---|---|---|---|---|---|---|
| 21 (12) Elementary | 10 | 25 | 8 | 20 | 4 | 10 | 6 | 15 | 5 | 13 | 4 | 10 | 3 | 8 | 40 | 100 |
| 16 (9) Sec. public | 8 | 32 | 4 | 15 | 1 | 3 | 2 | 7 | 3 | 12 | 6 | 24 | 2 | 7 | 26 | 100 |
| 13 (7) Sec. private | 7 | 35 | 4 | 20 | 2 | 10 | 1 | 5 | 2 | 10 | 2 | 10 | 2 | 10 | 20 | 100 |
| 18 (10) College | 6 | 33 | 6 | 33 | 1 | 6 | 2 | 11 | | | 1 | 6 | 2 | 11 | 12 | 100 |
| 11 (6) Grad. and prof. | 4 | 50 | 2 | 25 | 1 | 13 | | | | | 1 | 13 | | | 8 | 100 |
| 7 (4) Bus. school | 4 | 27 | 3 | 20 | 2 | 13 | 2 | 13 | 1 | 7 | 2 | 13 | 1 | 7 | 15 | 100 |
| 14 (8) Unknown | 7 | 40 | 4 | 24 | 1 | 6 | 1 | 6 | 1 | 6 | 2 | 12 | 1 | 6 | 17 | 100 |
| 100 (56) Totals: | 46 | | 31 | | 12 | | 14 | | 12 | | 18 | | 11 | | 144 | |

tant, head of a family and educated at only the elementary level. But these characteristics also describe a non-philanthropic millionaire.

The only variable which seems to have had a pronounced influence on the propensity of a millionaire to be a philanthropist was the method by which he acquired his fortune. *The "self-made men" in the sample were much more philanthropic than were those who inherited their wealth.* There were 56 per cent more known philanthropists in the "self-made" category (Table XI, line 4) than in the other acquisition group (line 1), although there were twelve more subjects who inherited their money. Among those who inherited their fortunes, we found that 46 per cent of those gainfully employed became donors. Only 22 per cent of those who were not so employed or who held only minor jobs were philanthropists. Of the 27 subjects not gainfully employed (line 3) only six could even tentatively be called donors and this gives the benefit of the doubt to Hugh Baxter, contributor of the prize for the "Baxter Mile" in a New York City track meet. The remaining five non-employed, endowed philanthropists were all women, and this number, out of a total of 15 woman millionaires, is relatively close to the average for the entire sample, 56: 124. On the other hand, 80 per cent of the subjects known to be entirely responsible for their own wealth were philanthropists (line 5). The few subjects who worked for their money but inherited a position, such as the presidency of a company, (line 6) were less generous than those entirely self-made but more so than the inheritors of wealth.

Source of fortune usually made no difference in allocation to specific fields of philanthropy, which approximate the general average (see Table IV). The sole exception was the sharp drop in donations to vocational and technical education among the 34 per cent who had inherited their million. Table XI shows the major results of asking our data the question, "What relation did source of fortune have on philanthropy?"

### Table XI—Philanthropy and Acquisition of Wealth

| | Identified Givers | | Non-Givers Unknowns | | Total | |
|---|---|---|---|---|---|---|
| | No. | Per Cent | No. | Per Cent | No. | Per Cent |
| 1. *Inherited Wealth* | 18 | 34 | 35 | 66 | 53 | 100 |
| A. (20 percent) own work and/or position, ie., starting with family connections | 12 | 46 | 14 | 54 | 26 | 100 |
| 41 percent | | | | | | |
| B. (21 percent) no work or minor jobs only. | 6 | 22 | 21 | 78 | 27 | 100 |
| 2. *Self-Made Wealth* | 32 | 78 | 9 | 22 | 27 | 100 |
| A. (28 percent) own work only | 28 | 80 | 7 | 20 | 35 | 100 |
| 33 percent | | | | | | |
| B. (5 percent) own work plus position | 4 | 67 | 2 | 33 | 6 | 100 |
| 3. *Source of Wealth Unknown* | 6 | 20 | 24 | 80 | 30 | 100 |
| 26 percent | | | | | | |
| 100 percent          Totals | 56 | | 68 | | 124 | |

A more meaningful expression of the relation between self-made men and heirs as philanthropists may be arrived at by computing the "generosity ratio" for each group. Dividing the ratio of self-made donors (line 4) to endowed donors with jobs (line 2) or 28:12 by the ratio of self-made non-philanthropists (line 4) to their endowed counterparts (line 2) or 7:14 gives the "generosity ratio" between these groups, which is 14:3. In other words the propensity of a self-made millionaire's being a donor was more than four times greater than than that of a man who inherited his wealth but was also employed. *It would seem, therefore, that the most significant differences in philanthropic habits existed between the possessors of self-made and inherited wealth.*

One factor in making the self-made millionaire more philanthropically inclined than those who inherited their wealth or position was the opportunity his lowly start gave him to become acquainted firsthand with conditions on the lower social and economic levels. The problems he himself faced, and overcame, were constant reminders of the needs philanthropy could serve. Such a man was also aware of the importance of providing the less fortunate individual with access to education, books, medical care, works of art, and fresh air. With such opportunities the chances of his improving his condition were increased. To the self-made man, philanthropy did not dampen initiative but provided an incentive to self-improvement. His benefaction helped open the door of success to more of his kind. Conversely, those born with the proverbial silver spoon had difficulty seeing beyond its handle or, if they could, were less sensitive to the problems of the needy than those responsible for their own success.

Another factor in the philanthropic habits of those who worked for their wealth and those who inherited it was the nature of the responsibility engendered by the possession of a million dollars or more. The self-made man was less apt to take his wealth for granted. Having made his money actively and, as it were, taken it from society, he was highly susceptible to influence by the concept of stewardship of wealth. Like Carnegie, he was inclined to feel that after providing for his family he owed society a debt that could be paid with philanthropy. Merely to pass his money on to his heirs was a violation of the trust great wealth entailed. Society had a claim to his fortune of which the self-made millionaire was sometimes apt to be aware.[20] As an example of this attitude, George F. Peabody, generous American philanthropist to many causes, once made a forceful statement of the motives which impelled him to give.[21]

Twenty-five years ago I realized that I had considerable wealth and it dawned upon me that the money was the result of other men's labors. I had been a banker for a quarter of a century and during that time I fear that I had forgotten that the only way a dollar can be actually produced is by real work. But when I came to see that the money which I had amassed was the work of others, I then and there decided to retire from business and become my own executor, to administer for the people that which rightfully belonged to them.

Of course not all rich Americans agreed with Peabody, but his statement suggests that for a self-made man the claims of society to his fortune could have a special meaning.

It is also likely that some self-made men found it desirable to give to respectable and worthy causes in order to improve their own social status. Concern for one's standing in the community certainly figured in the mental outlook and behavior of some men who had come up the hard way from humble beginnings, and although quantification is obviously impossible, biographical data suggest that status considerations entered into the complex motivation of many donors, including Andrew Carnegie.

On the other hand, many of these considerations were irrelevant to the man who inherited his million. He owed only his benefactor, most probably his parents, for this fortune. Of course at one time someone must have made the money with his own hands, but the beneficiary was less conscious of any debt to society that may have existed. Stewardship of wealth was not a pressing obligation. After all, his father, not his God, had given him his money. Moreover, being wealthy was something he took for granted, a commonplace with which he had usually grown up. The man who was given his money often felt a responsibility to *his* heirs and was inclined to pass it on to them rather than to the public, thereby perpetuating the pattern from which he benefitted. Obviously, too, status considerations were much less important among those who inherited their fortunes than among many self-made men.

Our second project was an analysis of large-scale gifts and bequests in the *New York Times*.[22] We checked every year from 1851 through 1879 but were forced by reason of the newspaper's greatly increased coverage to limit our study to only four years in the subsequent two decades. We chose 1885, 1887, 1890, and 1897 as years least likely to be affected by cataclysmic events such as depressions and wars. We then studied the *Times* for 1913 to see whether the trends continued to the dislocations of World War I and the income tax authorized by the Sixteenth Amendment to the Constitution.

Working through the *New York Times* index we assigned all reported gifts and bequests to the eleven categories used in the *New York Tribune* study of millionaires. The results of our study of long-range trends in philanthropy through the *New York Times* study were disappointing. We had hoped that the use of a single, reasonably reliable source would yield a fair basis for comparing philanthropic habits of a broader category than millionaires over a long period. Regrettably, the daily exigencies of newspaper publishing and changes in editorial policy over the years had distorting effects for which we could not compensate.

On the one hand, a donation might have been considered newsworthy one day but might be slighted the next. Then, the coverage of the *Times* was naturally heavier for New York City and the metropolitan area; only the most important or impressive donations from other sections of the country were reported. The proportion of gifts to the field of welfare, for example, was much heavier for New York, while that for universities and other regional and national institutions was greater in the rest of the country. Furthermore, as the *Times* became larger and more national in scope, habits of reporting donations to the several fields of philanthropy changed also.

A few tentative conclusions may, however, be drawn. *The fields of welfare and liberal arts education dominated the attention of American philanthropists in this period.* Outside of general contributions to education, interest in scholarly research was negligible in the nineteenth century. Research in natural science grew to 10 per cent of the total donations by 1913, but then only five contributors (3 per cent) accounted for the $2,573,000 contributed to this field. Support for research in the social sciences was also negligible, for in the entire period we found only one contributor in the 1860s of $150,000 and two in 1913 of $108,000. With the exception of missionary activities, donations to areas outside the country were higher in 1896 and 1913 but still small both in number of contributors and amounts given. The dollar amounts of gifts to libraries apparently hit a peak in the 1860s, with $1,057,000 or 18 per cent of the total amount contributed and 8 per cent of the total number of donations. Philanthropic interest in libraries declined for the rest of the century and were only 1 per cent of the total number of donations in 1913.

The *New York Times* study uncovered some data on benefactions to Negro education. Although it is known that many churches and missionary societies in the North contributed to this cause, in the South after the Civil War one would have to generalize that interest in this cause was slight if one depended on the *New York Times* record alone. In the decade after Appomattox a New Haven Negro laundress bequeathed her life savings of $5,000 to the Yale Theological School for a scholarship for a Negro student. This decade also witnessed a gift of $50,000 to Fisk University. Since our study included only two years in the 1880s (1885 and 1887), the $1,000,000 gift of John Slater in 1882 for Negro education in the South did not come into the range of the *New York Times* data. Mrs. John Jacob Astor bequeathed $25,000 to Hampton in 1886 and the 1897 survey yielded two bequests, one of $40,000 to a girls' school and one of $100,000. The Rosenwald gift of $202,000 in 1913 was, of course, only a small part of what one generous philanthropist did for the Negro.

The proportion of numbers and amounts of gifts to religion were comparatively high but no trend was noticeable. Gifts to social welfare and health, on the other hand, increased in the depression years clustered between 1870 and 1885 and thereafter replaced the liberal arts in numbers of donations.

In the field of education, the *New York Times* study indicated that donations to vocational and technical institutions increased somewhat irregularly up to the 1880s and 1890s, *while the general interest in liberal arts education fell off after a high in the 1870s of 35 per cent both in amount and numbers of donations.* Important exceptions to this general trend in liberal arts education were the endowments of three universities established in the 1880s: Stanford ($20,000,000), Clark, ($1,500,000), and DePauw ($1,250,000), accounting for 60 per cent in amounts given in that decade.

In concluding the summary of the *New York Times* study it may be useful to include a list of the three leading philanthropies for each

**Table XII—Top Three Philanthropies by Percentage of Dollar Amounts and Total Number of Contributors**

| Time span | Per cent of dollars | | Per cent of numbers | |
|---|---|---|---|---|
| 1850s | Liberal Arts Ed. | 59 | Liberal Arts Ed. | 19 |
| | Religion | 12 | Civic | 19 |
| | Civic | 9 | Welfare | 14 |
| 1860s | Liberal Arts Ed. | 36 | Liberal Arts Ed. | 29 |
| | Libraries | 18 | Welfare | 21 |
| | Welfare | 14 | Religion | 18 |
| 1870s | Liberal Arts Ed. | 35 | Liberal Arts Ed. | 35 |
| | Welfare | 27 | Welfare | 26 |
| | Religion | 12 | Religion | 21 |
| 1885, 1887 | Liberal Arts Ed. | 61 | Welfare | 32 |
| | Welfare | 10 | Religion | 26 |
| | Libraries | 9 | Liberal Arts Ed. | 11 |
| 1890, 1897 | Religion | 30 | Welfare | 28 |
| | Welfare | 23 | Religion | 26 |
| | Liberal Arts Ed. | 21 | Liberal Arts Ed. | 20 |
| 1913 | Liberal Arts Ed. | 24 | Welfare | 42 |
| | Voc.-Tech. Ed | 20 | Religion | 22 |
| | Art | 20 | Liberal Arts Ed. | 17 |

decade both with respect to dollars given and number of contributors. Table XII gives this list.

Because of statistical difficulties involved in both the *New York Times* and the *New York Tribune* studies it is difficult to make any really valid comparison between the findings of the two studies. Nonetheless, our investigation led us tentatively to believe that *the interests of philanthropic millionaires, despite the preferences of a few for liberal arts education, the arts and civic improvement, was not substantially different from those of most donors of their time.*

In retrospect, the study we made might have proved more positively revealing had it been undertaken and executed along different lines. It might, for example, have been more profitable to have made an exhaustive investigation, in terms of the total universe or by random sample, of wills probated in one city. Or, had we chosen to study a period later than the one we did choose, it might have been possible to have obtained permission from the Commissioner of Internal Revenue to examine the estate tax records available at the Federal Records Center at Alexandria, Virginia for some part of the period since 1916 when the Federal estate tax first went into effect. But this study, while it might have yielded more positive results, would have thrown no light on the earlier period in which the generosity of millionaires was under special discussion. It is precisely this early period for which we have hitherto had no quantitative study in which an effort was made to control variables. It is nevertheless to be hoped that the path broken by F. Emerson Andrews and Frank Dickinson in quantitative studies of philanthropy in the period since 1916 may be followed back to the nineteenth and twentieth centuries. Whether it is possible to project into the period before that date an investigation such as we undertook and succeed better than we did depends on the ability to uncover a complete record of the lives and philanthropic habits (or lack of them) for a group of Americans. This we found an extremely difficult task despite the use of available research tools including personal investigation in and hundreds of written inquiries to the surrogate courts, historical societies, and libraries of the communities in which our sample of millionaires lived and in some cases gave. The effort might nevertheless be worth pursuing, for our results, limited though they are in many respects, do suggest that the available impressionistic writings, biographies, and even the efforts of a more systematic sort made by the *New York Tribune*, the *New York World*, and *Appleton's Cyclopaedia* leave a great deal to be desired in precise knowledge. Moreover, our study has yielded significant results on the anatomy of the giving habits of a random sample of millionaires. It has given the first precise information on the categories of philanthropic causes which millionaire donors favored. It is also clear that sex, religion, family, education, and place of birth and residence did not have more than a slight relationship to the decision of millionaires to donate to philanthropic causes; on the other hand, contrary to expectations, the self-made men were much more philanthropic than those who inherited their wealth. Hopefully we may some day know whether these generalizations hold for both men and women of wealth in other periods, and whether the same factors figure in the giving habits of the less well to do, and of how the anatomy of giving in American compares with that of other countries.

# Machine Programming and Information Retrieval / *James W. Perry and John L. Melton*

"Knee-deep in paper and facing a rising tide, what, then, is the historian to do?" The answer, according to Dean Jesse H. Shera of the library of Western Reserve University, is in the mechanized information retrieval systems equipped to deliver specific data and conceptual relationships of a minimal sort.[1]

According to Shera, such systems can perform the tedious, repetitive operations of literature searching and document analysis more rapidly, more accurately, and at a lower cost than traditional library methods. They must be able to relate, compare, and otherwise correlate the information fed to them in ways comparable to those functions of the human brain. They must not be subject to the human error of forgetfulness. They must be able to deal with both specific and generic terms and to relate one to the other. They must operate on several semantic levels, for though much of the meaning of documents is conveyed by isolates, relations are also important. They must be mechanically dependable, and they must be available at a cost that is within reach of at least the larger research centers. One may assume that in the not distant future they will be within the budget of the average college library.

"But to turn to the other side of the coin, what is it that these machines are not? Certainly they are not substitutes for the human brain, and they will not free any scholar from the burden of concentrated thinking. They will search, but they will not perform research. They will answer the scholar's questions only when those questions are properly framed and expressed. They will not put the librarian or the bibliographer out of business, but on the contrary, they can raise his profession to new levels of intellectual achievement. But by the same token, the librarians and bibliographers of the future must prepare themselves to meet the new challenge of these machines—automotive engineering did not grow out of the livery stable."[2]

The interest in machines such as the one described in the article re-

James W. Perry and John L. Melton, "Principles of Machine and System Design with Special Reference to the Indexing and Analysis of Historical Literature," *American Documentation*, X (1959), 278–85. Reprinted by permission.

1. "New Tools for Easing the Burden of Historical Research," *American Documentation*, X (October, 1959), 274–77.
2. *Ibid.*

printed below is keenest among librarians who have been concerned traditionally with storing data, classifying it, and making it available. This is primarily a technical problem and mechanization is an extension of this facet. Such a machine as described below, if programmed correctly, can handle relatively simple concepts.

Despite Dean Shera's account of what machines can and cannot be expected to do, historians may be more skeptical than librarians of the value of the machine processes herein described. This selection is included not because of the belief that machines are necessarily part of the wave of Clio's future but as suggestive of a possible relationship between cybernetics and historiography.

Emphasizing the importance of documents to historians would indeed be carrying coals to Newcastle. The same doubtless would be true of any discussion of the desirability of improvements in library facilities and in the ability of libraries to provide services to support and to expedite research.

Recorded knowledge and related library facilities and services are equally important to other professions. A lawyer deprived of his library could scarcely hope to provide reliable advice to his clients. A chemist must use the record of past experimental investigations if his future research is to be well planned and efficiently executed. A similar situation prevails whenever a large body of specialized information and knowledge is recorded for future use.

## A Practical Problem

A familiar example of a large body of specialized information and knowledge is that monumental compilation of the official records of the Union and Confederate armies, *The War of the Rebellion*, commonly called the *O.R.* The 130 volumes of this work are at once the joy and the despair of those who must use them: joy at the enormous mass of information; despair at the difficulty of finding what we are looking for in such a mass. It is not much more difficult to find a reasonably large needle in a reasonably small haystack than to find, shall we say whether or not the Confederate forces were still holding the Weldon and Wilmington railroad in May of 1862.

But modern science can enable us easily to find our needle in the haystack—simply make it radioactive and use a Geiger counter. Likewise modern science can facilitate the finding of the Weldon and Wilmington railroad in the *O.R.* In both instances, of course, highly sophisticated techniques must be used to establish the situation in which the search can be made easy, but once this has been done, the rest of the process is exceedingly rapid.

To illustrate: let us assume that we are interested in the changing policy of the major Union military leaders toward slavery, and that at the moment we are investigating the *O.R.* to find what data are available on the attitude of General Ambrose B. Burnside, of the noble whiskers.

The conventional procedure would be to check first in the general index. Here we might hopefully look for such an entry as *Slavery, Burnside's Attitude Toward*, or *Attitude Toward Slavery*. Naturally we do not find any such entries. We do, however, find the entry, *Burnside, Ambrose E.*, with 46 references, the entry, *Slavery*, with 8 references, and the entry, *Slaves*, with 46 references. We could, of course, check each of those 101 listings, in the hope that one might have some bearing on our problem. But the work can be lessened by comparing the references for Burnside with those for slaves. The required information is likely to appear only where those two listings coincide.

Comparison shows us that the references do coincide in 36 instances. This, to be sure, means only that in 36 volumes there are references to Burnside and references to slaves. But the field has been cut down by 70 percent—we know where not to look.

Let us now examine one of the volumes—in our example, Volume Nine of Series One. Turning to its own index, we find no *Burnside, Attitude Toward Slavery*, but *Burnside, Ambrose E.*, and *Slaves and Slave Property*. There are 54 references to Burnside and 20 references to slaves, seven of these common to both.

Upon turning to these seven references, we find that two are to letters written to Burnside, one is to a letter which mentions Burnside only incidentally, and one has no direct reference to Burnside, whose name simply happens to appear on the same page with an order discussing contraband employment. The remaining two citations are indeed statements by Burnside about slavery. One of these is a proclamation to the people of North Carolina, which includes the remark that to say that the Federal forces intended to free the slaves is ridiculous and false. This tells us nothing about Burnside's personal attitude. The second reference is to a report in which Burnside remarks that in his next report he hopes to give a definite policy on fugitive slaves. This seems promising, but Burnside's next few reports do not mention the subject at all.

At this point it would be reasonable to assume that this volume has nothing of value to the particular problem being investigated. The tenacious research worker, however, would be aware of the possibility of Burnside's name appearing on one page as the signature to a letter which mentions slavery on another page, and would therefore investigate the volume a little further before giving up. In this instance, the added effort would be rewarded. There is a listing for Burnside on page 391, and a reference to slaves on page 390. Upon investigating this near coincidence, we discover something really useful. Not only does Burnside here report his policy on fugitive slaves—promised back on page 199—but also he draws a connection between the institution of slavery and the resistance of the South.

In this particular search we have been successful, but only as the consequence of a happy coincidence of effort, thoughtfulness, and good fortune. The element of chance might be greatly reduced—perhaps even eliminated—by a complete alphabetical index. But there is no complete alphabetical index to the *O.R.*, nor would one be practicable, for it would require at least as many volumes for the index as for the rest of the work

One should remember, too, that our search has exhausted only one volume of the 36 in which Burnside and slaves are both mentioned. The process will have to be repeated for every one of the others. Even after that, we will have the whole procedure to go through again for each of the other Union leaders. It is very clear that we have a long job before us.

Now, suppose it were possible to program a mechanical device to do this work for us. Suppose we could ask for every single reference to the subject of slavery, slaves, slave owners, or contrabands by any Federal officer above the rank of colonel, and that this information could be made available in a matter of hours, with every reference included, even those which were not included in the general or individual indexes. The value of such a device is obvious.

The *O.R.*, of course, has been available for nearly eighty years; the events which it records took place nearly a century ago. Yet there is scarcely a week—perhaps not even a day—which passes without there being produced a new book or article on the Civil War. In science and technology, the field with which I am most familiar, the information problem is also serious. There, new discoveries, new processes, and new techniques are continually being developed. Indeed, in science and technology, continuing success in research has generated new knowledge in such amounts that traditional library methods are becoming, year by year, less and less satisfactory in providing needed information services. Inevitably, the mounting costs of locating such information by using alphabetized indexes or conventional classification systems have come to the attention of research management. The contrast between steady advances in laboratory instruments and the lack of corresponding innovations in library techniques has become too great to be ignored.

An examination of library operations leads one to the conclusion that they involve two radically different types of tools. One type is composed of concepts and the terminology and symbols used to represent concepts. These intellectual tools are produced by the genius of the experts in the various disciplines. The second type of tools involved in library operations consists of certain mechanical devices such as card catalogs, pigeonholes and shelves for grouping documents and books, and listings of various kinds, e.g. alphabetized subject indexes. It is perhaps evident that changes in the second type of tools can be made so as to make more effective use of our intellectual tools. During the past fifteen years, a wide range of new mechanical and electronic devices have been used to extend and to expedite information services in various fields. These devices range from simple hand-sorted punched cards, and various card-operated business machines, to computers and electronic selectors.

Several books and many papers have been written to make available a wide range of experience in applying these new tools to various information problems.[1] Experience has demonstrated that a great variety of mechanical and electronic devices can be used to provide information services. To achieve the maximum margin of benefits over costs requires an understanding of the limitations and capabilities of these various devices. In many situations a combination of them, both old and new, provides maximum advantage. In our project work for the American Society for Metals, we are processing the world's metallurgical literature to provide (1) descriptive abstracts for periodical publication (2) annual author and subject indexes of conventional design (3) encoding of the individual published papers for hand-sorted punched cards, as well as (4) encoding of standardized informative abstracts for high speed searching and correlating by automatic electronic selecting equipment. Coordination of these different forms of processing scientific and technical literature permits important economies to be achieved.

These economies apply to preparatory processing, that is to say, to operations which are performed in the reviewing of documents and the preparation of abstracts, indexes, and various codes which make it possible to use automatic or semi-automatic equipment to accomplish selecting and correlating operations.

Such processing of documents must be regarded as a means to an end, namely, providing information services as required for research and other professional purposes. Part of this processing would appear to be of doubtful value in connection with the *O.R.* Specifically, the possible advantage of preparing abstracts of all the reports and correspondence in the *O.R.* appears to be meager. Abstracts—such as those once published in *Social Science Abstracts*—are invaluable for rapidly informing the scientist or scholar of new advances and findings in his field of interest. For primary source material, on the other hand, abstracts are, as a rule, inadequate—even useless.

The utility of extensive subject indexes is limited by the time and effort required to use them. More specifically, such indexing, though convenient and effective for locating information pertaining to a single subject of a highly specific nature is tedious and difficult to use when the information sought pertains to a combination of subjects, one of which is broad in scope, as exemplified by "Union Commanders above the rank of colonel."

The third type of processing, that of encoding for hand-sorted punched cards, is of course, strongly influenced by the inherent limitations of those simple devices. With regard to hand-sorted punched cards, the number of holes, that is to say, the number of coding positions, is restricted. It is true that different coding schemes permit one to vary somewhat the manner of coding but regardless of such variations, there are severe restrictions either (1) in the number of headings available for coding purposes or (2) the number of headings that may be used to designate the important characteristics of any one document.

Limitations of hand-sorted punched cards are overcome by the use of continuous tapes as the medium for recording characteristics of subject matter, or information symbols. The length of tape that may be used for recording characteristics is subject to no restriction other than such practical considerations as cost and scanning time. Because tapes are relatively cheap and high speed equipment is able to scan at least 350 feet of tape per minute, the degree of detail in the code that can be recorded in a practicable fashion provides plenty of leeway for detailed characterization of the subject matter of documents.

Furthermore, with selecting equipment of appropriate design, the subject matter characteristics recorded on the tape may be organized so as to constitute, in effect, a standardized form of informative abstract. Such an abstract, as recorded on the tape to be scanned by the selector, may indicate various relationships of the type specified in natural language by formation of phrases, sentences, and paragraphs. Great latitude exists for formulating these relationships in a syntactical pattern.

With the standardized informative abstract, or *telegraphic abstract*, we have a device which not only serves the purpose of informing us as to the nature of the material abstracted, but also can be searched and cor-related by high speed automatic selecting equipment. It performs all the functions of a very elaborate indexing system, which can be used to find very complex information with great rapidity. And it enables one to correlate information so widely separated and diversified that only by accident would it be likely to come to one's attention through conven-tional procedures.[2]

To illustrate, let us again return to the O.R. and to the letter from General Burnside which we discovered through the conventional index and a little thought. The portion of this letter which contains the required information is that part which reads:

There is much true loyalty here, and all the people are heartily sick of the war, and are very much exercised lest their own State should be made the next battle ground. They have been taught that the institution of slavery, which their leaders have made them believe is a great element of strength, is in fact an element of weakness. Wherever the Union arms have made a lodging they have lost the entire control of their slaves, and they are quite convinced that, if the slave States formed a recognized government independent of the North, we would not make war upon them with the same leniency that we do now, but would use this element against them with very great success. . . .

In the absence of definite instructions upon the subject of fugitive slaves, I have adopted the following policy:

*First.* To allow all slaves who come to my lines to enter.

*Second.* To organize them and enroll them, taking their names, the names of their masters, and their place of residence.

*Third.* To give them employment as far as possible, and to exercise toward old and young a judicious charity.

*Fourth.* To deliver none to their owners under any circumstances, and allow none of them to leave this department until I receive your definite instructions.

The telegraphic abstract of this passage would read as follows:

*Beginning of sentence—Beginning of phrase*

| | |
|---|---|
| Person acted upon | Confederates |
| Location | North Carolina |

*End of phrase, beginning of phrase*

| | |
|---|---|
| Action | Appraisal |
| By means of | Burnside |

*End of phrase, beginning of phrase*

| | |
|---|---|
| Characteristic determined | Loyalty |
| Characteristic determined | Attitude |
| | *War |
| | *Slavery |
| | *Confederacy |

*Beginning of sentence—Beginning of phrase* (cont.)

| | |
|---|---|
| Characteristic determined ) | |
| Characteristic influenced  ) | Strength |
| Characteristic determined ) | |
| Characteristic influenced  ) | Weakness |
| Influenced by | Slavery |

*End of sentence, end of phrase, Beginning of sentence, beginning of phrase*

| | |
|---|---|
| Person acted upon | Slaves |

*End of phrase, beginning of phrase*

| | |
|---|---|
| Action negative | Control |
| By means of | Owners |
| By means of | U.S. Army |

*End of phrase, end of sentence, beginning of sentence, beginning of phrase*

| | |
|---|---|
| Person acted upon | Slaves |
| | *Fugitive |

*End of phrase, beginning of phrase*

| | |
|---|---|
| Action | Crossing |
| Location | Lines |
| | *Union |
| Direction from | Masters |
| Action | Organizing |
| Action | Enrolling |
| Action | Registering |
| Action | Employment |
| Action | Treatment |
| Action negative | Returning |
| Direction to | Masters |
| Action | Detaining |
| By means of | U.S. Army |
| By means of | Burnside |

*End of phrase, end of sentence.*

Even this short example of the telegraphic abstract should make clear the quantity of information contained in such abstracts. Remember that the conventional index, with reference to this passage, contained only the words "Slave and slave property." Viewed simply as an index, the abstract is considerably more complete, containing as it does 27 words Moreover, it should be noted that each of those words in prefaced by a word or phrase which indicates its relationship to the passage and to the other words in the same phrase. The asterisks indicate that the word so marked is to be understood as modifying in some way the preceding word. By this means the actual usage of the word—its role in the subject passage—is made clear. The combination of words and "role indicators" may be thought of as analogs to the grammar and syntax of the original passage.

## Encoding of Example Abstract

But the processing of the telegraphic abstract for high speed automatic searching and correlation does not end here. It is now encoded, not only to make it available to machine processing, but to render it even more useful and flexible.

In the encoding of such abstracts, the meanings of individual terms may be expressed by codes which indicate the relationship of specific terms to more generic concepts. Here wide latitude exists as to (1) the selection and definition of a set of generic concepts which are used in generating codes for specific terms, (2) the designation of various types of relationships between specific terms and generic terms or semantic factors, as they are sometimes called, (3) symbolism, that is to say, the code symbolism used to designate semantic factors and also relationships between specific terms being encoded and assigned semantic factors. Thus, in establishing codes for terminology, their relationship to broader generic concepts may by specified in much the same way that the derivation of certain English words indicates their relationship to generic ideas. Examples of such English words are *phonograph telegraph telephone*, where the roots *phone tele graph* correspond to semantic factors in code. It should be emphasized however, that in setting up codes, the generic concepts may be defined in any way that may be appropriate. Although the derivation of English words may provide suggestions as to how to proceed in establishing semantic factors, the observed derivation of words in natural language does not, of course, impose limitations as to our formulation and definition of semantic factors.

An abstract completely encoded does not convey much meaning to one unfamiliar with the semantic code, or "machine language," in which it is written. To take a single phrase from the abstract we are using for an example, the phrase "person acted upon: slaves *fugitive," would be encoded as "KEP. LYST.PAPL.001* PAPL. RQLS. 020x.001." Expressing this code completely, it might be read as "*Person acted upon:* a member of the class *people,* characterized as *livestock,* the *first* member of this group of which cognizance has been taken by the system; *namely,* a member of the class *people,* making use of a form of *release,* specifically of *escape,* escape being the twentieth member of this group of which cognizance has been taken by the system, the *first* member of this group of which cognizance has been taken by the system." It is hardly necessary to point out that the encoded abstracts are never completely interpreted in this fashion, as this is not essential to their exploitation.

One will observe that the role indicators have been encoded as three-letter groups, while the words are encoded as combinations of four-letter groups and numbers. There are a relatively limited number of standardized role indicators, but there are as many words as there are concepts, In the semantic code, each word is composed of one or more four-letter groups know as "semantic factors." Each semantic factor is composed of three consonants—the first, third, and fourth letters—which represents a generic concept. Those semantic factors necessary to express the semantic content of the word are then supplied with a letter in the second space, indicating the relationship between the semantic factor and the specific concept represented by the word.

The encoding of standardized abstracts, that is to say, the replacement of the terms in an encoded abstract by the corresponding codes has been reduced to clerical routines in which automatic machines preform the task of looking up individual terms in the code dictionary. Both processing costs and reliability of encoding are favorably influenced by such encoding procedures.

## Searching and Selecting Capabilities

The encoding of standardized abstracts provides an enormous amount of flexibility in searching procedures. In the instance just cited, suppose a machine were programmed to detect all instances of the word combination FUGITIVE SLAVE. The appearance of FUGITIVE SLAVES, of FUGITIVE, of SLAVE, of SLAVES, of RUNAWAY SLAVES, of ES-CAPED SLAVES, and so on would go quite undetected, since the slightest change is sufficient to throw a machine off completely. Every possible combination would have to be considered and programmed into the machine, with resultant loss of time and machine capacity. However, depending upon the programming of the machine, the use of the semantic code would bring out our *slaves °fugitive* so long as any one of those semantic factors L-ST, P-PL, or R-LS, were called for. Depending on the degree of specification, of course, many other items might also appear. For example, simply searching of P-PL would bring out every reference in which human beings were mentioned. Naturally this would not usually be particularly helpful. Specifying also L-ST would decrease the number of references very sharply, though, in addition to *slaves* one would also get the references to *cavalryman, cowboy, shepherd,* and the like. This might also well be useful. Suppose one were concerned with the productive capacity of the Confederacy. In this, slaves were at least equally as important as horses, as cattle-breeders, as mules, and so forth. Thus a search for any combination of L-ST with the semantic factor D-MN.900, would bring all of these to light. The numbers, of course, serve to provide additional focus of specification where this is desirable.

When encoded abstracts recorded on tapes are scanned by searching mechanisms, the latter may be programmed to select all abstracts that have any one characteristic or any combination of characteristics. Thus, one might select those abstracts which are characterized by a single characteristic, such as a single semantic factor; or by designating a single combination of code elements, the selection might be programmed to select all abstracts which are characterized by a single term. Specification of combinations may be varied within wide limits depending on search requirements. For example, a combination of semantic factors may be specified to select those abstracts which contain any one of the required terms. The code dictionary is, in fact, a form of thesaurus the exploitation of which, by specifying combinations of semantic factors, makes it possible for the machine to be readily programmed so as to base selection on the relationship of meaning existing among synonyms and near-synonyms. One may cite more complex combinations in searching. Thus, one might specify that those abstracts be selected that contain at least one term for which the code contains a combination of certain semantic factors, for example, LYST.MYLT.NWML.PAPL:001, and in addition, at least, one term that contains another combination of semantic factors, for example, DYMN.900X.MYLT.GARP.901. Our example here would give us all references to Confederate cavalry. An additional possibility is to specify that one or more of such terms should be associated with one or another of the role indicators. In basing searches on such combinations one may specify, if appropriate, that a certain combination of terms— with or without role indicators, depending on scope of search—should be detected within a single phrase. Furthermore, combinations of such phrases may be specified to be found within a single sentence, and sentences so characterized may be specified as being detected within individual paragraphs.

It might be noted here that our first problem—whether or not the Confederates still held the Weldon and Wilmington railroad in May of 1862—could be determined easily by this process, even though it would be quite difficult by ordinary means, since the index to the *O.R.* does not even mention the Weldon and Wilmington railroad. A search which specified an abstract in which the semantic factors for *Confederate Army* appear in combination with the words, *Weldon and Wilmington*, the semantic factor for *railroad* and the dates *May* and *1862* would bring to light the very abstract which we are using for an example, for General Burnside mentions that the Confederates were in considerable force along the road.

The search for the second problem—the attitude of major Union military leaders toward slavery—could be determined by specifying abstracts in which the semantic factors for *General* appeared in combination with the role indicator for *author*, or in a sentence; in either instance in combination with the semantic factors for *U.S. Army* and the semantic factors for *slave*. Naturally, it would be easy enough to specify particular generals, or particular aspects of slavery, in order to form the search to the degree desired.

Enough has been said, perhaps, to make the point that selection of abstracts may be specified in terms of a widely varying range of individual code elements, and their combinations, and that relationships of a syntactical nature may—or may not—be specified as may be appropriate in designating the scope of a search.

Electronic selectors are designed to provide additional capabilities as follows: A multiplicity of searches may be performed simultaneously. For example, the WRU Searching Selector has been designed to conduct 10 simultaneous searches.[3] This makes it possible to interpret a research question more or less narrowly and to set up the different interpretations of a single information requirement as separate searches to be performed simultaneously by the selector. It is possible, by a sharply defined interpretation of an information requirement, to select those abstracts which are of greatest pertinent interest and that are, so to speak, "on the nose." A broader, less precise, interpretation of an information requirement makes possible concurrently performed searches to select simultaneously those items that may be relevant, though they may not correspond to strictly defined search requirements. A series of definitions of a given information requirement thus permit simultaneously performed searches to fractionate the selected abstracts problem. Again, there is a virtually limitless number of different combinations of code elements that may be specified in designating alternate interpretations of a given information requirement. One of the machine features which may also be used to advantage in designating alternate searches are circuits for detecting "near misses." Such a special case arises when the highest degree of pertinency would correspond to abstracts containing all of several specified characteristics where the absence of one or more characteristics from the full complement would correspond to documents of lesser probable relevancy.

## Man–Machine Teamwork

Enough has been said, perhaps, to indicate that appropriate formulation of searches enables their scope to be defined in virtually any desired combination of specific and generic concepts and that such formulations of scope of searches, relationships of a syntactic nature, may be taken into account. This provides a powerful tool for research but the nature of this tool should not be misunderstood. Specifically, one should not forget that a prerequisite to using this new library tool is the interpretation of a research assignment, or an information requirement, in terms of the specific searches to be performed by the machine. This interpretation requires considerable human skill and may often require the combined effort of a subject matter expert and a skilled machine programmer. As in any form of research, considerable thought and ingenuity will be required to exploit the full potential of these new library techniques. In particular, the ability to use combinations of generic and specific ideas provides a challenge to the subject matter expert.

Once selection has been performed, evaluation of the information as to its significance must also be a task for the subject expert. It may well be, in many cases, that the results of an initial search may serve to formulate one or more subsequent searches. In working out a research problem, changes in the orginal plan of investigation may become necessary as various searches are performed to answer the questions posed by subject experts.

Judgment and understanding of the subject matter of documents is also required during preparatory processing to provide abstracts that are properly classified, indexed, and coded. The first step in these diverse types of processing is that same, namely the making of decisions respecting the important features of the subject contents of the documents. Once such decisions have been made the characteristics determined to be important will guide the subsequent processing steps. In preparing abstracts, appropriately concise and readable statements must be written, an important criterion of excellence. In classification, the determination of important characteristics of the subject content guides and controls the assignment of a given item to one—or possibly more—groups. In punched card coding the determination of important characteristics guides and controls the assigment of code designations and the corresponding punching of the cards. In coding for searching by electronic selectors, the determination of important characteristics guides and controls the formulation of standardized abstracts for subsequent encoding and recording on tapes to be scanned by the automatic equipment.

## Coordination of Methods—Old and New

It is evident that abstracting, indexing, classifying, and coding have a common intellectual basis, namely the examination of documents to determine their important characteristics. This is vital for several reasons. In the first place, as already noted, it is possible to coordinate abstracting, indexing, classifying, and coding and, specifically, this range of processing operations may be based on a single reading, understanding, and evaluation of the subject contents of documents. Considered from another point of view, the common intellectual basis for the diverse operations of processing reveals that encoding for searching by semi-automatic or automatic devices is closely related to traditional indexing and classification procedures. In fact, the newer coding procedures may be regarded as an extension of previously developed indexing methods, therefore selecting and correlating capabilities of automatic and semi-automatic devices may be exploited in efficient and economical fashion. A close relationship between subject indexing and coding for machine searching also opens the possibility of reprocessing previously compiled subject indexes into a form amenable for machine searching. Such reprocessing would involve the following steps: (1) The dealphabetizing of previous subject indexes to draw together into a single group all the index entries pertaining to a given document. (2) Encoding the index entries so that the relationship of specific terminology to generic concepts would be recorded, thus making both specific terms and generic concepts available for searching and selecting operations. (3) Recording on an appropriate search medium, for example magnetic tape, the encoded sets of index entries. In processing subject indexes in this fashion it may be advisable to consider whether, and to what extent, it may be advantageous and advisable to submit the alphabetized sets of index entries to editorial review particularly for checking purposes or for supplying role indicators.

## Conclusions

Although the introduction of new mechanical and electronic devices into the library cannot be expected to perform creative thinking or to reduce the need for the expert understanding, evaluation, and judgment, of well-trained library specialists, these new devices have proved highly useful, particularly in the field of science and technology, and the principles developed in these areas suggest the practicability of their expansion into other disciplines in which the problems are similar. The new methods can relieve subject matter experts of much of the drudgery previously unavoidable when using conventional indexes and classification systems to identify the documents of pertinent interest for a given research problem. Utilizing the new library tools to fullest advantage provides a stimulating challenge to the imagination and resourcefulness of scholars in any field of professional activity in which information and knowledge recorded in large numbers of documents play an important role.

# Part V

# Beyond Social Science

# Moral Factors / *John Higham*

A PERENNIAL DILEMMA of historical scholarship is its need to use the resources of the present to discover what is not present, but past. The creative historian lives a double life, responsive on one side to the questions and issues of his own age, faithful on the other side to the integrity of an age gone by. Too feeble an involvement in the life of the present makes for a slack and routine grasp of the past. But present commitments that are too parochial imprison our imagination, instead of challenging it. At one extreme, historical thought is sterile, at the other tendentious. How can historians, by the strength of their detachment, rise above a constricting present, and, by the amplitude of their commitment, enter a living past?

If this is a perennial problem, it has a special pertinence for the American historian today. He usually works in a vast educational system that rewards its employees with prestige and security for predictable quantities of passionless research. The institutional setting, therefore, encourages much routine and mechanical history. On the other hand, the ideological conflicts of the twentieth century have, until now, swept many of our best historians in the opposite direction, entangling them in rather partisan commitments.

For a long time institutional restraints and ideological pressures seemed to offset and balance one another in a fairly effective way. The pull of neutrality and the push of commitment seemed enough adjusted to serve the pursuit of truth. As long as our present concerns remained fundamentally stable, a cumulative pattern of research could be observed. Conventional monographs followed easily in paths marked out by the major interpretive studies, and confidence in the progress of knowledge kept criticism within manageable bounds. Now, however, that working balance has been upset. The old ideological positions have broken down, so that the kind of present-mindedness that seemed to illuminate American history twenty years ago has largely outlived its usefulness. Many of the values and allegiances that guided our historical writing now seem unduly restrictive. There is, consequently, a danger and an opportunity: the danger of a largely negative scholarship, revisionist in motive but routine or merely clever in result; the opportunity of discovering, with the help of our newer present, a history of unsuspected richness and power.

John Higham, "Beyond Consensus: The Historian as Moral Critic," *American Historical Review*, LXVII (April, 1962), 609–25. Reprinted by permission.

Until very recently, two contemporary commitments dominated the interpretation of American history. First, many of the best American historians felt a close identification with particular sections or social groups. Secondly, progressive and pragmatic ideas had an extraordinary control over historical thinking. Both of these circumstances have altered.

In an increasingly homogeneous society, historians cannot be as urgently motivated by sectional, class, and ethnic ties as they were a quarter of a century ago. Then militant southerners, confident westerners, defiant Brahmins, and the first self-conscious representatives of various ethnic minorities were turning up facets of our history reflective of their claims or grievances and championing regionalism. Puritanism, or cultural pluralism, as the case might be. There is much less of this now. Younger scholars are not impelled to vindicate their respective subjects as ardently as Samuel Eliot Morison championed the Puritans, Walter Prescott Webb, the Great Plains, Carl Wittke, the immigrants, or Ulrich B. Phillips and E. Merton Coulter, the South.[1] One wonders how these various groupings in the American past will look to a new generation of historians, which is not anchored very securely in any of them.

While social changes were eroding the group loyalties of many historians, their generally progressive assumptions about American history were also breaking down. The two trends worked together. Just as progressive assumptions encouraged scholars to emphasize the struggle of contending groups in society, so the reaction against progressive historiography has discouraged such emphasis and has undermined the intellectual foundations of a group-centered point of view. We may, therefore, get to the heart of our current problem and opportunity when we understand what has happened to the progressive school of American historians.

From the American Revolution to the Second World War the great majority of our historians assumed that the underlying movement of American history was in the direction of improvement or betterment, not only in wealth but in freedom or happiness. In this movement, setbacks and even reverses had occurred, of course, when the American people were temporarily faithless to their basic principles. Such interludes were pronounced "Repressible Conflicts," "Great Abberrations," or "Great Betrayals,"[2] to indicate that they arose from mutual misunderstandings, irrational mistakes, and moral holidays, not from any fundamental defect in American culture. Even the fashionable disillusion of the 1920's left very little impress on professional historians. A President of the American Historical Association affirmed a law of progress in history in 1923, and in 1929 a leading authority on American social history urged his colleagues to synthesize their data by asking how every event or influence had checked or accelerated social evolution.[3] Attitudes such as these meant that historians were continually asking what each period "contributed" or "added" to the world of today. History was fundamentally aggregative, and even scholars devoted to the study of lost causes and vanished frontiers refused to draw pessimistic conclusions. They felt sure that the passing experience they cherished had left a permanent heritage of fruitful values.[4]

In the twentieth century these pervasive assumptions gave a strategic importance to historians who had a hardheaded explanation of the dynamics of change—historians who rendered the progressive faith realistically by explaining how and why human effort sometimes overcame human inertia and sometimes succumbed to it. Change, these scholars said, takes place through struggle, and progress occurs when the more popular and democratic forces overcome the resistance to change offered by vested interests. And so American history became a story of epic conflict between over- and underprivileged groups. Whether this strife was chiefly between sections, as with Frederick Jackson Turner, or between opposing economic groups, as with Charles Beard, or between Hamiltonian and Jeffersonian ideologies, as with Vernon Parrington, a fundamental dualism cut through the course of American history.[5]

In polarizing history vertically, the progressive realists also secured a principal of periodization. With eyes focused on the climactic moments in the continuing struggle, they dramatized the turning points when power had presumably shifted from one side to the other. Through revolution and counterrevolution, through reform and reaction, beat the rhythm of an exciting and meaningful history. Here indeed was a grand design, flexible, capacious, immediately relevant to the present interests of the 1920's and 1930's, capable of elaboration in a multitude of researches, yet simple in outline. In 1939 Arthur Schlesinger, Sr., could compress a generation of historiography and the whole span of American political history into a single sentence: "A period of concern for the rights of the few has [regularly] been followed by one of concern for the wrongs of the many."[6]

Twenty years later, to most American historians, the grand design probably looked more like a grand illusion. Many of them in the 1950's had devoted their best energies to shattering the design. It had, without question, proved wanting. Too much of the mounting data of cultural, intellectual, and economic history overflowed the dialectical categories of liberal versus conservative. The groups to whom these labels were attached proved much less persistent and cohesive in identity and aim than the design allowed. The theory that change is effected through domestic social conflict took too little account of the role of accommodation and compromise in American political history, too little account of the kind of innovation emphasized in American business history, too little account of the international influences so important to diplomatic and intellectual history.

Yet the design might have held together after a fashion—by stretching and squeezing, it might have contained a good measure of new research —if the social attitudes that went into the design had remained intact. After World War II, however, historians found themselves in a new era, much less tractable and less responsive to progressive values. Some of those values now seemed too simple and too limited in their relevance to human experience. The vaunted realism of the progressive historians no longer seemed realistic enough.

As far as historians were concerned, one of the principal casualties of the postwar world was the faith in progress itself. Few of them became prophets of doom, but fewer still remained oracles of hope. Their disenchantment owed something to the powerful polemic of Reinhold Niebuhr but more to their own sharpened awareness of America's dependence on a precarious civilization. Walter Prescott Webb's *The Great Frontier* (Boston, 1952), although too extreme in its conclusions to win general acceptance, showed how an international perspective could cast a somber light on the epic theme of American progress: the frontier thesis became an explanation of the temporary and declining vitality of modern Western civilization. Other postprogressive scholars, such as George Kennan, studied American wars and diplomacy with an eye for the tragic and with a sense of the limits of American capacities.[7] The revisionist school of Civil War history declined when its thesis that partisan statesmen had willfully ignored constructive alternatives to a "needless" war and a "vindictive" peace began to look naïvely optimistic.[8]

Perhaps the most widespread effect of the sober postwar mood was to deflate progressive confidence in social change. Instead of endorsing change, or distinguishing between more and less desirable kinds of change, many historians grew cautious if not distrustful toward change as such. In the work of Ralph Gabriel, Clinton Rossiter, Louis Hartz, Daniel Boorstin, Robert E. Brown, Edmund Morgan, and others, a new appreciation of continuity in American history emerged. Neither in love with modernity nor entranced by the antique, many historians now emphasized the enduring uniformities of American life, the stability of institutions, the persistence of a national character.[9]

Thus, a conservative trend of historical interpretation set in, and as it gathered momentum it displayed other attitudes often found in conservative quarters. In contrast to the progressive historians' confidence in mass democracy, one notices among historians today a skeptical attitude toward the comman man and a reluctance to give full sympathy to the underdog. Such democratic heroes as Roger Williams, Nathaniel Bacon, Andrew

Jackson, and Thorstein Veblen are now portrayed as less democratic or less heroic than earlier biographers saw them.[10] On the other hand, such nondemocratic figures as John Winthrop, Alexander Hamilton, Nicholas Biddle, George Fitzhugh, and John D. Rockefeller have risen several notches in historical reputation.[11]

This shift away from democratic affirmations should not be exaggerated. It has not, among many reputable historians, made heroes of the privileged and villains of their popular opponents. Such a reversal of progressive sympathies would preserve the progressive dichotomy between the many and the few, the haves and the have-nots. The deeper tendency in contemporary thought is to dissolve the old polarities. Skeptical especially of economic and ideological antitheses, historians nowadays are blending them together. Where the terms liberal and conservative still remain in use, we are finding that liberal movements were after all conservative[12] and that almost all Americans have really been liberal.[13] Instead of the two-sided nation enshrined in progressive history—a nation eternally divided between a party of the past and a party of the future, between noble ideals and ignoble interests—recent general interpretations show us a single homogeneous culture, or perhaps a balanced interplay between three elements. The trinitarian approach lends itself neatly to a reconciliation of contrasts within a final synthesis.[14] Not conflict, therefore, but consensus is now taken as the normative reality of American life.

It is not hard to understand why this should be so. Unlike the progressive historian, his conservative successor does not feel much at odds with powerful institutions or dominant social groups. He is not even half alienated. Carried along in the general postwar reconciliation between America and its intellectuals, and wanting to identify himself with a community, he usually reads the national record for evidence of effective organization and a unifying spirit.[15]

Often the strength of this uniformitarian bent is obscured by the conservative historian's delighted attention to the abundant variety of American life. Far from professing any love of conformity, he may conceive of the American whole as an infinite number of freely related parts.[16] In his more critical moments, he may fear that the process of centralization, bureaucratization, and standardization are going too far today, and he embraces the variations and complexities in American experience all the more readily because they seem to him so innocuous and impermanent. He discovers an immense variety of economic interests represented at Philadelphia in 1787, instead of only two. In restudying the Second Bank of the United States, Reconstruction, or the progressive movement, he fragments into a welter of factions what the progressive historian had thought of as "the business community."[17] Immersed in fluid experience, he is often quite pragmatic in his antipathy to formal ideologies and clearly defined categories. His sense of the unity of America, therefore, is largely unspecific and rests on a description of its multiplicity. His motto is *e pluribus unum*.

That this general approach to American history contains a large measure of truth, few will deny. Having much in common with our national mythology, it induces sympathies that are perhaps more general and less partisan than those of the progressive school. Although suffused by present attitudes, the historian of consensus is not involved so immediately and urgently in the struggles of his own time; he may be able more easily to project himself into the past on something like its own terms. The desire to see things whole, in the sense of understanding the working relationships between groups, should prove especially useful in the study of social history, which for too long was preoccupied with reform movements and social problems.

Yet the positive achievements of the conservative school seem less impressive, to date, than its attack on the old progressive formulas. Has it produced any master works of great strength and enduring significance? Perhaps, if Allan Nevins' retelling of the Civil War belongs to this school; but it is significant that Nevins' work seems to derive from an older conservative culture and to owe little to the contemporary mood. Of the outstanding books of the last ten years some have retained a modified progressive outlook, like C. Vann Woodward's *Origins of the New South, 1877–1913* (Baton Rouge, La., 1951). Some have expressed a disillusioned liberalism, like Richard Hofstadter's *The Age of Reform: From Bryan to F.D.R.* (New York, 1955) and Henry Nash Smith's *Virgin Land: The American West as Symbol and Myth* (Cambridge, Mass., 1950). The historians of consensus, on the other hand, have scored chiefly in restricted monographs or in highly generalized interpretive essays.

All in all, recent historians have been more successful in breaking down the interpretations of their predecessors than in building anew. The emphasis on consensus and continuity has softened the outlines and flattened the crises of American history. A certain tameness and amiability have crept into our view of things; perhaps the widespread interest in myths comes partly from a feeling that the realities are simply not as interesting. The conservative frame of reference is giving us a bland history, in which conflict is muted, in which the classic issues of social justice are underplayed, in which the elements of spontaneity, effervescence, and violence in American life get little sympathy or attention. Now that the progressive impulse is subsiding, scholarship is threatened with a moral vacuum.

To speak, perhaps extravagantly, of a moral vacuum is to raise afresh an old question that too many of us have regarded as long since settled. Since the rise of scientific history, the legitimacy of moral judgments in historical writing has been under official disapproval. By the end of the nineteenth century, the manuals of historical method had summarily banished moral evaluation from the proper sphere of historical science; the latest handbooks continue to ignore it.[18] But the present cultural situation has reopened this question. From English and German scholars we begin to hear warnings that academic history, by shrinking from evaluation of right and wrong, has helped to weaken the spirit of personal responsibility.[19] The warning applies with special force to the current state of American historiography. With the decline of progressive values, the principal source of moral energy on which American historians have drawn in recent decades is drying up. There is no substitute in the complacent empiricism of the conservative school. Yet the present situation offers a third alternative. We have today a major opportunity for revitalizing the moral relevance of historical scholarship.

Until history became professionalized, its practitioners felt no misgivings about teaching moral lessons. History, to them, exhibited universal laws of human nature and so comprised a vast repository of political and moral example. The nineteenth-century faith in progress put a supreme confidence into such moralizing; for the historian's assumption that he stood at the summit of history, and could therefore truly judge the actions and standards of earlier times by those of his own, expunged any doubt about his moral authority. He might exercise it with advantage in any field of history, although the study of one's own country was particularly improving. "That study," said the president of Harvard University in 1884, summing up a common conviction,

shows the young the springs of public honor and dishonor; sets before them the national failings, weaknesses, and sins; warns them against future dangers by exhibiting the losses and sufferings of the past; enshrines in their hearts the national heroes; and strengthens in them the precious love of country.[20]

The same year in which Charles W. Eliot spoke, the American Historical Association was established by men who were retreating from moral commitment in the name of science. The scientific historian aspired to be a flawless mirror reflecting an independent, external reality. By freely pronouncing judgments he would distort the picture. Yet the scientific historians, in denying themselves a judicial function, did not intend to lessen history's didactic usefulness. Secure in their faith in progress, they commonly supposed that objective history would reveal the evolution of morality in the march of events without intrusive comment by the writer.[21] Surely, over the long run, history displayed the gradual advance of wisdom and virtue. If the historian took care of the facts, the values would take care of themselves. In practice, of course, the early professional historians could not suppress moral rhetoric completely, but they could in principle forswear it without any sense of risk or anxiety, since scientific history emerged in America in a humane milieu, unperplexed by deep frustrations.

The new style progressives of the twentieth century, rebelling against the conservative implications of scientific history, were less complacent. They were activists, whose expectations of progress depended on the use of historical knowledge in order to control history. They felt less comfortable about the present than their conservative predecessors had, and they determined to link the past to current needs for reform.[22] They recognized a legitimate place for values in historical interpretation. By renouncing an unattainable objectivity, they hoped to arrive at usable truths.

In progressive hands American history became not only a struggle between the many and the few but a realm of clashing values. Once more, the American historian consciously played the role of moral critic, now with a pragmatic emphasis on the consequences of policies and ideas, instead of the easy dogmatism of a George Bancroft or a Francis Parkman. Unfortunately, however, the restoration of moral urgency in historical scholarship occurred on too narrow a front and too precarious a basis. The same progressive spirit that stirred the heart and conscience of historians also, in other aspects, severely limited their moral vision. For one thing, the range of moral concern contracted from the whole life of man to certain political and economic issues. The progressive historian did not ordinarily search the past for light on personal codes of behavior, the great sphere of private as opposed to public morality. Nor did he show much interest in studying the resolution of incompatible loyalties, or the nature of responsibility, greatness, initiative, and the like. His view of history remained largely impersonal: he concentrated on "social forces" as the earlier scientific historians had concentrated on "institutions." The only kind of ethics that engaged the progressive historian's interest was the ethics of democracy,[23] and even here he was pretty exclusively concerned with the actualization of democratic values rather than their relation to other good.

This tendency to dwell on means rather than ends—on the attainable results of an ideal rather than its intrinsic nature—reflected the progressive scholar's reluctance to venture much beyond the accustomed limits of scientific objectivity. He wanted his values, but he wanted them in the shape of facts. Tough-minded, realistic, disdainful of nineteenth-century pieties and platitudes, he tried to be pragmatic in his moral judgments. The practical results of any historical situation—the tangible action it produced—dominated and restricted his evaluation of it. Progressive historians ordinarily retained too much confidence in progress to doubt that the course of history would vindicate their democratic and pragmatic ethics.[24]

From these antecedents, the younger conservative historians of today have come. While reacting against a reformist bias, some of them continue to measure the past by pragmatic standards. What remains for them of the moral function of the historian now that the inspiration of social progress has dimmed, and the age of reform that lasted for half a century has passed? Now that stability rather than change has become the national objective, what values can pass the pragmatic test? Only what is snugly enmeshed in the texture of American experience has clearly proved its practical worth. Deprived of an active commitment to progress, the pragmatic approach tends to endorse sheer success and survival. Having lost its critical edge, pragmatism has tended to deteriorate into retrospective piety.

On the other hand, the present situation can give rise to a very different kind of historical scholarship, a scholarship engaged in a more widely ranging and a subtler moral criticism than American professional historians have yet undertaken. A lively critical impulse has clearly survived in many quarters. It is seeking a new field of expression now that the grand design of progressive historiography no longer contains and directs it. That impulse can draw today on a richer knowledge of human motivation than scholars have ever had at their disposal before; it can achieve a sympathetic understanding of a greater variety of human types. Having learned something of the relativity of values, today's historians can exercise a morally critical function with tentativeness and humility, with a minimum of self-righteousness, and with a willingness to meet the past on equal terms.

How can this come about? Let us look first at the pitfalls to be avoided; here the record of American historiography to date can guide us. None of the formal postures that American historians have conventionally adopted seem adequate today, either morally or historically. Neither the dogmatic moralist, nor the pure scientist, nor the pragmatist offers a satisfactory model.

Surely scholars may not, without corrupting history, revert to the judicial stance of a century ago. We are now too well aware of the wide disparities between ethical systems, and too ignorant of their relation to one another, to impose our own arbitrarily on another time and place. Let us beware of the easy temptations of moral judgment in essaying the difficult adventure of moral criticism. Let us operate on any subject with a conviction of its dignity and worth. Let us grant to every actor in a moral drama the fullest measure of his particular integrity; let us not destroy the drama by hastening to condemn or to absolve. The serious historian may not wrap himself in judicial robes and pass sentence from on high; he is too much involved in both the prosecution and the defense. He is not a judge of the dead, but rather a participant in their affairs, and their only trustworthy intermediary.

For these tasks, the moral neutrality of the scientific position has likewise proved wanting. In addition to the standard complaints—that it is unattainable, that it dehumanizes history, that it encourages fatalism and gives us nothing to admire—one may suggest a further difficulty. Scientific history, so far as it achieves neutrality, leaves an unbridged gulf between the subject and the reader. The scientific historian, in liberating his readers from moral absolutism, apparently assumed that they could make their own fair and independent judgments if given an unobstructed view of the past. On principle, therefore, the scientific historian did not address himself to the sensibilities of a particular audience. He did not deliberately connect its needs and perplexities with those of another time and place. Indeed, he was scarcely conscious of having an audience. Whereas the historical judge coerced the reader, the historical scientist ignored him. To write as a critic, however, is to assume an active responsibility both to a phase of the past and to a contemporary public, and to engage one with the other.

Our third model—the historical pragmatist—more nearly approximates that kind of role. He is very much aware of present needs, and his pronouncements are tentative and undogmatic. But his sympathies are limited, and his criticism does not go deep. Criteria that rest on a program of practical action takes account of a restricted present as well as a restricted past. A morality confined to social engineering emphasizes results at the expense of intentions. In a progressive age, it becomes a partisan in the struggle for results. In a conservative age, it celebrates results already largely achieved.

Once the pragmatic test is suspended, historians will still analyze the results of a situation in order to discover its causes and to learn how those particular results came to be, but a moral appraisal of the situation need not depend upon its outcome. A truly sensitive critic will go beyond the practical consequences of the process he describes. He may criticize his subject, not on the ground of its present relevance, but for its intrinsic value as a gesture of the human spirit.

One may well ask, however, for more specific directions. What strategies can the historian legitimately employ without compromising the integrity of his craft? What criteria may he apply in performing the office of moral critic? How much real change in historical scholarship is implied? These questions lead us into an aspect of historiography ignored by the standard manuals and treatises on method. Discussion has not ordinarily gone beyond the point of recognizing that the historian's own values inevitably color his writing. At best, we have acknowledged this coloring as a mark of our humanity.[25] Professional historians have hardly begun to consider moral insight as something they can gain by skilled and patient historical study, not merely as something they cannot keep out of it. Historical method acquires a new dimension when we begin to speak of the criticism of life in addition to the technical criticism of documents. Then moral evaluation becomes a professional task, not just a predilection of our unprofessional selves.

A comparison with analogous developments in literary studies during the last generation may help to clarify the present opportunity in historical scholarship. The reign of the literary historian—exclusively preoccupied with historical and biographical backgrounds to literature, with sources, influences, and social conditions—was challenged by the incursion of literary critics into academic circles.[26] Various schools of literary criticism proliferated, but all subordinated factual description and historical explanation to a close evaluation of the work of art. For a time, criticism went to absurdly antihistorical extremes; English departments split into factions—literary historians versus New Critics. But the ferment invigorated literary history enormously; in the hands of men like F. O. Matthiessen, Lionel Trilling, and Harry Levin, the study of literature profited from the interplay of critical and historical perspectives.

Possibly the professional study of history would benefit at least as much from the challenge of a similar movement, directed at the criticism of life rather than the criticism of art. On this analogy, we may look forward to something more noteworthy than the recent fruitless debate over the legitimacy of those present-centered judgments that inescapably condition all historical knowledge. Instead, we may look forward to the development of a partial distinction between the kind of historical inquiry that is familiar and traditional and a newer kind that is only beginning to appear in professional circles. The older type aims chiefly at knowledge of causal relationships in a particular phase of the past; the newer type aims chiefly at knowledge of the elements of good and evil discoverable in a particular historical setting. The former type holds moral appraisal in check in the interest of causal synthesis. The latter type, with equal propriety, subordinates causal interpretation to moral interpretation. Both endeavors will inevitably reflect the historian's own commitments. Both must accept the distinctively historical obligation to deal with a whole situation in its authentic complexity. But causal history should have a form appropriate to the actual *course* of experience; whereas moral history, proceeding with a similar drive for discovery, will take whatever shape seems best suited to elaborate the problematical *qualities* of experience.

This distinction, like any classification of historical studies, should not be pressed too far, though it can serve some useful purposes. It calls attention to the need for a thoroughgoing moral criticism, in contrast to the impressionistic moral judgments that creep into historical writing at every turn. A working distinction between causal history and moral history also guards against pragmatic confusion between facts and values. Moreover, it helps to equalize the legitimacy and importance of two great objectives: the reconstruction of history as objective reality (most appropriate to causal history), and the participation in history as subjective experience (essential to moral history).[27] Causal history and moral history at their best, however, are reciprocal modes of understanding, each of which suffers from neglect of the other. Let us distinguish between them as friendly rivals in order to overcome a destructive enmity.

A closer look at the nature of moral history will suggest how it can supplement and enrich existing scholarship. One may discern, within the wide domain of moral history, two general types. The first type deals with the whole quality of a life, a complex of lives, or an age. It enables us to grasp the moral tone of a particular time and place—to feel the involuntary drift and pressure of its values against a background of alternatives delivered in other times and places. How has the notion of honor changed since the Middle Ages? What did men mean in the nineteenth century when they spoke of "character" and put implicit confidence in leaders or associates who had it? To what sorts of people did the virtue of "character" appeal and attach? What tangled combinations of courage and weakness, or of love and hate, do we find pervading a career, a movement, or a period? Similarly, moral insight may reveal fundamental polarities in history that are more illuminating than class or sectional divisions. Is the great cleavage in American history the outward one between haves and have-nots, which twentieth-century progressives observed in society, or is it rather an inward opposition, which progressives strove to reconcile within themselves, between an ethic of communal responsibility and an ethic of unrestrained individualism?

These questions point to an extended kind of moral history that shades imperceptibly into causal history, and differs only in having somewhat more interest in the intrinsic meaning of the experience and somewhat less in explaining its development. Professional historians seem to be venturing increasingly into this genre, though more readily in casual essays than in their formal, full-dress works. Carl Becker was probably the first American professional historian to become adept at an intellectualized moral history, which may help to account for his great and continuing vogue in recent years. It remains true, however, that the major works of this kind are still written mostly by literary and cultural critics like Wilbur J. Cash, Hannah Arendt, and Lewis Mumford.[28] The amateur in history plunges instinctively and often rashly into moral criticism. A quickened interest among professional scholars would surely help academic history to find its rightful place in the republic of letters.

A second kind of moral history concentrates on particular acts of choice. Here we confront not involuntary or cumulative processes, but rather the moments of important human initiative, and we ponder the moral responsibility of the agents of decision. In the 1760's the British Parliament adopted a disastrous policy of spasmodic coercion toward the American colonies. A generation ago American scholars debated the constitutionality of that policy, and British scholars are still arguing about the exact nature of English government at the time;[29] but the momentous decision that precipitated the American Revolution has not yet had close attention as a problem in political ethics. Given the political and social institutions of the day, what real alternatives were present? Who erred most culpably? What balance of folly, insight, and constructive purpose can we discern in each of the major participants?[30] The study of moral responsibility remains crude unless each of the elements contributory to a situation fully exhibits its distinctive abilities, limitations, and dilemmas. Ideally, each element should effect a criticism of the others. As the author's design unfolds, the situation becomes luminous with unexpected contingencies.

In similar fashion it should be possible to study afresh the turning points in the lives of well-known individuals: Robert E. Lee's painful decision to cast his lot with the Confederacy in 1861, William James's famous affirmation of free will in 1870, Franklin D. Roosevelt's acceptance of a third term in 1940. Seizing upon the event, the historian can undertake to clarify the degree and quality of initiative suggested by a close comparison with other individuals similarly circumstanced (James with Henry Adams, for example), and by analyzing the other choices that might conceivably have been made.

In all such studies of an act of decision, as in larger studies of the moral climate, criticism cannot do without some causal analysis. We hold people responsible only to the degree that we think them free to choose their course. The imaginable range of choice within a particular situation guides our moral criticism, which must therefore include an appreciation of the unalterable conditions that bulk large in causal history. Yet moral criticism not only borrows from causal analysis, but also contributes to it. By enlarging our awareness of the latent possibilities of a situation, criticism will suggest new causal hypotheses. Perhaps it would be better to speak, not of causal history and moral history as separate types, but of two kinds of attention, each of which contributes to historical wisdom.

There remains the difficult question of the criteria that the critic of the past may legitimately employ. Surely one must have standards. Just as surely, the only proper standards are ones common to the historian and to the world he is studying. But to try to lay down exact criteria is, I think, to misconceive our opportunity and to narrow our prospect. The historian is not called to establish a hierarchy of values, but rather to explore a spectrum of human potentialities and achievements. While maintaining his own integrity, while preserving the detachment that time and distance afford, he must participate in variety, allowing his subjects as much as possible to criticize one another. In fact, the obligation of the historian to become a moral critic grows out of the breakdown of ethical absolutes. If no single ethical system, even a pragmatic one that trusts the piecemeal results of history, does justice to all situations, a complex awareness must take the place of systematic theory. Instead of depending on fixed canons or rules, the moral critic must learn from the great dramatists, like Shakespeare, from novelists, like Tolstoy, and from the matchless example of Thucydides.

In the simplest sense, the historian commits to moral criticism all the resources of his human condition. He derives from moral criticism an enlarged and disciplined sensitivity to what men ought to have done, what they might have done, and what they achieved. His history becomes an intensive, concrete reflection upon life, freed from academic primness, and offering itself as one of the noblest, if also one of the most difficult and imperfect, of the arts.

This discussion, instead of continuing the current argument about the interpretation of American history, has turned outward toward a wider horizon. But perhaps the original issue has undergone a partial resolution. When the historian's quest for understanding reaches beyond pragmatic and empirical concerns, he need not strain to find patterns of conflict or of consensus. He will have plenty of both. He will study, as the most meaningful kind of consensus, the moral standards of an age—what, distinctively, it assumed about the conduct of life. He will find conflict wherever those moral standards clash or break down, and so force men to make a choice. In confronting all that is unstable and precarious in human values, he can discover the profoundest struggles and conflicts that the drama of history affords.

# Causality / Cushing Strout

A SPECTER HAUNTS American historians—the concept of causality. After nearly a hundred years of passionate and dispassionate inquiry into "the causes of the Civil War" the debate is still inconclusive. Even more discouraging, according to the editor of a recent anthology of historical writings on the problem, "twentieth-century historians often merely go back to interpretations advanced by partisans while the war was still in progress."[1] Despite the impasse, historians are not often discouraged. Some take refuge in professional patience or the firm confidence that their opponents have simply hardened their hearts to truth. Others are reconciled to skepticism by the historical relativism, defended by Carl Becker and Charles Beard, which characterizes all historical interpretations as determined products of a temporary, dominant "climate of opinion." A few, like Beard himself, have drastically tried to cut the knot by surgical removal of the causal category itself from history, though his own practice of economic determinism flatly contradicted this Draconian proposal. When the investigation of the answer to a question has led to such frustrating difficulties, it is necessary to re-examine the question, even if it leads the historian into philosophical territory where he naturally fears to tread.

Historians are often vulnerable to Henry Adams's charge that their causal assumptions, "hidden in the depths of dusty libraries, have been astounding, but commonly unconscious and childlike,"[2] yet they can find no real help from the eccentric results of his own search for a historical physics which would unify the course of events under one abstract formula, "a spool upon which to wind the thread of the past without breaking it."[3] For all his brilliance his speculative theory has quite rightly struck most historians as an exotic hybrid of history and science, spoiling the integrity of each. The "scientific school of history" ended either in fanciful speculation about historical laws or a naive cult of fact-finding as the essence of scientific method. If even the scientist, at the level of sub-atomic particles, must substitute statistical probability for causal universals, the historian has always been embarrassed by the effort to discover conditions which invariably produce certain results not otherwise accounted for. He cannot discriminate with exactness constants and vari-

Cushing Strout, "Causation and the American Civil War," History and Theory, I (1961), 175–185. Reprinted by permission.

ables by experimentation on a past forever gone, nor can he always confidently turn to social scientists for causal rules when their findings, even when valid and relevant, are limited historically to particular times and places. Grateful as the historian may be for generalizations about, say, the voting behavior of Americans, he is ruefully aware that recurring evidence for the behavior of Americans in civil wars is fortunately not available.

The historian conventionally speaks of "multiple causes" because he knows he has no monistic formula to explain the course of history and no single generalization to cover all the necessary and sufficient conditions for a civil war. This fashion of speech is, however, misleading because he cannot escape his difficulties by multiplying them. If he does not believe that each of the many "causes" could have produced the Civil War by itself, then he must assume that the whole collection of them acted together as one in bringing about that effect. He is then left with the familiar problem of accounting for this causal relationship by reference to confirmed generalizations. What he cannot do for one "cause," he cannot do for a set of them acting as one.

Historians sometimes seek to avoid the problem of generalized causal rules by talking of a necessary chain of events.[4] Yet the events which are put into the so-called chains clearly have more determinants than are recognized by so placing them, and the same event can be put into a number of possible chains. The election of Lincoln, produced by a large number of small events, might well appear in two alleged chains of events which suggest quite different interpretations of the coming of the war. The chains are not, furthermore, really "necessary" unless their linkage is explained by theories or generalizations which the makers of chains seldom make clear, even to themselves.[5]

A deeper difficulty of the causal query is that it may be defined so as to conflict with the historical attitude itself. If the historian were to deduce consequences from antecedents, there would be nothing in the former not found in the latter. How then could he speak of anything new happening at all? The special sensitivity of the historian is to the novel elements, the discontinuities, emerging in a situation. He discovers the relevant antecedents retrospectively with the help of the illumination of the consequences, which call out for a past. Looking backwards, he discerns a process that does not logically or inevitably follow from certain antecedents, but takes its life and form only from its development. There is no point at which the historian can declare that the Civil War became inevitable, even though he might find it increasingly probable. Those who have said it was inevitable have either deduced it from a dogmatic general proposition about the "necessary" conflict of classes in society,

according to the determinism of historical materialism, or they have
pointed instead to the stubbornness of the slavery problem and the moral
and ideological imperatives which made certain policies humanly "necessary" (granted their premises), rather than historically inevitable in terms
of an impersonal process.[6] In studying the Civil War the historian must
know about such antecedents as the origins and expansion of slavery, for
example, but he cannot deduce the war from the existence of that institution. "American historians have been too clever by half", Carl Becker
once said, "In finding other causes of the Civil War,"[7] but the cleverness
has been stimulated by knowledge of the fact that slavery existed and
was eliminated elsewhere without civil war.

The serious difficulties of exact causal determination have led some
thinkers to suggest that the historian make reasonable estimates of causes,
based upon his judgment of what *would* have taken place in the absence
of a particular factor being tested for causal relevance.[8] If the course of
events would have been much the same, the factor is assumed to have
had no causal significance. Some critics have replied that history is, as
Beard maintained, "a seamless web"; but surely it is not so seamless that
historians must follow Beard in believing that there is no more reason to
explain American intervention in the First World War by reference to the
German policy of unlimited submarine warfare than by reference to the
Kaiser's moustaches.[9] This extreme position denies to the historian that
realistic sense of relevance which the study of history and direct experience of human affairs have traditionally provided. Many explanations in
history certainly do reflect and depend upon this trained sense of relevance.[10] Modern historians have stressed slavery rather than states rights
in explaining the crisis of 1860 because they know that the legal position
of states rights has often sheltered Northerners and Southerners alike, depending on the more substantial interests it has been designed to protect.
Beard himself rejected Turner's stress on the importance of free land to
American development on the ground that though slavery, capitalism, and
free land were "woven in one national mesh," yet "slavery would have
been slavery and capitalism capitalism in essence even had there been
no free land with its accompaniments."[11] He could only arrive at this
conclusion by imaginatively breaking the web he considered "seamless."
(Even so, this procedure does not convincingly support Beard's thesis of
the Civil War as a necessary conflict between capitalism and agrarianism,
not only because the economic issue of the tariff had been gradually composed since 1832, but because it was during the competition for and debate over the western territories that relations between the sections became
embittered to a state of crisis out of which the war came.)

Sidney Hook has persuasively argued for the importance of hypotheticals contrary to fact in establishing the interrelation of events. Yet he admits that though we have the right to make such predictions when they rest upon valid generalizations about individual and social behavior, still "we have no logical guarantee that they will continue to hold or that something new and completely unforeseen will not crop up . . ."[12] The difficulty is that in dealing from a hypothetical point of view with a particular series of events we are assuming that it will not be intersected by other seemingly unrelated series of events. For this reason our calculations, even at their best, may be "well grounded and reliable but not certain." Is the process sound enough to justify our saying that slavery was the cause of the Civil War if by assuming its absence we could reasonably demonstrate there would have been no armed conflict? We would then have to show that none of the other issues between the sections was intractable or explosive enough to generate war. The problem is that slavery was so entangled with the other grievances of a political, economic, and social character that it is artificial to separate it out, nor do we have at hand a confirmed set of generalizations about the causes of war to apply. Whatever our calculations might be, we could not satisfy the unknowns in the formula "if *a* and *only a,* then *b* and *only b.*" We might well grant that though the North fought for the Union, and the South for the right of secession, still it was slavery which menaced the Union and needed Southern independence to protect its growth; even so, we could only conclude that the war was essentially fought *about* slavery, not that it was *produced* by it.

The hypothetical method of discovering causal relevance has awkward difficulties whenever the issues become complex. The historian is trained to think with respect to documentary evidence, which exists only for what did happen, not for what would have happened. He can reflect upon what might have happened in order better to evaluate what actually did happen, but to speculate on what would have happened often puts him in the position of building his hypothesis on a nest of bottomless boxes of untestable hypotheses. It is clear that the historian may sensibly ask if slavery might have expanded into the newly acquired territories in the 1850's and after. Whether or not Americans were quarrelling about "an imaginary Negro in an impossible place" has turned on a discussion of the relevance of a staple-crop system inappropriate to the arid lands of the West, the potential use of slavery in mining, the expansionist ambitions of Southerners, or the fears of some future technological invention as potent as the cotton gin in bolstering slavery.[13] The question serves to highlight the possibilities contained within the situation of crisis, and it has a bearing on the historian's appreciation of the Republicans' position of containment of slavery.

Doubt over the significance of an event tends to generate the conditional query as a way of resolving it. If the historian wonders why the South seceded after Lincoln's election, he might ask himself what would have happened if Senator Douglas had been elected. Since Southern Democrats had already rejected Douglas at the Charleston Convention, they *might* have found him intolerable as president. The historian cannot be sure, but the question points up the South's demands and highlights the importance to Southern eyes of Lincoln's being the leader of a sectional party committed to containment of slavery. Since men who act in history must calculate the possible consequences of various alternatives, the historian in trying to understand them is led to do the same. Questions of what would have happened can be answered, of course, only by judgments of probability based on knowledge of the actual situation. They emphasize the significance of certain happenings without pretending to an impossible certainty, specificity, or scope.

A merely utopian conditional question allows equally plausible but contradictory answers. It has, for example, been argued that if the North had let the South secede in peace, the two nations would have enjoyed future friendly relations, thus saving the terrible costs of war.[14] It is not surprising that a Southerner might find this assumption convincing, but it clearly includes too many imponderables to justify any firm judgment. To raise questions that cannot be reasonably answered is an exercise in futility unless they are treated only as the indirect means of drawing attention to elements of an actual situation. Asking what would have happened if the North had "let the erring sister go," only serves to force a weighing of Lincoln's policy reasons for holding a symbol of federal authority in the South, as well as of the nationalistic sentiments of the Northerners who supported him. Provided the historian maintains his primary interest in what actually did happen, he may with propriety, under certain conditions, ask what might have happened or what would have happened. Such questions are especially useful for evaluating policy.

The most frequent type of historical explanation usually appears in causal disguise, which helps account for the historian's reluctance to banish the idea of cause. *Cause* often functions as *reason* or *purpose*. Explanation in terms of purpose is the natural way participants in a situation account for what happens. Thus the interpretations of the Civil War that prevailed at the time were couched by the North in terms of the aims of a "conspiracy" of aggressive slave-holders and by the South in terms of the ambitions of a radical group of abolitionist "Black Republicans." These simple theses were too obviously partisan charges of blame to find acceptance by later historians, whose professional confidence is rightly based on the principle that those who come after an event can.

with the help of emotional distance, awareness of consequences, and wider perspective, know more about it than any participants. But even later historians have extensively used the language of purpose. The "revisionist" thesis of a needless war produced by "blundering states-manship" essentially interprets the war in that way, as the consequence of human judgments and passions, though it condemns them as "irrational."

The historian cannot dispense with "cause" in this sense because, as Becker put it, "men's actions have value and purpose; and if we write his-tory in such a way as to give it meaning and significance we have to take account of these values and purposes, to explain *why* men behave as they do, what they aim to accomplish, and whether they succeed or not."[15] The critic might well say that a man's purpose may not be the cause of his action—yet apart from this "humanistic" concern history threatens to become a merely impersonal process which "might have occurred at any time and in any place, given a sufficient number of person to operate the events."[16] It is this intense commitment to the purposive dimension of history which leads many historians to feel a strong sympathy with literature and a sullen suspicion of social science. The occasional philistinism and arrogance of some propagandists for the social sciences have made many historians understandably defensive.

Yet in cooler moments the humanistic historian must acknowledge that this purposive dimension does not exhaust history. Historians have also been keenly interested in the explanatory relevance to American history of such relatively impersonal factors as De Tocqueville's "equality of condition," Turner's "frontier hypothesis," Beard's "capitalism and agrari-anism," Potter's "abundance," and Hartz's "atomistic social freedom." These explanations need not be antagonistic when they are formulated without monistic claims. Turner, despite the dogmatism of his famous essay, was committed in principle to a "multiple hypothesis" approach; Beard was increasingly led to modify the monistic and deterministic implications of his economic interpretation; and both Potter and Hartz have explicitly repudiated the sufficiency of a single-determinant explana-tion.[17] The force of these various theories lies in their capacity to illumi-nate structure and continuity in American history, as demonstrated by specific historical illustrations, numerous enough to give significance to the generalizations. As such, they are not so much "causes" of specific events as they are ways of segregating out long-term conditions and tendencies of American culture and development. They give contour and meaning to the stream of events insofar as the historical evidence supports the generalizations.

The causal problem becomes acute when the historian faces the task of explaining a complex series of events which have the ideal unity of a

single event, like the Civil War. The general causal question is then
propounded: what was "the fundamental cause" of the event? The notorious disparity of opinion on the answer to this question should suggest
that there is some fallacy in seeking to find a prime mover that can be
abstracted from the process to account for it, like slavery, rival economic
systems, or the "blundering statesmanship" of agitators and leaders. None
of these alleged fundamental causes can be understood apart from their
specific historical context, nor could any person be said to understand
the Civil War who only knew that its fundamental cause was any or all
of these things. Otherwise history would merely be a cook-book for those
sworn to fasting. These judgments of fundamental causality are only retrospective assessments of a reconstructed story and never a substitute for
it. Actually they should be taken only as clues to the story being told.
The pragmatic meaning of the assertion that slavery was "the fundamental cause" is only that the institution was so deeply entangled in the
issues that divided the sections that provides a valuable focus for examining the skein of events which culminated in war.

The historian does his work in good conscience, despite the difficulties
of causality, because so much of his labor does not depend upon causal
judgment. Whatever some philosophers may say, he knows that explanation is broader than causal explication. He may tell his readers much
about the issues between Lincoln and Douglas, the legal status of
slavery, the structure of classes in society, the economic interests of the
sections, the character of the abolitionist movement, the balance of power
in the Senate, the social and ideological differences between North and
South, and the chronology of events without venturing beyond descriptive
analysis into causal judgment. Characteristically, the historian explains
by showing how a certain process took shape, answering the "why" with
more of the "what" and "how." The careful, thorough and accurate answer
to the question How," writes the English historian C. V. Wedgwood,
"should take the historian a long way towards answering the question
Why . . ."[18] The historian is inescapably committed to narrative.

The relativists may quickly point out that the stories historians have
told clearly reflect the "climate of opinion" in which they were constructed. Beard's economic interpretation grew out of a Progressive
milieu in which the critics of industrial America had been drawn increasingly to economic analysis of contemporary problems; the "revisionism"
of J. G. Randall betrayed some of the liberals' disillusionment with World
War I and the fear of involvement with World War II; Arthur M.
Schlesinger, Jr.'s criticism of the "revisionist" thesis of "a needless war"
openly compares the Nazi and Southern threats to an "open society" and
reflects the post-war "hard" policy towards Soviet imperialism; and Avery

Craven's latest analysis, a modified "revisionist" view, strikes a Cassandra pose by comparing the Civil War crisis to the frightening "cold war" situation of today, where huge power-blocs compete for "satellites" and are deeply estranged from mutual understanding.[19] Inevitably, the historian's experience of present history will suggest questions and hypotheses, and in the attempt to relate his story to his public he will naturally try to find terms appropriate to his own age. Yet he must always be on guard against the insidious tendency of analogy to blur the important nuances of difference between a past age and his own. His fundamental premise as a historian must be that human experience significantly changes in its form and meaning, that his present is only a phase of a process which calls for historical analysis precisely because it is not uniform and continuous. The historian may believe that while one generation passes away and another generation comes, the earth abides forever, but it is his special obligation to note that the sun also rises on a new day.

The relativism of Becker and Beard was a valuable attack on the pretensions of nineteenth-century historical positivism, but its force was blunted by remnants of the same determinism they challenged. Becker considered historical judgments transient and arbitrary because he saw the mind of the historian as a mere product of the social forces active in his setting, projecting onto the blank screen of the past his own image, shaped by the hopes and fears generated by his "climate of opinion." Beard was nostalgic for the dream of an omniscient grasp of the totality of all happenings. He knew the dream was utopian; therefore, he settled instead for an "act of faith" in historical progress towards a specific future as the basis for interpretation of the past, a prediction which future history would validate or refute. But one must reply: if involvement in present history gives the historian his need to know the past, it does not necessarily prevent him from having enough detachment to apply articulate and impersonal standards to the evidence he examines; if the historian cannot know everything, it does not follow that he cannot know anything of historical importance; if the future is opaque, the past cannot be illuminated from a source which, being still indeterminate, will not furnish any light; if the historian is truly honored, it is because of his power of hindsight, not his power of prophecy.

If historians seem to have rented out a large hotel of "rooms with a view" in order to tell their story of the Civil War, it should be remembered that the sign out front should often read, "philosophy, not history, spoken here." Much of the recent debate over the Civil War centers on philosophical issues about economic determinism or rationalist politics. The historical materialists reduce the political, ideological, and moral questions to the "inevitable" conflicts of classes in society; the "revisionists" assume that violence is abnormal and that an event as bloody and tragic as civil war must have been avoided by "rational" men; their critics point to the intractability of moral issues and the normality of non-rational factors in history.[20] Historians cannot escape such philosophical questions, but they need not entail a skepticism about historical truth.

The philosophy of history in America, as Morton G. White has pointed out, has been a very poor relation indeed. (Not even the Pragmatists, who did much to stimulate interest in history, paid it the honor of systematic attention. It is therefore encouraging that Mr. White should seek to lead philosophers to consider the "special kind of discourse" which is narration.)[21] The causal problem would be greatly clarified if both historians and philosophers realized that in telling a story the historian is committed to the "logic" of drama. In explaining the Civil War he necessarily seeks to recreate the strife of opposing forces out of which the war came. The connective tissue of his account then has a dialectical form: a person or group takes a position and performs an action because of and in relation to the position or action of another person or group. The historian's story becomes a narrative of this reciprocal response. Thus, by a crude sketch, the explanation of the event would have this character: Lincoln saw in the South's pro-slavery position a threat to the democratic traditions of the American community; the South saw in his election the menace of future interference with their "peculiar institution" and growing domination by an industrial North; Lincoln and the North saw in Southern secession a challenge to federal authority and the prestige of national union; the South saw in the provisioning of Fort Sumter an intolerable danger to independence of the Confederacy . . . In such terms, but with much greater riches and concreteness, the historian tries to reconstruct the dramatic "logic" of a sequence of events which demands to be humanly understood rather than scientifically explained.

This dialectical method does not entail any Hegelian scheme or "bloodless dance of the categories"; on the contrary, it keeps the historian in touch with the familiar existential world of human action, too concrete and passionate for final abstract accounting. Like the action of a novel or play, it can be imaginatively experienced as a meaningful plot in which character, events, and circumstances are woven together in a process made intelligible in human terms of tradition, interest, passion, purpose, and policy. This kind of historical action is understood in the same way as a novel's plot is understood, though the former must be faithful to given evidence and the latter to aesthetic standards. To ask the question "why?" is then meaningful only as a demand for enlightenment on some particular passage of the story which does not "make sense." The general causal question remains at worst an irrelevant basis for interminable disagreement, at best a generator of hypotheses to stimulate research which may promote understanding by leading to a richer, more coherent story.

In reconstructing the dramatic "logic" of a situation which eventuated in civil war, historians cannot expect to achieve a flawless coherence in their stories. They have no warrant for making history neat and tidy when experience itself has ambiguities. Often there is uncertainty about motives, even for the actor himself, because the flaw lies not in the historian's impotence but in the documents or life itself. Even if historians cannot agree, to cite a classic controversy created by conflicting evidence, whether Lincoln sent a relief ship to Sumter in the cunning expectation that the South would commit aggression by firing on the fort, or, on the contrary, discovered by the attack how inaccurately he had measured the secessionist temper, nevertheless, they can still reach a common understanding of his policy reasons for risking war in the first place, whatever he expected or hoped would happen, after he had done what he felt had to be done.[22] Historians will never escape the need for critical debate on their findings to help them move towards a consensus of understanding, but this fate is no ground for despair. It is rather the dogmatic insistence on scientific explanations, especially when they are beyond historical competence, that dooms historians to endless and fruitless contention.

Mr. White prophesies "a new era in the philosophy of history" when "the tools of linguistic philosophy" shall be brought to bear on "clarifying the logic of narration."[23] Sharp as these instruments are, however, they involve the risk that the operation may kill the patient. In explaining narration it may be forgotten that narration is a form of explanation, which aims not at logical rigor of implication but at dramatic comprehensibility, appropriate to the untidy, passionate, and value-charged activities of men. Historians may be said to be engaged in constantly teaching that lesson, yet, as much of the long inconclusive debate about "the causes of the Civil War" makes clear, without really knowing it. It is time they directly confronted the specter that haunts them.

# Sociologist as Historian / *Carl N. Degler*

I T SEEMS TO BE either the fate or the opportunity of historians to be checking on how others use history. For it is the non-historians who write the broad interpretations of the American past. In the 1940s it was philosophers like Herbert Schneider and Ralph Barton Perry who ranged over the whole of American history and told us what it meant. More recently, in the 1950s, the sociologists have taken their turn. The most notable of several works by sociologists[1] is *The Lonely Crowd*, by David Riesman and others.[2] It is true, of course, that the primary object of that book is to analyze the nature of modern American society, not to reconstruct our past. Yet in the course of the work, if only as a bench mark from which to triangulate, as it were, the social dimensions of our own time, Riesman has set forth, or assumed, a rather definite picture of the society of the nineteenth century.

Because the book has become widely known—it is now available in at least two paperback editions—its presentation of the American past invites examination. After all, for the many Americans who have read it, Riesman's conception *is* the past. For that reason alone it is worth asking whether his conception has historical validity. Furthermore, since one of Riesman's conclusions is that the American character has changed between the nineteenth and twentieth centuries, an examination of the validity of his view of the nineteenth century has an important bearing upon the nature of the national character. At the outset, though, it should be understood that this examination is not concerned with the book's primary interest in the nature of the twentieth-century Americans; it deals only with the society of the nineteenth century as depicted in *The Lonely Crowd*.

As is well known, *The Lonely Crowd* describes a new type of social personality emerging in America and in the rest of the modern industrialized world. This is the other-directed man. In the nineteenth century, the argument goes, the ruling social character of people was innerdirection. The book deals with "the way in which one kind of social

Carl N. Degler, "The Sociologist as Historian: Riesman's The Lonely Crowd," American Quarterly, XV (Winter, 1963), 483–97. Reprinted by permission.

character, which dominated America in the nineteenth century is gradually replaced by a social character of quite a different sort."[3] To be
perfectly accurate, and despite this quotation, it should be said that the
inner-directed person, as Riesman conceives of him, is not strictly a historically rooted figure, limited to the nineteenth century. Inner-directed
people exist today and there were other-directed personalities in the
nineteenth century. But as the foregoing quotation and other material
in the early pages of the book makes clear, Riesman sees Americans of
the nineteenth and twentieth centuries differing to the degree they are
dominated by inner- or other-direction. Hence, for all intents and purposes, and despite the admitted and deliberate looseness with which
Riesman applies his categories, he sees a change through time in the
American character. The inner-directed personality dominated the nineteenth century and the other-directed has increasingly dominated the
twentieth.

One other general statement needs to be made before we turn to an
examination of Riesman's conception of nineteenth-century American
society. Despite the breadth of Riesman's canvas, he writes about and
confines his assertions to the American middle class. The culture of the
working class is ignored and, even though he is dealing with a nineteenth-
century society that was largely agricultural, he limits his attention almost
entirely to urban life. Such a restriction raises the question of whether
his description of nineteenth-century life is representative. But that is
another question; the analysis here is addressed to those aspects of the
nineteenth century he has elected to deal with.

Since Riesman at no one place in his book sets forth his conception of
the society of the nineteenth century, his view has to be pieced together
from scatered references throughout the book. At times, especially in
discussing Riesman's conception of nineteenth-century politics, it will be
possible to offer, concomitantly, some criticisms of his interpretation. In
any case, once his image of the nineteenth century had been delineated,
then it will be examined for its congruency with the historian's conception of that period.

Riesman's view of the past is on a grand scale. During the era of the
Renaissance and Reformation, he writes, there was a transition from the
tradition-directed man to the inner-directed. The former is a person
guided and channeled in his activities and thought by his society; simply
because things have always been done in a given way they should still
be performed that way. Tradition-directed man has played little part in
America because the colonies were settled only after the emergence of
the inner-directed man. This second type of social personality is typically
self-reliant, self-confident, clear about his goals and objects in life. Seven-

teenth-century Puritans are the classic examples of inner-directed persons: outwardly energetic, tough-minded, self-determined, yet inwardly concerned with moral renovation. "They tend to feel, throughout life that their characters are something to be worked on."[4] Because they derive the justification for their actions from within themselves (hence the term inner-directed), "loneliness and even persecution are not thought of as the worst of fates. Parents, sometimes even teachers may have crushing moral authority, but the peer-group has less moral weight, glamorous or menacing though it may be."[5] Translated into more familiar words, the inner-directed personality is individualistic and self-reliant.

In *The Lonely Crowd* the decisive, ruthless, brusque, self-confident robber baron is taken as typical of the nineteenth century. If an inner-directed person "founded a firm, this was his lengthened shadow."[6] In those days, Riesman writes, "it is fair to say that the human mood of the work force was not yet felt to be a major problem." Instead employers concerned themselves with getting out the goods and not with the people who worked or consumed the goods. In short, as a society, the inner-directed were more concerned with production than consumption, more with things than with people. "It was the product itself, . . . not the use made of it by the consumer that commanded attention. Despite what Mark called 'the fetishism of commodities,' the inner-directed man could concern himself with the product without himself being a good consumer; he did not need to look at himself through the customer's eyes."[7] In substance, the economy of the nineteenth century was "quite loose-jointed and impersonal and perhaps seemed even more impersonal than it actually was."[8]

It was the involvement with things, instead of people, which underlay the pervasive impersonality of the nineteenth century. That century was symbolized, Reisman contends, by the bank account, while the modern business world is summed up in the expense account.[9] The glad hand has taken the place of the old devotion to craftsmanship and the product. Instead of the corps of public relations advisors, labor counselors, and advertising men that modern business requires in dealing with people, "business firms until World War I," Riesman explains, "needed only three kinds of professional advice: legal, auditing, and engineering." And significantly, all three, he adds, were impersonal services.[10]

The inner-directed person of the nineteenth century was "job-minded" and clear about his goals.[11] The old Latin motto of the nineteenth century: "*Ad Astra Per Aspera*" has become, in our day, a "Milky Way" of multiple and changing goals.[12] Simply because his standards were internal, failure for the inner-directed man was possible without feelings of total inadequacy. Edison's example of trying again and again (presumably for the best substance for a light bulb filament) is the archetype of the inner-directed man.[13]

Work was hard, important, and different from play. As Riesman puts it: "The inner-directed businessman was not expected to have fun; indeed, it was proper for him to be gloomy and even grim."[14] Thus literature and other forms of entertainment were escape from work and problems; the other-directed man, however, cannot escape and so he uses popular culture for group adjustment.[15]

Since Riesman attaches great importance to upbringing in fixing social character, the life of the child in the age of inner-direction is discussed at some length. He sums up the differences in child-rearing practices in the three types of society by saying that in the tradition-directed home the child "propitiates" its parents; in the inner-directed age, he "fights or succumbs to them," and in the other-directed era, he "manipulates them and is in turn manipulated."[16] Like the man, the inner-directed child is "job-minded, even if the job itself is not clear in his mind." Today, "the future occupation of all moppets is to be skilled consumers."[17] The demand made of inner-directed children was that they work, study, pray, and save.[18] "Even boys from comfortable homes were expected until recently to hit the sunrise trail with paper routes or other economically profitable and 'character-building' chores."[19] The large size of the family in the era of inner-direction resulted in the older children harmlessly hazing the young ones and thus psychically toughening them.[20] But a large family did not mean that group activity was paramount in the life of the child. Instead, the inner-directed child was more likely to go off and read a book, for, as Riesman says, "in contrast with the lone reader of the era of inner-direction, we have the group of kids today, lying on the floor reading and trading comics and preferences among comics, or listening to 'The Lone Ranger.'"[21]

The school of the nineteenth century reflected the stern character of the home environment. The instructional emphasis was on intellectual activities and there was little emotional involvement for teacher or pupil. "The teacher is supposed to see that the children learn a curriculum, not that they enjoy it or learn group cooperation."[22] As befits a society bent upon production, the whole emphasis is on accomplishment and not on "internal group relations," or morale.[23]

Undoubtedly to anyone with a spark of inner-direction in his personality the nineteenth century as depicted in *The Lonely Crowd* is almost too good to be true. Riesman, to be sure, explicitly denies that he is making comparisons between paradise and paradise lost.[24] Nevertheless there is a golden glow suffusing the past, which is absent when the present is discussed; the trenchant realism with which the present is limned rarely penetrates the portrait of the past. Sometimes the past is almost shamelessly romanticized as in this passage: "As recently as 1920 an American boy of the middle class was not too worried about the problem of committing himself to a career. . . . He could dream of long-term goals because the mere problem of career entry and survival was not acute; that he might for long be out of a job did not occur to him."[25]

There was an integration and a meaning to life in those days absent in our own. Men were not under constant public scrutiny then as they are today and consequently they could be more themselves. "The inner-directed person reading a book alone, is less aware of the others looking on; moreover he has time to return at his own pace from being transported by his reading—to return and put on whatever mask he cares to."[26] Even sexual experience was more soundly grounded in the nineteenth century. Today, comments Riesman, sex is of engrossing interest to an other-directed person largely in order to afford him "reassurance that he is alive. The inner-directed person driven by his internal gyroscope and oriented toward the production problems of his outer world, did not need this evidence."[27]

It is in fitting the politics of the nineteenth century in his scheme that Riesman most romanticizes the past and in the process exaggerates its difference from the present.[28] In delineating the political outlook of the inner-directed, Riesman draws a picture of the nineteenth century that is at best misleading and, at worst, inaccurate. According to him the political apathy so characteristic of our day was wholly absent in the nineteenth century. "Cynicism toward politics as a whole (as against cynicism about democracy or bossism or other specific political form or usage) was virtually unknown. Indeed, a feeling prevailed in many circles that the millenium was near."[29] This picture, which has certain relevance for the age of Jackson, is hard to reconcile with the description of political life between the years 1865 and 1896 that emerged from the autobiography of Henry Adams, Ostrogorski's *Democracy and the Organization of Political Parties*, and Woodrow Wilson's *Congressional Government*.

Almost by definition in Riesman's analysis, William McKinley, because he was in office at the end of the nineteenth century, must be made out to be among the last of the inner-directed political leaders. As a consequence, in making the decision to take the nation into war in 1898, McKinley is contrasted with Franklin Roosevelt, who, in the age of other-direction, was in no position to make the decision himself, as McKinley had been, but was forced to wait upon the action of the enemy.[30] That McKinley's decision for war should be considered an example of inner-direction strikes the historian as strange. After all, wasn't it Theodore Roosevelt who said McKinley possessed no more backbone than a chocolate eclair? That description hardly comports with our image of the inner-directed man. And even in the particular instance of the decision to declare war McKinley does not emerge as a man of self-confidence and will. It is true that McKinley was in a position to make a decision between peace and war in a way that Franklin Roosevelt was not, but that was simply the result of different historical circumstances in the two instances. The manner of the decision had nothing to do with the approach to politics of two different character structures, as Riesman contends. It would seem more to the point that McKinley, for all his alleged inner-direction, acceded to the demands for war from his party and the public, despite his own wishes to preserve peace.[31] In short, in this instance McKinley acted like a man with an other-directed personality.

The style of Franklin Roosevelt's domestic leadership is also said to conform to that of the other-directed character structure. Today, Riesman argues, "what is called political leadership consists, as we could see in Roosevelt's case in the tolerant ability to manipulate coalitions."[32] That may be true, but the implication that such manipulation is a twentieth-century phenomenon is certainly false. American politics has always involved the creation and manipulation of coalitions, from Jefferson's with Aaron Burr, through Jackson's and Lincoln's down to John Kennedy's. Coalitions and their manipulation have been a function of our geographical extent and of the local character of our party structure rather than an innovation introduced by a change in the character structure of Americans.

One more observation on Riesman's analysis of nineteenth-century politics. "The bullet that killed McKinley," he writes, "marked the end of the days of explicit class leadership."[33] Presumably he means that business interests dominated politics in the forty years prior to McKinley's death, which may well be true, but the implication that leadership was carried on in the name of class is certainly not true. One has only to recall the changes which were rung upon James G. Blaine's presence at the millionaire's dinner at Delmonico's in 1884 to see how dangerous it was for a politician to seem to ally himself openly with the wealthy classes.

The ordinary citizen during these years, Riesman goes on, grounded his politics in self-interest and did not, as the other-directed man would, consult his "preferences and likings" in the voting booth.[34] Here, too, he seems to be wandering from the historical facts. If there is one thing we have learned about the Jacksonian period, for example, it is that the enthusiastic popular support of Jackson is largely inexplicable except in the language of charisma and mystique.[35] Moreover, as Richard Hofstadter has pointed out,[36] it was not until the utopian nostrums of Populism were defeated in 1896 that the farmer turned to a realistic appraisal of his own needs and came out for frankly self-interested devices like price supports and parity. And while we are on the subject of self-interest in politics, it is worth observing that probably no era has been more notable in this regard than the years since 1932, with appeals to labor, farmers, Negroes, senior citizens. And the reason is that our political parties, after all, for most of our history, not just in the nineteenth century, rather than being based on a few grand, differentiating principles, have been composed of diverse interest groups, frankly held in common allegiance by concrete appeals to self-interest. Was there really any more self-interest in the waving of the bloody shirt by the Republicans during the two decades after the Civil War than in the waving of the tattered shirt by the Democrats in the twenty years since the Great Depression? In substance, then, in attempting to highlight the other-directedness of our modern political practice, Riesman has felt compelled to see the practices of the nineteenth century in a relatively dimmer light. To the historian, though, the broad features of our political practice seem, at least since the day of the democratic upheaval associated with the name of Andrew Jackson, remarkably similar and persistent.

As the foregoing remarks imply, my dissatisfaction with the image of the nineteenth century portrayed in the pages of *The Lonely Crowd* is not simply its lack of realism. It extends to Riesman's assertion that there is a clear difference in social characteristics between the nineteenth and mid-twentieth centuries. The two periods simply are not that sharply differentiated. As is evident from the discussion on politics, the social characteristics of our time are often found to be present in the nineteenth century. The question therefore arises whether the origins of other-direction do not really go back much farther in our history than Riesman has been willing to recognize. I hesitate to put myself in the position of emulating those medievalists who have been pulling the Renaissance back into the Dark Ages, century by century, but, in effect, that is what I am suggesting. Let us look into other areas of nineteenth-century life for further evidence that other-direction began before the twentieth century.

Anyone who is familiar with Tocqueville's *Democracy in America* must, when he first examines Riesman's book, ask himself, "What is the difference between the other-directed man of the twentieth century and the majority-dominated man of the nineteenth of whom Tocqueville was so fearful?" As we read in Riesman's pages the persuasive descriptions of our own other-directed world, the observations of Tocqueville keep nagging at the periphery of our minds. We are tempted to ask, "Is not this other-directed man an old story in America?"

Riesman, to be sure, recognizes that Tocqueville may have seen the type first. He believes, however, that Tocqueville was describing not an other-directed man, but an inner-directed one who was being controlled by outside forces. In Jackson's time, he writes, the need for seeking the opinions of one's peers had not yet been internalized by society and parents.[37] Indeed, in two different places Riesman takes the evidence of Tocqueville and turns it to the support of his own thesis, observing that Jacksonian America was a kind of training ground, a beginning, as it were, for the later development of other-directed man.[38] The question immediately arises, how does Riesman know? From the printed word it is hard to tell whether these people of Tocqueville's time were "merely practising" or whether their attitudes were "embedded in their character."[39] Furthermore, the type was so common that Tocqueville was only the most perceptive of the travelers who reported it. But even if we leave this question aside, Riesman's casual disposal of Tocqueville's majority-dominated man is not quite convincing. If the men of Jacksonian America were in training for other-direction, as he suggests, what happened to them in the subsequent age of the robber barons, which, we have been assured, was the heyday of the inner-directed man?

Once possible answer, as has been suggested, is that in describing other-direction, Riesman is actually picturing the American character for most of its history; that the other-directed personality has dominated since at least Tocqueville's day and that it continued to do so even in that age of so-called rugged individualism—the second half of the nineteenth century. Lord Bryce, it is true, in his *American Commonwealth* denies that the fears of Tocqueville had been realized in the 1880s,[40] but elsewhere in his book he describes the American in a manner that gets very close to Riesman's conception of other-direction.[41] Furthermore, if we look at the number of traits that Riesman picks out as peculiar to the nineteenth century, inner-directed society, we see that, for almost all of them, large qualifications from the historical evidence have to be made.

Solidity of work and attention to production were certainly elements of the Old America, but the land speculator, the wildcat banker, the projector in general were as much a part of the American business scene as the better-remembered stodgy banker and the tight-fisted entrepreneur who sweated his laborers because he cared mainly for production. Was the primary form of entertainment in the nineteenth century really solitary reading? Were not the tears that flowed so profusely when Little Eva was lifted to heaven in performances of "Uncle Tom's Cabin" as much the result of a sentimental peer culture as are analogous reactions in our own time? Nor is the manipulation of children by parents and of husbands by wives novel or more acceptable today than it was in the nineteenth century. Tom Sawyer was beloved for his skill at getting a fence painted by manipulation and the point of James M. Barrie's play "What Every Woman Knows" was clearly that men are generally manipulated by their women. To say, as Riesman does,[42] that the inner-directed person of the nineteenth century "pursued clear acquisition and consumption goals with a fierce individualism," is to ignore the suffocating popularity of Currier and Ives prints and Rogers statuary groups of that day. Furthermore, as Russell Lynes has shown, the mediocrity of taste so common in the nineteenth century was often deliberately cultivated as well as pervasive.[43] And what, one must ask, was the mission of the celebrated Sir Joseph Duveen but the education of "individualistic" robber barons to appreciate the "right" things in art?

Although Riesman's description of the child in the age of inner-direction, aside from its somewhat unrealistic tone, comports with that generally held by many today, it squares not at all with the picture drawn by historians of the American family. The research which has been done in this field, it is true, is slight indeed. It is now almost half a century since Arthur Calhoun produced his three-volume *Social History of the American Family*, and, though for its time it was a remarkable piece of work, it is now clearly unsatisfactory, both in its naive approach to social forces and in its inept synthesis of the materials. Calhoun's chapter on "The Career of the Child"[44] has almost no point of contact with the view of the inner-directed child presented by Riesman. Freedom of the child from parental control is the theme of Calhoun's chapter, and that freedom began before the Civil War. Almost all of his numerous excerpts from sources speak of the lack of discipline in the American family of the period and of the great attention and consideration given children by adults. This lack of discipline in the family is evident in Hugo Münsterberg's *American Traits*,[45] published at the turn of the century. His chapter on education in America seems to belie the picture of strictness of discipline and attention to the curriculum that Riesman spreads on his pages. Indeed, Münsterberg's chapter reads like Arthur Bestor discussing modern progressive education. The family is urged by Münsterberg to be stern enough to support the discipline of the school. And, as in our own time, the parents are strongly cautioned against complaining to the teacher that the amount of homework is excessive—a clear indication that parents were doing just that. At best such examples are no more than suggestive. One of the obvious tasks of social historians for the future would be a study of the American family in the age of alleged inner-direction. At the moment, though, my suspicion is that the similarity of practices in the nineteenth century with those today in our so-called other-directed society would be startling and quite disturbing to those who discern a sharp social distinction between the two periods.

One of the distinctive marks of the other-directed society, Riesman asserts, is the self-restraint placed on the exercise of power.[46] By implication, then, the nineteenth century was the age when power was frankly and freely used. But was it? Certainly from the private correspondence of business leaders of the time we know that some men, in a position to do so, often refused to use their power. In his book *Railroad Leaders*, Thomas Cochran gives a striking example. In the 1850s, long before there were threats of government regulation, railroad presidents settled damage suits outside of court for more than was necessary merely to keep public good will[47]—just as a corporation might do today when other-direction and concern for consumers supposedly rule. Moveover, as Edward Kirland has suggested, the much discussed robber barons were not as thick-skinned and steady of nerve as our conventional history makes them out to be.[48]

Perhaps the most significant insight that Riesman has brought to a comparison of the nineteenth and twentieth centuries is that the former was concerned with production and the latter is largely oriented toward the consumer. In large part, that conception of the nineteenth century has been fostered by historians themselves, who, in their texts, have emphasized, in discussions of the economy, steel mill construction, railroad building and the like. Too often, though, they have ignored the enormous expansion of consumer industries in the last thirty years of the nineteenth century.

One piece of evidence for thinking that the late nineteenth-century economy was concerned with consumption is the boom in advertising. As David Potter has pointed out,[49] advertising is the classic institution of the consumer society. Advertising in newspapers alone tripled between 1867 and 1880 and then doubled by 1890. In 1900, almost $96 million was being spent on advertising in newspapers, an increase of over 1,000 per cent since 1867.[50] Many firms by the 1890s were already devoting substantial proportions of their revenues to advertising. Monarch bicycle, then in the midst of the advertising-created bicycle craze, spent between 4 and 5 per cent of its income on advertising; in the dry goods industry, 2.5 to 5 per cent was a common figure. Packaged cereals were the creation of advertising in the 1880s; thus it is not surprising that a reported 28 per cent of sales revenues went into advertising.[51] One contemporary authority on advertising in the period estimated that in 1898 something like half a billion dollars was spent on advertising in the United States each year.[52] Of a gross national product of about $17.3 billion, advertising thus constituted 2.8 per cent; in 1956, advertising expenditures were $9.9 billion in a GNP of $419 billion, or 2.4 per cent—a smaller proportion, it will be noted, than the figure for the late 1890s. The continuity between that period and our own is brought home by two examples of advertising. One was a complaint against advertising published in 1900: "Many are the instances in which the demand for new goods or for a particular brand of old goods has been built up from nothing by continuous advertising. The advertiser cultivates wants."[53] The other was a caption under an advertisement for porcelain-lined bathtubs in 1890. It read: "Ask your wife if she would like to bathe in a china dish, like her canary does."[54] When the percentages of GNP and lapses in grammar then and now are so similar, the differences between the periods cannot be as great as we have supposed.

The importance of advertising is one indication that attention to production was not the overriding consideration Riesman would lead us to believe; another is the history of consumer industries at the end of the nineteenth century. As Alfred Chandler Jr. has shown, the growth of a great firm like the American Tobacco Company under J. B. Duke was dependent upon close attention to the consumer. Tobacco production by the 1880s was far outrunning demand and only the reorganization of marketing procedures and large-scale advertising made possible the expansion of the business. Armour and Swift with their imaginative attention to distribution created a market for frozen beef where none existed before; William Clark, to name only one more of a number that could be cited, did the same for Singer Sewing Machine.[55] The emphasis on the consumer is further evident in the famous slogans and trademarks of the day, some of which are still potent and familiar and all of which were vital in the development of their respective enterprises: "99 44/100 Per Cent Pure," "Children Cry For it," "The Beer That Made Milwaukee Famous," "Uneeda Biscuit," and above all, Eastman's "Kodak," and the slogan, "You Press the Button and We Do the Rest."[56]

The question which this essay sought to answer was simply: "is the picture of the nineteenth century which Riesman presents historically valid?" To that question, the answer must be "no." At the very least, Riesman confuses several tendencies of the nineteenth century. Thus the commitment to political activity of the Jacksonian era is projected without warrant through the rest of the century while the individualistic "the public be damned" stereotype of the robber baron of the 1880s is, equally without warrant, taken as typical of the American character in the previous seventy-five years. Furthermore, the historical evidence just does not sustain the kind of sharp division between the political, social, and economic practices of the society of the nineteenth and twentieth centuries; instead there is a marked continuity.

That conclusion, though, raises some further questions. That there are marked similarities between the social character of the two centuries suggests that perhaps the kind of categories that Riesman advances— inner-direction and other-direction—may be totally inadequate for purposes of historical analysis and should therefore be discarded. Riesman himself, by saying that the two character structures co-exist in both periods, has encouraged us, in a sense, to reach such a conclusion. Indeed, that admission has caused some historians to argue that his thesis, therefore, is not a historical thesis at all. But from the way that Riesman actually employs these terms in his book—he consistently, for example, attaches one of them to evidence drawn from the nineteenth century and the other to evidence from the twentieth—it is clear that he is dealing with change. And change is certainly one of the primary concerns of all historians. But, it might be objected, even if the historical character of Riesman's approach is conceded, can the historian validly use such broad categories to describe a nation that is made up of many different regions, classes, and ethnic groups? Here, too, I think Riesman's approach must be judged worthwhile for the historian. The reason for thinking so, without going into any detail, is the same as that which justifies the conception of national character. Not all students of American society, to be sure, accept that conception, but there certainly are a sufficient number who do to make it meaningful and worth exploring.[57]

If one accepts the concept of national character but rejects Riesman's assertion of a significant difference between the social character of the nineteenth and twentieth centuries, what conclusion is one to draw? As has been suggested, the soundest conclusion seems to be that what Riesman has called the central feature of the modern American character —other-direction—is, in fact, the dominant element in our national character through most of our history. There may be some accentuation of certain aspects of it in our own time, but what Tocqueville designated in the 1830s as "*democratie*" is essentially what Riesman means by other-direction. Rather than a changing American character, the evidence suggests a remarkably stable one, at least since the early years of the nineteenth century.

# The Limits of Social Science / *Arthur Schlesinger, Jr.*

Lᴇᴛ ᴍᴇ, first, express my great pleasure in being here. An historian among sociologists, I fear, is a case of an inferior Daniel cast into a den of superior lions; but my natural anxiety in facing this assemblage is outweighed tonight by the satisfaction I have in being permitted to join this tribute to your president—a tribute which the humanist claims the right to share along with the card-holding empirical social researcher. However much one may occasionally differ with Paul Lazarsfeld—and even more, on occasion, with the Lazarsfeldians—one must acknowledge both the brilliance and charm of the man and the notable stimulus the sociologist has provided to all students, humane as well as behavioral, of social processes. I might add that whenever I encounter Paul Lazarsfeld, I recognize the truth of an old adage much cherished by historians: that, inside every sociologist, there is an humanist struggling to get out.

As an historian, I am naturally strongly prejudiced in favor of empirical social research. If I understand this term correctly, it refers, I take it, to two things: first, to gaining the most complete possible factual knowledge about events which have already taken place; and, second, to devising inquiries and experiments which, by enlarging our knowledge about present and future events, may enlarge our understanding of social and human processes in general. No historian can possibly deny the value of empirical social research in both senses: such research is the stuff by which historians live—and by which, I may add, we too often live carelessly and irresponsibly. I am well aware how dismally written history lacks in rigor, how impressionistic the historian's analysis so often is, how imprecise his generation, how loose his language, how literary his whole style of attack. Insofar as empirical social research can drive historians to criticize their assumptions, to expose their premises, to tighten their logic, to pursue and respect their facts, to restrain their rhetoric—in short, insofar as it gives them an acute sense of the extraordinary precarious-

"The Humanist Looks at Empirical Social Research" by Arthur Schlesinger, Jr. *American Sociological Review*, XXVII (December, 1962), 768–771. Reprinted by permission. Remarks presented before the fifty-seventh annual meeting of the American Sociological Association in Washington D.C., August 31, 1962.

ness of the historical enterprise—it administers a wholly salutary shock to a somewhat uncritical and even complacent discipline.

I would wish everything else I have to say this evening about empirical social research to be construed in the light of this *cri de coeur*. But I know that you have not come tonight to hear how wonderful empirical social research is. Let me therefore conclude this part of my remarks by quickly entering these two points into the record: first, my indebtedness as an historian to the sociologists who have so vastly broadened my own intellectual horizons and refined my own conception of the historical enterprise; and, second, my own intense awareness of the shortcomings, epistemological and methodological, of the enterprise. Let me now pass on to the question whether, granted all this, empirical social research in the sense used by sociologists is *the* key to social knowledge.

This question, it should now be clear, has to do, not with the value of empirical social research *per se,* but with what one must call the *mystique* of empirical social research—the notion that it is, not one of several paths to social wisdom, but the central and infallible path. And this question derives particularly from the extent to which empirical social research is taken by its practitioners to mean, above all, *quantitative* research—that is, research which deals in quantifiable problems and yields numerical or quasi-numerical conclusions.

Again I do not want to be misunderstood. No historian can deny that quantitative research, complete with IBM cards and computers, can make an important contribution to historical understanding—no historian, that is, who has examined, for example, a recent production by the historical branch of the Lazarsfeld family *Massachusetts Shipping, 1697–1714,* by the Bailyns. Yet the problem remains: does quantitative research provide the best way of solving significant historical problems?

Your president raised one aspect of this question in a stimulating article in the Winter 1950–1951 issue of the *Public Opinion Quarterly* entitled "The Obligations of the 1950 Pollster to the 1984 Historian." Paul Lazarsfeld proposed here that public opinion data can be of inestimable use to the future historian in defining the 'prevailing values' of a society and in charting the interaction between ideas and social action as well as in analyzing specific events like elections. Similarly, Hadley Cantril in his indispensable survey *Public Opinion, 1935–1946* suggests how useful historians would have found a similar compilation of public opinion polls covering such confused and turbulent epochs of history as the American or French Revolution or the Civil War.

At first, the thought of the availability of such materials is deeply attractive. Yet, on reflection, I wonder whether the existence of public opinion data would, in the end, cause us to write the history of these epochs very differently. What does a public opinion poll report? It reports essentially, I would suppose, what people think they think. It does not report what people really think, because people ordinarily don't know what they really think in advance of a situation which compels them to act on the basis of their thoughts. Public opinion polling, in short, elicits essentially an *irresponsible* expression of opinion—irresponsible because no action is intended to follow the expression. The expression of opinion is not given weight or substance by a sense of accountability for consequences; when that sense of accountability enters, then the expression may very likely be different.

Irresponsible opinion is certainly of interest. It may well tell us a great deal about the general atmosphere of a period. But it is responsible opinion—opinion when the chips are down, opinion which issues directly in decision and action—which is relevant to the historical process and of primary interest to the historian. And public opinion polls do not add greatly to our own knowledge of the evolution and distribution of responsible opinion. The measure of responsible opinion is not answers, but acts. As an experienced student of these matters, Harry S Truman, once put it, "I think the best poll there is is the count after election."

Polls catch public opinion in a plastic, unfinished, and superficial state, while the historian is concerned with opinion under the stress of decision, opinion as it is crystallized by events and leadership and brought to bear at points of political and intellectual action. The difference between expression without responsibility and expression under responsibility raises problems which go to the root of the whole question of assent. Cardinal Newman's old distinction between "notional assent" and "real assent" represents one salient aspect of the problem involved in the difference between "public opinion" in the polls and "public opinion" in the historical process.

Why does a political leader make a decision? The decision is generally the result of an accommodation between his own views of what is wise and the *felt* pressures on him as to what is possible. The crux of the matter is that the pressures are felt; they are politically kinetic pressures, not inert or latent attitudes. Only a crude politician construes felt pressures in terms of lobbies and pressure groups; a statesman is attuned by his own radar to a whole turmoil of public sentiment; he knows that, by action and by leadership, he can to some degree generate the pressures which will propel him along the course he has already chosen to go. Public opinion data can no doubt provide a kind of measure of his success in marshalling opinion. But his actions and the effective response to them provide a far more reliable measure. Nor do current attempts to evaluate the intensity with which opinions are held really meet the question, since they do not abolish the essential difference between responsible and irresponsible opinion. For this reason, I doubt whether full Gallup, Roper,

Michigan, and Harris dossiers on the American or French Revolutions would radically change the historian's view of these historic events. The best poll there is remains the count after election—not what people say they think, but what they do.

Polls represent only one aspect of the attempt to quantify historical data. A number of excellent historians—Sir Lewis Namier and his followers in Great Britain and certain American scholars under the spell of behavioral sciences—have mounted more general attacks on classic historical questions in a formidable effort to make them surrender to quantitative soutions. This effort has a pervading complex of assumptions —that the role of human purposes, ideas and ideals in social action is vastly overrated; that history can, in effect, be reduced to a set of social, ethnic, and economic tropisms; and that the quantitative method can transform the historian into a detached and "scientific" observer. But there seem to me two main troubles with this effort—with an effort, for example, to solve quantitatively the problem of the causes of the Civil War. One is that most of the variables in an historical equation are not susceptible to commensurable quantification; the other is that the observer is too mixed up with the phenomena observed to eliminate the subjective element.

When Sir Lewis Namier condemns the tendency to exaggerate "the importance of the conscious will and purpose in individuals," he holds forth the possibility of a form of historical certitude—but he does so by dismissing a whole range of historical issues which happen not to be susceptible to quantification. This seems to me the essential trick of the quantitative approach. That approach claims a false precision by the simple strategy of confining itself to the historical problems and materials with which quantitative techniques can deal—and ignoring all other questions as trivial. The *mystique* of empirical social research, in short, leads its acolytes to accept as significant only the questions to which the quantitative magic can provide answers. As an humanist, I am bound to reply that almost all important questions are important precisely because they are *not* susceptible to quantitative answers. The humanist, let me repeat, does not deny the value of the quantitative method. What he denies is that it can handle everything which the humanist must take into account; what he condemns is the assumption that things which quantitative methods can't handle don't matter.

I would suggest that these are the things that matter most. Nor can one accept the answer that it is all a temporary shortcoming of method— that improvements in technique will soon extend the sway of the quantitative approach until it can subdue all problems. My old friend Professor B. F. Skinner tells us that this is so—and warns us that we must face the consequences. I would not assume that Professor Skinner speaks for all behavioral scientists, but I do feel that he has pursued the logic of the behavioral approach with admirable candor to an ultimate conclusion. His conclusion is briefly that "the application of the methods of science to human affairs" is increasingly and irrevocably "at odds with the traditional democratic conception of man" and "the so-called 'democratic philosophy' of human behavior." The more we understand about human behavior, Professor Skinner tells us, the less we can credit to man himself:

as such explanations become more and more comprehensive, the contribution which may be claimed by the individual himself appears to approach zero. Man's vaunted creative powers, his original accomplishments in art, science and morals, his capacity to choose and our right to hold him responsible for the consequences of his choice—none of these is conspicuous in this new self-portrait.

Where the democratic view assumes a measure, however limited, of free choice and individual responsibility, science, Professor Skinner suggests, refutes such fancies and absorbs everything in a system of comprehensive determinism.

If this is so, then it is so; but the proof does not lie in assertion—or in extrapolation. It can lie only in demonstration—and in a demonstration that has not yet been made. Until it is made, those who accept this view accept it on faith. Science in such terms ceases to be a system of provisional hypothesis and becomes instead a form of poetic myth, almost of religion.

The defenders of behavioral science are sometimes given to the doubtful practice of trying to dispose of its critics by advancing theories about the personal or status insecurities which impel them to criticism. I do not wish to emulate this form of reductionism, and I will refrain, therefore, from speculating about the impulses which divide the world into what William James called the tender-minded and the tough-minded—the impulses which make some people monists and others pluralists. The point is not the psyche of the individuals, but the merit of the arguments.

The key is the demonstration—and one is compelled to doubt whether the necessary demonstration is likely to be made in the near future. For one thing, the vision of comprehensive determinism remains a psychological impossibility in the sense that no human being could conceivably act upon it or live by it. As Sir Isaiah Berlin has put it, "If we begin to take it seriously, then, indeed, the changes in our language, or moral notions, our attitudes toward one another, our views of history, of society and of everything else will be too profound to be even adumbrated." We can no more imagine what the universe of a consistent determinist would be like than we can imagine what it would be like to live in a world without time or one with seventeen-dimensional space. And it is more than a psychological impossibility: it is also a quite illegitimate extension of existing evidence. Until the omnipotence of determinism can be demonstrated by infallibility of prediction and control, one must surely stick with the provable facts and accept the existence of intractable elements in experience which may well, in the future as in the past, continue to defy quantification.

In this belief, I am encouraged by the testimony of Dr. Norbert Wiener, who has done as much as any one to invent the devices which make modern quantitative research possible. Dr. Wiener has noted the contention of behavioral scientists that the main task of the immediate future is "to extend to the fields of anthropology, of sociology, of economics, the methods of the natural sciences, in the hope of achieving a like measure of success in the social fields. From believing this necessary, they come to believe it possible. In this, I maintain, they show an excessive optimism, and a misunderstanding of the nature of all scientific achievement." Success in exact science, Dr. Wiener points out, has come where there is a high degree of isolation of the phenomenon from the observer—as in astronomy or atomic physics. But the social sciences deal with short statistical runs, and observers are deeply, inextricably and indeterminately involved in what they observe. He concludes:

Whether our investigations in the social sciences be statistical or dynamic . . . they can never be good to more than a very few decimal places, and, in short, can never furnish us with a quantity of verifiable, significant information which begins to compare with that which we have learned to expect in the natural sciences. . . . There is much which we must leave, whether we like it or not, to the "unscientific," narrative method of the professional historian.

I would qualify Dr. Wiener's conclusion only by expanding it. There is much, I would add, which we must leave, whether we like it or not, not just to historians but to poets, novelists, painters, musicians, philosophers, theologians, even politicians, even saints—in short, to one form or another of humanist. For an indefinite future, I suspect, humanism will continue to yield truths about both individual and social experience which quantitative social research by itself could never reach. Whether these truths are inherently or merely temporarily inaccessible to the quantitative method is a question which only experience can answer.

In the meantime, this humanist is bound to say that, as an aid to the understanding of society and men, quantitative social research is admirable and indispensable. As a guide to the significance of problems, it is misleading when it exudes the assumption that only problems susceptible to quantitative solutions are important. As a means of explaining human or social behavior, it is powerful but profoundly incomplete. As the source of a theory of human nature and of the universe, it is but a new formulation of an ancient romantic myth.

# Notes

## THE CONCEPTUALIZATION OF AMERICAN HISTORY

1. Richard Hofstadter, "History and the Social Sciences" in Fritz Stern, ed., *The Varieties of History* (New York, 1957), 361.

2. Carl Bridenbaugh, "The Great Mutation," *Amer. Histor. Rev.*, LXVIII (January, 1963), 315–31.

3. Johann Huizinga, "Historical Conceptualization," in Stern, *Varieties, op. cit.*, 297; James Ford Rhodes, *Historical Essays* (New York, 1909), 4, 20, 22; David M. Potter, "Explicit Data and Implicit Assumptions," in Louis Gottschalk, ed., *Generalization in the Writing of History* (Chicago, 1963), 182.

4. Huizinga, *Conceptualization, op. cit.*, 299.

5. Arthur Schlesinger, Jr., "The Humanist Looks at Empirical Social Research," *American Sociological Review*, XXVII (December, 1962) 768; Henry J. Young, in *Mississippi Valley Historical Review*, XLIX (June, 1962). Bridenbaugh, "Mutation," *op. cit.*; S. M. Pargellis, "Clio in a Straightjacket," *Amer. Quart.*, XI (Summer, 1959), 225–31.

6. J. C. Charlesworth, ed., "The Limits of Behavioralism," (Philadelphia, October 1962), 17; David Easton, "Introduction: The Current Meaning of 'Behavioralism' in Political Science," *Ibid.*, 1–25.

7. Leo Strauss, *Natural Right and History* (Chicago, 1953).

8. Howard White, "The New Political Science Reexamined: A Symposium," *Social Research*, XXIX (Summer 1962), 127–56.

9. Evron M. Kirkpatrick, "The Impact of the Behavioral Approach on Traditional Political Science," in A. Ranney, ed., *Essays on the Behavioral Study of Politics* (Urbana, 1962), 6–7.

10. Hannah Arendt, "Understanding and Politics," *Partisan Review*, XX (July–August, 1953), 377–92.

11. Peter H. Odegard, "A New Look at Leviathan" in Lynn White, Jr., ed., *Frontiers of Knowledge in the Study of Man* (New York, 1956), 94.

12. A. L. Kroeber, *Culture: A Critical Review of Concepts and Definitions* (Cambridge, Mass., 1952), 35.

13. Robert A. Dahl, *Who Governs?* (New Haven, 1961).

14. For a critique of Dahl, see *supra.*, 211.

15. C. Wright Mills, *The Sociological Imagination* (New York, 1959), 154.

16. See, especially, the devastating review by an economic historian, Julius Rubin, of David C. McClelland, *The Achieving Society* (Princeton, 1961), in *J. Econ. Hist.*, XXIII (March, 1963), 118–21.

17. Gardner Lindzey, *Handbook of Social Psychology* (Reading, Mass., 1954), 175.

18. Bruce Mazlish, ed., *Psychoanalysis and History* (New York, 1963), esp. Introduction.

19. Dexter Perkins, et al., *The Education of Historians in the United States* (New York, 1962), 169.

20. David Potter, *Amer. Quar.*, VII (Spring, 1955), 79–81.

21. Letter from Bernard Wishy, *Columbia Forum* (Winter, 1963), 52.

22. Corinne L. Gibb, "Should We Learn More About Ourselves?" *Amer. Histor. Rev.*, LXVI (July, 1961), 990; Anne Roe, *The Psychology of Occupations* (New York, 1956).

23. *Theory and Practice in Historical Study: A Report of the Committee on Historiography* (1946); *The Social Sciences in Historical Study* (1954); Gottschalk, *Generalization, op. cit.*

24. Lee Benson, *The Concept of Jacksonian Democracy* (Princeton, 1961), viii.

25. Sidney Goldstein, et al., *The Norristown Study* (Philadelphia, 1961), vi.

26. *American Studies*, V (December, 1962), 4.

27. Review of *The Social Sciences in Historical Study, American Quarterly*, VII, (Spring, 1955), 80.

28. H. P. Fairchild, ed., *Dictionary of Sociology* (Paterson, 1961), 317.

29. Herman Ausubel, *Historians and their Craft: A Study of the Presidential Addresses of the American Historical Association, 1884–1945* (New York, 1950), 189–255.

30. *Ibid.*, 191.

31. *Ibid.*, 189–91; Edward N. Saveth, *American Historians and European Immigrants* (New York, 1948), 32–42.

32. Ausubel, *Historians, op. cit.*, 203.

33. Carl Becker, "Some Aspects of the Influence of Social Problems and Ideas upon the Study and Writing of History," *American Sociological Society Publications*, VII (June, 1913), 95–96. For a similar point of view see Frederick Jackson Turner, "Social Forces in American History," *American Historical Review* XVI, (1911) 217.

34. I. L. Bernard and Jessie Bernard, *Origins of American Sociology* (New York, 1943), 763.

35. Hans Meyerhoff, ed., *The Philosophy of History in Our Time* (New York, 1959), 17, 42. This kind of reductionism is attacked by Popper in *The Open Society and its Enemies* (Princeton, 1950) Ch. 14, which argues that the social sciences are relatively independent of psychological assumptions and that psychology is not the basis of social science, but is one social science, among others. Reference to Dilthey is based upon a conversation with Salomon.

36. Ausubel, *Historians, op. cit.*, 223–24.

37. Becker, "Some Aspects," 105–106.

38. Phil L. Snyder, ed., *Detachment and the Writing of History: Essays and Letters of Carl L. Becker* (Ithaca, 1958), 21.

39. Fred A. Shannon, *Critiques of Research in the Social Sciences: III, An Appraisal of Walter Prescott Webb's The Great Plains* (New York, 1940), 237.

40. Raymond O. Rockwood, ed., *Carl Becker's Heavenly City Revisited* (Ithaca, 1958), 65.

41. Carl Becker, *Saturday Review of Literature*, II (August 15, 1925), 38–40.

42. Karl R. Popper, *The Poverty of Historicism* (Boston, 1957), 27–28.

43. George Clinton Burr, "The Freedom of History," *American Historical Review*, XXII (1917), 253–71.

44. Frederick Jackson Turner, *The Significance of Sections in American History* (New York, 1932), 20. Quoted sections written in 1904.

45. John W. Burgess, "On Methods of Historical Research in Columbia University," in G. Stanley Hall, ed., *Methods of Teaching History* (Boston, 1883), 220.

46. A. L. Kroeber, "An Anthropologist Looks at History," *Pacific Historical Review*, XXVI (August, 1957), 281–87; Allen Gilmore, "Trends, Periods, and Classes," in H. S. Hughes, ed., *Teachers of History* (Ithaca, 1954), 309 asserts: "The meanings of historical usage are partly the meaning of ordinary language"; Potter, "Explicit Data," 187.

47. David Levin, *History as Romantic Art* (Stanford, 1959), 50.

48. Henry Adams, *The History of the United States during the Jefferson and Madison Administrations* (9 vols., New York, 1889–1891), IV, 289.

49. Max Weber, *The Theory of Social and Economic Organization* (New York, 1942), 90, 92, 109.

50. Edward Augustus Freeman, *Comparative Politics* (London, 1873), 302.

51. Edward N. Saveth, *American Historians and European Immigrants, 1875–1925* (New York, 1948), 18, 26.

52. F. C. Lane and J. C. Riemersma, eds., *Enterprise and Secular Change* (Homewood, Ill., 1953), 507.

53. Quoted in Meyerhoff, *Philosophy, op. cit.*, 98.

54. Roy C. Macridis, *The Study of Comparative Government* (New York, 1956), 5.

55. Sir John Neale, "The Biographical Approach to History," *History*, n.s., XXXVI (October, 1951), 193–203.

56. Edward N. Saveth, ed., *Henry Adams* (New York, 1963), 54, 66, 165–71.

57. Bernard, *Origins, op. cit.*, 792.

58. *Wisconsin Domesday Book. Town Studies*, vol. 1 (Madison: 1924). *Wisconsin Magazine of History* IV (1921), 61–74; "The Microscopic Method Applied to History," *Minnesota History Bulletin*, IV (1922), 3–20.

59. Roy F. Nichols, *The Disruption of American Democracy* (New York, 1948), 20.

60. Oscar and Mary Handlin, *The Di-*

mensions of Liberty (Cambridge, Mass., 1961).

61. W. H. B. Court, "Economic History," in H. B. R. Finberg, ed., Approaches to History, (Toronto, 1962), 20, 22, 24, 27, 28, 30.

62. William R. Taylor, "Historical Bifocals in the Year 1800," New England Quarterly (June, 1950), 172–86.

63. Arthur Schlesinger, Sr., "An Editor's Second Thoughts" in W. E. Lingelbach, ed., Approaches to American Social History (New York, 1937), 84.

64. J. H. Hexter, Reappraisals in History (Evanston: 1961), 14–25.

65. Roland Berthoff, "The American Social Order: A Conservative Hypothesis," American Historical Review, LXV (April, 1960), 495–514.

66. H. J. Perkin in Finberg, "Social History," op, cit., "Foreword" to Hexter, Reappraisals, op. cit.

67. "American Social Order," op. cit., 497.

68. Ibid., 499–500.

69. J. H. Hexter, Reappraisals in History, op. cit., 16–17.

70. Ibid., xvi.

71. Louis Gottschalk, Generalization, op. cit., 74–75.

72. G. W. Pierson, "The Frontier and American Institutions: A Criticism of the Turner Theory," New England Quarterly, XV (June, 1942), 224–55; Pierson, "The Frontier of Turner's Essays," The Pennsylvania Magazine of History of Biography, LXIV (October, 1940).

73. Lee Benson, Turner and Beard (New York: The Free Press of Glencoe, 1960), 167–74; Robert P. Sharkey, Money, Class and Party (Baltimore, 1959), 276–311.

74. Talcott Parsons, "On the Concept of Influence," [with replies by J. S. Coleman and R. A. Bauer] Public Opinion Quarterly, XXVII (Spring, 1963), 37–92.

75. Robert A. Dahl, "The Concept of Power," Behavioral Science, III (July, 1957), 202.

76. David Potter, American Quarterly, VII (Spring, 1955), 80.

77. For the inability of theory alone to define a concept see Donald W. Olmsted, Social Groups, Roles and Leadership: An Introduction to the Concepts (East Lansing, Michigan, 1961), 46; Charles M.

Bonjean, "Community Leadership: A Case Study of Conceptual Refinement," American Journal of Sociology, LXVIII, (May, 1963), 672–81.

Reference group theory and its implications have been developed less adequately than have their specific application. See, especially, Richard B. Sherman, "The Status Revolution and Massachusetts Progressive Leadership," Political Science Quarterly, LXXVIII (March, 1963), 59–65.

78. Social Sciences, op. cit., 34–35.

79. Louis Wirth, "The Social Sciences" in Merle Curti, ed., American Scholarship in the Twentieth Century (Cambridge, 1953), 40–45; E. K. Francis, "History and the Social Sciences: Some Reflections on the Reintegration of Social Science," Rev. Politics, XIII (April, 1951), 355–58; F. N. House, The Development of Sociology (New York, 1936).

80. Social Sciences in Historical Study, 13–14. W. W. Rostow has remarked that American graduate schools "have a peculiar power to denature problem-oriented thought . . . and to tame it to departmentally organized disciplines; for a real problem, involving whole people, rarely if ever breaks down along lines into which the study of human affairs is professionally fragmented." Supra, 28.

81. Eric Lampard, "American Historians and the Study of Urbanization", American Historical Review, LXVII (October, 1961), 49–61; Oscar Handlin and John Burchard, The Historian and the City (Boston, 1963).

82. James C. Malin, The Grasslands of North America: Prolegomena to its History (Ann Arbor, 1947), 316–30; Malin, "Ecology and History" The Scientific Monthly, LXX (May, 1950), 295–98; Roy F. Nichols, "Kansas Historiography: The Techniques of Cultural Analysis", Amer. Quart. (Spring, 1957), 85–91.

83. Ranney, ed., Behavioral Study of Politics, Richard C. Snyder, "Some Recent Trends in International Relations Theory and Research," 114.

84. George G. Iggers, "The Image of Ranke in American and German Historical Thought," History and Theory II, 17–40; Herbert Butterfield, George III and the Historians (New York, 1959), 213.

85. Benedetto Croce, *Logic as the Science of the Pure Concept* (London, 1917).

86. Snyder, *Detachment and History*, 14–17.

87. Charles Winick, *Dictionary of Anthropology* (New York, 1956), 128; J. T. Zadrozny, *Dictionary of Social Science* (Washington, 1959), 60; Leland E. Hinsie and Robert J. Campbell, *Psychiatric Dictionary* (New York, 1960), 145; Henry Pratt Fairchild, ed., *Dictionary of Sociology* (Paterson, 1961), 56; Philip L. Harriman, *The New Dictionary of Psychology* (New York, 1947), 80; Dagobert D. Runes, *Dictionary of Philosophy* (Ames, Iowa, 1959), 61; H. B. English and A. C. English, *A Comprehensive Dictionary of Psychological and Psychoanalytical Terms* (New York, 1958), 105. Hans Sperber and Travis Trittschuk, *American Political Terms: An Historical Dictionary* (Detroit, 1962) does not define the related concepts.

88. Heinrich Rickert, *Science and History* (New York, 1962), 37.

89. David Easton, "The Current Meaning of 'Behavioralism' in Political Science," 17, in Charlesworth, *Behavioralism, op. cit.*

90. Louis Gottschalk *Generalization, op. cit.* Reviewed by John William Ward, *American Quarterly*, XV (Fall, 1963), 467.

91. Ernest Nagel, Typological Procedures in the Natural and Social Sciences" in "Symposium; Problems of Concept and Theory Formation in the Social Sciences," *Science, Language, and Human Rights* (Philadelphia, 1952), 63. The idea of a science of history is advanced by Max Savelle. He identifies it as "a science of two variable subject-matters—the individual human being and the human group. It would be a science of human indeterminacy. One might hazard an analogy with Heisenberg's principle of indeterminacy in physics were it not for the fact that the historical atom, the individual human being, is far more unpredictable than the electron precisely because it is self-conscious, enjoying a wide range of freedom of choice. . . ." Historical laws would be "laws of indeterminacy." "The Functions of History in the Age of

Science," *The Historian*, XXII (August, 1960), 359–60.

92. Rickert, *Science, op. cit.*

93. Gottschalk, *Generalization, op. cit.*, 137.

94. Bray Hammond, *Banks and Politics in America from the Revolution to the Civil War* (Princeton, 1957), vii; Lee Benson, *The Concept of Jacksonian Democracy* (Princeton, 1961); Stanley Elkins, *Slavery: A Problem in American Institutional and Intellectual Life* (Chicago, 1959).

95. Charlesworth, *Behavioralism, op. cit.*, 17, 18, 23, 24, 43.

96. Gottschalk, *Generalization, op. cit.*, 74.

97. John C. Wahlke, "Behavioral Analyses of Representative Bodies" in Ranney, ed., *Essays on the Behavioral Study of Politics*, 174–75.

98. L. B. Namier, *The Structure of Politics at the Accession of George III* (London, 1929).

99. W. O. Aydelotte, "A Statistical Analysis of the Parliament of 1841: Some Problems of Method," *Bulletin of the Institute of Historical Research*, XXVII (1954), 141.

100. Talcott Parsons, *The Structure of Social Action* (New York, 1937), 39; Morton B. King, Jr., "Some Comments on Concepts," *Social Forces*, XXXIV (October, 1955), 1–4; Arnold Brecht, *Political Theory* (Princeton, 1959), 59.

101. Gottschalk, *Generalization, op. cit.*, vi–vii n.

102. Aspects of the micro-macro problem are discussed by Heinz Eulau, "Segments of Political Science Most Susceptible to Behavioristic Treatment," in Charlesworth, *Behavioralism, op. cit.*, 44. See also Stern, *History, op. cit.*, 372.

103. Harold A. Nelson, "A Tentative Foundation for Reference Group Theory," *Sociology and Social Research*, XLV (April, 1961), 274–80, discusses "the complex network of concepts and empirically derived interrelationships which must be a part of reference group theory as theory."

104. Saveth, *American Historians, op. cit.*, 21–22.

105. E. W. Phifer, "Slavery in Microcosm: Burke County, North Carolina,"

*Journal of Southern History* XXVIII (May, 1962).

106. Joseph Schumpeter, *Imperialism and Social Classes* (New York, 1951), 158.

107. F. T. Wainright, "Archaeology and Place-Names," in Finberg, *Approaches, op. cit.,* 201–14.

108. Talcott Parsons and Edward A. Shils, eds., *Toward A General Theory of Action* (Cambridge, 1952), 30.

109. See especially the definitions of social science in Zadrozny, *Dictionary, op. cit.,* 315; Fairchild, *Dictionary, op. cit.,* 292.

110. Charlesworth, *op. cit.,* 22–3; Marshall White, *The Nature of Scientific Thought* (Englewood Cliffs), 147–8; Rollo Handy and Paul Kurtz, "A Current

Appraisal of the Behavioral Sciences" in *Bulletin of the Behavioral Research Council* (1963), 9.

111. A. M. Schlesinger, Jr., "The Historian and History," *Foreign Affairs,* XLI (April 1963), 493.

112. Bernard Bailyn and Lotte Bailyn, *Massachusetts Shipping, 1657–1714* Cambridge, 1959), 135–41.

113. J. G. A. Pocock in *History and Theory* III (1963), 130.

114. Glenn Tinder, "The Necessity of Historicism," *American Political Science Review,* LV (September, 1961), 564; Popper, *Poverty, op. cit.,* 147.

115. David Potter, "Explicit Data and Implicit Assumptions in Historical Study," 187.

## ECONOMICS

1. We can, of course, track our ancestry to Adam Smith, in which case we have done briefs for both sides on the issue of free trade, as indeed we (and other historians) have done on most major issues of public policy.

2. The upper turning point in modern business cycle theories, for example, is usually traced back to a short-period rise in saving (reflecting the diminished relative marginal utility of consumption with a rise in income); to supply bottlenecks and cost increases (reflecting short-period diminishing returns); to a short- or long-period exhaustion of avenues for profitable investment adequate to sustain full employment (again reflecting diminishing returns); or to some combination of these factors.

3. For further discussion see the author's *Process of Economic Growth* (London, 1953), pp. 5–6.

4. This case could, of course, be reversed; that is, it could be regarded as a debate between those who held to classic assumptions and those who faced the long-period reality of inflexible money wage rates. Politically, the Keynesians were the

men of the short-period; in theory, the Pigovians.

5. See, for example, *The First Indian Five-Year Plan* (New Delhi, 1951), Ch. ii.

6. See R. S. Eckaus, "The Factor Proportion Problems in Underdeveloped Areas", *American Economic Review,* XLV (Sept. 1955), 539–65.

7. See, for example, T. Haavelmo, *A Study in the Theory of Economic Evolution* (Amsterdam, 1954).

8. See *Capital Formation and Economic Growth* (Princeton: Princeton University Press, 1955).

9. S. Kuznets, W. E. Moore, and J. J. Spengler, *Economic Growth: Brazil, India, Japan* (Durham: Duke University Press, 1955).

10. See, notably, D. Rustow, "New Horizons for Comparative Politics," *World Politics,* IX (July 1957), 530–49. See also George McT. Kahin, Guy J. Pauker, and Lucian Pye, "Comparative Politics of non-Western Countries," *American Political Science Review,* XLIX (Dec. 1955), 1022–41.

## SOCIOLOGY

1. *Aofsätze zur Soziologie,* by Joseph A. Schumpeter. Tübingen: J. C. B. Mohr (Paul Siebeck), 1953, p. 232. Paper DM 15.80, Bound DM 18.80.

2. J. A. Schumpeter, *Imperialism and Social Classes,* transl. by H. Norden, ed. by P. M. Sweezy (New York: Kelley, 1951).

3. R. Bendix and S. M. Lipset, *Class,*

Status, and Power: A Reader in Social Stratification (New York: The Free Press of Glencoe, 1953), pp. 75–81.

4. Samuel Lubell, The Revolution in World Trade and American Economic Policy (New York: Harper, 1955), pp. 110–23.

5. Page 89. Schumpeter's italics. The translations given here and elsewhere in this and the following section differ somewhat from the Norden translation, referred to in note 2, above.

6. See pp. 172–73 and 183–201 for the former; and pp. 139–45 in the preceding essay for the latter.

## ANTHROPOLOGY

1. Eleven years ago the American Historical Association devoted several sessions to a consideration of the cultural approach to history, which was later issued in a volume edited by Caroline Ware, The Cultural Approach to History (New York: Columbia University Press, 1940). The volume included an excellent summary by Geoffrey Gorer of existing theory in cultural anthropology. In my discussion I have relied on this volume as a kind of bench mark, taking its suggestions into account and attempting to add to it in the light of growth in anthropological theory over the last decade, experience in working in inter-disciplinary teams which did not include historians, and experience (especially in Columbia University Research in Contemporary Cultures and in the American Museum of Natural History project "Studies in Soviet Culture") in working closely with historians and with members of the culture being studied, who had been well-grounded in the history of some aspect of their own culture. These last two experiences are distinct and differently rewarding—at least for the anthropologist.

2. G. Bateson and M. Mead, Balinese Character: A Photographic Analysis (New York: New York Academy of Sciences, 1942).

3. For systematic discussions of these distinctions, cf. Gregory Bateson, Naven (Cambridge University Press, 1936); Co-operation and Competition Among Primitive Peoples, edited by Margaret Mead (New York: McGraw-Hill Book Co., 1937); Ralph Linton, The Study of Man (New York: D. Appleton-Century Co., 1936); A. R. Radcliffe-Brown, "On Social Structure," Journal of Royal Institute of Anthropology, LXX (1940), 1–12.

4. The work of Bronislav Malinowski in the Trobriands, my work in Samoa, Ruth Bunzel's work in Zuni, and the series of studies carried on under Radcliffe-Brown at the University of Sydney, are examples of this shift of emphasis from attempts to reconstruct the culture of a bygone period to work with whole communities as they exist.

5. Philip Mosely's studies of the Zadruga are pioneer studies in this combination of the historical approach with the case studies of actual communal joint families. Cf. "The Zadruga: or Communal Joint Family in the Balkans and its Recent Evolution," in Ware, op cit. pp. 95–108.

6. For example, Ruth Benedict's treatment of the material on the Kwakiutl Indians in Patterns of Culture (Boston: Houghton Mifflin, 1934) and R. K. Lamb's work in which hitherto unemphasized connections through family and clique membership among statesmen and landed and merchant families are providing a new basis for the analysis of early American entrepreneural history. See "Entrepreneurship in the Community" in Explorations in Entrepreneural History, Vol. II, No. 3, 114–127.

7. Cf. Arnold Gesell and Frances L. Ilg, Infant and Child in the Culture of Today (New York: Harper and Bros., 1943); David Riesman, The Lonely Crowd (New Haven: Yale University Press, 1950); E. H. Erikson, Childhood and Society (New York: W. W. Norton, 1950); M. Mead, "On the Implications for Anthropology of the Gesell-Ilg Approach to Maturation," American Anthropologist (Jan.–Mar. 1947), Vol. 49, No. 1, 69–77; Gregory Bateson, "Social Planning and the Concept of Deutero Learning," part of Chap. iv, Second Symposium

on *Science, Philosophy and Religion* (New York, 1942); John Dollard, *Criteria for the Life History* (New Haven: Yale University Press, 1935).

8. Gregory Bateson, "Cultural Determinants of Personality," in McVeigh Hunt, *Personality and the Behavior Disorders* (New York: Ronald Press, 1944), 714–735.

9. W. L. Warner and others, *Yankee City Series,* I–IV (New Haven: Yale University Press, 1941, 1942, 1945, 1947).

10. Gregory Bateson, "Bali: The Value System of a Steady State" in *Social Structure: Studies Presented to A. R. Radcliffe-Brown.* ed. by Meyer Fortes (Oxford: Clarendon Press, 1949), 35–53; Jurgen Ruesch and Gregory Bateson, "Structure and Process in Social Relations" in *Psychiatry* (May 1949), Vol. XII, No. 2, 105–124; Eliot D. Chapple and Carleton S. Coon, *Principles of Anthropology* (New York: Henry Holt and Co., 1942); L. F. Richardson, "Generalized Foreign Politics," *British Journal of Psychology* Monograph Supplement XXIII (1939); J. A. Schumpeter, *The Theory of Economic Development* (Cambridge: Harvard University Press, 1934); Frank Tannenbaum, "The Balance of Power in Society" in *Political Science Quarterly* LXI (December 1946), 481–504.

11. T. H. Huxley and Julian Huxley, *Touchstone for Ethics* (New York: Harper and Row, 1947).

12. G. Bateson and M. Mead, *Balinese Character: A Photographic Analysis, op cit.*

13. How dangerous it can be to surrender the detachment provided by a lapse of time without replacing it with some new ethic, is only too vividly demonstrated in Dorothy Thomas and Richard Nishimoto: *The Spoilage* (Berkeley and Los Angeles: University of California Press, 1946). Overtly the study lacks value judgments, but a covert bias is displayed in the choice—as subject matter—of the 10 per cent of the interned Japanese for whom the experience was disastrous.

14. Report of the Committee on Ethics, *Human Organization* (Spring 1949), Vol. 8, No. 2, 20–21. For a history of some of the thinking in this field, cf. Margaret Mead, "The Comparative Study of Cultures and the Purposive Cultivation of Democratic Values, 1941–1949," in *Perspectives on a Troubled Decade: Science, Philosophy, and Religion, 1939–1949, Tenth Symposium,* ed. by Lyman Bryson, Louis Finkelstein, R. M. MacIver (New York: Harper and Row, 1950); 87–108.

## PSYCHOLOGY

1. *Journal of Social Issues,* XVII (1961).

2. This view still informs historians with a taste for the heroic, even though their idea of the historic process may have become more complex. It can be clearly discerned, for instance, in the evolutionary mythology which inspired Spengler's *Decline of the West.*

3. The jolt reverberates in many speculations about the possibility that the past might in some way endure. It is reflected in the Greek image of the nether world (Hades) and reaches its most explicit form in St. Augustine. The same idea and the same wishful motive underlie the modern fantasy of a Time Machine.

4. "In the nature of things no historical analysis can ever be brought up to date" (Simpson, 1959.)

5. It must not be confounded with another kind of anti-historicism of which Nietzsche's *Vom Nutzen und Nachteil der Historie* is probably the most incisive manifesto. The attitude which I dispute here comes from a kind of one-track empiricism as well as from a deep-rooted wariness of the past. Nietzsche's argument is in reaction against a powerful cultural trend, the historicism of the nineteenth century.

6. There is, for instance, no mentioning of the conceptual problems of *social* or *historical change* in Mandler and Kessen's (1959) otherwise broadminded and detailed book on the Language of Psychology.

## PSYCHOANALYSIS

1. Sigmund Freud, *Moses and Monotheism* (New York: Alfred A. Knopf, 1949), p. 109.

2. John Stuart Mill, "Grote's Plato," in *Dissertations and Discussions* (New York: Henry Holt & Co., 1847), p. 230. Freud in 1879, at twenty-three, translated the twelfth volume of a collected edition of Mill's writings, which included the essay "Grote's Plato," in which Mill comments on the Platonic theory of anamnesis. Cf. my "The Meaning of History and Religion in Freud's Thought," *Journal of Religion*, XXXI, No. 2 (April, 1951), 414–31.

3. Otto Gierke, *Political Theories of the Middle Ages* (Cambridge University Press, 1927), pp. 7–8.

4. See, for a history of analogy in social thought, A. Meyer, "Wesen und Geschichte der Theorie vom Mikro- und Makrokosmos," *Berner Studien zur Philosophie und ihrer Geschichte*, XXV (1900), 1–122; F. W. Coker, "Organismic Theories of the State," *Studies in History, Economics and Public Law* (Columbia University, 1910), XXXVIII, No. 2, 259–463; and George Perrigo Conger, *Theories of Macrocosms and Microcosms in the History of Philosophy* (New York: Columbia University Press, 1922).

5. Freud had read Fechner with great admiration. Freud, *Beyond the Pleasure Principle* (London: International Psycho-Analytical Press, 1922), pp. 2–4.

6. *Moses and Monotheism*, pp. 116–17.

7. *Ibid.*, p. 104.

8. *Ibid.*, p. 117.

9. Freud, "Totem and Taboo," in *Basic Writings* (New York: Modern Library, 1938), p. 829.

10. *Moses and Monotheism*, pp. 105–6. Freud's italics.

11. *Ibid.*, p. 120.

12. *Ibid.*, p. 108.

13. *Ibid.*, p. 109.

14. *Ibid.*, p. 89. The regular attempt to read *Totem and Taboo* out of its important place in the Freudian corpus ignores the fact that the assumptions Freud projected in that book remained basic in his writings after 1912. Cf. Harold D. Lasswell, *The Analysis of Political Behavior* (London: Routledge & Kegan Paul, 1948), p. 287.

15. Freud, *Collected Papers* (London: Hogarth Press, 1949), II, 33.

16. *Ibid.*, II, 25.

17. *Ibid.*, I, 319–23.

18. For a constructive discussion of the problem see a review article by Alan Gewirth, "The Psychological Approach to Politics," *Ethics*, LIX No. 3 (April, 1949), 211–20.

19. An adequate example of the psychoanalytic treatment of political history is to be found in Fritz Wittels, "Economic and Psychological Historiography," *American Journal of Sociology*, LI, No. 6 (May, 1946), 527–32.

20. See Lasswell, *Psychopathology and Politics* (Chicago: University of Chicago Press, 1930), pp. 75–76.

21. See, for a view of Freud and Kant as opposite, Franz Alexander, *Fundamentals of Psychoanalysis* (New York: W. W. Norton, 1948), p. 17. For a view of the relation of Freud and Kant similar to our own see Roland Dalbiez, *Psychoanalytical Method and the Doctrine of Freud* (London; Longmans, Green & Co., 1941), II, 326–27. Dalbiez closes his two-volume work with an evocation of the relation between Freud and Kant: "Freud, who professes that he does not read philosophy [the profession is somewhat misleading; Freud read a good deal of philosophy], and has probably not read Kant, gives us to understand that the science of psychopathology is the legitimate heir of the liquidation of Kant's doctrines."

22. *Collected Papers*, V, 173. The source of Freud's Copernican image of Darwin and himself was Haeckel: "Haeckel liked to compare Darwin's reform of biology with the reform of cosmology achieved by Copernicus three hundred years before" (cf. E. Haeckel, *Natürliche Schopfungsgeschichte* [1868], quoted in Ernest Cassirer, *The Problem of Knowledge* [New Haven: Yale University Press, 1950], p. 160).

23. Freud, *Outline of Psychoanalysis* (New York: W. W. Norton, 1949), p. 106.

24. Of course, Freud knew that all

epileptics did not become *homo religiosi.* In his famous paper "The Psychogenesis of a Case of Homosexuality in a Woman" (1920) Freud conceded that "so long as we trace the development from its final stage backwards, the connection appears continuous, and we feel we have gained an insight which is completely satisfactory or even exhaustive. But if we proceed the reverse way, if we start from the premises inferred from the analysis and try to follow these up to the final result, then we no longer get the impression of an inevitable sequence of events which could not be otherwise determined. We notice at once that there might have been another result, and that we might have been just as well able to understand and explain the latter. The synthesis is thus not so satisfactory as the analysis; in other words, from a knowledge of the premises we could not have foretold the nature of the result." Moreover, the identical causal factors might not produce the same result in another person. But, Freud concluded: "It is very easy to account for this disturbing state of affairs. Even supposing that we thoroughly know the aetiological factors that decide a given result, still we know them only qualitatively, and not in their relative strength." The missing knowledge that blocked prediction forward but did not prevent understanding backward was simply another kind of knowledge about individual psychological mechanisms. The psychoanalytic microscope was not yet refined enough to perceive the phenomena in the way necessary for prediction but only in the way necessary for retrospection. "We never know beforehand which of the determining factors will prove the weaker or the stronger. We only say at the end that those which succeeded must have been the stronger. Hence it is always possible by analysis to recognize the causation with certainty, whereas a prediction of it by synthesis is impossible" (*Collected Papers,* II, 226–27). Freud could not accept the possibility that the missing knowledge which prevented the prediction of a Paul from a Saul was of the objective and the historical rather than of individual and psychological factors.

25. Mario Praz, *The Romantic Agony* (London: Oxford University Press, 1951), p. viii.

26. Although, at the beginning of his *Leonardo,* he specifically disclaims any intention of analyzing Leonardo's art qua art, Freud, like all Platonists, seems to deny that there is a realm of autonomous aesthetic experience. Wherever Freud dealt with the problem, he derived creative impulse from individual pathology and aesthetic sensation from the general forms of sexual sensation. (Thus, Freud thought that all men were capable of being spectators, but not all men could be creators.) But even if the aesthetic is permitted autonomy, what is important is that Freud supplements the problematically autonomous aesthetic with psychological rather than historical knowledge. Historical knowledge says no more about what made Rubens or Leonardo great artists than psychological, but what it says may provide better data on the genesis, mode, and intention of their work. Both historical and psychological knowledge are extra-aesthetic, answering questions of origin and consequence that aesthetic knowledge cannot legitimately encounter. There are two traditional approaches to, say, that favorite object of psychoanalysis, *Hamlet,* which are excluded by a consideration of the play qua play. One moves historically (e.g., Hamlet themes in the earlier literature, the social ideals of Elizabethan society, the mechanics of the theater, Shakespeare's social status, etc.). The other moves psychologically: the work of art is more powerfully a catharsis for the artist than for the audience; the relevant data are the known and inferred events of the artist's life (e.g., Shakespeare's naming of his son Hamnet, the death of Shakespeare's father, his relations with Anne Hathaway, etc.). See, for examples of the Freudian aesthetics, Paul Schilder, "Psychoanalytic Remarks on 'Alice in Wonderland' and Lewis Carroll," *Journal of Nervous and Mental Diseases.* LXXXVII, No. 2 (February, 1938), 159–68; Ernest Jones, "The Influence of Andrea del Sarto's Wife on His Art," *Essays in Applied Psycho-Analysis* (London: International Psychoanalytical Press, 1923), pp. 227–44.

27. Freud, *Leonardo da Vinci: A Study*

in *Psychosexuality* (New York: Random House, 1947), p. 96.

28. *Ibid.*, p. 120.

29. "Totem and Taboo," in *Basic Writings*, p. 864.

30. G. W. F. Hegel, *The Philosophy of History* (rev. ed.; New York: Colonial Press, 1900), pp. 31–32.

31. Nor is the "basic-personality-types" school of cultural anthropology less immune to similar criticism. It still sees the objective social contexts, e.g., "values, ideals, religion," as "complicated end products" of individual development. It is the individual, not the social, that is the object of analysis. The elements of the social are simply the "currency of the . . . life of man" (see Abraham Kardiner, *The Psychological Frontiers of Society* [New York: Columbia University Press, 1945]; p. 22).

32. Karl Marx: *Capital* (Chicago: Charles H. Kerr, 1906), I, 648.

33. Hegel, *op. cit.*, p. 30.

34. Here is the place to note a difference for Marx. Marx substituted false consciousness for unconsciousness. His insight into psychological problems was defined by his ethical aim: to eliminate false consciousness by rational consciousness. Reason was understood by Marx as an ongoing critique of what was given objectively as false consciousness, which was an unconscious response of the action-demands of specific historical situations.

35. Talcott Parsons and Edward A. Shils (eds.), *Toward a General Theory of Action* (Cambridge: Harvard University Press, 1951), p. 52.

36. Louis Wirth, "Social Interaction: The Problem of the Individual and the Group," *American Journal of Sociology*, XLIV, No. 6 (May, 1939), 966, in the symposium on "The Individual and the Group."

37. Ernest R. Hilgard and Daniel Lerner, "The Person: Subject and Object of Science and Policy," *The Policy Sciences*, ed. Daniel Lerner and Harold D. Lasswell (Stanford: Stanford University Press, 1951), p. 16. The entire book is a useful and self-critical compendium on the present state of the social sciences.

38. Wirth, *op. cit.*, p. 966.

39. Hilgard and Lerner, *op. cit.*, pp. 17–19.

40. *Ibid.*, pp. 39–40.

41. Wirth, *op. cit.*, p. 967 (my italics).

## MOTIVATION

1. I deliberately refrain from citing specific works and authors. In suggestions as tentative as mine, I have not thought it profitable to take issue with individuals. One point I do wish to make clear is that I am not suggesting *all* historians have viewed the abolitionists without sympathy or understanding. Men such as Louis Filler, Dwight Dumond, Irving Bartlett, Leon Litwack, Ralph Korngold, Louis Ruchames, Oscar Sherwin, and David Davis have, in varying degrees, demonstrated their sympathy. But they have not, in my view, as yet carried the majority of historians along with them.

2. Gordon W. Allport, *Becoming, Basic Considerations for a Psychology of Personality*, Clinton, 1960, 23.

3. Allport, *op. cit.*, 65–68.

4. Based largely on what people think Freud said, rather than what he actually said. See Philip Rieff, *Freud: The Mind of the Moralist*, N. Y., 1959.

5. See, for example, O. Hobart Mowrer, "Psychiatry and Religion," *The Atlantic*, July, 1961.

6. Allport, *op. cit.*, 45.

7. It is interesting that in its original form, the aphorism read: "Is this the exception which probes the rule?"

8. Erich Fromm, *Psychoanalysis and Religion*, Clinton, 1959, 12.

## THE SUBCONSCIOUS

1. The most common meeting ground of the two has been biography. See John A. Garraty, "The Interrelations of Psychology and Biography," *Psychological Bulletin*, LI (Nov. 1954), 569–582, and the same author's *The Nature of Biography* (New York, 1957). The 1957 presidential address to the American Historical Association con-

tains a cogent plea to historians to extend their psychological investigations, and touches on a number of the problems with which we have been particularly involved. See William L. Langer, "The Next Assignment," *American Historical Review,* LXIII (Jan. 1958), 284–288.

2. See *The Campaign in Virginia, 1781: an Exact Reprint of Six Rare Pamphlets on the Clinton-Cornwallis Controversy,* ed. Benjamin F. Stevens, 2 vols. (London, 1888).

3. *The American Rebellion: Sir Henry Clinton's Narrative of His Campaigns, 1775–1782, with an Appendix of Original Documents,* ed. William B. Willcox (New Haven, 1954), p. xv. These memoirs are the principal printed source for Clinton's career.

4. Clinton, *American Rebellion,* p. xxvi; see also pp. 61–62.

5. Clinton, *American Rebellion,* pp. xliii–xliv, 318–319.

6. For a detailed and instructive example see Alexander and Juliette George, *Woodrow Wilson and Colonel House: a Personality Study* (New York, 1956).

7. Psychoanalytic biography has value only if a solution can be found to the problem with which we are here concerned, of how a person's unconscious motives can be inferred from written and other records without the self-correcting and continuous process of therapy. Clinical interpretation *outside* therapy cannot be checked and modified by its own results, as it continually is *in* therapy. When a technique is shifted from its native ground, the conclusions that it suggests are always, in one of Clinton's favorite phrases, *sujets á caution.* For a sanguine attempt to solve this problem see Phyllis Greenacre, *Swift and Carroll: a Psychoanalytic Study of Two Lives* (New York, 1955); and the cautions of reviewers see Frederick Wyatt, Deborah Bacon, and Arthur W. Eastman in *Literature and Psychology,* VI, No. 1 (1956), 18–27, and Frederick Wyatt, "Psychoanalytic Biography," *Contemporary Psychology,* I, No. 4 (1956), 105–107.

8. But see below, note 17.

9. *The American Rebellion* and the three following articles by Willcox, which are based primarily upon the Clinton papers: "Rhode Island in British Strategy, 1780–1781," *Journal of Modern History,* XVII (Dec. 1945), 304–331; "British Strategy in America, 1778," *ibid.,* XIX (June 1947), 97–121; "The British Road to Yorktown: a Study in Divided Command," *American Historical Review,* LII (Oct. 1946), 1–35.

10. Sigmund Freud, "Some Character-Types Met with in Psycho-Analytic Work," *Collected Papers* (London, 1953), IV, 318–344.

11. Clinton, *American Rebellion,* pp. 120 and note, xxxii, 142–143 and note.

12. *Ibid.,* pp. xix–xx.

13. See Otto Fenichel, *The Psychoanalytic Theory of Neuroses* (New York, 1955), pp. 268–310 and passim; Herman Nunberg, *Principles of Psychoanalysis* (New York, 1955), pp. 53–178 and especially pp. 157–173.

14. His belief, according to his memoirs, was founded on enemy letters intercepted in the late spring. In fact, however, these letters were not deciphered until months later, and in any case provided no basis for his idea; the episode therefore looks like another case of his falsifying the record. But the evidence is inconclusive. We are indebted to Mr. K. L. Ellis, of Hatfield College, Durham, for pointing out that a similar belief seems to have been current in British governmental circles as early as the autumn of 1780, in which case Clinton may have acquired his misconception from London. See Clinton, *American Rebellion,* pp. 305–306 and n. 14; [William Knox], *Extra Official State Papers Addressed to the Right Hon. Lord Rawdon, and Other Members of the Two Houses of Parliament, Associated for the Preservation of the Constitution and Promoting the Prosperity of the British Empire* (London, 1789), pp. 27–28 and note.

15. Clinton, *American Rebellion,* p. 333.

16. *Ibid.,* pp. 317–318, 321, 324, 327.

17. New evidence has appeared after this article was in draft. The Clements Library has just acquired a hitherto unknown collection of Clinton's papers which includes much private correspondence. We therefore have an unexpected opportunity to check our conclusions against fresh data. Already one relevant datum has come to light: the only known instance, aside from that discussed in

the text, of Clinton's distorting the words of a letter. The episode, we believe, strengthens our hypothesis of an inner psychic conflict as the cause of distortion.

One of the early indications of such a conflict is Clinton's state of mind after the Battle of Bunker Hill. During the battle he had disobeyed the letter of his instructions in order to assist the British attack, and for months afterward he was haunted by worry over this disobedience. In fact he had nothing to fear; his gallantry won high praise. (Clinton, *American Rebellion*, p. xvii.) We had therefore concluded that what disturbed him was not his actual conduct, objectively considered, but a sense that independent initiative transgressed against authority. On this point the recently discovered papers have enlightening evidence.

When the news of Clinton's conduct in the battle reached the Duke of Newcastle, his cousin and patron, the Duke reproached him gently by letter, and urged him to content himself in future "with doing what is *right*, for volunteering is not *necessary*." Clinton's answer was a furious complaint that the Duke had called him "an idle, wanton volunteer." New-castle apologized in some confusion for a phrase that he believed—quite correctly —that he had never used. (Newcastle to Clinton, July 28, Clinton to Newcastle [ca. Oct. 11], and Newcastle to Clinton, Nov. 28, 1775). In a mood of self-distrust, in short, Clinton read into a letter words that were highly unwelcome and that had never been written; he exaggerated his cousin's rebuke in order to make it fit his own charge against himself. The episode, although not completely comparable with the later and more complex episode of Germain's instructions, does give further indication that Clinton could externalize his battle with himself by putting words into another man's pen.

18. During this period, it has been contended, Clinton was intermittently blind. This he was not; but he unquestionably suffered from severe eyestrain, which may have been psychosomatic in origin. Although the evidence is suggestive, it warrants nothing more than conjecture. See Randolph G. Adams, "A View of Cornwallis's Surrender at Yorktown," *American Historical Review*, XXXVII (Oct. 1931), 36, 38; Willcox, "The British Road to Yorktown," p. 24 and note.

## GROUP STRUCTURE AND CAREER-LINE ANALYSIS

1. The table of leaders and the Note on Method and Sources in the original article have been omitted here. Ed.

2. Tucker to Wirt, Sept. 25, 1815, *William and Mary Quarterly*, 1st Ser., XXII (1914), 252–257.

3. Bailyn, "Politics and Social Structure in Virginia," *Seventeenth-Century America: Essays on Colonial History*, ed. James Morton Smith (Chapel Hill, 1959), pp. 98–102.

4. No information was found on the dates of arrival of the ancestors of four of the 110.

5. Sydnor, *Gentlemen Freeholders: Political Practices in Washington's Virginia* (Chapel Hill, 1952), pp. 78–93.

6. See Carl Bridenbaugh, *Myths and Realities: Societies of the Colonial South* (Baton Rouge, 1952), pp. 2–6.

## INTERGROUP CONFLICT

1. For an alternative to the method followed in this article, see John Higham's perceptive essay, "Another Look at Nativism," *Catholic Historical Review* (Washington), XLIV (July, 1958), 147–58. Higham rejects the ideological approach to nativism and stresses the importance of concrete ethnic tensions, "status rivalries," and face-to-face conflicts in explaining prejudice. Though much can be said for this sociological emphasis, as opposed to a search for irrational myths and stereotypes, the method suggested by Higham can easily lead to a simply "stimulus-response" view of prejudice. Awareness of actual conflicts in status and self-interest should not obscure the social and psychological functions of nativism, nor distract attention

from themes that may reflect fundamental tensions within a culture.

2. For a brilliant analysis of Mormon-Gentile conflict, see Thomas F. O'Dea, *The Mormons* (Chicago, 1958).

3. Freemasons were blamed for various unrelated economic and political grievances, but anti-Masonry showed no uniform division according to class, occupation, or political affiliation. See Charles McCarthy, "The Anti-Masonic Party," American Historical Association, *Annual Report for the Year 1902*, Vol. I (Washington, 1903), 370–73, 406–408. I am also indebted to Lorman A. Ratner, whose "Antimasonry in New York State: A Study in Pre-Civil War Reform" (M.A. thesis, Cornell University, 1958) substantiates this conclusion.

4. For a detailed analysis of the issues and development of anti-Catholicism, *see* Ray A. Billington, *The Protestant Crusade, 1800–1860* (New York, 1938).

5. It should be noted, however, that national attention was attracted by the Mountain Meadows Massacre and by Albert Sidney Johnston's punitive expedition to Utah.

6. For anti-Catholic references in *The Book of Mormon*, see I Nephi 13:4–9; II Nephi 6:12, 28:18. Parallels between Masons and the "Gadianton robbers" have been frequently discussed.

7. *Anti-Masonic Review and Magazine* (New York), II (October, 1829), 225–34. It was even claimed that Jesuits had been protected by Frederick the Great because they were mostly Freemasons and shared the same diabolical designs. See *Free Masonry: A Poem, In Three Cantos, Accompanied with Notes, Illustrative of the History, Policy, Principles, &c. of the Masonic Institution; Shewing the Coincidence of Its Spirit and Design with Ancient Jesuitism . . . By a Citizen of Massachusetts* (Leicester, Mass., 1830), 134.

8. William Hogan, *Popery! As It Was and as It Is: Also, Auricular Confession: and Popish Nunneries*, two books in one edition (Hartford, 1855), 32–33.

9. Jedidiah Morse, *A Sermon Preached at Charleston, November 29, 1798, on the Anniversary Thanksgiving in Massachusetts* (Boston, 1799); Vernon Stauffer, *The New England Clergy and the Bavarian*

*Illuminati* (New York, 1918), 98–99, 233, 246–48.

10. In Ned Buntline's *The G'hals of New York* (New York, 1850) the Jesuits seem to be connected with all secret conspiracies, and their American leader, Father Kerwin, is probably modeled on Brown's Carwin. George Lippard admired Brown, dedicated a novel to him, and was also fascinated by secret societies and diabolical plots to enslave America. In *New York: Its Upper Ten and Lower Million* (New York, 1853), the Catholic leaders are Illuminati-like atheists who plan revolutions, manipulate public opinion, and stop at no crime in their lust for wealth and power. These amoral supermen were clearly inspired by such characters as Brown's Ormond, as well as by the anti-Catholic writings of Eugène Sue and others.

11. Though the term "nativist" is usually limited to opponents of immigration, it is used here to include anti-Masons and anti-Mormons. This seems justified in view of the fact that these alarmists saw themselves as defenders of native traditions and identified Masonry and Mormonism with forces alien to American life.

12. For a lucid and provocative discussion of this "restoration theme," see Marvin Meyers, *The Jacksonian Persuasion* (Stanford, 1957), 162–64.

13. Hiram B. Hopkins, *Renunciation of Free Masonry* (Boston, 1830), 4–7.

14. Jacob Lefever of Hagerstown appealed to regional loyalty and urged citizens of Maryland to forget their differences and unite against "foreign influence" from an area notorious for its "tricks and frauds." *Free-Masonry Unmasked: or Minutes of the Trial of a Suit in the Court of Common Pleas of Adams County, Wherein Thaddeus Stevens, Esq. Was Plaintiff, and Jacob Lefever, Defendant* (Gettysburg, 1835), pp. xiii-xiv.

15. *The Cloven Foot: or Popery Aiming at Political Supremacy in the United States, By the Rector of Oldenwold* (New York, 1855), 170–79.

16. William Mulder and A. Russell Mortensen (eds.), *Among the Mormons: Historic Accounts by Contemporary Observers* (New York, 1958), 76–79. The quotation is from the minutes of an anti-

Mormon meeting in Jackson County, Missouri, July 20, 1833.

17. John H. Beadle, *Life in Utah: or, the Mysteries and Crimes of Mormonism* (Philadelphia, [1872]), 5.

18. *Anti-Masonic Review*, I (December, 1828), 3–4.

19. Letter of May 4, 1831, printed in *The Anti-Masonic Almanac, for the Year 1832*, ed. by Edward Giddins (Utica, 1831), 29–30.

20. *Anti-Masonic Review*, I (December, 1828), 6–7; Lebbeus Armstrong, *Masonry Proved to Be a Work of Darkness, Repugnant to the Christian Religion; and Inimical to a Republican Government* (New York, 1830), 16.

21. *The Anti-Masonic Almanack, for the Year 1828: Calculated for the Horizon of Rochester, N.Y. by Edward Giddins* (Rochester, 1827), entry for November and December, 1828; Armstrong, *Masonry*, 14.

22. Hogan, *Popery*, 32–33.

23. Edward Beecher, *The Papal Conspiracy Exposed, and Protestantism Defended, in the Light of Reason, History, and Scripture* (Boston, 1855), 29.

24. *Anti-Masonic Review*, I (February, 1829), 71.

25. Mulder and Mortensen (eds.), *Among the Mormons*, 407; Jennie Anderson Froiseth (ed.), *The Women of Mormonism: or, the Story of Polygamy as Told by the Victims Themselves* (Detroit, 1881–1882), 367–68.

26. It is true that anti-Catholics sometimes stressed the inferiority of lower-class immigrants and that anti-Mormons occasionally claimed that Mormon converts were made among the most degraded and ignorant classes of Europe. This theme increased in importance toward the end of the century, but it seldom implied that Catholics and Mormons were physically incapable of being liberated and joined to the dominant group. Racism was not an original or an essential part of the counter-subversive's ideology. Even when Mormons were attacked for coarseness, credulity, and vulgarity, these traits were usually thought to be the product of their beliefs and institutions. See Mrs. B. G. Ferris, "Life among the Mormons," *Putnam's Monthly Magazine* (New York),

VI (August, October, 1855), 144, 376–77.

27. Hogan, *Popery*, 35.

28. *Free Masonry: A Poem*, 55–58.

29. Hogan, *Popery*, 7–8; *Auricular Confession*, 264–65.

30. Froiseth (ed.), *Women of Mormonism*, 285–87, 291–92.

31. *Free Masonry: A Poem*, 29–37; *Anti-Masonic Review*, I (June, 1829), 203–207. The charge was often repeated that higher degrees of Freemasonry were created by the "school of Voltaire" and introduced to America by Jewish immigrants. Masonry was also seen as an "auxiliary to British foreign policy."

32. This question was most troubling to anti-Masons. Though some tried to sidestep the issue by quoting Washington against "self-created societies," as if he had been referring to the Masons, others flatly declared that Washington had been hoodwinked, just as distinguished jurists had once been deluded by a belief in witchcraft. Of course Washington had been unaware of Masonic iniquities, but he had lent his name to the cause and had thus served as a decoy for the ensnarement of others. See *Free Masonry: A Poem*, 38; *Anti-Masonic Review*, I (January, 1829), 49, 54; *The Anti-Masonic Almanac, for the Year of the Christian Era 1830* (Rochester, 1829), 32.

33. Beecher, *Papal Conspiracy Exposed*, 391.

34. Beadle, *Life in Utah*, 30–34.

35. *Ibid.*, 332–33. According to Beadle, religious error and sexual perversion were related "because the same constitution of mind and temperament which gives rise to one, powerfully predisposes toward the other."

36. *Cloven Foot*, 294–95.

37. Froiseth (ed.), *Women of Mormonism*, 113.

38. Though Horace Greeley was moderate in his judgment of Mormonism, he wrote: "I joyfully trust that the genius of the Nineteenth Century tends to a solution of the problem of Woman's sphere and destiny radically different from this." Quoted in Mulder and Mortensen (eds.), *Among the Mormons*, 328.

39. It should be noted that Freemasons were rarely accused of sexual crimes, owing perhaps to their greater degree of inte-

gration within American society, and to their conformity to the dominant pattern of monogamy. They were sometimes attacked, however, for excluding women from their Order, and for swearing not to violate the chastity of wives, sisters, and daughters of fellow Masons. Why, anti-Masons asked, was such an oath not extended to include *all* women? David Bernard, *Light on Masonry: A Collection of all the Most Important Documents on the Subject* (Utica, 1829), 62 n.

40. Anthony Gavin, *A Master-Key to Popery, Giving a Full Account of All the Customs of the Priests and Friars, and the Rites and Ceremonies of Popish Religion* (n.p., 1812), 70–72. Such traditional works of European anti-Catholicism were frequently reprinted and imitated in America.

41. *Cloven Foot*, 224. The Mormons were also alleged to regard the wives of infidels "lawful prey to any believer who can win them." Beadle, *Life in Utah*, 233.

42. Hogan, *Auricular Confession*, 289.

43. Ann Eliza Young, *Wife No. 19: or, the Story of a Life in Bondage, Being a Complete Exposé of Mormonism* (Hartford, 1875), 433, 440–41, 453.

44. Maria Ward, *Female Life among the Mormons: A Narrative of Many Years' Personal Experience, By the Wife of a Mormon Elder, Recently Returned from Utah* (New York, 1857), 24; Beadle, *Life in Utah*, 339.

45. Ward, *Female Life among the Mormons*, 68, 106, 374.

46. The Mormons, for instance, were imagined to engage in the most licentious practices in the Endowment House ceremonies. See Nelson W. Green (ed.), *Fifteen Years among the Mormons: Being the Narrative of Mrs. Mary Ettie V. Smith* (New York, 1857), 44–51.

47. Hogan, *Auricular Confession*, 254–55; *Cloven Foot*, 301–304.

48. This point is ably discussed by Kimball Young, *Isn't One Wife Enough?* (New York, 1954), 26–27.

49. *Ibid.*, 311.

50. Quoted in Mulder and Mortensen (eds.), *Among the Mormons*, 274–78.

51. George Bourne, *Lorette: The History of Louise, Daughter of a Canadian Nun, Exhibiting the Interior of Female Convents* (New York, 1834), 167–77; Hogan, *Auricular Confession*, 271; Frances Stenhouse, *A Lady's Life among the Mormons: A Record of Personal Experience as One of the Wives of a Mormon Elder* (New York, 1872), 77.

52. *Anti-Masonic Review*, I (December, 1828), 24 ff.; *Cloven Foot*, 325–42, 357–58; Froiseth (ed.), *Women of Mormonism*, 317–78; Ward, *Female Life among the Mormons*, 428–29.

53. Armstrong, *Masonry*, 22.

54. *Free Masonry: A Poem*, p. iv.

55. *Ibid.*, pp. iii, 51; Hopkins, *Renunciation of Free Masonry*, 5, 9–11; *Anti-Masonic Almanac*, 1830, pp. 28–29; Bernard, *Light on Masonry*, p. iii.

56. Stenhouse, *Lady's Life among the Mormons*, 142–43.

57. Hogan, *Auricular Confession*, 226–29, 233, 296–97.

## STATUS REVOLUTION AND REFERENCE GROUP THEORY

1. Richard Hofstadter, *The Age of Reform* (New York, 1955), Chap. IV, "The Status Revolution and Progressive Leaders," 131–172.

2. Alfred D. Chandler, Jr., "The Origins of Progressive Leadership," in Elting E. Morison, ed., *The Letters of Theodore Roosevelt* (Cambridge, Massachusetts, 1954), VIII, app. III, 1462–1465; George E. Mowry, *The California Progressives* (Berkeley and Los Angeles, 1951), Chap. IV, 86–104. See also George E. Mowry, *The Era of Theodore Roosevelt* (New York, 1958), Chap. 5, 85–105.

3. Data have been obtained from stand-ard references such as *Who's Who in America*, *Who's Who in New England*, *National Cyclopaedia of American Biography*, and several other similar works, newspapers and a few manuscript collections.

4. See Richard B. Sherman, "Augustus Peabody Gardner: The Conservative as Insurgent," *Essex Institute Historical Collections*, XCVII (October, 1961), 261–276.

5. Note comments about Lodge's "intelligent conservatism" by John A. Garraty, *Henry Cabot Lodge* (New York, 1953), 225–229; see also 284–285.

6. In 1910, 31.5 per cent of the population of Massachusetts was foreign-born, but, as noted, not even the Democrats had a significant number of foreign-born political leaders. See Massachusetts, *Report of the Commission on Immigration on the Problem of Immigration in Massachusetts* (Boston, 1914), 29.

7. Hofstadter, 135.

8. Mowry, *Era of Theodore Roosevelt*, 87 ff.

9. Richard B. Sherman, "Charles Sumner Bird and The Progressive Party in Massachusetts," *New England Quarterly*, XXXIII (September, 1960), 328–329.

10. See Richard M. Abrams, "A Paradox of Progressivism: Massachusetts on the Eve of Insurgency," *Political Science Quarterly*, LXXV (September, 1960), 379–399.

## CLASS

1. *The Historian's Craft* (New York, 1953), p. 158.

2. Quoted in Zoltan Haraszti, *John Adams and the Prophets of Progress* (Cambridge, 1952), p. 248.

3. Autobiography," *The Life and Selected Writings of Thomas Jefferson*, eds. Adrienne Koch and Walter Peden (New York, 1944), p. 38.

4. Asa Briggs, "The Language of Class in Early Nineteenth-Century England" in *Essays in Labor History*, eds. A. Briggs and J. Saville (London, 1960); Ralf Dahrendorf, *Class and Class Conflict in Industrial Society* (Stanford, 1959), pp. 3–7.

5. *Ibid.*, pp. 76, 153.

6. *The Historian's Craft*, p. 176. For the multiple definitions of class see Leonard Reissman, *Class in American Society* (Glencoe, Ill., 1960), passim; Joseph Kahl, *The American Class Structure* (New York, 1957).

7. Rowland Berthoff, "The Working Class," in *The Reconstruction of American History*, ed. John Higham (New York, 1962).

8. Lee Benson, *Turner and Beard* (Glencoe, Ill., 1960), pp. 108, 111; Robert P. Sharkey, *Money, Class and Party* (Baltimore, 1959), p. 293.

9. "The Concept of Power," *Behavioral Science*, III (July, 1957), 201–15.

10. Joseph Schumpeter, *Imperialism and Social Classes* (New York, 1951), p. 148; Talcott Parsons, "Social Classes and Class Conflict in the Light of Recent Sociological Theory," *Essays in Sociological Theory* (Glencoe, Ill., 1954), p. 328.

11. Kahl, *The American Class Structure*, p. 189.

12. Francis Biddle, *A Casual Past* (New York, 1961). p. 17.

13. Michael Chevalier, *Society, Manners and Politics in the United States*, edited with an introduction by John William Ward (New York, 1961), p. 398; G. W. Pierson, *Tocqueville and Beaumont in America* (New York, 1938), p. 603.

14. Oscar Handlin, "A Note on Social Mobility and the Recruitment of Entrepreneurs in the United States," *Explorations in Entrepreneurial History*, Winter Supplement (1956), pp. 1–5; Bernard Bailyn, *New England Merchants in the Seventeenth Century* (Cambridge, 1955), pp. 87–91, 135–58; John A. Munroe, *Federalist Delaware, 1775–1815* (New Brunswick, 1954), p. 199.

15. "Theodore Roosevelt's Ancestry, A Study in Heredity," *New York Genealogical and Biographical Record*, LXXV (1954), 196–205.

16. "By covert culture we refer to traits of culture rarely acknowledged by those who possess them." B. Bowron, L. M. Marx and A. Rose, "Literature and Covert Culture," *American Quarterly*, IX (Winter 1957), 377.

An example of the private satisfactions of genealogy is offered by the late Myron C. Taylor who took great pride in his descent from a vigorous personality named Captain John Underhill, a pioneer settler of Oyster Bay in the early seventeenth century. So devoted was Mr. Taylor to this ancestor that he sponsored and financed a four-volume genealogy of his Underhill ancestors. (J. C. Frost, *Underhill Genealogy* [New York, 1932]). He was also the prime mover of the Underhill Society, composed of the descendants of Captain

John Underhill (*New York Genealogical and Biographical Record*, XC, 92).

17. Introductory "Note" to Kenneth E. Hasbrouck and Ruth P. Neidgerd, *The Deyo (Deyoe) Family* (1958). See the review of this volume by A. D. Keator in the *New York Genealogical and Biographical Record* (October 1959).

18. Anthony R. Wagner, *English Genealogy* (London, 1960), pp. 178–205, 304–54.

19. Lester J. Cappon, "Genealogy, Handmaid of History," *Special Publications of the National Genealogical Society*, XVII, 3, 8. Some idea of the scope of genealogical literature, indexed as to family, may be obtained from Freeman Rider, ed. *The American Genealogical Index* (Middletown, Conn., 1942–52) and *The American Genealogical-Biographical Index to American Genealogical, Biographical and Local History Materials* (Middletown, Conn., 1952-date). See also Cappon, "Bibliography of American Genealogical Periodicals, *Bulletin of the New York Public Library*, LXVI (January 1962), 63–66; Capon, *American Genealogical Periodicals A Bibliography* . . . (New York, 1962).

20. Merle Curti et al., *The Making of An American Community A Case Study of Democracy in a Frontier County* (Stanford, 1959), pp. 1–11; Stanley Elkins and Eric McKitrick, "A Meaning for Turner's Frontier," *Political Science Quarterly*, LXIX (September 1954), 349.

21. *Imperialism and Social Classes*, p. 169.

22. (Chapel Hill, N. C., 1956), preface and author's note.

23. "The Beekmans of New York: Trade, Politics and Families," *William and Mary Quarterly*, XIV (October 1957), 605–6; *Idem*, XI (January, 1954), 98–104.

24. *The Degradation of the Democratic Dogma* (New York, 1949), p. 93.

25. Henry F. Pringle, *The Life and Times of William Howard Taft* (New York, 1939), I, 19.

26. Peter de Mendelssohn, *The Age of Churchill* (New York, 1961), p. 56.

27. The Great Mutation," *American Historical Review*, LXVIII (January, 1963), 323.

28. *The Social Sciences in Historical Study*, Bulletin 64 of the Social Science Research Council (New York, 1954), p. 96.

29. "The Kinship System of the Contemporary United States," *Essays in Sociological Theory*, p. 185.

30. "The Break-Up of Family Capitalism," *Partisan Review*, XXIV (Spring 1957), 317–20.

31. The real type differs from the ideal type construct of Max Weber. Writing of the ideal type as "formed by the one-sided accentuation of one or more points of view and by the synthesis of a great many diffuse, discrete, more or less present and occasionally absent *concrete individual* phenomena, which are arranged according to these one-sidedly emphasized viewpoints into a unified *analytical* construct," Weber seems to be outlining the process whereby fictional types are created. (My position on Weber follows closely that of Gabriel Kolko, "A Critique of Max Weber's Philosophy of History," *Ethics*, LXX [1959], 21–36; "Max Weber on America: Theory and Evidence," *History and Theory* [1961], 243.)

Not that fiction and aesthetics are without value for social science research, as Karl Deutsch has indicated. The semi-fiction of the ideal type meets and resembles the semi-reality of the fictional image of the patrician drawn by such careful hands as Marquand, Wharton, Holmes Sr., Auchincloss, Glasgow, and Faulkner. ("Summary statement on Results of the Conference on the Social Sciences in Historical Study," [mimeo, June 20–22, 1957], p. 19; A. Arnold, "Why Structure in Fiction: A Note to Social Scientists," *American Quarterly*, X [Fall 1958], 135). See also the interesting statement by A. J. Toynbee, "History, Science and Fiction," *The Philosophy of History in Our Time*, ed. Hans Meyerhoff (New York, 1959), pp. 117–18.

32. Clara Longworth de Chambrun, *The Making of Nicholas Longworth* (London, 1933), pp. 46–47. Other references to the big house in patrician personal literature include Julia Davis, *Family Vista* (New York, 1958), p. 9; Elting E. Morison, *Turmoil and Tradition* (Boston, 1960), p. 11; E. S. Ives and H. Dolson, *My Brother Adlai* (New York, 1956), p. 22; Herman Hagedorn, *The Roosevelt*

Family of Sagamore Hill (New York, 1954), pp. 38–40; W. E. Smith, The Francis Preston Blair Family in Politics (New York, 1933), I, 186; Eleanor Roosevelt, This is My Story (New York, 1939), pp. 117–23.

The big house and its significance is discussed in Edward C. Kirkland, Dream and Thought in the Business Community (Ithaca, N.Y., 1956), pp. 29–49 and by E. L. Godkin, "The Expenditures of Rich Men," Scribner's Magazine, XX (October 1896), 495.

33. Family Letters of the Three Wade Hamptons, ed. Charles E. Cauthen (Columbia, S. C., 1953), p. 14. The letter is dated February 6, 1811.

34. Planters and Business Men The Guignard Family of South Carolina 1795–1930, ed. Arney R. Childs (Columbia, S. C., 1957), pp. 17, 38–39; The Lides Go South . . . And West, The Record of a Planter Migration in 1835, ed. Fletcher M. Green (Columbia, S. C., 1952), p. v.

35. Ruth K. Nuermberg, The Clays of Alabama (Lexington, Ky., 1958), pp. 77–78, 85, 93, 103; Allen Tate, "A Southern Mode of the Imagination," Studies in American Culture, eds. J. J. Kwiat and M. C. Turpie (Minneapolis, 1960), p. 104.

36. Chambrun, The Making of Nicholas Longworth, p. 47.

37. Simpson, The Cokers of Carolina . . . , p. 291.

38. "The Kinship System of the Contemporary United States," p. 185.

39. Power Without Property (New York, 1959), p. 74.

40. "The Break-Up of Family Capitalism," pp. 317–20.

41. Ralph Hewins, The Richest American (New York, 1960), pp. 17, 20, 39, 391–92, 395.

42. "How Joe Kennedy Made His Millions," Life, January 25, 1963.

43. Tyler Dennett, John Hay (New York, 1933), p. 101.

44. Osborn Elliot, Men at the Top (New York, 1959), pp. 37, 67–68. For executive continuity along family lines in Russia see David Granick, The Red Executive (New York, 1960), p. 53.

45. Closest to such an account is A. W. Calhoun, A Social History of the American Family (3 vols.; Cleveland, 1917–19).

This is more than a half-century old and inadequate on many levels.

Without such a history, the tendency is to flounder in controversy that cannot be readily resolved. Witness the current sociological dispute over whether the American family is characteristically "extended" or characteristically "nuclear." Ruth Cavan, The American Family (New York, 1959), pp. 119–47; A. B. Hollingshead, "Class and Kinship in a Middle Western Community," American Sociological Review, XIV (1949), 469–75; John Sirjamaki, The American Family (Cambridge, 1959), pp. 141–43; Eugene Litwak, "Occupational Mobility and Extended Family Cohesion," American Sociological Review, XXV (February, 1960), 9–21; "The Use of Extended Family Groups in the Achievement of Social Goals: Some Policy Implications," Social Problems, VII (Winter, 1959–60), 177–87; Marvin B. Sussman, "The Isolated Nuclear Family: Fact or Fiction," Social Problems, VI (Spring, 1959).

Theoretical studies of the American family, not solidly grounded in history, have caused Richard Titmuss to exclaim: "much of the nonsense that is written in the subject [of family structure] to-day requires challenging." Especially, he added, "the theoretical studies of family emanating from the United States." Preface to Michael Young and Peter Willmott, Family and Kinship in East London (Glencoe, Ill., 1957).

There is an echo of this controversy in historical literature, Bernard Bailyn, Education in the Forming of American Society. . . . (Chapel Hill, N. C., 1960), p. 250.

46. Turmoil and Tradition (Boston, 1960).

47. See especially David C. McClelland, The Achieving Society (Princeton, 1961).

48. See, for example, William J. Parish, The Charles Ilfeld Company (Cambridge, 1961) and other volumes of the Harvard Studies in Business History.

49. Lewis B. Namier, England in the Age of the American Revolution (London, 1930), pp. 22–23; H. J. Habakkuk, The European Nobility in the Eighteenth Century, ed. A. Goodwin (London, 1953), p. 2.

50. "Family Structure and Economic Change in Nineteenth-Century Europe," Journal of Economic History, XV (1955), 1, 4.

51. There is, for example, ample material in the debates of the various state legislatures and the proceedings of the state constitutional conventions.

Wills, as sources of insight into family structure and also into family relationships, have been much neglected. There was a time when the making of a will was not the cut-and-dried procedure that the legal profession has made of it. Wills were more personal documents than they now are; individuals not only disposed of property but told why they acted as they did, and it is the whys which are of interest to the student of family history. Eugene E. Prussing. *The Estate of George Washington Deceased* (Boston, 1927), p. 3. Washington declared that in the construction of his will, "it will readily be perceived that no professional character has been consulted, or has had any agency."

52. James W. Hurst, *Law and Social Process in United States History* (Ann Arbor, 1960), p. 10.

53. (Boston, 1944).

54. *Advice to the Privileged Orders* . . . , p. 29.

55. "Primogeniture and Entailed Estates in America," *Columbia Law Review* (1928).

56. Unpublished doctor's thesis, University of Chicago, 1927.

57. "Politics and Social Structure in Virginia," *Seventeenth Century America*, ed. James M. Smith (Chapel Hill, 1959), pp. 110–11.

58. *Studies in the History of American Law* (New York, 1930).

59. Carl Bridenbaugh, *Cities in Revolt* (New York, 1955), p. 138.

60. Bailyn, "Politics and Social Structure in Virginia," pp. 110–11.

61. Sigmund Diamond, *The Reputation of the American Businessman* (Cambridge, 1955).

62. R. Richard Wohl, "Three Generations of Business Enterprise in a Midwestern City: The McGees of Kansas City," *Journal of Economic History*, XVI (December, 1956), 514–28.

63. G. W. Pierson, *Tocqueville and Beaumont in America*, pp. 117, 368, 603; *Journey to England and Ireland*, ed. J. P. Mayer (New Haven, 1958), p. 70.

64. *Imperialism and Social Classes*, p. 169. Schumpeter's conclusion as to the mobility of the European aristocracy, that the class could be likened to a "bus whose

passengers are always changing," avails us little because there is almost no society without some mobility. The problem is not whether there is mobility, but its extent and rate; the relationship of mobility rates to time and place; whether the passengers change more rapidly in America than in Europe and in one period of history rather than another; and, finally, the circumstances of the change.

65. *Elsie Venner* (Boston, 1861), pp. 1–2.

66. Professor Richard B. Morris, referring to mobility in colonial America, affirmed the applicability of "the expression from shirtsleeves to shirtsleeves in three generations." "Class Struggle and the American Revolution," *William and Mary Quarterly*, XIX (January 1962), 27. N.S.B. Gras speaks vaguely of the "chronic tendency of mercantile families to dry up." *Business and Capitalism* (New York, 1946), p. 162.

67. Certain problems involved in historians' concern with mobility are noted by Oscar Handlin, "Ethnic Factors in Social Mobility," *Explorations in Entrepreneurial History*, IX (October 1956), 1–7; *Class, Status and Power*, eds. R. Bendix and S. M. Lipset, pp. 5–6; Oscar and Mary Handlin, *The Dimensions of Liberty* (Cambridge, 1961), pp. 133–54.

68. Catherine S. Crary, "The Humble Immigrant and the American Dream, 1746–1776," *Mississippi Valley Historical Review* (June 1959).

69. Schumpeter, *Imperialism and Social Classes*, pp. 140, 149, 166, 169.

70. William T. Whitney Jr., "The Crowninshields of Salem 1880–1808," *Essex Institute Historical Collections* (April and June 1958).

71. H. R. Trevor-Roper, "The Gentry 1540–1640," *The Economic History Review Supplements* (n.d., Cambridge), pp. 6, 31 and *passim*; Alan Simpson, *The Wealth of the Gentry 1540–1660* (Chicago, 1961), p. 21.

72. W. L. Warner et al., *Social Class in America* (Chicago, 1949), pp. 16–17.

73. See especially the criticisms by Ruth R. Kornhauser, "The Warner Approach to Social Stratification," in *Class, Status and Power*, eds. Bendix and Lipset; Harold W. Pfautz and Otis D. Duncan, "A Critical Evaluation of Warner's Work in Community Stratification," *American Sociological Review*, XV (April, 1950), 205–

15; Oscar Handlin, *New England Quarterly*, XV (1942), 554; XVIII (1945), 523; *Journal of Economic History*, VII (1947).

74. C. Wright Mills, *The Sociological Imagination* (New York, 1959), p. 154.

75. *Who Governs? Democracy and Power in an American City* (New Haven, 1961), p. 11. The book contains no reference to important historical studies such as Leonard W. Labaree, *Conservatism in Early American History* (New York, 1948), and M. M. Klein, "Democracy and Politics in Colonial New York," *New York History*, XL (July, 1959), 221–46, that could have contributed depth to the earlier chapters. For additional references that could have improved Dr. Dahl's understanding of power and its exercise in the colonial period see Bernard Bailyn, "Political Experience and Enlightenment Ideas in Eighteenth-Century America," *American Historical Review*, LXVII (January, 1962), 341, n2. See also Roger Champagne, "Family Politics versus Constitutional Principles: The New York Assembly Election of 1768 and 1769," *William and Mary Quarterly*, XX (January, 1963), 57–79.

76. Eric E. Lampard, "American Historians and the Study of Urbanization," *American Historical Review*, LXVII (October, 1961), 49–61.

77. "A Meaning for Turner's Frontier," *Political Science Quarterly*, LXIX.

78. "Local History Contributions and Techniques in the Study of Two Colonial Cities," *Bulletin of the American Association for State and Local History*, II (February, 1959), esp. the comment by Bayrd Still, pp. 246–50, which has important bearing upon the integration of local history and community sociology. See also Philip D. Jordan's survey, *The Nature and Practice of State and Local History* (Washington, 1958).

79. Heinz Eulau, *Class and Party in the Eisenhower Years* (Glencoe, Ill., 1962), p. 19; Reissman, *Class in American Society*, 203–5.

80. *The Power Elite* (New York, 1956).

81. *Top Leadership U.S.A.* (Chapel Hill, N. C., 1959).

82. E. Digby Baltzell, *Philadelphia Gentleman* (Glencoe, Ill., 1958), p. 21.

83. Lawrence Bloomgarden, "Our New Elite Colleges," *Commentary* (February, 1960).

84. "The Introduction of Industrialists into the British Peerage: A Study in Adaptation of a Social Institution," *American Historical Review* (October, 1959), pp. 1–16.

85. *Feudal Society*, pp. 283–85.

86. R. R. Palmer, *The Age of the Democratic Revolution* (Princeton, 1959), pp. 508–17.

87. Not that an establishment or even a vestigial establishment is an infallible guide. Compilations such as Burke's *Peerage* and the *Almanach Da Gotha* and its successor, the *Genealogisches Handbuch Des Adels*, are by no means decisive in establishing antiquity and continuity in family lines. (Wagner, *op. cit.*, p. 84). Even so, they are rough indices of class belonging which, with all their faults, are probably more useful as a finder for European aristocracy than is the *Social Register* for the American patriciate. (My observations as to the *Social Register* are based on a conversation with Norton Mezvinsky who is preparing a study of Boston and New York aristocracy between 1875 and 1925. He has compared *Register* data with other materials and places less reliance upon the *Register* than does Baltzell.)

88. H. H. Gerth and C. Wright Mills, *From Max Weber* (New York, 1958), pp. 180–95; Kahl, *American Class Structure*, p. 16.

89. Arthur B. Ferguson, *The Indian Summer of English Chivalry* (Durham, N. C., 1960), pp. 119–20, 182; Lewis Namier, *The Structure of Politics at the Accession of George III* (London, 1957), p. 10; Frank Freidel, "The Education of Franklin Delano Roosevelt," *Harvard Educational Review*, XXXX (Spring, 1961), 158–67.

90. William B. Hesseltine, "Four American Traditions," *Journal of Southern History*, XXVII (February, 1961), 4.

91. Robert A. Dahl, "A Critique of the Ruling Elite Model," *American Political Science Review*, LII (1958). The literature on the nature of community power is a large one. The extent to which power is concentrated or diffused has been shown to be much influenced by the researcher's

procedure. (R. E. Wolfinger, "Reputation and Reality in the Study of 'Community Power,'" *American Sociological Review*, XXV [October, 1960], 636–44; David B. Truman, "Theory and Research on Metropolitan Political Leadership: Report on a Conference," *Items, Social Science Research Council*, March, 1961, p. 3).

Using one type of research design, Floyd Hunter developed an elitist conception of power. Other approaches to power, like that employed by Dahl in his study of New Haven, see power as more diffused than concentrated with the balance likely to shift with the issue being decided N. W. Polsby, "The Sociology of Community Power: A Reassessment," *Social Forces*, XXVII (March, 1959), 232–36.

92. *The History of Political Parties in the Province of New York, 1760–1776* (Madison, Wis., 1909).

93. *Gentlemen Freeholders* (Williamsburg, Va., 1952).

94. *Conservatism in Early American History* (New York, 1948), pp. 1–31.

95. See, for example, Robert P. Sharkey, *Money, Class and Party* (Baltimore, 1959), 290–311; Forrest McDonald, *We The People* (Chicago, 1958), pp. 358–99.

96. Klein, *New York History*, XL, 240; Champagne, "Family Politics. . . ."

97. J. E. Neale, "The Biographical Approach to History," *History*, New Series, XXXVI (October, 1951), 193–203.

98. Herbert Butterfield, "George III and the Namier School," *Encounter*, 1957, pp. 70–76; *George III and the Historians* (New York, 1959); Lee Benson, *Turner and Beard*, pp. 159, 195.

99. The difficulties involved in establishing cause are dealt with by Sidney Hook in *Theory and Practice in Historical Study* (New York, 1946), pp. 110–15. Among the better more recent accounts is

Cushing Strout's in *History and Theory*, I (1961), 175–85.

100. David Donald, "Toward a Reconsideration of the Abolitionists," in *Lincoln Reconsidered: Essays on the Civil War* (New York, 1956); Richard Hofstadter, *The Age of Reform* (New York, 1960); Alfred D. Chandler Jr., "The Origins of Progressive Leadership," in Elting E. Morison, ed. *The Letters of Theodore Roosevelt* (Cambridge, 1954), VIII, appendix III, 1462–65; George E. Mowry, *The California Progressives* (Berkeley and Los Angeles, 1951), pp. 86–104; Ari Hoogenboom, *Outlawing the Spoils. A History of the Civil Service Reform Movement* (Urbana, Ill., 1961), pp. 190–97; Gerald W. McFarland, "The New York Mugwumps of 1884: A Profile," *Political Science Quarterly*, LXXVIII (March, 1963), 40–65. Critiques of this method include R. A. Skotheim, "A Note on Historical Method. . . ," *Journal of Southern History*, XXV (1959), 356–65; Richard B. Sherman, "The Status Revolution and Massachusetts Progressive Leadership," see above.

101. Robert K. Merton, *Social Theory and Social Structure* (Glencoe, Ill., 1957), pp. 50–51.

102. Herbert H. Hyman, "Reflections on Reference Groups," *Public Opinion Quarterly* (Fall 1960), pp. 383–96.

103. Edward N. Saveth, "Henry Adams: Waning of America's Patriciate," *Commentary*, October 1957.

104. Rowland Berthoff, "The American Social Order: A Conservative Hypothesis," *The American Historical Review*, LXV (April 1960), 511.

105. Seymour M. Lipset, *Political Man* (New York, 1959), p. 301.

106. C. Vann Woodward, "Populist Heritage and the Intellectual," *American Scholar*, XXIX (Winter, 1959), 70.

107. *George III and the Historians*, passim.

## MOBILITY

1. James Morton Smith, ed., *Seventeenth-Century America* (Chapel Hill [1959]), 10ff.; Oscar Handlin, ed., *American Principles and Issues* (New York, 1961), viff., 31ff.

2. See, e.g., Francis Higginson, *New-*

*England's Plantation* (London, 1630); Edward Johnson, *Wonder-Working Providence*, ed. J. F. Jameson (New York, 1910), 198ff.; Cotton Mather, *Pietas in Patriam, the Life of His Excellency Sir William Phips* (London, 1697), 28–30.

3. See Andrew Carnegie, *Triumphant Democracy* (New York, 1893), 139ff.; James Willard Hurst, *Law and the Conditions of Freedom* (Madison, 1956); David M. Potter, *People of Plenty* (Chicago [1954]).

4. E. A. J. Johnson, *American Economic Thought in the Seventeenth Century* (London, 1932), 98ff.; Bernard Bailyn, "The Apologia of Robert Keayne," *William and Mary Quarterly*, VII (1950), 568ff.

5. Richard McKeon, "The Development of the Concept of Property in Political Philosophy," *Ethics*, XLVIII (1937-38), 302ff., 344.

6. See above, 76; Francis Bowen, *Principles of Political Economy* (2d ed., Boston, 1859), 27.

7. See Henry C. Carey, *Principles of Political Economy* (Philadelphia, 1837-1840); Bowen, *Principles of Political Economy*, 127, 128, 545, 546; William G. Sumner, *What Social Classes Owe to Each Other* (New York, 1883), 112ff.; Joseph Dorfman, *Economic Mind in American Civilization* (New York, 1949), III, 258ff.

8. John Taylor, *Inquiry into the Principles and Policy of the Government of the United States* (Fredericksburg, 1814), 274, 275; McKeon, "Concept of Property," 360.

9. Daniel Webster, "First Settlement of New England," *Works* (4th ed., Boston, 1853), I, 34ff.; Edward Everett, *Address Delivered Before the Mercantile Library Association* (Boston, 1838), 13.

10. George Frederic Parsons, "The Labor Question," *Atlantic Monthly*, LVIII (1886), 98–99. See also above, p. 184, n. 13.

11. Russell H. Conwell, *Acres of Diamonds* (New York, 1915), 17ff.

12. Seymour M. Lipset and Reinhard Bendix, *Social Mobility and Industrial Society* (Berkeley, 1959), 28ff.; Kaare Svalastoga, *Prestige, Class and Mobility* (Copenhagen, 1959), 356ff.; Natalie Rogoff, "Social Stratification in France and the United States," Reinhard Bendix and Seymour M. Lipset, *Class, Status and Power* (Glencoe [1953]), 577ff.; David V. Glass, *Social Mobility in Britain* (London [1954]).

13. Oscar and Mary F. Handlin,

"Memorandum on the History of Social Mobility" (International Sociological Association, Subcommittee on Stratification Research, September 17, 1959).

14. The Center already has under way two extensive statistical studies: one of colonial New England college graduates, their parents and children; the other of the career lines of Americans high in achievement.

15. On these problems, see in general Pitirim Sorokin, *Social Mobility* (New York, 1927), 117ff., 141ff., 164ff., 414ff., 463ff. For community studies that bear upon the problem, see Lipset and Bendix, *Social Life of a Modern Community* (New Haven, 1941), I, II.

16. See above, 114. For material on licensing, see Henry L. Taylor, *Professional Education in the United States* (Albany, 1900), I, 216ff., 496ff., II, 813ff., 1002ff., 1284ff.; Oscar and Mary F. Handlin, *Commonwealth* (New York, 1947), 72ff., 223fl.

17. Oscar Handlin, *John Dewey's Challenge to Education* (New York [1959]), 37. On the general problem see Lipset and Bendix, *Social Mobility*, 91ff., Sorokin, *Social Mobility*, 169ff., 187ff., Svalastoga, *Prestige, Class and Mobility*, 399ff.

18. Robert F. Seybolt, *Apprenticeship and Apprenticeship Education in Colonial New England and New York* (New York, 1917).

19. Robert F. Seybolt, *The Evening School in Colonial America* (Urbana, 1925); Handlin, *John Dewey's Challenge*, 21ff.; Paul H. Douglas, *American Apprenticeship and Industrial Education* (New York, 1921); Perry W. Reeves, *Digest of Development of Industrial Education* (Washington [1932]); Frederick E. Bolton and John E. Corbally, *Educational Sociology* (New York [1941]), 412ff.; Charles A. Prosser and Charles R. Allen, *Vocational Education in a Democracy* (New York, 1925), 220ff.; Charles A. Bennett, *History of Manual and Industrial Education* (Peoria [1926-37]), I, 266ff., II.

20. Thomas Woody, *Educational Views of Benjamin Franklin* (New York, 1931), 115ff., 142ff., 151ff.; Bernard Bailyn, *Education in the Forming of American Society* (Chapel Hill [1960]), 33ff.

21. See Omar Pancoast, Jr., *Occupational Mobility* (New York, 1941), 124ff. Some of these problems are treated for the recent period by Byron S. Hollinshead, *Who Should Go to College* (New York, 1952), 28ff., 135ff.

22. See, e.g., Frederick Rudolph, *Mark Hopkins and the Log* (New Haven, 1956), 65ff.; Bolton and Corbally, *Educational Sociology*, 76ff., 86ff.

23. See, e.g., Carter Goodrich and Sol Davidson, "The Wage Earner in the Westward Movement," *Political Science Quarterly*, L (1935), 161ff.; Joseph Schafer, 'Safety Valve for Labor," *Mississippi Valley Historical Review*, XXIV (1937), 299ff.

24. See B. H. Hibbard, *History of Public Land Policies* (New York, 1924); Roy M. Robbins, *Our Landed Heritage* (Princeton [1942]); George Nadel, *Australia's Colonial Culture* (Melbourne [1957], 10ff.

25. See Merle Curti, *Making of an American Community* (Stanford, 1959), 57, 77ff., 141ff., 179ff.; Sorokin, *Social Mobility*, 43ff.; Bowen, Political Economy, 493ff.

26. See Bowen, *Political Economy*, 104ff., 129ff.

27. See Lipset and Bendix, *Social Mobility*, 101ff., 114ff.

28. Curti, *Making of an American Community*, 222ff.; Lewis E. Atherton, *The Pioneer Merchant in Mid-America* (Columbia, 1939); Lewis E. Atherton, *Southern Country Store* (Baton Rouge, 1949); Lewis E. Atherton, *Main Street on the Middle Border* (Bloomington, 1954). See also Svalastoga, *Prestige Class and Mobility*, 394ff.

29. See, e.g., Seymour M. Lipset, *The Political Man* (Garden City, 1960), 367ff.

30. Arthur W. Calhoun, *Social History of the American Family* (Cleveland, 1917), I, 37ff. See also Lipset and Bendix, *Social Mobility*, 250ff.

31. See, e.g., Catherine E. Reiser, *Pittsburgh's Commercial Development* (Harrisburg, 1951), 125ff.; Richard C. Wade, *The Urban Frontier* (Cambridge, Mass., 1959), 203ff.; Natalie Rogoff, *Recent Trends in Occupational Mobility* (Glencoe [1953]), 64ff., 75ff.; Lipset and Bendix, *Social Mobility*, 104ff.; Oscar and Mary F. Handlin, "Ethnic Factors in Social Mobility," *Explorations in Entrepreneurial History*, IX (1956), 1ff.

32. Mather, *Pietas in Patriam*; Benjamin Franklin, "The Way to Wealth," *Works*, ed. Jared Sparks (Boston, 1836), II, 87ff.; Lipset and Bendix, *Social Mobility*, 81ff.; Kenneth S. Lynn, *The Dream of Success* (Boston, 1955); R. R. Wohl, "The Rags to Riches Story," Bendix and Lipset, *Class, Status and Power*, 388ff.

33. See Richard D. Birdsall, *Berkshire County* (New Haven, 1959), 25ff.; Dixon R. Fox, *Decline of Aristocracy in the Politics of New York* (New York, 1919); David M. Ellis, *Landlords and Farmers in the Hudson-Mohawk Region* (Ithaca, 1946); Neil A. McNall, *Agricultural History of the Genesee Valley* (Philadelphia, 1952).

34. Earl of Bellomont to the Lords of Trade, May 13, 1699, E. B. O'Callaghan and Berthold Fernow, *Documents Relative to the Colonial History of the State of New York* (Albany, 1856–87), IV, 516. For the professions generally, see Taylor, *Professional Education*; A. M. Carr-Saunders and P. A. Wilson, *The Professions* (Oxford, 1933).

35. Handlin, *Commonwealth*, 104, 138–139, 223–224; Handlin, *John Dewey's Challenge*, 35; Carr-Saunders and Wilson, *Professions*, 65ff.; Lawrence Bloomgarden, "Who Shall Be Our Doctors?" *Commentary*, XXIII (1957), 506ff.; Lawrence Bloomgarden, "Our Changing Elite Colleges," *ibid.*, XXIX (1960), 150ff. See also, for England, Charles Newman, *Evolution of Medical Education in the Nineteenth Century* (London, 1957).

36. See George G. Mercer, *The American Scholar in Professional Life* (Philadelphia [1889]), 13ff.; Birdsall, *Berkshire County*, 214ff.; Carr-Saunders and Wilson, *Professions*, 55ff.

37. For expressions of the ideology see Henry Adams, *Degradation of the Democratic Dogma* (New York, 1919); Irving Babbitt, *Democracy and Leadership* (New York, 1925); Ralph A. Cram, *The Nemesis of Mediocrity* (Boston, 1917); Ralph A. Cram, *End of Democracy* (Boston, 1937); Paul Elmer More, *Aristocracy and Justice* (Boston, 1915). See also David Spitz, *Patterns of*

*Anti-Democratic Thought* (New York, 1949). The first effort at analysis, E. D. Baltzell, *Philadelphia Gentleman* (Glencoe, 1958) suffers from the inclination to accept the self-evaluations of the group.

38. Oscar and Mary F. Handlin, "Cultural Aspects of Social Mobility" (International Sociological Association, Working Conference on Social Stratification, December, 1957); Curti, *Making of an American Community*, 440, 441.

39. See Lipset, *Political Man*, 48ff.;

Thomas W. Shea, Jr., "Barriers to Economic Development in Traditional Societies," *Journal of Economic History*, XIX (1959), 504ff.; Herbert Kisch, "The Textile Industries in Silesia and the Rhineland," *ibid.*, XIX (1959), 541ff.; Sorokin, *Social Mobility*, 508ff.; A.N. Whitehead, *Adventures of Ideas* (New York, 1933), 353ff.; John S. Mill, *On Liberty*, ed. R. B. McCallum (Oxford, 1946), 50ff.; H. M. Kallen, ed., *Freedom in the Modern World* (New York, 1928), 25.

## SOCIAL STRUCTURE

1. Philip Alexander Bruce, *Social Life of Virginia in the Seventeenth Century* (Richmond, 1907), pp. 15, 17–18; "The Virginia Census, 1624–25," *Virginia Magazine of History and Biography*, VII (1899–1900), 364–67; Edward Channing, *A History of the United States* (New York and London, 1905–25), I, 204–5.

2. See, e.g., Alexander Brown, *The Genesis of the United States* (Boston and New York, 1897), I, 142, 180, n. 1, 244–45, 393–99; II, 595–96, 738, 741; *Calendar of State Papers and Manuscripts Relating to English Affairs . . . in the Archives and Collections of Venice . . .*, Vol. XI, Nos. 52, 466, 794, 821; Carl Russell Fish (ed.), *Guide to the Materials for American History in Roman and Other Italian Archives* (Washington, 1911), pp. 150ff.; Henry Chandlee Forman, *Jamestown and St. Mary's* (Baltimore, 1938), pp. 37, 38; Alexander Brown, *The First Republic in America* (New York and Boston, 1898), pp. 48, 50, 51–52, 62, 79–80, 121, 123, 125, 152, 160, 184–85, 218–19.

3. Brown, *Genesis*, II, 700–706.

4. Quoted in Louis B. Wright, *The First Gentlemen of Virginia* (San Marino, 1940), p. 109.

5. Susan Myra Kingsbury (ed.), *Records of the Virginia Company* (Washington, 1906–35), III, 21.

6. "Minutes of the Council and General Court," *Virginia Magazine of History and Biography*, XXIII (1915), 138.

7. Wesley Frank Craven and Walter B. Hayward, *The Journal of Richard Norwood, Surveyor of Bermuda* (New York, 1945); Brown, *Genesis*, I, 442;

"London's Lotterie," *William and Mary Quarterly*, V (3d ser., 1948), 259–64.

8. Herbert Levi Osgood, *The American Colonies in the Seventeenth Century* (New York and London, 1904—1907), I, 32–34; II, 30–32; Philip Alexander Bruce, *Economic History of Virginia in the Seventeenth Century* (New York and London, 1896), I, 3–4.

9. Wesley Frank Craven, *Dissolution of the Virginia Company* (New York, 1932), p. 24. For an account of the structure of the Company see William Robert Scott, *The Constitution and Finance of English, Scottish and Irish Joint-Stock Companies to 1720* (Cambridge, 1910), II, 247–59, 266–88.

10. A *Declaration of the State of the Colonie and Affairs in Virginia* (London, 1620), in Peter Force (ed.), *Tracts and Other Papers, Relating . . . to the . . . Colonies in North America* (Washington, 1836–46), III, 5; Brown, *Genesis*, I, 357.

11. John Smith, *Description of Virginia and Proceedings of the Colonie* (Oxford, 1612), in Lyon Gardiner Tyler (ed.), *Narratives of Early Virginia* (New York, 1907), p. 178.

12. Susan Myra Kingsbury, "A Comparison of the Virginia Company with the Other English Trading Companies of the Sixteenth and Seventeenth Centuries," *Annual Report of the American Historical Association for the Year 1906* (Washington, 1907), pp. 162–63.

13. Quoted in Keith Glenn, "Captain John Smith and the Indians," *Virginia Magazine of History and Biography*, LII (1944), 231, n. 12.

14. Wesley Frank Craven, "Indian Policy in Early Virginia," *William and*

*Mary Quarterly*, I (3d ser., 1944), 65–82.

15. John Smith, *Description of Virginia*, in Tyler (ed.), *op. cit.*, pp. 125–26, 140–41, 159–60; Thomas Jefferson Wertenbaker, *Patrician and Plebeian in Virginia* (Charlottesville, 1910), pp. 5–9; Bruce, *Social Life*, pp. 39–43.

16. The quotations are in Osgood, *op. cit.*, I, 46–47; Smith, *Generall Historie*, in Tyler (ed.), *op. cit.*, pp. 331–32; John Smith, *The Proceedings of the English Colonie in Virginia* (Oxford, 1612), in the A. G. Bradley edition of Edward Arber (ed.), *Travels and Works of Captain John Smith* (Edinburgh, 1919), I, 149. See also Osgood, *op. cit.*, I, 50, 54–55; Bruce, *Economic History*, I, 197.

17. Channing, *op. cit.*, I, 204.

18. *Calendar of State Papers, East Indies, 1571–1616*, No. 432; Brown, *Genesis*, I, 252–54; E. Ribton-Turner, *A History of Vagrants and Vagrancy* (London, 1887), 141; Kingsbury (ed.), *Records*, I, 304–6, 270, 359; III, 259; *Acts of the Privy Council of England, Colonial Series*, Vol. I, No. 42; Abbot Emerson Smith, *Colonists in Bondage* (Chapel Hill, 1947), pp. 147–49; Richard B. Morris, *Government and Labor in Early America* (New York, 1946), p. 385.

19. A. E. Smith, *op. cit.*, pp. 94–95; Morris, *op. cit.*, p. 323.

20. Kingsbury (ed), *Records*, I, 520, II, 108; A. E. Smith, *op. cit.*, pp. 139–40.

21. Craven, *Virginia Company*, pp. 29–33; Scott, *op. cit.*, II, 250–52; Philip Alexander Bruce, *Institutional History of Virginia in the Seventeenth Century* (New York and Lonon, 1910), II, 237–41.

22. A. E. Smith, *op. cit.*, pp. 44–46.

23. Brown, *Genesis*, I, 355.

24. *Ibid.*, I, 356.

25. *A Sermon Preached in London before the Right Honourable Lord la warre, Lord governor and Captaine Generall of Virginia* (London, 1610), quoted in Perry Miller, "Religion and Society in the Early Literature: The Religious Impulse in the Founding of Virginia," *William and Mary Quarterly*, VI (3d ed., 1949), 31; Brown, *Genesis*, I, 364.

26. James Curtis Ballagh, *White Servitude in the Colony of Virginia* ("Johns Hopkins University Studies in Historical and Political Science, 13th Series," Vols. VII–VIII [Baltimore, 1895]), pp. 15–17;

Craven, *Virginia Company*, pp. 29–33; Craven, *Southern Colonies*, pp. 85–90; A. E. Smith, *op. cit.*, pp. 8–10; Kingsbury, "Comparison," *op. cit.*, pp. 163–69.

27. *The New Life of Virginea . . . Being the Second Part of Nova Britannia* (London, 1612), in Force (ed.), *op. cit.*, I, 17–18; *Nova Britannia*, in Force (ed.), *op. cit.*, I, 26.

28. *A True and Sincere Declaration* (London, 1609), in Brown, *Genesis*, I, 352.

29. Quoted in Craven, *Southern Colonies*, p. 64.

30. Appendix to *A True and Sincere Declaration*, in Brown, *Genesis*, I, 352.

31. *For the Colony in Virginea Britannia, Lawes Divine, Morall and Martiall, &c* (London, 1612), in Force (ed.), *op. cit.*, III, 68.

32. Kingsbury (ed.), *Records*, III, 216–19.

33. *Ibid.*, p. 15.

34. *Ibid.*, p. 27.

35. *Ibid.*, p. 22.

36. For the full text of the code see *For the Colony in Virginea Britannia. Lawes Divine, Morall and Martiall &c* (London, 1612), in Force (ed.), *op. cit.*, Vol. III.

37. *For the Colony in Virginea Britannia*, in Force (ed.), *op. cit.*, III, 44, 55, 61–62.

38. Kingsbury (ed.), *Records*, III, 173, 160.

39. Appendix to *A True and Sincere Declaration* (1609), in Brown, *Genesis*, I, 352; *Virginia Company* broadside of 1610, in Brown, *Genesis*, I, 439.

40. Quoted in Charles M. Andrews, *The Colonial Period of American History* (New Haven, 1934–38), I, 113–14.

41. Brown, *Genesis*, II, 648–49.

42. Morris, *op. cit.*, pp. 169–71.

43. Ballagh, *op. cit.*, pp. 22–23; Osgood, *op. cit.*, I, 75–77; Bruce, *Economic History*, I, 212–15; Craven, *Southern Colonies*, pp. 116–17; A. E. Smith, *op. cit.*, pp. 10–11.

44. Quoted in Miller, "Religion and Society," *op. cit.*, p. 37.

45. Craven, *Virginia Company*, *passim*, but esp. pp. 168–71; Craven, *Southern Colonies*, pp. 145–47; Scott, *op. cit.*, II, 266–88; Susan Myra Kingsbury, *An Intro-*

duction to the Records of the Virginia Company of London (Washington, 1905), pp. 34–35, 40–41, 94–95.

46. "Instructions to Governor Yeardley, 1618," Virginia Magazine of History and Biography, II (1894–95), 161–62; Bruce, Economic History, I, 226–33, 511–14; Ballagh, op. cit., pp. 25–28, 31; Craven, Virginia Company, pp. 50–57; Craven, Southern Colonies, pp. 127–29.

47. A. E. Smith, op. cit., pp. 11–17; Ballagh, op. cit., pp. 28–30; Bruce Economic History, II, 41–48; Morris, op. cit., p. 395.

48. Kingsbury (ed.), Records, III, 115, 493–94, 505.

49. Thomas Jefferson Wertenbaker, Virginia under the Stuarts (Princeton, 1914), pp. 38–39; Craven, Virginia Company, pp. 70–80; Craven, Southern Colonies, pp. 127–29; "Proceedings of the First Assembly in Virginia, Held July 30, 1619," in Colonial Records of Virginia (Richmond, 1874).

50. Samuel H. Yonge, "The Site of Old 'James Towne,' 1607–1698," Virginia Magazine of History and Biography, XI (1903–4), 399–400.

51. A Declaration of the State of the Colony (1620), in Force (ed.), op. cit., III, 5–6.

52. Kingsbury (ed.), Records, IV, 59, 61–62, 239, 234; see also ibid., pp. 41–42, 232, 235–36.

53. Ibid., pp. 235–36, 312–32; III, 417; see also ibid., III, 456.

54. Proclamation of Governor Wyatt, June, 1622, in Kingsbury (ed), Records, III, 659.

55. Act of March, 1623/24 (ibid., IV, 584).

56. Act of March, 1623/24 (ibid., IV, 582).

57. Ibid., IV, 564, 581; Smith, Generall Historie, in Tyler (ed.), op. cit., p. 356; George Sandys to John Ferrar, April 11, 1623, in Kingsbury (ed.), Records, IV, 110–11.

58. The figures are derived from the muster rolls in John Camden Hotten, The Original Lists of Persons of Quality; Emigrants, Religious Exiles . . . Who Went from Great Britain to the American Plantations, 1600–1700 (London, 1874).

59. A. E. Smith, op. cit., pp. 226–29; Kingsbury (ed.), Records, IV, 128–30.

60. Kingsbury (ed.), Records, IV, 473.

61. Pory to Carleton, September 30, 1619, in Tyler (ed.), op. cit., p. 285; Kingsbury (ed.), Records, III, 469.

62. Kingsbury (ed.), Records, III, 263.

63. Ibid., IV, 38–39.

64. Ibid., pp. 71, 237; see also ibid., pp. 455–57.

65. The Rights of the British Colonies asserted and proved (Boston, 1764), in Samuel Eliot Morison (ed.), Sources and Documents Illustrating the American Revolution . . . (2d ed.; Oxford, 1929), p. 8.

66. Quoted in Paul F. Lazarsfeld, "Public Opinion and the Classical Tradition," Public Opinion Quarterly, XXI, No. 1 (Spring, 1957), 53.

67. Kingsbury (ed.), Records, IV, 411, 417, 424–25, 416, 419.

## LEADERSHIP

1. Henry James, Hawthorne (1956 Reprint), 34.

2. 8 Julian Boyd, ed., The Papers of Thomas Jefferson, 635.

3. 26 J. C. Fitzpatrick, ed., Writings of George Washington, 483.

4. The Crisis, no. 13.

5. Jefferson, First Inaugural Address.

6. 9 Life and Works of John Adams, 420.

7. Memorial, quoted in R. E. Delmage, "American Idea of Progress," 91 Proceedings of the American Philosophical Society, 314.

8. 26 Writings of Washington, 227.

9. 3 Clarence E. Carter, ed., Territorial Papers, 264.

10. K. M. Rowland, I Life of George Mason, 166.

11. 10 P. L. Ford, ed., Writings of Thomas Jefferson, 378.

12. William Tudor, Life of James Otis, 144.

13. Josiah Quincy, Memoir of the Life of Josiah Quincy, 289.

14. "Dissertation on Canon and Feudal Law," 3 Works, 448. When in 1785 Adams recommended his son John Quincy to Professor Waterhouse at Harvard College, he noted that while the boy was

"awkward in speaking Latin," in "English and French poetry I know not where you would find anybody his superior, in Roman and English history, few persons of his age. He has translated Virgil's Aeneid, Suetonius, the whole of Sallust and Tacitus Agricola, his Germany and several books of his Annals, a great part of Horace, some of Ovid and some of Caesar's Commentaries . . . besides a number of Tully's Orations. . . . In Greek . . . he has studied morsels of Aristotle's Poetics, in Plutarch's Lives of Lucian's Dialogues . . . and lately he has gone through several books in Homer's Iliad." 9 Works, 530. An elaborate appreciation of the unifying role of the study of the classics on this generation is Douglass Adair, "Intellectual Origins of Jeffersonian Democracy," unpublished Ph.D. dissertation, Yale University, 1943.

15. Quoted in Saul K. Padover, The World of the Founding Fathers, 173.

16. Karl Lehmann's observation of Jefferson's historical-mindedness might apply equally to most of the Founding Fathers. "Patrick Henry seemed to speak like Homer, and Homer's language could not fail to be imbued with a new and concrete vitality after listening to Henry, with that analogy in mind. General Arnold's famous march to Quebec was a parallel to Xenophon's retreat in Asia Minor as narrated in his Anabasis. John Adams, like Themistocles in Athens, had been the constant advocate of the 'wooden walls' of a navy. And the King of England would welcome American-Tory-traitors as the Persian King had given refuge to the fugitive aristocracy of Greece. Burr was the Cataline of the American Republic." (Thomas Jefferson, Humanist, 93.)

17. "What does it matter to me," wrote Madame du Châtelet to her friend Voltaire, "to know that Egil succeeded Haquin in Sweden, and that Ottoman was the son of Ortogrul? I have read with pleasure the history of the Greeks and the Romans; they offered me certain great pictures which attracted me. But I have never yet been able to finish any long history of our modern nations . . . a host of minute events without connection or sequence, a thousand battles which settled nothing . . . which overwhelms the mind

without illuminating it." It was the cri de coeur of that whole generation.

18. Quoted in Carl Becker, Heavenly City of the Eighteenth-Century Philosophers, 91.

19. The Farmer Refuted.

20. Quoted in Ernst Cassirer, The Philosophy of the Enlightenment (Beacon Press edn.), 216.

21. So John Adams concluded his Defence of American Constitutions with the observation that "all nations from the beginning have been agitated by the same passions. The principles developed here will go a long way in explaining every phenomenon that occurs in history of government. The vegetable and animal kingdoms, and those heavenly bodies whose existence and movements we are as yet only permitted faintly to perceive, do not appear to be governed by laws more uniform or certain than those which regulate the moral and political world."

22. The comment of Helvetius on the factual evidence which Montesquieu included to support some of his arguments in The Spirit of the Laws, illuminates this attitude. "What the deuce does he want to teach us by his treatise on feudal tenure," said Helvetius. "What new forms of legislation can be derived from this chaos of barbarism that has been maintained by brute force, but must be swept away by reason? He should have tried to derive some true maxims from the improved state of things that is at hand." (Quoted in J. W. Thompson, II History of Historical Writing, 63.)

23. The literature on this subject is large, but it is sufficient to suggest here Edwin T. Martin, Thomas Jefferson, Scientist, Daniel Boorstin, The Lost World of Thomas Jefferson, and Gilbert Chinard, "Eighteenth Century Theories on America as a Human Habitat," 91 Proc. Am. Phil. Society, 27 ff., and the references which they give.

24. 3 L. W. Labaree, ed., Papers of Benjamin Franklin, 412 ff.

25. "Notes on Virginia," Query 14.

26. Lectures on History, 75–76.

27. John G. Zimmerman, Essay on National Pride (London, 1797 edn.), 241 ff.

28. "History," said the omniscient Dr. Priestly, "by displaying the sentiments and

conduct of truly great men, and those of a contrary character, tends to inspire us with a taste for solid glory and real greatness, and convinces us that it does not consist in what the generality of mankind are so eager in pursuit of. We can never again imagine, if we derive our instruction from history, that true greatness consists in riches. . . ." And he concluded, "We conceive more clearly what true greatness of mind is, at the same time that our hearts are more filled with admiration for it, by a simple narration of some incidents of history than by the most elaborate and philosophically exact description of it." *Lectures on History and General Policy* (Philadelphia, 1803 edn.), first lecture.

29. From Pericles' Funeral Oration. Jefferson had four copies of Thucydides' *History* in his library.

## POWER

1. And electors for President of the United States.

2. See letter of John Clopton, Sr., early 1797, in Clopton mss., Duke University.

3. See F. Hamilton to David Campbell, January 16, 1808, Campbell mss., Duke University.

4. McCrae to John Clopton, Sr., May 9, 1806, Clopton mss.

5. William Cabell Bruce, *John Randolph of Roanoke, 1773–1833: A Biography Based Largely on New Materials* (New York and London, 1922), I, 142.

6. Richmond *Enquirer*, May 9, 1823.

7. Charles S. Sydnor, *Gentlemen Freeholders: Political Practices in Washington's Virginia* (Chapel Hill, N.C., 1952), p. 41.

8. John Clopton, Jr., to William Armistead, February 17, 1826, Clopton mss.

9. "Roane Correspondence," *The John P. Branch Historical Papers of Randolph-Macon College*, II (June, 1905), 125–126.

10. Powhatan Bouldin, *Home Reminiscences of John Randolph of Roanoke* (Danville and Richmond, 1876), p. 42.

11. Undated draft in the Campbell mss.

12. Lyon G. Tyler, *The Letters and Times of the Tylers* (Richmond, 1884), I, 308.

13. See note 11.

14. Letter of April 19, 1812, Clopton mss.

15. "Letters of John Taylor of Caroline County, Virginia," *The John P. Branch Historical Papers of Randolph-Macon College*, II (June, 1908), 338.

16. Letter of March 14, 1812, Clopton mss.

17. Arthur Campbell to David Campbell, April 4, 1816, Campbell mss.

18. Letter of April 19, 1812, Clopton mss.

19. John Campbell to his sister, April 7, 1816, Campbell mss.

20. Letter to his son, April 13, 1812, Clopton mss.

21. See letters of December 23, 1798, and March 28, 1802, Clopton mss.

22. See John Clopton, Sr., to his son, May 11 and 13, 1812, Clopton mss.

23. Bouldin, *Home Reminiscences of John Randolph*, p. 122.

24. John Campbell to David Campbell, April 7, 1813, Campbell mss.

25. Edward Campbell to David Campbell, August 12, 1812, Campbell mss.

26. *Calendar of Virginia State Papers*, ed. H. W. Flournoy, IX (Richmond, 1890), 111–112.

27. John Campbell to David Campbell, May 4, 1816, Campbell mss.

28. David Campbell to his wife, April 25, 1816, Campbell mss.

29. "Roane Correspondence," *The John P. Branch Historical Papers of Randolph-Macon College*, II (June, 1905), 125–126.

30. John Clopton, Sr., to his son, April 13, 1812, Clopton mss.

31. Richmond *Enquirer*, April 16, 1824.

32. Sydnor, *Gentlemen Freeholders*, Appendix I, "Numbers of Voters in Virginia Elections, 1741–1843."

33. *Ibid.*

34. Letter of June 22, 1816, Campbell mss.

35. John Clopton, Sr., to his son, April 19, 1812, Clopton mss.

36. John Campbell to David Campbell, December 3, 1811, Campbell mss.

37. *Ibid.*, December 7, 1811, Campbell mss.

38. *Ibid.*, February 1, 1811, Campbell mss.

39. *Ibid.*, January 20, 1812, Campbell mss.

40. *Ibid.*, November 30, 1824, Campbell mss.

41. *Ibid.*, November 30, 1824, Campbell mss.

42. Letter of December 31, 1811, Clopton mss.

43. John Campbell to his mother, December 4, 1810, Campbell mss.

44. John Campbell to David Campbell, January 18, 1827, Campbell mss.

45. *Ibid.*, December 3, 1814, Campbell mss.

46. David Campbell to Arthur Campbell, January 24, 1821, Campbell mss.

47. John Campbell to David Campbell, January 20, 1812, Campbell mss.

48. *Ibid.*, January 20, 1812, Campbell mss.

49. *Ibid.*, February 1, 1811, Campbell mss.

50. W. C. Gooch to David Campbell, January 20, 1820, Campbell mss.

51. *Ibid.*

52. John Campbell to David Campbell, May 8, 1828, Campbell mss.

53. David Campbell to his wife, December 22, 1822, Campbell mss.

54. Letter to David Campbell, December 6, 1814, Campbell mss.

55. Charles Henry Ambler, *Sectionalism in Virginia from 1776–1861* (Chicago, 1910), p. 88.

56. John Campbell to David Campbell, November 24, 1814, Campbell mss.

57. Hugh A. Garland, *The Life of John Randolph of Roanoke* (New York and Philadelphia, 1850), II, 225.

58. [William Wirt], *The Letters of the British Spy*, 4th ed. (Baltimore, 1811), p. 127.

59. Barton H. Wise, *The Life of Henry A. Wise of Virginia, 1806–1876* (New York, 1899), p. 30.

60. *Ibid.*, p. 31.

61. [George Tucker (?)], *Letters from Virginia Translated from the French . . .* (Baltimore, 1816), p. 54.

62. John P. Kennedy, *Memoirs of the Life of William Wirt, Attorney General of the United States* (Philadelphia, 1849), I, 227.

63. James Mercer Garnett, *Biographical Sketch of Hon. Charles Fenton Mercer, 1778–1858* (Richmond, 1911), pp. 6, 23.

64. John Clopton, Jr., to William Armistead, February 17, 1826, Clopton mss.

65. Day Book, February 23, 1830, Clopton mss.

66. Kennedy, *Memoirs of the Life of William Wirt*, I, 227.

67. *Ibid.*, I, 228.

68. *Ibid.*, II, 56.

69. Bouldin, *Home Reminiscences of John Randolph*, pp. 70, 158.

70. Bruce, *John Randolph of Roanoke*, II, 648.

71. Letter of November 22, 1808, Clopton mss.

72. Letters of November 24, 1813, and December 7, 1813, Clopton mss.

73. John Campbell to David Campbell, December 1811, Campbell mss.

74. Probably the unambitious Edward had never thought of any such idea.

75. John Campbell to David Campbell, January 7, 1810, Campbell mss.

76. *Ibid.*, December 1811, Campbell mss.

77. *Ibid.*, January 20, 1812, Campbell, mss.

78. *Ibid.*, June 21, 1812, Campbell mss.

79. *Ibid.*, July 12, 1812, Campbell mss.

80. David Campbell to Edward Campbell, January 30, 1814, Campbell mss.

81. See letters from John Campbell to David Campbell, December 3, 1814, and January 21, 1815, Campbell mss.

82. John Campbell to David Campbell, July 4, 1815, Campbell mss.

83. John Campbell to David Campbell, January 20, 1817, Campbell mss.

84. *Ibid.*, February 20, 1817, Campbell mss.

85. *Ibid.*, March 10, 1817, Campbell mss.

86. David Campbell to John Campbell, January 5 and 24, 1821, Campbell mss.

87. John Campbell to David Campbell, February 20, 1825, Campbell mss.

88. David Campbell to James Campbell, March 29, 1827, Campbell mss.

89. General Smyth to David Campbell, November 6, 1827, Campbell mss.

90. John Campbell to David Campbell, February 20, 1829, Campbell mss.

91. *Ibid.*, April 11, 1829, Campbell mss.

92. [Wirt], *British Spy*, pp. 110–111.

93. Charles Henry Ambler, *Thomas Ritchie, A Study in Virginia Politics* (Richmond, 1913), p. 111.

94. *Gentlemen Freeholders.*

## VOTING BEHAVIOR

1. Samuel J. Eldersveld, "Theory and Method In Voting Behavior Research," in Heinz Eulau, et al., *Political Behavior*, 268, and 267–274, *passim*.

2. The Turner and Beard theses usually are treated as fundamentally opposed; in my opinion, they stem from the same source and, closely examined, make the same economic determinist assumptions. In his *Economic Interpretation of the Constitution of the United States* (Macmillan Co., 1954 printing) XIX, and 239–241, Beard explicitly acknowledged his heavy dependence upon Turner and the work of the latter's students. The European origin of Turner's and Beard's versions of economic determinism is discussed in Lee Benson, *Turner and Beard*.

3. Beard was quoted to this effect in Howard K. Beale, "What Historians Have Said About the Causes of The Civil War," *Bulletin 54, Theory and Practice in Historical Study: A Report of the Committee On Historiography* (Social Science Research Council, New York, 1946), 55.

4. Richard Hofstadter, *The American Political Tradition* (New York, 1948), VII–VIII, and *passim*.

5. Louis Hartz, *The Liberal Tradition in America* (New York, 1955), *passim*. Another book, "The American Civil War: A War Against National Unification," will try to show how that hypothesis facilitates a more credible explanation of the Civil War.

6. George Sabine, *A History of Political Theory* (New York, 1956, rev. ed.) 529.

7. Clinton Rossiter, *Conservatism in America* (New York, 1955), 67. The fact that this quotation is from a self-styled conservative's view of "the American Political Tradition" suggests the fundamental agreement which exists between "liberals" and "conservatives" in the United States. For an analysis of the wide areas of agreement on political fundamentals in the United States, in contrast to the deep disagreement on "great principles" in Europe, see *New York Tribune* (w.), July 26, 1851, p. 4.

8. My thinking concerning the relationships between the American governmental and party systems has benefited considerably from reading a draft of a forthcoming book, Morton Grodzins, *American Political Parties and the American System*.

9. I have developed this argument at greater length in an essay called "A critique of Beard and His Critics." See *Turner and Beard*.

10. For the advantages of qualitative classification systems, see Paul F. Lazarsfeld and Allen H. Barton, "Qualitative Measurement in the Social Sciences: Classification, Typologies, and Indices," in Daniel Lerner and Harold Lasswell, eds., *The Policy Sciences* (Standford, Cal., 1951), 155–182.

11. William James, *The Principles of Psychology* (Dover Publications, Inc.: United States, 1950 ed.), 1: 488.

12. Henry James, *The Spoils of Poynton*, New York, 1922 printing, V–VI.

13. *New York Tribune* (w.), March 22, 1851, p. 5. Although unsigned, the editorials quoted here have all the hallmarks of Greeley's style and I am reasonably certain that he wrote them. But the points made in the text do not depend upon correct identification of the editorial's author.

14. *Ibid.*, September 11, 1852, p. 2.

15. Theodore M. Newcomb, *Social Psychology* (New York, 1956 printing), 280. In discussing and using the social role concept, I have considerably benefited from reading the relevant chapters in this text on social psychology.

16. Robert K. Merton, *Social Theory and Social Structure*, 234. American historians in particular, I believe, would benefit heavily from the two chapters dealing with reference group theory. *Ibid.*, 225–386.

## IMAGE

1. Alexis de Tocqueville, *Democracy in America*, ed. by Phillips Bradley (2 vols., New York, 1945), II, 74.

2. In the light of such pioneering studies as Albert K. Weinberg, *Manifest Destiny: A Study of Nationalist Expansion*

in *American History* (Baltimore, 1935); Carter Goodrich and Sol Davison, "The Wage Earner in the Westward Movement," *Political Science Quarterly* (New York), L (June, 1935), 161–85, and LI (March, 1936), 61–116; Henry Nash Smith, *Virgin Land: The American West as Symbol and Myth* (Cambridge, 1950); John W. Ward, *Andrew Jackson: Symbol for an Age* (New York, 1955); and Arthur K. Moore, *The Frontier Mind: A Cultural Analysis of the Kentucky Frontiersman* (Lexington, Ky., 1957), this may well seem an ungracious if not an inaccurate statement. Yet while this essay owes much of its conceptual framework and many of its citations to their inquiries, its main focus is the development of a characteristic eastern perspective on the territorial possessions of the United States, which in one fashion or another each tends to neglect. Weinberg's focus is on attitudes toward territories outside our national boundaries. Goodrich and Davison are concerned with the "safety-valve" concept of our western lands to the exclusion of other matters. Ward concentrates on Andrew Jackson as popular hero reflecting fundamental American values, and Moore is concerned with the transfer of ancient stereotypes of Nature to the American experience of Kentucky. Even Smith, whose *Virgin Land* constitutes the main work in the field, and who had dealt with a wide range of literary and political ramifications of the American West, tends rather to pursue the development of a western literature and politics than to establish the perspective in which eastern spokesmen visualized the West.

Needless to say, my point in making these comments is not to deprecate the achievements of these scholars, but to identify my own somewhat different purposes more clearly. I should add that two other essays bear with particular relevance upon the problem I am dealing with here. One is Arthur E. Bestor, "Patent-Office Models of the Good Society: Some Relationships between Social Reform and Westward Expansion," *American Historical Review* (New York), LVIII (April, 1953), 505–26; the other, Barry Marks, "The Concept of Myth in *Virgin Land*," *American Quarterly* (Philadelphia), V (Spring, 1953), 71–76.

3. Timothy Dwight, *Travels in New-England and New-York* (4 vols., New Haven, 1881–1822), II, 459, 473, and compare p. 458.

4. "An Estimate of the Present and Future Physical, Civil, and Moral Power of the West, Including the Country Watered by the Mississippi and Its Tributaries," *Quarterly Journal of the American Education Society* (Boston), I (April, 1828), 64.

5. "Claims of the West," *Quarterly Christian Spectator* (New Haven), 3rd series, VI (December, 1834), 513–24.

6. [G. B. Bishop], "Requisite Qualifications of a Ministry Adapted to the Wants of the West," *Biblical Repertory and Theological Review* (New York), VIII (July, 1836), 382. This magazine later came to be better known as the *Princeton Review*.

7. *Quarterly Christian Spectator*, 3rd series VI (December, 1834), 514.

8. *Quarterly Journal of the American Education Society*, I (April, 1828), 63; *Biblical Repertory and Theological Review*, VIII (July, 1836), 382.

9. Lyman Beecher, *A Plea for the West* (Cincinnati, 1835), 11–12.

10. "Condition and Wants of the West," *Christian Review* (Boston), I (June, 1836), 254.

11. *North American Review* (Boston), XLIII (July, 1836), 28, and compare Smith, *Virgin Land*, 217. At the time of his review, it should be said, Clarke had been living in Kentucky for approximately three years, and was to remain for four more. But it is clear in the text that he is an eastern commentator at heart.

12. *North American Review*, LXXX (January, 1855), 96.

13. Charles C. Tansill (ed.), *Documents Illustrative of the Formation of the Union of the American States* (Washington, 1927), 357, 375, 638.

14. *Debates and Proceedings in the Congress of the United States*, 8 Cong., 1 Sess., cols. 465, 443, 34 (October 25 and November 2, 1803).

15. Fisher Ames to Thomas Dwight, October 26, 1803, Seth Ames (ed.), *Works of Fisher Ames* (2 vols., Boston, 1854), I, 328.

16. Dwight, *Travels*, II, 470, 461, 462.

17. *North American Review*, XXIII (October, 1826), 355, 356.

18. *American Quarterly Review* (Philadelphia), V (June, 1829), 357.

19. *North American Review*, XXVIII (January, 1829), 82.

20. *Ibid.*, LV (October, 1842), 511.

21. Smith, *Virgin Land*, 218.

22. James H. Lanman, "The Progress of the Northwest," *Hunt's Merchants' Magazine* (New York), III (July, 1840), 39; and see *ibid.*, V (September, 1841), 219–20.

23. Dwight, *Travels*, II, 458, 469.

24. *Debates and Proceedings in Congress*, 8 Cong., 1 Sess., cols. 34, 443.

25. *North American Review*, XXIII (October, 1826), 356.

26. *Biblical Repertory and Theological Review*, VIII (July, 1836), 381–82.

27. *American Quarterly Review*, V (June, 1829), 355–56.

28. Rev. Charles White, "Influence of Colleges, Especially on Western Education and Civilization," *Biblical Repository and Classical Review* (New York), 3rd series, IV (July, 1848), 383.

29. *Register of Debates in Congress*, 21 Cong., 1 Sess., 521 (January 13, 1830).

30. William H. Seward, *The Elements of Empire in America* (New York, 1844), 26.

31. *Congressional Globe*, 32 Cong., 1 Sess., Appendix, 729 ff., 390 (April 22 and March 30, 1852).

32. *Ibid.*, 31 Cong., 2 Sess., 213 (January 10, 1851).

33. [E. Judson], "The Evangelization of the West: How Shall It Be Affected? And by Whom?" *New Englander* (New Haven), IV (January, 1846), 38.

## TYPE

1. Max Weber, *The Methodology of the Social Sciences*, trans. and ed. Edward A. Shils and Henry A. Finch (Glencoe, Ill., 1949), 90; I have discussed the theoretical problems involved at greater length in "A Critique of Max Weber's Philosophy of History." *Ethics*, LXX (1959), 21–36.

2. Max Weber, *The Theory of Social and Economic Organization*, trans. A. R. Henderson and Talcott Parsons, and ed. Talcott Parsons (New York, 1947), 92.

3. Max Weber, *The Protestant Ethic and the Spirit of Capitalism*, trans. Talcott Parsons with foreword by R. H. Tawney (New York, 1930), 182. The tour was reported in Marianne Weber, *Max Weber: Ein Lebensbild* (Heidelberg, 1950), 316–45. A selected translation of Weber's American letters can be found in Walter Henry Brann, "Max Weber and the United States," *Southwestern Social Science Quarterly*, XXV (1944), 18–30.

4. Weber, *Protestant Ethic*, 55–56.

5. *Ibid.*

6. *Ibid.*, 276.

7. See Perry Miller, *The New England Mind: The Seventeenth Century* (Cambridge, 1954), 383 ff, 387–392; Perry Miller, *The New England Mind: From Colony to Province* (Cambridge, 1953), Chap. III; Perry Miller, *Errand into the Wilderness* (Cambridge, 1956), Chaps. III, V.

8. Weber, *Protestant Ethic*, 62. My italics.

9. Quoted in E. A. J. Johnson, *American Economic Thought in the Seventeenth Century* (London, 1932), 89; also 86–100 for an excellent summary of Puritan economic doctrine, Johnson concludes, in reference to Weber's Protestant Ethic, that "There is little significant evidence to support this thesis in the writings of the American Puritans . . . There is no more idealization of wealth accumulation than there is in the Catholic economic literature." (92). The American Puritan position was that "the care of the publique must oversway all private respects, by which not onely conscience, but meare Civill pollicy doth binde us; for it is a true rule that perticuler estates cannott subsist in the ruine of the publique." John Winthrop, "Model of Christian Charity," *The Puritans*, Perry Miller and Thomas H. Johnson, eds. (New York, 1938), 197.

10. Miller, *From Colony to Province*, 51; Bernard Bailyn, "Kinship and Trade in Seventeenth-Century New England," *Explorations in Entrepreneurial Hist.*, VI (1954), 197–206.

11. Bernard Bailyn, *The New England Merchants in the Seventeenth Century*

(Cambridge, 1955), 40 ff.; see Miller, *The Seventeenth Century*, 370 ff., for a discussion of Antinomianism.

12. Arthur Henry Hirsch, *The Huguenots of Colonial South Carolina* (Durham, N.C., 1928), 90. For Boston, see Bailyn, *New England Merchants*, 135–139; for New York, see Virginia D. Harrington, *The New York Merchants on the Eve of the Revolution* (New York, 1935), 17.

13. Max Weber, *The Religion of China*, trans. and ed. Hans H. Gerth (Glencoe, Ill., 1951), 136.

14. H. M. Robertson, *Aspects of the Rise of Economic Individualism* (Cambridge, 1933), 115–117; also see Johnson, *American Economic Thought*, 213–223, for a discussion of usury and Puritanism. Throughout the colonial period, and in most colonies, interest was strictly regulated by law at low rates, and with the general provision that contracts in excess of the legal maximum were void. Massachusetts in 1641 restricted the rate of interest to eight percent so that there would not be "usury amongst us contrary to the law of God." (Quoted in J. B. C. Murray, *The History of Usury*, Philadelphia, 1866, 77.) In 1693 the rate was reduced to six percent.

15. Richard B. Morris, *Government and Labor in Early America* (New York, 1946), 84–89; Leila Sellers, *Charleston Business on the Eve of the American Revolution* (Chapel Hill, 1934), 21–24; Joseph Dorfman, *The Economic Mind in American Civilization* (New York, 1946), I, 45–46; Johnson, *American Economic Thought*, 26–32; Harrington, *New York Merchants*, 282–284; William B. Weeden, *Economic and Social History of New England 1620–1789* (Boston, 1890), II, 526; Harold C. Syrett, "Private Enterprise in New Amsterdam," *William and Mary Quarterly*, 3rd Ser., XI (1954), 536–550; see David J. Saposs, "Colonial and Federal Beginnings," *History of Labour in the United States*, John R. Commons, ed. (New York, 1918), I, 25–137, for the role of government not only as the protector of labor and controller of quality, wages and prices, but as the subsidizer and promoter of economic activity.

16. Weber, *Protestant Ethic*, 41; also see *China*, 245–246.

17. For South Carolina, see Hirsch, *Huguenots*, 156, 170, 182–185; for New York, see Harrington, *New York Merchants*, 30ff.; for New England, see Weeden, *History of New England*, II, 742–744; Victor S. Clark, *History of Manufacturers in the United States, 1607–1860* (Washington, D.C., 1916), I, 119; for Philadelphia, see Frederick B. Tolles, *Meeting House and Counting House: The Quaker Merchants of Colonial Philadelphia, 1682–1763* (Chapel Hill, 1948), Chap. VI; also Carl Bridenbaugh, *Cities in Revolt: Urban Life in America, 1743–1776* (New York, 1955), Chap. IX.

18. Arthur Meier Schlesinger, *The Colonial Merchants and the American Revolution, 1763–1776* (New York, 1918), 25.

19. James Truslow Adams, *Provincial Society, 1690–1763* (New York, 1927), 160–161; also see 94–5, 311; Weeden, *History of New England*, I, 188.

20. Weber, *Protestant Ethic*, 278.

21. Wesley Frank Craven, *The Southern Colonies in the Seventeenth Century* (Baton Rouge, 1949), 69, 141–142, 228.

22. Clark, *History of Manufactures*, 31–32, 70–71; Philip Alexander Bruce, *Economic History of Virginia in the Seventeenth Century* (New York, 1895), II, 486–491ff.

23. Clark, *History of Manufactures*, 152; also 169; for Virginia, see Bruce, *Economic History of Virginia*, II, 135, 440–442, 486–491ff.

24. Clark, *History of Manufactures*, 67.

25. *Ibid.*, 70–71; Bruce, *Economic History of Virginia*, II, 412–413, 478–481ff.

26. Bailyn, *New England Merchants*, 71–74; Craven, *Southern Colonies*, 211–213; Clark, *History of Manufactures*, 169, 195–200.

27. Clark, *History of Manufactures*, 76–77, 88.

28. Caroline F. Ware, *The Early New England Cotton Manufacture* (Boston, 1931), passim.

29. Kathleen Bruce, *Virginia Iron Manufacture in the Slave Era* (New York, 1931), passim.

30. Arthur Cecil Bining, *British Regulation of the Colonial Iron Industry* (Philadelphia, 1933), 13ff.; for the abortive Massachusetts iron-mill, see Bailyn, *New England Merchants*, 62–71.

31. Bining, *British Regulation*, 15–19, 122, 129–134.

32. Weber, *China*, 247; also see 242–249, and *Protestant Ethic*, 17–18.

33. Harrington, *New York Merchants*, 78 ff., describes the problems of purchasing sight unseen. For the West Indies trade, see Richard Pares, *Yankees and Creoles* (Cambridge, 1956), passim.

34. *History of New England*, II, 661.

35. *Colonial Merchants*, 40.

36. *Ibid.*, 46; Clark, *History of Manufactures*, 200-205; Bining, *British Regulation*, 86–92; Hirsch, *Huguenots*, 151–152; for a general survey, see Charles M. Andrews, *The Colonial Period of American History [England's Commercial and Colonial Policy]* (New Haven, 1936), IV.

37. *China*, 86.

38. *Protestant Ethic*, 173–174.

39. Morris, *Government and Labor*, 372–373, 393, 402, 416–419, 437–441, 463–476, 506; for bounties, see Adams, *Provincial Society*, 98; for war captives, see Bailyn, *New England Merchants*, 68, and Bruce, *Economic History of Virginia*, I, 608–610.

40. Craven, *Southern Colonies*, 214; Bruce, *Economic History of Virginia*, I, 594, II, 81; Hirsch, *Huguenots*, 170–171. For merchant origins of large landowners see Thomas J. Wertenbaker, *The Shaping of Colonial Virginia: Patrician and Plebian in Virginia* (Charlottesville, 1910). On slavery, see Oscar and Mary F. Handlin, "Origins of the Southern Labor System," *William and Mary Quarterly*, VII (1950), 199–222.

41. *Protestant Ethic*, 51ff.; Marianne Weber, *Lebensbild*, 387–390.

42. *Protestant Ethic*, 53.

43. Quoted in Lewis J. Carey, *Franklin's Economic Views* (New York, 1928), 150; also 140–142. Franklin was also something of a plagiarist. His concepts of value and interest were printed, almost verbatim, from William Petty. The *Almanac* was, predictably, primarily a collection of English proverbs, written mainly by Anglicans, suitably doctored by Franklin. See Robert H. Newcomb, "The Sources of Benjamin Franklin's Sayings of Poor Richard," Unpublished Ph. D. thesis, University of Maryland, 1957; also Carey, Chap. II.

44. Bernard Fay, *Franklin, The Apostle of Modern Times* (Boston, 1929), 96–114, 136–140, 155–161.

45. Carl Van Doren, ed., *Benjamin Franklin's Autobiographical Writings* (New York, 1945), 54–56.

46. *Protestant Ethic*, 263; Fay, *Franklin*, 454–456, 461–469; see his letter on mistresses in L. Lincoln Schuster, ed., *A Treasury of the World's Great Letters* (New York, 1940), 160–162. Colonial sexual habits, in general, fail to sustain Weber's assertion on Puritanism and sex. See Edmund S. Morgan, "The Puritans and Sex," *New England Quarterly*, XV (1942), 591–607; and Adams, *Provincial Society*, 158–161.

47. Carey, *Franklin's Economic Views*, 6–7, 15–16; Dorfman, *Economic Mind in America*, I, 179.

48. Fay, *Franklin*, 330–331; 348–350; Dorfman, *Economic Mind in America*, I, 187; Shaw Livermore, *Early American Land Companies* (New York, 1939), 113ff.; Clarence Walworth Alvord, *The Mississippi Valley in British Politics* (Cleveland, 1916), I, 321ff.

49. *China*, 86, 103.

50. Clark, *History of Manufactures*, 71.

51. Livermore, *Early Land Companies*, 38. Also see Oliver M. Dickerson, *The Navigation Acts and the American Revolution* (Philadelphia, 1951), Chap. 11, for this point and merchant support for government economic regulation.

52. For Vermont debt riots, see Chilton Williamson, *Vermont in Quandry 1763–1825* (Montpelier, 1949), 19–20; for New Hampshire, see Jeremy Belknap, *The History of New-Hampshire* (Dover, 1831, I, 396–403; for the Massachusetts crisis, see Oscar and Mary Handlin, *Commonwealth: A Study of the Role of Government in the American Economy* (New York, 1947), Chap. 2; for the general scene, see Merrill Jensen, *The New Nation, 1781–1789* (New York, 1950); for earlier conflicts, see Curtis P. Nettels, *The Roots of American Civilization* (New York, 1938), Chap. 13.

53. Livermore, *Early Land Companies*, 67; also 80; Adams, *Provincial Society*, 244–247; Alvord, *Mississippi Valley in British Politics*, Chap. XI. Land, and the possibilities of fortunes based on it, was the key factor in attracting the colonial

bureaucracy to the colonies in the 17th century. See Edward Channing, *A History of the United States* (New York, 1905), I, Chap. 17 and *passim*. Examples of the exploitation of politics to accumulate offices, and their fees, can be found in Ellen E. Brennan, *Plural Office-Holding in Massachusetts, 1760–1780* (Chapel Hill, 1945), 32–35, 110–116; and, to 1750, Evarts B. Greene, *The Provincial Governor* (Cambridge, 1898), Chap. III, 112–124, 157–159. Also see W. T. Baxter, *The House of Hancock: Business in Boston, 1724–1775* (Cambridge, 1945), 95–110, 120–123, Chap. IX; Bernard Bailyn, "Politics and Social Structure in Virginia", *Seventeenth-Century America*, James M. Smith, ed. (Chapel Hill, 1959), 90–115.

54. Livermore, *Early Land Companies*,

134, 139, 155–156, 162–164; Robert A. East, "The Business Entrepreneur in a Changing Colonial Economy", *Journal of Economic History*, Supplement VI (1946), 19; Robert A. East, *Business Enterprise in the American Revolutionary Era* (New York, 1938), *passim*; Oscar Handlin, "Laissez-Faire Thought in Massachusetts, 1790–1880", *Journal of Economic History* Supplement III (1943) 55–65; Louis Hartz, "Laissez-Faire Thought in Pennsylvania, 1776–1860", *Journal of Economic History*, Supplement III (1943), 66–77; Joseph S. Davis, *Essays in the Earlier History of American Corporations* (Cambridge, 1917), II, 328ff. The role of the state in the distribution of public land is exhaustively discussed by Alfred N. Chandler, *Land Title Origins* (New York, 1945).

## ROLE

1. Edmund P. Learned, David N. Ulrich, Donald R. Boos, *Executive Action* (Boston: Division of Research, Graduate School of Business Administration, Harvard University, 1951), p. 58.

2. See p. 108.

3. See p. 110.

4. J. M. Forbes, Dir., C. B. & Q., to P. Forbes, cousin, September 6, 1865 (*JMF*).

5. J. Joy, Dir., M. C., to E. Corning, Dir., January 21, 1851 (*EC*).

6. G. Watrous, Pres., N. Y. N. H. & H., to J. Wilson, Pres., N. Y. & N. E., November 29, 1882 (*NYH*).

7. C. E. Perkins, Pres., C. B. & Q., to T. Potter, Vice-Pres., August 13, 1885 (*CBQ*).

8. J. Brooks, Pres., B. & M., Neb., to G. Harris, Land Commissioner, March 9, 1871 (*CBQ*).

9. H. Ledyard, Pres., M. C., to Rev. G. Worthington, March 22, 1886 (*MC*).

10. Jenks in *Journal of Economic History* LV (1944), 10.

11. J. M. Forbes, Pres., C. B. & Q., to J. Sanborn, June 10, 1878 (*CBQ*).

12. Matthew Josephson, *The Robber Barons* (New York, Harcourt, Brace and Company, 1934).

13. C. E. Perkins, Pres., C. B. & Q., to J. M. Forbes, Chr., January 19, 1888 (*CBQ*).

14. R. Harris, Pres., C. B. & Q., to C. E. Perkins, Vice-Pres., December 7, 1876 (*CBQ*).

15. Grodinsky, *The Iowa Pool*.

16. See T. Cochran, "Entrepreneurial History," *Bulletin of the Business Historical Society* XXIV (September 1950), 116–117.

## TURNER THESIS: PREDICTIVE MODEL

1. "The Significance of the Frontier in American History", read at the annual meeting of the American Historical Association at Chicago in July 1893.

2. See Henry Nash Smith, *Virgin Land: The American West as Symbol and Myth* (Cambridge, 1950) for proof that on a poetic level the frontier idea still has its fascinations. See also Walter Prescott

Webb's *The Great Frontier* (Boston, 1952).

3. *The Frontier in American History* (New York, 1920), p. 293.

4. Benjamin F. Wright, Jr., "Political Institutions and the Frontier", in D. R. Fox, ed., *Sources of Culture in the Middle West* (New York, 1934), p. 36.

5. An excellent symposium of these

critical views, containing all the subtleties denied them here, may be found in *The Turner Thesis*, Number 2 of the Amherst *Problems in American Civilization*, George R. Taylor, ed. (Boston, 1949). The criticism is well summarized in Richard Hofstadter, "Turner and the Frontier Myth", *American Scholar*, XVIII, 433–43 (Oct., 1949).

6. The "textual" approach has been used with more success in the analysis of modern poetry and is the principal tool of the "New Criticism." There are indications, however, that even here the method's shortcomings are beginning to be felt. See "The New Criticism", a forum discussion by William Barrett, Kenneth Burke, Malcolm Cowley, Robert Gorham Davis, Allen Tate, and Hiram Haydn, *American Scholar*, XX, 86–104, 218–31 (Jan.-Apr., 1951).

7. This would involve principally the claim for institutional "novelty" (which puts an extra burden on the theory) and the "safety valve" (which isn't necessary). For that matter, although the frontier assuredly had little to say to the "underprivileged," its *real* "safety valve" aspect is all too seldom stressed. To the part-time real estate operator, whether tobacco planter of the early Tidewater or wheat farmer of the pre-World War Middle Border, the frontier as a safety valve against agricultural bankruptcy has always made perfect sense.

8. "Not only is leadership limited objectively by given patterns of authority but the will to lead of the leader is vitiated if what he stands for cannot command a following. . . . [The leader's] effectiveness in no small measure derives from how much loyalty he can count upon." Jeremiah F. Wolpert, "Toward a Sociology of Authority", in Alvin W. Gouldner, ed., *Studies in Leadership* (New York, 1950), p. 681. This is the point made by Guglielmo Ferrero in his discussion of "legitimacy"; see *The Principles of Power*, trans. by Theodore Jaeckel (New York, 1942), p. 23.

9. *Democracy in America* (Oxford Galaxy Ed., New York, 1946), p. 320.

10. The study's working title is *Patterns of Social Life: Explorations in the Sociology of Housing*, by Robert K. Merton, Patricia S. West, and Marie Jahoda.

We are greatly indebted to Mr. Merton for his generosity in allowing us to examine the material in manuscript.

11. Mr. Merton offers various graphs and tables to establish this. In one of them, 88 per cent of the early comers were found to be more highly active in Craftown organizations than in their former communities; only 8 per cent had had the same degree of participation in both communities.

12. Two other communities, each of which underwent a similar experience in similar circumstances, were Park Forest, Illinois, and Shanks Village, New York, described in William H. Whyte, Jr., "The Future, c/o Park Forest", *Fortune*, June 1953, pp. 126–31, 186–96; and Bernard Horn, "Collegetown: A Study of Transient Student Veteran Families in a Temporary Housing Community" (unpub. M.A. thesis, Columbia University, 1948).

13. Thus "homogeneity"—in the total sense which we have given that concept—did not exist in Hilltown. There was a clear distinction—to extend the analogy—between "the rulers and the ruled."

14. These facts seem to go together. An illuminating Craftown anecdote concerns a woman who was fined $5 by one of the locally elected judges for letting her dog run loose. "Well, that's just like working men," she declared. "A rich man wouldn't be so interested in money. . . . I don't think any working man should mix in politics. I think a man that has money is better able to rule." It is at the same time quite possible to imagine the same woman making *this* statement (also recorded at Craftown): "I never voted in the city for mayor or things like that. I just didn't have the interest. In the city they get in anyhow and there's nothing you can do about it. Here they're more connected with people."

15. Mr. Merton points out that this phenomenon was taken as a concrete cultural fact by Malinowski, who called it "phatic communion." Each utterance is an act serving the direct aim of binding hearer to speaker by a tie of some social sentiment or other . . . language appears to us in this function not as an instrument of reflection but as a mode of action." Bronislaw Malinowski, in C. K. Ogden and I. A. Richards, *The Meaning*

of *Meaning* (New York, 1923), pp. 478–79. The connection between this kind of thing and the folklore of democracy is seldom appreciated: consider, for example, the typical American reaction to disaster —the ease with which the traditions of the frontier are converted into spontaneous organizational techniques for coping with the emergency. The community response to the tornado which struck Flint, Michigan, in 1953 provides a perfect case in point; examples like it are numberless.

16. "When the time comes, and the forces collect togeather, a captain is appointed, and the men divide into proper sections, and [are] assigned to their several duties." Henry B. Curtis, "Pioneer Days in Central Ohio", *O. State Arch. and Hist. Pubs.*, I, 245 (1887). Almost any state or county history or pioneer memoir will refer to or describe this familiar social function; see, e.g., William T. Utter, *The Frontier State* (Columbus, 1942), pp. 138, 139–41; W. C. Howells, *Recollections of Life in Ohio* (Cincinnati, 1895), pp. 144–51; etc., etc.

17. There is a vivid contemporary description of a combined logrolling and political rally in Baynard Rush Hall, *The New Purchase*, James A. Woodburn, ed. (Princeton, 1916), pp. 202–205. See also Logan Esarey, *History of Indiana* (Indianapolis, 1915), pp. 421, 425–26.

18. Beverly W. Bond, Jr., *The Civilization of the Old Northwest* (New York, 1934), pp. 249, 268, 351, 357. "The shrill whistle of the fife and the beat of the drum, calling to arms for the defense of their countrymen, was answered by many a gray-haired sire and many a youthful pioneer." H. W. Chadwick, comp., *Early History of Jackson County* (Browntown, Ind., 1943), p. 14. The War of 1812 in the Northwest, particularly in Ohio, had as much or more to do with hostile Indians as with the British, and defense was typically handled by the raising of local militia. See "Ohio and the War of 1812," ch. iv in Utter, *op. cit.*, pp. 88–119.

19. Elias P. Fordham, *Personal Narrative*, ed. by Frederic Ogg (Cleveland, 1906), pp. 154–55; Hall, *op. cit.*, p. 196; Charles Francis Ingals, "A Pioneer in Lee County. Illinois", ed. by Lydia

Colby, *Ill. State Hist. Soc. Jour.*, XXVI, 281 (Oct., 1933).

20. As soon as conditions were favorable the pioneers of the neighborhood constructed a rude cabin schoolhouse. . . . There was no school revenue to be distributed, so each voter himself had to play the part of the builder. The neighbors divided themselves into choppers, hewers, carpenters, and masons. Those who found it impossible to report for duty might pay an equivalent in nails, boards, or other materials. The man who neither worked nor paid was fined thirty-seven and one-half cents a day." William F. Vogel, "Home Life in Early Indiana", *Ind. Mag. of Hist.*, X, 297 (Sept., 1914).

21. The "interfaith chapel" was invariably the early solution to this problem (there was one in Craftown, also in Park Forest and Shanks Village). "The first church . . . was free to all denominations, and here, for miles and miles came the pioneer and family on the Sabbath day to worship God." Chadwick, *op. cit.*, p. 35. See also Vogel, *loc. cit.*, p. 291; Morris Birkbeck, *Letters from Illinois* (London, 1818), p. 23; John D. Barnhardt, Jr., "The Rise of the Methodist Episcopal Church in Illinois from the Beginning to the Year 1832", *Ill. State Hist. Soc. Jour.*, XII, 149–217 (July, 1919).

22. C. H. Rammelkamp, ed., "The Memoirs of John Henry: A Pioneer of Morgan County", *Ill. State Hist. Soc. Jour.*, XVIII, 55 (Apr. 1925).

23. In a history of the town of Lancaster, Ohio, which was founded in 1800, there is a longish series of biographical sketches of its "leading pioneers." Twenty-seven of these sketches concern settlers who arrived within the first ten years of the town's existence and who held office, and of these 27, age data are given for 15. For what such a haphazard sample is worth, the average age of this group at the date of the town's founding was twenty-four. C. M. L. Wiseman, *Centennial History of Lancaster* (Lancaster, 1898).

24. The county histories make every effort to secure the immortality of their leading citizens by reciting as many of their accomplishments as are known. Thus if the biographical sketches make no mention of public office held elsewhere, it

should be safe to assume that at least in most of the cases their civic careers began in the new settlement.

25. Frank S. Heinl, "The First Settlers in Morgan County," *Ill. State Hist. Soc. Jour.*, XVIII, 76–87 (Apr., 1925); Remmelkamp, *loc. cit.*, pp. 39–40 and *passim*; George Murray McConnel, "Some Reminiscences of My Father, Murray McConnel," *Ill. State Hist. Soc. Jour.*, XVIII, 89–100 (Apr., 1925).

26. The seemingly fabulous Wesley Park—who was the first settler at Auburn, Indiana, and DeKalb County's first sheriff, road commissioner, road supervisor, jail commissioner, and clerk of the first county board—was actually a figure quite typical. We see blacksmith-judges and carpenter-sheriffs everywhere. See S. W. Widney, "Pioneer Sketches of DeKalb County," *Ind. Mag. of Hist.*, XXV, 116, 125–26, 128 (June, 1929). "Few of the officials prior to 1850 [in Parke County, Indiana] were men of education. For years it was the custom to elect a coroner from among the stalwart blacksmiths. . . ." Maurice Murphy, "Some Features of the History of Parke County," *Ind. Mag. of Hist.*, XII, 151 (June, 1916).

27. Bond, *op. cit.*, pp. 102, 124.

28. Quoted in Solon J. Buck, *Illinois in 1818* (Springfield, 1917), p. 260. Consider again the power of "phatic communion": in the 1952 presidential election the governor of that same great state of Illinois might have been seen blandly kissing babies.

29. Hall, *New Purchase*, p. 178.

30. *Ibid.*, pp. 200–201, 177.

31. Vogel, *loc. cit.*, p. 309. "Our candidates certainly sweat for their expected honours", Hall remarks. ". . . Nay, a very few hundreds of rival and zealous candidates would, in a year or so, if judiciously driven under proper task masters, clear a considerable territory." *Op. cit.*, p. 205.

32. *Civilization of the Old Northwest*, pp. 321–32.

33. Buck, *op. cit.*, pp. 47, 54–55. "The situation was so serious that the matter was taken up with the secretary of state, and the president issued a proclamation directing that after a certain day in March, 1816, all squatters on the public lands should be removed. Against the execution of this proclamation, Benjamin Stephen-son, the delegate from Illinois territory, protested vigorously. . . . The marshal of the Illinois territory actually made preparations to remove the intruders; but the secretary of the treasury wrote him on May 11, 1816, recommending 'a prudent and conciliatory course'; and nothing seems to have been accomplished." *Ibid.*, p. 54.

34. Notably the Congressional legislation of 1796, 1800 and 1804.

35. Bond, *op. cit.*, pp. 337–38.

36. A special situation in Illinois added to the difficulty of amassing large absentee holdings; actual sales of public land could not begin there until 1814 owing to the perplexity of the French claims, and the result was a growing population of squatters and slim pickings for speculators. Buck, *op. cit.*, p. 44.

37. Symmes had sold, in advance, a number of tracts outside his 1792 patent, expecting to take them up at 66⅔ cents an acre. Subsequently the price rose to $2.00, on which Symmes could not possibly make good. An original contract for 1,000,000 acres had been partly paid for in Continental certificates, and the patent of 1792 gave him title to those lands for which he had paid. Neither his influence nor that of Harrison was ever able to guarantee the entire claim of 1,000,000 acres. Meanwhile the Scioto Company had completely collapsed, and the representations of the Illinois and Wabash companies met with even less success than did those of Symmes.

38. McConnel, *loc. cit.*, p. 95.

39. Heinl, *loc. cit.*, p. 84. See also *supra*, note 15.

40. Thurman Arnold in his *Folklore of Capitalism* (New Haven and London, 1937) makes a parallel point in suggesting that the "traditions" of American business have been derived from a primitive phase in its development; Richard Hofstadter, in a forthcoming work on Populism and Progressivism, notes the same interesting fact with respect to our agriculture. These writers in each case stress the conceptual difficulties which the "myths" of an earlier stage impose upon the realities of a later, much-advanced one. Mr. Hofstadter metaphorically characterizes this polarity as "soft" and "hard." It might be added that a humane view of American culture would

recognize a need, on the part of both the business man and the farmer, for "folklore": the need of each for dramatizing to himself his own role, for maintaining his self-respect.

41. For years the late Professor Schumpeter maintained a theory of this sort. "History," he wrote, "clearly confirms this suggestion: historically, the modern democracy rose along with capitalism, and in actual connection with it. But the same holds true for democratic practice: democracy in the sense of our theory of competitive leadership presided over the process of political and institutional change by which the bourgeoisie reshaped, and from its own point of view rationalized, the social and political structure that preceded its ascendancy: the democratic method was the political tool of that reconstruction." Joseph Schumpeter, *Capitalism, Socialism, and Democracy* (New York, 1947), pp. 296–97.

42. The very gaps in available statistics are dramatic. We have no early figures for the Southwest, but by 1853 there were in Alabama only thirty towns with a population of over 200 and only twenty-nine in Mississippi. On the other hand as early as 1833 Indiana, with less than one-half Alabama's 1853 population, had seventy-seven such towns, and Illinois, with one-fifth the 1853 population of Alabama, had thirty-four. By 1847, when Indiana's population had reached the 1853 level of Alabama, it had 156 towns whose population exceeded 200. If complete figures were available for towns of over 500 population the difference would be even more striking: while towns of this size were quite common in the Northwest, they were, aside from the port cities and state capitals, very rare in Alabama and Mississippi. As early as 1821 Ohio, with a population of 581,434, had sixty-one towns with a population of over 200, twenty-nine of 500 or more, and twenty-two of over a thousand. J. D. B. DeBow, *Statistical View of the United States . . . being a Compendium of the Seventh Census . . .* (Washington, 1854); John Scott, *Indiana Gazeteer,* (Indianapolis, 1833); J. M. Peck, *A Gazetteer of Illinois* (Jacksonville, 1834); E. Chamberlain, *Indiana Gazeteer* (Indianapolis, 1850); John Kilbourn; *Ohio Gazeteer* (Columbus, 1821).

43. William V. Pooley, *The Settlement of Illinois from 1830 to 1850* (Madison, 1908), p. 564.

44. In 1836, lots in Peoria sold as high as $100 per front foot while good neighboring farm land was still to be had at the standard price of $1.25 an acre. R. Carlyle Buley, *The Old Northwest: Pioneer Period* (Indianapolis, 1950), II, 116.

45. This is very clear from an illuminating survey made by James W. Silver of land operations in Tate and Tippah counties, Mississippi, between 1836 and 1861. Most impressive in his findings are (1) the huge amounts of land in which the successful speculator had to deal, and (2) the lengths of time that these men customarily held their land before selling it. In these two counties alone, 337,000 acres were held by single investors, eight of whom held between 3,000 and 4,000 acres, six holding from 4,000 to 5,000 acres, four from 5,000 to 6,000, and three between 6,000 and 7,000; one owned between 10,000 and 15,000 acres, two between 15,000 and 20,000, and one over 25,000. Averages were struck for thirty-one individual speculators owning a total of 197,376.5 acres at an investment of $267,-382.19 with profits of $244,824.24. But the average length of time held was 18.6 years; the profit must thus be figured in terms not of quick killings but of average annual return. For a majority this came to less than 5 per cent. James W. Silver, "Land Speculation Profits in the Chickasaw Cession", *Jour. of South. Hist.,* X, 84–92 (Feb. 1944). This may be called "speculation", but it was speculation on an order quite different from that typically occurring in the Old Northwest.

46. Here are two typical cases: Wesley Park, who in 1836 laid out the town of Auburn, Indiana, gave one third of the lots to the county, "receiving no compensation," as he piquantly admits, "but the assurance that it would be permanently the county seat." Widney, *loc. cit.,* p. 128. In that very same year, Bolivar County, one of the rich counties of the Delta, was being organized in Mississippi. The proceedings of the Board of Police (a year later) "show the acceptance of the offer of William Vick to sell five acres of land, including the overseer's residence, for the Seat of Justice," at a price of $100

an acre and $300 for the improvements. Florence Warfield Sillers and others, *History of Bolivar County, Mississippi* (Jackson, 1948), p. 12.

47. A comparison of the two sections in 1840 with respect to primary and common schools is shown in accompanying table.

48. *Democracy in America*, p. 109.

49. *Ibid.*, p. 152.

50. In Crawford County, when the seat was first relocated, tradition says that the citizens of Fredonia went in a body to Mount Sterling and forcibly removed the records. "If the records were carried away by force," notes a chronicler, "it was only the first time; they have been carried away from each of the later county seats by force." What more excellent instance of democracy could be found than this ardent and universal participation in the concerns of the community? H. H. Pleasant, "Crawford County", *Ind. Mag. of Hist*, XVIII. 146 (June 1922). See also Ernest V. Shockley, "County Seats and County Seat Wars in Indiana", *Ind. Mag. of Hist.*, X, 26 (Mar. 1914).

51. The story is best told by the Census figures in accompanying table.

52. Max Weber was much impressed by the later counterpart of the master placator, the American urban political boss. The boss was thoroughly responsible but not quite respectable. See *From Max Weber: Essays in Sociology*, trans. and ed. by H. H. Gerth and C. Wright Mills (New York, 1946), pp. 109–110.

53. The Board of Public Works advised in its report "that nothing short of the extension of the canal navigation to every considerable district in the state will satisfy that public will, which justly claims that benefits conferred shall be co-extensive with the burthens imposed; and that, in those districts, where canals cannot be made, an approximation to equality should be obtained by aid in constructing roads." The warning, in short, was that there must be something for everyone. Ernest L. Bogart, *Internal Improvements and State Debt in Ohio* (New York, 1924), p. 55.

54. "The role of local government was typically not the planning of a great system of transportation. It was an attempt to gain a favorable competitive position for the particular community. . . ." Carter Goodrich, "Local Government Planning of Internal Improvements", POLIT. SCI. Q., LXVI, 442 (Sept. 1951).

55. Esarey, *History of Indiana*, pp. 352–73.

56. Theodore C. Pease, *The Frontier State, 1818–1848* (Springfield, 1918), pp. 194–219. Interesting unpublished material on the Illinois system exists: Alan Heimert, "The Internal Improvement Act of 1837: An Introduction to the Study of Illinois Politics in the 1830s" (M.A. thesis, Columbia University, 1950), and John Henry Krenkel, "Internal Improvements in Illinois, 1818–1848" (Ph.D. thesis, University of Illinois, 1937).

57. The state of Mississippi sought in vain to make a modest loan of $200,000 for internal improvements, backed by its 3 per cent fund, future land grants, and the faith of the state. Dunbar Rowland, *History of Mississippi* (Chicago-Jackson, 1935), I, 553–54. Alabama likewise did next to nothing, and when the Northwest's improvement systems collapsed with the panic of 1837, the governor even con-

TABLE FOR NOTE 47

| | Alabama | Miss. | Ohio | Indiana | Illinois |
|---|---|---|---|---|---|
| Population | 590,756 | 375,651 | 1,519,467 | 685,866 | 476,183 |
| No. primary & common schools | 659 | 382 | 5,186 | 1,521 | 1,241 |
| Scholars in common schools | 16,243 | 8,236 | 218,609 | 48,189 | 34,876 |

Abstracted from *Sixth Census*, U. S. Census Office (Washington, 1841).

TABLE FOR NOTE 51

| | Alabama | Miss. | Ohio | Indiana | Illinois |
|---|---|---|---|---|---|
| Population | 590,756 | 375,651 | 1,519,467 | 685,866 | 476,183 |
| No. persons in commerce | 2,212 | 1,303 | 9,201 | 3,076 | 2,506 |
| No. persons in mfg. & trade | 7,195 | 4,151 | 66,265 | 20,590 | 13,185 |

Abstracted from *Sixth Census* (1840).

gratulated his state for having remained inactive. As late as 1851 Alabama's Committee on Internal Improvements noted bitterly that there had been "not one serious effort on the part of the Legislature to advance the great interests of agriculture, commerce, or manufactures. . . . Other states are rich because they are old, but our destiny seems to be to grow old and poor together." William E. Martin, "Internal Improvements in Alabama", *Johns Hopkins Studies in Hist. and Polit. Sci.*, XX, No. 4 (1902), 40, 73.

58. Baynard Rush Hall, the first professor at Indiana University, was unpleasantly aware of this. "With our own eyes we saw Cash! handled it with our fingers: heard it jingle with our ears! and all at once 'high larning' became as popular as common schools. . . . Only show that a school, an academy, a college, or, a church, will advance the value of town lots—bring in more customers—create a demand for beef, cloth, pepper and salt, powder and shot; then, from vulgar plebian dealing in shoe leather, up to the American *nobleman* dealing in shops, and who retails butter and eggs, we shall hear one spontaneous voice in favour!" *New Purchase*, p. 400.

59. This connection between *practical* tolerance and business (ceremonial "tolerance" comes later) can hardly be too much emphasized. In 1849 there was a remarkable act of cultural assimilation in Jacksonville, Illinois. In that year 130 Portuguese exiles from the island of Madeira were brought there, civic committees having undertaken to find accommodations and situations for them, and urged that in coming the exiles "would thus learn our manners, our habits (we hope our good ones only), and our way of doing business of all kinds—and become useful to themselves, and in time amalgamated with us." It was a transaction managed with great efficiency by local groups, including the ladies of Jackson-

ville, and was highly beneficial to all. George R. Poage, "The Coming of the Portuguese," *Ill. State Hist. Soc. Jour.*, XVIII, 100–135 (Apr. 1925).

60. Max Weber insisted that this was still true at a much later stage of development. "Industrial monopolies and trusts are institutions of limited duration; the conditions of production undergo changes, and the market does not know any everlasting valuation. Their power also lacks the authoritative character and the political mark of aristocracies. But monopolies of the land always create a political aristocracy." Gerth and Mills, eds., *From Max Weber*, p. 383.

61. Edward Thornton Heald, *The Stark County Story* (Canton, 1949), I, 42–50, 52–55; John Danner, *Old Landmarks of Canton and Stark County* (Logansport, 1904), pp. 43, 470.

62. Heald, op. cit., p. 66. County organization at that time called for three or more justices of the peace, tax commissioners, a sheriff, a coroner, a recorder, a treasurer, a license commissioner, and justices and clerks of the various courts. Ohio Historical Records Survey Project, Inventory of the County Archives of Ohio, No. 76, Stark County (Columbus, 1940), p. 23.

63. Edward T. Heald, *Bezaleel Wells, Founder of Canton and Steubenville, Ohio* (Canton, 1948).

64. "All of them except Tuscaloosa were situated in agricultural communities; and Tuscaloosa was not really an exception, inasmuch as the mineral resources in the vicinity had not then been developed." Thomas H. Owen, *A History of Alabama and Dictionary of Alabama Biography* (Chicago, 1921), II, 265.

65. Heald, *Stark County Story*, pp. 12, 94–96, 217.

66. Heald, *Bezaleel Wells*, pp. 113–14, 118–19, 122, 126; Danner, *Old Landmarks*, p. 451; Heald, *Stark County Story*, pp. 6, 94–114, 119–123, 126–33, 135.

## PARTY: COMPARATIVE MODEL

1. See Max Weber, "Politics as a Vocation", in *From Max Weber: Essays in Sociology*, edited by H. H. Gerth and C. Wright Mills (New York, 1946), 102–103.

2. See, e.g., the recent summary history of English parties by Sir Ivor Jennings, *Party Politics: The Growth of Parties* (Cambridge, England, 1961), 6–26.

3. Charles A. Beard, *An Economic In-*

terpretation of the Constitution of the United States (New York, 1913); Economic Origins of Jeffersonian Democracy (New York, 1915); and his brief history, The American Party Battle (New York, 1928).

4. For the politics of ratification, Forrest McDonald, We the People: The Economic Origins of the Constitution (Chicago, 1958), which also offers remarkable coverage of the actual state politics of the time; for the fresh origins of the parties of the 1790s, Joseph Charles, The Origins of the American Party System (Williamsburg, Virginia, 1956), which makes the point most effectively.

5. M. Ostrogorski, Democracy and the Organization of Political Parties, 2 volumes (New York, 1902); Edgar E. Robinson, The Evolution of American Political Parties: A Sketch of Party Development (New York, 1924), 69–71; Avery Leiserson, Parties and Politics: An Institutional and Behavioral Approach (New York, 1958), 43–44, 48–50. See also the suggestive review of the literature and summary by Neil A. McDonald, The Study of Political Parties, Short Studies in Political Science (New York, 1955), 9–36.

6. Truly durable and significant party organization was established on the American scene only with the advent of the Jacksonian Democrats in the 1820s and 1830s. Cf. Ostrogorski, op. cit., II, 39–79, despite his treatment of earlier patterns of structure or action in the late 1700s as "the germs of . . . organization", ibid., 3–38.

7. Wilfred E. Binkley, American Political Parties: Their Natural History, third edition (New York, 1958).

8. The phrase originated with Ralph M. Goldman, but has been given currency by V. O. Key, Jr., Politics, Parties, and Pressure Groups, fourth edition (New York, 1958), 181–182 ff.

9. Binkley, op. cit., 3, 11, 14, 18, 22, 27–28, 29, 45–46. passim.

10. Weber, loc. cit., 99–102.

11. Maurice Duverger, Political Parties: Their Organization and Activity in the Modern State (New York, 1954), xxiv, xxvii–xxviii, xxix.

12. Charles O. Paullin, "The First Elections Under the Constitution," Iowa Journal of History and Politics, II (1904), 3–33.

13. George D. Luetscher, Early Political Machinery in the United States (Philadelphia, 1903).

14. See, e.g., portions on early politics in Harry M. Tinkcom, The Republicans and Federalists in Pennsylvania, 1790–1801: A Study in National Stimulus and Local Response (Harrisburg, Pennsylvania, 1950), and in Russell J. Ferguson, Early Western Pennsylvania Politics (Pittsburgh, 1938); also Forrest McDonald, op. cit., 163–172.

15. See Dixon Ryan Fox, "The Decline of Aristocracy in the Politics of New York," Studies in History, Economics and Public Law, LXXXVI, Columbia University (New York, 1919), and biographies such as E. Wilder Spaulding, His Excellency George Clinton (New York, 1938), or Nathan Schachner, Alexander Hamilton (New York, 1946); also, Forrest McDonald, op. cit., 283–300.

16. It was Burke, of course, who praised "Honourable connexion[s]" as means by which men could "act in concert," and "act with confidence," because they were "bound together by common opinions, common affections, and common interests," or "practiced friendship and experimented fidelity"—but it was also Burke who defined "party" as "a body of men united, for promoting by their just endeavours the national interest, upon some particular principle in which they are all agreed," and who argued the necessity of party as a "proper means towards . . . the proper ends of government," in "public life" as "a situation of power and energy" (Edmund Burke, Thoughts on the Cause of the Present Discontents, ed. F. G. Selby [London, 1902], 78–84). In short, Burke is a traditional figure, familiar in practice with old-style "connexions," but concerned with possibilities of political action which could be realized only in parties, and remarkably principled parties at that.

17. For faction politics in the early American states, cf. Elisha P. Douglas, Rebels and Democrats: The Struggle for Equal Political Rights and Majority Rule During the American Revolution (Chapel Hill, North Carolina, 1955); Frederick W. Dallinger, Nominations for Elective

Office in the United States (New York, 1903); Ralph Volney Harlow, *The History of Legislative Methods in the Period Before 1825* (New Haven, 1917); Allan Nevins, *The American States During and After the Revolution* (New York, 1924); Charles Henry Ambler, *Sectionalism in Virginia from 1776 to 1861* (Chicago, 1910); Walter R. Fee, *The Transition from Aristocracy to Democracy in New Jersey* (Somerville, N.J., 1933); Fox, "The Decline of Aristocracy in the Politics of New York," *loc. cit.*; also, Forrest McDonald, *op. cit.*, 113-346.

18. For the English contrast, and politics, "parties," connexions, and factions in the eighteenth century, cf. Charles B. Realey, *The Early Opposition to Sir Robert Walpole, 1720-1727* (Lawrence, Kansas, 1931); Keith Feiling, *The Second Tory Party, 1714-1832* (London, 1938); Lewis M. Wiggin, *The Faction of Cousins: A Political Account of the Grenvilles, 1733-1763* (New Haven, Connecticut, 1958); L. B. Namier, *The Structure of Politics at the Accession of George III*, second edition (London, 1957), and *England in the Age of the American Revolution* (London, 1930), esp. Chapters II, III; John Brooke, *The Chatham Administration, 1766-1768* (London, 1956), esp. 218-294; Herbert Butterfield, *George III, Lord North and the People, 1779-80* (London, 1949). For recent discussions of the subject, cf. also Namier, "Monarchy and the Party System," in *Personalities and Powers* (London, 1955), and Herbert Butterfield, *George III and the Historians*, revised edition (New York, 1959), esp. 193-299; Jacob M. Price, "Party, Purpose, and Pattern: Sir Lewis Namier and His Critics," *Journal of British Studies*, I (1961), 71-93. The insights of Ostrogorski, *op. cit.*, I, 6-134, into eighteenth-century English politics as a kind of pre-party politics should also be noted.

19. Indeed, "this spirit, unfortunately, is inseparable from our nature . . . It exists under different shapes in all governments . . . but in those of the popular form it is seen in its greatest rankness and is truly their worst enemy . . . in governments purely elective, it is a spirit not to be encouraged." (George Washington, "Farewell Address," September 17, 1796, in

Henry Steele Commager, ed., *Documents of American History*, third edition [New York, 1946], I, 172). Given Washington's hidden patrician value premises, there are interesting empirical suggestions here— perhaps Hamilton's—about the nature and operations of party, particularly as they may be related to mass or democratic politics and the potential effect of party on differential advantages in power.

20. Charles, *op. cit.*, 4-53, 74-90. Despite some over-argument and other flaws, Charles' volume remains a provocative treatment of the main themes of early American party development. See also the present writer's study, *Parties in a New Nation: The American Experience, 1776-1809* (New York, 1963).

21. Schachner, *op. cit.*; John C. Miller, *Alexander Hamilton; Portrait in Paradox* (New York, 1959), and *The Federalist Era, 1789-1801* (New York, 1960), 33-69, 84-125; also, if it is read constructively for insights into actual Congressional behavior and not simply for its polemic, *The Journal of William Maclay* (New York, 1927), covering the beginnings of Hamilton's ascendency. Despite his capacity for strictures on the idea of "the spirit of party," broadly directed against the opposition, Hamilton in practice was initiating party action.

22. Manning J. Dauer, *The Adams Federalists* (Baltimore, 1953), 3-34, 275-287, contains a systematic treatment of the Federalist power base; see also Binkley, *op. cit.*, 29-51.

23. Quoted in Charles, *op. cit.*, 39.

24. For the Republican development generally and Madison's and Jefferson's roles, see the leading and thorough monograph, Noble E. Cunningham, Jr., *The Jeffersonian Republicans: The Formation of Party Organization, 1789-1801* (Chapel Hill, North Carolina, 1957); Irving Brant, *James Madison: Father of the Constitution, 1787-1800* (New York, 1950); and Dumas Malone, *Jefferson and the Rights of Man* (Boston, 1951); also, Charles, *op. cit.*, 74-140.

25. H. H. Brackenridge, frontier philosopher in Pittsburgh, quoted in Marcus Cunliffe, *The Nation Takes Shape, 1789-1837* (Chicago, 1959).

26. Eugene Perry Link, *Democratic-*

*Republican Societies, 1790–1800* (New York, 1942).

27. See Philip M. Marsh, "John Beckley, Mystery Man of the Early Republicans," *Pennsylvania Magazine of History and Biography,* LXXII (1948), 54–69; Noble E. Cunningham, Jr., "John Beckley: An Early American Party Manager," *The William and Mary Quarterly,* Third Series, XIII (1956), 40–52; also, Charles, *op. cit.,* and Cunningham, *op. cit.*

28. Charles, *op. cit.,* 103–140; Cunningham, *op. cit.,* esp. 76–85; see discussions and data concerning trends toward party voting in Congress in above, and in Dauer, *op. cit.,* esp. 288–331. For the consolidation of Republican party structure generally and in the states, see *inter alia* Harry Ammon, "The Formation of the Republican Party in Virginia, 1789–1796," *Journal of Southern History,* XIX (1953), 283–310; Dice Robins Anderson, *William Branch Giles: A Study in the Politics of Virginia and the Nation from 1790 to 1830* (Menasha, Wisconsin, 1914); W. P. Cresson, *James Monroe* (Chapel Hill, North Carolina, 1946); Delbert H. Gilpatrick, *Jeffersonian Democracy in North Carolina, 1789–1816* (New York, 1931); Lewis Leary, *That Rascal Freneau: A Study in Literary Failure* (New Brunswick, New Jersey, 1941); Samuel Eliot Morison, "Squire Ames and Doctor Ames," *New England Quarterly,* I (1928), 5–31; William A. Robinson, *Jeffersonian Democracy In New England* (New Haven, Connecticut, 1916); Nathan Schachner, *Aaron Burr* (New York, 1937); Raymond Walters, Jr., *Albert Gallatin: Jeffersonian Financier and Diplomat* (New York, 1957), and *Alexander James Dallas: Lawyer—Politician—Financier, 1759–1817* (Philadelphia, 1943); Charles Warren, *Jacobin and Junto: or Early American Politics as Viewed in the Diary of Dr. Nathaniel Ames 1758–1822* (Cambridge, Massachusetts, 1931); John H. Wolfe, *Jeffersonian Democracy in South Carolina* (Chapel Hill, North Carolina, 1940); also party monographs previously cited, Notes 14, 15, 17.

29. E. E. Robinson, *op. cit.,* 73–75.

30. Robert Michels, *Political Parties: A Sociological Study of the Oligarchical Tendencies of Modern Democracy* (New York, 1915), 21–90, 365–392.

31. The term "plebiscitarian" is Weber's; it is used here, however, in a restricted sense as indicated above, to connote a politics of mass dependence, mass appeals, limited mass action often through manipulation, and elections as plebiscites —as contrasted with a "democratic" politics of popular representation, active popular initiative or participation, free public opinion, and elections as open choices.

32. Cunningham, *op. cit.,* 62–66.

33. Benjamin Disraeli, *Coningsby, or the New Generation* (London, 1844).

34. See, e.g., Norman Birnbaum, "The Sociological Study of Ideology," *Current Sociology,* IX (1962), 91, 116, passim; it may also be noted that my approach here has points in common with the more extended treatment by Michael Walzer, "Puritanism as a Revolutionary Ideology," in the present symposium.

35. Charles, *op. cit.,* esp. 92–103 ff., and Dauer, *op. cit.,* 288–331.

36. For a provocative though sometimes provoking recent discussion of democracy as choice, see E. E. Schattschneider, *The Semisovereign People: A Realist's View of Democracy in America* (New York, 1960), 129–142, passim.

37. Even the short-lived third parties of American history have generally looked forward to continuation, in which case they may be called parties, or strictly, proto-parties. Where they have not, they may be written off as quasi-parties.

38. Thomas H. Eliot, *Governing America: The Politics of a Free People* (New York, 1960), 272.

39. The specific form structure takes for any given party at a particular time is conditioned by the total context (social system, political culture, ideology, and situation) in which the party has evolved and acts. Thus, American parties today are not quite the same as the Federalist or Republican parties of the 1790s; parties in Great Britain or France differ from American parties; and party in the U.S.S.R. or Ghana is something else again. Yet—and the point will be argued more fully later—certain broad features will be found in common.

40. Weber, *loc. cit.,* 99–104.

41. Duverger, *op. cit.,* 151–168.

42. Key, *op. cit.,* 181–182.

43. Binkley, *op. cit.,* passim.

44. Weber, *loc. cit.,* 107–108.

45. For the vexed problem of historical

explanation, I have found particularly interesting Carl Hempel, The Function of General Laws in History," *Journal of Philosophy*, XXXIX (1942), 35–48; Patrick Gardiner, *The Nature of Historical Explanation* (London, 1952); William Dray, *Laws and Explanation in History* (London, 1957); Maurice Mandelbaum, "Historical Explanation: the Problem of 'Covering Laws,'" *History and Theory*, I (1961), 229–242.

46. Cf. Leiserson, op. cit., 39–81, *passim.*

47. Louis Hartz, *The Liberal Tradition in America: An Interpretation of American Political Thought Since the Revolution* (New York, 1955), 3–23, esp. 17, 20, 21, 22.

48. See, e.g., Samuel H. Beer, "The Representation of Interests in British Government: Historical Background," *American Political Science Review*, LI (1957), 613–650; also his "Great Britain: From Governing Elite to Organized Mass Parties," in Sigmund Neumann, ed., *Modern Political Parties: Approaches to Comparative Politics* (Chicago, 1956), 9–56; and "New Structures of Democracy: Britain and America," in William N. Chambers and Robert H. Salisbury, eds., *Democracy in the Mid-Twentieth Century: Problems and Prospects* (St. Louis, 1960), 30–59. Again, cf. the treatment of English politics in the eighteenth century by Ostrogorski, op. cit., I, 6–134, and the contrast with politics after the Reform Bill of 1832, *passim.*

49. The almost immediate futility of John Adams' painful efforts to establish Harringtonian mixed government through the "Oceana" constitution of 1780 in Massachusetts underscores the point.

50. For recent valuable summaries of early American development relating to these points, see Edmund S. Morgan, *The Birth of the Republic, 1763–1789* (Chicago, 1956), and Cunliffe, op. cit.,; also Hartz, op. cit., 35–96.

51. It is the frank recognition of this free play of pluralism which gives point to Madison's statement that in modern societies a variety of interests will "grow up of necessity," where "liberty is to faction what air is to fire," and which differentiates his American conception of politics from Harrington's or Montesquieu's conceptions of a balance of fixed ranks, estates, orders, or classes.

52. An intra-American comparison is also suggestive here, and "fits." Of all the American states in the 1780s, Pennsylvania and New York probably exhibited most fully the general conditions noted above as facilitative to party development. They differed, however, in that New York also exhibited some of the factors noted as obstacles, particularly in the old-established patterns of family dominance which sustained an old-style clique and faction politics, whereas these factors had substantially disappeared in Pennsylvania by the 1780s. Thus, Pennsylvania produced state parties early, New York followed (concomitantly with national party development) in the 1790s as the obstacle conditions rapidly broke down, and other states moved still more slowly toward party formations as adjuncts of the national parties.

53. Morgan, op. cit., 93–94; see also 7–8.

54. Paullin, loc. cit., 27–31, and Luetscher, op. cit.; Bureau of the Census, *Historical Statistics of the United States 1789–1945* (Washington, 1949), esp. 289–290; Richard P. McCormick, "New Perspectives on Jacksonian Politics," *American Historical Review*, LXV (1960), 288–301.

55. Cunliffe, op. cit., 11–39, 150–180.

56. Noting that his interpretation will be called "a 'single factor' analysis," Hartz, op. cit., 20, says that "probably the only way of meeting this charge is to admit it." The matter may not be so easy, however, in the immediate case or particularly in the whole panoply of theory or explanation in history or political science.

57. Karl Mannheim, *Ideology and Utopia: An Introduction to the Sociology of Knowledge* (New York, 1954), 64–70.

58. See, e.g., Jennings on "Joe's Caucus" in Birmingham and related patterns of action, op. cit., 134–143.

59. Weber, loc. cit., 99. In his discussion of the development of American parties as the fullest expression of the "plebiscitarian principle," Weber adumbrates important aspects of the general hypothesis of party origins proposed here, as does Ostrogorski in a different way in his discussion of American and British parties.

60. Duverger, op. cit., 17–40, 62–71.

61. See, *inter alia*, Max F. Millikan and Donald L. M. Blackmer, *The Emerging*

Nations: Their Growth and United States Policy (Boston, 1961); Gabriel A. Almond and James S. Coleman, eds., The Politics of the Developing Areas (Princeton, 1960); John H. Kautsky, et. al., Political Change in Underdeveloped Countries: Nationalism and Communism (New York, 1962).

62. Cf. the different comparative analyses by Seymour Martin Lipset, Political Man: The Social Bases of Politics (New York, 1960), 45–72, and Harry Eckstein, "A Theory of Stable Democracy," Research Monograph, Center of International Studies (Princeton, 1961, passim.

## NATIONAL CHARACTER

1. Frederick Jackson Turner, The Frontier in American History (New York: Henry Holt and Co., 1920), p. 4.

2. Robert Lynd, "The People as Consumers," writes that there is "probably today a greater variation from house to house in the actual inventory list of family possessions . . . than at any previous era in man's history." Recent Social Trends in the United States (New York: McGraw-Hill, 1933), pp. 857–911.

3. In 1957, of the 21,000,000 women in the work force, 11,000,000 were wives. Female employment was highest (45 per cent in the age brackets 20 to 24, declined to 39 per cent in bracket 25 to 44, rose to 40 per cent in the bracket 45 to 64, and declined to 10 per cent in the bracket 65 and over.

4. Harper's Magazine, Vol. 223 (Nov., 1961), p. 23.

5. David Riesman, "The Lonely Crowd: A Reconsideration in 1960" in Seymour Martin Lipset and Leo Lowenthal, eds., Culture and Social Character: The Work of David Riesman Reviewed (New York; The Free Press of Glencoe, 1961), p. 428, discusses an investigation by Michael S. Olmstead which showed that Smith College girls regarded themselves as more other-directed than men and regarded other girls as more other-directed than their group, but Riesman does not state what his own belief is in this matter.

6. Probably the best of the literature which emphasizes the sex frustration of the modern American woman is found in professional publications in the fields of psychology and psychoanalysis which do not

reach a popular audience. In the literature for the layman, probably the best presentation of this point of view is Simone de Beauvoir's excellent The Second Sex (New York: A. A. Knopf, 1953), but other items have enjoyed a circulation which they hardly deserve. Two cases in point are Ferdinand Lundberg and Marynia F. Farnham, Modern Woman: The Lost Sex (New York: Harper, 1947) and Eric John Dingwall, The American Woman: an Historical Study (New York: Rinehart and Co., 1958). Denis W. Brogan's judicious and yet precise evaluation that Dingwall's book is "strictly for the birds" would be equally applicable to Lundberg. For an able argument that the condition of modern woman must be understood partly in social terms, and that the concept of "genital trauma" has been overdone, see Mirra Komarovsky, Women in the Modern World: their Education and their Dilemmas (Boston: Little, Brown and Company), pp. 31–52.

7. Komarovsky, Women in the Modern World, pp. 127–153.

8. Experiments on the rate of eye-blink, as conducted by James M. Vicary, a leading exponent of motivation research, were reported in Vance Packard, The Hidden Persuaders (New York: David McKay Co., 1957), pp. 106–108.

9. Sylvia Wright, "Whose World? and Welcome to It," in Harper's Magazine, vol. 210 (May, 1955), pp. 35–38.

10. John P. McKee and A. C. Sheriffs, "Men's and Women's Beliefs, Ideals, and Self-Concepts," in American Journal of Sociology, LXIV (1959, 356–363.

## ECONOMETRICS

1. See, for example, Charles D'Avenant, An Essay Upon the Probable Method of Making a People Gainers in the Balance of

Trade (London, 1699); John Graunt, Natural and Political Observations Mentioned in a Following Index and Made

*Upon the Bills of Mortality* (London, 1662); Gregory King, *Natural and Political Observations and Conclusions Upon the State and Condition of England 1696* (London, 1810); Charles H. Hull, ed., *The Economic Writings of Sir William Petty* (Cambridge, Mass., 1899).

2. William Newmarch, "An Attempt to Ascertain the Magnitude and Fluctuations of the Amount of Bills of Exchange (Inland and Foreign) in Circulation at One Time in Great Britain, in England, in Scotland, in Lancashire, and in Cheshire, Respectively, During Each of the Twenty Years 1828-1947, Both Inclusive; and Also Embracing in the Inquiry Bills Drawn Upon Foreign Countries," *Journal of the Statistical Society of London*, XIV (1851), 143-92.

3. Frank W. Taussig, *The Tariff History of the United States* (New York and London; G. P. Putnam's Sons, 1888); Walter B. Smith and Arthur H. Cole, *Fluctuations in American Business 1790-1860* (Cambridge, Mass.: Harvard University Press, 1935); Arthur H. Cole, "Seasonal Variation in Sterling Exchange," *Journal of Economic and Business History*, II (Nov. 1929) 203-318; Arthur H. Cole, "Evolution of the Foreign Exchange Market of the United States." *Journal of Economic and Business History*, I (1928), 384-421.

4. See, for example, Simon Kuznets, *National Product Since 1869* (New York: National Bureau of Economic Research, 1946); or Simon Kuznets, *Secular Movements in Production and Prices; Their Nature and Bearing Upon Cyclical Fluctuations* (Boston and New York: Houghton Mifflin, 1930); or "Long-Term Changes in the National Income of the United States Since 1870," *Income and Wealth of the United States Trends and Structure*, Series II, pp. 10-246.

5. Robert C. O. Matthews, *A Study in Trade Cycle History; Economic Fluctuations in Great Britain, 1833-1842* (Cambridge, England: University Press, 1954); Alfred H. Conrad and John R. Meyer, "The Economics of Slavery in the Ante Bellum South," *Journal of Political Economy*, LXVI (April, 1958), 95-130.

6. Newmarch, "Circulation."

7. Jonathan R. T. Hughes and Stanley Reiter, "The First 1,945 British Steamships," *Journal of the American Statistical Association*, LIII (June, 1958), 360-81.

8. Newmarch, "Circulation," p. 149.

9. Lance E. Davis, "Sources of Industrial Finance: The American Textile Industry, A Case Study," *Explorations in Entrepreneurial History*, IX (April 1957), 189-203.

10. Lance E. Davis, "Stock Ownership in the Early New England Textile Industry," *The Business History Review*, XXXII (Summer, 1958), 204-22.

11. Hughes and Reiter, "1,945 Steamships."

12. Lance E. Davis, "The New England Textile Mills and the Capital Markets: A Study of Industrial Borrowing, 1840-1860," *The Journal of Economic History*, XX (March, 1960), 1-30.

13. Lance E. Davis and Jonathan R. T. Hughes, "A Dollar Sterling Exchange 1803-1895," *Economic History Review* (August, 1960).

14. W. Allen Wallis and Harry V. Roberts, *Statistics, A New Approach* (New York: The Free Press of Glencoe, 1956), p. 20.

## SAMPLING AND CORRELATION

1. For examples see Merle Curti, "American Philanthropy and the National Character," *American Quarterly*, X (Winter, 1958), 420-37.

2. James Bryce, *The American Commonwealth* (3d ed.; 2 vols.; New York, 1909), II, 723.

3. Arthur M. Schlesinger Sr., "The True American Way of Life," *St. Louis Post-Dispatch*, December 13, 1953, Part II, 3.

4. Shepard E. Clough, "Philanthropy and the Welfare State in Europe," *Political Science Quarterly*, LXXV (March, 1960), 87.

5. For example, the completed and recently published book-length study of American giving overseas by Merle Curti and the investigation in progress on the impact of philanthropy on American colleges and universities by Curti and Roderick W. Nash; Jesse B. Sears, *Philanthropy in the History of American Higher Education*, "Department of Interior, Bu-

reau of Education, Bulletin No. 26"
(Washington, 1922); Robert Bremner,
*American Philanthropy* (Chicago, 1960);
Merle Curti, "Tradition and Innovation
in American Philanthropy," *Proceedings
of the American Philosophical Society*,
CV (April 1961), 146–56; Edward C.
Jenkins, *Philanthropy in America* (New
York, 1950); and Arnaud C. Marts,
*Man's Concern for his Fellow Man* (New
York, 1961).

6. W. K. Jordan, *Philanthropy in England, 1480–1660* (New York, 1959), *The
Charities of London, 1480–1660* (London,
1960), and *The Charities of Rural England,
1480–1660* (New York, 1962).

7. F. Emerson Andrews, *Philanthropic
Giving* (New York, 1950), *Corporation
Giving* (New York, 1952), *Attitudes toward Giving* (New York, 1953), and *Philanthropic Foundations* (New York, 1956).
The forthcoming study of American philanthropy sponsored by the National Bureau of Economic Research similarly concentrates on the recent period.

8. "American Millionaires: The Tribune's List of Persons Reputed to be
Worth a Million or More," *Tribune
Monthly*, IV, No. 6 (June, 1892). Sidney
Ratner has reprinted the *New York Tribune* list and discussed it in an informing
introduction: *New Light on the History
of Great American Fortunes: American
Millionaires of 1892 and 1902* (New York,
1953).

9. George P. Watkins, "The Growth
of Large Fortunes," *Publications of the
American Economic Association*, VIII, 3d
series (1907), 875 ff. For other favorable
judgments on the care with which the
Tribune list was compiled and on its general reliability see Ratner, *New Light on
the History of Great American Fortunes*,
p. xix.

10. The *New York World's* list of
3,561 millionaires living in 1902 is also
included in the Ratner volume.

11. For a recent edition of this and
other essays bearing on the problem of
wealth see Andrew Carnegie, *The Gospel
of Wealth*, ed. Edward C. Kirkland (Cambridge, 1962).

12. *Review of Reviews*, VII (February,
1893), 48–60.

13. Attention was called to the generosity of several Cleveland millionaires
to Western Reserve University, to the
$1,000,000 gift of William J. Gordon for
a park and to the donations of Mrs. Samuel Mather and her late husband for several causes.

14. George J. Hagar, "Magnitude of
American Benefactions," *Review of Reviews*, XXIX (April, 1904), 464–65. The
yearly totals as well as an itemized listing
of the contributions appeared in *Appleton's Annual Cyclopaedia and Register
of Important Events* under the heading
"Gifts and Bequests" from 1893 to 1902.
Hagar's figure for 1903 appears only in
his article.

15. Hagar, *Review of Reviews*, XXIX,
465.

16. It seems not improbable that the
records for outstandingly large gifts (and
bequests) are fairly complete. Table II
presents figures which may have some
general interest.

17. For what limited value it may have,
the authors compiled a table of dollar
amounts for their own reference which is
on file at the Wisconsin Project on the
History of American Philanthropy.

18. These figures and percentages give
only a rough indication of the areas which
interested philanthropists. The table gives
no indication of actual dollar amounts or
of proportion of dollar amounts.

19. In these and some subsequent tables
percentage components do not add to total
because of rounding.

20. Hagar, *Review of Reviews*, VII, 49,
argued in 1893 that millionaires are the
product not only of their own efforts but
of "the unearned increment in expanding
land values, the productive value of railway
and other franchises, and the other forms
of wealth that arise out of conditions
which Society itself creates. . . ." For
this reason he concluded, the wealthy
should give generously to public purposes.

21. *New York Times*, July 26, 1931.

22. We appreciate the careful and time-
taking work of Sharon Smith and John
Tomsich, research assistants on the University of Wisconsin Project, in collecting
data on donations as reported in the *New
York Times* in selected years.

## MACHINE PROGRAMMING AND INFORMATION RETRIEVAL

1. See, for example, *Punched Cards, Their Application to Science and Industry,* 2nd Edition, edited by Robert S. Casey, J. W. Perry, M. M. Berry, and Allen Kent. New York, Reinhold Publishing Co., 1958.

2. For details as to the preparation of standardized informative abstracts, their encoding, recording and selective searching by automatic electronic equipment, see *Tools for Machine Literature Searching,* by J. W. Perry, Allen Kent, and John L. Melton. New York, Interscience Publishers, 1958.

3. See Chapter 18, "The Western Reserve University Searching Selector," in *Tools for Machine Literature Searching,* op. cit.

## MORAL FACTORS

1. Samuel Eliot Morison, *The Puritan Pronaos: Studies in the Intellectual Life of New England in the Seventeenth Century* (New York, 1936); Walter Prescott Webb, *The Great Plains* (Boston, 1931); Carl Wittke, *We Who Built America: The Saga of the Immigrant* (New York, 1939); Ulrich B. Phillips, *Life and Labor in the Old South* (Boston, 1929); E. Merton Coulter, *The South during Reconstruction, 1865–1877* (Baton Rouge, La., 1947). Negro historians and students of labor history seem also increasingly irenic; even business history may be losing an apologetic tone.

2. Avery Craven, *The Repressible Conflict, 1830–1861* (Baton Rouge, La., 1939); Samuel Flagg Bemis, *A Diplomatic History of the United States* (New York, 1950), 463–75; Thomas A. Bailey, *Woodrow Wilson and the Great Betrayal* (New York, 1945).

3. Edward P. Cheyney, *Law in History and Other Essays* (New York, 1927), 22–24; Dixon Ryan Fox, "A Synthetic Principle in American Social History," *American Historical Review,* XXXV (Jan., 1930), 256–66.

4. Frederick Paxson, *When the West Is Gone* (Boston, 1930).

5. The economic interpretation of history, Charles A. Beard wrote in 1913, "rests upon the concept that social progress in general is the result of contending interests in society—some favorable, others opposed to change." (*An Economic Interpretation of the Constitution,* rev. ed., New York, 1935, 19.)

6. Arthur Schlesinger, Sr., "Tides of American Politics," *Yale Review,* XXIX (Dec. 1939). 220.

7. George F. Kennan, *American Di-* *plomacy 1900–1950* (Chicago, 1951).

8. The gradual revision, since World War II, of Avery Craven's revisionism has often been remarked upon. See T. N. Bonner, "Civil War Historians and the Needless War Doctrine," *Journal of the History of Ideas,* XVII (Apr., 1956), 193–216.

9. Ralph Gabriel's *The Course of American Democratic Thought: An Intellectual History Since 1815* (New York, 1940) anticipated a point of view that has become much more common since World War II in books such as Clinton Rossiter's *Seedtime of the Republic: The Origin of the American Tradition of Political Liberty* (New York, 1953), Louis Hartz's *The Liberal Tradition in America: An Interpretation of American Political Thought Since the Revolution* (New York, 1955), Robert E. Brown's *Middle-Class Democracy and the Revolution in Massachusetts, 1691–1780* (Ithaca, N.Y., 1955), and Edmund S. and Helen M. Morgan's *The Stamp Act Crisis: Prologue to Revolution* (Chapel Hill, N.C., 1953). Perhaps the most provocative analysis of the "togetherness" of American society and the continuity of American history is Daniel J. Boorstin's *The Americans: The Colonial Experience* (New York, 1958). See also David Potter's interpretation of the unifying influence of economic abundance in American history, *People of Plenty: Economic Abundance and the American Character* (Chicago, 1954). I have criticized this trend at greater length in "The Cult of the 'American Consensus': Homogenizing Our History," *Commentary,* XXVII (Feb., 1959), 93–100, an article from which some of the remarks in the next few paragraphs are drawn.

10. Allan Simpson, "How Democratic Was Roger Williams?" *William and Mary Quarterly*, XIII (Jan., 1956), 53–67; Wilcomb E. Washburn, *The Governor and the Rebel: A History of Bacon's Rebellion in Virginia* (Chapel Hill, N.C., 1957); Bray Hammond, *Banks and Politics in America from the Revolution to the Civil War* (Princeton, N.J., 1957); David Riesman, *Thorstein Veblen: A Critical Interpretation* (New York, 1953).

11. Edmund S. Morgan, *The Puritan Dilemma: The Story of John Winthrop* (Boston, 1958); Broadus Mitchell, *Alexander Hamilton, Youth to Maturity, 1755–1788* (New York, 1957); Thomas P. Govan, *Nicholas Biddle, Nationalist and Public Banker* (Chicago, 1959); C. Vann Woodward, "George Fitzhugh, Sui Generis," in *Cannibals All!* by George Fitzhugh (Cambridge, Mass., 1960), vii–xxxix; Allan Nevins, *Study in Power: John D. Rockefeller* (2 vols., New York, 1953).

12. Richard Hofstadter, *The Age of Reform: From Byran to F.D.R.* (New York, 1955); Marvin Meyers, *The Jacksonian Persuasion* (Stanford, Calif., 1957); Cecelia Kenyon, "Men of Little Faith: The Anti-Federalists on the Nature of Representative Government," *William and Mary Quarterly*, XII (Jan., 1955), 3–43.

13. Hartz, *Liberal Tradition*.

14. For example: Will Herberg, *Protestant-Catholic-Jew: An Essay in American Religious Sociology* (New York, 1955); R. W. B. Lewis, *The American Adam: Innocence, Tragedy, and Tradition in the Nineteenth Century* (Chicago, 1955); Gabriel, *Course of American Democratic Thought*. In sketching another version of the unity of American history, William B. Hesseltine has adopted a quadruple rather than a triple calculus. See his presidential address, "Four American Traditions," *Journal of Southern History*, XXVII (Feb, 1961), 3–32.

15. Allan Nevins, *The War for the Union* (2 vols., New York, 1959–1960), I, v; Rowland Beethoff, "The American Social Order: A Conservative Hypothesis," *American Historical Review*, LXV (Apr., 1960), 495–514.

16. Boorstin, *The Americans*, 185–205.

17. Forrest McDonald, *We the People: The Economic Origins of the Constitution* (Chicago, 1958); Hammond, *Banks and Politics*; Robert P. Sharkey, *Money, Class and Party: An Economic Study of Civil War and Reconstruction* (Baltimore, 1959); Robert H. Wiebe, "Business Disunity and the Progressive Movement, 1901–1914," *Mississippi Valley Historical Review*, XLIV (Mar., 1958), 664–85.

18. Charles V. Langlois and Charles Seignobos, *Introduction to the Study of History* (London, 1898), 279; Oscar Handlin et. al., *Harvard Guide to American History* (Cambridge, Mass., 1954); Jacques Barzun and Henry Graff, *The Modern Researcher* (New York, 1958). One exception is Allan Nevins, *The Gateway to History* (Boston, 1938), 235—a book written with unprofessional gusto and addressed to a wide audience.

19. Isaiah Berlin, *Historical Inevitability* (London, 1054); Friedrich Meinecke, "Values and Causalities in History," *The Varieties of History*, ed. Fritz Stern (New York, 1956), 267–88; C. V. Wedgwood, *Truth and Opinion: Historical Essays* (London, 1960), 47–54; David Knowles, *The Historian and Character* (Cambridge, Eng., 1955); A. J. P. Taylor, *Rumours of Wars* (London, 1952), 9–13. The most cogent arguments on the other side of the issue—denying to the professional historian an ethical function—are also by Europeans: Herbert Butterfield, *History and Human Relations* (London, 1951), 101–30; Marc Bloch, *The Historian's Craft* (New York, 1953), 139–41; Geoffrey Barraclough, "History, Morals, and Politics," *International Affairs*, XXXIV (Jan. 1958), 1–15. A valuable essay by an American philosopher, defending the exercise of moral judgment by historians, came to my attention too late for use in this paper: Arthur Child, "Moral Judgment in History," *Ethics: An International Journal of Social, Political, and Legal Philosophy*, LXI (July, 1951), 297–308.

20. Charles W. Eliot, *Educational Reform: Essays and Addresses* (New York, 1909), 104–106.

21. Henry C. Lea, "Ethical Values in History," *Annual Report, American Historical Association*, 1903 (2 vols., Washington, D.C., 1904), I, 53–69. This was the classic rebuttal, by an American scientific historian, to Lord Acton's famous protest in 1895 against the prevailing spirit of scientific neutrality: "I exhort you . . . to

try others by the final maxim that governs your own lives, and to suffer no man and no cause to escape the undying penalty which history has the power to inflict on wrong." On this controversy, see Andrew Fish, "Acton, Creighton, and Lea: A Study in History and Ethics," *Pacific Historical Review*, XVI (Feb. 1947), 59–69, and John Emerich Edward Dalberg Acton, *Essays on Freedom and Power*, ed. Gertrude Himmelfarb (London, 1956), 41–52, 329–45.

22. Frederick Jackson Turner, "Social Forces in American History," in *The Frontier in American History* (New York, 1920), 323–32; James Harvey Robinson, *The New History: Essays Illustrating the Modern Historical Outlook* (New York, 1912).

23. For a parallel trend among philosophers, see Jay William Hudson, "Recent Shifts in Ethical Theory and Practice," *Philosophical Review*, XLIX (Mar., 1940), 105–20.

24. Although beset by such doubts in the 1930's, Beard fell back on an ultimate "act of faith" that history was moving "on an upward gradient toward a more ideal order." (Charles A. Beard, "Written History as an Act of Faith," *American Historical Review*, XXXIX [Jan., 1934], 226.)

25. Louis Gottschalk, *Understanding History* (New York, 1950), 10–13.

26. René Wellek, "Literary Scholarship," in *American Scholarship in the Twentieth Century*, ed. Merle Curti (Cambridge, Mass., 1953), 111–45.

27. For a balanced summary of these competing views of history, see W. H. Walsh, *An Introduction to Philosophy of History* (rev. ed., London, 1958).

28. Wilbur J. Cash, *The Mind of the South* (New York, 1941); Hannah Arendt, *The Human Condition* (Chicago, 1958); Lewis Mumford, *The City in History: Its Origins, Its Transformations, and Its Prospects* (New York, 1961). Two recent efforts by professional historians are C. Vann Woodward, *The Burden of Southern History* (Baton Rouge, La., 1960), and William R. Taylor, *Cavalier and Yankee: The Old South and American National Character* (New York, 1961).

29. Charles H. McIlwain, *The American Revolution: A Constitutional Interpretation* (New York, 1923), and Robert L. Schuyler, *Parliament and the British Empire* (New York, 1929); Herbert Butterfield, *George III and the Historians* (London, 1957). A reviewer of the last book observed: "It is perhaps the strangest thing of all to find so impressive a controversy reared on the insoluble, and to some extent uninteresting question of what exactly were the relationships between George III, the Duke of Newcastle, and the Earl of Bute in the years following 1760." (*Times Literary Supplement*, Nov. 22, 1957).

30. For an unusual and pioneering inquiry of this kind, see Eric L. McKitrick, *Andrew Johnson and Reconstruction* (Chicago, 1960).

## CAUSALITY

1. Kenneth M. Stampp, *The Causes of the Civil War* (Englewood Cliffs, N.J., 1959), vi.

2. *The Education of Henry Adams* (New York, 1931), 382.

3. *Ibid.*, 472.

4. Adams described his own history of the United States as an effort to state "such facts as seemed sure, in such order as seemed rigorously consequent," so as to "fix for a familiar moment a necessary sequence of human movement." *Ibid.*, 382.

5. Mario Bunge, *Causality: the Place of the Causal Principle in Modern Science* (Cambridge, Mass., 1959), 126.

6. Arthur M. Schlesinger, Jr. sees the Civil War as a "log-jam" which had to be "burst by violence," a common feature of the "tragedy" of history; but surely only commitment to policy positions deemed necessary and worth the price of force explains the "log-jam" he describes. See his "The Causes of the Civil War: a Note on Historical Sentimentalism," *Partisan Review*, 16 (1949), 969–81. Pieter Geyl, who also attacks the "revisionist" thesis of a "needless war," carefully avoids mak-

ing the claim that it was inevitable, leaving the issue moot. See his "The American Civil War and the Problem of Inevitability," *New England Quarterly*, 24 (1951), 147–68.

7. Letter to Louis Gottschalk, Sept. 3, 1944, in C. Becker, *Detachment and the Writing of History*, ed. Phil L. Snyder (Ithaca, 1958), 88.

8. See Max Weber, "Critical Studies in the Logic of the Cultural Sciences," reprinted in English in *The Methodology of the Social Sciences*, ed. Edward A. Shils and Henry A. Finch (Glencoe, Ill., 1949), esp. 164–88.

9. See his *The Discussion of Human Affairs* (New York, 1936), 79, where he characterizies causal judgments as subjective, arbitrary ruptures of the "seamless web" of history.

10. The relevance of training to the use of "guarded generalizations", neither purely analytic nor purely synthetic, is argued convincingly by Michael Scriven, "Truisms as the Grounds for Historical Explanations," in *Theories of History*, ed. Patrick Gardiner (Glencoe, Ill., 1958), 463–68.

11. Letter to Frederick Jackson Turner, May 14, 1921, Box 31, Turner Papers, The Huntington Library.

12. *The Hero in History: a Study in Limitation and Possibility* (New York, 1943), 132.

13. See Harry V. Jaffa, "Expediency and Morality in the Lincoln-Douglas Debates," *The Anchor Review*, 2 (1957), 199–204.

14. Richard H. Shyrock, "The Nationalistic Tradition of the Civil War: A Southern Analysis," *South Atlantic Quarterly*, 32 (1933), 294–305. There is a useful extract in Stampp, *op. cit.*, 45–9.

15. Letter (n. above,) 87.

16. Becker, "Harnessing History", *New Republic*, 22 (1920), 322.

17. For Turner and Beard see my *The Pragmatic Revolt in American History: Carl Becker and Charles Beard* (New Haven, 1958), 21–3, 105–6. For the others see David M. Potter, *People of Plenty: Economic Abundance and the American Character* (Chicago, 1954), 165; Louis Hartz, *The Liberal Tradition in America* (New York, 1955), 20–3.

18. *Truth and Opinion: Historical Essays* (London, 190), 14.

19. Schlesinger specifically refers to the problem of dealing with a "closed society" in both periods in "The Causes of the Civil War: a Note on Historical Sentimentalism", in *Partisan Review*, 16 (1949), 969–81; and the "cold war" analogy is extensively developed in Avery O. Craven, *Civil War in the Making, 1815–60* (Baton Rouge, La., 1959), esp. xiii–xiv.

20. Illustrative examples of these three positions can be found in Stampp, *op. cit.*, 56–65, 83–7, 113–22.

21. "A Plea for an Analytic Philosophy of History," in Morton G. White, *Religion, Politics, and the Higher Learning* (Cambridge, Mass., 1959), 74.

22. The best discussion of this controversy is in David M. Potter, *Lincoln and His Party in the Secession Crisis* (New Haven, 1962), xxiii–xxxii and 371–75. The author makes a strong case for Lincoln's pacific intentions, pointing out that those who argue for the deliberately provocative nature of the Sumter policy fail to indicate what nonprovocative course could have been followed, granted Lincoln's aim to preserve a symbol of federal authority in the South. The provocative theory mainly rests on the hindsight testimony of those who had partisan reasons for making a miscalculation look like a clever stroke. The debate is a good example of the usefulness of asking questions about alternatives.

23. *Loc. cit.*

## SOCIOLOGIST AS HISTORIAN

1. At one time in working on this paper I included a study of two other sociological works that have helped to delineate modern conceptions of the American past, namely, W. H. Whyte Jr., *The Organization Man* (Garden City, N.Y., 1956) and C. Wright Mills, *White Col-* lar, *The American Middle Classes* (New York, 1956). But a close examination of these two works revealed that though they assumed a view of the nineteenth-century American past that was similar in many respects to that of Riesman, their explicit description was small and therefore not

really worth inclusion on a level with the very full and explicit discussion to be found in *The Lonely Crowd*. Hence I have concentrated here only upon that book. Furthermore, *The Lonely Crowd* is so much more subtle and sensitive in its depiction of the nineteenth century that any critique of that superior work can also serve as a criticism of the less complete view of the nineteenth century to be found in the works of Whyte and Mills.

2. David Riesman, Nathan Glazer and Reuel Denney, *The Lonely Crowd* (New York, 1953). Riesman is the principal author and I have attributed to him alone, for the sake of simplicity, any ideas I have cited from the book. Hereafter cited as *LC*.

Throughout this paper I have used the paperback edition, even though it is abridged, simply because it was the form in which most readers would see the book. Inasmuch as the abridgment was done by the authors and the amount cut out is less than 70 pages and those largely concerned with methodological matters, there is not much difference between the popular and the scholarly versions. I have collated the two and only once did I find anything in the original edition which caused me to qualify, and then only slightly, a conclusion I had drawn from the paperback edition. The paperback edition, in reality, is a second edition rather than a simple abridgment since it contains some restatements of ideas, rearrangements of materials and, occasionally, new material.

3. *Ibid.*, p. 17.
4. *Ibid.*, p. 62.
5. *Ibid.*, p. 90.
6. *LC*, p. 165.
7. *LC*, p. 136.
8. *Ibid.*, p. 138.
9. *Ibid.*, p. 161.
10. *Ibid.*, p. 159
11. *Ibid.*, p. 151.
12. *Ibid.*, p. 165.
13. *Ibid.*, p. 150.
14. *Ibid.*, p. 161.
15. *Ibid.*, p. 184.
16. *Ibid.*, p. 70.
17. *Ibid.*, p. 101
18. *Ibid.*, p. 72–73.
19. *Ibid.*, p. 67.
20. *Ibid.*, p. 76.

21. *Ibid.*, p. 122.
22. *Ibid.*, p. 78.
23. *Ibid.*, p. 85.
24. Riesman is careful to point out that one must not unthinkingly value the inner-directed man over the other-directed simply on the grounds of his seeming independence. For, as he points out, the inner-directed man is "no less a conformist to others than the other-directed person, but the voices to which he listens are more distant, of an older generation, their cues internalized in his childhood." *LC*, p. 48. In any case, it is clear that a fourth type, the autonomous person, is the ideal toward which Riesman looks.

25. *LC*, p. 140.
26. *Ibid.*, p. 186.
27. *Ibid.*, p. 173.
28. This is not to say that he has nothing important to contribute, for he has. His observation, for example, that the other-directed man is typically an "inside-dopester" in political behavior is an apt and accurate characterization of the contemporary pseudo-realist who, in political discussions knows all the angles and is ever ready to divulge some story of hidden motives behind political behavior or to attribute Machiavellian slyness to straightforward acts of human sympathy. Similarly, Riesman's attribution of the name "moralizer" to the inner-directed strikes a note of rightness in the mind of anyone who has read the speeches of someone like William Jennings Bryan. See *LC*, pp. 200–17. But there is a vast difference between having insight into political types and characterizing an age as being dominated by one of them.

29. *Ibid.*, p. 203.
30. *Ibid.*, p. 244.
31. Margaret Leech, *In the Days of McKinley* (New York, 1959), pp. 184–85.
32. *LC*, p. 244.
33. *Ibid.*, p. 241.
34. *Loc. cit.*
35. John William Ward, *Andrew Jackson, Symbol For an Age* (New York, 1955) is largely devoted to showing this aspect of Jackson; see also, Marvin Meyers, *The Jacksonian Persuasion* (Stanford, 1957), chap. 1.
36. Richard Hofstadter, *The Age of*

*Reform* (New York, 1955), chap. 3.

37. *LC*, pp. 35, 40.

38. *Ibid.*, pp. 254, 293. After referring to Tocqueville's comments, Riesman writes on p. 254: "very likely what was mere practice in his day has become embedded in character in ours."

39. In the original edition, *The Lonely Crowd* (New Haven, 1950), p. 20, in a footnote which does not appear in the abridged edition, Riesman seems to discount the testimony of Tocqueville. He writes: "I have tried to discover, by reading the eyewitness social observers of the early nineteenth century in America, whether Tocqueville 'saw' or "foresaw' it, to what extent he was influenced—as visiting firemen of today also are—by American snobs who take their image of Europe as the norm in describing their own countrymen. And to what extent, in establishing America's polarity with Europe, he tendentiously noticed those things that were different than those that were the same. From conversation with Phillips Bradley and Arthur Schlesinger, Jr., and from G. W. Pierson, *Tocqueville and Beaumont in America* . . . I got the impression that all these qualifications must be put on Tocqueville's picture of America in the 1830's." It is not clear whether the deletion of this footnote, when others were retained, results from an alteration in his thought or from a simple desire to save space. In any event, this passage suggests that Riesman recognized the problem which Tocqueville's report presented.

40. James Bryce, *The American Commonwealth* (London, 1888), II, 312–13.

41. Majority rule, Bryce pointed out, weakens the sense of individualism. A man "cannot long hold that he is right and the multitude wrong. An American submits more readily than an Englishman would do, ay, even to what an Englishman would think an injury to his private rights. . . . It may seem a trivial illustration to observe that when a railway train is late, or a waggon drawn up opposite a warehouse door stops the horse-car for five minutes, the passengers take the delay far more cooly and uncomplainingly than Englishmen would do. . . . It is all in the course of nature. What is an individual that he should make a fuss be-

cause he loses a few minutes, or is taxed too highly." *Ibid.*, II, 304. When he asked a conductor on an elevated railroad how he was able to enforce the rule against smoking when all other trains permitted smoking, the conductor replied. "I always say when anyone seems disposed to insist, 'Sir, I am sure that if you are a gentleman you will not wish to bring me into difficulty' and then they always leave off." *Ibid.*, II, 607n. See also his conclusions on the lack of individualism in the "inner life of men" in America, *Ibid.*, II, 678–79.

42. *LC*, p. 100.

43. Russell Lynes, *The Tastemakers* (New York, 1955), pp. 16–17.

44. Arthur W. Calhoun, *A Social History of the American Family* (Cleveland, 1917–19), III, chap. 7.

45. Hugo Münsterberg, *American Traits from the Point of View of a German* (Boston and New York, 1902), chap. 2.

46. *LC*, pp. 246 ff.

47. Thomas C. Cochran, *Railroad Leaders, 1845–1890* (Cambridge, 1953), pp. 157–58. W. H. Vanderbilt, it is true, said in a fit of pique, in 1882, "the public be damned," but a few years earlier he had written privately to a business associate, "we must be conservative and keep the public with us." At another time, according to Professor Cochran, he "recommended a minor change in policy because 'we don't want to get the public excited.'" *Ibid.*, p. 157.

48. Edward Chase Kirkland, *Dream and Thought in the Business Community, 1860–1900* (Ithaca, N.Y., 1956), pp. 8–10.

49. David M. Potter, *People of Plenty* (Chicago, 1954), chap. 8.

50. Frank Presbrey, *The History and Development of Advertising* (Garden City, N.Y., 1929), p. 591.

51. Sidney A. Sherman, "Advertising in the United States," *Quarterly Publications of the American Statistical Association*, n.s. VII (December 1900), 154.

52. *Loc. cit.*

53. *Ibid.*, p. 159.

54. Presbrey, *History of Advertising*, p. 426.

55. Alfred D. Chandler Jr., "The Beginnings of 'Big Business' in American

Industry," *Business History Review*, XXXIII (Spring, 1959), 4–14.

56. James Playsted Wood, *The Story of Advertising* (New York, 1948), pp. 263–64.

57. See, for example, Walter P. Metzger, "Generalizations about National Character. An Analytical Essay" in Louis Gottschalk (ed.), *Generalization in the Writing of History* (Chicago, 1963) and David M. Potter, *People of Plenty* (Chicago, 1954), Pt. I. In effect, also, Elting E. Morison (ed.), *The American Style* (New York, 1958) is a collection of papers assuming the existence of national character, though there it is called "style." See also Seymour Martin Lipset and Leo Lowenthal (eds.), *Culture and Social Character* (Glencoe, Ill., 1961) for an examination by sociologists and others of this question with particular reference to the work of Riesman.

# Index